2nd Edition

Real Estate Brokerage

A Guide to Success

By Dan Hamilton

**Real Estate Brokerage
A Guide to Success**

Dan Hamilton

Executive Editor: Sara Glassmeyer

Project Manager: Elizabeth King, Cenveo Publisher Services

Product Specialist: Deborah Miller

Manager, Creative Services: Brian Brogaard

Cover Images: monkey businessimages/iStock/GettyImages

kitzcorner/iStock/GettyImages

SolisImages/iStock/GettyImages

undrey/iStock/GettyImages

© 2018 OnCourse Learning

ALL RIGHTS RESERVED. No part of this work covered by the copyright herein may be reproduced, transmitted, stored, or used in any form or by any means graphic, electronic, or mechanical, including but not limited to photocopying, recording, scanning, digitizing, taping, web distribution, information networks, or information storage and retrieval systems, except as permitted under Section 107 or 108 of the 1976 United States Copyright Act, without the prior written permission of the publisher.

For product information and technology assistance, contact us at
OnCourse Learning and Sales Support, 1-855-733-7239.

For permission to use material from this text or product, please contact **publishinginfo@oncourselearning.com**.

Library of Congress Control Number: 2018943462

ISBN 13: 978-1-62980-955-7

ISBN 10: 1-62980-955-1

OnCourse Learning
20225 Water Tower Blvd
Brookfield, WI 53045
USA

Visit us at **www.oncoursepublishing.com**

Printed in the United States of America
1 2 3 4 5 6 22 21 20 19 18

This book is dedicated to my daughter, Brittany, who taught me:

- how to love those who are unlovable, which I can be (far too often)
- to live each moment to the fullest because she DID grow up too fast, just as my mom said she would
- that angels are real; for when I look into her face I see the face of an angel
- that egotism and self-worth are as far apart as the East is from the West (She loves herself, and that allows her to love others immensely.)
- the true meaning of unconditional love (I would lay down my life for her without hesitation or question, unconditionally.)
- that no matter how old she gets, she will always be my little girl
- that the word "Daddy" is the greatest word ever spoken

And she taught me all this with no books, no marker boards, and no big screens. I learned all this from simply seeing her smile up at me. She is my legacy.

Brief Contents

Introduction   xiii

About the Author   xix

1. Real Estate Industry   1
2. Starting a Brokerage Business   17
3. Ethical and Legal Business Practices   59
4. Analyzing the Market and the Competition   139
5. Managing Risk   181
6. Financing a Real Estate Brokerage Business   219
7. Negotiating a Commercial Lease   255
8. The Marketing Plan   289
9. Management Style and Structure   347
10. Employment Law and Compensation Management   387
11. Recruiting Sales Agents   421
12. Professional Brokerage Competency and Associate License Holder Productivity   479
13. Evaluating the Real Estate Brokerage Business   541
14. Growth Opportunities   563

Answer Key   589

Appendix   593

Credits   635

Index   639

Contents

Introduction xiii

About the Author xix

1 Real Estate Industry 1
  Pros and Cons of Being a Broker 5
  Brokerage Outlook and Trends 8
  Chapter Summary 11

2 Starting a Brokerage Business 17
  Reasons Real Estate Brokerages Fail 18
  Initial Planning 20
  Start Up or Purchase an Existing Brokerage 30
  Choosing a Business Type 35
  Choosing a Business Structure 42
  Naming the Brokerage 46
  Configuring the Brokerage 48
  Chapter Summary 53

3 Ethical and Legal Business Practices 59
  Ethics Defined 60
  Canons of Ethics 60
  Ethics Thoughts 64
  Business Ethics (Corporate Ethics) 67
  Real Estate License Law 71
  Deceptive Trade Practices Act 76
  Real Estate Associations 81
  Responsibility of the Real Estate Brokerage 83

Unfair Competition Laws   85
Unfair Business Practices   89
Americans with Disabilities Act   90
Agency and Representation   92
Prospecting Laws   100
Contracts   106
Disclosures   108
Sherman Antitrust Act   113
The Clayton Act   117
Do-Not-Call, Do-Not-Fax, and Antispam Laws   118
Fair Housing   120
Real Estate Settlement Procedures Act   124
Chapter Summary   125

4   Analyzing the Market and the Competition   139
What Is the Real Estate Market?   140
Analyzing the Market   144
Analyzing Competition   146
Analyzing an Organization   149
Writing a Business Plan   151
Chapter Summary   173

5   Managing Risk   181
Theory of Risk Management   182
Protecting the Institution   184
Policies and Procedures: Privacy Policy   197
Oversite Transaction and Compliance Review   200
Methods of Loss Control   209
Business Insurance   211
Chapter Summary   212

6   Financing a Real Estate Brokerage Business   219
The Financials   220
How Much Money Is Needed?   226
Financial Resources   229
General Operating Budget   246
Chapter Summary   247

7   Negotiating a Commercial Lease   255
Buying Versus Renting   256
Leasehold   258

Typical Lease Clauses 259
Factors in Selecting a Facility 262
Virtual Office Versus Physical Office 266
Facilities Management 268
Communications and Information Systems 281
Chapter Summary 282

8 The Marketing Plan 289
Marketing Properties 293
Direct Marketing 301
Marketing Budget 306
Marketing Campaign 307
Advertising 311
Types of Advertising 317
Protecting the Company's Image 337
Chapter Summary 339

9 Management Style and Structure 347
Scope of Activities and Authorization 348
Leadership 350
Managing People 354
Manager Development Program 358
Management Styles 368
Management Structure 374
Chapter Summary 378

10 Employment Law and Compensation Management 387
Employment Relations 388
Federal Employment Guidelines 390
State Employment Guidelines 391
Compensation Management 396
Salespersons 403
Employment Process 409
Chapter Summary 413

11 Recruiting Sales Agents 421
Selecting Potential Recruits 423
Top Reasons License Holders Choose a Broker 424
Brokers Should Recruit the Best Salespersons 425
Recruiting Actions 428
Tips for Speaking with a Recruit 431

Categories of Recruits   433
AWOC Action Plan   436
Calling on an AWOC   437
The Broker Should Watch for Events   441
Additional Ways to Improve Recruiting Efforts   441
Advertising for Recruits   442
Potential Recruiting Opportunities   446
Recruit Interview   447
Recruit Interview Hints   450
The Interview   450
Recruit Presentation   454
Main Topics of a Recruiting Presentation   454
Recruiting Packet   455
Costs of Recruiting   455
Objection-Handling Techniques   456
Objection-Handling Worksheets   460
Closing Techniques   461
Chapter Summary   468

12 **Professional Brokerage Competency and Associate License Holder Productivity   479**
Texas Real Estate Commission (TREC) on Rule 531.3 Competency   480
Managing Employees and Independent Contractors   480
License Holder Operations   482
Performance Management   486
Orientation Programs   489
Performance Appraisals   491
Training Programs   492
Business Meetings and Retreats   500
Personal Interaction   508
Retention   509
Resignation and Termination   513
Productivity Management   515
Agent Business Plan   519
Personal Marketing Plan   523
Time Management Plan   525
Chapter Summary   532

13 Evaluating the Real Estate Brokerage Business 541
*Financial Controls 543
Monitoring the Business 545
Management of Information 550
Maximizing Income 551
Minimizing Expenses 553
Chapter Summary 556*

14 Growth Opportunities 563
*Horizontal Expansion 564
Vertical Expansion 569
Organic Growth 572
Inorganic Growth (Mergers and Acquisitions) 577
Looking Toward the Future 581
Chapter Summary 583*

Answer Key 589

Appendix 593

Credits 635

Index 639

Introduction

Real Estate Brokerage is a book designed to be the end all, be all book of real estate brokerage. The concepts in the book are for the startup real estate brokerage, a midsized brokerage, and the buyout of an existing brokerage. This book is beneficial for the real estate license holder, the associate broker who is contemplating owning or managing a real estate brokerage, and the veteran broker who is looking for a better way to make money with fewer complications.

A large percentage of real estate license holders have dreamed of owning a real estate brokerage. Like any business, it is exciting! But it is also stressful. The broker has to worry not only about his/her actions but also about the actions of all of his/her sponsored license holders. This can be a nightmare if the broker has hundreds of sponsored license holders. Brokers work harder and longer than most real estate license holders, and most struggle to make ends meet. When a broker begins to hate the brokerage business, the broker needs to look to another occupation for the benefit of his/her agents and all others involved.

Brokers are recognized and respected in the local community where they operate. Brokers provide opportunities for individuals to make a respectable living and, in some cases, even become wealthy. The best real estate brokers receive more satisfaction from seeing others succeed than they do seeing themselves succeed.

The Texas Real Estate Commission (TREC) requires all brokerages to be registered and approved. The TREC regulates the basic operations of a brokerage. It tends to be stricter on brokers than agents because the broker is responsible for the actions of his/her sponsored license holders.

The real estate brokerage business is an exciting and rewarding business if handled properly. This book is designed to help the designated broker with brokerage and all that that entails. Real estate brokerage, like all other businesses, is based on fidelity, integrity, and trustworthiness as well as good work habits and a true concern for the customer. If you want to own a real estate brokerage in your future, you must incorporate what you learn from this book into your overall philosophy when it is time to open the doors of your real estate brokerage.

New to This Edition

Chapter 1 now addresses the issue of the Common Law of Agency and the fiduciary relationship a license holder has with a client.

Chapter 2 expands the need for detailed planning of a real estate brokerage's operations. The chapter addresses the need to have goals for the brokerage and the benefit for completing those goals. It takes a new look into configuring the brokerage, the office identity, signage, and high-speed internet.

Chapter 3 has the real estate brokerage student walk-through: several ethical scenarios to determine the best course of action. The chapter now includes case studies that delve into the necessity for a broker to have the highest level of integrity through the proper ethical code. The information about the Deceptive Trade Practices Act (DTPA) is expanded to include the definition of an unconscionable action and the danger of acting in such a manner. The discussion goes on to differentiate between knowingly acting and intentionally acting and how the DTPA treats both actions. The chapter elaborates on the National Association of REALTORS® (NAR) activities. It adds a look at prospecting laws and has in-depth coverage of the Fair Housing Law including a description of each protected class and how the broker must educate his/her sponsored license holders on fair housing laws. The contracts portion of the material now includes 16 contract-writing hints to help the broker in evaluating contracts that his/her license holders are writing. Predatory pricing is now addressed in the material. Also added in this chapter is a set of questions about antitrust to test the student's current knowledge of the Sherman Antitrust Act. The chapter ends with a quick hit section of applicable laws, including:

- trademark infringement
- misappropriation of trade secrets

- trade libel
- tortious interference
- Fair Credit Reporting Act
- Gramm-Leach-Bliley Act
- Children's Online Privacy Protection Act

Chapter 4 now includes bulleted coverage of the characteristics of a buyer's market and a seller's market as they relate to the real estate industry. The chapter now addresses the NAR's research on the Pending Home Sales Index, the Housing Affordability Index, and the Metropolitan Median Home Prices and Affordability report. The chapter takes a quick look at the Real Estate Center and the quality information that is produced by the Real Estate Center for the real estate broker.

Chapter 5 has some important changes, but the biggest is the section on business insurance. This chapter addresses the need for business insurance, including the risks that may be too much to survive if no business insurance is acquired. This chapter identifies multiple types of business insurance and the benefits of each. The chapter closes with a discussion on the need for a periodic audit of the current insurance, any new insurance needs, and how to determine whether the current insurance is the best insurance for the needs of the brokerage.

Chapter 7 has a new, updated look into a brokerage office layout. The chapter references the reception area, conference rooms, bathrooms, the bullpen, semi-private offices, private offices, the equipment room, storage, operational offices, and break rooms.

Organization

The Real Estate Brokerage: A Guide to Success is organized around the two main functions of a real estate broker: recruiting new and experienced salespeople and retaining them once they join. These two functions are the basis of real estate brokerage success.

Brokers in today's real estate companies have a multitude of exhilarating and challenging roles simply because of the way the industry is evolving. Technology and the internet, which have touched virtually every aspect of the business, are constantly changing and evolving. Additionally, economic, geopolitical, social, and legal climates create opportunities that challenge the management skills of today's brokers. Running a brokerage in this environment most likely means an attitudinal shift to move away from traditional practices.

Becoming a real estate broker appeals to individuals' desires to be imaginative and to influence, lead, and inspire others. The reward is that the brokerage does more than simply exist; rather, it thrives. Most gratifying of all for brokers is the exhilaration of seeing the people they manage grow in their professional successes.

Operating a real estate brokerage firm can be an intimidating and humbling experience. *The Real Estate Brokerage: A Guide to Success* helps brokers with their responsibilities, as everything that happens in an organization rises or falls on their decisions. Today's brokerages are complex sets of systems, processes, and people that function in a fluid or changing business environment, an understanding of which requires the education provided by this book.

Perhaps the most significant word in this book's title is *guide*. Today's real estate companies don't fit into one model. Each company is unique, and each broker is an individual. There are, however, certain basic principles for running a real estate company and coaching salespeople that are the foundation of a well-run brokerage. The purpose of this book is to help brokers understand the fundamentals of management and develop the ability to apply those fundamentals in ways that best fit their situation and company.

The Real Estate Brokerage: A Guide to Success provides a framework within which to manage in any environment. Whether the book is used for classroom study and certification or as preparatory reading prior to opening a brokerage, the book is an indispensable resource in any real estate library. The book is well designed and formatted for easy reference during challenges and expansion of any real estate company.

You may be embarking on a new career or already have real estate brokerage experience. You may be a salesperson who is not yet involved in management but seeking an inside look into the operation of a brokerage company. In any case, *The Real Estate Brokerage: A Guide to Success* is useful for gathering the tools of today's management trade and seizing new opportunities that are on the horizon.

To most people, the real estate brokerage business seems concerned largely with salesmanship, with success depending only upon the listing and selling abilities of the sales force. While these activities are important, and they have a lot to do with individual success, real estate brokerage is also a business and must be run with profit in mind. In today's competitive market, the ability to operate a brokerage firm as an efficient business is just as significant as the quality of the service the firm provides. It is this aspect of the real estate brokerage business that this book addresses.

These pages contain little about the activities of salespeople. Rather, we are concerned here with the management of the business: planning, organization, control, and financial well-being. In every field, a great many new businesses are formed every year, and most of them eventually fail. While the reasons for failure are many, much of the time it is because of improper management and the confusion, inefficiency, and money troubles that result. For the same reason, many that are able to survive do so far below their potential.

This book is arranged as a text, but it is not intended only for classroom use. The working broker and sales manager will be able to find plenty of use and value in these pages. Furthermore, anyone considering owning and/or operating a real estate brokerage business should learn and apply the ideas and concepts contained here. Because most states require that an individual's broker's license be preceded by a period of licensure as a salesperson, this book assumes that someone interested in the operation of a brokerage company will have acquired some knowledge of the real estate selling process. This allows the book to concentrate on the management and organizational aspects of the real estate brokerage business.

Acknowledgments

I would like to thank several people for their help on this book: Sara Glassmeyer of OnCourse Learning for believing in me from the beginning; Elizabeth King of Cenveo Publisher Services for working many hours on making this book a success; Krystyna Budd for all her copyediting efforts, which helped to make this book readable; and also Heather Dubnick for her editing help. In addition to being invaluably helpful, all have generously given their time and knowledge. Special thanks to my family, who has given me the time and space to complete this project. And all my gratitude goes out to my students who have let me "experiment" on them in class as I perfected this material.

About the Author

Dan Hamilton has held a broker's license since 1989 and has had decades of experience as a full-time real estate brokerage owner. During this time, he has earned a reputation for integrity, honesty, trustworthiness, competence, and fidelity both with his peers and with his clients.

He purchased his first office, Century 21, Main St. in Azle, Texas, and within one year it was recognized as a Top-Ten Office out of more than 50 real estate offices in the Southwest Region for Century 21. He bought Century 21, Main St. in Burleson, Texas, and within one year it was recognized as the fourth-ranked real estate office in the region. This office went on to receive the coveted Quality Service Award for Outstanding Customer Service from Century 21. Hamilton then started Century 21, Main St. Southwest in Fort Worth, Texas. This office is recognized as one of the fastest growing diversified companies in the Century 21 system for the Southwest Region.

Dan Hamilton developed the Hamilton Real Estate Education School. This school helped numerous real estate professionals obtain and maintain their real estate education for their real estate career. He is a certified by the Texas Real Estate Commission as a lead trainer for licensure and renewal and is certified to teach all qualifying courses. He has logged over 30,000 hours teaching Real Estate SAE Courses and over 15,000 hours in Real Estate CE courses.

In addition to being author of this book, *Real Estate Brokerage: A Guide to Success*, Dan Hamilton is the author of the *Real Estate Marketing and Sales Essentials: Steps for Success*, *Perfect Phrases for Real Estate Agents & Brokers*, *Texas Real Estate Law*, and *Real Estate Agency Law*. He is also co-author of *Texas Real Estate License Exam Prep*.

He is the president/founder of InveSTAR's real estate investment group. He has been the guest speaker for many real estate meetings and conventions including the Texas Association of REALTORS®, and he has served on the education committee for multiple associations. He has the Graduate Realtor Institute (GRI), Instructor Training Institute (ITI), and Certified Real Estate Instructor (CREI) designations. He served on the board of the national Real Estate Educators Association (REEA) and was president of the Texas Real Estate Teachers Association (TRETA).

The Texas Association of REALTORS® recognized Dan Hamilton for his Risk Management Series as the Most Innovative Local Association Education Program. The Risk Management Series was outlined by small and large brokerage offices to give real estate professionals tips and techniques to manage risk.

Dan Hamilton is currently the Texas agency representative with Alliant National Title, pursuing his talents in teaching and writing. Mr. Hamilton is relentless in his pursuit of knowledge in real estate as well as communicating that knowledge to others. He has the courage to take on the tough subjects and make them understandable. He believes in the individual, and he believes everyone can make it if he/she follows his/her passions.

Dan Hamilton welcomes email at Mainbroker@aol.com.

CHAPTER 1
Real Estate Industry

Real estate brokerage is the business of real estate sales in its many forms. The real estate industry is an exciting business in general. Everyone wants to talk about real estate—it is part of the "American dream." People are interested in buying and selling their homes; in investing in rental property, new construction, commercial property, leasing, property management, farms, ranches, condominiums, townhomes, row houses; and in purchasing vacation property. The list is endless. Buying or leasing a place to live can be one of the most complex and important financial events in one's life. Buyers and sellers want help with these important decisions from educated, regulated, and talented real estate professionals. That is the main reason why and how the real estate industry has evolved.

Most people entering the real estate field as a career want to become the broker of a real estate business. They want to have their own company. They get their broker license and buy some yard signs, and "BAM!"—they have their brokerage, without training, financial backing, or experience. That is what far too many do, and that is the reason some joke it is "Broke-er" because being a broker makes a person broke. Many brokers will state that they made more money selling real estate as an agent than they did as a brokerage owner. Some figure the real estate brokerage business out through the "School of Hard Knocks," making many costly errors. Those actions waste time and the lessons are expensive. A person needs to be aware of the complications of brokerage before entering that world, and that is the reason for this book.

Real estate brokers are licensed, independent businesspeople who sell real estate owned by others. The relationship between the buyers and the sellers of real estate and the real estate broker was originally established by reference to the English Common Law of Agency. The relationship is a fiduciary relationship in which both parties owe duties to the other. A fiduciary relationship is a "higher"-than-normal relationship. In a fiduciary relationship agents must place the interests of their clients above their own. Agents generally earn their commission when they perform their function of matching a real estate buyer with a real estate seller or a tenant with a landlord. This "earns when" is being paid by a "contingency." With the internet providing the people interested in real estate with all the information, competent real estate professionals are figuring out ways to be paid in the real estate business other than on a contingency basis. These open-minded brokers will survive and thrive into the future.

Real estate brokers and their salespersons assist owners in pricing, staging, marketing, advertising, promoting, presenting, negotiating, contract writing, making repairs, closing the real estate transaction, and following up after. They also can assist buyers in the same real estate processes. There will be minor differences in performance, but the representation is still a fiduciary relationship.

Brokers supervise real estate salespersons (also called real estate agents, license holders, and professionals, terms that will be used throughout the material interchangeably), who sell real estate owned by others. Brokers hire office managers to manage their own offices: They advertise properties, review contracts, coach agents, hold office meetings, monitor progress, do the accounting, arrange for office maintenance, and handle all other business matters. Some brokers combine this arrangement with other types of work, such as leasing, property management, mortgage, and insurance. Most real estate brokers and salespersons sell residential property. A much smaller number sell commercial, industrial, agricultural, farm and ranch, and/or special-purpose real estate. Every specialty requires knowledge of the specialty's particular type of property and particular type of client. Leasing property requires an understanding of leasing practices, business trends, and available-property locations. Salespersons who sell or lease industrial properties must understand the region's infrastructure, transportation, utilities, laws, regulations, and labor supply. Whatever the type of property, the salesperson or broker must know how to meet the client's particular requirements.

Once a person becomes a real estate broker, it feels great for him/her to hold sales meetings and to know that all the salespersons are looking to the broker for leadership; to walk in front of several hundred peers to receive an award for a top-producing real estate office; to mentor a rookie real estate salesperson and create a star! Money is a reward in and of itself; but rather than claim all the limelight for themselves, the great brokers want to see others succeed as a result of their efforts. The love of helping others succeed is the prime reason a broker makes a great broker.

The real estate industry was ultimately developed to fulfill a need of buyers and sellers of real property. The need developed because real estate can be a complicated business, and without the help of experienced real estate professionals, the ordinary consumer could be at a disadvantage. Real estate has been around since dirt, pun intended. The real estate industry has had to adapt to keep up with current changes

and demands, and these changes and demands have had a profound effect on the real estate brokerage business: Regulators began limiting the role of the broker, the age of information altered the role of the broker, and the advent of the computer completely changed the direction of the real estate industry. The formation and widespread use of the internet changed the way the real estate industry found clients and moved information. Many brokers have changed their entire philosophy because their salespersons no longer need a "bricks-and-mortar" office to work from. These salespersons now work from home or from their vehicle. Despite these changes, however, a real estate salesperson still makes money by bringing buyers and sellers together, and that will never change.

Most real estate firms are relatively small; some are one-person businesses. By contrast, some large real estate firms have several hundred real estate salespersons operating out of numerous branch offices. Many brokers have franchise agreements with national or regional real estate organizations.

Real estate brokers deal frequently with other specialists in the real estate business: competing brokers, investors, property managers, commercial brokers, leasing agents, appraisers, surveyors, engineers, financial institutions, title companies, architects, contractors, inspectors, attorneys, and accountants. A broker should establish and maintain good working relationships with these professionals.

Real estate brokers and salespersons have a thorough knowledge of the real estate market they serve. They know how to find the right neighborhoods that will best fit their clients' wants and needs. They are familiar with the laws and regulations affecting a real estate transaction. They know where to obtain the best financing options.

Pros and Cons of Being a Broker

Becoming a broker is prompted by many reasons that are great and many that are heartbreaking. The talented long-term broker strives to lessen the cons and accentuate the pros. The broker's job is never done, working weekends and holidays and all hours of the day. However, when brokers see one of their sponsored license holders become wealthy by selling real estate, the brokers gain a powerful sense of satisfaction.

Advantages of Being a Broker (Pros)

The advantages of being a broker are many. Some of the advantages are easily recognizable, the result of the money earned through real estate sales: affording the new house, buying the best car, and traveling the world. The disadvantages are also many, like not having the time to enjoy the new house or fancy car and never traveling. Becoming a broker/owner of a brokerage has a multitude of advantages including:

- *financial income*–A real estate brokerage can be a money maker if operations are executed properly. The wise broker has reserve accounts for fluctuations in income. The wise broker knows that the financial stream in the real estate brokerage business is very volatile and changes daily. Without the reserve account (at least six months' expenses), the broker could be out of business right before the big business hits. Many brokerages make the broker/owner several hundred thousand dollars per year, and the business net worth can run into millions of dollars.
- *prestige*–It is honorable to be the broker/owner of a real estate brokerage. People look up to brokers and want to be like them. Kids may not dream of becoming a real estate brokerage owner, but the business professionals in the community know the power and prestige that the position brings.
- *pride of ownership*–A broker/owner should be proud every time he/she walks through the door of the office. It is the broker who

created this brokerage, and its success is directly attributable to the broker.
- *leadership*—The broker is the designated leader of a brokerage. New agents look up to the broker for mentoring and hand-holding, and experienced agents rely on the broker for guidance and recommendations.
- *office philosophy*—Every office is different, and the broker determines the philosophy of the office. If the broker is a go-getter, the office will tend to be the same. If the broker is big on education, the agents will tend to be the same.
- *decision maker*—The broker has the privilege to make the important decisions. Having this honor is disposed only upon the leader, the broker, the person in charge.
- *mentoring*—Mentoring is one-to-one in-depth training through field experience and personal involvement. The broker is the ultimate mentor. The more time the broker can spend on developing the agents, the better the agents will be. The better the agents, the more money they will earn for themselves and the brokerage. Mentoring is also an advantage because it builds loyalty.
- *teaching*—Teaching could be one-to-one or in a group. It lacks the in-depth field training that mentoring involves. Brokers could train on any number of topics that are relevant to their real estate agents. The broker who trains is the broker who retains agents. The broker should not delegate too much training to others because the current agents will bond with the trainer and then that trainer could leave to form his/her own brokerage, taking the newly trained agents with him/her.
- *determining direction*—The broker should have a vision that the brokerage will follow. When the broker's direction allows the brokerage to become a financial powerhouse, the broker gets the credit.
- *hiring*—The broker creates jobs for others. The broker gets to hire the license holders who fit into the brokerage philosophy.
- *office design*—The broker is the person who designs and implements the office layout. The broker gets to determine room functionality and desk placement, for example, and whether the brokerage will offer agents computers to use or expect each agent to have a laptop.
- *community involvement*—The broker will be invited to local community events. As the face of the brokerage, the broker should attend as many community functions as time allows.

- *stability of employment*–No one can fire the broker/owner. Thus brokers know their employment is assured.
- *cost control*–The broker should control all costs or delegate this responsibility to a trusted person. Cost control is an advantage because, if handled properly, it can result in the retaining of brokerage funds that contribute to the bottom-line profit.

Disadvantages of Being a Broker

- *financial income*–The broker should not be but typically is paid last. Many brokers have to put their own real estate sales earnings back into the brokerage just to keep it afloat. The financial risks of any small business is typically great. The broker should not open unless the brokerage is well funded.
- *prestige*–Prestige is fleeting if the brokerage is failing. No one will look up to the broker of a failing brokerage. In fact, the broker will find that people are now avoiding *contact with him/her just in case the bad luck rubs off.*
- *pride of ownership*–There is nothing to be proud of if the agents are not working and the business is failing. Pride does not last if the ship is sinking.
- *leadership*–Leadership is not given; it must be earned. The broker who fails to attain the position of leader will never have the brokerage that was dreamed about. If the broker delegates leadership, the broker is no longer a broker but an employee. Eventually the brokerage will fail without a powerful broker leader.
- *office philosophy*–If a broker cannot control the office philosophy or ignores it, that broker will wake up to find a party office or one in which no one shows up.
- *decision maker*–The broker is the decision maker; however, if the decisions the broker makes continually fail, the broker will have everyone around doubting his/her ability to make decisions. Eventually the brokerage will fail because of the bad decisions.
- *mentoring*–If the broker does not know how to mentor or the license holders who are mentored fail, the broker loses credibility and no one will trust the broker.
- *teaching*–Many brokers teach their own agents and think themselves great teachers, but the agents may not agree. The brokers may finally discontinue training because no agents are showing up for classes and business drops off because of the agents' lack of training.

- *firing*–The broker must make the tough decision to fire staff and agents who are not performing or who are underperforming. Doing this is not easy, and it is certainly not an advantage, but if action is not taken, employees will figure out that the broker does not fire an underperformer. So they will not feel threatened that if they fail to perform, they will lose their job.
- *office design*–The broker may not have the ability to design an office, and because of this failure the brokerage will not run as efficiently as a properly designed office. The broker could hire a designer but expenses would now escalate.
- *community involvement*–If the broker is not good in public situations, the broker could hurt the brokerage. A drunk broker at a prestigious event, for example, will mark that brokerage forever.
- *stability of employment*–Stability of employment is available only to brokers who are successful. Those who fail will be looking for a job.
- *cost control*–Failure by a broker to control the costs of a brokerage is the fastest way to the brokerage closing.

Brokerage Outlook and Trends

The outlook for real estate and the real estate brokerage business is continually improving. The economic fundamentals of the real estate climate are strong, but rising technology costs are putting pressure on the profitability of real estate brokerage offices.

The competition in the real estate sector is increasingly stiff and harsh. As more and more real estate license holders enter the real estate industry, the competition for the sale will also increase. The brokerage firms must provide the services demanded by the consumer and the real estate license holder.

Consistent growth in population and economic production, along with low mortgage rates, has produced a strong base for home sales. This trend should continue well into the future. Interest rates are creeping up, but the overall 20-year average is still extremely affordable. The biggest issue now and in the future is low house inventory levels. Property prices are escalating, and if they do not level off, the real estate market could get upside down. If this happens then another real estate collapse may follow.

Because interest rates are currently at a low level, investments in real estate have been increasing steadily. However, the inventory of investment properties is dropping because owners no longer have to sell at an investment level to get a property sold. Investments will always be available, but the investor may have to be more patient than in past years.

The business is and has been breaking into two main segments over the past few decades. The first segment is the mom-and-pop shop, a single broker working from home. Overhead is so small that the mom-and-pop shop will survive any change in the real estate market. The broker will typically deal only with clients from past years and referrals, so no advertising is needed. If this broker has only a handful of real estate transactions in a year, the operation is sustainable.

The second segment is the megafirm. This type of company is so large that it operates on economies of scale. The megafirm has hundreds of real estate license holders and several offices. The ability to buy large quantities of supplies at a discount and to negotiate large discounted contracts with service providers allows this company to survive almost any change in the real estate market. Watch for the consolidation of middle real estate companies for many years into the future.

Trends indicate that these are the most likely types of real estate brokerage firms to survive and thrive in the near future. The middle firms, the ones with one or two offices with 10 to 50 real estate license holders, will be squeezed until they cannot continue in business. The real estate salesperson is demanding more on a commission-split and

expects the broker to pay for all the necessary services associated with selling real estate. The profit margins in the real estate industry have been shrinking for the past 15 years and will continue to dwindle until all the middle firms are gone. The problem with this approach to business is that "everyone" wants to be the owner of his/her own real estate company, and the most frequent type formed is the middle firm. These middle firms will form and dissolve many times in the next several years.

An approach that has faded is the purchase of residential real estate brokerage firms by nonbrokerage real estate companies, holding companies, or financial services companies, such as title insurance firms or banks. The entry of nonbrokerage firms with unlimited capital could change the brokerage industry quickly because they can acquire existing brokerages with the largest market share and broadest reach, but so far they have languished. Also, holding companies have discovered that regulatory approval would be required to acquire existing brokerages and that is difficult.

Some pundits believe that the internet will replace the need for real estate professionals. There is no chance that will ever happen, however. The internet can do a lot of things, but it cannot give the feel of actually walking through a house. Even a 360° virtual tour cannot duplicate the feel of a buyer's first walkthrough of a house. Those in the real estate profession like to say that the house "talks" to the buyer. A buyer walks through a house and simply pauses for a second in complete silence, then smiles. It is then that the house just "talked" to the buyer and the buyer listened. How can the internet "talk" to a buyer? It cannot!

The internet has revolutionized the way real estate license holders communicate. But the biggest trend that has surfaced is the way a real estate brokerage business uses the internet to advertise for clients. Most real estate brokerage businesses have rerouted their advertising funds from print media to the internet, and this trend will continue. Social networking is used religiously in the real estate industry for keeping up with clients and developing new clients.

Fluctuations in oil and gas prices has a critical effect on real estate purchases. If the price drops too low, many jobs will be lost and Texas could see foreclosures. If prices remain stable or rise, the housing industry will also remain stable or improve. Expectations are that somewhat stabilized prices in an area will not affect real estate either way.

Another trend of the past few years is low interest rates, which will continue to stimulate sales of real estate and result in the need for more agents and brokers. With low rates, growing families will be in a better position to buy a new home. Baby boomers are now retiring and seeking alternative living arrangements. The trend for retirees is not to settle down but to look for an active lifestyle and living arrangement. Through the internet and Facebook, Twitter, and other social media, millennials are buying property and communicating in ways that traditionalists did not, and real estate professionals must adapt to their ways to thrive. All these changes are opportunities for the real estate company that is alert, aware, and willing to adapt. Although the future is never certain, the willingness to adapt to change will help the pioneers in this business grow and prosper.

CHAPTER SUMMARY

Real estate brokerage is the business of real estate sales in its many forms. Everyone wants to talk about real estate—owning one's own home is, after all, associated with the "American dream." People are interested in buying and selling their homes; in investing in rental property, new construction, commercial property, leasing, property management, farms, ranches, condominiums, townhomes, row houses; and in purchasing vacation property. Buying or leasing a place to live or selling one's house can be one of the most complex and important financial events in an individual's life. Buyers and sellers want help with these important decisions from educated, regulated, and talented real estate professionals. That is the main reason why and how the real estate industry has evolved.

Most people entering the real estate field as a career want to become the broker of a real estate business. Many brokers will state that they made more money selling real estate as an agent than they did as a brokerage owner. Some figure the real estate brokerage business out through the "School of Hard Knocks," making many costly errors. This approach wastes time, and the lessons learned in this way are expensive.

The relationship between the buyers and the sellers of real estate and the real estate broker was originally established by reference to the English Common Law of Agency. A fiduciary relationship is a relationship that is "higher" than normal. In a fiduciary relationship, agents must place the interests of their clients above their own.

Real estate brokers and their salespersons assist owners in pricing, staging, marketing, advertising, promoting, presenting, negotiating, contract writing, making repairs, closing the real estate transaction, and following up after. They also can assist buyers in the same real estate processes.

Brokers supervise real estate salespersons (also called agents, licensees, professionals, terms that will be used throughout the book interchangeably), who sell real estate owned by others. Most real estate brokers and salespersons sell residential property. A much smaller number sell commercial, industrial, agricultural, farm and ranch, and/or special-purpose real estate.

The love of helping others succeed is the primary reason a broker makes a great broker.

Real estate has had to adapt to keep up with current changes and demands, and these have had a profound effect on the real estate brokerage business: Regulators have begun limiting the role of the broker, the age of information has changed that role, and the advent of the computer has completely changed the direction of the real estate industry.

The formation and widespread use of the internet has changed the way the real estate industry finds clients and moves information.

Becoming a broker/owner of a brokerage has a multitude of advantages and disadvantages in the following areas:

- financial income
- prestige
- pride of ownership
- leadership
- office philosophy

- decision making
- mentoring
- teaching
- determining direction
- hiring/firing
- office design
- community involvement
- cost control

Consistent growth in population and economic production, along with low mortgage rates, has produced a strong base for home sales.

The real estate sales business is and has been breaking into two main segments over the past few decades. The first segment is the mom-and-pop shop, which comprises a single broker working from home; and the second segment is the megafirm, a company with hundreds of license holders and many offices.

Although the future is never certain, the willingness to adapt to change will help the pioneers in the real estate industry grow and prosper.

CHAPTER QUESTIONS

1. Real estate is:
   A. always a bad investment
   B. only for people with cash
   C. is the American dream
   D. best only if held for longer than three years

2. Buying or leasing a place to live can be:
   A. complex
   B. the biggest financial event in a person's life
   C. an important life-changing decision
   D. all of the answer choices

3. In general, who can make the most money in the real estate business?
   A. real estate salespersons
   B. real estate assistants
   C. real estate brokers
   D. real estate instructors

4. What is the problem with learning the brokerage business through the "School of Hard Knocks"?
   A. It is costly and wastes time.
   B. It is a requirement of any good entrepreneur.
   C. It is the recommended by the Texas Real Estate Commission (TREC).
   D. All of the answer choices are valid.

5. Most license holders sell what type of real estate?
   A. residential
   B. commercial
   C. agricultural
   D. industrial

6. License holders who sell or lease industrial properties must:
   A. understand the laws that could affect industrial properties
   B. understand the regulations that could affect industrial properties
   C. know about the local labor supply
   D. all of the answer choices

7. No matter the recent changes, which of the following is still the best way to make money in the real estate business?
   A. spending a great deal of money on print advertising
   B. sitting at home watching TV and waiting for potential buyers to call
   C. bringing buyers and sellers together
   D. all of the answer choices

8. Becoming a broker/owner has which of the following advantages?
   A. mentoring
   B. hiring
   C. determining the brokerage direction
   D. all of the answer choices

9. Which of the following could lead to a real estate market collapse?
   A. steady income levels
   B. property price escalation
   C. low mortgage interest rates
   D. rapid increase in the number of real estate license holders

10. Where are most real estate brokers spending the largest amount of advertising dollars?
    A. the internet
    B. print advertising
    C. mailers
    D. telemarketing

CHAPTER 2

Starting a Brokerage Business

Starting a real estate brokerage business is an exciting yet frightening process. The typical brokerage owner has little knowledge of business ownership and little knowledge of risk management. To become a brokerage owner, there is no requirement to obtain a business degree. There is only the requirement for a broker to obtain a broker's license, and this involves an additional 30-hour brokerage course. With a broker's license, a person can open a brokerage and hold licenses. Where would a broker look to seek more education? This book is a starting point, designed to provide the knowledge necessary to help a broker become a success to whatever level desired. This book is applicable for the newest broker and the most veteran broker. The broker's only question should be is, "Will I have the courage to learn and grow, or will I do this the hard way and learn on my own?"

Reasons Real Estate Brokerages Fail

Real estate brokerage owners will fail in their endeavors if they approach their role as broker in the same way they did in their previous career. One broker would periodically interview each of his sponsored license holders to see how they were doing. One of the questions he asked was, "Have you ever thought about owning or managing a real estate office?" Over 60% of them answered, "Yes." This approach is peculiar because a majority of brokers were not running their real estate sales businesses efficiently. How did they feel they could train and help other real estate license holders with their real estate sales business? What happens when real estate salespersons feel they can do better than their current broker and open up their own offices? Quickly they find out they cannot do that either, and the office suffers. So lack of planning is the first reason a broker/owner fails.

Other reasons a broker/owner fails are:

- lack of funds, or undercapitalization
- lack of management experience
- lack of focus
- lack of specialization

These reasons are considered next.

Lack of Funds, or Undercapitalization

Lack of funds, or undercapitalization, as the accountants say, is a typical problem. A great many new real estate offices are under pressure from the moment they open because they do not have the funds to last until the money starts dropping into the till. Lack of funds is not new to the entrepreneur; as a matter of fact, it is one of the top reasons that small businesses fail. However, in real estate, it is an even bigger dagger to the heart of a successful real estate business because a listing taken today may take six months to sell, and it may take another 60 days to finalize the sale and get the fee. Translated, this means that a real estate company should have at least a full year's worth of money to operate the business at startup and then at least six months of income for reserves. This does not include any capital expenditures, such as office equipment.

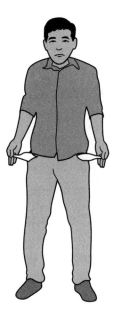

Lack of Management Experience

Another leading indicator of failure in a real estate enterprise is lack of management experience. Being a successful real estate salesperson does not translate into a being successful real estate broker/owner. A very successful real estate salesperson, for example, was "promoted" to a manager's position. She knew nothing about real estate management, and soon the office failed and the doors closed. After a review, the real estate corporation she worked with determined that it had decided to "promote from within." Because it had followed that hard-and-fast rule, the company suffered, losing a real estate office as well as a top producer (the promoted salesperson was upset because her office failed, so she left for another real estate company).

Lack of Focus

Lack of focus is evident in owners of a real estate brokerage who try to save money by doing everything themselves. These owners are at the office 23½ hours a day (they take a nap for 30 minutes in the storage room), seven days a week. They serve as managers, accountants, marketers, trainers, judges, friends, mentors, leaders, and janitors. There simply are not enough hours in a day to do everything required. With all this to do, most small broker/owners also have to sell real estate for commission income to stay above water. They cannot concentrate on the main objective of a real estate office, and that is to make a profit.

Lack of Specialization

The real estate company that fails for lack of specialization is a company that tries to be all things to all people. Such companies are not big enough to departmentalize, so they close a transaction without the expertise to consistently do it responsibly. They close a residential deal here, a commercial deal there. They dabble in property management and investments. Because they choose not to specialize, they do everything. Eventually they make a critical error, and after all the litigation they have nothing left. A broker should specialize in one field and become the best at it.

Initial Planning

The most important aspect of any business is the initial planning. To take on the risks and responsibilities of owning a real estate brokerage company would be foolish without weeks of planning. Thinking about and planning every aspect of the business is critical. During the initial planning stage a potential broker/owner will need to determine if he/she has what it takes (including the finances to make it) and if the market will afford another competitor. The initial planning stage is the prerequisite to the business plan. The business plan takes the thoughts and feelings considered during the initial planning stage and puts them into a formal document. A few things that need to be thought through include but are not limited to purpose, positioning, profitability, location, services offered, number of staff, number of agents, type of real estate to be practiced, agency policies, office operation, fees, compensation, and the characteristics necessary to become a qualified broker.

Characteristics of Talented Brokers and Owners

A broker must have certain characteristics and skills to be successful in the real estate industry. A broker who has certain characteristics and skills will have an easier time recruiting agents and retaining his/her current agents. People want to work with someone who is skillful and yet caring. If a broker is not proficient in one area, that broker could develop the skill, hire someone who has that skill, or overcome the deficiency by making more effort. A broker does not need all the characteristics explained in the following sections, but without most the broker will experience a tough career. So the question is, "What makes a good and productive real estate broker?"

There are basic characteristics of really talented brokers, and these are discussed next.

Emotionally Stable

Being emotionally stable means that the broker is generally neither too happy nor too sad. The broker is neither too optimistic nor too pessimistic. Good brokers must be able to tolerate frustration and stress without freaking out. They cannot allow themselves the pleasure of getting personally involved in salespersons' disputes. The broker cannot ever take one agent's side over another's. Overall, brokers must be well adjusted and have the psychological maturity to deal with anything they are required to face. The brokerage business changes every day, and the broker who is emotionally stable will be able to adjust and thrive during the process.

Commanding

A commanding broker is one who takes control and asserts power when necessary. Commanding brokers are often competitive, enthusiastic, and decisive, and they usually enjoy overcoming obstacles. These are not mean people; they are strong people, strong with integrity and purpose. Overall, they are assertive in their thinking style as well as their attitude in dealing with others. The commanding broker is a leader because people want to follow a person who has a commanding, powerful personality. No one wants to follow or believes in a weak person who is afraid of making the tough decisions.

Enthusiastic

Enthusiasm is many things. An enthusiastic broker is one who is excited about the future success of the brokerage. An enthusiastic broker is usually seen as active, expressive, and energetic. An enthusiastic broker is a cheerleader when needed and a supporter when needed. An enthusiastic broker leads through the power of motivation. Such brokers are often very optimistic and open to change. Overall, they are generally quick and alert and tend to be uninhibited.

Conscientious
Conscientious brokers are often dominated by a sense of duty and tend to be exacting in character. Conscientious brokers are thoughtful and concerned about every one of the agents of the brokerage. The conscientious broker is less concerned with self and more concerned about the community that the brokerage serves. Conscientious brokers usually have a high standard of excellence and an inward desire to do their best. They see the big picture and operate on a higher plane. They also have a need for order and tend to be self-disciplined. They understand that all their actions are being watched and are therefore extremely vigilant.

Socially Bold
Socially bold brokers tend to be spontaneous risk takers. These brokers are not reckless, but they are not afraid of taking an educated chance. They are usually socially aggressive and generally thick-skinned. They will not back down from the doubters and are not concerned with the incorrect opinions of others. Socially bold brokers are good at building powerful relationships with staff, agents, and members of the local community. Overall, they are responsive to others and tend to be high in emotional stamina.

Tough-Minded
Tough-minded brokers are practical, logical, and to-the-point. Tough-minded brokers tend to have a vision that they alter only when overwhelming evidence requires that vision to change. Tough-minded brokers never let their guard down and will stand up to anyone who threatens their brokerage. They tend to be individuals low in sentimental attachments and comfortable with criticism. They are usually insensitive to hardship and always remain poised. Tough-minded brokers will continue their education to be the best in their business.

Self-Assured
Self-assured brokers are confident, and that confidence creates strong bonds between the broker and the broker's agents. Confidence is the silent factor that all leaders possess. A self-assured broker believes that his/her opinion is correct and makes a difference. Self-assured brokers are excited to lead, and they believe that the success of the brokerage is a result of their leadership. Self-assured brokers confront negative issues without blame and handle those issues in a professional manner.

Self-assurance and resilience are common traits among almost all great brokers. These brokers tend to be free of guilt and have little or no need for approval. They are generally secure and are usually unaffected by earlier mistakes or failures.

Composed
Composed brokers are controlled and precise in their social interactions. Composed brokers perform well in public situations. There is never a fear of social embarrassment resulting from a public remark from the composed broker. Overall, they are very protective of their integrity and reputation; consequently, they tend to be socially aware and careful when making decisions or determining specific actions.

Highly Energized
Long hours and few days off are usually prerequisites for leadership positions, especially as the brokerage company grows. Remaining attentive and maintaining focus are two of the most important traits for a broker to have. Highly energized brokers have the drive to keep going when the going gets tough. Highly energized brokers never quit but keep going until they succeed and all those who are with the broker also succeed. Energized brokers never feel it is too late or too early. Their energy is so contagious that their agents become energized.

Intuitive
Intuitive brokers learn to listen to their intuition. Brokers have a great deal of information available to them, but that still might not be enough. Having good judgment in situations is invaluable, especially in interpersonal relationships. Intuitive brokers can sense if a direction is not right and will have the courage to make a course change for the brokerage. Intuitive brokers can feel if a transaction is not acceptable and will avoid that agency or terminate that agency when it occurs.

Mature

Mature brokers have sufficient maturity to earn respect from their agents, who will respect them enough to seek their advice. Mature brokers do not react haphazardly but act meticulously and scrupulously. To be a good broker/owner, the individual must ensure that personal power and recognition are secondary to the development of the employees. In other words, maturity is based on recognizing that more can be accomplished by empowering others than by ruling others. As a matter of fact, good brokers enjoy the successes of the people they lead more than they enjoy their own successes.

Team-Oriented

Good brokers today put a strong emphasis on teamwork. In any real estate office, working as a team and helping each other are prerequisites. Real estate salespersons are independent contractors, but they also want to feel part of something bigger and more important than themselves. Team-oriented brokers enjoy doing real estate work in teams. The team-oriented broker knows that teams build enthusiasm and almost always lead to success for the brokerage.

Empathetic

Good brokers will have empathy, but not sympathy, for their salespersons. In other words, a broker should be able to know how others feel without crying with them. Without empathy, trust is difficult to build. And without trust, a broker will never be able to get the best effort from the brokerage's salespersons. Empathetic brokers will listen to the agents and help those agents work through the situation. Empathetic brokers understand the difficulties of the real estate business but do not let these difficulties prohibit them from moving on and pursuing success.

Charismatic
People usually perceive real estate brokers as larger than life. Charisma plays a large part in this perception. Brokers who have charisma are able to arouse strong emotions in their salespersons, staff, and clients by defining a vision that unites and captivates them. Using this vision, brokers motivate all those involved to reach toward a future goal by tying the goal to substantial personal rewards and values.

The following is an additional list of characteristics that make a quality owner/broker:

persistent	honest	trustworthy
patient	good communicator	opportunistic
organized	problem solver	exudes integrity
educator	mentor	mediator
pleasant	neat in appearance	ethical
tactful	understanding	motivator
detail oriented	great memory	business savvy

A majority of these characteristics are traits that one either has or does not have—they cannot easily be developed. If a person has never been honest, for example, it would be hard to believe that once he/she becomes a broker, that person would suddenly become honest. This does not mean that people cannot change. These traits are in everyone, and so the question for the broker is, "Can I develop these characteristics and become the best broker I can possibly be?"

Initial Planning: Rules and Regulations
In real estate, as in other businesses, a broker must follow the rules and regulations of the land as set forth by the government. The broker must treat others with respect, and the broker must have a real estate service for which the public is willing to pay. Specifically, before a broker begins operations as a real estate company, the broker must do the following:

- ***Obtain business name approval.*** A start-up real estate company must have a business name approved by the state real estate commission. Most companies use a "doing business as" (DBA) name as

well as their own name. DBAs are filed at the county courthouse. The broker/owner needs to check the local regulations on how to handle this. Also, the broker needs to be sure to check with the state real estate commission before filing the name of the company because some commissions will not accept a proposed company name that may mislead the public into thinking they are not dealing with a real estate brokerage company.
- *File legal paperwork.* The real estate company must file all the paperwork required by the state real estate commission. The broker should not take this obligation lightly because some of the filings can take a great deal of time and cost more money than imagined.
- *Create an evidence-of-trust account.* A trust account is a bank account that holds monies of others. This is not the broker's operating account. Not all brokerages are required to open a trust account, but if the brokerage chooses to open the account, then the broker must abide by the strict and complex rules established.
- *Offer financial protection for the consumer.* A real estate commission could require the broker to be bonded to protect consumers. In Texas, the Texas Real Estate Commission (TREC) has set up a recovery fund to compensate aggrieved persons if the real estate broker fails to do so.
- *Pay appropriate fees for company registration.* The primary purpose of a real estate commission is to protect the public from errors, omissions, and violations of the Real Estate License Act by real estate license holders. TREC is funded by the dues and fees charged to license holders, including applications and renewal fees. The Commission uses these funds to regulate the industry.
- *Obtain a license.* Every state requires a real estate broker to have a real estate license. The legal requirements for becoming a real estate broker vary from state to state but generally require the candidate to have experience in the real estate industry as a real estate salesperson. Other requirements include completing additional education and passing the broker's exam. Generally, a college degree is not required to become a real estate broker, but some college courses in the fields of finance and management would be extremely valuable. In Texas, for a person to become a real estate broker, he/she must:
  - be a citizen of the United States or lawfully admitted alien;
  - be 18 years of age or older;

- be a resident of Texas, unless the applicant:
  - was licensed in Texas as a sales agent or broker in the past two years, or
  - is licensed as a broker in another state; and
- meet TREC's qualifications for honesty, trustworthiness, and integrity.

Qualifying Education Requirements

All broker license applicants must complete the required qualifying education for a total of 270 classroom hours (18 semester hours or nine courses). The Real Estate Brokerage course must be completed not more than two years before the application date. An additional 630 classroom hours (for a total of 900 classroom hours) in related qualifying courses are required.

Filing a Broker License Application

An applicant should submit a broker license application and any fees due to become a broker using the TREC online services tab or send in a paper application, which typically takes longer.

License Exam

The broker is also required to take and pass a broker exam for Texas. These exams are administered by an independent testing service company. The broker will be sent a notice with instructions for scheduling the exam and obtaining a copy of the exam *Candidate Handbook*. If the broker fails the exam three times, the broker will be required to take additional courses before reapplying.

After completing all of the above items, the brokerage entity must now act in accordance with the structure that was designed. Any major changes in owners or structure must be reported to the TREC before the changes occur.

Applicants have one year from the date the application is filed to meet all license requirements. Once met, TREC will send an active broker license via email. Licensed real estate brokers can sponsor and supervise real estate sales agents.

Business Plan

Many business owners have no business plan. They allow the business to happen to them rather than taking an active part in shaping and directing their own progress. They wait for problems to arise and then try to deal with them. Instead of being proactive, they are reactive to the happenings around them. Business owners who make a plan and *work* the plan take control of their business and their careers. They do not allow themselves to get discouraged because they know where they are going and what they have to do to get there. That is the purpose of the business plan.

A broker needs to determine his/her own strengths and weaknesses, as well as the brokerage's strengths and weaknesses. The broker needs to determine what the brokerage's own special competencies are and plan how to capitalize on them. The brokerage must be competitive.

A new broker needs to analyze the market of the predictable outside forces that the broker can manage. The broker must look at the possible environmental changes such as economic, social, political, and any other sources that could affect the broker herself and the new brokerage business. The broker should have a plan (or many plans) as to how to deal with everything that will be coming up. The broker should not wait and be unprepared. It is best to go with the old saying, "Hope for the best and plan for the worst." Those real estate brokers who are truly professional make plans. And more often than not, when they do, they succeed!

Business Goals

Real estate brokers who make goals with a plan and complete those goals take control of their own careers. They stay motivated and do not get discouraged when things are not happening as quickly as they would like. The reason? Because they know where they are going and how they are going to get there. However, a written goal without a plan of action for reaching the goal is nothing more than a piece of paper. The broker must determine what he/she wants as a goal because that is the first thing that needs to be done. Writing the goal down is the second thing. By writing the goal down, the broker gives the goal meaning. The act of writing the goal down is an act of further committing to accomplishing the goal. The broker needs to develop a plan of action that will help accomplish the goal.

Having goals to meet is the basis of the initial planning segment. It sets up the business plan. Having goals tells others that the broker is serious and has a vision, a purpose. Setting goals and then making every effort to see those goals through to fruition prove to others the broker is qualified and here to stay.

Brokers (new or experienced) always need to be involved in the initial planning of a brokerage. Either the brokerage makes sense, or maybe another route should be taken. The broker needs to ask the following critical questions:

- How much money do I want to make this year from this brokerage?
- How many closings does the office need this year?
- How many listings does the office need this year?
- How many buyers do my agents need to be working with this year?
- What segments of the market should the brokerage focus on?

Many questions could be asked during the initial planning stage, but it is best for a broker to start small and think through these five questions thoroughly before asking a multitude of other questions. Making this process more complicated than necessary can overburden the effectiveness of the planning.

The answers to the questions set up the writing of goals, which sets the writing of the business plan. Annual goals will be considered by some to be long-range goals and by others to be short-range goals. Long-term goals are typically longer than one year. Goals can be set as long-term objectives or short-term objectives. A long-term goal allows the broker to dream and allows the broker to think far into the future of what would bring self-fulfillment and happiness out of life. A long-term goal allows the broker to envision the ultimate ending of what is to be accomplished out of life. Now is the time for the broker to *dream* that goal of self-fulfillment.

Start Up or Purchase an Existing Brokerage

The initial planning stage should have addressed whether to start a brokerage or to purchase an existing brokerage. A startup is where the broker is starting from scratch. There was no real estate business in place, and now the broker has created one. A purchase is simply the buying out of a current operating brokerage. The terms of the buyout should be written by an attorney to be sure the rights and obligations of all parties are spelled out correctly and fairly.

Startups and existing brokerages each have their own advantages and difficulties. These must be weighed separately and then together to determine which has the most merit. Frequently, a real estate broker will take whatever is offered. If the broker is offered a buyout, then that is what the broker takes. If it is a startup, then the broker simply opens the doors and is ready for business.

There are a great many factors that must be weighed to determine which is right for a particular brokerage. Such things as location, cost, equipment, leases, name recognition, and long-term viability are important considerations.

The broker should have or develop a checklist to remember to consider each important aspect of forming a new startup or purchasing an existing brokerage.

Start Up a Brokerage

A startup is generally the first type of brokerage that a broker/owner will form. The startup brokerage is typically run on a tight budget. A broker who opened an office with less than a thousand dollars sold it five years later at a significant profit. Brokerages like this tend to specialize in the area where they are located. The reason for this is that they typically do not have the money to advertise outside their own small area. This is a great place for a broker to learn the brokerage business. As long as the broker does not violate a law, the risks are small. Not many mistakes this broker can make will be catastrophic. If he/she does make a marketing mistake, the total loss will be small enough for recovery.

The startup brokerage can be a large-scale startup, but it is extremely rare. If a broker has a great deal of money to invest, why start out with nothing? No agents, no place of business, and no equipment. Most large-scale brokerages get their start through acquisitions.

Small-scale startups usually involve just a single person, the broker, who runs the operation. The business can have partners, though it is rare with startups.

Starting a Brokerage Business

A broker/owner of a small-scale startup must determine the answers to the following questions to be sure that everything has been taken into account.

- Why open a real estate brokerage company?
- Does the market need another real estate brokerage company?
- Is there a completed business plan?
- Who are the owners? Investors?
- Who is to manage the brokerage? Outside advisors?
- Will the brokerage need to seek additional financing? Equity sharing?
- What is the office philosophy? The atmosphere?
- What is the experience level of the broker?
- Are there enough capital reserves to last 12 months?
- What should the business structure be?
- Has a location been chosen? Safety? Security? Room for expansion?
- Has a name been chosen?
- Who is the target market?
- Will the market expand or contract? Other acquisitions?
- What types of agents will be hired? Number? Experience level?
- What types of commission-splits will be offered? Bonuses? 100%?
- Will teams be allowed to form under the brokerage?
- Has a marketing budget been formed?
- What training will be provided? Staff? Agents? Manager?
- Have equipment requirements been specified?
- Will the equipment be new or used?
- How should the office be laid out?
- Is the business current with the national, state, and local regulations? TREC?
- Will the brokerage lease or buy a building?
- Will the brokerage consider a virtual office?
- How large a business should be acquired? Amenities? Parking? Landscaping? Cleaning?
- In what technology should the brokerage invest?
- Is the company for profit or capital gain? Both?
- Will the brokerage purchase in bulk or just in time for office supplies?
- Will the broker be full time, or will the broker need to engage in real estate sales to supplement income?
- Has a financial budget been completed? When will the company be profitable?

- What services will be offered to the public?
- What services will be offered to the brokerage agents?
- What type of staff will be needed? Temporary or permanent?
- What price should be applied to the customer services offered?
- Is there an exit strategy?

Purchasing an Existing Brokerage
A broker/owner of a buyout or purchase of an existing brokerage must answer the same questions, with the addition of the following questions:

- Why does the owner want to sell? What is the "real" reason?
- Why do you want to acquire this brokerage?
- What do the past five years of tax returns indicate?
- What are the assets that are being sold?
- What is the business structure? Corporation? Sole proprietorship? Partnership?
- How many agents are currently with the brokerage? What percentage of agents will leave? Are the agents who stay quality agents? What is the current commission-split structure?
- Are expenses in line with revenue?
- Is the local real estate market moving up? Down? Stable?
- Does the current broker/owner want a premium for "name recognition"?

A general assumption is that a buyer needs cash for a down payment to purchase an existing real estate brokerage. This is not always true, however. One broker negotiated to buy out a current brokerage with no money down, for example, and the owner financed the entire purchase. The current broker/owner had had enough and was willing to sell no matter how the deal was structured. The brokerage was a national franchise, and the ranking of that particular brokerage was 47th out of 49 offices in the region. The brokerage had been sent a termination notice. The new broker/owner bought it and within a year had turned the company around, paid off the seller finance, earned a large six-figure income, and ranked 8th out of the 49 regional offices. As a result, the franchisor no longer wanted to terminate the brokerage.

Real estate brokerages are a lot like other opportunities. If the broker must sell, that brokerage is virtually worthless; however, if another wants to buy a brokerage, that brokerage is worth millions.

Starting a Brokerage Business

Case Study

Suppose you are the broker/owner of the brokerage company mentioned above. You purchased the company (owner financed) for $75,000 with no money down. The company was in dire straits. Agents had no motivation because all of them knew that the owner was closing the doors in three months if he could not sell. You have no money for advertising or marketing. You seriously wonder if you will be able to pay next month's bills. You have to terminate the receptionist (the only staff member) because you will not be able to pay her. The national franchisor will soon terminate the franchise, and the brokerage will close.

But instead of accepting the fate of failure, you motivate the current agents to succeed. You train them in the ways to make real money in the real estate business. You teach them how to "close" the deal and make large commissions while at all times protecting your clients. After approximately four months of struggling, you begin to see profits, which steadily grow through the year end.

You have succeeded! You took a failing company and made it hugely profitable, the franchisor no longer wants to terminate, and you are now number 8 in the region out of all other real estate offices. It is so great that the franchisor wants to give you a trophy for making it into the Top Ten in the Region.

At the award ceremony, you are asked to come up on stage to receive your award for being in the Top Ten in the Region for the year—a year YOU created! How does that make you feel? How proud do you feel at this moment?

You get back to the office table and show all your agents the award. Every one of them, to a person, stated, "Look what WE did!" The same people who were failing before your training and efforts are now claiming, "Look what WE did!"

How Do You Respond?

Consider the ways you could respond to your agents. You could:

1. respond silently, not to create a scene. However, you resent their taking of your award and the moment in time that was yours.
2. take your trophy (because it is yours!) and walk off, stating, "This was given to me, and this is mine!"

3. explode and declare, "Without me you would have failed! I was the only difference in the year and I saved your sorry hides!"
4. politely explain to them that it was your training and efforts that made the difference. You should therefore be respected for that effort.
5. tell them what they want to hear: "You all were so great this year! And this is proof! Congratulations everyone on a job well done!"

Which Should You Choose? To motivate and encourage your agents, there is only one way to respond. The only answer is to tell them what they want to hear: "You all were so great this year! And this is proof! Congratulations everyone on a job well done! This may hurt, but it is the thing for a good broker to do. Indeed, the most important reason that a broker/owner turns into a successful broker/owner is wanting to inspire success in other people!

If a broker truly has that goal in his/her heart then the broker feels joy in seeing others succeed from his/her efforts. Yes, it would be great to get that recognition, but it is great to see others get that recognition. A broker must always act for and on behalf of his/her agents and place them first above self. This is the same fiduciary duty that the agents owe to their clients.

Method of Purchasing an Existing Brokerage

Probably the best way to learn how to run a real estate brokerage is by successfully owning and operating a startup brokerage company. The knowledge and experience gained in this way give the broker an advantage when negotiating for the purchase of an ongoing brokerage business. How does a broker find another broker who may want to sell?

A broker who wants to purchase an existing brokerage should start by asking every one of the local brokers out to lunch. It does not matter whether the target broker has shown any interest in selling. During the conversation, if the target broker indicates dissatisfaction in owning the brokerage, that would open the door for further discussion. If the target broker does not indicate interest in selling, two things have been accomplished: establishing rapport with a competitor and positioning oneself for a possible future purchase should a broker decide to sell later.

Rapport with a Competitor Too many times brokerages consider competition to be negative. Competition is negative, however, only if the broker lets it become negative. Most brokers have their own different goals and do not really compete head-to-head. One broker may be specializing in upper Fort Worth, whereas another brokerage is in Westside. These two brokers do not compete directly, but if they merge, the merged brokerage now has an interest in both areas. Competition does not need to be negative, of course; it should be positive and breed creativity.

They May Sell Later The second reason to take competitive brokers to lunch is to be their first option when they do begin to think of selling. It may happen soon or it may be years before a competitive broker decides to sell, but at least the startup broker is positioned to be the competition's first option when he/she does want to sell. During lunch the competitor may also state that he/she is not interested in selling but knows of a broker who would be willing to talk. No matter what the outcome, this action is "working the business," and that always leads to success.

Choosing a Business Type

Selecting a type of office is one of the most important aspects of beginning a real estate brokerage office. Choosing the right office type could give a broker the boost to become a leader in the real estate industry. Choosing the wrong office type could ruin the brokerage business's chances or at best cost the broker thousands of dollars. Many individuals enter the real estate brokerage business and never think about the type of office they want and should have. There are several types to examine.

Mom-and-Pop Shops

The mom-and-pop shop usually comprises a single broker working alone or with his/her spouse. These brokers work out of their home, so their overhead is minimal. They usually are veterans in the real estate industry and now sell only to their friends and past clients. Because of their low overhead, these types of brokerages will always be around. These mom-and-pop shops have few services and are not technologically savvy. They survive only because people love to do business with

them. The real estate business is a relationship business, and the mom-and-pop shops are best at relationships.

Individually, mom-and-pop shops represent a very small number of sales, but when grouped all together they can make up a huge force. Gathered together in "associations," they have a more powerful voice and referral networks.

Niche Offices

Niche offices (also called boutiques) are quite similar to mom-and-pop shops, except that they usually have an office separate from their home. These offices will specialize. They may specialize (i.e., have a "niche") in the sale of fine homes in a specific area. They may make a "point of interest" their "niche." such as the Alamo Agents. They may be the designated real estate company for a local business corporation, such as Hamilton Corporation Real Estate. Whatever their niche, they rarely venture outside it because they cannot serve a huge community as well as they do their niche.

Single Office with a Broker and Fewer Than Five License Holders

A single office with a broker and fewer than five license holders is generally a start up real estate office. This may begin when a broker-associate of a real estate office believes he/she can do a better job than that office and rents office space, buys some yard signs, and starts up his/her own real estate office. On the way out the door, the broker-associate takes some friends along, angering the previous broker/owner (this is one reason why the real estate brokerage business is considered cutthroat.) This type of brokerage is usually an independent office with no support from any other source. It is also usually underfunded, so the marketing and advertising budget is small or non-existent. The single-office firms require little capital to begin, and their limited access to capital may inhibit growth opportunities associated with investment in technology and infrastructure.

The reason this type of office can succeed is that these brokerages can specialize in one particular area or one particular type of real estate. They tend to specialize in buyer brokerage, fine homes and estates, or the like.

A smaller independent broker is able to implement changes faster than bigger franchised brokerages; pay commissions on the day of settlement; and keep overhead low. And the broker tends to be more of a friend, not a dictator.

Single Office with a Broker and More Than 5 License Holders but Fewer Than 50

A single office with the broker and more than five license holders but fewer than 50 is an agency that has grown from only a handful of people to a midsize real estate office. The office will begin to specialize in the services offered to its license holders, such as providing a real estate trainer to help the salespersons make more money. Then it may hire a recruiter to go out and build the office. Accounting functions will become more centralized, and the broker/owner will begin to concentrate on the direction the company is to take instead of focusing on day-to-day operations. The broker/owner will continue this process until the office grows into the next type.

Single Office with a Broker and More Than 50 License Holders

A single office with the broker and more than 50 license holders is a large office, and there are usually several people managing the office. The space occupied must accommodate the large number of salespersons. This type of office can balloon to have more than 1,000 real estate salespersons under one roof. Because of the large number of real estate salespersons, these offices are typically found in large metropolitan areas. The services offered to their salespersons are highly specialized, with numerous support staff. These large-market single firms are more likely to be franchised brokerages and use this affiliation to offer larger-firm services.

The advantage of a single firm is that the company can negotiate for floor space for only one office instead of negotiating for multiple offices in remote locations. Keeping all operations under one roof is a huge cost savings. All the services to the community and to the sales force are located in one place. The disadvantage is that the company may be a considerable distance from some of the communities it serves.

Two to Five Offices Owned by One Broker with Fewer Than 100 License Holders

Having two to five offices owned by one broker with fewer than 100 license holders illustrates the theory that it is better to have several small to midsize offices in several areas than one centrally located large office. Each type of brokerage has its own advantages and disadvantages. The large, centralized office has many economies of scale and can buy and move supplies around with ease. The multi-office setup can serve the community from within the community.

The services offered to the license holders are usually offered at the local offices. Each office works independently, with the company providing marketing and support. The two-to-five-office system can still be managed by one broker/owner by employing office managers in each office to handle the day-to-day operations.

More Than Five Offices and More than 100 License Holders

Once a real estate company achieves the status of having more than five offices and more than 100 license holders, it has usually formed a corporation. These companies control major segments of the sales process. Most have huge advertising budgets and expensive marketing materials, and they may even venture into television. Almost all real estate offices are constantly hiring real estate salespersons, but in these types of offices hiring new salespersons becomes their lifeblood. Without a steady stream of new real estate salespersons, these companies cannot afford the structure they have put in place. The top 250 firms (there are over 30,000 real estate firms) represent 24% of all real estate salespersons and one in six home sales. This number represents the impact the megafirms have on the real estate industry.

Some real estate salespersons believe a bigger office offers more opportunity once the brokerage is established. These salespersons did not want to be the "big fish" in the small pond; they would rather be a little fish and still have room to thrive and achieve.

To grow and prosper, these vertically expanded firms have broadened their operations and product lines to include ancillary services. *Ancillary services* are real estate-related businesses that turn into profit centers for the brokerage business. These services will be discussed later.

Marketing Companies

A real estate marketing company is a nontraditional real estate company that does not represent a party to the transaction but, rather, helps the sellers market their property. The marketing company offers services on smorgasbord-type packages. Each service can be paid for separately or in bundles at a discount. These services are paid for upfront, and the seller pays only a commission to the selling salesperson who finds a buyer. These marketing companies appeal to the price-conscious consumer and do-it-yourself home sellers who are willing to conduct some aspects of the real estate transaction themselves. Customers of marketing companies are likely to be drawn from the For Sale by Owner (FSBO) clientele, who represent less than 20% of transactions in any given year. New construction is another source of potential clientele (i.e., the builders) for the marketing company.

The marketing companies rarely provide representation for a client; rather, they provide the marketing that is difficult for individual sellers. Some of the services could include:

print advertising	internet exposure	open houses
office tours	mortgage support	contract forms
buyer qualification	access to multiple listing service (MLS)	title support
key boxes		color graphics
sign info boxes	broker luncheons	home warranties
property staging	property showing	seller's net sheets
price determinations	contract negotiations	inspections
yard signs	appraisals	closing details

Typically the marketing company will group these services into packages and offer their clients a discount if they order a package. If they chose access to MLS, the clients would have to ensure that the selling salesperson who brought the buyer would be compensated separately. The "marketing" concept is growing in status, but it will be mostly concentrated in a few sellers who have the time and patience to sell their own homes.

Independent Offices

Independent offices are real estate brokerages owned by a person or an entity not associated with a national franchise. These companies survive and thrive because they can act and react on a moment's notice. They tend to serve niche markets and specialize in their marketing. Their size is typically small, but some dominate multistate regions. These companies operate as a family business, and their corporate structure is very flat, with the owner/broker making the decisions. Generally, the owner/broker knows every salesperson in the company and knows the families of the salespersons as well. The independent office is the easiest and least expensive real estate operation to start up and as such is the most frequently used type. Independent offices can survive the future, but they must remain on the cutting edge and be open to the changes their clients demand.

National Franchise Offices

The national franchise office is part of a group of brokers who have national ties with a larger company. The national franchiser does not usually own individual offices but, rather, offers services and systems to the local franchisee. The advantages of this type of company include proven brokerage systems and an advertising budget into tens of millions of dollars.

Most actual real estate offices have very little contact with their corporate franchise. Instead, they manage their day-to-day operations just the same as independent offices. The advantages include marketing on an international level, real estate systems that have a proven track record, and the support of a team of real estate professionals that only big money could buy. The disadvantage of the franchise is that there are certain franchise rules the franchisee must abide by. Most of the rules are determined to be the best for all franchisees, but occasionally they limit the quick response that this business demands. Second, not all these services are provided for free. The cost to the franchisee could be staggering.

International Franchises

The national franchise and the international franchise operate in virtually the same way, except that the international franchise has real estate offices in foreign countries. That being said, international operations bring countless new challenges. The laws, regulations, and customs will vary drastically from country to country and pose critical problems and opportunities. The "big boys" are the only ones to tackle this type of real estate company. There are no independent international operations.

Neighborhood Offices
A neighborhood office is usually a small office with sights set on being the experts in a localized area. These offices specialize in knowing the area, people, and events in that specific neighborhood. The neighborhood office is almost always an independent office with no ties to a national franchise.

Unlike a "niche" office, the only thing these offices specialize in is location. They are located in a particular neighborhood, and that is their market. Their marketing efforts are solely targeted at their neighborhood. Most of their business comes by referrals and "word-of-mouth," so a huge advertising budget is unnecessary. Any listings or sales outside their market come up only by chance. These offices are highly visible, always present in the area. They participate in and often lead neighborhood activities and events.

Community Offices
Community offices serve a wider area than the neighborhood offices, often encompassing an entire community. These offices take pride in being a centerpiece of the community. Several members of the office usually have prominent places in the local government or on school boards. The salespersons are active in charity events, sporting events, and school activities. Very little advertising outside the community ever takes place because it is not necessary for this type of office.

Community offices generally start off as neighborhood offices that expand their reach until they have encompassed the entire community. These offices work hard to earn the respect of the community they serve.

City Offices
City offices are located within a city and concentrate their efforts on the entire city. In many cases, this type of operation will have multiple offices to cover the entire city. The marketing is not as fixed on communities as it is on exposure throughout the entire city. There is less and less of marketing to events and activities and more and more of a "shotgun" approach, appealing to the masses. Local marketing is left to the salespersons.

These companies receive a great deal of their business from the media, and their salespersons usually work with clients they are meeting for the first time. This needs to be explained to their salespersons because it is tempting to "sell 'em and leave 'em," meaning simply that the salesperson makes a sale and never contacts the client again. If a city office is ever to succeed, its salespersons must make a concentrated effort to build referral business.

Multistate Offices

As mentioned, a real estate company could consider its market in multiple states. The company must have licenses in each state it is to serve. Generally, where the transaction actually occurs is the state of record. The coordination of this type of operation is complex. The "home"-state salespersons may feel that they are superior to all other salespersons. The events that occur must include all members, and no matter what, some will feel left out. If operations are not monitored carefully, there might be a mutiny.

Most national franchises started out as a single office. They grew in stature and wealth. They then expanded markets and bought or developed surrounding offices. That expansion continued even into neighboring states. And finally, they formed a franchise and sold the rights to the organization across the globe. So if there is a multistate operation, it may be the next international franchise.

Regional Offices

Regional offices focus on an entire region. A real estate brokerage company in California may take the region of southern California as its market area. A broker in Texas may take the north Texas region. A company near a state's border may select a tristate area as its market area. Each of these choices brings with it any number of problems and scenarios. The coverage can almost always be obtained only by the use of multiple offices. Marketing in this type of real estate company is twofold. First, the company must market each separate office locally. Second, it must market itself as a total entity to the region.

Choosing a Business Structure

The real estate brokerage business can be operated using several different business structures. Determining the type of business structure should be well thought out, possibly with the advice of an attorney, because it is difficult to change the business structure at a later date. The most common types of brokerage business structures include:

- sole proprietorship
- partnerships
- limited liability corporations (LLCs)
- corporations

Real estate brokers need to know the laws and rules that govern any business structure they are considering. This is the reason that an attorney is suggested, so that the broker can discuss what the broker wants and needs and how the business structure can aid or hinder these goals. Each business type is seen differently under the law. The business structure affects everything from tax status to disposition upon death and the liability of the broker in a legal proceeding involving the brokerage.

Sole Proprietorship

A sole proprietorship is the ownership of a brokerage by one person. The brokerage is held under the name of the broker unless the broker files a fictitious name with the state. The business is the owner. If more than one owner wants to own the brokerage, then a partnership would be a more likely choice. This type of business structure is the easiest to set up and the fastest to get operational. The owner of the brokerage must have an active broker's license or hire a licensed broker to be able to hold other real estate licenses.

Texas has no state regulations requiring a sole proprietorship to file for compliance. The only issue is if the business name must be registered with the state by filing for a "Doing Business As" (DBA). A DBA is used so the state can find the owner. For example, if Dan Hamilton wanted to start a brokerage business and name it Hamilton Real Estate, Mr. Hamilton would need to obtain a DBA that would read, Dan Hamilton DBA Hamilton Real Estate and file that DBA with TREC. Dan Hamilton now has two names for which he is totally liable. No reports are due to the commission monthly, quarterly, or yearly. The broker has to keep his/her broker's license active and pay the broker license dues, but no dues or fees are necessary for the brokerage to pay.

These sole proprietorship–type brokerages typically remain small with only a few license holders active. Rarely does a sole proprietorship become large because the brokerage will change structure before that happens. To terminate a sole proprietorship the broker must notify any licensed agents and notify TREC of the termination.

Partnerships

A partnership can be two people or multiple people who form a brokerage for the mutual benefit of all the parties involved. A partnership gives all partners the ability to own a brokerage together. Partnerships allow for the synergy of people together, and people working together can achieve more than the same as individuals working alone. The partnership should help extend the reach of the brokerage, enabling it to find, market, and obtain business from a wider area than could be possible with each person working individually.

There are two main types of partnerships, general and limited.

General Partnerships

A general partnership is formed when all members of the partnership are full partners. Each has the ability to bind the partnership to agreements, and all share in the profits and losses. A general partnership is assumed if no partnership agreement that states otherwise is in place.

Limited Partnerships

Limited partnerships allow for one or more general partners to operate a brokerage business, and they involve multiple limited partners who invest in the business. The general partners are the ones who make business decisions for the partnership and are the only ones who are personally liable for the partnership. The limited partners are liable only for their investment. Suppose a brokerage was formed using a limited partnership. One general partner and three limited partners put up $35,000 each. The brokerage was sued and lost $250,000. The limited partners would lose their investment but would have no further liability. The general partner is responsible for everything now and into the future.

Limited Liability Corporation

An LLC is a business structure that requires each member of the LLC to be a real estate–licensed broker. Each broker works separately and is responsible only for his/her own business. No income is shared, and no liability is shared. Each member shares in the cost of the brokerage—for example, sharing the cost for a receptionist to handle all of the members' incoming calls, sharing in the cost of the office space, and sharing in any other expense that benefits all members. Members could agree to share in marketing and have a better marketing campaign working together than separately. Each member is allowed to make as much money as each can without sharing the income. A member who wants to leave the LLC would be allowed to do so without any real issue. If all agree to dissolve the LLC, then it terminates. If a new broker wants to join the LLC, then upon a vote the new broker is in or out.

If a member violates the law and is sued, that broker is the only one who is liable and the LLC is held separate. For this reason, each LLC member must be a Texas real estate broker, or this advantage is lost. The LLC should become a more popular business structure in the brokerage industry.

Corporation

The corporate structure is used frequently in the real estate business, especially for the larger brokerages. A corporation can hold a real estate broker's license as long as a person working for the corporation is a designated broker. The corporate business structure has several important characteristics:

1. Ownership is determined by shares of interest. Each share has a value and a percentage of ownership. These shares can be held by only a few or can be offered to the general public.

2. Because a corporation is an entity itself, it creates limits of liability for shareholders. This limitation is not complete. A corporate charter can be broken by a court order, and then the directors of the corporation could be liable.
3. A corporation is perpetual. It continues on no matter who owns shares or whether there is a management change. A corporation can be dissolved, but until it is dissolved it remains an entity.

The corporate structure takes care of a major issue in the real estate business, and that is the death or incapacitation of the broker. With a sole proprietor business structure, all employment agreements (listing agreements and buyer representation agreements) are the property of that particular broker. All the license holders under that broker are directly tied to that broker. If the proprietary broker dies suddenly, then all the employment agreements die also: All license holders become inactive. The license holders must find another broker, and the sellers (or buyers) must create an agency relationship with another broker.

With the corporate business structure, if the designated broker dies, the corporation remains active; the corporation is perpetual and lasts forever. The employment contracts are in the name of the corporation and do not have to be altered.

Naming the Brokerage

The right name can sometimes make all the difference when it comes to propelling a brokerage to success. Names are quite powerful. Each one is distinct. The right name will enable branding to be easier and more effective. A business name cannot be changed easily. The name is the broker's choice, and agents should not be involved in deciding what to call the brokerage. This action of involving agents, even though it may seem like a good idea, will ultimately alienate more agents than those made happy.

Here are a few things to consider:

1. *The name needs to sound good.* Many people will say the brokerage name, and so it should be easy to pronounce. It should not tie the tongue in knots. If the broker wants his/her name in the brokerage name, it too should be easy to pronounce. A name like Pheounastras Real Estate may not be appropriate. A name like DaWong Numba Realtors many send the wrong

message when answering the brokerage office telephone. Also, some names can be modified into some really awkward words.

It is best not to use the broker's name for two other reasons. First, when it comes time to sell, the brokerage will be much more difficult to sell if the broker/owner will leave. It could also lead to misunderstandings from the public if the brokerage sign reads, for example, Dan Hamilton Real Estate and there is no Dan Hamilton anywhere to be found. Second, some names could be judged to be a certain national origin and could lead to potential discrimination.

2. *The name needs to have a meaning and convey a benefit.* When a person hears or reads the brokerage name he/she should know immediately what the business is about. A name like Mansfield Real Estate is simple, but anyone in Mansfield will know what that business does. Make sure the name is not too generic. Best Real Estate Company shows no distinction. The broker should not try to be everything to everybody with the brokerage name: Commercial, Residential, Farm and Ranch, Property Management, Leasing, and Industrial Real Estate are far too long and too much to generate any business.

3. *The name should not be too clever.* Names for brokerage companies should be professional. A name such as Houses 4 U will confuse some people. Real Estate Frum Frum (so named because the broker's name is Alice Frum), is clever but not effective for a brokerage. Avoid any name that appears too clever.

4. *The name should be complete and without abbreviations.* A name like B.S. Realty may not communicate Bob Smith Realty. If it is important enough to have in a name, it is important enough to spell it out. However, the name should not be too long; otherwise it will be a beating to the consumer. The name The Best Real Estate Company for Mansfield, Texas, and Surrounding Area may be descriptive, but it would probably give consumers a tired head to recall or repeat.

5. *The name cannot be used by another.* Every name must be searched in the office of the Texas Secretary of State. The broker should not try to "steal" a name, one too similar to that of another brokerage, because a lawsuit later could ruin the brokerage's finances. A name such as IBM Real Estate may be descriptive of the clients served but also may be a name infringement and

may result in a lawsuit. Dan Hamilton Realtors may be a violation of the National Association of REALTORS®.

6. *The name should not be the name of a city.* The simple reason for this is expansion. It is very difficult to use a brokerage name of one city in another without changing the name and losing the synergies of multiple offices. Naming the brokerage after a city may be a good idea initially for a small independent, but expansion will be difficult.
7. *The name should make sense to the people using the brokerage.* It may be clever to have the name "We Are the Number One Brokerage" in Latin, as Numerus Unus Sumus Brocur! However, not many people understand Latin, so the meaning will be lost on most of the people interested in engaging the services of the business.
8. *The purchase of an existing brokerage has naming considerations.* If a broker already owns a brokerage and purchases another brokerage, should the broker change the name to the match the existing company? Doing this could lose all the name recognition earned by the purchased company. The acquired agents may leave because of the name change. Changing a name has inherent costs (e.g., signs, marketing materials, etc.). However, if the previous name is kept, the brokerage may lose the synergy that two brokerages would obtain. Members of one office could feel that they are the favored office, and internal fighting could occur.

The broker should take all these suggestions and then consult a trademark attorney, a marketing expert, to verify that the name is legal and impactful.

Configuring the Brokerage

The configuring of the brokerage is another step to get ready to open for business. A properly configured brokerage business has the correct equipment for business and has it in the correct place. Everything in the office and surrounding the office should be considered. The brokerage will run more effectively and efficiently when the brokerage is configured correctly. The flow of the office makes work less laborious and monotonous. Taking the configuration of the brokerage office into account is of utmost important because once set, configuration becomes much more difficult, if not unfeasible, to alter.

The broker should consider a number of factors when opening a new real estate brokerage; these are explained next.

Office Identity

Identity must be consistent throughout a brokerage. Lack of consistency in a broker's message will dilute the brokerage and its recruiting effectiveness. A broker decides he/she wants to project an office image in which the salespersons are empowered to make decisions on their own and have a great deal of autonomy. But in action, the broker rules with an iron fist. The broker is now sending mixed messages to his/her salespersons and the real estate community. Frequently a broker just lets the office identity develop on its own. This could lead to disaster. A broker must plan what type of identity he/she wants and then systematically engage in behaviors that enhance the opportunity for the identity to develop.

A broker should consult with potential customers and others to get their visions of how they see the brokerage's identity. A broker should ask local city council members how the city government views the brokerage's identity. Finally, a broker should meet with every agent in the brokerage to find out their perception of the brokerage's identity.

Signage

A real estate office should have some sort of outside signage. The signage alerts the general public to the presence of the brokerage and identifies the services provided. The outside sign should be elevated on a pole or rooftop—the higher and bigger, the better. The broker wants people from as far away as possible to see the brokerage sign. This is business, and bigger is better. The broker should consult someone from the city to be sure of the signage restrictions and consult the owner of the building for signage restrictions if the broker is leasing space.

The best and most expensive signs are lighted. A lighted sign is not only visible during the day, but because it is lighted it is a sales tool even through the night and stormy weather. The sign should be simple and be seen from both directions. The colors should match the colors of the brokerage. The sign should not have a lot of information on it because it will be too busy, and busy signs will not be read by cars passing by. The sign should have the name of the brokerage, the logo of the brokerage, and the main telephone number of the brokerage, and that is it.

The broker should drive by the brokerage monthly and be sure no tree branches block the view of the sign. If a light bulb in the sign goes out, that light bulb needs to be replaced as soon as possible. Once the sign begins to wear and fade, the broker needs to replace it, no matter the cost. The only thing worse than no sign is a sign in disrepair. That indicates that the broker is not successful or that the broker simply does not care. The front door should have signage to indicate the brokerage and the business hours. This can be lettering or a professional separate sign.

The front window should have the brokerage name, logo, and the telephone number. Some brokers place listing sheets in the windows of currently held listings. This is a great marketing idea if there is a high number of walk-by traffic. The listing sheet must be professionally displayed, framed, and current. Again, if the display looks sloppy, then the brokerage is viewed as the same.

High-Speed Internet

The real estate office should provide high-speed internet service to its license holders. Real estate license holders use the computer to search the internet or a multiple listing service (MLS). They search listings to determine properties their clients may want to view. They search the internet for listing and buyer leads. They search listings to help sellers determine the best possible price for their property. Without high-speed internet, these searches would take forever.

Brokerages are more of a stop-by place than a place to conduct business. Brokerage offices are smaller than they were 10 years ago because real estate professionals are no longer tied to the office. The internet allows real estate licensees to do business on the move or from their house. This is not an excuse for a broker not to have the latest in high-speed access to the internet. The brokerage office should be a haven for the license holder. Licensees should be able to trust that if they need to stop by the office to do some work, the internet is sufficiently fast for them to be able to get the work completed. Nothing is more embarrassing for a license holder than to have a client next to him/her in the office and be unable to get an internet connection.

Parking

A broker should not discount the importance of parking and should not forget to negotiate adequate parking in any lease. The brokerage company will need parking for the license holders, staff, and clients.

Too little parking can result in a drastic drop in sales because, if there is not enough parking, people will find another brokerage. The broker can make estimates or hire a space planner to design the parking needs the brokerage will have over the next 10 years. Again, trying to get additional parking after a lease is signed is expensive and may not be possible.

The broker needs to consider where the parking area is located. Is it on the property, across the street, or in a separate lot? If it is in town, is there adequate free parking in front of the building, or is all the parking in a parking garage that requires payment? If the brokerage validates the latter type of parking, how much will it cost the brokerage each month? This may not seem like a big deal, but there are real estate brokerages struggling because they have limited parking in front of their office, so their license holders have to park in back to leave adequate parking spaces for the public. An additional problem is that when there are no customers in an office as a result of inadequate parking, the office looks closed.

A broker may choose to mark the parking spots with signs that read, "Parking for Acme Real Estate, All Others Will Be Towed." This keeps spaces open for customers but can create ill will toward the brokerage within the community that the brokerage is serving. Also, will the broker actually call for a car to be towed? Most brokers would not want that negative public image.

The broker will need to determine the condition of the parking area. Are there holes and cracks in the parking lot? Are the painted lines visible? It is best to have these concerns addressed and repairs made before a lease is signed because, after the fact, parking may be difficult to be remedied without costing the broker a great deal of money.

Outside Break Area
The broker needs to consider building an outside break area for license holders. This break area allows license holders to meet in an informal setting. It enables license holders to eat outside the office, rather than inside, at their desks. It is unprofessional for license holders to eat at their desks. The food inside makes the entire office smell. The license holder may not clean up after eating, and clients can see the mess. None of this is acceptable or professional.

An outside break area is ideal for the license holders who smoke cigarettes or vapor pipes. This activity should not be allowed in any office. Some people have a really negative view of smoking, and others have respiratory issues; in some areas, smoking is a violation of city code. Having an outside break area gives these license holders a place to smoke without causing offense. The break area need not be air conditioned or heated, but such climate control would be best if the expense is not unbearable. The break area should have tables and chairs and some sort of cover to protect against the sun and rain.

Landscaping

Landscaping is one of those expense items that is most often forgotten or neglected. However, if the property the broker is buying or leasing has neglected landscaping, the broker may have to compensate. Landscaping may be the first impression a potential client will receive. If that is impressive, the brokerage is impressive. If that impression is dead, so is the brokerage.

The broker should regularly stroll around the brokerage property—at least twice a day—and take along a checklist to make notes on additions and subtractions that should be made to the exterior landscaping. The exterior is easily overlooked and neglected.

If the broker owns the property, the broker should consider adding trees to give shade and add beauty to the property. The trees should be hearty so that replanting is not a factor. The trees purchased should be consistent with the temperatures in the local area. The trees should not be planted too close to any buildings because the roots can cause major damage to the foundation, and the limbs can cause damage to the roof of a building. Trees can be set in large planters and appear very decorative and inviting to the general public.

If there is no land for landscaping, the broker should hire a company to provide plants in planters and to maintain those plants. A brokerage looks cold and uninviting if there are no plants or flowers. Hanging plants are perfect for this type of brokerage. Finally, too much of anything is not good either. If there is a plant on every square inch of the brokerage, then the brokerage no longer looks like a brokerage business but like a flower business. Landscaping can be expensive, but in general it is worth the investment.

The foregoing are just a few of the considerations a broker needs to make when configuring the brokerage. Configuring a brokerage business is simply thinking through everything that is necessary to open the brokerage. The more time the broker spends thinking through the requirements of opening the brokerage, the better.

CHAPTER SUMMARY

Real estate brokers will fail in their endeavors if they approach the broker's position as they did their previous career. The first reason a broker/owner fails is lack of planning. Here are some others:

- lack of funds, or undercapitalization
- lack of management experience
- lack of focus
- lack of specialization

The most important aspect of any business is the initial planning. During the initial planning stage a potential broker/owner will need to determine if he/she has what it takes, has the finances to make it, and enters a market that will afford another competitor.

A broker must have certain characteristics and skills to be successful in the real estate industry. There are basic characteristics of really talented brokers, such as being:

emotionally stable	empathetic	enthusiastic
conscientious	commanding	tough minded
self-assured	composed	highly energized
intuitive	mature	team oriented

When a broker begins operations as a real estate company, the broker must do the following:

1. obtain business name approval
2. file legal paperwork
3. create an evidence-of-trust account
4. provide financial protection for the consumer
5. pay appropriate fees for company registration
6. obtain licensing:
    a. meet qualifying education requirements
    b. meet experience requirements
    c. file a broker license application
    d. pass the license exam

Real estate brokers who make goals with a plan and complete these goals take control of their own careers. Brokers needs to ask the following critical questions:

- How much money do I want to make this year from this brokerage?
- How many closings does the office need this year?
- How many listings does the office need this year?
- How many buyers do my agents need to be working with this year?
- What segments of the market should the brokerage focus on?

The answers to these questions set up the writing of goals, which in turn initiates the writing of the business plan.

The initial planning stage should have addressed whether to start a brokerage or to purchase an existing brokerage. Startups and existing brokerages each have their own advantages and difficulties. However, a startup is generally the first type of brokerage that a person will form.

Selecting a type of office is one of the most important aspects of beginning a real estate brokerage office.

The mom-and-pop shop is usually a single broker working alone or with his/her spouse.

Niche (also called boutique) offices are quite similar to the mom-and-pop shops, except that they usually have an office separate from their home.

A single office with the broker and fewer than five license holders is generally a start up real estate office. This type of office is usually an independent brokerage with no support from any other source.

A single office with the broker and more than five license holders but fewer than 50 is an agency that has grown from only a handful of people to a midsize real estate office. The office will begin to specialize in the services offered to its license holders.

A single office with the broker and more than 50 license holders is a large office and usually has several people managing the office.

Two to five offices owned by one broker with fewer than 100 license holders practices the theory that it is better to have several small to mid-size offices in several areas than one centrally located large office.

Once a real estate company achieves the status of having more than five offices and more than 100 license holders, the company has usually formed a corporation.

A real estate marketing company is a nontraditional real estate company that does not represent a party to the transaction but, rather, helps sellers market their property.

Independent offices are real estate brokerages owned by a person or an entity not associated with a national franchise.

The national franchise office is part of a group of brokers who have national ties with a larger company.

A neighborhood office is usually a small office with sights set on being the experts in a localized area.

Community offices serve a wider area than the neighborhood offices, often encompassing an entire community.

City offices are located within a city and concentrate their efforts on the entire city.

Regional offices focus on an entire region.

The real estate brokerage business can be operated using several different business structures. The most common types of brokerage business structure include:

- sole proprietorships
- partnerships
- LLCs (limited liability corporations)
- corporations

Real estate brokers need to know the laws and rules governing any business structure the broker is considering.

A sole proprietorship is the ownership of a brokerage by one person.

A partnership can be two people or multiple people who form a brokerage for the mutual benefit of all the parties involved.

A general partnership is formed, and all members of the partnership are full partners.

Limited partnerships allow for one or more general partners to operate a brokerage business and multiple limited partners who invest in the business.

An LLC is a business structure that requires each member of the LLC to be a real estate–licensed broker.

A corporation can hold a real estate broker's license as long as a person working for the corporation is a designated broker. The corporate business structure has several important characteristics:

- Ownership is determined by shares of interest. Each share has a value and a percentage of ownership. These shares can be held by only a few or can be offered to the general public.
- Because a corporation is an entity itself, it creates limits of liability for shareholders. This limitation is not complete. A corporate

charter can be broken by a court order, and then the directors of the corporation could be liable.
- A corporation is perpetual. It continues on no matter who owns shares or whether there is a management change. A corporation can be dissolved, but until it is dissolved it remains an entity.

The right name can sometimes make all the difference when it comes to propelling a brokerage to success. The name:

- needs to sound good
- needs to have a meaning and convey a benefit
- should not be too clever
- should be complete and without abbreviations
- cannot be used by another
- should not be the name of a city
- should make sense to the people using the brokerage

Furthermore, the purchase of an existing brokerage has naming considerations.

The broker should consider the following when opening a new real estate brokerage:

- The office identity must be consistent throughout a brokerage.
- A real estate office should have some sort of outside signage.
- The real estate office should provide its license holders with high-speed internet service.
- The broker should not discount the importance of parking and should not forget to negotiate adequate parking in any lease.
- The broker needs to consider building an outside break area for the license holders.

CHAPTER QUESTIONS

1. What is the typical broker lacking when starting a brokerage business?
   A. real estate knowledge and closing techniques
   B. business knowledge and risk management
   C. listing and selling skills
   D. appraisal knowledge and inspection knowledge

2. What are some reasons that brokers fail in the brokerage business?
   A. lack of management experience
   B. lack of focus
   C. lack of specialization
   D. all of the answer choices

3. Which of the following is NOT needed to be thought through when opening a brokerage?
   A. purpose of the brokerage
   B. racial makeup of the office's surrounding area
   C. positioning the brokerage will take
   D. all of the answer choices

4. What is it called when the broker that takes control and asserts power when necessary?
   A. commanding
   B. resourceful
   C. stubborn
   D. intimidating

5. Where should a broker file a DBA (Doing Business As)?
   A. local sheriff's office
   B. county courthouse
   C. federal courthouse
   D. DBAs do not need to be filed to be valid

6. Which of the following courses is NOT required for real estate license application?
   A. Real Estate Principles I
   B. Real Estate Principles II
   C. Real Estate Principles III
   D. Real Estate Law of Contracts

7. Which of the following questions should a broker never ask when planning a brokerage?
   A. How many buyers do my agents need to be working with this year?
   B. What segments of the market should the brokerage focus on?
   C. How much profit should the brokerage make next year?
   D. Which racial group should the brokerage concentrate on marketing to?

8. Which of the following questions should be asked on a small-scale start up brokerage?
   A. What types of commission-splits will be offered? Bonuses? 100%?
   B. Will teams be allowed to form under the brokerage?
   C. Has a marketing budget been formed?
   D. All of the answer choices are valid.

9. What is typically the best attitude toward competitors?
   A. resent them
   B. sabotage them
   C. build rapport with them
   D. disparage them

10. What type of office is owned by a person or an entity not associated with a national franchise?
    A. Century 21 Real Estate Corporation
    B. medium-sized brokerages
    C. independent offices
    D. single office with fewer than five license holders

CHAPTER 3

Ethical and Legal Business Practices

All real estate business falls under the purview of the state's real estate commission. The commission regulates the operations and activities of real estate brokers and their license holders. The regulations have become more stringent because of pressure from consumers to be treated in an honest manner. Agency laws have defined the relationships of the real estate brokerage business. The agency laws spell out how brokers and salespersons should represent their clients and the duties they should perform. The real estate broker must know these laws and how they can affect the real estate business.

Ethics Defined

Ethics refers to "moral character." The major principle of ethics comes from the Latin *primum non nocere,* meaning "First, do no harm." The words "legal" and "ethical" mean different things. Legal is the lowest standard—for example, everyone must obey the law—and personal ethics is the highest standard. Personal ethics is how a person acts when no one is around. Forcing real estate salespersons to be ethical does not work. They must realize the importance of ethics. Ethics leads to the most vital ingredient in any relationship: trust. Of all the strategies to attract consumers, nothing is as powerful or as profitable as ethics. It takes courage to follow high ethical standards, to place the interests of consumers first. In the long term, however, the rewards to consumers and salespersons are magnificent.

Canons of Ethics

The sections that follow introduce some overall ethics standards brokers should incorporate in their brokerage firm operations and apply to their relationships with clients.

Legal Law

Real estate salespersons will at all times obey the legal law and regulations applicable to real estate license holders in their state. The real estate salesperson should keep current with any changes in the laws by taking classes and attending seminars on important topics. These regulations also apply to the rules established by their broker. This is a legal matter, but the ethics of the broker will not allow any real estate license holder to get around the law. Some people believe that as long as a person is not caught, getting around the law is no big deal.

Ethics states the opposite. Getting around the law is a violation; it is a big deal. A person should not even consider violating or even skirting a law or regulation.

Moral Law

Real estate license holders should apply moral law based on "doing the right thing" by all people with whom they do business and with whom they work. The real estate license holder should follow the National Association of REALTORS® (NAR) main ethics rule: the "Golden Rule." Everyone is familiar with the "Golden Rule" (Matt. 7:12):

> *Do unto others as you would have them do unto you.*

Real estate license holders are expected to use their character and good judgment to know what is morally right. If, in their opinion, the transaction they are involved with will lead to unacceptable results, they must excuse themselves from that transaction.

Staff

Real estate license holders must treat all staff at the real estate office with respect and will expect the same from staff members toward each other. Staff will not tolerate disrespect from any license holder. Real estate license holders will not tolerate rudeness toward any client by any staff members. These rules should be in place by the broker. Too many times a staff member or a license holder is in a bad mood and then he/she takes it out on a consumer. Such behavior should never be tolerated by a broker. This can lead to consumers' choosing another real estate brokerage. The broker should send home anyone in a bad mood so that he/she does not disrupt the brokerage business.

Presentation

Real estate license holders must make sure that their actions and appearance are always professional. This includes professional business attire, a clean and tidy car, and an office or work area that is well maintained. Even if license holders are only in the office for a short period of time, the broker should insist on compliance. It is difficult for a real estate agent to maintain a professional image if another agent is walking around the office in a ratty T-shirt and shorts. The presentation to the consumer of the brokerage is only as good as the lowest common denominator.

Client Care

Real estate license holders must, at all times, give priority to the interests and welfare of their clients. Numerous lawsuits have been filed and lost because the real estate license holders were looking out for themselves and not for their clients. In the event that a real estate agent is incapable of servicing a client, the agent will refer the client to another real estate sales professional. Client care begins the moment there is an agreement between the agent and the client and lasts until the transaction is concluded. The agent should continue to follow up after closing even after the agency terminates.

No Risk

Real estate license holders must never create a situation in which the brokerage can profit while the clients of the brokerage suffer financial loss. If the license holder is not confident of selling the property, the license holder should decline to accept the client. If the license holder believes an offer for a seller is not the best for the client, the license holder must say so. The agent must protect his/her client and not place the client at risk. Real estate can be a risky endeavor, but real estate agents must nonetheless protect their clients. If a situation becomes risky, the agent should disclose the issue that may be risky.

Inspections by Licensed Inspectors

Real estate license holders will make sure that all people who are interested in a property have had a professional inspector inspect the property before purchase. A real estate inspector reduces the liability of all parties. Real estate license holders should not ever inspect a property for any individual. This should be left to the professionals. If the agent notices a structural defect, then the agent should disclose the possibility of a defect and insist on real estate inspections. If a buyer refuses to hire an inspector, the agent should seek the broker's advice before proceeding.

Seller's Disclosure Notice

A Seller's Disclosure Notice (SDN) is a notice to the buyer from the seller about the condition of the property. The SDN gives the seller the opportunity to disclose any defect the seller knows about or suspects. A property disclosure is required by Texas statute, and the agent should protect the seller-client by providing the SDN for the seller to complete. The agent should not aid in the completion of the SDN.

Information Provided by the Government
A license holder can provide any party information by the government.

Qualifying of Homebuyers
Real estate salespersons will make sure that all buyers are fully qualified before being shown properties for sale. The real estate salesperson should not prequalify the buyers but should have a mortgage professional prequalify them. Real estate salespersons should make showing appointments at a time to suit the buyers and not create stress for the sellers. Real estate salespersons should be sure that all property shown is secure afterward.

Marketing
Real estate salespersons are required to study and have knowledge of marketing and to make sure they are always aware of the most cost-efficient and effective ways of marketing real property. The real estate salesperson should contact his/her clients and keep them up-to-date on the progress of their marketing campaign.

Negotiation
Real estate salespersons are required to study and have knowledge of professional negotiation. Negotiation is an important aspect of the real estate business. The salesperson should be able to successfully negotiate real estate contracts and sales.

Training
Real estate salespersons are required to study the real estate industry and salesmanship. In addition, real estate salespersons should at all times discover new ways to do business. Training should never be neglected. The real estate professional should read, go to classes and seminars, and seek knowledge from other real estate professionals.

Disclosures
Real estate salespersons are required to make sure that they explain all relevant points of a real estate transaction to clients before the clients make a decision to list or sell their property. Real estate salespersons must advise clients of all offers made on their properties. Disclosures must be made to buyers on the property's condition.

Prospecting
Real estate salespersons are to be courteous and considerate when looking for business. If a homeowner requests no contact, the real estate salesperson will respect the request. The real estate salesperson should not solicit other professional real estate salespersons' current listings.

Confidentiality
A real estate salesperson must keep confidential the personal information provided by a client. Disclosures must be made, but not about confidential information. Confidential information is information about a party in a transaction rather than information about the property.

Advice
Real estate salespersons must take care not to give investment or legal advice without advising the recipient of such advice to seek independent advice, preferably from a lawyer or a qualified investment advisor. The real estate license holder should give advice on pricing, marketing, and negotiating.

Civic Duty
Real estate license holders have a civic duty to their local area and should always be ready to help their community. Real estate license holders are expected to be examples of good corporate citizens.

Ethics Thoughts

The student should answer the following using only his/her ethical thoughts; therefore, there is no absolute, correct answer:

1. You are showing a client a house and the client makes flirtatious comments and gestures. Not openly and not excessive. What should you do?
   A. You refer the client to another salesperson.
   B. Nothing is wrong as long as it does not get out of hand.
   C. You call the police and press charges. (It starts here but could end in assault.)
   D. You take another salesperson with you the next time.

One person's "being nice" is another person's sexual harassment. If you chose:
"A," then you could lose most of your commission
"B," then it could escalate
"C," then this could escalate in the opposite way

Given the scenario, "D" is probably the best answer.

2. You promised to buy a home warranty for your buyers at the beginning of a buyer-broker agreement. These buyers have hassled you from the start, and finally you had to cut your commission by several hundred dollars just to make them happy and close the deal. At closing you notice that the title company has not recorded a home warranty and the buyers have not asked for one. What should you do?
   A. Nothing. The buyers have made that much by your commission cut and obviously did not want it if they could not remember it.
   B. Bring it up and pay for it. The buyers' being jerks does not release you of your promise.
   C. Ask to be excused from the closing table and quickly draw up a disclosure statement that states: "The buyers in this transaction have received $XXX.XX in monies from the real estate broker as a rebate. For consideration of this money, the buyers release the broker from any and all further liabilities in this transaction." If they sign it, you are safe.
   D. Call the title officer out of the room to see if he/she will split the cost with you. You will both make money, so both of you should take the hit.

   This one is a little easier.
   "A" Generally ignoring a problem is not the right answer.
   "B" This is probably the best answer to save your integrity.
   "C" The statement is true, but your intentions are wrong.
   "D" The title officer had nothing to do with your first agreement.

3. You are two listings short to be the top-listing agent for the company. Your manager comes to you on the last day and tells

you he/she will give you two "phantom listings" to make your award. After the awards, the manager will release those two listings. What should you do?
- A. Report the manager to the designated broker. If that broker does not do anything, report the manager to the Texas Real Estate Commission (TREC). This kind of thing must be stopped.
- B. Take the listings. It is your manager who will be in trouble if anything happens, and probably nothing will. Not only that, everyone does this.
- C. Refuse the listings. You want to win the award ethically or not at all. Of course the winner would get his/her name and photo in the newspaper, and that would help your sales if you win.
- D. Take the listings. Your manager told you to, and you must listen to your manager. You do not want to be known as a troublemaker.

This one has two correct answers but only one that is best.
"A" is definitely the correct answers if the manager is frequently being unethical, but it may not be the best answer normally.
"B" is unethical, so do not do it. It is not how you would want to be treated if you were the one who actually should have won.
"C" is probably the best answer. By doing this you avoid trouble while keeping your personal ethics.
"D" is simply unethical.

4. You are sitting with a fellow real estate salesperson. The salesperson says that he/she is going to be transferring to a new office in three days. You know that the salesperson has not told the broker yet. What do you do?
- A. Tell your broker. It would be far worse for you if you did not and the broker found out after the fact. You have no loyalty to the other salesperson.
- B. Negotiate with the broker: You will tell about the agent who is leaving if you get the agent's listings for yourself.
- C. Do nothing. The agent told you that in confidence, and your honor is greater than any corporation.

D. Sell your silence. Tell the agent that if he/she does not give you one hundred dollars, you will tell the broker. All is fair in business, and if that agent is stupid enough to give you information, you are smart enough to sell it back to the agent.

This one is tricky because two of the answer seem correct.
"A" is probably the best answer. The other person needs to tell the broker by rules of TREC, and to wait takes advantage of the broker.
"B" is unethical.
"C" is right to the agent but wrong to the broker.
"D" is unethical.

Business Ethics (Corporate Ethics)

Business ethics, also known as corporate ethics, are a code of ethics set up by business associations or groups for their members to follow. Business ethics are more stringent than government regulations and laws. Generally, business ethics stem from transactions that did not end in a manner deemed proper by the profession. As a result, ethical rules were established to prevent future transactions from following the same direction. These rules are a way professionals want everyone in the industry to act so that the industry has the general public's respect and trust.

Business ethics may not be the best for the organization in the short term, looking at profit only, but it is critical for businesses that are looking out for the long-term benefit to the consumer. Consumers want to be treated ethically and will return to businesses that conduct their operations in that manner. To respond to this demand, in 1980, the Society for Business Ethics was formed in an effort to bring together professionals with a high degree of interest in business ethics.

Texas real estate license holders who are also members of the NAR have two sets of ethics they are required to follow: the NAR Code of Ethics® and the TREC Canons of Professional Ethics and Conduct. Each of these sets of ethics aims to ensure that all real estate professionals act in a professional, moral, and "client-first" manner. Failure to do so could result in loss of membership privileges to loss of the real estate license and disciplinary actions.

National Association of REALTORS® Code of Ethics

NAR was founded as the National Association of Real Estate Exchanges (NAREE) on May 12, 1908, "to unite the real estate men of America for the purpose of effectively exerting a combined influence upon matters affecting real estate interests." NAREE was established because at that time real estate brokers were not licensed, were writing contracts on sheets of paper. In 1916, the NAREE name was changed to the National Association of Real Estate Boards (NAREB).

The term "REALTOR®," identifying real estate agents as members of the NAREB and subscribers to its code of ethics, was first used in 1916. Not all real estate license holders are REALTORS®; only those who belong to NAR can use this designation. To claim to be a REALTOR® and not be a member of NAR is an ethical violation. This code of ethics is a requirement for membership.

The main reason NAR has a code of ethics is to further the positive reputation of the real estate professional in the market. Deceptive and dishonest actions by one real estate license holder are projected on all real estate license holders. The NAR Code of Ethics is intended to help make a difference by giving guidelines for performance. NAR membership is not a requirement, but it is highly recommended for those real estate companies that desire ethical and fair treatment for their customers.

NAR's Code of Ethics and Standards of Practice are more extensive than the TREC Canons of Professional Ethics and Conduct. They contain 17 articles covering three broad categories: Duties to Clients and Customers (Articles 1–9), Duties to the Public (Articles 10–14) and Duties to REALTORS® (Article 15–17). The Code is imposed only on NAR members who "pledge to observe its spirit in all their activities and to conduct their business in accordance with the tenets."

Texas Real Estate Commission Canons of Professional Ethics and Conduct

The TREC Canons are a code of ethics with three main canons (i.e., rules or laws): fidelity, integrity, and competency. These are broad and encompassing to allow TREC wide-reaching power to protect the public from improper actions of license holders.

Let's look at the three canons in their entirety.

§531.1 Fidelity

A real estate broker or salesperson, while acting as an agent for another, is a fiduciary. Special obligations are imposed when such fiduciary relationships are created. They demand:
1. *that the primary duty of the real estate agent is to represent the interests of the agent's client, and the agent's position, in this respect, should be clear to all parties concerned in a real estate transaction; that, however, the agent, in performing duties to the client, shall treat other parties to a transaction fairly;*
2. *that the real estate agent be faithful and observant to trust placed in the agent, and be scrupulous and meticulous in performing the agent's functions; and*
3. *that the real estate agent place no personal interest above that of the agent's client.*

§531.2 Integrity

A real estate broker or salesperson has a special obligation to exercise integrity in the discharge of the license holder's responsibilities, including employment of prudence and caution so as to avoid misrepresentation, in any way, by acts of commission or omission.

DEFTERIOS V. DALLAS BAYOU BEND, LTD., 350 S.W.3D 659 (TEX.APP.-DALLAS 2011, PET. DENIED)

A developer, Nussbaum, received a call from Defterios, a broker, stating that his client, Flaven, was interested in purchasing the developer's properties. Defterios told the developer that Flaven was the beneficiary of a trust fund and wanted to use those trust funds to purchase the properties. Flaven signed contracts to buy nine of the properties. The contracts initially called for an August 2004 closing, but the closings were rescheduled a number of times. Defterios told the developer that the reason for the delays was that the trust fund was not releasing the funds.

Defterios told Nussbaum that he had verified the existence of the funds and that the closings were imminent. Over a year after the contracts were signed, however, the deals still had not closed. As it turned out, Flaven was a Massachusetts truck driver and was not the beneficiary of a multimillion-dollar trust fund; he never closed on the contracts.

> Eventually, some of the properties were deeded to the lender in lieu of foreclosure, and others were sold for a loss. Many of the individual investors in the properties lost all the savings they had invested in the properties. The jury found no direct benefit-of-the-bargain damages, but awarded over $12 million in consequential damages to the developer and investors for fraud and negligent misrepresentation.
>
> This case demonstrates the need for integrity!

§531.3 Competency

It is the obligation of a real estate agent to be knowledgeable as a real estate brokerage practitioner. The agent should:
1. *be informed on market conditions affecting the real estate business and pledged to continuing education in the intricacies involved in marketing real estate for others;*
2. *be informed on national, state, and local issues and developments in the real estate industry; and*
3. *exercise judgment and skill in the performance of the work.*

The Consumer Information Form requires each active real estate broker to display prominently this form at each place of business. This rule facilitates a TREC directive to establish methods whereby consumers who have been or feel they have been wronged can obtain TREC's mailing address and telephone number so that they can register a complaint.

The Discriminatory Practices canon mirrors the Federal Fair Housing Act. No license holder shall inquire about or make a disclosure that indicates a preference, limitation, or discrimination based on race, color, religion, sex, national origin, ancestry (Texas Fair Housing), familial status, or handicap of an owner, previous or current occupant, potential purchaser, lessor, or potential lessee of property. The term "handicap" includes anyone who has had or may have AIDS, an HIV-related illness, HIV infection, or a mental illness.

The first three canons (fidelity, integrity, and competency) were the initial rules formally adopted by TREC. A real estate broker was sued for breach of fiduciary duty. The broker failed to tell the owner that her listed property had been posted for foreclosure. The broker knew of the foreclosure. The broker contended that his conduct was governed exclusively by the listing agreement. The court disagreed. Rules and regulations promulgated within an agency's authority have the force and effect of law. The law existing at the time of the transaction becomes part of the contract (Kinnard v. Homann, 750 S.W. 2d 30 [1988]).

Real estate license holders should want to follow these business ethics. Doing so should not be a struggle. Building a real estate career around sound ethical practices means a long and fruitful career that a person would be proud to claim. Those who choose another route will not last long in the real estate industry.

Real Estate License Law

Every state has some type of real estate license law. These laws were enacted to protect the public from unscrupulous business practices by real estate license holders. The laws regulate the relationship between real estate agents and their principals (i.e., their clients), as well as the duties that are expected to be performed. The laws regulate the brokerage companies and the registration process to practice real estate. Each state will have certain laws for that particular state, but in general the laws limit the activities the real estate broker and license holders can perform. The laws generally prohibit a list of activities, such as:

- payment of fees to unlicensed persons
- material misrepresentation of a significant property defect
- felony conviction, especially for fraud
- fraudulent procurement of real estate
- dishonesty
- failure to cooperate with the state's real estate commission
- false advertising
- maintaining undisclosed agency relationships
- commingling, or mixing personal funds with those of another
- conversion, or using funds of others for a use other than that intended
- negligent or incompetent behavior

These activities are prohibited to protect the consumer. The broker should obey the real estate license laws and make sure the office personnel understand and act in accordance with them.

The real estate license law that presides in Texas is under the state Occupations Code, Title 7 Practices and Professions Related to Real Property and Housing, Subtitle A. Professions Related to Real Estate, Chapter 1101. Real Estate Brokers and Sales Agents.

The first part of the regulation deals with definitions, as follows:

Broker *means a person who, in exchange for a commission or other valuable consideration or with the expectation of receiving a commission or other valuable consideration, performs for another person one of the following acts:*

(i) *sells, exchanges, purchases, or leases real estate;*
(ii) *offers to sell, exchange, purchase, or lease real estate;*
(iii) *negotiates or attempts to negotiate the listing, sale, exchange, purchase, or lease of real estate;*
(iv) *lists or offers, attempts, or agrees to list real estate for sale, lease, or exchange;*
(v) *auctions or offers, attempts, or agrees to auction real estate;*
(vi) *deals in options on real estate, including a lease to purchase or buying, selling, or offering to buy or sell options on real estate;*
(vii) *aids or offers or attempts to aid in locating or obtaining real estate for purchase or lease;*
(viii) *procures or assists in procuring a prospect to effect the sale, exchange, or lease of real estate;*
(ix) *procures or assists in procuring property to effect the sale, exchange, or lease of real estate;*
(x) *controls the acceptance or deposit of rent from a resident of a single-family residential real property unit;*
(xi) *provides a written analysis, opinion, or conclusion relating to the estimated price of real property if the analysis, opinion, or conclusion:*
   (a) *is not referred to as an appraisal;*
   (b) *is provided in the ordinary course of the person's business; and*
   (c) *is related to the actual or potential management, acquisition, disposition, or encumbrance of an interest in real property; or*
(xii) *advises or offers advice to an owner of real estate concerning the negotiation or completion of a short sale; and includes a person who:*
   (a) *is employed by or for an owner of real estate to sell any portion of the real estate; or*
   (b) *engages in the business of charging an advance fee or contracting to collect a fee under a contract that requires the person primarily to promote the sale of real estate by:*
      (i) *listing the real estate in a publication primarily used for listing real estate; or*
      (ii) *referring information about the real estate to brokers.*

That is the definition of one word, "broker." The Real Estate License Act—once included in the Occupations Code—has such lengthy definitions because if under legal pretenses the Act does not cover everything, then everything can be argued in court. The definition continues to expand every time a person states that he/she was not practicing real estate and the case ends up in court.

A person needs to apply to TREC to become a licensed real estate broker. The person has one year from the date the application is filed to meet all license requirements. Once the person has met all the requirements of the broker's license, TREC will email an active broker license to the new broker.

License holder [Licensee] means a broker or sales agent licensed under the Real Estate License Act.

Real estate means any interest in real property, including a leasehold, located in or outside Texas.

Sales agent means a person who is sponsored by a licensed broker for the purpose of performing an act described by the Real Estate License Act.

Subagent means a license holder who represents a principal through cooperation with and consent of a broker representing the principal and is not sponsored by or associated with the principal's broker.

Real Estate Brokerage

The term "real estate brokerage" is defined both by what a brokerage is and by what it is not within the Real Estate License Act:

(a) A person is engaged in real estate brokerage if the person, with the expectation of receiving valuable consideration, directly or indirectly performs or offers, attempts, or agrees to perform for another person any act described by the Real Estate License Act, as a part of a transaction or as an entire transaction.

(b) A person is not engaged in real estate brokerage, regardless of whether the person is licensed under the Real Estate License Act, based solely on engaging in the following activities:
   1. constructing, remodeling, or repairing a home or other building;
   2. sponsoring, promoting, or managing, or otherwise participating as a principal, partner, or financial manager of, an investment in real estate; or
   3. entering into an obligation to pay another person that is secured by an interest in real property.

Applicability of the Real Estate License Act
This Act does not apply to:

1. an attorney licensed in Texas;
2. an attorney-in-fact authorized under a power of attorney to conduct not more than three real estate transactions annually;
3. a public official while engaged in official duties;
4. a licensed auctioneer licensed while conducting the sale of real estate by auction if the auctioneer does not perform another act of a broker;
5. a person conducting a real estate transaction under a court order or the authority of a will or written trust instrument;
6. a person employed by an owner in the sale of structures and land on which structures are located if the structures are erected by the owner in the course of the owner's business (builder);
7. an on-site manager of an apartment complex;
8. an owner or the owner's employee who leases the owner's improved or unimproved real estate; or
9. a transaction involving:
    a. the sale, lease, or transfer of a mineral or mining interest in real property;
    b. the sale, lease, or transfer of a cemetery lot;
    c. the lease or management of a hotel or motel; or
    d. the sale of real property under a power of sale conferred by a deed of trust or other contract.

National Regulations

There are a number of national laws and regulations that affect the real estate industry. The laws passed on a national level include the Real Estate Settlement Procedures Act and the Federal Fair Housing Act. These laws apply to all who engage in the real estate industry and overrule any laws and regulations on the state and local level. Here are a few of the national laws that affect real estate:

CAN-SPAM Act—regulates marketing real estate to consumers

Community Reinvestment Act (CRA)—requires banks to loan in all areas in which they collect deposits

Do Not Call Act—regulates marketing real estate to consumers

Dodd-Frank Wall Street Reform and Consumer Protection Act—prohibits coercion, requires disclosures, and regulates compensation

Equal Credit Opportunity Act (ECOA)—prohibits discrimination in credit transactions

Fair Credit Reporting Act (FCRA)—makes free credit reports available and protects consumer privacy

Financial Institutions Reform, Recovery and Enforcement Act (FIRREA)—regulates appraisers and appraisal standards

Home Ownership and Equity Protection Act (HOEPA)—prohibits equity stripping

Junk Fax Prevention Act—regulates marketing real estate to consumers

Mortgage Acts and Practices—regulates information about lender's loan products

Mortgage Assistance Relief Services (MARS)—regulates promotion of business involved in short sales or loan modifications

Mortgage Reform and Anti-Predatory Lending Act (MRAPL)—governs lender compensation and requires risk retention

National Flood Insurance Program (NFIP)—requires flood insurance in designated areas

Real Estate Settlement Procedures Act (RESPA)—regulates disclosure of affiliated businesses and estimated costs

Residential Lead-Based Paint Hazard Reduction Act—requires disclosure of lead-based paint

Secure and Fair Enforcement for Mortgage Licensing Act (SAFE)—regulates and requires mortgage licensing of loan originators

Title VIII of the Civil Rights Act (Fair Housing)—prohibits discrimination in housing transactions

Truth-in-Lending Act (TILA)—regulates disclosure of anticipated credit costs

USA Patriot Act—regulates reporting of earnest-money deposits

State Regulations

Most major laws and regulations for individual real estate offices are passed on the state level. These laws include abiding by the rules of the state real estate commission. The Texas Property Code is a major law that affects the real estate profession.

Local Regulations

Again, there are few local real estate regulations that apply only to real estate brokerage and no other business. Such laws are usually formed on the state level. Regulations like zoning laws apply not only to a real estate company but also to all businesses in that specific area.

General Law

The real estate business has certain general law issues, including contract law, truth-in-advertising, and agency law.

Deceptive Trade Practices Act

The Deceptive Trade Practices Act (DTPA) is probably the best protection available to consumers in business transactions. Its provisions ensure that real estate license holders behave professionally and serve their clients knowledgeably and honestly. The DTPA is a means of eliminating the real estate license holders who seek to take advantage of consumers of real estate services. However, the DTPA applies to any businessperson, not just to real estate license holders.

The provisions of the DTPA are believed by many to unfairly disadvantage real estate license holders by making them responsible for things not always under their control. A real estate license holder could be in violation of the DTPA by failing to disclose property defects that he/she knew or should have known were present. The DTPA asks two questions:

- Did you know?
- Should you have known?

If the answer to either question is "yes," then the license holder could be in violation of the DTPA. The dangerous question is, "Should you have known?" The reason: A good attorney can make it look like the real estate professional should have known almost anything about the real estate business. If something went wrong, accordingly, the agent should have known it would go wrong.

The law protects the consumer when the license holder has made a misrepresentation concerning a transaction. Representation as used here means a "statement of fact," not "representation of a client." So a misrepresentation is a false statement of fact. Misrepresentation can occur by commission or omission. Commission is making a mistake or error, and omission is leaving out information. For example:

> A real estate professional was working with a buyer named Dan Hamilton. The buyer wanted to go on contract to purchase a property. The agent wrote the buyer's name as Dan Hampton. The agent may have done that because he/she was in a hurry, the buyer mumbled his name, or the agent may have had a friend with the last name Hampton. No matter, it is still misrepresentation. The agent misrepresented the buyer's name.

Now, perhaps it won't be an issue. If the agent or buyer catches the misrepresentation, the agent can make the correction. In legal terms, this is called "remedying" the misrepresentation. No harm here, no intention, but still an error.

Suppose a broker lists a townhome for sale. The sellers know there is $120 per month in association dues. The broker knows of the dues but fails to tell the buyers about the dues. Because the broker failed to disclose the dues, the broker has made a misrepresentation by omission. Just because the buyers should have realized that someone needs to be paid for maintaining the townhome community does not relieve the broker of misrepresentation for failing to disclose.

If any situation cannot be remedied in a timely manner or without damage, the broker should have errors and omissions (E&O) insurance to protect the brokerage from such misrepresentations. The broker could agree to settle with the person who was damaged. The broker needs to be careful about going too far into a settlement without involving his/her E&O insurance carrier; however, because they have professional negotiators and if the broker escalates the situation into something worse, the E&O insurance carrier could void the policy.

Misrepresentation can also involve fraud. Fraud is the intentional misleading of a person. A misrepresentation that results in fraud will cancel any E&O insurance that the broker may have obtained. Certain factors must be in place for fraud, including *reliance*, *intent*, and *damage*.

- *reliance on the information provided*. The consumer who has been the victim of fraud must have relied on the statement of fact as fact and as a reliable fact. Suppose the broker claims to a buyer that "I'm the greatest real estate broker who has ever lived!" No one would have any reason to believe that this is a fact to be relied on. This is an example of puffing, and puffing is not actionable.
- *intent to commit fraud*. Intention is not difficult to understand. The license holder knew what was right and intentionally took action that was wrong.
- *damage to the individual*. The consumer must be able to prove damage. Damage is easy to prove. If a person spills a cup of hot coffee in her lap and can receive over $600,000 in damages, obviously damage is easy for an attorney to prove.

The Act enables a consumer who prevails in a DTPA action to receive actual damages. If it is found that the license holder committed fraud knowingly, the award may be three times the amount of actual damages, called punitive damages. Punitive damages have been awarded even though the buyers would have discovered the misrepresentations had they exercised reasonable diligence. A buyer does not have to do anything; the license holder should have disclosed the information. Furthermore, it is not required that the consumer actually buy the real estate in question, only that the consumer must be seeking or inquiring about a property.

There is no defense from the DTPA that will work every time, but the next three will "probably" work most of the time; "probably" is inserted here because most DTPA cases are settled without a ruling. These defenses should be used to protect the license holder as much as possible:

- *inspections by licensed inspectors.* It is the job of licensed inspectors to find out what is potentially wrong with a property. Once they give their professional opinions on an inspection report, they are liable for their opinions.
- *written SDN.* An SDN is a document that describes the property in detail. It allows the seller to note anything about the property and indicate whether systems are functioning properly.
- *information from the government.* Information is given by the government that a license holder has no reason to believe is false.

The following three defenses under the DTPA will not work even though many real estate professionals always try to use them:

- *waiver.* A person cannot waive his/her right to sue before the event happens.
- *"as is."* This phrase means the buyer is stating that he/she will not sue the seller even though the buyer is not fully aware of the property and any problems it could have. The law says problems must be disclosed; it does not, however, require that a person repair the problems.
- *caveat emptor* (let the buyer beware). Under the DTPA, the buyer does not have to show due diligence.

The DTPA applies to all business transactions. License holders should be especially concerned with how the DTPA applies in transactions involving the sale or rental of real estate, including the actions of real estate license holders engaging in the practice of real estate brokerage. The DTPA provides a laundry list of deceptive practice that the real estate broker should be keenly aware of. Here is a partial list of practices that are clearly deceptive:

- Passing off goods or services as those of another
  Ex. A real estate broker states that "Hamilton Builders" built a particular home when the broker knows it was built by a different builder.

- Causing confusion or misunderstanding as to the source, sponsorship, approval, or certification of goods or services
  Ex. A real estate broker stating that a building has a certified appraisal when the broker knows it did not have the appraisal done.

- Causing confusion or misunderstanding as to affiliation, connection, or association with, or certification by, another
  Ex. A broker claiming that he/she is a REALTOR® when the broker is not.

- Using deceptive representatives or designations of geographic origin in connection with goods or services
  Ex. A broker states that the house has Italian marble when the broker knows the marble came from a Lubbock, Texas, quarry.

- Representing goods or services that claim to have sponsorship, approval, characteristics, ingredients, uses, benefits, or quantities but do not; or claiming to have a sponsorship, approval, status, affiliation, or connection but not having it
  Ex. A broker stating that once the buyers purchases the house, they get access, as members, to an exclusive country club when the broker knows the purchase does not include club membership.

- Representing that goods are original or new if they are deteriorated, reconditioned, reclaimed, used, or secondhand
  Ex. A broker claiming that a roof is new when the broker knows that the roof is over 20 years old.

- Representing that goods or services are of a particular standard, quality, or grade, or that goods are of a particular style or model, if they are of another
  Ex. A broker makes the assurance that the stove is a "Hamilton Exclusive" brand when the broker knows it is actually some generic knockoff.

- Disparaging the goods, services, or business of another by false or misleading representations of facts
  Ex. A broker claims that the competing broker is a drunk and should be arrested when, in fact, the competing broker does not abuse alcohol.

- Advertising goods or services with intent not to sell them as advertised
  Ex. A broker advertises that if a person lists with the brokerage, all commissions will be waived when the broker knows that he/she would be charging a commission.

- Advertising goods or services with intent not to supply a reasonable, expectable public demand, unless the advertisement disclosed a limitation of quantity
  Ex. A broker representing a landlord advertises that a three-bedroom, two-bath apartment can be rented for $450 per month. The area market rent for such a place is three times that amount. The broker has made only one of the 80 units available at that price.

- Making false or misleading statements of fact concerning the reasons for, existence of, or amount of price reductions
  Ex. A broker tells a buyer that the seller is desperate to sell because this is his parents' house and they both died recently in an airplane crash. This is why the price is so low. In reality, the seller's parents live in Montana, but the broker does not want to tell the truth about the foundation issues with the property.

Unconscionable Action

A consumer may maintain an action for damages based on breach of an express or implied warranty or for any unconscionable action. An unconscionable action is defined as an action that takes advantage of the lack of knowledge, ability, experience, or capacity of a person to a grossly unfair degree or one in which there is a gross disparity between the value received and the consideration paid. That basically states that if a broker could do such a thing, the broker must not have a conscience. Before buying or selling a real estate property, a real estate professional must disclose that he/she is a license holder. Failing to do so could be a violation of the DTPA, an unconscionable action. Also, by listing a property with a net listing, a broker could trigger an investigation into an unconscionable act. A net listing is one wherein the owner wants a net amount of the sales price and the broker can keep any amount above that. Suppose a broker took a net listing for $100,000 and then sold it for $250,000. Clearly, there is a gross disparity between the value received and the consideration paid. Net listings are very dangerous because now the broker is working for himself/herself and not for the client.

Knowingly
The broker may have been actually aware at the time of an action or practice complained of, of the falsity, deception, or unfairness of an action or practice giving rise to the consumer's claim. Any knowing broker who fails to take action or remains silent is subject to the DTPA prohibitions against deceptive practices.

Intentionally
The broker may have actual awareness of the falsity, deception, or unfairness of the act or practice, or the condition, defect, or failure constituting a breach of warranty giving rise to the consumer's claim, coupled with the specific intent that the consumer acts in detrimental reliance on the falsity or deception or in detrimental ignorance of the unfairness.

The DTPA is a formidable law, but with the proper training and control, brokers can lessen their liability. The broker should use the information that the local real estate association provides on the DTPA. The Association provides a great deal of education training and information.

Real Estate Associations

The National Association of REALTORS® (NAR), "The Voice for Real Estate," is America's largest trade association, which includes institutes, societies, and councils involved in all aspects of the residential and commercial real estate industries.

Membership is composed of residential and commercial REALTORS®, who are brokers, salespersons, property managers, appraisers, counselors, and others engaged in all aspects of the real estate industry. They are pledged to the strict NAR Code—its Code of Ethics and Standards of Practice.

Working for America's property owners, the NAR provides a facility for professional development, research, and exchange of information among its members and to the public and government for the purpose of preserving the free enterprise system and the right to own real property.

Annual Report

Each year, the NAR works tirelessly to show the people of America what is a fundamental right, and that is property ownership, whether residential, commercial, or ranchland, and it showcases the real estate professionals who put the parties together and make it all possible. The NAR Annual Report details what the Association has accomplished over the past year to make a difference.

In 2015, the NAR worked to achieve a record-breaking grassroots advocacy and REALTORS® Political Action Committee fundraising, continued its commitment to the safety of real estate professionals, created a new national advertising campaign, and partnered with the brokerage community on an initiative to streamline listing data entry and syndication.

The 2015 annual report, "Thriving through Change," demonstrates that the REALTOR® brand remains a recognized and respected symbol of the professionalism shown in the rapidly evolving real estate industry.

Community Programs

Real estate professionals not only help make the dream of homeownership a reality; they also help their local area through community programs, including the Smart Growth and Housing Opportunity programs.

The NAR offers a multitude of programs through which its members can further their role in facilitating home ownership and affordable housing for more Americans.

April 2016 marks the 48th anniversary of the 1968 Fair Housing Act. Each year REALTORS® recognize the significance of this event and reconfirm their commitment to upholding fair housing law as well as their commitment to offering equal professional service to all in their efforts to help individuals achieve their dream of home ownership.

Each state has its own association to represent its members, and each state association is subsumed under the NAR. In addition, most large cities have a local association. For example, Texas has the Texas Association of REALTORS® (TAR), and Fort Worth, Texas, has the local association, the Greater Fort Worth Association of REALTORS® (GFWAR) State and local associations offer training and information to support their REALTORS® on the local level.

Responsibility of the Real Estate Brokerage

A brokerage should have classes on the laws and regulations governing its real estate salespersons. Without providing these classes, the broker is at risk. The real estate commission will hold the real estate broker responsible for the lack of training. The meeting could be yearly risk-reduction seminars for the entire company. Or the education could take 15 minutes at a weekly sales meeting. The approach does not matter, as long as the information is disseminated.

TREC rules delineate the responsibilities assigned to real estate brokers in §535.2 Broker Responsibility:

- *A broker is required to notify a sponsored sales agent in writing of the scope of the sales agent's authorized activities under the Act. Unless such scope is limited or revoked in writing, a broker is responsible for the authorized acts of the broker's sales agents, but the broker is not required to supervise the sales agents directly. If a broker permits a sponsored sales agent to conduct activities beyond the scope explicitly authorized by the broker, those are acts for which the broker is responsible.*
- *A broker owes the highest fiduciary obligation to the principal and is obliged to convey to the principal all information known to the agent which may affect the principal's decision unless prohibited by other law.*
- *A broker is responsible for the proper handling of trust funds placed with the broker.*
- *A broker is responsible for any property management activity by the broker's sponsored sales agents that requires a real estate license.*
- *A broker may delegate to another license holder the responsibility to assist in administering compliance with the Act and Rules, but the broker may not relinquish overall responsibility for the supervision of license holders sponsored by the broker. Any such delegation must be in writing. A broker shall provide the name of each delegated supervisor to the Commission on a form or through the online process approved by the Commission within 30 days of any such delegation that has lasted or is anticipated to last more than six months. The broker shall notify the Commission in the same manner within 30 days after the delegation of a supervisor has ended. It is the responsibility of the broker associate or newly licensed broker to notify the Commission in writing when they are no longer associated with the broker or no longer act as a delegated supervisor.*
- *Listings and other agreements for real estate brokerage services must be solicited and accepted in a broker's name.*

- A broker is responsible to ensure that a sponsored sales agent's advertising complies with the Real Estate License Act.
- Except for records destroyed by an "Act of God" such as a natural disaster or fire not intentionally caused by the broker, the broker must, at a minimum, maintain the following records in a format that is readily available to the Commission for at least four years from the date of closing:
  - disclosures;
  - commission agreements such as listing agreements, buyer representation agreements, or other written agreements relied upon to claim compensation;
  - work files;
  - contracts and related addenda;
  - receipts and disbursements of compensation for services subject to the Act;
  - property management contracts;
  - appraisals, broker price opinions, and comparative market analyses; and
  - sponsorship agreements between the broker and sponsored sales agents.
- A broker who sponsors sales agents or is a designated broker for a business entity shall maintain, on a current basis, written policies and procedures to ensure that:
  - Each sponsored sales agent is advised of the scope of the sales agent's authorized activities subject to the Act and is competent to conduct such activities.
  - Each sponsored sales agent maintains their license in active status at all times while they are engaging in activities subject to the Act.
  - Any and all compensation paid to a sponsored sales agent for acts or services subject to the Act is paid by the sponsoring broker.
  - Each sponsored sales agent is provided on a timely basis, before the effective date of the change, notice of any change to the Act, Rules, or Commission promulgated contract forms.
  - In addition to completing statutory minimum continuing education requirements, each sponsored sales agent receives such additional educational instruction the broker may deem necessary to obtain and maintain, on a current basis, competency in the scope of the sponsored sales agent's practice subject to the Act.
  - Each sponsored sales agent complies with the Commission's advertising rules.
- All trust accounts, including but not limited to property management trust accounts, and other funds received from consumers are maintained by the broker with appropriate controls in compliance with the Act.

- A broker or supervisor must respond to sponsored sales agents, clients, and license holders representing other parties in real estate transactions within three calendar days.
- A sponsoring broker or supervisor shall deliver mail and other correspondence from the Commission to their sponsored sales agents within 10 calendar days after receipt.
- When the broker is a business entity, the designated broker is the person responsible for the broker responsibilities.

Unfair Competition Laws

Unfair competition laws are simply laws that help protect against unfair business practices. Unfair competition in real estate law refers to a number of areas of law involving acts by one competitor or group of competitors that harm another in the field and may give rise to criminal offenses and civil causes of action. The most common areas falling under the banner of unfair competition include trademark infringement, passing off, stealing of trade secrets, trade libel, false light, and tortious interference.

Trademark Infringement

Trademark infringement can occur when a real estate company uses a name, logo, or other company-specific characteristics to deceive consumers into thinking that they are buying the real estate services of a competitor. In the United States, this form of unfair competition is prohibited under common law and by state statutes, and it is governed at the federal level by the Lanham Act. The Lanham Act, named for Texas Representative Fritz G. Lanham, is the primary federal trademark statute of law in the United States. The Act prohibits a number of activities, including trademark infringement, trademark dilution, and false advertising. Violation of the Lanham Act could result in treble damages.

Suppose an organization decides to open a real estate company and call it Century 22 Real Estate. That organization is exposing itself to a trademark issue with Century 21 Real Estate. Even though the names are different, they may be too similar for the consumer to tell the difference. Further, it may be argued, the only reason someone would name a company Century 22 Real Estate is to steal the goodwill of a reputable, national real estate company. Century 21 Real Estate has the right to challenge this trademark infringement.

The Anticybersquatting Consumer Protection Act (ACPA), 15 U.S.C. §1125(d), enacted in 1999, established a cause of action for using an internet domain name confusingly similar to a trademark name. The law was designed to prohibit registration of internet domain names containing trademarks by those with no intention of creating a legitimate website but who instead plan to sell the domain name back to the actual trademark owner.

Suppose that someone registers the following domain names on the internet:

- Century 21
- Century 21 Real Estate
- Century 21 Real Estate Services
- Century 21 Real Estate Company
- Century 21 Real Estate Corporation

Suppose also that the person doing this has nothing to do with the actual Century 21 company. Domain name registration on the internet is inexpensive. This person now waits until Century 21 company wants to register a domain name and then offers to sell one or all of the held names to the actual Century 21 company. Century 21 pays because of the fear that if the company does not use a name that the consumer will recognize, the site will not get the business desired. Currently, this problem is less of an issue because companies now register their trademark name and domain name at the same time, preventing theft of that trademark domain name.

Passing-Off Law

The common law of "passing off" (the tort of passing off) prevents one real estate agent from misrepresenting real estate services as being the services of another. If an independent broker claimed to be an owner of a national real estate franchise to get business and establish credibility, the action would create a claim of passing off.

This law also prevents a real estate agent from holding out his/her services as having some association or connection with another when this is not true. To claim to be a REALTOR® when the person is not a member of the NAR is a violation of passing off. A Texas real estate license holder is not automatically a REALTOR®. That Texas real estate license holder must belong to and pay dues to the NAR to claim the title of REALTOR®. The NAR protects this designation with fervor because to allow any variance, the organization could lose its trademark protection. Kleenex tissue is a prime example: When the public began to call all facial tissues kleenexes, it became a trademark dilution that could result in the loss of the trademark.

The passing-off law is meant to protect a person's right to the goodwill in providing services or products. Goodwill is the business value over and above the value of identifiable business assets brought about by good business relations with the community the business serves. Passing off is also a violation of the Texas Deceptive Trade Practices Act.

Misappropriation of Trade Secrets

Misappropriation of trade secrets occurs when one competitor uses espionage, bribery, or outright theft to obtain economically advantageous information in the possession of another. In the United States, this type of activity is forbidden by the Uniform Trade Secrets Act (UTSA) and the Economic Espionage Act (EEA).

The UTSA was enacted to provide a legal framework to better protect trade secrets for U.S. companies. The UTSA aims to create standards in common law and remedies regarding misappropriation of trade secrets on a state-to-state basis.

Suppose that a real estate company developed secure software that allowed access to property without requiring potential customers to make a telephone call and that was internet based and worked on a smartphone. Suppose also that a member of the real estate company that developed the software sold that software to another real estate company without the knowledge or permission of the first company. This could result in a violation of the UTSA.

The EEA deals with a wide range of issues, including espionage and stealing of trade secrets. Real estate companies have trade secrets, but these are difficult to recover if stolen and the law is difficult to enforce. Marketing campaigns, prospecting strategies, and market niches are not trade secrets and are therefore not protectable. However, if the building plans of a builder are stolen or if one brokerage has a contract to purchase another brokerage and that contract is copied and sold to a third competitor, these actions could constitute a violation of the EEA.

Trade Libel

Trade libel is the publishing of false information about the quality or characteristics of a competitor's real estate services. This constitutes a business tort and allows the injured party to seek both compensatory damages and punitive (i.e., punishing) damages. Real estate brokerages spend a great deal of time and money communicating to the public that their brokerage is reputable and ethically in good standing. Then a competitor makes a random false claim about the brokerage just to end the goodwill that has been generated in the community. This action by the competitor could be considered trade libel. Competition and true comparisons between competitors are not only allowed but encouraged by the courts. Purposeful lies are not tolerated.

Trade libel is prohibited by common law and the Texas Real Estate License Act (TRELA), the Texas Deceptive Trade Practices Act, and the NAR Code.

Under common law, to constitute defamation, a claim must generally be false and must have been made to someone other than the person defamed. Some common law jurisdictions also distinguish between spoken defamation, called "slander," and defamation in other media such as printed words or images, called "libel."

To potentially win a trade libel lawsuit, the plaintiff must have the following for a cause of action:

1. The defendant made a false statement about the real estate broker and/or license holders, the real estate brokerage, or the real estate brokerage services.
2. The statement was published.
3. The statement was published as a fact and not an opinion.
4. The plaintiff was monetarily harmed by the statement.

All four of these criteria must be met, or the plaintiff will probably not win a trade libel lawsuit.

False Light

False light laws protect against statements that are not technically false but that are misleading. A false light claim is usually easier to bring than a defamation claim. To be able to bring and potentially win a false claim lawsuit, the plaintiff must prove the following:

1. The defendant published information about the plaintiff.
2. The information is misleading.

3. The information is highly offensive.
4. The defendant must have published the information with reckless disregard.

Suppose that there is a story on how some real estate brokers are fraudulent. It has been proven through the records that certain brokers have lost their real estate broker's license because of fraudulent actions—all of which is true—but the story also runs a picture of a real estate broker in front of his office, clearly showing his face and the name of his company. This broker, however, has never committed fraud or even been accused of fraud. Because the picture of the broker was published with the article, the public would be misled into believing that this particular broker was one of those who committed fraud even though the article never accused him of fraud. This might blossom into a case for a false light lawsuit.

Tortious Interference

Tortious interference is when one competitor interferes with another competitor's contract or relationship with a third party. This interference could be by threat, libel, or coercion, and the interference could be to change or terminate the current situation. This tort is broadly divided into two categories, one specific to contractual relationships (irrespective of whether they involve business), and the other specific to business relationships or activities (irrespective of whether they involve a contract).

Suppose that a real estate agent contacts a seller who has an exclusive right to sell a listing agreement with a competing real estate brokerage. The agent convinces that seller to terminate the current listing agreement so that the seller can list with the second agent. This action would clearly be tortious interference. This action is also a violation of the NAR Code and the TRELA.

Various unfair business practices such as fraud, misrepresentation, and unconscionable contracts may be considered unfair competition if they give one competitor an advantage over others.

Unfair Business Practices

A real estate broker should never engage in business practices that could be construed as unfair business practices. The reputation of a brokerage is of utmost importance in this era of distrust. Many polls have been conducted, and the polls usually indicate that real estate professionals rank lower than 50% on trust. So more than half the population does not trust real estate professionals. The reason is that too many real estate brokerages engage in unfair business practices. Some get caught and pay the penalty and some do not, but all affect the public's trust in and the integrity of the real estate industry.

The Federal Trade Commission (FTC) handles almost all complaints regarding unfair business practices. The FTC's main focus is protecting America's consumers. The Commission's Bureau of Consumer Protection prohibits unfair, deceptive, and fraudulent business practices by:

- receiving complaints and conducting investigations
- bringing litigation against companies and people who violate the rules
- developing those rules to maintain a fair business environment
- educating consumers and businesspeople about their rights and responsibilities

The FTC collects complaints from people who feel they have been treated unfairly in the business community. The complaints number into the hundreds and range from cyber-security infiltration and deceptive advertising to fraud and identity theft. The FTC uses these complaints to bring litigation against the wrongdoers and provide law enforcement agencies worldwide with access to the information found in their investigation.

The FTC has eight regional offices—in Atlanta, Chicago, Cleveland, Dallas, Los Angeles, New York, San Francisco, and Seattle—that help to strengthen their access to the local and national community; this network allows them proximity to the entire United States.

Americans with Disabilities Act

The Americans with Disabilities Act (ADA) became law in 1990. The ADA is a civil rights law that prohibits discrimination against individuals with disabilities in all areas of public life, including jobs, schools, transportation, and all public and private places that are open to the general public. The purpose of the law is to make sure that people with disabilities have the same rights and opportunities as everyone else. The ADA gives civil rights protections to individuals with disabilities similar to those provided to individuals on the basis of race, color, sex, national origin, age, and religion. It guarantees equal opportunity for individuals with disabilities in public accommodations, employment, transportation, state and local government services, and telecommunications. The ADA is divided into five titles (or sections) that relate to different areas of public life.

Title III Public Accommodations and Services Operated by Private Entities

Title III, which is regulated and enforced by the U.S. Department of Justice:

- prohibits places of public accommodation from discriminating against individuals with disabilities (Public accommodations include privately owned leased or operated facilities like hotels, restaurants, retail merchants, doctor's offices, golf courses, private schools, day care centers, health clubs, sports stadiums, movie theaters, and real estate brokerage offices.)
- sets the minimum standards for accessibility for alterations and new construction of commercial facilities and privately owned public accommodations and also requires public accommodations to remove barriers in existing buildings where it is easy to do so without much difficulty or expense
- directs businesses to make "reasonable modifications" to their usual ways of doing things when serving people with disabilities
- requires that businesses take steps necessary to communicate effectively with customers with vision, hearing, and speech disabilities

Both a tenant and an owner of a place of public accommodation are subject to ADA compliance. Brokers representing parties to transactions involving places of public accommodations should recommend that their clients hire experts to conduct an ADA review.

Real estate brokers must make reasonable modifications in their policies, practices, or procedures to ensure their services and facilities are available to people with disabilities. Reasonable modifications range from widening doors, to installing ramps and bathroom grab bars, to writing contracts in Braille. Brokers could choose to arrange meetings at accessible locations where modifications have been made.

Although tenants and owners of a place of public accommodation are subject to ADA compliance, allocation of responsibility for these changes may be determined (or negotiated) in the lease. Paragraph 15C in the Texas Association of REALTORS® (TAR) "Commercial Lease" provides that the party designated in the lease (determined by a check box) to maintain and repair the item must complete and pay the expenses of any governmental-required modification, including ADA compliance.

The Americans with Disabilities Act Amendments Act (ADAAA) amended the ADA to include a broader list of disabilities, including caring for oneself, performing manual tasks, seeing, hearing, eating, sleeping, walking, standing, lifting, bending, speaking, breathing, learning, reading, concentrating, thinking, communicating, and working. The ADAAA also includes major bodily functions, among them functions of the immune system; normal cell growth; and digestive, bowel, bladder, neurological, brain, respiratory, circulatory, endocrine, and reproductive functions.

Agency and Representation

Agency law is derived from common law. This simply means that agency law applies to everyone. An agent is one who acts for and on behalf of another. The real estate broker/owner needs to establish an office policy for agency law, put it in writing, and make sure all the salespersons associated with the company are aware of and abide by these rules. The best way to protect the traditional real estate company is to have all real estate license holders associated with the company sign a notice stating that they have read and understand the agency policy manual.

There are several types of office policies that an office could adopt. These are examined next.

Seller Only

The *seller-only* office is referred to as a traditional office because for years real estate brokerages represented the seller only. With this type of agency policy, company license holders cannot represent buyers. This does not mean the license holder cannot work "with" a buyer, but it does mean he/she cannot work "for" the buyer. One broker remembers selling real estate during the time of seller-only agency; he said he never even thought about representing the buyer. He could show property, help with the paperwork, and monitor the closing process, but at all times he still represented the seller's best interest. Times have changed, however, and in today's market it is expected that the buyer will be represented.

Buyers have figured out the system of representing sellers only and are seeking representation for themselves. Because of this trend, seller-only real estate companies have had to adapt or lose business. Very few real estate offices today practice seller-only agency.

Buyer Only

Buyer-only offices represent buyers only. Under such an arrangement, the office must refuse seller representation. Just as with seller-only offices, buyer-only offices miss half the market. These offices specialize in representing buyers. They provide advice and advocacy to the buyers and help them make correct decisions in a real estate transaction. Buyer-only offices tend to be small mom-and-pop operations because of the reduction of the potential market. Again, very few real estate offices today practice buyer-only agency.

Seller Only with Buyer Representation

Seller only with buyer representation is a type of agency policy that is quite dangerous. With this type of policy, the real estate company represents sellers only. If a buyer wants to buy an office listing, the company must represent the seller and can work only with the buyer. However, if a buyer wants to buy a property not represented by the company, the buyer can be represented.

This arrangement is confusing, especially to the buyer prospect. A couple, for example, decide they want to buy a home and walk into an office that practices seller only with buyer representation. They look at the company's listings in which the real estate license holder is representing the seller only. They do not find anything they want to buy, so the license holder shows them listings from other offices. The buyers want to make an offer on one of the properties. The license holder, now representing the buyer, completes a competitive market analysis (CMA) to determine a fair price to offer to the seller and advises the buyer which types of repairs to request. The offer is negotiated but never consummated. The buyers now want to make an offer on a listing that is in-house. The license holder now represents the seller. The buyer asks for a CMA. The license holder must refuse because providing that might not be in the seller's best interest. The buyers asks the license holder what they should offer, and the license holder may only state the list price. Given this restriction, very few, if any, real estate companies practice seller only with buyer representation. Nonetheless, this type of representation must be discussed because it is a legal option.

Buyer Only with Seller Representation

Buyer only with seller representation is the opposite of the aforementioned agency policy. This will not be discussed in detail because by taking the previous discussion and substituting "buyer" for "seller," the reader will grasp the concept. Very few, if any, real estate companies practice buyer only with seller representation.

Intermediary

An *intermediary* office represents buyers and represents sellers. The only time there is a change is when a represented in-house buyer wants to buy a represented in-house seller's property. In this instance, the broker of record becomes an intermediary. An intermediary's position is to remain neutral and not favor either the buyer or the seller. The license holders involved still represent their respective clients 100%.

The advantages for a real estate company are many. First, the company can represent both buyers and sellers, thus appealing to more potential clients. Second, the broker remains neutral, which should be easy because a broker typically does not know confidential information about any one client. There are, however, disadvantages for smaller companies in which the broker both lists and sells; the broker cannot represent one party and also be the intermediary. In these cases, the broker must appoint a license holder to represent the client, and then the broker can become the intermediary. Most real estate brokerages in this market at this time are intermediary agency offices.

Dual Agency

Dual agency had its time, and that time has passed. When the real estate industry was going through the change from seller only to representing buyers, dual agency reared its ugly head. Dual agency involves representing both parties in one transaction. Doing this is not illegal, but it is extremely dangerous.

As discussed in the book *Real Estate Marketing and Sales Essentials*, when a broker represents a seller, it is the broker's duty to obtain the highest price and the best terms possible for the seller. If a broker represents a buyer, the broker's duty is to obtain the lowest price and best terms for the buyer. When the same broker represents two or more principals (i.e., buyers and sellers) in the same transaction, the result is a dual or divided agency, and a conflict of interest results. If the broker represents both principals in the same transaction, to whom is the broker loyal? Does he/she work equally hard for each principal? This is an unanswerable question; therefore, the law requires that each principal be told not to expect the broker's full allegiance, and thus each principal is responsible for looking after his/her own interest.

If a broker represents more than one principal and does not obtain their informed consent, the broker is in violation of *undisclosed* dual agency.

Dual agency is dangerous, for how can a person truly represent both parties in one transaction? The answer is that no one can. Dual agency is *restricted agency*, meaning that the license holder must not represent one party over another or disclose confidential information between the parties. This can be achieved, though not easily, and that is why dual agency is still legal. The only problem is that in practice it is difficult to handle dual agency: One mistake can lead to a legal nightmare. In contrast, intermediary agency allows the representation of both parties without the liability of dual agency, which is why most real estate companies practice an intermediary approach as their agency policy.

Non-Agency

Non-agency is a dream world where real estate brokerages are paid millions of dollars to make real estate transactions happen without the liability of representation. This is not a realistic scenario. If for the same amount of money buyers had a choice between one real estate professional to represent them and give them advice and another person who would help but cannot give any advice, the choice would be obvious. Brokers love non-agency, but consumers do not. Consumers will win this debate by spending their money for representation.

Non-agency simply means not representing anyone in the transaction. There is a place for non-agency in a limited-service agreement, for example. A minimum-service agreement (i.e., fee for service or limited service) is a smorgasbord of real estate services that a consumer could pay for. Each service that the consumer wants costs a certain amount of money. The fewer services desired, the less money spent.

To complete a minimum-service transaction, it is best to be a non-agent. Suppose that the sellers had found a buyer for their property. The sellers wanted a real estate professional to write up the contract. A license holder could do this but would want to be a non-agent so that neither buyers nor sellers think they are being represented, which could encompass a great deal more than just writing the offer. For clarity, no office policy or action can be attempted by any license holder without direct authorization and guidance from the designated broker. Some other terms synonymous with "non-agency" are "consultant," "counselor," "facilitator," and "transactional broker."

Minimum-Services Requirements

TRELA has established requirements for the minimum services a broker should provide, as follows.

> TRELA §1101.557 ACTING AS AGENT; REGULATION OF CERTAIN TRANSACTIONS
>
> A. A broker who represents a party in a real estate transaction or who lists real estate for sale under an exclusive agreement for a party is that party's agent.
> B. A broker described by Subsection (a):
>   a. may not instruct another broker to directly or indirectly violate the Texas Real Estate License Act (TRELA);
>   b. must inform the party if the broker receives material information related to a transaction to list, buy, sell, or lease the party's real estate, including the receipt of an offer by the broker; and
>   c. shall, at a minimum, answer the party's questions and present any offer to or from the party.
> B. For the purposes of this section:
>   a. a license holder who has the authority to bind a party to a lease or sale under a power of attorney or a property management agreement is also a party to the lease or sale;
>   b. an inquiry to a person about contract terms or forms required by the person's employer does not violate TRELA if the person does not have the authority to bind the employer to the contract; and
>   c. the sole delivery of an offer to a party does not violate TRELA if:
>   i. the party's broker consents to the delivery;
>   ii. a copy of the offer is sent to the party's broker, unless a governmental agency using a sealed bid process does not allow a copy to be sent; and
>   iii. the person delivering the offer does not engage in another activity that directly or indirectly violates TRELA.

Non-agency is also appropriate for the real estate counselor, who represents corporations buying property in the hundreds of millions of dollars. No one cares about paying $100,000 for the advice of a real estate counselor on a $400-million housing complex. But there might be trouble paying the same $100,000 on a single-family property valued at $75,000.

TREC Rules §535.2 (f) Listings and other agreements for real estate brokerage services must be solicited and accepted in a broker's name.

TREC Rules §535.2 (b) A broker owes the highest fiduciary obligation to the principal and is obliged to convey to the principal all information known to the agent which may affect the principal's decision, unless prohibited by other law.

Representation

Commonly, a real estate broker will enter into an agreement to represent a buyer, seller, landlord or tenant. While it is prudent for the broker and the client to have the agreement in writing, the agreement to represent another party may also be established by an oral agreement or by implication from the parties' actions. Once an agreement to represent a party exists, an agency relationship is created, and the broker has fiduciary obligations to the client.

General Fiduciary Duties In Texas

The general fiduciary duties a broker owes to his or her client are loyalty, good faith, honesty, refraining from self-dealing, integrity, fair and honest dealing, and disclosure.

Specific Duties

The specific duties a broker owes to his or her client, which are described in TRELA or the TREC Rules, may be summarized in the following categories.

- The broker must represent the interest of the client as his or her primary duty. The broker is to be faithful to the client and be observant (mindful) of the duty of trust. The broker may not place his or her personal interest above the client's interest.
- The broker must disclose to his or her client any conflict of interest or any matter that would affect the client's decision in a transaction.
- The broker must be clear to all parties in a transaction whom the broker represents.
  - When performing brokerage duties, the broker is to
  - act meticulously and scrupulously;
  - exercise integrity;
  - employ prudence and caution to avoid any misrepresentation;
  - exercise judgment and skill; and
  - not act negligently, in an untrustworthy or dishonest manner, or in bad faith.

- The broker is to keep informed about his or her practice, the market, and developments in the industry.
- The broker must keep the client informed of material information related to a transaction, including but not limited to the receipt of any offer.
- The broker must be available to answer the client's questions.
- The broker must give the client a proper accounting of all funds received in the transaction. The broker may not commingle any funds held for another with the broker's own funds.

TRELA and the TREC Rules also specify duties the broker has to other persons who may or may not be the broker's clients. For example, the broker must disclose to a buyer all known material defects of a property regardless of whether the buyer is the broker's client. Additionally, a broker may not publish advertisements that are misleading or that fail to include the required statutory disclosures. These obligations are more commonly known as compliance obligations and are not necessarily fiduciary in nature. If a dissatisfied client is successful in establishing a breach of a fiduciary duty in court, the remedies may include, but are not limited to:

- actual damages resulting from the breach (out-of-pocket losses or lost profits), as well as mental anguish damages foreseeable as a result of the breach;
- fee forfeiture; and
- exemplary damage when the breach is intentional or done willfully with no regard for the interest of the client.

Brokers must be aware of breaches of fiduciary duty. The lawsuits involving fiduciary duty can be very expensive, including a jury award over $750,000, attorney fees, and court costs in Markovich v. Prudential Gardner Realtors, a case in which a real estate license holder was found guilty of accepting a second offer while a counteroffer was still pending. The courts found that the actions of the real estate license holder were a breach of fiduciary duty.

"Fiduciary" is a term that is used frequently, but some license holders do not understand that it means to put their clients' interests ahead of their own. For another example, a real estate broker introduced a seller whose home had been on and off the market for four years to a buyer who offered him $70,900 in cash in addition to an ownership stake in another person's life insurance policy supposedly worth $638,100. A year later, the seller received $172,046 for the insurance policy after the buyer's "life settlement company" was placed in receivership by securities regulators and its assets liquidated. In this case, a jury found the broker guilty of breaching his fiduciary duty to his client and awarded the seller $25,000 in damages. The seller appealed the award as "grossly inadequate," but the decision was upheld by the Court of Appeals (Elgersma v. RE/Max of Grand Rapids Inc.).

Quiz on Agency Law

Answer the following questions on agency law. All are either true or false. Answers will appear at the end of the chapter.

1. An agent is a license holder who has been appointed and empowered to represent the interests of a client and acts on the client's behalf.
2. An agent owes no fiduciary duties to a customer.
3. A real estate salesperson license holder must have a sponsoring broker and is the general agent of that broker.
4. A written buyer representation agreement is the best way to establish buyer agency.
5. The agent owes fiduciary duties to the seller because the seller promises to pay the commission.
6. The seller informed the listing agent of termite damage, and the agent must inform all prospective buyers of this condition.
7. The duties of honesty, fairness, and disclosure of material facts about the property are owed to unrepresented buyers.
8. An intermediary agency relationship must be created in writing to comply with Texas statutes.
9. A fiduciary relationship exists between a seller and a buyer.
10. Janice, a licensed broker, represents Howard, the buyer. Janice locates Fred's property and Howard purchases the property. Janice is the agent and Fred is the client.

Prospecting Laws

Prospecting in the real estate industry is an integral part of the business for real estate license holders. There are laws on prospecting that brokers must be aware of and communicate to their agents. Failure to do so could result in fines and penalties that brokers and agents would not want to incur. All such understanding of laws and regulations starts with the broker, and that broker must inform and train his/her agents. TREC will first look at the broker if a violation occurs.

Brokerages also need to prospect. A broker who does not prospect acts as a determent to his/her agents because if they see no prospecting from their broker, they themselves have no impetus to prospect. Why should they? Broker prospecting could involve prospecting for agents to join the firm. Brokers could prospect certain areas of town where the brokerage needs more license holders to dominate. Brokers could prospect for sellers and buyers for the brokerage or for referrals for the licensees. Brokers could also prospect for acquisition of competing firms. Prospecting for a broker is an ongoing process. Broker prospecting laws are like those governing real estate license holders, and so the broker needs to be aware of these laws. The main law that limits and restricts prospecting deals with fair housing, the Fair Housing Act, is explained next.

The federal Fair Housing Act is to eliminate discrimination in housing. The Act requires the real estate professional to describe the property not the parties of the transaction. The broker is ultimately responsible for all the advertising that leaves the brokerage office. The standard policy should be for the broker to review all the advertising from the brokerage and from any license holder before it hits the media. Fair housing laws do not look at the broker's or license holder's intent. If advertisements indicate a discriminatory action, then there was a discriminatory action, and a violation of the federal fair housing laws occurred.

Advertising that limits occupancy should not be used if the limit restricts a protected class. Advertisements should reflect a worldview instead of a limited view. A landlord should not care about the type of person who wants to rent a unit as long as the person is financially qualified. Anything else could be an indication of discrimination.

Brokers are to protect their clients when it comes to fair housing. A broker should know the fair housing laws, such as Title VIII of the Civil Rights Act and the Fair Housing Act of 1968, and how they relate to prospecting, marketing, advertising, and promotions. Failure to know and enforce these laws will result in an increase of risk to the brokerage.

The U.S. Department of Housing and Urban Development (HUD) investigates any complaints about fair housing violations. The Fair Housing Act Sec. 804 (c) specifies:

> *To make, print or publish, or cause to be made, printed or published any notice, statement or advertisement with respect to the sale or rental of a dwelling that indicates any preference, limitation or discrimination based on race, color, religion, sex, handicap, familial status or national origin or an intention to make such preference, limitation or discrimination.*

HUD's advertising guidelines categorize discriminatory advertising into three groups:

1. advertising that contains words, phrases, symbols, or visual aids that indicate an illegal preference or limitation
2. advertising that selectively uses media, human models, logos, and locations to indicate an illegal preference or limitation
3. various types of discriminatory advertising practices condemned by the Fair Housing Act

Race, Color, or National Origin

Real estate advertisements both print and electronic should state no discriminatory preference or limitation on account of race, color, or national origin. Use of words describing the current or potential residents, or the neighbors or neighborhood, in racial or ethnic terms will clearly create liability. Phrases such as "master bedroom," "rare find," or "desirable neighborhood" are not in violation. Words such as "colored home," "Jewish home," or "Hispanic home" would all be direct violations. If in any doubt, the agent or broker should reword the advertisement or online publication or check the HUD website for further clarification. HUD publishes lists of acceptable words, cautionary words, and unacceptable words for use by real estate professionals.

Religion

Advertisements should not contain an explicit preference, limitation, or discrimination on account of religion. Advertisements that use the legal name of an entity containing a religious reference or those containing a religious symbol standing alone may indicate a religious preference. However, if such an advertisement includes a disclaimer (such as the statement "This home does not discriminate on the basis of race, color, religion, national origin, sex, handicap, or familial status"), it will not violate the act. Advertisements containing descriptions of properties or services that do not on their face state a preference for persons likely to make use of those facilities will not violate the Act.

The use of secularized terms or symbols relating to religious holidays, such as Santa Claus, the Easter Bunny, or St. Valentine's Day images or phrases such as "Merry Christmas," "Happy Easter," or the like, does not constitute a violation of the Act.

The broker should also inspect each advertisement for any terms that could remotely be challenged. Advertisements should be inclusive, not limited. Inclusive ads have a better chance to entice a transaction, and that is the goal of any advertisement.

Sex (Gender)

Advertisements for single-family dwellings or separate units in a multifamily dwelling should contain no explicit preference, limitation, or discrimination based on sex (gender). Use of the term "master bedroom" does not constitute a violation of either the "sex" provisions or the race discrimination provisions. Terms such as "mother-in-law suite" and "bachelor apartment" are commonly used as physical descriptions of housing units and also do not violate the Act. References to preference of gender on rental or sale would be a violation, however. Ads that restrict the selection of tenants based on the sex of the tenant would not be allowed. An ad that stated "This apartment complex is for females only" would be a violation.

Handicap

Real estate advertisements should not contain explicit exclusions, limitations, or other indications of discrimination based on a handicap. Advertisements containing descriptions of properties, services or facilities, or neighborhoods do not violate the Act. Advertisements may describe the amenities the property offers. Advertisements describing the conduct required of residents do not violate the Act. Advertisements containing descriptions of accessibility features are lawful.

Because prospecting also includes the showing of properties, a broker who is prospecting should be mindful not to discriminate. If the broker believes that someone who wants to see a property should not see it, perhaps because of a handicap, under no circumstances should the broker voice his/her opinion, because the broker is considering the person's handicap, and doing that is a violation. If the consumer wants to see a property, the broker has an obligation to show it; the consumer can then make the decision to accept the property or reject it.

Familial Status
Advertisements may not state an explicit preference, limitation, or discrimination based on familial status. Familial status refers to individuals under the age of 18 living with a parent or a guardian. Advertisements may not contain limitations on the number or ages of children, nor may they state a preference for adults, couples, or singles. Advertisements describing the property, services and facilities, or neighborhoods are not discriminatory and do not violate the Act. Any statements such as "no children allowed" would be a direct violation.

Fair Housing Wording Guidelines
The words and phrases in the following chart represent the position of HUD on advertising issues and are printed here to aid in writing advertisements that do not discriminate.

Acceptable wording	Questionable wording	Unacceptable wording
Close to schools	55 and older (restrictions)	Adults only
Den	Male roommate	(Blank) need not apply
View	Older persons	Catholic church
Play area	Female roommate	Couples only
Secluded	Executive neighborhood	Ethnic landmarks
Family room		Handicap limitations
Walking distance to . . .		No family problems

This chart is by no means conclusive. Each word in an advertisement should be reviewed for compliance. Advertisement is not meant to be difficult to compose, but it should also not limit the availability of a property based on a protected class under the fair housing laws. HUD is the best source for any questions regarding compliance. For more information visit the web page https://fairhousing.com/node/17572.

Advertisements That Comply with Regulation Z

TILA, the Truth-in-Lending Act, was enacted to "assure the meaningful disclosure of credit terms so that the consumer would be able to compare more readily the various credit terms available to him/her to avoid the uninformed use of credit." The Act, which refers to Regulation Z, has been merged with the Real Estate Settlement Procedures Act (RESPA) to create TILA and RESPA Integrated Disclosures, or TRID. TRID has furthered the informed use of credit and the necessary disclosures to help the consumer.

One of the specific forms of credit requiring disclosures is residential mortgage transactions. Special rules exist for advertising of mortgages, which apply to any ad for the sale of real estate containing financing information.

Facts About Advertising and Regulation Z

Regulation Z, popularly referred to as Reg Z, applies only to the advertising on one- and two-unit residential real property. Reg Z applies only to advertising of property the potential consumer will use as a principal dwelling.

Advertisements to sell the following types of properties must comply with Reg Z:

- single-family detached housing
- duplex (Each side is considered separate.)
- two detached units on one legal description
- townhouses (each unit)
- condominiums (each unit)
- houseboats that are used as such
- cooperative housing unit (proprietary lease)
- farms and ranches used primarily for residential purposes, not as working property
- mobile homes and trailers (also applies if these are considered personal property)

If advertisements promote the sale of the following types of real property, the ads do not need to comply with Reg Z:

- vacant land or vacant lots
- business or commercial real estate
- industrial real estate
- residential rentals with three or more units
- farms and ranches primarily used for agricultural purposes

For fixed-rate loans, if a broker advertises any one of the following, then all of these must be included:

- annual percentage rate
- simple interest rate
- down payment amount
- monthly payment (exact amount)
- loan term (i.e., length)

The Reg Z laws and regulations aim to protect the consumer from being discriminated against or taken advantage of in a business or consumer transaction. A broker must be aware of these laws and communicate them to the sales force. If a real estate license holder wants to use advertising to prospect, he/she should check that the advertising is in compliance with the rules of Reg Z.

Suppose that a rental unit is located in an area where rents are over $2,000 a month. The following advertisement is placed on the internet. If its contents are *true*, is there a violation?

> Call today to get this wonderful four (4) bedroom, three (3) bath apartment in the prestigious Brittany Bay community. It is close to excellent schools and top end shopping. The rent is only $220 a month!

The advertisement is indeed true, so the advertiser cannot be prosecuted for fraud. Because of Reg Z, however, the advertiser is in violation of federal law. The apartment complex is offering only one of the 200 units at this rental price, and all other units are $2,800 per month. The ad is intended to attract callers and then move them to other, more expensive properties. This bait-and-switch strategy is illegal.

Such deceptive ads were numerous before 1968 when Reg Z of TILA became law. One of Reg Z's main objectives was to ensure truthfulness in advertising, requiring the advertising of the time to be less deceptive and more factual and complete.

Mortgage Acts and Practices

Mortgage Acts and Practices Is another law that can affect prospecting performed by real estate brokerages. Real estate license holders who make commercial ads about mortgage credit products are prohibited from making misrepresentations about the products and also must keep records of the ads for two years. The rule does not include informational materials about mortgage credit products. Real estate license holders should include a disclaimer on all advertisements.

Truth-in-Advertising Laws

It is a violation of federal and state law for any real estate brokerage to make false or deceptive claims when advertising real estate services. The FTC enforces false advertising laws at the federal level, and individual states have agencies.

Consumer Protection Laws

Each state has consumer protection laws with the purpose of preventing businesses, including real estate brokerages, from using misleading marketing campaigns to increase business sales. It is a violation for a real estate brokerage to offer a specific commission rate and then not honor that rate at the time of listing.

Contracts

Real estate contracts are a critical aspect of the real estate business. Contracts are in every sector of the real estate industry. There are contracts between license holders and the broker, contracts between brokers and clients, and contracts between buyers and sellers. Virtually every day a real estate brokerage will be handling, completing, revising, and following a contract of some type.

    The law of contracts is one of the most complex areas of common law to study. This section does not delve into that complexity because it is expected that a broker has been introduced to contract law in other courses. This section will, however, discuss writing contracts in a manner that will give a broker and his/her brokerage a professional appearance. Contracts normally used in real estate include listing agreements, earnest-money contracts, leases, deeds, mortgages, liens, and partnership agreements. For the purposes of this book, the discussions of contract law are centered on the creation and construction of contracts.

> A contract is a voluntary agreement between legally competent parties to perform or refrain from performing some legal act, supported by legal consideration.

This definition includes the four elements for any contract: voluntary agreement, legally competent parties, legal consideration, and legal objective.

- Voluntary agreement means agreement to all the terms of a contract by all the parties of the contract. This agreement could also be called "mutual assent" or "meeting of the minds." The contract must be entered into freely and voluntarily. The following would not be considered voluntary:
  - *Misrepresentation* is an error in the contract. Some errors can be remedied easily, but others could cause a party to no longer want to be a party to the contract.
  - *Fraud* is intentional misrepresentation. Fraud does not automatically terminate a contract but allows the nondefaulting party certain rights, including the right to terminate.
  - *Duress* refers to the use of force. If a person is forced to sign a contract, it would not be enforceable.
  - *Menace* is the threat of violence. If a person is threatened to sign a contract, it would not be enforceable.
  - *Undue influence* refers to the use of one's power. If a person uses his/her position of power to push someone into signing a contract, it would not be enforceable.
- Legally competent parties must have the mental capacity to be held to the terms of a contract and must be at least 18 years of age.
- Legal consideration means something is given in exchange for something else. It could be a promise in exchange for a promise. Valuable consideration is something of actual value like money or personal property. Good consideration is love or affection, and gratuitous consideration is a free promise.
- Legal objective refers to purpose. Every contract must be of legal purpose. Contracts cannot violate the law.

The Statute of Frauds requires all contracts for the sale of real property to be in writing to be enforceable. The Statute also requires all leases for more than one year to be in writing to be enforceable.

Earnest money is:

- *a good-faith down payment*. It means that the buyer is serious about purchasing the property.
- *liquidated damages*. These are damages agreed to in advance. In a court of law, liquidated damages have a great deal of power with a judge when determining how much the damages should be if there is a default of contract. Acceptance of the earnest money releases the parties from further obligations to each other.

The Statute of Limitations for a written contract is four years from the date of the breach; for an oral contract it is two years.

The broker should review every contract the brokerage sends out or receives. This may take time but is a good safety measure. The TREC highly recommends this procedure. Failure to check every contract makes the broker liable to situations that may have been corrected had those contracts been reviewed. If the broker has too many contracts to review, he/she could assign this duty, but the broker cannot assign the risk and liability, which remains the broker's alone.

The broker has the responsibility of ensuring that all contracts that leave the brokerage are correct and legal. (See Chapter 5 for more about writing and presenting contracts that should help.)

An addendum is any addition annexed to a document and made a part of the document by reference. An addendum is usually a TREC-promulgated addendum and attached to the document. It is required to have the parties to the document write their signatures on the addendum to demonstrate their knowledge and acceptance of the addition. Addendums are also known as riders or attachments and carry the same legal standing as the primary document.

Brokers are burdened by a great many liabilities, and contract writing is one of the most dangerous. Brokers would be wise to continue their education on contract law and stay up-to-date on the latest changes to the law, as well as informed of any currently available "best practices" regarding contract writing. Brokers will be less liable if the proper actions and procedures are taken in the office to prepare and review all contracts.

Disclosures

Disclosures to the buyers and sellers of real estate are probably the best defense for a real estate broker involved in a lawsuit. If there is any doubt, the broker should disclose. (Examples of disclosures follow.)

Failure to disclose is the reason many brokers have lost large sums of money. The only disclosures the broker should not make are those that violate a law.

Seller's Disclosure Notice

The SDN is a disclosure of the seller's knowledge of the condition of the property as of the date signed by seller. This notice is not a substitute for any inspections or warranties the buyer may wish to obtain. It is not a warranty of any kind by the seller, seller's agents, or any other agent.

Environmental Hazards Disclosure

The Addendum for Seller's Disclosure of Information on Lead-Based Paint and Lead-Based Paint Hazards as Required by Federal Law is an addendum approved by the TREC. This Addendum states:

> *Every purchaser of any interest in residential real property on which a residential dwelling was built prior to 1978 is notified that such property may present exposure to lead from lead-based paint that may place young children at risk of developing lead poisoning. Lead poisoning in young children may produce permanent neurological damage, including learning disabilities, reduced intelligence quotient, behavioral problems, and impaired memory. Lead poisoning also poses a particular risk to pregnant women. The seller of any interest in residential real property is required to provide the buyer with any information on lead-based paint hazards from risk assessments or inspections in the seller's possession and notify the buyer of any known lead-based paint hazards. A risk assessment or inspection for possible lead-paint hazards is recommended prior to purchase.*

Intermediary Relationship Notice

TAR 1409 Intermediary Relationship Notice is the disclosure form used to notify buyers and sellers of a real estate property for which their broker is now an intermediary. The form requires the written authorization for the broker to proceed in this transaction.

Agency Notice

All license holders are required to give the information about their brokerage services to prospective buyers, tenants, sellers, and landlords. The Agency Notice form is in fact entitled *Information About Brokerage Services*. The form spells out the main duties a broker or license holder must perform, depending on the type of representation taking place.

Information About Special Flood Hazard Areas

TAR 1414 Information About Special Flood Hazard Areas is a TAR form disclosing flood areas as defined by the Federal Emergency Management Agency (FEMA). The form indicates that flood insurance is typically available for all houses. It specifies the ground floor requirements that elevate a home above the potential flood level and indicates flood insurance rates for properties in special flood hazard areas.

Notice to Purchasers: Importance of Home Inspections

TAR 1928 HUD Notice to Purchasers: Importance of Home Inspections is a HUD notice to disclose to the buyers the necessity to obtain property inspections. It notifies the buyers that appraisals are different from inspections and that the buyers must ask for a home inspection to be conducted. The form discusses radon gas testing and closes by telling buyers that it is their responsibility to be informed buyers.

Notice to Prospective Buyer

Approved by TREC, the TAR 2505 Notice to Prospective Buyer addendum discloses that buyers should have the abstract examined by an attorney or the buyers should have furnished to them a policy of title insurance. The addendum further discloses that buyers should receive the statutory notice if the property is situated in a utility district.

Disclosure of Relationship with Residential Service Company

Any time a real estate brokerage has a monetary relationship with a residential service company, that relationship must be disclosed to the buyer and to the seller. The broker usually receives some sort of compensation, usually a small fee, for performing part of the inspection for the residential service company.

A residential service contract is a product under which a residential service company, for a fee, agrees to repair or replace certain equipment or items in a property. Copayments typically apply to most service calls. Residential service companies are licensed and regulated by the TREC. The extent of coverage and the cost of coverage will vary. Before buying a residential service contract, the buyer should read the contract and consider comparing it with the extent of coverage and costs from several other residential service companies. The buyer can choose any company, and it is not mandatory to buy a residential service contract.

Compensation is not contingent on a party to the real estate transaction purchasing a contract or services from the residential service company. Compensation is the fee for the services that the listing broker or other broker, either directly or through an agent, provides to the company. As required by the RESPA and HUD Regulation X, any fees paid to a settlement services provider are limited to the reasonable value of services actually rendered.

Addendum for a Property in a Propane Gas Service Area

If the real property that the buyer is about to purchase is located in a propane gas system service area, which is authorized by law to provide propane gas service to the properties in the area, the buyer is to receive the Texas Addendum for Property in a Propane Gas Service Area pursuant to Chapter 141, Texas Utilities Code.

If the property is located in a propane gas system service area, there may be special costs or charges that the buyer will be required to pay before he/she can receive propane gas service. There may be a period required to construct lines or other facilities necessary to provide this service to the property.

The buyer is advised to determine if the property is in a propane gas system service area and contact the distribution system retailer to determine the cost that the buyer will be required to pay and the period, if any, that is required to provide propane gas service to the property.

Consumer Notice Concerning Hazards or Deficiencies

TAR 2504 Texas Real Estate Consumer Notice Concerning Hazards or Deficiencies is a TREC-approved disclosure form that cautions buyers on the following:

- malfunctioning, improperly installed, or missing ground-fault circuit protection devices for electrical receptacles in garages, bathrooms, kitchens, and exterior areas;
- malfunctioning arc-fault protection devices;
- ordinary glass in locations where modern construction techniques call for safety glass;
- malfunctioning or lack of fire safety features, such as smoke alarms, fire-rated doors in certain locations, and functional emergency escape and rescue openings in bedrooms;
- malfunctioning carbon monoxide alarms;
- excessive spacing between balusters on stairways and porches;

- improperly installed appliances;
- improperly installed or defective safety devices;
- lack of electrical bonding and grounding; and
- lack of bonding on gas piping, including corrugated stainless steel tubing.

Inspector Information

TAR 2506 Inspector Information discloses to the buyers that the list of licensed property/pest inspectors provided by the license holder is not a recommendation by the license holder; it is simply an aid to buyers to help them in selecting a real estate inspector.

Protecting Your Home from Mold

Mold growth problems can adversely affect many homeowners in Texas. Homeowners who act quickly and appropriately can prevent or correct conditions that may cause mold growth. The Texas Department of Health and Texas Department of Insurance have prepared a publication called *TAR 2507 Protecting Your Home from Mold* to help buyers understand the concerns related to mold growth and to provide some effective steps homeowners can take to help prevent mold growth. The information will help protect homeowners' investments in their home and may prevent the possibility of health risks related to mold exposure.

Information About Property Insurance for a Buyer or Seller

The availability and the affordability of property insurance may affect both the buyer and the seller. Typically a buyer will seek to insure the property. Most mortgage lenders require that the property be insured in an amount not less than the loan amount. The failure to obtain property insurance at or before closing may delay the transaction or cause it to end, either of which can impose both inconvenience and cost to both the buyer and the seller.

Information About Mineral Clauses in Contract Forms

Historically, buyers and sellers of property near urban areas have not been concerned about the conveyance or retention of mineral interests. Mineral interests for such properties may have been severed in the past, or the value of the mineral interests may have been relatively insignificant. There has historically been little risk that the owner of the mineral interests under property near urban areas could or would access the surface of the property to drill or excavate for minerals (perhaps, because the property was too small to support such activity or because such activity may have been heavily regulated by a city). In recent years, the discovery of large mineral deposits near urban areas and advances in drilling technologies have led to increased exploration and drilling activities in and near urban areas. In turn, buyers and sellers of property in urban and suburban areas have raised questions as to whether it is best to convey or retain all or part of the mineral interests in a particular sale.

Owners of property in or near urban areas typically are not aware of the precise extent of the mineral interests they may own. One may own all or only a portion of the mineral interests. Further, the mineral interests may have been leased. Determining who owns the mineral interests, whether the mineral interests have been leased, and who holds rights under any leases requires an expert—such as an oil-and-gas attorney—to review the chain of title and formulate an informed opinion.

The residential contract forms promulgated by the TREC and the commercial contract forms published by the TAR provide that the seller will convey to the buyer all of the seller's rights associated with the property, including all mineral interests and any rights held under any mineral leases by the seller. If a seller wishes to reserve all or a part of the mineral interests and rights held by the seller in a residential transaction, the seller must use the TREC's Addendum for Reservation of Oil, Gas, and Other Minerals (TREC No. 44-2, TAR No. 1905). If the Addendum is not attached to the sales contract, the seller conveys to the buyer all the mineral interests and rights held by the seller at the time of the transaction. In a farm-and-ranch transaction, the seller may use the TREC-promulgated form, but he/she may also use any addendum prepared by an attorney or by either party.

Sherman Antitrust Act

The Sherman Antitrust Act prohibits any type of collaboration of businesses to the detriment of consumers. Section 15 of the Act states that:

> *Every contract, combination in the form of trust or otherwise, or conspiracy, in restraint of trade or commerce is declared to be illegal. Every person who shall make any contract or engage in any combination or conspiracy hereby declared to be illegal shall be deemed guilty of a felony, and, on conviction thereof, shall be punished by fine not exceeding $10,000,000 if a corporation, or, if any other person, $350,000, or by imprisonment not exceeding three years, or by both said punishments, in the discretion of the court.*

Antitrust prohibits price-fixing. Price-fixing is the act of two or more competitors joining together to force consumers to pay a higher amount than they would pay if competition were unrestrained. If any two real estate brokers get together and agree to charge a certain commission, that would be price-fixing. Commissions are and will remain negotiable between the brokerage company and the client. This can happen almost unintentionally. A number of competing real estate brokers, for example, are sitting around complaining about not making enough money. One of the brokers comes up with the great idea that if everyone raised commission rates to the same amount, all brokers would make more money. If a broker even hears such a discussion, the broker must leave immediately or repudiate the statement and change the topic. It is not a defense for the broker to declare after the fact that he/she was not the one making the suggestion. A price-fixing violation can be inferred from the similar commission rates received by members, even if no written or oral agreement is evident.

Case Study

United States v. Foley

Facts During a dinner party hosted by John Foley (President, Jack Foley Realty) at a local country club, he stood up and announced that his firm was raising its commission rate across the board, from 6% to 7%, regardless of what the other firms did. Within the following months, several other firms that had had representatives at the dinner party also raised their commission rate to 7%.

Notable Facts

- There was evidence of efforts to force other firms to raise their rates from some of the defendants,
- The real estate market was down, and many real estate brokers were losing money.
- There was sufficient evidence to find that several other corporate defendants had also stated that they were raising their commission at the dinner.
- Foley was head of the trade association.

Analysis
- It was easy for the real estate brokers to change commissions charged from 6% to 7%.
- Because every real estate transaction involved firms for both the buyer and the seller, it would have been extremely difficult to charge 6% without all the other brokers finding out.
- Entry into the field is quite difficult and exclusion is simple, because real estate firms can refuse to deal with new real estate license holders.
- Evaluating the economic sense of a potential agreement has made economic principles part of the plus factors.

Summary
A U.S. grand jury found all nine defendants (Foley and the eight others at the dinner party) guilty.

Predatory Pricing

Antitrust violations constituting unfair competition can occur when one competitor attempts to force others out of the market (or prevent others from entering the market) through tactics such as charging low commissions that drive other brokerages out of the business and then raising those commissions higher than they would have been if the market was balanced. It also includes obtaining exclusive purchase rights to elements of the real estate business needed to offer a competing real estate service. Suppose that a broker is able to pay the multiple listing service (MLS) fee and then not allow certain competitor brokerages access to the MLS data, thereby eliminating them as competitors. These actions clearly limit competition, which is best for the consumer in a consumer-driven economy such as ours.

It is usually difficult to prove that commission fees dropped because of deliberate predatory pricing rather than legitimate price competition. The real key is a significant reduction in the commission charged rather than market fluctuation in pricing.

Predatory pricing is difficult to accomplish in large markets but not so in small towns with only one big real estate company. When another competitor decides to enter the market in a small town, the large established firm can take some losses for a while and cut its commission to the consumer to unfair levels. The new company does not have the funds to survive for long under this condition and must raise its commissions to keep the business going. Because the new company has a higher commission rate, the consumer does business with the established company. This continues until the new company closes its doors, leaving the market to the big real estate company, thereby eliminating competition.

Boycotting and Other Prohibited Strategies

The Sherman Antitrust Act also prohibits *boycotting*, which is the collaboration of a group of businesses to avoid doing business with another business. A group of real estate brokers agreeing not to show the properties of another broker to force said broker out of business is an example of boycotting. Boycotting that rises to the level of a violation would also include forcing competitors to raise commission rates or refusing to do business with them.

Antitrust includes the allocation of customers as a violation. If two brokers agreed to split an area in half and not do business in the other area, that would be the allocation of customers and clearly a violation. An agreement among members of an association or group to divide customers is in itself a criminal act. The antitrust laws prohibit any understandings or agreements between competitors or members of an association that involves the division or allocation of customers.

If a broker is a part of an association or is thinking of forming a trade group, the broker should thus be careful not to prohibit membership of certain people or companies to avoid competition. A basic assumption about every trade association is that its members derive an economic benefit from membership. Denial of membership to an applicant may therefore constitute a restraint of trade in that such denial of an economic benefit limits the rights of an applicant to compete. Thus, membership criteria must be carefully drafted to avoid antitrust problems.

Antitrust Questions

Answers will appear at the end of the chapter.

1. True or false? Two or more companies can get together to create a new pricing structure as long as it results in lower prices for consumers.
2. True or false? Although competitors cannot directly do so, an MLS can require a certain minimum term for listings.

Ethical and Legal Business Practices

3. If a license holder is at a meeting in which two or more competitors agree to boycott another, the license holder should:
   A. openly and affirmatively repudiate the statement
   B. demand to see evidence why the company should be boycotted
   C. remain silent
   D. put his/her hands over his/her ears
4. It is acceptable to refuse to cooperate with a competitor if the:
   A. competitor is rude
   B. competitor was found guilty of an ethics violation in the past
   C. client instructs the license holder not to cooperate because cooperation is not in the client's best interest
   D. license holder receives MLS approval to do so
5. Punishments for antitrust violations include:
   A. treble damages
   B. imprisonment
   C. court supervision of the license holder's business
   D. public apologies
6. True or false? Only the U.S. Department of Justice Antitrust Division can file suits for antitrust violations.
7. True or false? It is acceptable for two or more competitors to jointly decide never to use a particular inspector because the inspector is not a direct competitor.
8. True or false? Within the same firm, two agents can charge different fees for the same service.
9. True or false? A real estate license holder can publish his/her fees on the internet.
10. True or false? It is considered an antitrust violation if more than three companies independently decide to stop advertising in the newspaper after an ad-rate hike.

The Clayton Act

The Clayton Antitrust Act of 1914 expanded the Sherman Antitrust Act. Section 15 of the Clayton Act states that "it shall be unlawful for any person engaged in commerce to discriminate in price between different purchasers of services and where the effect of such discrimination may be substantially to lessen competition or tend to create a monopoly in any line of commerce, or to injure, destroy, or prevent competition with any person who either grants or knowingly receives the benefit of such discrimination, or with customers of either of them." The main aspects of the Clayton Act are the prohibition of price-fixing and collaboration between brokers, both of which are also prohibited under the Sherman Antitrust Act, as discussed earlier.

Do-Not-Call, Do-Not-Fax, and Antispam Laws

The do-not-call, do-not-fax, and antispam laws were adopted to limit the numerous unwanted telephone, fax, and email sales communications and spam sent to consumers. Some of these laws have been around for years with very little enforcement. Those days are gone, however. These antinuisance laws are not difficult to follow, but brokers must be sure their license holders are following the rules because a violation by even only one license holder can be very expensive.

History of the Do-Not-Call Rules

In 1991, Congress passed the Telephone Consumer Protection Act. The Act aimed to protect the privacy of residential telephone users. It was to create a national do-not-call registry. A great idea, but it was not developed because of cost and technological limits. The main setbacks concerned who would maintain the registry and how. The law did define when telemarketers may call, and it required telemarketers to maintain internal no-call lists. Real estate license holders were exempt from these rules. There was very little enforcement of the laws, however.

In 2002, the FTC amended the Act by expanding the rules to include real estate license holders. It created the first true National Do Not Call Registry.

In 2003, the Federal Communications Commission (FCC) amended its rules that required telemarketers to use the National Do Not Call Registry maintained by the FTC and gave an "established business relationship" exemption so that:

- rules apply to calls that contain a commercial solicitation (most cold calls); and
- the no-call rules do not apply to calls made when an established business relationship exists.

Under federal rules, an established business relationship exists when the:

- caller had a transaction with the receiver within the past 18 months; or
- customer has made an inquiry with the caller's firm in the past three months.

Generally, to make a prospecting call, the real estate license holder must "scrub" the number against the National Do Not Call Registry and the firm's internal no-call list. If the number does not appear on either list, the license holder may call.

- The real estate license holder may make calls between 9 a.m. and 9 p.m. on weekdays and Saturdays and between 12 p.m. and 9 p.m. on Sundays.
- The caller must identify himself/herself before making the solicitation, must identify it as a solicitation call, and must disclose all material information related to the solicited service.
- The caller may not use caller-ID blocking.

Violators potentially face an $11,000 fine by the federal government for calling a number on the registry, and the state attorney general may bring a civil suit for $500 per call. The federal government does not actually want to cause real estate license holders trouble. The government's main target is the massive telephone canvassing banks through which several hundred people are on the telephone calling consumers. Chances are that if a license holder accidentally calls a number on the National Do Not Call Registry, he/she will not be fined. As the broker, make sure to maintain the internal no-call lists and to have correct procedures in place.

For the observant broker, this law benefits the real estate brokerage business. The law does not prohibit prospecting calls. It only prohibits the call to someone on the National Do Not Call Registry. In the real estate industry, the law has resulted in a great deal of fear and a great deal of relief: fear of being fined for calling the "wrong" person, and relief because of this fear that real estate salespersons can no longer make calls. In other words, if the brokerage's salespersons "scrub" their prospecting lists and continue to call those consumers not on the "Do Not Call" list, they and the broker will make a great deal of money because most real estate salespersons are no longer calling.

> **Case Study**
>
> In Dallas, a real estate broker received a letter in the mail notifying him that he would be brought up on a lawsuit in Minnesota under the do-not-call law if he did not pay the plaintiff $15,000 now. The letter went on to state that the plaintiff had called one of this broker's offices (the broker owned 18) and asked for a copy of the broker's written procedures on how to comply with the Do Not Call Registry rules to be sent to him in Minnesota. The person answering the telephone did not know what to do and dismissed the call as "crazy." By rule, the broker then had 10 days to send the information to the caller or he would be in violation. This broker was now in violation. After lengthy discussions with an attorney, the broker paid.

History of Antispam Rules

The CAN-SPAM Act prohibits the sending of unsolicited email with commercial advertisements unless the subject line is preceded with "ADV" for *advertisement*. It requires the sender to provide the recipient with a means to unsubscribe, which must be honored within ten days. This law also places requirements on senders of spam and imposes penalties for violations.

This Act prohibits the falsification of routing information or sending information. It also prohibits any false, misleading, or deceptive information in the subject line. A fine of $10 per unlawful message or $25,000 for each day, whichever is less, can be issued.

The do-not-call, do-not-fax, and antispam laws are constantly changing, and so it would benefit any real estate brokerage to stay abreast of the latest changes.

Fair Housing

Fair housing pertains to the equal treatment of all people with similar financial means in the purchase or rental of real property. The federal fair housing laws—the Fair Housing Act and the Fair Housing Act Amendments discussed earlier—are designed to allow everyone an opportunity to living in the place of his/her choice by creating an open and unbiased market. The first fair housing law was passed in 1866 and only protected the class of race. A person who experienced racial discrimination in housing was required to bring a suit in federal court to seek relief under this law. In 1968 another fair housing law was adopted as part of the Civil Rights Act. The 1968 law prohibited unequal treatment in housing based on sex, color, national origin, race, or religion. In 1988 familial status and handicap were included as protected classes. Familial status refers to the makeup and relationship of people within a family (e.g., a family with minor children). The Act provides for handicapped persons to make minor modifications to allow their access and use of the property. People with hearing, mobility, and visual disabilities, chronic alcoholism, mental illness, and AIDS are considered handicapped. Complaints for unequal treatment are filed with HUD-FHA. In some circumstances, there is no limit to the damages obtained under the fair housing laws.

Protected Classes

The seven protected classes under the fair housing laws are:

- race
- color
- sex (gender)
- religion
- national origin
- handicap (physical or mental handicap that substantially limits one or more major life activities)
- familial status (under the age of 18, living with parent or guardian; also someone pregnant)

The Supreme Court in Jones v. Mayer ruled that discrimination on the basis of race is strictly prohibited. There are no exceptions with regard to race.

The Fair Housing Act and its amendments do not specifically include sexual orientation and gender identity as prohibited bases for discrimination. However, a lesbian, gay, bisexual, or transgender person's experience with sexual orientation or gender identity housing discrimination may still be covered by the Fair Housing Act. The Act applies to almost all housing in the United States.

Violations

The Fair Housing Act prohibits discrimination in residential real estate transactions and makes it illegal to coerce, intimidate, threaten, or interfere with people exercising their rights under the Act or assisting others in exercising their rights. To comply with the Fair Housing Act, a seller, landlord, lender, insurance agent, realtor, and the like, may not:

- deny housing, offer different terms and conditions to an applicant, or refuse to rent, sell, or negotiate with an applicant because of one or more of the prohibited bases cited above;
- use discriminatory advertising or make discriminatory statements in connection with housing;
- falsely deny that housing is available;
- deny access to or membership in an MLS or real estate broker's organization; and
- discriminate in making loans for, or secured by, residential real estate.

In addition, landlords, condominium boards, homeowner associations, or other entities that exercise control over individual residences or common spaces within a development may not:

- refuse permission for residents with disabilities or their families to make reasonable modifications to housing, at their own expense, if the changes are necessary for a resident to fully enjoy the premises. However, in some instances, the resident may be required to restore the property to its original condition before moving out; and
- refuse to make reasonable accommodations in rules, policies, practices, and services to provide equal opportunity to residents with disabilities to use and enjoy their homes, as long as it does not interfere with the rights of others to use and enjoy their homes.

The Fair Housing Act also prohibits the adoption and enforcement of discriminatory zoning and land use ordinances.

Familial status protections do not apply to certain housing for older people. Such housing is exempt under the law if it is intended for, and solely occupied by, residents 62 years of age or older, or if 80% of the units are occupied by at least one person 55 years of age or older and the housing facility has the intent to have housing for older persons.

Most multifamily dwellings of four or more units are required to be designed and built so that the units are accessible to persons with disabilities.

Best Practices

A broker needs to protect the brokerage against a fair housing complaint. There are several best practices the broker can employ to achieve this end, documenting each time he/she does employ them. The broker should:

- have a written office policy that mirrors the fair housing laws and make clear that even the hint of a violation will not be tolerated by the brokerage
- put a system in place to monitor the activities of each license holder of the brokerage (Have each license holder document every buyer, seller, landlord, and tenant he/she is working with and each property listed or shown. This documentation is critical for a defense against a fair housing complaint.)
- have a reporting procedure for any license holder who believes another license holder is potentially violating a fair housing law
- have quarterly mandatory education courses for the brokerage and document which courses were held and who among the license holders attended
- post a sign that states, "It is against company policy as well as state and federal laws to offer any information on the race, national origin, or religious makeup of a neighborhood or to restrict the showing of a property because of a protected class living or wanting to live in any area."
- prominently display the HUD Equal Housing Opportunity Poster, which can be found on HUD's website
- always act in the appropriate manner and treat every person with respectful, honest, and fair treatment (The broker must also demand the same actions from the license holders.)

Fair Housing Enforcement

Any person who believes he/she has been discriminated against may file a complaint with HUD within one year from the alleged act. The plaintiff (i.e., complainant) has two years to file a civil suit for discrimination. HUD will try to reach a settlement, called "conciliation," between the plaintiff and the defendant (i.e., respondent). If none can be obtained, the case will be referred to an administrative law judge (ALJ), and if the ALJ decides that discrimination has occurred, the defendant could be ordered to:

- compensate the plaintiff for damages, including but not limited to humiliation, pain, and suffering
- provide the housing available to the plaintiff

- pay a civil penalty to the federal government as punishment
- pay reasonable attorney's fees and court costs

Questions for Fair Housing Compliance

1. What would you say if the sellers asked you not to show their home to a protected class?
2. If a person from another country wanted to live in an area where there are like people, how would you address that?
3. Would you show a house to a person in a wheelchair if you knew that the only way to access that house was by a staircase with hundreds of steps?
4. As a property manager, would you allow a woman and her 11 kids to occupy a three-bedroom apartment? Does she fall under the protected class of "familial status"?

Real Estate Settlement Procedures Act

RESPA, first passed in 1974, requires consumer disclosures and specifies distinctive roles for real estate professionals and related service companies. One of its purposes is to help consumers become better shoppers for settlement services. Another purpose is to eliminate kickbacks and referral fees that unnecessarily increase the costs of certain settlement services. RESPA requires that borrowers receive disclosures at various times. Some disclosures make clear the costs associated with the settlement, outline lender servicing, describe escrow account practices, and portray business relationships between settlement service providers.

Section 8 of RESPA prohibits a person from giving or accepting anything of value for referrals of settlement service business related to a federally related mortgage loan. It also prohibits a person from giving or accepting any part of a charge for services that are not performed. Section 9 of RESPA prohibits home sellers from requiring home buyers to purchase title insurance from a particular company.

Generally, RESPA covers loans secured with a mortgage placed on a one- to four-family residential property. These include most purchase loans, assumptions, refinances, property improvement loans, and equity lines of credit. HUD's Office of Consumer and Regulatory Affairs Interstate Land Sales/RESPA Division is responsible for enforcing RESPA.

Ethical and Legal Business Practices

CHAPTER SUMMARY

Ethics refers to "moral character." The major principle of ethics comes from the Latin *primum non nocere,* meaning "First, do no harm."

Here are some overall ethics standards of practice that brokers should incorporate in their brokerage firm:

legal law	moral law
staff	presentation
no risk	inspections by licensed inspectors
seller's disclosure notice	
qualifying of home buyers	information provided by the government
negotiation	
disclosures	marketing
confidentiality	training
civic duty	prospecting
	advice

Business ethics are a code of ethics set up by business associations or groups for their members to follow.

The main reason the National Association of REALTORS® (NAR) has a code of ethics is to further the positive reputation of the real estate professional in the market. NAR's Code of Ethics and Standards of Practice (collectively, the Code) are more extensive than the Texas Real Estate Commission (TREC) Canons of Professional Ethics and Conduct. They contain 17 articles covering three broad categories: Duties to Clients and Customers (Articles 1–9), Duties to the Public (Articles 10–14), and Duties to REALTORS® (Article 15–17). The Code is imposed only on NAR members who "pledge to observe its spirit in all their activities and to conduct their business in accordance with the tenets."

The TREC Code incorporates three main canons (i.e., rules or laws). These are broad and encompassing to allow the TREC wide-reaching power to protect the public from improper actions by license holders. These three important canons are:

1. §531.1 Fidelity
2. §531.2 Integrity
3. §531.3 Competency

Real estate laws generally prohibit specific activities such as:

- payment of fees to unlicensed persons
- material misrepresentation of a significant property defect
- felony conviction, especially for fraud
- fraudulent procurement of real estate
- dishonesty
- failure to cooperate with the state's real estate commission
- false advertising
- maintaining undisclosed agency relationships
- commingling, or mixing of personal funds with those of another
- conversion, or using funds of others for a use other than intended
- negligent or incompetent behavior

Here are some terms and their meanings as used in the real estate industry:

- ***Licensee*** (also called license holder) is a broker or sales agent licensed under the Texas Real Estate License Act (TRELA).
- ***Real estate*** is any interest in real property, including a leasehold, located in or outside Texas.
- ***Sales agent*** is a person who is sponsored by a licensed broker for the purpose of performing an act described by TRELA.
- ***Subagent*** is a license holder who represents a principal through cooperation with and consent of a broker representing the principal and is not sponsored by or associated with the principal's broker.

The TRELA does not apply to a(n):

- attorney licensed in Texas;
- attorney-in-fact authorized under a power of attorney to conduct not more than three real estate transactions annually;
- public official while engaged in official duties;
- licensed auctioneer licensed while conducting the sale of real estate by auction if the auctioneer does not perform another act of a broker;
- person conducting a real estate transaction under a court order or the authority of a will or written trust instrument;
- person employed by an owner in the sale of structures and land on which structures are located if the structures are erected by the owner in the course of the owner's business (builder);

Ethical and Legal Business Practices

- on-site manager of an apartment complex;
- owner or the owner's employee who leases the owner's improved or unimproved real estate; or
- transaction involving the:
  - sale, lease, or transfer of a mineral or mining interest in real property;
  - sale, lease, or transfer of a cemetery lot;
  - lease or management of a hotel or motel; or
  - sale of real property under a power of sale conferred by a deed of trust or other contract

There are many national laws that affect real estate. A few of these are:

CAN-SPAM Act
Community Reinvestment Act (CRA)
Do Not Call Act
Dodd-Frank Wall Street Reform and Consumer Protection Act
Equal Credit Opportunity Act (ECOA)
Fair Credit Reporting Act (FCRA)
Truth-in-Lending Act (TILA)
USA Patriot Act

The Deceptive Trade Practices Act (DTPA) is probably the best protection available to consumers in business transactions. Its provisions ensure that real estate license holders behave professionally and serve their clients knowledgeably and honestly. The DTPA asks two questions:

- Did you know?
- Should you have known?

Intentionally misleading a person is fraud. A misrepresentation that results in fraud will cancel any E&O insurance that the broker may have obtained. Certain factors must be in place for an action to be considered fraud, including:

- reliance
- intent
- damage

These defenses should be used to protect the license holder as much as possible:

- inspections by licensed inspectors

- written Seller's Disclosure Notice (SDN)
- information from the government

The following defenses under the DTPA will not work:

- waiver
- "as is"
- *caveat emptor* (Let the buyer beware.)

The DTPA provides a "laundry list" of practices that are clearly deceptive:

- passing off goods or services as those of another
- causing confusion or misunderstanding as to the source, sponsorship, approval, or certification of goods or services
- causing confusion or misunderstanding as to affiliation, connection, or association with, or certification by, another
- using deceptive representatives or designations of geographic origin in connection with goods or services
- representing goods or services that claim to have sponsorship, approval, characteristics, ingredients, uses, benefits, or quantities but do not; or claiming to have a sponsorship, approval, status, affiliation, or connection but not having them
- representing that goods are original or new if they are deteriorated, reconditioned, reclaimed, used, or secondhand
- representing that goods or services are of a particular standard, quality, or grade or that goods are of a particular style or model if they are of another
- disparaging the goods, services, or business of another by false or misleading representations of facts
- advertising goods or services with intent not to sell them as advertised
- advertising goods or services with intent not to supply a reasonable, expectable public demand, unless the advertisement disclosed a limitation of quantity
- making false or misleading statements of fact concerning the reasons for, existence of, or amount of price reductions

Some important definitions of actions associated with DTPA prohibitions are these:

- *unconscionable action.* An unconscionable action is defined as any action that takes advantage of the lack of knowledge, ability,

experience, or capacity of a person to a grossly unfair degree or one in which there is a gross disparity between the value received and the consideration paid.
- *knowingly*. To act knowingly is to have actual awareness; in this context, to have awareness that an action is prohibited.
- *intentionally*. To act intentionally is to have actual awareness of the falsity of a claim.

The NAR, "The Voice for Real Estate," is America's largest trade association, which includes institutes, societies, and councils involved in all aspects of the residential and commercial real estate industries.

TREC rules delineate the responsibilities assigned to real estate brokers in TREC Rules §535.2 Broker Responsibility. Under these rules, a broker:

- must notify a sponsored sales agent in writing of the scope of that agent's authorized activities under the Act
- "owes the highest fiduciary obligation to the principal"
- is responsible for properly handling trust funds held by the broker
- takes responsibility for the property management activity of his/her sponsored sales agents
- may have another licensee assist in administering compliance
- must accept the real estate brokerage services agreements in his/her own name
- must ensure that advertising complies with TRELA rules

In addition, the TREC requires brokers to:

- keep records for at least four years
- maintain written policies and procedures to ensure that each sponsored agent:
  - is advised of the scope of the sales agent's authorized activities
  - maintains their license in active status
  - is paid compensation owed by the sponsoring broker
  - receives notice of any change to TRELA
  - receives the additional educational instruction required
  - complies with TREC' advertising rules
- maintain all trust accounts received from consumers
- respond to sponsored agents, clients, and licensees within three business days
- deliver TREC correspondence from sponsored agents within 10 business days

In addition, under TREC rules, when the broker is a business entity, the designated broker is the person responsible for compliance with all TREC requirements.

Certain business practices may be construed as unfair and therefore illegal. These include trademark infringement, passing off, misappropriation, trade libel, false light, and tortious interference.

A real estate broker should never engage in any business practices that could be construed as unfair business practices.

The Fair Credit Reporting Act, which ensures the accuracy and privacy of information kept by credit bureaus and other consumer reporting agencies, gives consumers the right to know what information these entities are distributing about them to creditors, insurance companies, and employers.

The Gramm-Leach-Bliley Act requires financial institutions to ensure the security and confidentiality of customer information, provide notice to consumers about their information practices, and give consumers an opportunity to direct that their personal information not be shared with certain non-affiliated third parties.

The Children's Online Privacy Protection Act is meant to give parents control over information online companies can collect about their children and how such information can be used.

The Federal Trade Commission's (FTC) Division of Privacy and Identity Protection operates the Identity Theft Data Clearinghouse, which houses the federal government's centralized repository for consumer identity theft complaints. The Division analyzes identity theft trends, promotes the development and efficacy of identity fraud prevention strategies in the financial services industry, and identifies targets for referral to criminal law enforcement.

The FTC Division of Advertising Practices protects consumers from unfair or deceptive advertising and marketing practices that raise health and safety concerns, as well as those that cause economic injury.

The FTC Division of Enforcement litigates civil contempt and civil penalty actions to enforce federal court injunctions and administrative orders in FTC consumer protection cases; coordinates FTC actions with criminal law enforcement agencies through its Criminal Liaison Unit; develops, reviews, and enforces a variety of consumer protection rules; coordinates multipronged initiatives to address current consumer protection issues; and administers the Bureau of Consumer Protection's bankruptcy program.

The FTC Division of Marketing Practices responds to ever-evolving problems of consumer fraud in the marketplace.

The FTC Division of Consumer Response & Operations collects and analyzes data to target law enforcement and education efforts and measure the impact of activities related to the FTC's consumer protection mission.

The FTC Financial Practices Division promotes truthfulness and fairness in the provision of these services by entities within the FTC's jurisdiction so that consumers can make better-informed decisions.

The FTC Division of Litigation Technology and Analysis plays a central role in the bureau's investigation and litigation of consumer protection matters.

The Americans with Disabilities Act (ADA) is a civil rights law that prohibits discrimination against individuals with disabilities in all areas of public life.

Agency law is derived from common law. This simply means that agency law applies to everyone. An agent is one who acts for and on behalf of another.

An intermediary office represents buyers and also represents sellers.

In Texas, a broker owes general fiduciary duties to his/her client. These duties are loyalty, good faith, honesty, refraining from self-dealing, integrity, fair and honest dealing, and disclosure.

The specific duties a broker owes to his/her client are:

- representing the interest of the client as the primary duty: being faithful to the client and observant (mindful) of the duty of trust and not placing personal interest above the client's interest
- disclosing to his/her client any conflict of interest or any matter that would affect the client's decision in a transaction
- communicating clearly to all parties in a transaction whom the broker represents
- when performing brokerage duties,
  - acting meticulously and scrupulously
  - exercising integrity
  - employing prudence and caution to avoid any misrepresentation
  - exercising judgment and skill
  - not acting negligently, in an untrustworthy or dishonest manner, or in bad faith
- keeping informed about his/her practice, the market, and developments in the industry

- keeping the client informed of material information related to a transaction, including but not limited to the receipt of any offer
- being available to answer the client's questions
- giving the client a proper accounting of all funds received in the transaction; not commingling any funds held for another with the broker's own funds

The Fair Housing Act was founded on the belief that any real estate professional should describe the property, not a principal, in the transaction.

A contract is a voluntary agreement between legally competent parties to perform or refrain from performing some legal act, supported by legal consideration. This definition includes the four elements for any contract:

- *voluntary agreement.* All parties must agree voluntarily to all the terms of the contract. There must be no:
  - misrepresentation
  - fraud
  - duress
  - menace
  - undue influence
- *legally competent parties.* All who sign the contract must have the mental capacity to be held to the terms of a contract. The parties must be at least 18 years of age.
- *legal consideration.* Something is given in exchange for something else. It could be a promise in exchange for a promise. Valuable consideration is something of actual value like money or personal property. Good consideration is love or affection, and gratuitous consideration is a free promise.
- *legal objective.* The contract must be of legal purpose. The contract cannot violate the law.

The Statute of Frauds requires all contracts for the sale of real property to be in writing to be enforceable. It requires all leases for more than one year to be in writing to be enforceable.

Earnest money is given in good faith and may involve liquidated damages.

The Statute of Limitations for a written contract is four years from the date of the breach; for an oral contract, two years.

The Seller' Disclosure Notice (SDN) is a disclosure of seller's knowledge of the condition of the property.

The Intermediary Relationship Notice is used to notify the buyers and sellers that the broker is now an intermediary. The form requires the written authorization for the broker to proceed in this transaction.

All license holders are required to give prospective buyers, tenants, sellers, and landlords information about brokerage services.

TAR 1414 Information About Special Flood Hazard Areas discloses flood areas as defined by the Federal Emergency Management Agency (FEMA).

TAR 1928 HUD Notice to Purchasers: Importance of Home Inspections discloses to buyers the need to obtain property inspections.

TAR 2505 Notice to Prospective Buyer discloses that the buyers should have the abstract examined by an attorney or the buyers should have furnished to them a policy of title insurance.

Any time a real estate brokerage has a monetary relationship with a residential service company, that relationship must be disclosed to the buyer and to the seller.

If the real property that the buyer is about to purchase is located in a propane gas system service area, the buyer is entitled to receive the statutory notice.

The Sherman Antitrust Act prohibits any type of collaboration of businesses to the detriment of consumers. Antitrust prohibits price-fixing, which is the act of two or more competitors joining together to force consumers to pay a higher amount than they would pay if competition were unrestrained. In addition, antitrust prohibits the allocation of customers, which is a violation of the Act.

The do-not-call, do-not-fax, and antispam laws were adopted to limit the numerous unwanted telephone, fax, and email communications sent to consumers.

Fair housing refers to federal laws pertaining to the equal treatment of all people with similar financial means in the purchase or rental of real property. The seven protected classes under fair housing are:

- race
- color
- sex (gender)
- religion
- national origin

- handicap (physical or mental handicap that substantially limits one or more major life activities)
- familial status (under the age of 18, living with parent or guardian; also someone pregnant)

The Fair Housing Act prohibits discrimination in residential real estate transactions and makes it illegal to interfere with people exercising their rights under the Act. To comply with the Fair Housing Act, a professional may not:

- deny housing
- use discriminatory advertising or make discriminatory statements in connection with housing
- falsely deny that housing is available;
- deny access to or membership in an MLS or real estate broker's organization
- discriminate in making loans
- refuse permission for residents with disabilities or their families to make reasonable modifications to housing at their own expense
- refuse to make reasonable accommodations in rules, policies, practices, and services to provide residents with disabilities equal opportunity to use and enjoy their homes

The Real Estate Settlement Procedures Act (RESPA) requires consumer disclosures and specifies distinctive roles for real estate professionals and related service companies.

Answers to Quiz on Agency Law

1. True
2. True
3. True
4. True
5. False (Promise to pay is NOT a primary element in the creation of an agency relationship.)
6. True
7. True
8. True
9. False (A fiduciary relationship exists when a license holder acts as an agent for another person.)
10. False (Janice is the agent of Howard, the client whom she represents.)

Answers to Antitrust Questions

1. False
2. False
3. A
4. C
5. A, B, C
6. False (The FTC, state attorney general, and private parties can file suits.)
7. False
8. True
9. True
10. False

Answers for Fair Housing Compliance

1. *Best Answer*: Overcome that objection by asking questions.
   Good Answer: Walk away from the listing.
   Wrong Answer: Agree with the seller.

2. *Best Answer*: Overcome that objection by asking questions.
   Good Answer: Say that would be a violation.
   Wrong Answer: Know areas by class standards.

3. *Best Answer*: Yes—The buyer must deny the showing.
   Good Answer: Yes—After describing the property.
   Wrong Answer: No—They could not get in.

4. *Best Answer*: No—Texas Property Code states three persons per room.
   Good Answer: No—This goes against standard operating policy.
   Wrong Answer: Yes—It would be a violation.

CHAPTER QUESTIONS

1. The major principle of ethics comes from the Latin *primum non nocere*, meaning:
   A. First, do no harm.
   B. It is senseless.
   C. Do not unto others.
   D. This is the prime directive.

2. A code of ethics set up by associations or work groups for their members to follow is called business:
   A. law
   B. morals
   C. ethics
   D. code

3. To obtain a broker's license, a candidate must show:
   A. honesty
   B. integrity
   C. trustworthiness
   D. fidelity

4. What does the National Do Not Call Registry regulate?
   A. promotion of business-involved loan modifications
   B. the reporting of earnest-money deposits
   C. marketing real estate to consumers
   D. disclosure of affiliated businesses

5. The broker is responsible for which of the following?
   A. highest fiduciary obligation to the principal
   B. proper handling of trust funds
   C. property management activity by his/her sponsored sales agents
   D. all of the answer choices

6. What is it called when one competitor interferes in another competitor's contract or relationship with a third party?
   A. contract blocking
   B. tortious interference
   C. conversion
   D. boycotting

7. Which agency policy allows a brokerage to represent both buyers and sellers in a single transaction?
   A. seller-only agency
   B. buyer-only agency
   C. intermediary
   D. complete agency

8. Which law was founded on the belief that an agent should describe the property and not the parties involved?
   A. Fair Housing Act
   B. Real Estate Settlement Procedures Act (RESPA)
   C. Deceptive Trade Practices Act (DTPA)
   D. Sherman Antitrust Act

9. Which is not a protected class under the National Fair Housing Act?
   A. race
   B. color
   C. religion
   D. age

10. Which document discloses the seller's knowledge of the property condition?
    A. Owner's Realty Announcement
    B. Seller's Disclosure Notice
    C. Buyer's Acknowledgment of Property Condition
    D. Property Defects and Remedies

CHAPTER 4

Analyzing the Market and the Competition

A real estate broker must be aware of the market and of the competition. The broker needs to understand the real estate market and how it is trending. A broker once took this for granted and expanded her offices. She acquired several offices, but the market was changing. At one point she was losing over $100,000 a month. The market had indications of change, but she ignored them and it cost her dearly.

The broker must also be aware of the competitors of his/her brokerage and his/her license holders. One broker failed to monitor the competition, and the competition moved in down the road with the latest, greatest office and took over half of his license holders. He never did recover. He is still in business, but he never regained the market share and is continually fighting just to break even.

No one wants to own a real estate brokerage and fight to break even. A brokerage needs to be a profitable business, or it should never be opened. Knowing the market and what the competition is contemplating is crucial for survival as well as profit.

What Is the Real Estate Market?

The real estate market is composed of all types of real estate in all locations at any price. As the definition is limited, the market becomes smaller. The real estate market could be limited by type. There are several categories of property, including residential, farm and ranch, commercial, industrial, fine homes and estates, and vacation property.

Each of these real estate markets can be subdivided into smaller real estate markets. Take residential; it could be subdivided by price

range, square footage, age, location, amenities and many others, each creating its own market. They can also be classified according to buyer's and seller's markets.

Residential Market

The residential market is made up of single-family homes, duplexes, triplexes, and quads. Typically anything bigger than a quad would be considered commercial. A single-family residence is the most common type of residential sale. A single-family home could range from less than 100 square feet—popularly called a "Tiny House"—to as large as 20,000 square feet. The single-family home can be located in a city or in the country. A duplex is an attached housing property with a party wall. A party wall is the wall that separates both units. A triplex is three units, and a quadruple unit (quad) is a building with four separate units. Any of these housing units can be multistory. Quads can have two units up and two down or all four units on the ground level.

Farm-and-Ranch Market

The farm-and-ranch market is made up of properties with acreage usually outside any city jurisdiction. The farm is generally referred as to a crop-growing type of property, and a ranch is a livestock-raising type of property. A farm-and-ranch property is usually 5 acres or more and may be as large as several thousand acres. A ranchette is usually 5 acres or less with a country setup but typically not production. Issues of farm and ranch include determining the owner of the annual crops in the field and the livestock present. Other issues include determining the value of such things as cross fencing, pipe fencing, cable fencing, barns, barndominium (i.e., house inside a barn), stock ponds (i.e., tanks), chutes, and more. The use of the farm and ranch is also in question: Will it be production or a showplace? Will it be leased as hunting land or farm land? All are questions that factor into the farm-and-ranch market. A farm-and-ranch broker may have to market worldwide to find just the right buyer for a particular farm or ranch.

Commercial Market

The commercial market is made up of income-producing commercial properties and properties intended "for business." Income-producing properties include shopping malls, apartment complexes, and office buildings.

Industrial Market

The industrial market is similar to the commercial market in the aspect of income-producing properties. However, because these properties are used for industry, the real estate properties are specific in nature, conforming to the needed use of the building by the specific industry. Some may have refrigeration capabilities, some may have extremely high-factor floors for cranes, and some may have shipping bays to move product out to the consumers.

Fine Homes and Estates Market

The market for fine homes and estates is generally considered a residential property market of houses that are valued at over $500,000. These properties are unique in their amenities. A special licensee, with knowledge of this type of property, is needed to sell fine homes and estates. The buyers for this type of property, like those for farm and ranch, may hail from all over the world. The commission on a multimillion-dollar luxury estate may be high, but an actual qualified buyer may be rare.

Vacation Property Market

A true specialty in the real estate sales business is the vacation property market. Most often thought of as resort properties because they are usually around a lake, recreation area, or area of high interest. The buyers for these types of properties must be able to afford their current residence while also affording the payments on their vacation property.

Some vacation properties are of the "timeshare" variety. A timeshare has multiple owners, each having one or two weeks per year when the property is "theirs." The rest of the year the property belongs to each of the other owners. The reason timeshare properties work is that most resorts are for the vacationer who has a week or two away from work and wants to spend these weeks relaxing and enjoying some time off.

The real estate market could be divided by location. Subdivisions typically create their own real estate markets. Real estate is local, which simply means that most of the variations in price occur on the local level and are rarely affected by national or international issues.

Buyer's Market

A buyer's market is when there are few buyers and a great number of sellers. This market drives prices down and places the buyer in the best negotiating position. In this market, sellers may be desperate to sell, and a buyer who does not like the negotiation process for a particular property will simply find another property down the street. Buyers offer significantly less than the asking price; they ask for everything and give nothing. The buyers ask and get personal property, have insignificant repairs made, and require the sellers to pay the buyer closing costs. The seller has not had a showing in weeks, and this is the first offer in months.

Real estate brokers should be aware of the specific characteristics of a buyer's market:

- few offers
- long market time
- buyer's demand for everything
- low earnest-money deposits
- lowball offers

Real estate brokers in this market will tend to look to help sellers. Sellers are anxious to sell, and real estate professionals have the ability to market a property on a wider scale than an individual seller. That additional exposure may entice another buyer to actually buy.

Seller's Market

A seller's market is when there are few sellers and a great number of buyers. This market drives prices up and places the seller in the best negotiating position. Buyers are desperate to buy, and the seller who does not like the negotiation process will simply accept a different buyer's offer. In one seller's market, a listing agent put a property on the market at fair market value on Friday. By Monday, just three days later, the seller had 57 showings and nine offers. Two of the offers were full price, but seven were over the asking price! Buyers ask for nothing extra in this market, and their offer will not even be considered if they do.

Real estate brokers should be aware of the specific characteristics of a seller's market:

- multiple offers
- short market time (just a few days)
- prequalified or cash offers
- no contingencies to hinder the sale
- high earnest-money deposit
- no personal property included
- full price or higher offers

Real estate brokers in this market tend to specialize in buyer representation. Buyers need help finding and negotiating to get a property. The buyers need coaching on being patient and yet reacting quickly when a potential property does become available.

Analyzing the Market

The real estate market should be analyzed daily because it can change so drastically in a short period of time on local issues. Suppose a large conglomerate moves into a local area. The market may jump drastically overnight just because of the announcement. Hundreds of jobs are created, bringing in new workers who need places to live, thereby driving up prices.

Case Study

Rhome, Texas, is a sleepy little town outside the Dallas/Fort Worth metroplex. Intel Corporation announced that it would be moving its entire international operations to Rhome. Land in Rhome had been going for about $5,000 per acre. After the announcement, the property values started to skyrocket. Not only will Intel need land, but workers will need land for houses, and parasite companies— those totally dependent on the big corporation that will follow the corporation wherever it goes—will need land. At one point after the announcement, the land was selling for $25,000 per acre. After all this real estate action, Intel announced that sales of microprocessors were down and therefore the company would no longer relocate. The price of land in Rhome, Texas, returned to its previous price of approximately $5,000 per acre.

The reason for the drastic changes in real estate property prices in Rhome is known as the "Principle of Anticipation." However, real estate markets are slow to adjust to national or international events. The local real estate market does not vary with interest rates as much as the media would like to portray. After the World Trade Center was attacked by terrorists, the local real estate market was not adversely affected. Only a few transactions fell out, and those were quickly back, sold to waiting buyers.

To analyze the real estate market, the broker should use multiple sources to help in the analysis. These should include the National Association of REALTORS® (NAR).

The NAR researches a wide range of topics of interest to real estate brokers, including market data, commercial and international trends, home buying and selling, and technology. Brokers can use the data NAR provides to improve their business through knowledge of the latest trends and statistics as long as the broker is a member of NAR.

NAR publishes a guide for brokers called "NAR Research Resource Guide." This is a guide to the surveys, reports, data, and products that NAR Research has created, updated for the current year. The broker can use the information to plan the future of his/her brokerage.

Pending Home Sales Index

A leading indicator for housing activity, the Pending Home Sales Index is released each month and measures housing contract activity. If the broker notices that the existing home sales report shows level activity but the pending report indicates an increase in the market, there might be change coming. The reason the Pending Home Sales Index may be greater than the existing home sales is that the market is increasing.

Housing Affordability Index

The Housing Affordability Index measures whether or not a typical family earns enough income to qualify for a mortgage loan on a typical home at the national and regional levels based on the most recent monthly price and income data. With this information brokers can market their area based on the index. This information is also critical for use at a client presentation to indicate why individuals in the local market are renting or buying homes.

Metropolitan Median Home Prices and Affordability

The NAR releases statistics on metropolitan-area housing affordability and metropolitan-area median home prices each quarter. This price report reflects sales prices of existing single-family homes by metropolitan statistical area. This report is similar to the Housing Affordability Index except that it looks at larger metropolitan cities and how those major hubs are reacting to the market.

Real Estate Center

The Real Estate Center comprises a group of economists commissioned by the Texas Real Estate Commission (TREC) to track real estate data and report those data to the public. The economists travel the state giving lectures and presenting the latest data they have obtained. The information is always relevant and worthwhile. The Center is the nation's largest publicly funded organization devoted to real estate research of which most of that money is from real estate license fees. The Center's staff conducts research on financial, socioeconomic, public policy, trade, land use, and local market analysis issues related to real estate.

The Real Estate Center offers publications with current data on a wide range of real estate topics; some are Texas-specific publications such as *News Talk Texas*, and others are general real estate publications like the quarterly magazine *Tierra Grande*. The Center is probably the single best source of real estate statistical information in the state of Texas.

Analyzing the Competition

A wise broker will always be in touch with what the competition is doing. The broker should analyze the local competition by monitoring their advertising campaigns, recruiting efforts, and any type of expansion. The broker should be aware of any national franchise wanting to place a new office in the broker's market area. Being aware of the competition allows the broker sufficient time to adequately respond to a competitor's challenge to the broker's market share. The broker should research local competitors as well as outside competition.

Research Local Competitors

Researching local competitors requires looking at the specific factors explained here:

- *market share*—The broker needs to know how much market share each local competitor holds. The broker should determine if one competitor holds a large share of the market. This could mean that there is room for another, or it could mean that one competitor is so good that no other brokerage is worthy. If there are many competitors and a slow or limited market, there may not be enough business for yet another competitor. Frequently, a broker will claim that he/she can take on any competitor. This may not be the best strategy. A broker may be wise not to financially fight a competitor but to look for an area that is underserved and dominate that area quickly.
  - *number of license holders*—The broker needs to know how many license holders each competitor has on his/her roster. If one brokerage has a majority of the license holders, it may be hard to recruit against that brokerage. If a brokerage has only a few license holders, that brokerage may be a good candidate for acquisition.
  - *production of license holders*—The broker should research local competitors to determine how much each license holder produces for the brokerage. If a brokerage has a significant number of license holders but few are quality producers, that brokerage may be struggling. If the brokerage has a few license holders but high producers, that brokerage may be tough to compete against, so the broker may want to find a new location.
  - *years in business*—The broker should want to know how many years any competing broker has been in the business and how many years the brokerage company has been in the business. If the competing broker is new, he/she may be prone to mistakes, mistakes a good competitor could capitalize on. If the competing broker is a long-time real estate veteran, perhaps he/she is not up-to-date on the latest trends and technology—this could be another gap that enables the new broker to compete.
  - *marketing campaigns*—The broker needs to find out if any of the competition is conducting extensive marketing campaigns to obtain customers. A broker is wise not to get into a spending competition with another broker; doing so can be very

costly. However, if no brokerage has a major marketing campaign, then the broker may be able to gain market share if he/she implements one.
- *recruiting efforts*—The broker needs to determine if any competing brokers have continuous recruiting efforts. This could be potentially dangerous to a broker if the brokerage opens its doors and all of the brokerage's license holders are recruited out.
- *number of locations*—Real estate companies with multiple offices can have a decided advantage over single offices. The advantage also comes with challenges that can, if not handled properly, lead to disadvantages. Multiple offices typically require a management staff and duplication of all office supplies, equipment, and accounting. A well-run, multiple-office brokerage will have economies of scale and a larger marketing budget. However, only one office brokerages can respond quickly to market changes and create competitive, productive niches in the real estate industry.
- *expansion*—The broker needs to know if any brokerage is contemplating expansion. One small brokerage is not much competition, but if that same brokerage expands to five offices in the market area, that may be enough to end all other brokerages.

Research Outside Competitors

Plans to Enter the Local Market
The broker needs to be aware of any new brokers contemplating entering the local real estate market. A broker should never be surprised by the entry of a new broker. When a new broker is entering the local market, all other brokers need to be keenly aware of their current license holders. The new broker brings excitement, and that excitement is a prime recruiting tool for the new brokerage. A broker who believes that all his/her license holders are happy and will never leave will soon be lonely.

New Office Location
The broker needs to know where the new brokerage will be located. If that brokerage locates in a progressive area, that brokerage may see a great deal of business go its way when the business could have gone to

the current local brokers. Wise brokers will preempt the new brokerage by arranging an aggressive marketing campaign around the new brokerage's location.

Marketing Campaigns

New brokerages may decide to announce a new location by using a marketing campaign. Brokers needs to be aware of such marketing campaigns and challenge them by creating marketing campaigns of their own.

Advancements of New Office

A broker needs to know what the new brokerage will offer to local license holders. If the brokerage is entering the market with a large amount of spending capital, this broker will have the latest, greatest office. One broker entered a local market with a marble entry, the best technology, and multiple services offered to license holders. This brokerage decimated all other local brokerages because each lost multiple license holders to the new, "*awesome*" brokerage.

Analyzing an Organization

The best way to analyze an organization is to let the professionals handle it. A professional accountant or business attorney will be the best avenue to obtain a detailed analysis of an organization. The professionals can make an overall examination as well as provide detailed reports on a real estate brokerage. This analysis is expensive but well worth it. If a business is struggling, these data would be key to restructuring the organization to become profitable. If a broker is looking to buy an existing brokerage, these data would be crucial to making a wise investment.

A broker himself/herself can gather the information to analyze an organization, but doing so is time consuming and the data may be tainted by the broker's bias. The broker would need to procure the following types of data:

- *overall profitability report*—The balance sheet is the most important here because it shows itemized accounts and overall balances in each income and expense category.

- *total number of listings taken*—This number indicates the future of the brokerage. Listings taken shows the brokerage will be profitable well into the future. If this number is low, the brokerage may be heading to lean times.
- *average price range of listings*—This number is an indication of the amount of the commissions that will be earned. If the average price range of brokerage listings is high, the money will follow. If the price range of the brokerage listings is low, the license holders will spend as much time but receive considerably less as income.
- *average days on market*—This number indicates the market pace and the ability of the brokerage to sell real estate. If the number is high, more effort needs to be spent on pricing and marketing.
- *total number of sales completed*—This number includes the buyer-side sales as well as the listings. This number will show progress from the past or failures in the present.
- *total commissions earned*—This is the total amount of the commissions earned by the brokerage.
- *total commissions retained*—This is the amount of the commissions that remains with the brokerage. If this number is too high the brokerage may not be able to survive because the brokerage is paying too much to the current in-house license holders.
- *agent report*—This includes the number of current license holders, the number of license holders recruited, and the number of license holders lost.

Developing and Implementing a Business Plan

Any business that has a chance to survive begins with business planning. Good real estate brokers plan their business and then execute the plan. Planning may be avoided for any number of reasons, including not knowing how, fear, and too much enthusiasm that blinds reason. This chapter will teach the reader how to begin to plan to run a real estate brokerage business. Any business that fails to plan is bound to fail.

Writing a Business Plan

Writing a business plan is one of the most important aspects of starting a real estate business in today's changing environment. Starting a real estate brokerage is a challenge in itself. So many people looking for a change are jumping into the real estate brokerage business without first planning their new venture. The importance of spending time planning for any business venture cannot be overemphasized.

The real estate brokerage business plan should convey the business's overall goals from the viewpoint of the broker. It should also entail the core values of the business. It should be written in a way to help the business succeed today, tomorrow, and far into the future.

By taking an unbiased look at the business, the broker can identify areas of weaknesses and strengths that the broker might otherwise overlook. Planning can mean the difference between success and failure.

The idea of a plan is to help keep the broker mentally focused. In a sense, it is like setting a goal: First the goal must be desired, it must be written it down, and it must be followed. If changes and updates are needed, those changes are adopted. Doing so will help the broker keep everything in proper perspective; because without a step-by-step business plan, there is no way a broker can keep the real estate brokerage business running successfully.

Writing a business plan is simply the process the broker will use to organize business goals and strategies. The plan document is a written expression of the business ideas, and it also provides information needed for others to evaluate the business. A thorough business plan will show any investors that the broker is prepared for the real estate business and that money invested in this business is money well invested.

When it comes to preparing a business plan, the broker is going to organize it to fit the particular circumstances that currently exist. A business plan should be one of the first things a new real estate broker implements before getting too involved in the real estate brokerage business. It is best to plan a business before starting it.

A broker should keep in mind the required elements of a written business plan, explained next.

Cover Page

The cover page tells what business is being planned and how to reach the writer. The cover page should read "Business Plan" and should include the broker's:

- personal name
- business name
- business logo
- business trademark
- business charter
- address
- telephone number
- fax number (if needed)
- email address
- license number

The date should also be included on the cover page.

Table of Contents

The table of contents should be one page and should give details of the contents of the business plan. The table of contents indicates how well the broker has organized the entire plan and should make it easy to navigate through the plan.

The table of contents provides a quick and easy way to find particular sections of the plan. All pages of the business plan should be numbered, and the table of contents should include the page numbers. After the broker assembles the plan and numbers the pages, the broker should go back to the table of contents to insert correct page numbers. The broker should be sure to list headings for major sections, as well as for important subsections.

Executive Summary

The executive summary is a brief statement summing up the purpose of the business and covering the substance or main points of the brokerage business; it determines what kind of first impression the broker will make on any readers. The executive summary should answer the following questions:

- What is the brokerage's distinct service?
- What are the broker's personal goals?
- What are the broker's personal objectives?
- What is the broker's business or previous job history?

Although the executive summary is the first part of the plan, it should be written last. As the broker creates the other sections of the business plan, the broker should designate sentences or sections for inclusion in the Executive Summary. The Executive Summary should be between one and three pages and should include the business concept, financial features, financial requirements, current state of the business, date when the business was formed, and principal owners and key personnel of the business, as well as the major achievements of the business. Brokers should use industry association statistics, market research from other sources, and other documenting information to back up statements they make.

The broker should keep the Executive Summary short, interesting, and polished. The broker should have several people read it—both those who know the business and those who do not—to check for clarity and presentation.

Mission Statement

The discussion of the business should begin with the brokerage's mission statement, which comprises one or two sentences describing the purpose of the business and to whom the real estate services are targeted. Not being clear in the mission statement indicates that the broker is not clear about the purpose of the business.

Vision Statement

Too many real estate brokers make the mistake of operating without a vision—a situation that hampers the ability of their business to grow and prosper. A real estate broker without a vision will have difficulty describing his/her business. A concise, easy-to-understand description of the business will not only help the broker write the business plan but also benefit the broker in any number of other day-to-day situations.

> *The vision has about it the suggestion of prophecy and the tacit implication that it will be acted upon. A vision must not be wasted. The vision quest is in some sense a covenant between the seeker and the sought. The seeker does not necessarily know what it is that he seeks, but he knows that it is a relation that will change his life and give it strength, direction, purpose, and meaning.*
>
> *N. Scott Momaday*

A real estate broke should write a vision statement for the brokerage. The vision statement should follow these guidelines:

- A vision statement must be based in reality to be meaningful.
- To be relevant, a vision statement must be believable to the entire company, including the salespersons. It should inspire everyone associated with the organization.
- A vision statement must be inclusive and make people want to be part of the future of the company. It should allow people to feel as if they are part of a greater whole and to see how their work contributes to the welfare of the entire company.
- A vision statement focuses on the future. A good vision should orient the company toward the future.
- A vision statement should help in the development of strategies that will lead to future success.
- A vision statement should make it easier for everyone to make the right decisions the very first time.
- A vision statement should point out any unproductive behavior patterns not aligned with the vision statement.
- A vision statement should be modifiable as the culture and environment changes.

Strategy
The strategy is developed as an integral part of a comprehensive framework that encompasses the vision, the execution, and the attainment of the desired results. A company strategy is designed to thoroughly plan out the ways to achieve the brokerage goals. The strategy should motivate the people of the organization to carry out the strategy. Personal

issues are fully taken into account, deadlines are easily identified, and solutions developed.

One specific type of strategy is an exit strategy. An exit strategy is a plan to sell the real estate business even before operations have begun. Planning for the exit of the current ownership assures that the company is heading in the right direction. Some owners believe it is creepy to think of selling at such an early stage in business, but waiting will create even more issues and problems should selling become a necessity.

Continuous Improvement

A broker should believe in the theory of "continuous improvement" of the company's services and business operation. Continuous improvement is the belief that effort should be spent to look at all the services and business operations of a real estate company and begin to make small changes to improve them. Continuous improvement involves:
- planning and implementing process-based improvements
- gaining enthusiastic support of all real estate license holders and staff
- systematically aligning the whole organization behind the broker's program
- systematically identifying activities with the highest impact on the brokerage
- institutionalizing a culture of continuous improvement
- attacking the activities that are the easiest, quickest to implement, most significant, and highly visible

Defining the Brokerage's Customers

It is important to be thorough and specific when creating a description of the target customer for the brokerage's real estate services. This description defines the characteristics of the people to whom the broker wants to sell to and should indicate, among other things, whether the customers are cost or quality conscious, under what circumstances they buy or sell, and what types of concerns they have. If the company is an existing brokerage business, the broker should list the current customers and the how the brokerage sells to them.

To create a customer definition, describe the target customers in terms of common, identifiable characteristics. For example, the broker could target professional couples in the metro Dallas area who need to move out of the city. Or the broker could target people relocated by their company to the local area.

A common mistake is to describe customers in general terms, such as "all people who want to buy a house" or "anyone who needs a real estate professional." To avoid this stumbling block, the broker should make a list of the characteristics of the people or companies that will be interested in the brokerage's real estate services. The broker should be sure to include details of the geographic region where the broker plans to sell. When determining the characteristics of the target people, the broker should never use a Fair Housing–protected class as a criterion.

The Market

Identifying the market is one of the most important parts of the plan, taking into account current market size and trends, and may require extensive research. Many of the sections that follow—from prospecting, to marketing, to the amount of money brokerage needs—will be based on the sales estimates created here.

When the broker is writing about the real estate market, the broker should be sure to consider factors affecting market growth, such as industry trends, socioeconomic trends, government policy, and population shifts. The broker should show how these trends will have a positive or negative impact on the brokerage. The broker should cite all sources for the data and should state the credentials of the people providing these data.

Sales and Marketing

This section of the brokerage business plan describes both the strategy and the tactics the broker will use to get customers to use the brokerage's real estate services. Sales and marketing are the weak link in many business plans. A strong sales and marketing section can serve as a map for the broker, and so the broker should have a workable plan and the resources for promoting and selling the brokerage's services.

Sales and Marketing Strategy

Important elements for a sales and marketing strategy include identifying the broker's target customer in the initial push and the customers the broker has designated for follow-up phases. Other elements of a sales and marketing strategy include:

- how the broker will find prospects, and once found, how the broker plans to educate them about the brokerage's real estate services
- what features of the brokerage's service the broker will emphasize to get customers to notice

- any sort of innovative marketing or sales techniques the broker will employ
- whether the broker will focus on efforts locally, regionally, nationally, or internationally, and whether the broker plans to extend beyond the initial region (and, if so, why)

Marketing Plan

The marketing plan explains:

- how the business will differ from that of the brokerage's competitors
- who the customers are
- where the market is
- how long this market will need the brokerage's service
- the characteristics of the average customer
- the environmental factors of the business
- who the brokerage's competition is
- what competitive advantage the brokerage has over competitors
- the best way to sell the brokerage's real estate service
- how the broker will promote and market the brokerage's service

The Service

The broker should describe each of the services the brokerage offers to customers, with a particular focus on how it will help the client achieve his/her goal. The broker should go into as much detail as necessary and underscore the specific features or variations that the brokerage services provide.

The broker should emphasize the activity that sets the brokerage's service apart from the competition. Why will the brokerage's services be successful in the marketplace? If there is a chance the competition will begin offering services that also have unique features, the broker needs to devise new ways to offer something valuable and special.

The broker should be specific in describing the brokerage's competitive edge. The broker should not say something like "We intend to provide better service." The broker should explain how it will be done and why this sets the brokerage apart from the competitors.

Positioning

Position is the brokerage's identity in the marketplace: how the broker wants the market and the competitors to perceive the brokerage's service. The brokerage's positioning is based on the customers and competition. The brokerage could position itself as the brokerage "having shortest marketing time," "being the most dependable," "having the best rates," or "providing the best service." The broker could emphasize cost, convenience, flexible services, unique services, or some combination of these. The brokerage may be positioned as a boutique, a traditional enterprise, or an aggressive real estate office. Positioning is based on image. The broker should develop the brokerage's position by answering the following questions with brief, direct statements:

- What is unique about the brokerage's service?
- How dos the broker want people to view the brokerage's services?
- How do the competitors position themselves?

Information About the Business

Information about the business includes general information about the business's formation, like:

- the brokerage form (sole proprietorship, partnership, limited liability business, or corporation)
- a statement identifying all the brokerage's business licenses
- a statement outlining the business insurance requirements
- descriptions of any other laws and regulations that affect the business

Business Description

The broker must be able to present a clear portrait of what the brokerage business does. The business description furthers the corporate vision and defines who the brokerage is, what the brokerage will offer, what the market needs and how the brokerage will address that need, and why the brokerage business idea is viable. A typical business description section includes:

- an overview of the real estate industry
- a discussion of the brokerage's particular real estate business
- the brokerage's position in the real estate industry

The business description should begin with a brief overview of the real estate industry. Ultimately, the broker should want to demonstrate that real estate is a great industry with an excellent long-term outlook. The broker is also setting the stage for the business description by showing where the brokerage fits in the marketplace.

The broker should discuss both the present situation in real estate as well as future possibilities. The broker should provide information about the various market segments within the industry, with a particular focus on their potential impact on the brokerage. The broker should include any new services or other developments that will benefit or possibly hurt the brokerage.

The broker should describe the real estate industry as if telling a story. The broker needs to grab attention with strong, exciting language that will get readers interested in the real estate industry and the broker's business. Answering "why" makes any description stronger. Saying, "The market will grow at 9% annually" may sound impressive, but what will cause that rate of growth? Adding, "because a growing number of baby boomers are now in the real estate market either moving up or down in the cycle" makes the answer stand out.

Many business plans make the mistake of basing their market observations on their beliefs. Instead, the broker will want to research the real estate industry and back up the observations with facts. The broker should note all sources. Trade associations such as NAR are excellent sources of information about trends in the real estate industry.

The broker should not be afraid to include negative information about the real estate industry. Discussing the possible roadblocks the business might face shows that the broker has a realistic view of the market.

The broker should also include the more technical aspects of the real estate business. The broker should remember that this is a story and that even though there are specific areas to cover, the broker will want to keep the narrative lively and interesting. Some questions the broker should answer include:

- When was the business founded?
- When did the broker get a broker's license?
- What is the brokerage's legal structure? Sole proprietorship? Corporation? Partnership?
- Who are the business's principals, and what pertinent experience do they bring?
- What market needs will the brokerage meet? Whom will the brokerage sell to? How will the service(s) be sold?
- What support systems will be utilized? Customer service? Advertising? Promotion?

The business focus often depends on the market. A small-town real estate brokerage can sell residential, commercial, and farm and ranch properties because the brokerage may be the only real estate company that sells the properties in the area. A larger market would require greater specialization to set itself apart from the competition.

Operations

The operations section explains how the broker plans to actually run day-to-day operations, pay bills, and deliver quality customer service to clients. In this section, the broker should answer the following questions:

- Who are the brokerage employees?
- What are their credentials?
- How does the business make money?
- How does the broker price the brokerage services?
- What office supplies does the business use? (List the brokerage supplies and supplier.)
- How easy or difficult is it to obtain supplies?
- Are suppliers' prices steady and dependable?

Service Fees

The broker should discuss what the license holders will charge for the real estate services offered and how the broker derived the amount. Once the broker has briefly explained the service fees and rationale, the broker should discuss where this cost strategy places the brokerage in the spectrum of the other providers of real estate services. Next, the broker needs to explain how the fees will attract customers, maintain and possibly increase the brokerage's market share in the face of competition, and produce profits.

Costs tend to be underestimated. If the broker starts out with low costs and low fees, he/she may leave the brokerage with little room to maneuver, and so fee hikes will be difficult to implement. If the broker charges more than competitive existing services, the broker will need to justify the higher fees on the basis of quality, timeliness, and/or services offered.

If a fee will be lower than that of an existing, competing real estate service, the broker should explain how the brokerage will maintain profitability. This may happen through more efficient marketing and promotions, lower labor costs, lower overhead, and/or lower supplies costs.

Personnel Development

In this section the broker will describe the details of personnel development and training costs, location, and labor requirements. The broker should design, present, and discuss a personal development budget. This budget should include the cost of all education, seminars, and consultants. The broker should include labor, materials, consulting fees, and the cost of professionals such as attorneys.

Development Status

The broker should describe the current status of the brokerage's real estate services and what remains to be done to make these services ready to be marketed. The broker needs to include a schedule detailing when this work will be completed. Even though the business plan is for a service business, there is still a strong need for a development status section. Service companies have to set up offices, make plans for fielding calls, buy stationery and business cards, conduct market research, gather references, and complete a sample mailing of sales pieces, among other things.

Service Process

The broker should describe the process of delivering the service, from the first marketing step to the last step at closing. The broker should include such things as:

- *marketing*—The broker should describe the marketing efforts the brokerage will engage in to discover those who want to buy or sell real estate. The broker should explain the process but not make this a specific marketing campaign because there is an entire section in the written business plan for that. Here, the broker should give an overview of the company's goals and desires and state how marketing will help achieve these goals.
- *prospecting*—Similar to marketing, except that in this section the broker will describe the process of prospecting, which is actually going out and getting the business through the broker's direct efforts. Marketing, on the other hand, is making the effort to be known so that the client will contact the brokerage. Prospecting should be part of everyone's daily business. The real estate license holders should be prospecting for people who want to buy or sell real estate. As well, all staff and managers should be constantly prospecting for new recruits into the real estate profession.

- *listing*—The broker should explain the process of listing. The broker should explain the listing appointment and the sales and negotiation efforts that must be undertaken before the listing is taken. The broker should not miss a step here or overlook any small detail. Listings are the name of the game, so the broker should make sure that anyone reading the business plan could recognize that by the evident effort the broker made in detailing listings.
- *staging*—The broker needs to walk through the process of staging a house for sale. Staging is the moving of furniture, cleaning, and decorating a property for the most effective showings possible. Staging a property makes it appear to be the best to any consumer during a showing.
- *servicing*—The broker should completely describe the process of getting a property sold. The broker should determine the actions that will be taken and explain why these efforts are important. Servicing includes all the marketing actions taken, as well as communication with the client.
- *showing*—The broker should portray the process of showing a property to a buyer. The broker should detail the wants and needs analysis that must be completed with the buyer. The broker should include the actual property selection process.
- *selling*—The broker needs to describe the actual selling of the property to the buyer. The broker would want to include the sales techniques used and the time it takes. The broker may want to describe any incentives that the brokerage will use.
- *evaluating*—The broker should illustrate the process of evaluating a property to determine a fair market value. The broker must completely describe the steps taken in the appraising process. By using the "sales comparison" approach to value, the broker could demonstrate how subject properties are chosen and then evaluated. The broker would complete the process by describing the reconciliation procedure.
- *financing*—The broker should depict the process of obtaining financing for a property and the processing of the loan. The broker should discuss the possible types of financing a potential buyer could choose.
- *inspecting*—The broker would want to show the inspection process and the benefits for all parties in the transaction. The broker should determine how an inspector is chosen and who should pay the costs involved.

- *negotiating*—The broker should to discuss the nuances of negotiating in the real estate business. The broker should include negotiations between the license holders and their clients, as well as negotiations between each of the clients. Negotiations generally involve contracts, so the broker should be sure to analyze the negotiations carefully.
- *accounting*—A real estate broker must account for the client's funds involved in a real estate transaction. The broker must account for the earnest money and make sure it gets into the correct hands. He/she must review the "closing statement" to be sure all the items on the statement are correct and complete.
- *contracting*—Contracts are legal documents where two parties agree to do or not to do certain things. Contracts that are typically used are the "independent contractor" agreement between the broker and the salesperson. The listing agreement is between the broker and the seller. The buyer-broker agreement is between the broker and the buyer. The purchase agreement is between the buyer and the seller. With all these legal documents in place, the broker needs to describe how the brokerage office will deal with them.
- *closing*—The closing is the time that all the paperwork is signed and the funds are transferred. The broker should describe the procedures used during a closing. The broker should talk about how the license holders should behave and document that behavior. The closing should be a good time. The seller has the opportunity to move on with his/her life, and the buyer gets into the home of his/her dreams. However, it is also a time of tension. When there is tension, the broker needs to have policies and procedures in place to handle any situation.
- *tracking*—The brokerage office should have procedures in place to track and follow up on all the clients and license holders. These people need to remain in contact with the broker, or they will forget the broker. It is difficult to get new business, so the broker should be sure not to lose the current business through lack of communication.

Outsourcing Marketing

The section on outsourcing marketing should point out why and how the decision of whether to develop a marketing campaign or to outsource it was made. The strategy focuses on whether the broker will create a marketing campaign for the distribution of the brokerage marketing pieces or purchase a service that will do all that. This is a complicated and costly decision, so the broker needs to spend extra time and effort explaining this in the business plan. The broker should consider the following questions:

- Does the brokerage office have the capability to do a professional marketing campaign?
- How much would it cost to purchase the equipment to do the marketing campaign the broker has envisioned?
- How long would it take to recoup the capital cost of the equipment?
- What would it cost to maintain the equipment and purchase raw materials per year?
- What would it cost in work hours to do the marketing campaign in-house per year?
- What would it cost to outsource the marketing campaign (including any additional set-up charges)?
- In the long run, would developing the marketing campaign or outsourcing it be more efficient?

Location

The broker should discuss the geographic location for the brokerage firm. In real estate, location can be a huge bonus to the production numbers if the office has walk-up business. Choosing a location was previously discussed in this book, so the broker should use that information in this section. The broker can justify his/her location decision by talking about greater traffic flow, proximity to available staffing, or other factors important to the brokerage business.

Method of Sales

In the methods of sale section the broker should demonstrate the ability and knowledge to get the brokerage's real estate services into the hands of the target customers. The broker should not make the mistake of confusing sales with marketing. Sales focuses on how the broker gets the brokerage services out to the customers. Marketing is concerned with how the broker educates the potential customers about the brokerage's services.

Many real estate brokers who form brokerages assume that a sales team can be set up with minimal time, effort, and expense. This is not the case. It can take as long as a year for a license holder to become acquainted with the real estate industry. Even if the broker uses license holders who are intimately familiar with a territory and market, the broker should expect there to be ramp-up time.

Estimated Sales

Estimated sales for the real estate brokerage business are based on the broker's assessment of the advantages of the brokerage's services, the customers, the size of the market, and the competition. This estimate should include sales in housing units and dollars for the next three years, with the first year broken down by quarter. These numbers will be crucial to other financial documents the broker presents later in the plan.

The broker should write a one-paragraph summary to justify the projections. The broker should include a concise statement of what sets apart the brokerage's services from other real estate brokerages in the marketplace. The broker should state why he/she sees the customer base growing and indicate how he/she will go after this business.

The broker should not make outlandish projections. Such projections will ruin the broker's credibility as a reputable businessperson. A common mistake is assuming the brokerage business will have a few modest years and then a dramatic increase in sales when "the market takes off." The broker should use "best case," "worst case," and "likely" scenarios to create a spectrum of sales projections.

Advertising and Promotion

The broker's advertising and promotion campaign is how the broker communicates information about the brokerage's services. This section should include a description of all advertising vehicles the broker plans to use—newspapers, magazines, radio and television, telephone directory, and so on—as well as the broker's public relations program, sales/promotional materials (such as brochures and listing sheets), trade show efforts, and the like. If the broker is using an advertising and/or public relations agency, the broker should discuss the talents of its staff and what efforts it is contracted to make on the brokerage's behalf.

If the broker has a public relations plan in place, the broker should include a copy of the press kit and a list of targeted media in the business plan. These will further demonstrate that the broker knows exactly how to reach the target audience.

If trade shows will be an integral part of the broker's recruiting strategy, the broker should include a trade show schedule outlining at which expos the broker will be exhibiting. And the broker should explain why he/she chose those specific shows.

If advertising or promotion is a critical expense, the broker should include a budget showing how and when these costs will be incurred.

Management Description

The broker should use the management description section to detail the responsibilities and expertise of each person. If the brokerage is a one-person operation, the broker should detail how he/she has the expertise to function in each of the needed management areas. This may be difficult, but with a small operation it can be successfully done. The broker should detail future plans to hire additional management help as needed. The broker also needs to anticipate which positions will need to be filled, when the broker anticipates they will need to be filled, and why they will need to be filled.

If the brokerage operation is large and the broker has positions that have not been filled, he/she should detail the need to hire additional personnel to achieve the goals set out in the service development schedule. The broker should describe the talents any new employee needs to possess and how the addition of the person will help the business meet its objectives.

The broker should have major categories of business management covered, such as marketing, sales (including customer relations and service), quality assurance, accounting, and administration. The broker does not have to have personnel devoted to each of these areas, but the broker should have employees who will be able to assume these responsibilities as needed.

The broker should include relevant details in the management description, but he/she should save complete resumes as attachments to the plan. The broker needs to emphasize people who have already committed to working with the brokerage business.

Ownership

A short section on who owns and controls the business will help provide a better understanding of who will be making decisions. The broker should discuss the involvement of the owner or owners. Will the owners be an integral part of the business or be silent owners and let the management team operate the business? The broker should include the owners' resumes in the appendix.

Board of Advisors

The broker should form a board of advisors, having asked industry peers for the names of the best advisors in the real estate industry.

A board of advisors is a group of nonsalaried business talent available to the broker for business advice. This talent includes attorneys, appraisers, inspectors, accountants, and advertising professionals, as well as other real estate brokers, mortgage brokers, and title officers. The presence of such people on the board of advisors indicates the broker's ability to attract talent to the business. In the broker's description of each support service, the broker should describe the strengths each individual possesses, as well as the experience or contacts he/she brings to the brokerage business. The broker needs to outline each individual's employment, training, education, and expertise. The broker should also highlight each board member's experiences and how that board member will help the brokerage business thrive. The broker should include each board member's resume in the appendix of the business plan. If the board members have industry connections, good reputations, or the potential to raise capital for the brokerage, the broker should be sure to include these facts. A strong advisory board is an asset to a brokerage business: It can add credibility to the management team and increase the likelihood of success.

The broker should create a board that complements existing management. To do this, the broker should first create a chart to determine the kind of talent needed to move the brokerage business ahead. The broker should next list the skills of the management team. The broker can then make a list of the skills the broker needs to acquire from the people who possess those skills.

Competition

The business plan must include a section in it that analyzes the competition. This section should be full of research and quite lengthy. Each competitor in the real estate industry should be investigated and then detailed here. In a geographic area with multiple competitors, the broker should investigate a variety of competitors, but it may not be feasible to investigate them all. If possible, the broker should include their annual sales and their market share. Each assessment should include why these real estate companies do or do not meet their customers' needs. The broker should then explain why the broker thinks the brokerage can capture a share of their business.

Strengths and weaknesses can fall into a number of different categories. Market dominance, quality of service, service fees, marketing and advertising capability, image, size of company, company philosophy, and breadth of services are all ways real estate companies differentiate one company from another. The broker should ask himself/herself these key questions: Who is the cost leader? Who is the quality leader? Who has the largest market share? Why have certain brokerages recently entered or withdrawn from the market? These factors are critical to a successful competitive analysis.

The investigation should include:

- production numbers
- number of associates
- years in business
- number of locations
- business structure
- commission structure
- advertising strategy
- services offered
- areas served
- franchise/independent

The competition section should also include any other information the broker deems necessary to make the best decisions. Finding the information may be tricky, but the effort should be made. The broker could research the competitors by shopping their stores or calling them to see what they offer and what they charge for it. To create a list of the competitors' strengths and weaknesses, the broker should look at areas such as pricing, value, service, and timeliness. The broker's market research should look at commissions, add-on services, and reputation in the marketplace.

The competition section indicates where the brokerage's real estate services fit in the competitive environment. It should demonstrate that the broker is prepared to cope with the barriers to the success of the brokerage business. Many business plans fail to give a realistic view of their true competitive universe by defining the competitive field too narrowly. The broker should think as broadly as possible when devising a list of competitors by characterizing competitors as any business customers who may patronize similar services.

To determine the brokerage's competitors' strengths and weaknesses, the broker should evaluate why customers buy from them. Is it cost? Value? Service? Convenience? Reputation? Very often, it is perceived strengths rather than actual strengths that the broker will be evaluating.

The broker should consider describing who is not a competitor. For example, people may think that an attorney competes with a brokerage. The broker will want to stress that attorneys provide legal documents but rarely ever sell real estate and do not understand the market the way the broker does, so attorneys are not direct competition.

Financials

The section on financials deals with the development and implementation of a plan for the achievement of one's overall financial objective. It also describes how and where the broker plans to obtain money to get the brokerage business started and running. This section should answer the following questions:

- How will the broker finance the brokerage business?
- How will the broker manage the finances?
- What needs to be financed?
- Where will the brokerage finances come from?

Financials are used to document, justify, and convince. This is the section in which the broker makes the case in words and backs up what the broker believes with financial statements and forms that document the viability of the brokerage business and its soundness as an investment. It is also where the broker indicates that the broker has evaluated the risks associated with this real estate venture.

Financial Statement

The financial statement is, in fact, a financial report. It includes:

- a balance sheet
- an income statement

- accounts receivable
- accounts payable
- a debt schedule
- reconciliation of net worth

This statement should be included for new and existing businesses. Here, the broker should project the financial statements for the next three years (monthly for the first year, annually for second and third).

Income Statement

The income statement is where the broker proves that the brokerage business can and will generate cash. This document is where the broker records revenue, expenses, capital, and cost of services. The outcome of the combination of these elements demonstrates how much money the brokerage business made or will make, or lost or will lose, during the year. An income statement and a cash-flow statement differ in that an income statement does not include details of when revenue was collected or expenses paid.

An income statement for a business plan should be broken down by month the first year. The second year can be broken down quarterly, and each year thereafter can be broken down annually. The broker should analyze the results of the income statement briefly and include this analysis in the business plan. If the brokerage business already exists, the broker should include income statements for previous years.

The broker should avoid insufficiently documented assumptions about the growth of the brokerage business. In other words, if the broker states the brokerage firm will grow by 30% in the first year and 50% in the second, the broker needs to document why these numbers are attainable. It can be because similar real estate brokerages have had this growth path; because the industry is growing at this rate (cite the source for these data); or because of projections from a specific market researcher, industry association, or other source.

Cash-Flow Statement

A cash-flow statement shows readers of the business plan how much money the brokerage will need, when the brokerage will need it, and where the money will come from. In general terms, the cash-flow statement looks at cash and sources of revenue minus expenses and capital requirements to derive a net cash-flow figure. A cash-flow statement provides a glimpse of how much money a business has at any given time and when it is likely to need more cash. The cash-flow statement is critical for budgeting purposes. The broker should analyze the results of the cash-flow statement briefly and include this analysis in the business plan. As with all financial documents, the broker should have the cash-flow statement prepared or at least reviewed by a reputable accountant.

The broker should not fall into the common trap of underestimating cash-flow needs. This can lead to undercapitalization, which means the funds will prove inadequate for meeting the brokerage obligations.

Balance Sheet

Unlike other financial statements, a balance sheet is created only once a year to calculate the net worth of a business. If the business plan is for a new real estate business, the broker will need to include a personal balance sheet summarizing the broker's personal assets and liabilities. If the business exists already, include the past years' balance sheets up to the balance sheet from the brokerage's last reporting period. The broker should analyze the results of the balance sheet briefly and include this analysis in the business plan.

Operating Expenses

By creating a financial form called "Operating Expenses," the broker will pull together the expenses incurred in running the brokerage business. Expense categories include marketing, sales, and overhead. Overhead includes fixed expenses such as administrative costs and other expenses that remain constant regardless of how much business the brokerage has. Overhead also includes variable expenses, such as travel, equipment leases, and supplies.

A complete and thorough examination of every detail of every operating expense, both fixed and variable, should be conducted and included in this section. The broker should start by asking the following questions:

- Is this expense necessary?
- Could this expense be eliminated or reduced?
- Could some of these expenses be combined?
- Could these expense items be purchased in bulk to take advantage of economies of scale?
- Could the lease of the space be negotiated or reworked?
- Could any loans be negotiated or reworked?
- Could reducing the costs of utilities in any way attain savings?

- Could the broker outsource any marketing/advertising campaign at reduced cost?
- Could the broker outsource the accounting/payroll functions at reduced cost?
- Could policies/procedures be implemented to reduce or eliminate employee theft of office supplies?

Any and all of these suggestions could help the broker reduce expenses. Any reduction of expenses is a direct bonus to the bottom line of the financial statement.

Capital Requirements

The "Capital Requirements" form details the amount of money the broker will need to procure the equipment used to start up and continue the operations of the brokerage business. Capital equipment can be leased or purchased. For this section of the business plan, the broker should refer to capital equipment as those things the broker buys. A complete analysis of leasing versus buying the capital equipment the real estate office will need should be completed and included in the business plan. Leasing of equipment will be covered in the operating expense section. Capital requirements also include depreciation details of all purchased equipment. To determine the capital requirements, the broker needs to think about anything in the brokerage business that will require capital. For real estate sales this might be a moving van, fax machine, desktop and laptop computers, telephone system, and yard signs.

Cost of Services

For a real estate sales business, the cost of services is the cost incurred in the execution of the service. To generate a cost-of-services chart, the broker will need to know the total number of housing units the brokerage will sell for a year and the cost to produce that sale.

The cost-of-services chart allows the broker to see how much money is required per closing. It also allows the broker to determine the money the broker will have left over after a sale to use in the budget planning.

Risks

No business is without risks. The broker's ability to identify and discuss them demonstrates the broker's skills as a leader. The broker must show that he/she has taken the initiative to confront risk issues and is capable of handling them. The following list of problems is by no means complete, but it should alert the broker to some of the possibilities:

- The competitors cut their prices (i.e., lower their commissions).
- A key customer (such as a builder) cancels a contract.
- The industry's growth rate drops.
- Service costs exceed the broker's projections.
- The sales projections are not achieved.
- An important ad campaign flounders.
- Important ancillary businesses (such as lenders) fail to keep their promises.
- The competitors release a new, better service.
- Public opinion of the brokerage's services changes.
- The broker cannot find trained salespersons or staff.

The broker should evaluate the risks honestly. To generate a complete list of risks, the broker should examine all the assumptions about how the brokerage business will develop. The flipside of many of the favorable assumptions may be risks.

CHAPTER SUMMARY

The real estate market is composed of all types of real estate in all locations at any price.

Residential Market—The residential market is made up of single-family homes, duplexes, triplexes, and quads.

A single-family home could range from less than 100 square feet (popularly called a "Tiny House") to as large as 10,000–20,000 square feet. A duplex is an attached housing property with a party wall, which is the wall that separates both units. A triplex is three units, and a quadruple unit (quad) is a building with four separate units.

Farm-and-Ranch Market—The farm-and-ranch market is made up of properties with acreage usually outside any city jurisdiction. A farm-and-ranch property is usually 5 acres or more and may be as large as several thousand acres.

A ranchette is usually 5 acres or less with a country setup but typically not production, whereas a barndominium is a house inside a barn.

Commercial Market—The commercial market is made up of income-producing commercial properties and "for business" properties.

Income-producing properties include shopping malls, apartment complexes, and office buildings.

Industrial Market—The industrial market is similar to the commercial market in comprising income-producing properties.

Fine Homes and Estates Market—The fine homes and estates market is generally considered residential property that is valued at over $500,000.

Vacation Property Market—Usually vacation properties are thought of as resort-type properties because they are usually around a lake, recreation area, or an area of high interest.

A timeshare has multiple owners, each having one or two weeks per year in which the property is "theirs."

Buyer's Market—A buyer's market is when there are few buyers and a great number of sellers. The characteristics of a buyer's market include:

- few offers
- long market time
- buyers' demand for everything
- low earnest-money deposits
- lowball offers

Seller's Market—A seller's market is when there are few sellers and a great number of buyers. The characteristics of a seller's market are:

- multiple offers
- short market time (just a few days)
- prequalified or cash payments
- no contingencies to hinder the sale
- high earnest-money deposit
- no personal property included
- full price or higher offers

Real estate markets are slow to adjust to national or international events.

The Real Estate Center is a group of economists commissioned by the TREC to track real estate data and report those data to the public.

The broker should analyze local competitors by monitoring their advertising campaigns, recruiting efforts, and any type of expansion. The broker should research local competitors to find out:

- market share
- number of license holders
- production of license holders
- years in business

- marketing campaigns
- recruiting efforts
- number of locations
- expansion

The broker should likewise research outside competitors to find out:

- plans to enter the local market
- new office location
- marketing campaigns
- advancements of new office

Some important itemizations found in the business plan are these:

- The balance sheet is the most important element of the business plan because it shows itemized accounts and overall balances in each income and expense category.
- Total number of listings indicates the future of the brokerage.
- The average price range of listings is an indication of the amount of commissions that will be earned.
- The average days on market show the market pace and the ability of the brokerage to sell real estate.
- Total number of sales completed will show progress from the past or failures in the present.
- Total commissions earned is the total amount of commissions earned by the brokerage, whereas total commissions retained reflects the amount of commissions that remains with the brokerage.
- The Agent Report includes the number of current license holders, the number of license holders recruited, and the number of license holders lost.

Writing a Business Plan

Writing a business plan is one of the most important aspects of starting a real estate business in today's changing environment.

The cover page tells what business is being planned and how to reach the writer.

The table of contents should be one page and should give details of the contents of the business plan.

The executive summary is a brief statement summing up the purpose of the business and covering the substance or main points of the brokerage business.

The mission statement is one or two sentences describing the purpose of the business and to whom the real estate services are targeted.

A vision statement is a concise, easy-to-understand description of the business that will not only help the broker write the business plan but also benefit the broker in any number of day-to-day situations.

The strategy is designed to thoroughly plan out the ways to achieve the brokerage goals.

The target customer description defines characteristics of the people to whom the broker wants to sell.

The market includes industry trends, socioeconomic trends, government policy, and population shifts.

The sales and marketing section of the brokerage business plan describes both the strategy and the tactics the broker will use to entice customers to use the brokerage's real estate services. Sales and marketing strategy include whom the broker is targeting with the initial push and what customers the broker has designated for follow-up phases.

The marketing plan explains:

- how the business will differ from that of the brokerage's competitors
- where the market is
- how long this market will need the brokerage's service
- the environmental factors of the business
- what competitive advantage the brokerage has over competitors
- the best way to sell the brokerage's real estate service
- how the broker will promote and market the brokerage's service

The broker should describe each of the services the brokerage offers to customers, with a particular focus on how it will help clients achieve their goal.

Position is the brokerage's identity in the marketplace: how the broker wants the market and the competitors to perceive the brokerage's service.

The business plan includes general information about the business formation, including:

- the brokerage form (sole proprietorship, partnership, limited liability business, or corporation)
- a statement of all the brokerage's business licenses
- a statement of the business insurance requirements
- a description of any other laws and regulations that affect the business

The business description furthers the corporate vision and includes who the brokerage is, what the brokerage will offer, what the market needs and how the brokerage will address these needs, and why the brokerage business idea is viable.

The operations section of the business plan explains how the broker plans to actually run day-to-day operations, pay bills, and deliver quality customer service to clients.

The broker should discuss how much license holders will charge for the real estate services offered and how the broker derived the amount.

The section on personnel development includes details of personnel development and training costs, location, and labor requirements.

The broker should describe the process of delivering the service, from the first marketing step to the last step at closing. The broker should include such things as:

marketing	prospecting	listing
staging	servicing	showing
selling	evaluating	financing
inspecting	negotiating	accounting
contracting	closing	tracking

In the section on outsourcing marketing, the broker should point out why and how he/she made the decision of whether to develop a marketing campaign or to outsource that function.

The broker should discuss the geographic location of the brokerage firm.

The broker's advertising and promotion campaign is how the broker communicates information about the brokerage's services.

Management description describes the business management, including the responsibilities and expertise of each person.

A short section on who owns and controls the business will help provide a better understanding of who will be making decisions.

The broker should form a board of advisors comprising a group of nonsalaried individuals with business talent available to the broker for business advice.

The business plan must include a section in it that analyzes the competition. Each competitor in the real estate industry should be investigated and then detailed.

Whereas the financial section deals with the development and implementation of a plan for the achievement of one's overall financial objective, the financial statement is a financial report that includes:

- a balance sheet
- an income statement
- accounts receivable
- accounts payable
- a debt schedule
- reconciliation of net worth

By creating a financial form called "Operating Expenses," the broker will pull together the expenses incurred in running the brokerage business.

The Capital Requirements Form details the amount of money the broker will need to procure the equipment used to start up and continue operations of the brokerage business.

The income statement is where the broker proves that the brokerage business can and will generate cash. This document is where the broker records revenue, expenses, capital, and cost of services.

A cash-flow statement shows readers of the business plan how much money the brokerage will need, when the brokerage will need it, and where the money will come from.

A balance sheet is created only once a year to calculate the net worth of a business.

CHAPTER QUESTIONS

1. What is made up of single-family houses, duplexes, triplexes, and quads?
   A. the residential market
   B. the total real estate market
   C. the fine homes and estates market
   D. all of the answer choices

2. Which of the following is not a characteristic of a buyer's market?
   A. few offers
   B. long market time
   C. full-price or higher offers
   D. buyer's demand for everything

3. What is a brief statement summing up the purpose of the business?
   A. a customer profile
   B. the market
   C. a market plan
   D. an executive summary

4. A vision statement must:
   A. be based in reality
   B. be inclusive
   C. focus on the future
   D. all of the answer choices

5. What is the brokerage's identity in the marketplace?
   A. business description
   B. positioning
   C. competition
   D. market analysis

6. What is the nonsalaried business talent that is available to the broker for business advice?
   A. competition
   B. ownership group
   C. board of advisors
   D. staff

7. What document demonstrates the brokerage can and will generate cash?
   A. Income Statement
   B. Promissory Note
   C. Cash Deposits Account Notice
   D. Ancillary Generated Cash Disclosure Notice

8. What document shows itemized accounts and overall balances in each income and expense category?
   A. Account Management Report
   B. Balance Sheet
   C. Directory of Accounts
   D. Categories of Account Balances Annual Report

9. What group of economists provides information financial, socioeconomic, and local market analysis related to real estate?
   A. Texas Real Estate Commission
   B. Texas Legislature
   C. Texas Real Estate Center
   D. Texas Travel Agency

10. What market has few sellers and many buyers?
    A. local market
    B. seller's market
    C. buyer's market
    D. no market (it is an anomaly)

CHAPTER 5
Managing Risk

Managing risk aids the broker in making the correct decisions in his/her real estate brokerage to avoid risk and liability. It is unfortunate that many quality real estate brokers lose their license each year because of mistakes that could have been avoided. Texas has adopted special laws, rules, and regulations affecting professionals engaged in real estate sales and brokerage. These rules and regulations impose special requirements on the agency relationship in the context of real estate. They have the effect of limiting, redefining, and superseding the common and statutory laws that would otherwise apply in non–real estate situations.

Being clear on representation is one of the most important requirements of any sale of real estate. REALTORS® assume a position of trust with buyers and sellers when entering into an agency relationship. Managing this risk is a necessity for all brokers and license holders. Each broker has the right to set office policies, and any advice or recommendations made in this material should be verified and agreed to by the designated broker. This chapter explores the most significant litigation issues affecting real estate and aims to enable real estate professionals to develop sound business practices and minimize legal liability.

Theory of Risk Management

Risk is the possibility that an event will occur and adversely affect the achievement of real estate sales. Risk for a brokerage firm is also anything that disrupts the closing process. Risk management is the process that attempts to manage the uncertainty that influences the achievement of real estate sales, with the goal of reaching the closing and thus creating profit for the brokerage. A real estate broker must be aware of

all that negatively affects a real estate transaction. To accomplish this goal, it is necessary to constantly apply risk-management techniques throughout all aspects of a real estate transaction. Risk management attempts to identify risks and take appropriate action to diminish their impending effects on a brokerage.

The risk-management process is as follows:

1. The first step is to clearly state the objective to be achieved. Is it to protect the brokerage from client liability, regulatory risks, misrepresentations, omissions, or errors, for example? From the objective it is possible to derive what exactly is exposed to risk. The objective can involve a financial risk, a customer issue, or an internal process.
2. Based on what type of situation is exposed to risk, it is possible to identify the events that form a threat to the objective. The result of the identification is a list containing internal and external risks that form a threat to the brokerage.
3. To be able to compare risks, the next step should be the assessment of the likelihood and impact of each of the identified events.
4. Risks are prioritized by comparing individual risks.
5. After assessing relevant risks, a proper response to each of the risks must be implemented. Possible responses are avoidance, reduction, prevention, sharing, acceptance, separation, duplication, and diversification.

In risk management, the step that creates value for a brokerage is selecting the appropriate risk responses to counter risk. For financial risks, this choice is often a case of optimization, given that the goal is to find a balance between the cost of the reaction to be applied and the residual risk after application. It is important to note that the broker's attitude toward the impending risk has an influence on the process of choosing the suitable reaction to deal with the risk. Some brokers may be more lenient toward risk-taking than others and will tolerate more risk. When faced with the same risk, a broker with a more lenient attitude toward taking risks might be more likely to try to reduce the possible impact of the risk, whereas a more hesitant broker might see fit to completely terminate the risk.

Risk control is a key component in any sound company strategy. It is necessary to ensure long-term organization sustainability and profitability. Without proper risk-management implementation, the broker sets the brokerage up for failure. The broker should hire risk managers if he/she is unable or does not have the expertise to properly account for risks to the brokerage.

Protecting the Institution

Protecting the brokerage is one of the key elements in good broker management. The broker is ultimately responsible for the brokerage and all the sponsored license holders. Any qualified broker takes protecting the brokerage personally. The broker should not ever let any situation place the brokerage or any sponsored license holder at risk. Education and training on risk management are crucial to the process of risk management. There follow some suggestions on how brokers can protect their brokerage from risk.

License Holders Selling Their Own Property

When real estate license holders sell their own property or personally buy a property, they must use the term "agent-owner" in all advertising in print and on the internet and on listing information sheets and materials. If the real estate firm's sign is displayed in the yard of the property for sale and the firm's services are being used, "agent-owner" on the sign is not required. The Deceptive Trade Practices Act (DTPA) and the Texas Real Estate License Act (TRELA) require that license holders not deceive the public, and failing to disclose the real estate license would be considered deceptive.

This disclosure will be necessary no matter how much interest the license holder has in the property. This disclosure includes transactions in which the purchase or sale is with an investment group in which the license holder has a minor interest. As a further risk-reduction measure, the license holder should also disclose any interest that a close relative or friend has in a property.

Any license holder must inform his/her broker that he/she is intending to sell personal real estate property. There is no requirement to sell the property through the license holder's real estate company; the license holder could sell it as a "For Sale by Owner" transaction. Selling it in this way would not eliminate the risk to the brokerage. The broker must be aware of the sale, however, so that the broker has the ability to oversee the transaction to protect himself/herself, the sponsored license holder, and the brokerage.

Potential Risks for Selling Their Own Property
Real estate license holders who buy or sell their own real estate property without disclosing that they are licensed by the state of Texas are at risk for license suspension and financial loss. The DTPA prohibits this action because real estate license holders have an unfair advantage over the typical consumer and because it is a requirement that license holders must disclose their licensure to prevent this undisclosed advantage, the failure of which is called an "unconscionable action."

Dealing with Divorce
Real estate license holders will at some time encounter a situation in which they will have to deal with the topic of divorce and the real estate that is caught between two parties. The home may be the largest single asset of any married couple. Frequently, therefore, it becomes the major point of contention in a divorce. The home has a great deal of financial and emotional value. The couple has lived there in love, raised their children there, and had hope. All that now is in jeopardy, and the tension is high and often unbearable. All these factors could lead to irrational and inappropriate decision making. Individuals need advice from both a professional real estate license holder and a divorce attorney to help understand legal rights, financial risks, and long-term implications before making any decisions about the home during a divorce.

There are several key factors about real estate that affect the handling of the asset or the distribution of the net proceeds from the sale of the asset in a divorce. The factors are:

- identification of the type of real estate and the type of ownership interest each party possesses in the property
- ownership history of the real estate, including any prior interests by uninvolved third parties
- current income and future income potential from any real estate
- taxes on the real estate, including capital gain taxes
- loans on the properties or secured by the properties
- ability to continue to make the payments on the properties
- improvements that have been made and their cost depreciation claimed on any prior year's tax return as well as their increase in property value
- insurance proceeds received from any claim and whether the issue was repaired or was deferred and not repaired

Potential Risks on Determining the Real Estate in a Divorce

Before the client goes to see an attorney, the real estate professional should advise the client to gather all the necessary documents and records about each piece of real estate. The attorney will require the documents not only for the property titled in the client's name but also for all the property in which the couple has an ownership interest. This is important because all property should be included at this point, and the attorney will need to determine the possibility of an interest in it. Other types of real estate that a person may have an interest in are vacation properties, rental properties, commercial or office buildings, buildings on land leases, vacant land, ranch properties, and mineral rights/leases and other types of special-use real estate. The real estate professional should make sure his/her client is prepared for the attorney.

Division of the Real Estate in a Divorce

The house is an asset and therefore subject to division according to Texas property division law. In Texas, in a marriage the individuals are separate and yet one. Because of this, the community estate will be divided equitably. The percentage interest in the house is shared evenly, with each partner having a 50% interest. However, a Texas court could order the house conveyed to either party. The court could also divide the property unequally, awarding a disproportionate amount to one of the parties depending on the circumstances of the divorce.

Potential Risks on Division of the Real Estate in a Divorce

The real estate license holder must keep in mind that the court could make a decision that is not favored by one or both of the parties. The best option is for the license holder to assist the parties in making an agreement before the court makes the division of the couple's real estate assets. The license holder should even suggest a mediator if needed. In Texas, the courts will listen to a married couple's wishes as long as the wishes do not diminish one party's rights or create an undue hardship. These types of agreements are best dealt with through attorneys. The real estate license holder should not get involved in giving advice at this point but could offer assistance. The Texas Real Estate Commission (TREC) does not consider spousal negotiations to be a function of selling real estate but outside of a real estate license holder's expertise. Giving advice or negotiating between spouses could be viewed as a conflict of interest.

The real estate license holder can help the parties determine if either party can afford the property individually. If a new mortgage is necessary, a mortgage loan officer may need to become involved. If neither party can afford a loan, the property could be sold, the debt dissolved, and the proceeds divided. If a license holder persuades a client to sell when it may not be in the client's best interest, that license holder will have broken his/her fiduciary duty to their client.

Sometimes the easiest solution is to sell the house and split the proceeds. It is a difficult decision, but many couples choose this option when:

- there is a substantial amount of equity tied up in the house and selling the house would free up funds (Divorce is expensive.)
- the mortgage payments are too much for one of the parties to handle without the income from the other spouse
- selling the house relieves both parties and allows them to move on with their new life

At this point, the real estate license holder may have to meet separately with each party in the divorce. At no time should a decision be made without the complete understanding and written consent of both parties. Failing to involve both parties could place the real estate license holder in a fiduciary breach as well as pose financial risk.

Dealing with Foreclosures, Short Sales, and Bankruptcies

Foreclosures, short sales, and bankruptcies are an ongoing element of a real estate licensee's business during most real estate markets. Foreclosures could be "preforeclosures," in which the owner retains some decision-making responsibility. Foreclosures can take place so quickly that nothing may be able to be done to prevent a foreclosure.

A license holder may be wise to suggest that the owners discuss with the lender the possibility of a short sale. A short sale is when a lender agrees to take less for a property than the loan amount to get the property sold. Lenders do not want properties on their in-house inventory—called real estate-owned (REO) property—and vacant, foreclosed houses can cause numerous problems for a lender. With short sales the owner is still in control and the lender is considered a "contingency." The lender contingency is final approval of the short sale. The lender does not make up the terms of a short sale; terms are established only between the parties.

Bankruptcies are the responsibility of the real estate property owner. A bankruptcy does not necessarily require a property to be sold. An owner can have the property set aside from the bankruptcy by a judge. All this must be discussed with a qualified bankruptcy attorney.

License holders should take a careful look at the foreclosure marketplace before selling real estate foreclosures. The foreclosure marketplace is fraught with potential risks. Potential buyers are excited about the possibility of saving money on their real estate purchase, whereas the owners have lost their home and the entity that has foreclosed on the property is generally in the position of losing money. None of these events play well for real estate license holders who are unprepared. However, for those license holders ready for the challenges of dealing in the foreclosure marketplace, there can be a great deal of success.

Buyers have the perception that they will always save money when buying a foreclosure property. This clearly is not always true. Not all foreclosures are deals. The buyer had better be prepared for fix-up expenses, and the real estate license holder who fails to disclose the potential hazards of purchasing a foreclosed property could face financial liability.

Short sales have their own issues. A license holder dealing in short sales should be aware of the following situations that could be problematic:

The Buyer—The buyer is expecting to save a great deal of money and to be able to close on the property immediately. Generally, the lender is not on the same schedule. The real estate license holder should caution the buyer that the timetables may be overlong and inconvenient and, further, alert the buyer that this property may not be a steal. Failure to inform the client of these possibilities could result in a potential breach of fiduciary duty as well as financial loss.

The agents—Frequently, the buyer's agent will push the listing agent for a quicker response from the lender. This could create a rift between agents and put the transaction in jeopardy. The listing agent and the buyer's agent must remain professional in such a situation, keeping in mind that their clients and clear communication are key.

The current lender—A lender sees the short-sale transaction as a business transaction and not a personal deal. The buyer, though, does see the transaction as personal. The buyer can become agitated and frustrated with the process of waiting for an uninterested lender to take action. Working with lenders may make this transaction difficult to complete. Failing to do anything could result in the buyer charging the license holder with abandonment (this is a law of agency term—an agent has a fiduciary duty to perform. If the agent does not perform that duty, it is called "abandonment" and is actionable by the client). If such a thing happens, the license holder will certainly lose his/her commission.

The property—The seller could have undisclosed liens, judgments, and other issues that could stop or slow down closing. The real estate license holder should do his/her best to determine the potential risk from such situations.

The mortgage lenders—Short sales take a long time, and the buyer's mortgage company could remove a program, change a program, or simply change guidelines that now place the buyer in a "non-approval" status.

The following are typically needed before seeking a short sale:

1. hardship letter stating what happened to cause the borrower to fall behind, when it happened, and what the borrower is doing to fix the situation
2. financial worksheet that is a breakdown of all the borrower's income and expenses
3. last month of pay stubs or a recent profit-and-loss statement if self-employed
4. last two months of bank statements
5. last two years of tax returns (first two pages only)
6. purchase agreement if applicable
7. signed listing agreement
8. third-party negotiation authorization letter

The listing agent should be sure that all the proper documents are in order before seeking a short sale. Failure to do this could result in a considerable delay for their client. If the delay is excessive, the license holder may be liable if the property forecloses in the meantime. Real estate professionals should seek proper training and take classes to help educate themselves on the proper way to handle these types of transactions.

Dealing with Mineral Rights

Mineral rights are a hot topic right now and will be long into the future. Real estate license holders must themselves understand and help their clients understand the implications of mineral rights. The buyer wants the mineral rights and the seller wants the mineral rights, and this type of conflict is ripe with risk.

Background on Mineral Rights

In Texas, since 1876, a grantee of land has received all minerals unless they are expressly reserved. To the extent that a landowner also owns the minerals in his/her tract, that landowner may legally sever such minerals from the surface estates. The usual practice is for a lease to be executed by the mineral owner to an operator who undertakes to develop the minerals. Under a typical lease the operator assumes all expenses of operations to develop the mineral resources in return for a conveyance of a larger interest to them; the landowner or lessor retains a smaller interest free and clear of all costs. This interest of the mineral owner or lessor is what is known as "royalty." Royalties in Texas are negotiable and depend on a number of factors.

The real estate professional faces risk because these oil and gas leases are generating a great deal of wealth, and everyone, buyers as well as sellers, wants to capitalize on the oil and gas boom. A license holder who "forgets" or "neglects to inform" the client on the implications of mineral reservations could put himself/herself at severe financial risk.

Background on Determining Mineral Rights

Legally, oil and gas are minerals. The likelihood of minerals being conveyed with a tract of land depends on when the property was purchased and where it is located. For example, if the property is located in eastern Texas and the purchase occurred in the past 20 years, there is a good chance that the minerals were severed from the surface because there is a long history of drilling in the area. Likewise, in western Texas, there is a long history of drilling; if a person received any minerals with a purchase, it is likely that the person received only a portion of them. On the other hand, there are areas where drilling has not occurred, and so landowners are more likely to part with the minerals upon the sale of the property.

When dealing with mineral rights, a real estate license holder should have the owner:

1. *locate and hire a landman—someone who specializes in searching mineral ownership.* This is probably the most expensive choice but will provide the owner with the most accurate answers.
2. *contact a local abstract company/title company to ask the company to prepare a title search on the property.* The owners should ask the title company to provide all vesting documents and mineral easements or mineral deeds to the property going back as far as their title plant goes (a title plant comprises the recording documents of land in a certain area and can date back to the inception of deeds). Depending on the difficulty of the search, the search could run as little as a few hundred dollars or could cost much more. The title company will not provide the owner with an opinion, but it will provide most if not all of the documents that an attorney will need to analyze the ownership question.

NOTE: Title companies do not insure minerals. However, they do often provide information about the minerals (i.e., reference to mineral deeds) when they encounter the information during a search for a normal sales transaction.

The owner may also have the following documents that can have valuable information:

1. Title Policy Schedule A: If under the heading "Vesting" there is a reference to "surface only of the . . . ," there is a good chance that someone reserved the minerals before the current owner's possession.
2. Title Policy Schedule B: Under Schedule B, there may be a reference to mineral exceptions or mineral deeds. This will not reveal the exact status, but if there is a reference, someone has at least reserved a portion of the minerals. If there are multiple references, then there is a chance that all the minerals have been reserved by predecessors in title.
3. the deed: Check for specific language stating that "grantor reserves unto himself all minerals." A general reference such as "all mineral reservations being previously reserved or recorded" is not as significant because it is a relatively general and contained in most deeds.

The real estate license holder should distance himself/herself from addressing directly the issue of the owner's or buyer's rights to the minerals. By stating that the client will have the mineral rights when the client does not could place the license holder in a position to have to compensate the client for the loss of income.

In the real estate industry currently there is a great deal of confusion as how to address mineral rights in a contract. The safest way is to involve attorneys. This, of course, affects the transaction entirely, and some individuals cannot afford the expense of an attorney.

Real estate license holders need to be very careful writing mineral rights into a contract. License holders are not attorneys. Failure to correctly write mineral rights into a contract could make the license holder liable for the financial recovery of the client. The Texas Association of Realtors® has an addendum that provides information on mineral clauses but does not address the wording of the clause. TREC has a promulgated addendum required for use by license holders in any situation involving mineral rights. The form is designed to provide the wording necessary to address the question of mineral rights.

Dealing with Probate Law

Probate law is another area of frequent interest for real estate licensees. Probate can quickly affect the conditions of sale and could have extreme consequences if handled improperly. Who inherits real property under Texas law when someone dies intestate (i.e., without a valid will) is determined by the Texas Probate Code. Probate is the process in which a court directs the payment of a person's debts and the distribution of his/her assets upon the person's death. The court's role is to facilitate this process and protect the interests of all creditors and beneficiaries of the estate.

The real estate professional must disclose to any seller in a probate estate position that the taxes owed on the estate may drastically affect the return on sale of a property. Failing to disclose the possible consequences of a real estate sale during probate could lead the license holder into financial as well as legal trouble.

The first issue is to determine whether the deceased's property is separate or community property. If the deceased is not married, the property will be separate. If the deceased is married, the presumption in Texas is that all property is considered community property.

Community Property

- On the death of one spouse in a marriage, with no valid will, the community property passes to the surviving spouse if:
  - no child or other descendant of the deceased spouse survives the deceased spouse; or
  - all surviving children and descendants of the deceased spouse are also children or descendants of the surviving spouse.
- If a child or other descendant of the deceased spouse survives the deceased spouse, and that child or descendant is not a child or descendant of the surviving spouse, the spouse retains one-half of the community estate and the other half goes to the children or descendants of the deceased spouse.

Separate Property

- If both a spouse and children survive the deceased, the following conditions hold:
  - As to personal property, the spouse gets one-third and the children equally divide the remaining two-thirds.
  - As to real property (land), the ownership of the land goes to the children equally, subject to a life-estate in one-third of the land by the spouse.

The real estate license holder should never give advice as to the status of property that is probated by the state. If the license holder is wrong and causes the client financial harm, the license holder could be held liable.

Background on Documentation for Probate Law
Under most situations the parties involved in a probate should seek legal advice. The following is a list of documents that the attorney will need to further the probate process:

- death certificate of the deceased
- obituaries of any of the following if applicable:
  - the deceased
  - any spouse of the deceased
  - any deceased children of the deceased
- birth certificate of each child of the deceased and whether that child is living or dead
- driver's license numbers for the deceased and any living spouses, ex-spouses, children, parents, brothers or sisters
- Social Security numbers for the deceased, and any living spouses, ex-spouses, children, parents, brothers and sisters
- tax returns of the deceased
- any decrees of divorce of the deceased
- if there is a family Bible with birth information, copy the relevant pages
- list of names, addresses, and phone numbers of neighbors (previous and/or current), coworkers, or close friends who can speak about the family history of the deceased
- adoption papers if the deceased adopted any children
- any records, "baby books," or old photos that show the names of the children

By advising the client to gather the documents before visiting the attorney, the real estate license holder can save the client both time and money. Failing to advise the client could result in the license holder's having financial liability for lack of disclosure.

Dealing with the Seller's Disclosure Notice
The real estate professional should know the contents of and explain the Seller's Disclosure Notice (SDN) to all parties involved in a real estate transaction. The SDN protects all parties and license holders in a real estate transaction.

Background on Requirements for the Seller's Disclosure Notice

The SDN is a document that when filled in by the seller identifies the items in the house and whether those items are working properly or not. There is no required form, but most brokers use the one approved by the TREC. One of the most common sources of lawsuits is the lack of a properly completed SDN. The single, most effective defense against a buyer suing the seller after the sale of the home is a properly completed SDN.

Texas state law dictates that the seller of a one- to four-family residence must provide the buyer with a complete and accurate disclosure of the condition of the property. This requirement is to protect buyers from hidden or undisclosed defects that are known at the time of sale. The SDN actually protects everyone because of this disclosure.

Lawsuits typically arise out of disputes between the buyer and the seller over what the seller actually knew about the property at the time of the sale. If it can be proven that the seller knew or should have known about a defect that was not disclosed to the buyer, the buyer could sue the seller and potentially receive some level of compensation for the nondisclosure of the defect.

If a real estate license holder is involved in any transaction that results in a lawsuit, that lawsuit will involve the license holder and the broker. It is the license holder's responsibility to ensure that the SDN is filled in and, to the best of the license holder's ability, to be sure the information is correct. The best protection from a buyer claiming misrepresentation about the property condition is by having the buyer sign the SDN. The signature indicates that the buyer has had the opportunity to review the disclosure and react to the items on the SDN.

Background on Owners Not Required to Provide a Seller's Disclosure Notice

Some owners are not required to provide an SDN. Section 5.008(e) of the Texas Property Code states that the requirement to provide an SDN does not apply to a sale under these conditions:

- pursuant to a court order or foreclosure;
- by a trustee in bankruptcy;
- to a mortgagee by a mortgagor or successor in interest, or to a beneficiary to a deed of trust by a trustor or successor in interest;
- by a mortgagee or beneficiary under a deed of trust who has acquired the real property at a sale conducted pursuant to a power

of sale under a deed of trust or a sale pursuant to a court-ordered foreclosure or has acquired the real property by a deed in lieu of foreclosure;
- by a fiduciary in the course of the administration of a decedent's estate, guardianship, conservatorship, or trust;
- from one co-owner to one or more other co-owners;
- made to a spouse or to a person or persons in the lineal line of consanguinity of one or more of the transferors;
- between spouses resulting from a divorce or a decree of legal separation or from a property settlement agreement incidental to such a decree;
- to or from any governmental entity;
- of new residences of not more than one dwelling unit that have not previously been occupied for residential purposes; or
- of real property where the value of any dwelling does not exceed five percent (5%) of the value of the property.

The foregoing identifies sellers who are not required by law to provide an SDN. In all transactions, the real estate license holder would be wise to get owners to provide an SDN. Sometimes it is not possible, but the best answer is to always disclose. A license holder who was involved in a transaction in which the SDN was not provided and failed to check to be sure an exemption was in place would be at risk of financial and legal liabilities.

Texas Property Code § 5.008 requires a seller to complete an SDN and deliver it to the buyer on or before the effective date of a contract. If the seller (or agent of the seller) fails to deliver the notice in a timely manner, the buyer may terminate the contract for any reason within seven days after the buyer receives the notice. The license holder must therefore remain aware to make sure that the seller provides the correct disclosure.

The seller's disclosure notice statute requires the seller to use the form set out in the statute or a form that is substantially similar and, at a minimum, contains all the items in the statutory form. This allows:

- flexibility of the form;
- additions to the form that might not have been considered by legislators when the statute was passed; and
- changes to the form necessary to clarify questions posed in the form.

Considering that sellers have for decades been obliged to disclose known material defects to prospective buyers, the SDN statute does not include any additional disclosure requirements. The statute simply specifies the mechanism by which sellers must make disclosures.

Policies and Procedures: Privacy Policy

An office policies and procedures (P&P) manual is one of the best ways to protect a real estate brokerage from potential risks. The P&P manual should lay out all the brokerage's rules, regulations, and procedures and provide helpful hints for the real estate industry. The P&P manual should be a comfort for license holders because they no longer have to guess the procedures; they are all explained. The P&P manual can be a great recruiting tool because it gives a potential recruits an insight to what  is expected of them and shows the brokerage's professionalism. Most brokers never show a recruit their office P&P manual until the recruit has agreed to work with their company. If the recruit is from one of the brokerage's competitors, the new broker may impress the recruit if the recruit's current office does not have a P&P manual.

Suppose that two license holders in a brokerage office just found out they have both been working with the same buyers. A broker needs to have a policy or procedure to handle such a situation. The license holder's best option is to check the office P&P manual. The manual should explain the procedure to handle such a challenge. The broker might not make everyone happy, but the broker will have a clearly outlined, fair plan.

From handling "For Sale by Owner" transactions to settling commission issues, a well-designed P&P manual for the real estate office is a must because it avoids a lot of confusion and unnecessary disputes among the license holders as well as outlines the rules and regulations of the real estate commission.

The P&P manual should be given to each real estate license holder sponsored by the broker, and everyone should read it. Brokers understand that a license holder might not read every page, so a good practice is to have all license holders sign a document that indicates that they have read and understood the policy manual.

When writing a P&P manual, the broker should include at least all of the following:

Commission-splits	Bonuses
Errors and omissions (E&O) insurance	Administrative fees
Training	Production expectations
Office support	Independent contractor agreement
Agency rules	
Termination	Dress code
Corporate structure	Assistants
Contract writing	Ethics
Office hours	Membership in associations
Office functions	Office appearance
Lockup and security	Office maintenance/cleaning
Sales documentation	Personnel records
Sexual harassment	Front desk
Telephone operations	Advertising
Postal services	Office equipment
Personal items	Office files
Confidentiality	Food in the office
Property signs	Conflicts of interest
Smoking	Printed material
Offers	Types of listings
Referrals	Disclosures
Performance review	Sales meetings
Awards program	

Once the broker has written the P&P manual, the broker should get a second opinion from a professional real estate attorney on certain sections, such as settlement, regulatory compliance, and the process for terminations. The manual should be a fluid, responsive document; yet once issued, the document should not change unless the changes are absolutely necessary and thoroughly thought out. If the broker has to make a change, the broker should distribute it to every sponsored license holder and get their signatures to prove that they understand the changes. The broker could have a consultant write an office manual, but the cost is typically prohibitive. The TAR offers a generic one for sale that is very good and at a reasonable price. The broker would need to modify it, but it lays a good foundation.

Policies and Procedures and Privacy Policy: The Law

TREC Rule §535.2 stipulates that a broker who sponsors salespersons or is a designated broker for a business must maintain current written policies and procedures to ensure the following:

- Each sponsored salesperson is advised of the scope of the salesperson's authorized real estate activities and is competent to conduct such activities.
- Each sponsored salesperson maintains his/her license in active status at all times while he/she is engaging in real estate activities.
- Any compensation paid to a sponsored salesperson for real estate services is with written consent of the sponsoring broker.
- Each sponsored salesperson is provided notice of any change to the Act or to TREC Rules.
- Each sponsored salesperson receives additional necessary educational instruction to maintain competency.
- Each sponsored salesperson complies with the Commission's advertising rules.
- All trust funds received from consumers are maintained by the broker with appropriate controls.
- Records are properly maintained.
- Transactions in which a license holder is involved in buying or selling his/her own property should include:
  - a determination from the broker's E&O provider on coverage in such transactions;
  - disclosure of the license status; and
  - whether the license holder must be represented by another license holder in the firm when listing property owned by the license holder.

Sponsoring brokers are also required to have a policy or procedure that:

- specifies proper use of unlicensed assistants
- addresses the sudden cessation or break of sponsorship as a result of illness or death
- addresses safety issues
- complies with all federal regulations, including but not limited to the Real Estate Settlement Procedures Act (RESPA), Truth-in-Lending Act, do-not-call and do-not-fax laws, rules established by the Consumer Financial Protection Bureau, as well as state laws, such as the Texas Department of Insurance Procedural Rule 53.

Oversite Transaction and Compliance Review

A broker always needs to be aware of ways to reduce risk to the brokerage. One of the best ways to do so is to oversee all transaction in the brokerage firm and design a compliance review. "Oversite transactions" refers to the broker reviewing all listing contracts, buyer representation contracts, purchase agreements, property management agreements, advertising, publications, mailers, social media, internet advertising, and anything else that involves the public. Failure to monitor these activities puts the broker at considerable risk. The broker may not have the time in the day to monitor all these activities, so the broker can appoint a trusted license holder to take on this task.

> ### Case Study
>
> In a real estate brokerage company a license holder was going to send a letter to all the owners of real estate in a specific area because a house at the end of the block was being converted to a property that houses mentally handicapped children (a protected class under the federal Fair Housing Act). The letter read:
>
> > "Dear Homeowners,
> > I am sure you are aware of the home at the end of the block that is being converted to a home for mentally handicapped children. I am also sure you are aware that the home will decrease the home values in your area. If you would like to sell before this occurs, please give me a call."
>
> This is blockbusting—also called "panic pedaling," which is the inducement of owners to sell because of a protected class moving into an area—and it is in WRITING! If the broker had not have caught this action, who knows what the result would have been.

When a broker reviews a purchase agreement, the broker should be looking for contract errors and nonnegotiable items; the errors should be discussed with the agent handling the agreement. If the broker suspects a negotiation issue that is not best for the client, the broker should discuss the matter with the agent but not the client.

There are a few items a broker should put into a P&P manual about contract writing. The broker should review all contracts to be sure the license holder is complying with the following:

1. *A license holder acting properly should keep the contract neat.* If a license holder does not have neat and legible writing, that license holder should use a typewriter or word-processor computer forms. There have been contracts so sloppy that they put the real estate license holder in jeopardy. A contract that is difficult to read could lend itself to multiple interpretations. In a similar situation, a real estate license holder had a contract that was handwritten and had a random mark that made the sales price appear different than intended. The license holder who wrote the contract lost $5,000. If a contract appears to be confusing, it should be rewritten, and the new contract should be signed by all parties. A real estate professional should always keep the previous contract on file. The true real estate professional knows that when dealing with contracts, neatness counts. "A contract is ambiguous when its meaning is uncertain and doubtful or is reasonably susceptible to more than one interpretation" (Heritage Res., Inc. v. NationsBank, 939 S.W.2d 118, 121 [Tex. 1996]).
2. *A license holder acting properly should be sure that all the blanks are filled in correctly.* A license holder should not leave blanks in a contract even on unimportant details. The license holder should slow down and make sure each blank is addressed. Caution and thoroughness will make any license holder look more professional. All license holders should use "N/A" (Not Applicable) as needed and blue ink on originals to differentiate from copies if allowed. If the contract has a $ symbol before the blank, the license holder should write a dollar amount. A license holder should not get creative here and use a percentage even if doing so would make the negotiation easier. If TREC requires a dollar amount, the license holder should write a dollar amount in the blank. This may require more effort, but to change the contract fundamentally is to practice law.
3. *A license holder acting properly should always use full names for the parties of a contract.* A real estate professional should ask the parties their full names when filling out a contract. This makes

the contract clearer and helps the title company in doing its research. The license holder should not use Latin in describing a person—for example, *et ux.* (and wife), *et vir.* (and husband), *et al.* (and all), *femme sole* (single female), *baron sole* (single male), and the like. Real estate professionals are to build trust and confidence, and Latin will create distance.

4. *A license holder acting properly should always double-check all the numbers and figures.* Failing to add correctly could indicate to a buyer that the down payment, for example, is less than required. Generally, the difference is made up out of the real estate salesperson's pocket.

5. *A license holder acting properly should always double-check all the dates.* A real estate professional should make sure all dates match and that the closing is not on weekends or holidays. The license holder should make sure that the year is correct and the dates are agreeable to the client.

6. *A license holder acting properly should be sure to collect all personal checks necessary (earnest money, option money).* Any time a real estate license holder submits a contract with the first part of Paragraph 5 filled in, it indicates that an earnest-money check has been given. Trusting a buyer to give an earnest-money check tomorrow will put that license holder in a position to make that check good. A license holder once took an earnest-money check for $3,000 with the stipulation that the buyer would make the check good in three days. The buyer never made the check good. Because the license holder accepted the check and promoted it as good, the license holder was responsible for paying the $3,000 out of their own pocket. If a buyer does not have valid earnest money at the time of contract, a license holder should fill in the "additional earnest money" blank in Paragraph 5.

7. *A license holder acting properly should be sure the clients initial each page and any changes and sign the back.* Initials show agreement to all the terms on each page. The law does not require initials to make the contract valid, but the license holder should get them anyway for completeness. The signature of all the parties on the back page *is* required. It is surprising how many times contracts are submitted by real estate professionals that their clients have never signed. Every license holder should double-check the contract for initials and signatures.

8. *A license holder acting properly should be sure the clients receive a copy of everything signed and as soon as possible get them an original.* If possible, a licensee should immediately make a copy of anything the buyer or seller signs. Signing something without a copy makes people nervous, as it should. The license holder should make the clients comfortable by giving them copies. The license holder should also get both parties originals as soon as possible. A contract must have mutual assent (i.e., meeting of the minds) by all parties. The best way for a license holder to ensure that mutual assent has occurred is to give all parties an accepted original. An original is defined as having original signatures. So theoretically, multiple originals can exist as long as all have original signatures.
9. *A license holder acting properly should be sure all addendums necessary to the contract are with the contract.* A license holder could easily misplace an addendum on a contract because there is so much to do when writing a contract. The best way for a license holder to solve this problem is to pull out an addendum when it is discussed and not wait until the end and hope to remember to include the addendum. Failing to include the proper addendums could result in a TREC violation and possible financial liability.
10. *A license holder acting properly should always double-check the legal description to be sure it was written correctly.* A simple mistake here can be expensive. A real estate license holder wrote in a contract that the buyer was purchasing Lot B. After closing, the architect could not design plans to fit on the lot. The reason the architect could not design plans to fit the lot was that the license holder had sold the wrong lot—it should have been Lot A. Each lot was $200,000. Not a good day for that license holder or broker! All license holders should also double-check the listing with the tax records. If a discrepancy exists, the license holder should contact the listing agent for clarification before writing the offer.
11. *A license holder acting properly should explain the contract to the clients but should not interpret the legal ramifications of a contract.* Some license holders make stuff up because the clients asked them a question, and the license holder felt he/she should know the answer. All license holders should be sure the correct information is always given to all parties. The license holder should

research the correct information if necessary. The license holder should not assume the way it has always been done is the right way. If it has been done incorrectly for 10 years, it is still incorrect. The license holder needs to verify all information through some other reliable source.

12. *A license holder acting properly should not promise that real estate contracts do anything except put in writing the desires of the parties to sell real property.* If a client wants to have the property go to the spouse upon death, the real estate agent should have the clients seek legal advice through an attorney. Disbursement of property upon someone's death is the purpose of a will. Agents sell real estate; they should never attempt to do legal work. Some real estate salespersons do, on their own, put in the contract "rights of survivorship." This is not acceptable in Texas because it is a community property state. Doing this is construed as the practice of law, and the practice of law without a law license could land the real estate agent in prison.

13. *A license holder acting properly should not get creative in writing contracts.* "Creative" in this context means "practicing law." As mentioned above, the practice of law without a law license could expose the license holder to many problems both legal and financial. More real estate licensees lose their license and create liability for themselves because they become creative in writing contracts. Legal advice should be sought out on dodgy issues before writing the contract if the license holder is not absolutely sure of what is permissible. The license holder is not expected to know everything, but the license holder should care enough to find out the correct answer or procedure.

14. *A license holder acting properly should not use the term "as-is" but should use the term "no repairs" instead.* It could be assumed that "as-is" translates as nondisclosure. The real estate professional should always make sure that his/her clients disclose all that they know. Failure to disclose could result in liability. A seller could sell a house without repairs but must disclose what should be repaired on an Owner's Disclosure Statement.

15. A license holder acting properly should never use the word "sue." Real estate professionals are third-party negotiators and not involved in any one transaction as a principal. A real estate salesperson might pop off, "If I were you, I would sue them!" Saying this suggests to the principals that they should sue.

Agents are not judges; they are salespersons. License holders need to leave the judging to judges. License holders should be working to solve problems and not creating them. Anger can create liability. A license holder should never stand on principle but should work to make things better.
16. *A license holder acting properly should not accept poorly written contracts from other real estate salespersons because doing so puts all license holders at risk.* The license holder should rewrite the incorrect portions with the approval of the client. Claiming that it was the other agent who wrote the contract is not defensible in court.
17. *A license holder acting properly should have the seller use the SDN whenever applicable.* The SDN will help all parties to stay out of court. It helps the seller disclose what is necessary. It allows the buyer to determine the property condition from the seller's point of view.

Specific Areas of Contracts That Can Cause Risk

Notices Paragraph

The "Notices" paragraph of the TREC-promulgated residential contract is frequently overlooked as not that important, but in reality it is. The result could be drastic if the instructions in the paragraph are not followed correctly. This paragraph asks for the addresses of both the buyer and the seller so that information that is relevant to the transaction can get to the appropriate parties. Failure of a real estate license holder to fill in the address properly could result in lack of notification and possible license violations as well as legal liability.

Without completing the paragraph, the buyer or buyer's agent would not have a place to send important notices to the seller, such as the Notification of Termination of Contract. A license holder is advised not to fill in personal information in this section. If the listing agent places his/her personal information in the blank, that agent is now responsible for all communication.

Third-Party Financing Condition Addendum

The Third-Party Financing Condition Addendum should be added to any transaction that involves financing of any type. Failing to use this addendum could expose the agent to disciplinary actions.

Using the "contingency," the buyer must, within the time specified, give written notice to the seller that the buyer is not able to obtain financing approval. This must be presented for the contract to terminate and for the buyer to be refunded the earnest money. If the buyer does not give the notice within the time required, the contract is no longer subject to the financing contingency described in the addendum.

Financing approval occurs when the buyer has satisfied the lender's requirements related to the buyer's ability to borrow the money, which includes creditworthiness, credit history, income, assets, and the like.

> Loan approval is not financing approval, and the addendum uses the term "financing approval." Loan approval is the unequivocal statement by the lender that the lender is ready to fund without further conditions. To grant loan approval, the lender must be satisfied in two general areas: the buyer's ability to repay the loan—determined by creditworthiness, income, and assets—and the collateral, which is the property. The addendum defines financing approval to mean the first item, which is related to approval of the buyer, not the property. Ron Walker is past director of legal affairs for the Texas Association of REALTORS®.

Lender Underwriting Requirements

Real estate professionals should be careful to understand the lender's underwriting requirements on each transaction in which they are involved. Each lender can modify the requirements according to the lender's current standards. If a lender has a large sum of investment capital, the lender's requirements can get a little "looser"; and if the opposite happens, the money is more difficult to obtain because of many more strict requirements. Failure to understand each lender's underwriting requirements could result in delayed closings and possible loss of transactions. A listing agent must continue to communicate with the agent representing the buyer to be sure that the approval is obtained for the reasons mentioned earlier.

Misuse of the Designation "Single Family"

Many real estate license holders use the designation "single family" and do not understand the ramifications of their statement. A single-family home is a freestanding residential building with no common walls. It is not a duplex, where one family lives in one side and another family lives in the other. Claiming that a property is single-family but is attached could lead to charges of deception.

Homeowners' Association Documentation

According to the TREC-promulgated residential contract, the seller is required to notify the buyer that the property is located in a mandatory property owner's association. The restrictive covenants governing the use and occupancy of the property and a dedicatory instrument governing the establishment, maintenance, and operation of the residential community are recorded in the Real Property Records of the county where the property is located. Copies can be obtained from the county clerk. If the buyer (now owner) does not pay the mandatory membership in the Homeowner's Association, the Association has the right to set a lien against the property and eventually foreclose on the property. Failure for the buyer to know such things is considered a lack of disclosure of the agent involved and clearly a TRELA violation.

Real estate professionals involved in the sale of real property with a mandatory Homeowner's Association should use the promulgated addendum "Mandatory Membership in a Property Owner's Association."

Special Provisions

Violation of the "Special Provisions" paragraph is possibly the most frequent cause of disciplinary action against a license holder. Too many real estate professionals see the blank section and believe they should fill it in with something. The smart agent does not put anything in this paragraph. The contract states that any "factual statements and business details" are to be placed here, but a license holder should take time before writing in this paragraph and then seek someone else's opinion on the validity of what was written. Real estate salespersons should consult their broker. Brokers should consult a real estate attorney. It is that serious.

Declared Use of Property and Misuse of Property

Depending on the property, the declared use could define the actions of the new owner. Suppose that a buyer purchases a residential property to live in and also wants to operate a hair salon in the living room. The declared use is residential, and the proposed use is a commercial hair salon. If the license holder indicates at any time that this dual use is a possibility, but zoning in the area prohibits establishment of a commercial business, the license holder could be held liable to the new owner. The license holder should have asked the appropriate questions to find out the proposed use of the property before his/her client purchased the real estate property.

Proper Use of Dates
The typical real estate license holder does not realize the number of times the contract ties an action to a date. Failure to include, use, and monitor the dates of a contract will place the license holder in jeopardy of financial risk as well as place the license holder in a position to receive reprimands and face other disciplinary actions from the Commission.

Request for Repairs: Amendment to the Contract
One of the biggest areas of dispute in a contract is repairs. Buyers feel that the sellers should fix everything, and sellers think the buyers should take the home "as is." Real estate professionals are caught in the middle and if not careful could place themselves in a position of financial liability.

A buyer's agent should always use an itemized repairs list. If there are only a few items to be repaired, the agent could use the amendment form promulgated by the TREC. If the list is extensive, the agent could develop a separate list and note it in the form. The buyer's agent must be aware of the option period because if the sellers drag their feet, the buyer's agent must get the buyer to terminate the contract, extend the option, or certify in writing that the seller will not be required to make repairs past the termination date. Failure to notify the buyer could result in loss of license and financial responsibility by the agent.

The buyer's agent must also be certain that the seller has completed all the repairs prior to closing; this can be ascertained through the listing agent. If the seller is required to finish the repairs, a lawsuit may be required. Under the circumstances, if the buyer's agent failed to warn the buyer that repairs have not been completed, the agent will be held liable for those repairs if the seller refuses to do them.

Tracking Systems
One of the best ways to prevent violations and reduce risk is to have tracking systems in place that notify the real estate salespersons involved in a transaction of important dates. This system could evolve into a checklist of items involved in a real estate transaction. When an agent fails to complete the job and close the transaction, lawsuits begin. This system should help to alleviate the burden to the real estate professional.

A transaction management system (TMS) is one type of tracking system. The TMS will take a contract from start to finish with or without agent involvement. Most of the effort is conducted online, with very little interaction. Some key aspects of a good TMS are that it:

- manages scheduling, key dates, tasks, and reminders
- can access all transaction documents from any computer
- organizes documents in transaction files for quick retrieval
- enables document sharing by giving transaction parties online access rights
- forwards documents to other parties directly from the system via email
- provides property-showing confirmations and license holder feedback on listings
- has automated ordering of vendor services such as escrow, title, and inspections
- assures that vendor documents are received on time
- enables vendors to upload documents directly into the transaction file
- maintains a paper trail of all calls, notes, and messages in a transaction

Methods of Loss Control

There are several methods of loss control and risk reduction. Each of these has benefits and challenges.

Avoidance—completely shutting off all activities that cause the risk to exist. This happens when, for example, offering a service is no longer viable for profit. In this case, a brokerage can choose to stop offering the real estate service. Avoidance—that is, avoiding the risk completely—is the best means of loss control. If the broker's efforts at avoiding the loss have been successful, there is a 0% probability that the broker will suffer a loss (from that particular risk factor, anyway). This is why avoidance is generally the first of the risk-control techniques that is considered. It is a means of completely eliminating a threat.

Reduction—reducing either or both the impact or probability of the risk directly. For example, the risk of fire can be treated by reducing either the impact or the probability separately. To reduce the impact of the fire and destruction of critical records, a curative measure is taken, usually with no effect on the risk's probability. This could be accomplished by installing a sprinkler installation. On the other hand, a preventive measure can be taken to reduce the likelihood of a fire occurring. This is usually accomplished by the use of materials impregnated with fire-retardant agents. The preventive measure, in turn, does not always affect the risk's impact directly. Loss reduction not only accepts risk but also accepts the fact that loss might occur as a result of the risk. This technique will seek to minimize the loss in the event of some type of threat.

Prevention—limiting, rather than eliminating, loss. Instead of avoiding a risk completely, this technique accepts a risk but attempts to minimize the loss as a result of it. For example, completing contracts is a necessary risk for a real estate transaction. Any time a license holder fills in a contract, that license holder is responsible for any mistakes. A mistake is a serious risk for the brokerage. The broker limits the risk by training the license holder and by reviewing each contract written.

Sharing—fully or partially reducing the impact or probability of the risk by a full transfer or sharing of a risk. The best example of this response is an insurance policy. When a brokerage is not able to cover the impact of a risk, an insurer can be approached to cover the risk for a certain premium payment.

Acceptance—leaving the risk as is without taking any action. This can be done when a risk is of negligible size and is considered an acceptable risk. Otherwise, a risk of substantial size can be tolerated if the presence of the risk is vital for the existence and continuity of a brokerage. Any risks that remain and are tolerated should be subjected to monitoring, for they should not evolve from a tolerated acceptable risk into an unacceptable risk. A brokerage can choose which response or combination thereof should be employed to counter a specific risk. To determine the best-fitting response for a risk, the brokerage should consider risk tolerance and the effects of the available responses on the brokerage on a broad level.

Separation—a risk-control technique that involves dispersing key assets. This ensures that if something catastrophic occurs at one location, the impact to the business is limited to the assets only at that location. On the other hand, if all assets were at that location, the brokerage business would face a much more serious challenge. An example of this would be similar to the preceding example except another set of records is stored in another location.

Duplication—essentially involves the creation of a backup plan. This is a risk-control technique often necessary with technology. A failure with an information system's server should not bring the whole business to a halt. Instead, a backup or failover server should be readily available for access in the event that the primary server fails.

Diversification—allocates business resources to create multiple lines of business that offer a variety of brokerage services. With diversification, a significant revenue loss from one line of business will not cause irreparable harm to the company's bottom line.

Business Insurance

A brokerage should have insurance to pass some of the business risk to the insurance company. Insurance will not transfer all the risk, but it will help the broker mitigate (i.e., lessen) the damages if someone challenges the broker by mistake or because of an injury. Liability insurance helps pay for someone who is hurt on brokerage property. The brokerage office is a place of business, and anyone on the property could be a potential risk. The broker should take measures to be sure his/her brokerage office is as safe as possible and then have liability insurance to protect the brokerage further.

The brokerage should also have key person insurance. Key person insurance is coverage for a case when one of the key persons of the brokerage dies. The beneficiary can be anyone, but usually the brokerage itself is beneficiary to help in the transition from the previous key person to the next. The transition could include the hiring, training, and coordination with the staff of the brokerage. Other typical beneficiaries are the heirs of the key person. This type of transition occurs frequently with small brokerages that may not have enough money to cover the support of the family from the loss.

The brokerage should have the building insured. The building needs to be insured to protect the owners of the building from loss resulting from fire, acts of nature, vandalism, water penetration, or many other types of losses to the real property. This insurance should be audited for the entire building because the property value could change or the building could undergo improvements.

All types of insurance should be audited periodically to be sure the insurance covers what it should cover and the beneficiaries are correct. The insurance should be reviewed to verify the rates and be sure the insurance company is the best company for the type of insurance needed. Different insurance companies specialize in different types of insurance. No matter what the insurance provider states, it may be better to scout several insurance companies to obtain the best coverage. It is the broker's responsibility to perform this investigation and decide which insurance company to use. To have insurance with an inferior insurance company that could deny coverage when it is needed or make it difficult to collect insurance money if it is owed must be avoided.

The brokerage should have the contents of the business establishment insured. This insurance is to cover the personal property located in the building. This could be the furniture, copiers, computers, printers, and anything else that could be in a real estate brokerage. This type of insurance is frequently forgotten or put off because of the expense. A brokerage can be devastated if it takes a complete loss on all its personal property. Contents insurance is therefore a must from the first day.

The broker should insist that all license holders of the brokerage obtain liability insurance for their business cars. A car used in the course of real estate business may not be covered under personal auto coverage. Insurance companies usually require an additional rider (i.e., an additional policy extension to the current policy) or an altogether new policy for autos used in a business setting. If a person is struck by the automobile of a sponsored license holder or is riding in the automobile of a license holder at the time of an accident and is injured, the brokerage could be liable for the injuries. The best protection for such situations is for the license holder to pay the premium and allow the insurance company to take that risk.

E&O insurance is *imperative* for a brokerage to obtain. E&O insurance protects the license holder and the brokerage from honest mistakes (errors) and anything that a license holder should have disclosed to a client or customer (omission). This is an expenditure that must be budgeted for, paid for, and adjusted as needed.

CHAPTER SUMMARY

Risk is the possibility that an event will occur and adversely affect the achievement of real estate sales.

Risk management is the process that attempts to manage the uncertainty that influences the achievement of real estate sales, with the goal of reaching the closing and thus creating profit for the brokerage.

The risk-management process is as follows:

1. State the objective to be achieved.
2. Identify the events that form a threat to the objective.
3. Assess the likelihood and impact of each of the identified events.
4. Prioritize the risks.
5. Respond to each of the risks. Possible responses are avoidance, reduction, prevention, sharing, acceptance, separation, duplication, and diversification.

When real estate license holders sell their own property or personally buy a property, they must use the term "agent-owner" in all print and internet advertising and on listing information sheets and materials.

License holders must inform their brokers that they intend to sell their own property.

The Deceptive Trade Practices Act (DTPA) requires that if a license holder is selling his/her own property, it must be disclosed that the property belongs to the license holder. This disclosure is required because real estate license holders have an unfair advantage over the typical consumer. This unfair advantage is called an "unconscionable action" if not disclosed.

Individuals need advice from both a professional real estate license holder and a divorce attorney to help understand legal rights, financial risks, and long-term implications before making any decisions about the home during a divorce.

Before the clients go to see a lawyer, the real estate professional should advise them to gather all the necessary documents and records about each piece of real estate.

A short sale is when a lender agrees to take less for a property than the loan amount to get the property sold.

Probate is the process in which a court directs the payment of a person's debts and the distribution of his/her assets upon his/her death.

Community Property

- On the death of one spouse in a marriage who has no valid will the community property passes to the surviving spouse if:
  - no child or other descendant of the deceased spouse survives the deceased spouse; or
  - all surviving children and descendants of the deceased spouse are also children or descendants of the surviving spouse.

- If a child or other descendant of the deceased spouse survives the deceased spouse, and that child or descendant is not a child or descendant of the surviving spouse, the spouse retains one-half of the community estate and the other half goes to the children or descendants of the deceased spouse.

Separate Property

- If both a spouse and children survive the deceased:
  - As to personal property, the spouse gets one-third and the children equally divide the remaining two-thirds.
  - As to real property (land), the ownership of the land goes to the children equally, subject to a life-estate in one-third of the land by the spouse.

The Seller's Disclosure Notice (SDN) is a document that when filled in by the seller identifies the items in the house and whether those items are working properly or not. There is no required SDN document, but most brokers use the one approved by the Texas Real Estate Commission (TREC).

Texas state law dictates that the seller of a one- to four-family residence must provide the buyer with a complete and accurate disclosure of the condition of the property.

An office policies and procedures (P&P) manual is one of the best ways to protect a real estate brokerage from potential risks. The P&P manual should lay out all the brokerage's rules, regulations, and procedures and provide helpful hints for the real estate industry.

TREC Rule §535.2 stipulates that a broker who sponsors salespersons or is a designated broker for a business entity must maintain current, written policies and procedures to ensure that each of the following occurs:

- Each sponsored salesperson is advised of the scope of the salesperson's authorized real estate activities and is competent to conduct such activities.
- Each sponsored salesperson maintains his/her license in active status at all times while engaging in real estate activities.
- Any compensation paid to a sponsored salesperson for real estate services is with written consent of the sponsoring broker.
- Each sponsored salesperson is provided notice of any change to the Act or Rules.
- Each sponsored salesperson receives such additional educational instruction to maintain competency.

- Each sponsored salesperson complies with the Commission's advertising rules.
- All trust funds received from consumers are maintained by the broker with appropriate controls.
- Records are properly maintained.
- Transactions in which a license holder is involved in buying or selling his/her own property should include
  - a determination from the broker's E&O provider on coverage in such transactions;
  - a disclosure of the license status; and
  - whether the license holder must be represented by another license holder in the firm when listing property owned by the license holder.

Sponsoring brokers are also required to have a policy or procedure that:

- specifies proper use of unlicensed assistants
- addresses the sudden cessation or break of sponsorship as a result of illness or death
- addresses safety issues
- complies with all federal regulations, including but not limited to Real Estate Settlement Procedures Act (RESPA), Truth-in-Lending Act, do-not-call and do-not-fax laws, rules established by the Consumer Financial Protection Bureau, as well as state laws, such as the Texas Department of Insurance Procedural Rule 53.

"Oversight transaction" refers to the broker reviewing all listing contracts, buyer representation contracts, purchase agreements, property management agreements, advertising, publications, mailers, social media, internet advertising, and anything else that involves the public.

The broker should review all contracts to be sure the license holder is acting properly by:

- keeping the contract neat
- being sure all the blanks are filled in correctly
- always using full names for the parties of a contract
- always double-checking all the numbers and figures
- always double-checking all the dates
- being sure to collect all personal checks necessary (earnest money, option money)
- making sure the clients initial each page and any changes and sign the back

- ensuring that clients receive a copy of everything signed and receive an original as soon as possible
- being sure all addendums necessary to the contract are with the contract
- always double-checking the legal description to be sure it was written correctly
- explaining the contract to the clients but not interpreting its legal ramifications
- not promising that real estate contracts do anything except put in writing the desires of the parties to sell real property
- not getting creative in writing contracts
- not using the term "as is" but using the term "no repairs" instead
- never using the words "sue"
- not accepting poorly written contracts from other real estate salespersons because doing so puts all license holders at risk
- requiring the seller use the SDN whenever applicable

There are several methods of loss control and risk reduction. Each of these has benefits and challenges.

Avoidance
Reduction
Prevention
Sharing
Acceptance
Separation
Duplication
Diversification

A brokerage should have insurance to pass some of the business risk to the insurance company. It should also have key person insurance in case one of the key persons of the brokerage dies. Finally, the brokerage should have the building and its contents insured.

Brokers should insist that all license holders of the brokerage obtain liability insurance for their business cars.

Insurance that protects the license holder and the brokerage from honest mistakes (errors) and anything that a license holder should have disclosed to a client or customer (omission) is errors and omissions (E&O) insurance.

CHAPTER QUESTIONS

1. What is the possibility that an event will occur and adversely affect the achievement of real estate sales?
   A. competition
   B. risk
   C. adversity
   D. market drop

2. What must a license holder do when selling his/her own property?
   A. price the property under market
   B. sell only to a protected class
   C. disclose that he/she is a license holder
   D. ask another license holder to handle it

3. What factors need to be discovered when owners are going through a divorce?
   A. identification of all real estate owned
   B. current income potential from any real estate owned
   C. any loans on any real estate owned
   D. all of the answer choices

4. Which of the following refers to a person who dies without a valid will?
   A. testate
   B. intestate
   C. probate
   D. none of the answer choices

5. What document allows the seller to fill in information that identifies the items in the house and whether those items are working properly?
   A. Latent Defects Announcement
   B. Seller's Disclosure Notice
   C. Buyer's Agreement to Repairs
   D. Texas Property Condition Form

6. Which of the following is a good way to protect a brokerage from potential risks?
   A. have a written P&P manual
   B. hire only experienced license holders
   C. practice only property management
   D. hire a sergeant-at-arms

7. Which of the following is a TREC requirement for license holders?
   A. maintain the license
   B. pay commissions only through the designated broker
   C. engage in continuing education
   D. all of the answer choices

8. Which of the following is good contract advice to avoid risk?
   A. use full names
   B. double-check all numbers
   C. double check all dates
   D. all of the answer choices

9. What is a freestanding residential building with no common walls?
   A. a duplex
   B. a retail store
   C. a single-family home
   D. all of the answer choices

10. What type of loss control is "shutting off all activities that cause the risk to exist"?
    A. prevention
    B. sharing
    C. avoidance
    D. duplication

CHAPTER 6

Financing a Real Estate Brokerage Business

One of the most critical areas of concern for a real estate brokerage is finances. A majority of real estate brokerages start out without the proper capital to effectively operate. Once a company realizes its dilemma, it is usually too late for financial bailout. A broker needs to be keenly aware of the brokerage's financial situation at all times.

Borrowing money to begin operations as a real estate brokerage is difficult because lending institutions do not typically consider a brokerage viable when comparing the assets against the risks. The only tangible assets of an acquisition are some office equipment and supplies. The main assets are the license holders, and the company does not "own" them. The assets of a startup do not exist, therefore, except in the broker's personal finances. A broker should not feel too bad because this is the troubled path of almost all service industries.

The Financials

The financials are the lifeblood of the real estate brokerage business. The financials allow the broker to determine how the brokerage is performing and how the brokerage should perform well into the future. Knowing the brokerage's financials enhances the broker's decision-making ability. If the financials look good, the broker has options. The broker has the option to spend money on marketing. The broker has the option to expand the current location. The broker has the option to acquire additional offices. The broker has the option to make capital improvements. These all take considerable financial investment. If the broker does not have the finances to support such activities, then the brokerage suffers. If the financials are sluggish, the brokerage cannot expand and grow. If the financials crater, the brokerage may go under.

The broker needs financials to understand the performance or underperformance of the brokerage.

Horizontal analysis—compares ratios or line items over two or more years of financial data in both dollar and percentage form. It allows the broker to determine how a company has grown or declined over time. This analysis can be compared against competitors for growth rates.

Vertical analysis—shows each category of accounts on the balance sheet as a percentage of the total account. The difference between horizontal analysis and vertical analysis is that vertical analysis involves listing each item on a brokerage's financial statement as a separate column.

Ratio analysis—calculates statistical relationships between financial data. Ratio analysis is used to evaluate various aspects of a brokerage's operating and financial performance such as its efficiency, liquidity, profitability, and solvency. The trend of these ratios over time is evaluated to determine if the brokerage is improving or deteriorating.

Personal Financials

The primary consideration for a real estate brokerage is the broker/owner's financials. These personal financials will outline the broker's financial position at a given point in time. A personal financial statement will typically include general information about the broker, such as legal name and contact information. Personal financials will also include a breakdown of the broker's total assets and liabilities. Assets would include any account balances in checking or savings accounts, retirement account balances, trading accounts, and real estate. Liabilities would include credit card balances, personal loans, and mortgages. The broker will need to invest some or all of his/her personal finances to begin or buy out a real estate brokerage. The investment would be required by any lender to reduce the lender's risk into the brokerage. Generally, the broker will need to have 20% to 50% of the total investment in cash depending on the lender's view of the risk.

Personal Cash on Hand

Cash on hand is the money the broker can get quickly, also called "liquid assets." Liquid assets are cash or something that can be converted to cash in a timely manner without much hassle. Liquid assets would be cash, checking accounts, savings accounts, and money market funds. Most lenders will allow the broker to borrow cash from a relative or

friend. The broker could also take on partners but would lose ownership interest.

Personal Credit Cards

One source of additional cash would be borrowing cash from a credit card or multiple credit cards. The interest rates on this type of cash are extremely high but if it is paid in a short period of time, it might allow a broker to begin operations.

Personal Income

The broker will need to prove income and how that income will continue after the brokerage opens. This is a serious consideration for a broker. Some brokers want to continue earning income from real estate sales, but doing this leads to "broker competition," and frequently real estate license holders do not appreciate competing against their broker. It can make recruiting and retaining agents more difficult. Some brokers choose not to compete but instead work full time as a broker. This approach is better for the brokerage but puts a strain on the brokerage financials, especially if the broker lived a high-level lifestyle before buying the brokerage and now expects to continue to pull large amounts of cash from the brokerage.

Lenders like to see a broker who has an income source that can maintain the broker's current lifestyle without requiring income from the brokerage. This type of broker has earned personal wealth from previous businesses or investments and is now looking for another avenue for income through the brokerage but does *not* need income from it for some time into the future. This approach allows the brokerage to access cash at startup, when it is needed most, and hence lowers the risk to the lender. Of course, this is an age-old business truth: *Lenders love to lend to those who don't really need it.*

Personal Net Worth

Personal net worth is essentially everything a person owns of significance minus what the person owes in debts. Net worth shows any type of lender the broker's financial health. Basically, it is the amount of money a person would have left over after selling all his/her assets and paying off all debts. If the potential borrower has not maintained good financial health, the lender will not trust the borrower.

Personal assets includes things such as:

- real estate investments
- stocks
- bonds
- any retirement savings (e.g., IRAs)
- savings accounts
- personal home
- automobiles
- boats
- furniture
- jewelry
- collections
- art
- sports vehicles
- vacation homes
- business investments

The foregoing is not a complete list nor is it a promotion to buy "stuff," but if the broker has this stuff, then the broker should claim it as assets. Sometimes a broker can offset cash with collateral against the broker's assets.

Personal debts include virtually anything that the person owes, such as:

- child support
- loans of all types (e.g., personal, business, student, auto, and home)
- credit card balances

A negative personal net worth could indicate overborrowing. A person could have a large student loan that created the negative net worth, for example—not necessarily a bad thing if that same person is now working in a career supported by the student loan. As that student loan is paid down because of the income now earned, the individual's net worth will increase. However, if the negative net worth is because of credit card debt to buy "nice" things, there is no offsetting asset to compensate for the debt. Lenders fear the latter situation.

For a broker to increase his/her net worth, the broker should begin to spend less on consumables, entertainment, clothes, and toys and use that money to pay down on any debt. The better the net worth looks, the better the broker looks.

Business Financials

Business financials are those of the brokerage business. No longer are the broker's personal finances considered unless the broker intends to include them. Brokerage financials for a startup may require the broker's personal finances to be included in any calculations because a startup has no current financials to anticipate risk. If the brokerage has been operational, the brokerage financials should be easier to analyze than if the brokerage is just starting up.

Brokerage financials need to adhere to generally accepted accounting principles (GAAP) to maintain financial records retaining information from the past into the future. Because GAAP is universally applied, it also enables comparison between companies. Furthermore, if the brokerage records are audited by government agencies and accountants, GAAP ensures accuracy. Brokerage financials are also needed for tax liability determination and any further financing requirements.

Business Income Statement (Business Profit-and-Loss Statement)

The income statement is a financial statement that reports the brokerage's financial performance over a specific accounting period. Financial performance is assessed by giving a summary of how the business acquires its revenues and incurs its expenses through both operating and non-operating activities. It also shows the net profit gained or loss incurred over a specific accounting period. The income statement begins with sales and ends with net income. It also provides the broker with gross profit, operating profit, and net profit. The income statement allows the broker to easily see which expenses make up the largest portion of sales.

Operating activities—disclose information about revenues and expenses that are a direct result of regular brokerage operations.

Non-operating activities—disclose revenue and expense information about activities that are not directly tied to a brokerage's regular operations.

Business Balance Sheet

The balance sheet is a summary in time of the brokerage's assets, the brokerage's liabilities, and the broker's equity position. The balance sheet is used to analyze trends in assets and debts. A balance sheet must balance, hence the name. It follows this formula:

$$\text{Liabilities} + \text{Equity} = \text{Assets}$$

This formula reflects a basic financial report because a brokerage must pay for all things it owns (assets) by borrowing money (liabilities) or by taking it from profit (equity). Assets, liabilities, and equity are each composed of several additional accounts that get much more specific.

Assets are anything of value owned by the brokerage, including things of short- and long-term value:

- *short-term assets*—can be converted to cash in one year or less:
  - cash and cash equivalents–Treasury bills, certificates of deposit (CDs), cash
  - marketable securities–stock market
  - accounts receivable–clients who owe commissions to the brokerage
  - inventory–employment agreements (e.g., listing and buyer representation agreements)
  - prepaid expenses–insurance, rent
- *long-term assets*—will take longer than a year to convert to cash:
  - long-term investments–brokerage office building
  - fixed assets–land, equipment, buildings, and other capital assets
  - intangible assets–intellectual property and goodwill

Liabilities are money the brokerage owes to outside parties and include short- and long-term debts:

- *short-term liabilities*—those debts or obligations that must be paid within a year:
  - loans
  - rent
  - taxes
  - utilities
  - wages
- *long-term liabilities*—those debts that are payable at any point after a year:
  - loans

Equity (net assets) represents the broker/owner's investment in the brokerage minus the broker's withdrawals from the brokerage plus the net income since the business began. It is the amount of assets minus the amount of liabilities. It is the money that is attributable to the broker/owner. Equity can be retained by the brokerage as reserves, reinvested in the brokerage, used to pay off brokerage debt, or given to the broker/owner as a return on investment.

Business Cash-Flow Statements
The cash-flow statement provides an overview of the brokerage's cash flows from operating activities. Operating activities include any activity engaged in the primary purpose of making a profit. Cash flows from operations start with net income, and then all non-cash items are reconciled with cash items within business operations. The cash-flow statement deducts receivables from net income because it is not cash. Also included in cash flows from operations are accounts payable, depreciation, amortization, and numerous prepaid items booked as revenue or expenses but with no associated cash flow. Operating cash flow indicates whether a brokerage is able to generate sufficient positive cash flow to maintain and grow its operations.

Having proper personal finances in order is a requirement for a broker to start a brokerage. Having proper business financials provides the broker with the information needed to run the brokerage efficiently. Indeed, overlooking the need for proper financials until it is too late can leave an unwary broker in a great deal of trouble.

How Much Money Is Needed?

The purchase of a brokerage will cost money. The question is, how much?

The startup of a brokerage will cost money. The question is, how much?

The brokerage will need money to operate. The question is, how much?

The brokerage should return a profit. The question is, how much?

Brokers who do not ask these questions usually have no direction. It is critical to know how much money is needed to buy, operate, and make a profit from a brokerage. Many brokers continue to lose money year after year by owning a brokerage. For them, owning a brokerage is a point of pride when it should be business enterprise.

Purchase of a Brokerage

The purchase of a brokerage can cost very little or it can cost a fortune. A small, local, independent brokerage does not have much actual value, and so the broker who buys it may have to finance it himself/herself. Such brokerages have few license holders and do not generate much in sales. This situation can be of real value; however, if the new broker can motivate the license holders to produce and is able to recruit new agents. This can be a real drain, though, if the broker is unable to increase sales. These types of brokerages can range in price from free to no more than a few thousand dollars. The way a brokerage is acquired for free is to keep on the current broker and allow him/her to continue to engage in real estate business but not require the person to pay the brokerage any commissions (100%, no split). The broker may want some money paid out over time, of course. That is simply another negotiation point.

If this small local brokerage is franchised, the franchise has value. Wise brokers look for these types of vulnerable franchises and buy them up for less than what the franchise would cost new and obtain the franchise rights.

> CASE IN POINT: Suppose a franchise costs $45,000 and will last for 10 years before it will need to be renewed. A broker buys a franchise but after two years cannot make it work. That broker then sells the real estate brokerage and franchise—yes, franchises are generally transferable, though with limitations—to a "wise" broker for $20,000. The current broker at least got something back from the money pit of an investment. The "wise" broker just bought a brokerage that can be resurrected and has a franchise, all for much less than a single franchise would have cost and with eight years left before renewal.

The purchase of a medium-sized brokerage, one that has one or only a few office locations and 10–20 license holders at each location, involves a great deal of consideration. The cost for such a brokerage will vary greatly depending on the current broker's need to sell. If the broker is desperate, the price drops significantly. If the broker is not desperate, the price will escalate significantly. These brokerages are sold for several thousand dollars to several hundred thousand dollars.

A large, multi-office megafirm could cost millions of dollars to purchase. These types of purchases are frequently made through holding companies or large investment groups. The purchase of a megafirm brokerage requires months if not years of negotiations, groups of lawyers, and pages of contracts.

The downside to borrowing is creating another debt for the brokerage. This type of borrowing usually has favorable terms; if the debt is not repaid, however, then it has the potential to destroy personal relationships.

Working Capital

The amount of working capital required depends on the type and size of a brokerage. Brokerages vary in many aspects in addition to the amount of cash they need to operate. The broker also has a great deal to do with how much cash is spent. A frugal broker will spend less than a compulsive spender, who can run the brokerage completely out of money.

A small local brokerage, such as a mom-and-pop shop, may require very little in working capital to operate successfully. Small local operations spend what they make. If the money is not there, the brokerage must wait or find another solution to generate income. Mandatory bills are paid, but the purchase of a new computer may be delayed or it may never happen.

A small niche brokerage, in contrast, may require a great deal of working capital. If the niche is a high-end operation, buyers and sellers of real estate need to be courted, and the marketing needs to be highly professional.

Medium-sized brokers usually have larger offices than the mom-and-pop brokerages. Medium-sized brokers must employ staff, unlike the brokers of small local operations. And medium-sized brokers must have many more supplies to operate effectively. All of these needs require working capital. This is a real issue for brokers on a tight budget. Whereas the businesses that provide services or goods to the brokerage will require timely payment, the medium-sized brokers must wait 60, 90, or 180 days or longer to receive their earned commissions. This delay in receiving income is the main reason that large sums of working capital are required to effectively operate a brokerage.

The working capital requirements of megafirms could be several hundred thousand dollars per month. These large companies could have many layers of management and hundreds of employees. Each office within the megafirm, as well as the corporate office, has needs for working capital.

Profit

Profit is the financial benefit that is realized when the amount of revenue gained from a business activity exceeds the costs and taxes needed to sustain the activity. A brokerage should always operate with the goal of making a profit. A brokerage may start at breakeven or perhaps a loss, but the goal should always be to generate profit. Profit is the confirmation that the broker's business concept is sound. Profit should be paid out first. One more time with emphasis: **PROFIT SHOULD BE PAID FIRST.**

The reason for this emphasis is that otherwise all the money earned will be spent to cover expenses. If the first outlay of income is allotted to profit, all other expenses will somehow be covered. If profit is paid last, however, it will seldom be realized. Paying profit first may not be feasible at all times, but the broker needs to be aware that if at least a small percentage of income is not initially set aside as profit, the brokerage will find a use for all money allowed.

Financial Resources

The broker can provide the financial resources necessary to start up a brokerage or buy out an existing brokerage. However, frequently a broker may not have the amount of money necessary to open a brokerage. If that should be the case, a broker could look at other possibilities for funding.

One of the most obvious methods would be getting a commercial loan from a lending institution. Banks are in the business of lending money. Their main interest is the risk level of the loan. If a bank determines that offering a loan is risk free, the bank will lend every time. However, few loans are risk free, so the bank is going to demand certain provisions from the broker before a loan will be consummated.

Applying for a Business Loan

Borrowing money is one of the most common sources of funding for a small real estate business, but obtaining a loan is not always easy. Before a broker approaches a lender for a loan, it is a good idea for the broker to understand as much as possible about the factors the lender will evaluate when the lender considers making a loan. The lender will require a loan package before the lender will approve a loan. The loan package should include:

- contact information for the borrower
- completed application
- broker/owner's full credit report (usually ordered by lender)
- loan proposal letter

- full business plan
- separate executive summary
- all business financials
- business financial summary
- all personal financials
- personal financial summary
- amount, purpose, and collateral for loan
- purchase agreement, signed (if buyout)
- appraisal (if loan includes real property)

If the broker chooses to apply for a business loan, the broker should be aware of several factors the lending institutions will be concerned with, including the broker's ability to repay, available collateral, credit rating, management experience, equity, and detailed business plan. These are discussed next.

Ability to Repay

The ability to repay must be proven in the loan package. Lenders want to know that the broker will have the cash flow from the business to meet debt payments. To analyze the cash flow of the business, the lender will review its past financial statements. Lenders feel better with businesses that have been in existence for a number of years because they have a financial track record. If the brokerage has consistently made a profit and that profit can cover the payment of additional debt, then it is likely that the loan will be approved. It is much more difficult to obtain a loan if the business has been operating marginally or if that business is a startup.

Available Collateral

Collateral is anything of value that a lender could take to replace the loss of money in case of a default on a loan. The lender could attach a CD held in a bank or take a lien against real or personal property. The lender is looking to reduce its risk in making the loan.

Available collateral can be defined as those personal and business assets that can be sold to pay back the loan. Every loan program requires at least some collateral to secure a loan. If a potential borrower has no collateral to secure a loan, he/she will need a cosigner who has collateral to pledge. Otherwise, the borrower may have difficulty obtaining a loan. The value of collateral is not based on the market value but rather is discounted to take into account the value that would be lost if the assets had to be liquidated.

Credit Rating

Credit rating is the overall credit score that the broker has personally achieved. The broker's credit rating is based on past history of credit and the ability to repay that credit. The better the credit score, the better the credit the broker has and the less risk the lender is undertaking.

All brokers should have their credit checked out at least once per year. The credit bureaus must provide a full credit report yearly if requested. The broker will need to check whether there are any negative listings damaging the credit

score. This can happen quite easily, so the broker should not wait to check the rating until the credit is needed because clearing up even a minor mistake may take over a year. The broker does not need to hire a credit reporting company to obtain the report or to challenge any discrepancies. All the broker has to do is file a report with the credit bureau, which must then investigate. If the entity that filed the report does not respond, the credit bureau must eliminate the information from the record. Again, this process seems easy, but it will not happen overnight, so a broker must be patient. If the entity responds and confirms the credit problem, the broker must take up the issue with the entity that filed. Doing this will require more time and may cause aggravation, but the broker should remain persistent to finally have his/her credit restored. The broker will want to make sure that when the lender pulls the credit report, all the errors have been corrected and the credit history is up-to-date.

After receiving the credit report, the broker should be sure to check the proper spelling of the name, Social Security number, and address at the top of the page. The broker should make doubly sure these are correct. There are people who have found that they have received the credit information of another person because of mistakes in their identification information.

On the rest of the credit report, the broker will see a list of all the credit obtained in the past—credit cards, mortgages, student loans, and so on. Each credit item will be listed individually with information about how the broker paid that credit. Cases in which the broker has had a problem in paying the credit will be entered toward the top of the list. These are the credits that may affect the broker's ability to obtain a loan.

Having been late by a month on an occasional payment will probably not adversely affect the broker's credit a great deal. However, if the broker is continuously late in paying a bill, has an unpaid debt that was charged off, has a judgment filed against him/her, or has declared bankruptcy, foreclosure, or repossession in the past seven years, it is likely that the broker will have difficulty in obtaining a loan.

In some cases, a person has had a period of bad credit based on a divorce, medical crisis, or some other significant event. If that person can show that the credit was good before and after this event and has made an effort to pay back the debts incurred in the period of bad credit, the person should be able to obtain a loan. It is best if the person writes an explanation of the credit problems and how they have been rectified. This explanation should be attached to the credit report in the loan package. If the person needs assistance in interpreting or evaluating the credit report, he/she can ask an accountant or banker.

Research indicates that good personal credit history is one of the most important factors in identifying borrowers who will repay their commercial loans. Many loan programs require perfect personal credit to qualify. Being turned down from one institution does not prevent the broker from going to another. One broker, for example, once wanted financing for a real estate project and had to go to seven lenders before that broker was approved for the loan.

If the broker does not have the credit necessary to obtain a loan from a lending institution, the broker may have to seek out alternative financing sources.

Management Experience
A person who wants to open a business and has no experience in that business should not seek financing for that business. The person needs to hire those who know the business or to take on a partner who has the appropriate experience. Regardless, the person should be advised to take some time to gain experience in the business first and take entrepreneurial training classes.

A lending institution will need to know that the broker is prepared for business before applying for a loan. Bankers understand the importance of on-the-job training as well as book learning. The broker not only needs to show knowledge but also requires actual experience. It is best if the broker has served as a manager at another brokerage: This management experience will prove that the applicant is qualified to lead.

For a new business especially, it is important for the business owner to demonstrate that he/she has experience in the real estate industry and/or entrepreneurial experience. If the individual has never owned or operated a real estate brokerage before, he/she should research the industry and take some college classes before opening a brokerage.

Equity
Equity is the difference between what is owed on a business and its actual worth. Financial institutions want to see a certain amount of equity in a business before they feel comfortable lending money. Equity lowers the lender's risk because it is much more difficult to lose one's own wealth than that of others. Most banks want to see that the total liabilities or debt of a brokerage is not more than four times the amount of equity. Therefore, if the broker wants a loan, the broker must ensure that there is enough equity in the brokerage to leverage that loan. If the current debt to net worth is too great, it is unlikely that the business will be able to obtain any financing.

The broker should not be misled into thinking that startup businesses can obtain 100% financing through conventional or special loan programs. A business owner must usually put some of his/her own money into the business. The amount an individual must put into the business to obtain a loan depends on the type of loan, the purpose, and the terms. For example, most banks want the owner to put in at least 20% to 40% of the total request. A business owner who does not believe in a brokerage enough to risk his/her own money is a major blocking point for a loan.

Detailed Business Plan
Before any lending institution worth doing business with will loan a person money, the person must provide a detailed business plan. The two main functions of a business plan are:

1. to give direction and purpose to an organization; and
2. to provide information to lenders and investors about the company's viability and vision.

The business plan should already have been completed before the broker approaches the lender because formulating the plan is the first step required to open a real estate brokerage.

Brokers applying to lenders should focus on the presentation of this plan and should be sure to do the following:

1. *Have the business plan professionally bound with multiple copies.* Brokers should make multiple copies of their business plan. Brokers should go to the expense of making a quality presentation if they expect a lender to give them large sums of money. Brokers should understand that the loan process involves going through a loan committee, each member of which will need a copy of the business plan. The other elements of the loan package can be copied if needed. The business plan should consist of several hundred pages in a leather-bound or otherwise professional binder.
2. *Publish the business plan with plenty of time to spare.* Brokers do not want a presentation with a lender to be postponed simply because they are waiting for the plan to be printed. Brokers in need of a loan should demonstrate their professionalism by being organized and planning ahead.

The Loan Process

The following questions need to be asked and answered by the broker and/or the entire management group looking to obtain a loan. The questions are structured as if a business is in operation. If the broker is looking at a start-up operation, then use future projections to answer the questions:

1. Can the business repay the loan?

A lender wants to be sure the money it is loaning will come back. Do the numbers in the financial statement make sense? Do they show that the business will do well, or do they indicate that the venture might be a risk? Has the broker taken all things into consideration? Does the broker have current and future projections?

If the brokerage is an existing business that is profitable, there are demonstrated profits to repay some amount of new debt. If, however, a brokerage is not profitable, it becomes very important to prove how it will become profitable in the near future so that a loan can be repaid.

If the brokerage is a startup business, it is extremely important that the broker find as much data on comparable real estate brokerage business statistics as possible. These data will help the broker "prove" the revenues the broker intends to generate and the expenses the broker is anticipating are in line with current actual data.

2. Can the broker repay the loan if the business fails?

The lender wants to be sure the broker has enough assets in his/her personal funds or collateral to cover the debt if the business cannot. This is simple risk reduction by the lender. Most lenders will not require complete coverage of a business loan, but the more the borrower can cover, the lower the risk to the lender, and the more likely the loan will be approved.

3. Does the business pay its bills?

The brokerage needs enough revenue to cover all expenses and have enough left over to make payments to the loan. If the brokerage does not currently cover the expenses, what will happen once the loan payment comes due? If it is a startup business, will the brokerage have enough income to pay its bills?

4. Are the owners (any and all owners if more than just the designated broker) committed to the business? Do the owners have their real estate license? Do the owners have an occupation outside real estate? Will it be hard or easy for the owners to walk away from this business?

All these questions must be addressed before a loan is approved.

5. Does the brokerage have a profitable operating history?

The brokerage should show a profit and require money only to expand operations to make more money. The borrowed funds should not go to a brokerage that needs the money just to stay afloat. Desperation is not a good investment for a lender. If it is a startup brokerage, the broker needs to show that the real estate industry needs another competitor and that this brokerage can fill that void.

6. Are sales growing?

What are the trends for the real estate business? The brokerage should be able to show data that indicate a steady increase in profits.

Any slumps or drops in profits need to be explained in detail. The broker needs to indicate that the brokerage has corrected any of the situations that created any drop in profit. The broker needs to indicate an understanding of any increased profit of the brokerage and demonstrate that he/she knows how to continue that trend. If the trend is downward, the risk to the lender increases drastically. If the brokerage is a startup business, the broker should give examples of competitors in the real estate industry, explain their trends, and explain how he/she plans on improving the business.

7. Does the broker control expenses?

Some brokers spend money on everything. They overspend for the best location in town. They buy the latest in technology, and they overpay their sponsored license holders. All this spending shows lack of discipline in a broker and creates risk to a lender. All expenses should therefore be analyzed to determine if any of them could be reduced or eliminated. This is a difficult and time-consuming but necessary process. As owner of a startup brokerage business, the broker needs to lay out the systems that will be in place to control expenses.

8. Is there any discretionary cash flow?

Having discretionary cash flow will demonstrate the ability to take on another payment such as a loan payment. A real estate company that continually makes a profit will easily and quickly obtain a loan to expand operations.

9. What is the future of the real estate industry?

The future of the real estate industry should be strong. This includes both local and international markets. If the industry will not defend an expansion, the expansion should not be considered. Some brokers expanded their operations to excess and then fail or lose a great deal of money. Their real estate offices got so big that the area could not support the volume of sales that the real estate office required to stay viable.

10. Who are the competition, and what are their strengths and weaknesses?

The broker should know the brokerage competition and what they offer. A broker should never be caught sleeping and not notice that the competition have or are about to offer services that could be disastrous to the future of the current brokerage. The broker's knowledge of the competition shows the lender that the broker is prepared.

11. Has the broker filed all income tax returns and paid all taxes owed?

Lenders and government loan programs alike want to see that an individual has met his/her tax obligations for both filing and paying taxes. Many of the loan programs are offered in partnership with government agencies. These loan programs do not look favorably on individuals who have unpaid income taxes. Some brokers pay the taxes on the business last. The taxes should be paid second (remember, profit should be paid first).

12. Does your business have a positive net worth?

The business's net worth, which applies only to existing businesses, should be positive. The broker needs to have two net worth sheets: one for the broker personally, and one for the brokerage. The broker can combine the two if the brokerage operates as a sole proprietorship. The net worth statement helps the lender determine:

- progress toward financial goals
- plan for changes in assets or liabilities
- ability to keep tax liability down
- ability to chart financial progress

The broker should be sure the net worth statement takes a look at all current assets. Current assets of a real estate brokerage are the pending contracts for sale. The broker should examine the brokerage's fixed assets—those items that the brokerage owns, such as copy machines and office furniture. The last analysis with respect to assets are the deferred assets, and these are any investments the brokerage has made that cannot be converted to cash without a substantial penalty, such as a retirement plan for the broker.

13. Is the brokerage carrying too much debt?

Existing businesses that have too much debt will find that their profits are directed at paying back loans and not building equity in the business that can fund future growth. Consequently, banks and government loan programs look more favorably at loan requests that do not add too much debt to the business. Banks often look for a debt-to-net-worth ratio of 4 or less (total liabilities divided by equity).

14. Are you willing to personally guarantee a loan?

Most business owners are asked for a personal guarantee to obtain their first business loans. If the business fails, the lender can come after the business owner personally. Lenders do not lend to corporations unless the chairperson or other administrator is personally responsible.

15. Does the brokerage have qualified managers and advisors?

As existing real estate brokerages expand, they need more sophisticated management as it relates to strategic planning, marketing, recordkeeping, sales management, personnel, and so on. When the broker applies for a loan, the banker will consider the qualifications of the management team and advisors to determine whether they are capable of leading the business to the next level of growth.

If there are sectors of the brokerage business that need improvement or support, the broker should attend entrepreneurial training classes. The broker could check out the National Association of REALTORS® online, visit a business assistance center or small-business development center in the local area, or contact a regional Small Business Administration (SBA) office for information on local resources.

Any broker who cannot answer the foregoing questions in a positive manner should take the advice of business managers and realize that if he/she is in or attempting to open an enterprise that will not turn a profit, then he/she should not do it. This may be a difficult decision to make and may even hurt, but it is better to hurt now than when the doors are locked under foreclosure.

Preliminary Actions Before the Presentation

Now that the broker has a business plan and has answered all the preceding questions positively, it is time for the broker to go for a loan. Before the broker shows up at a lender's front door, there are a few things the broker should do:

The broker should write a proposal letter. A proposal letter is a simple, two-to-five-page letter describing the need for the loan and the ability to pay the loan back. The broker should be very specific in the letter about what the broker is actually asking for. Does the broker want a loan, or a line of credit, or a combination of both? Exactly how much money is necessary? The broker should not ask for too little because it will be evident that the broker cannot succeed without the necessary funds. The broker should not ask for too much because it will be perceived as imprudent on the broker's part. The letter should not go into details about the brokerage business or how the broker is to repay the loan because all that is found in the business plan. This is an expanded form of the executive summary that is in the business plan.

The broker should call first. Lenders like to be prepared for meetings, and a broker showing up unannounced will only give the broker poor results. The unannounced broker will be asked to return at a better time or the meeting will stall without resulting in a decision. The broker needs to build good relations with the lenders, and showing up and making them feel uncomfortable is not the best way. Some lenders demand to see the business plan before they meet with the applicant. They want to be more prepared.

Calling on Lenders

Calling on lenders takes a little courage, but the broker needs to remember that they want and need to make loans; otherwise they are out of business: This is a relationship, but at the same time it is business. If the broker is turned down, the broker should simply apply to another lender.

Before calling the first lender, the broker should read through the following script:

Receptionist: "This is First Bank of Brittany. How can I direct your call?"
Broker: "Who handles small-business loans?"
Receptionist: "That would be Bob Smith. Would you like me to connect you?"
Broker: "That would be great."
Loan Officer: "This is Bob Smith."
Broker: "Mr. Smith, my name is Dan Hamilton, and I would like to meet with you to discuss a business opportunity. I am available later today, or would tomorrow be better?"

Loan Officer: "Well, how about 2 p.m. tomorrow? I could set aside some time then."
Broker: "Great. Is there anything besides my business plan that you will need to see?"
Loan Officer: "Does your business plan cover your financial position?"
Broker: "Yes, it does."
Loan Officer: "Then that should be about it. See you tomorrow."

Most bankers are not as intimidating or mean-spirited as most people like to think. Bankers want these appointments because they never know which one is the moneymaker.

At the Appointment

The broker should dress as if already a success. Acting as if he/she has all the money in the world, the broker should be confident but not arrogant. The broker should dress in a professional business outfit and be there on time.

The broker should bring the following items:

- two writing pens
- a notepad
- the loan package and business plans
- business cards and business brochures

Once the broker is in front of the loan officer, the broker needs to begin by making small talk. The broker could mention that he/she likes the way the bank is laid out, for example. If the broker notices a picture of the loan officer's family on the desk, the broker could ask about them. The broker should not jump right into the presentation. The broker needs to remember that this first meeting initiates building a relationship.

After a few minutes of such small talk, the broker should begin the presentation. If the loan officer wants to take the lead, the broker should let him/her do so, but the broker needs to make sure that the presentation is on track.

The presentation should go through the following steps:

1. The broker should ask the loan officer to sign a nondisclosure statement. The broker should not be intimidated; they actually expect a professional to ask for one to be signed. If they

refuse to sign it (no reason why not), then the broker should ask to speak to someone else in the organization. The broker should not want the brokerage idea stolen. It should not happen, but the broker needs to protect the idea.

2. The broker should ask the loan officer the preliminary questions for a loan request, listed below. These questions help determine if the loan is the type the lending organization actually offers. Some lenders specialize; if the loan request is not in their specialty, the broker will not receive a loan. Also, they may not lend money in the amount needed. Some lenders will not lend money in amounts of less than $5 million, for example; so if the broker is applying for $100,000, they will not offer a loan.

   a. In what types of loans does your institution specialize?
   b. Do you frequently handle real estate brokerage loans?
   c. What other brokerages have you financed?
   d. How long has your institution been in business?
   e. What are your loan minimum and maximum limits?
   f. Do you offer any special small business–type loans?
   g. What do you look for in determining a potential loan?
   h. Are you able to make the loan today, or will it have to go through a committee?

3. If the broker has determined that the lender can offer the loan, the broker should go over the business concept. First, the broker should hand the business plan to the loan officer. The discussion should center on the executive summary and the proposal. The proposal explains why the broker wants the money, and the executive summary is all about the brokerage business and why the brokerage is a secure investment for the lender. The broker should mention the reasons for the brokerage and what is expected from a loan. The broker should not go into too much detail, and certainly the broker should not have the loan officer flipping pages in the business plan. Lenders tend to be numbers people, so the broker should let them absorb the idea.

4. The broker should ask the loan officer if he/she has any questions. If the answer is no, then the broker should ask for the loan. If the loan officer does have questions, the broker should answer them as well as possible and then should ask for the loan. The broker should not leave without asking for the loan.

Most loan officers cannot make a decision on the spot, however, and so the broker should not be concerned when the officer answers that he/she has to take this proposal to the loan committee for its approval. But the broker must ask nonetheless. Before the broker leaves, the broker should ask the loan officer, "If there is one thing about this loan request that would keep the loan committee from accepting it, what do you think that would be?" If the loan officer answers, the broker must be able to remedy that situation, or the proposal is doomed.

5. If it is time to leave, the broker should gather his/her things and ask when the next loan committee meeting will be. The broker should ask how many business plans they will need and then politely and professionally prepare to leave. The broker should offer a professional handshake and thank the loan officer for his/her time.
6. The very first thing the broker should do when back at the office is to write the loan officer a thank-you note and get it in the mail. Regular mail is more personal than email and will carry a lot more weight.
7. If the proposal is turned down, the broker should go meet with another lender. Persistence is the key.
8. Some lenders will have the broker mail the business plan to them, and they handle the entire procedure over the telephone or through the internet. This is not the best scenario, but it may be the only option.

The lending process and the types of loans on offer vary from lender to lender. The key for the broker is to find out as much information as possible about the lender before the presentation so that the broker can design the presentation to the requirements of that particular lender.

Alternative Sources of Loans

Not all loans are from traditional lenders. The broker should be sure of the quality of the lender before the broker originates a loan. A quick, uneducated decision could be the demise of the brokerage. The following are just a few lenders to whom the broker could send a "loan request":

Partners

Taking on partners is now only about obtaining a loan and not forming a long-term relationship with an equity position. A loan can be paid off, and once that occurs there is no more liability on the part of the business. The broker needs to be careful about taking on actual partners, though, because the broker cannot get rid of them as easily. Taking on a partner is viewed as a business marriage. Once the broker takes on a partner, the broker cannot dispose of him/her; if the broker does, it will cost the broker everything. Therefore the broker should only take on someone like an accountant or an attorney who brings something to the table. Anyone else had better be only a last resort. Why would a broker want to do all the work and have someone else share in the glory and profit? So for the purposes of the following discussions, these ventures are considered to be loans, even if the word "partner" is used.

Friends and Family

The broker can seek out friends and family for a real estate brokerage loan. They could be a great source of funding, but turning to our nearest and dearest could also be a disaster on many levels. The good side is that the relationships are already built and the qualification process is probably extremely easy. Many of the broker's current relatives and friends probably have money that is right now just sitting in the bank. The broker could use that money and if successful make everyone wealthy. The bad side is that if the broker does not succeed, he/she could lose not only the business but also the relationships with family and friends. With a lender, the brokers who go bankrupt can get on their feet again in a few years, whereas if the broker depends on friends and family, the broker has only one shot. In this situation, brokers who lose their savings once will not get another chance. Not only that, but a lender is not at family reunions or birthday parties.

Business Associates

Business associates are the people the broker engages with in the real estate business. If the broker has performed as a real estate license holder, these business partners know and most probably trust the broker. Some of these individuals may have a great deal of money and may be looking for a place to invest it with a better return than the bank is currently giving. The broker needs to provide them with the same proposal offered to a traditional lender. The good news, however, is that the broker already has a developed relationship with these individuals. Also note that these are associates and not actual partners. Once their investment is paid off with interest, these people are no longer associated with the brokerage financially. Here is a list of some possible associates:

- currently sponsored real estate license holders
- competitive license holders
- title attorneys
- real estate attorneys
- real estate instructors
- real estate managers of competitive brokerages
- staff
- mortgage officers
- inspectors
- marketing company owners
- owners of mortgage companies
- appraisers
- structural engineers
- real estate investors
- owners of title companies
- escrow officers
- surveyors
- current and past clients of the brokerage
- providers of residential services
- repair and remodel professionals
- insurance salespeople and owners

These people want the brokerage to succeed because when the brokerage succeeds, they succeed. The broker should not make a loan contingent on giving them business, however, even though they want to be associated with a growing brokerage—such a contingency could be a violation of the Real Estate Settlement Act. If the broker knows the owners of an associate company, not just the employees, the broker should go to them first. They probably have more discretionary income than those who work for them, and they probably started where the broker is today. They may want to help the broker because they know what it was like to be hungry for success.

Investment Group
If the people that the broker knows cannot finance the real estate brokerage project solely, the broker should think about forming an investment group. An investment group involves several individuals investing a specified amount in the brokerage business. These investors can be friends, relatives, or business partners. Each of them is paid back individually with interest. The broker alone will not have enough capital to begin a brokerage, but by combining several small investors, the broker can reach the goal. The broker needs to be aware of the laws that could affect investment groups, and the best way is to seek the legal counsel of an attorney.

Venture Capitalists
Venture capitalists are individuals, partners, or companies that have huge sums of money to loan to people who want to begin or expand their business but cannot obtain a loan from traditional sources. Venture capitalists generally specialize in pharmaceuticals and technology. However, there are some who specialize in the real estate industry. These people will give the broker money but want huge returns. They want such a large return because of the risk they are assuming. If brokerage venture were such a viable quality prospect, the broker would not need to turn to venture capitalists. They can be extremely valuable in the right circumstances, but the broker should turn to them only as a last resort.

Credit Cards
Credit cards can be borrowed against. The interest rates are high, so the amount borrowed should be paid off as quickly as possible. The good news here is that once the credit card is paid off, the credit company no longer has a financial interest in the business. Credit card loans for investment purposes actually makes sense.

Home Equity Loan
Brokers could use their current home as collateral for a loan by using a home equity loan.

Small Business Administration

The SBA should be high on a broker's list of considerations if the brokerage needs help with operating capital. Most banks have a relationship with the SBA and can help the broker in dealing with this matter. Most lenders, including the SBA, will want to see the business plan before offering any kind of a loan to the broker. The SBA loan has many advantages over the loans offered by conventional lenders. Those advantages are explained online at the SBA website (https://www.sba.gov).

Brokers can go online to the Texas Small Business Administration website to discover the wealth of information provided there to help brokers get started in a new brokerage. There is also a map showing where the SBA offices are located in Texas.

There are a variety of courses that the broker can take, some online and some not. Among the courses are Starting a Business, Business Management, and Marketing and Advertising. There are courses for Surviving in a Down Economy and Financing and Accounting. These are only a sampling of the courses that are available.

Additional assistance is available through the Texas SBA in either getting the broker started in business or helping the broker stay in business. Consultants and mentors and countless resources are there for the broker to take advantage of.

General Operating Budget

A general operating budget is a document set forth with projections of costs and income. These estimates are budgeted to provide enough money to make ends meet. A general operating budget is critical for a real estate brokerage. The real estate broker who has a general operating budget knows the financials and knows what can be spent and what cannot to maintain the integrity of the brokerage. The budget should not be so strict that it hinders growth, but it does need to limit uncontrolled spending.

A broker should use this form to prepare a dream budget for the real estate brokerage using the amount of money the broker intends to make (i.e., the projected annual and monthly income). As the broker proceeds, he/she should pencil in adjustments to the general operating budget.

Utilities, automobile, rent, and overhead are usually expenditures that are not very flexible. An area of expenditures that a broker tends to cut is advertising and promotions. However, this is the exact area the broker should not be short-sighted about and start cutting. Marketing activities and promotions earn money well into the future, and cutting their budget is akin to stepping over a dollar to pick up a penny.

After the broker has this proposed dream budget completed, the broker should track all the real expenditures for a month, comparing them against the dream budget. The broker should be able to see how closely the brokerage has come to adhering to the budget.

CHAPTER SUMMARY

One of the most critical areas of concern for a real estate brokerage is finances. The financials allow the broker to determine how the brokerage is performing and how the brokerage should perform well into the future. Knowing the brokerage financials gives the broker effective decision-making ability.

Horizontal analysis—compares ratios or line items over two or more years of financial data in both dollar and percentage form. It allows the broker to determine how a company has grown or declined over time. This analysis can be compared against competitors for growth rates.

Vertical analysis—shows each category of accounts on the balance sheet as a percentage of the total account. The difference between horizontal analysis and vertical analysis is that vertical analysis involves listing each item on a brokerage's financial statement as a separate column.

Ratio analysis—calculates statistical relationships in financial data. Ratio analysis is used to evaluate various aspects of a brokerage's operating and financial performance such as its efficiency, liquidity, profitability, and solvency. The trend of these ratios over time is evaluated to determine if the brokerage is improving or deteriorating.

Personal financials include a breakdown of the broker's total assets and liabilities.

Personal assets include any account balances in checking or savings accounts, retirement accounts, trading accounts, and real estate.

Personal liabilities include credit card balances, personal loans, and mortgages.

Cash on hand is the money the broker can get quickly, also called liquid assets.

Liquid assets are cash or something that can be converted to cash in a timely manner without much hassle. These include cash, checking accounts, savings accounts, and money market funds.

"Broker competition" is when brokers list and sell real estate and "compete" against their own sponsored license holders.

Personal net worth is essentially everything a person owns of significance minus what that person owes in debts. Personal debts include virtually anything that the person owes.

Business financials are those of the brokerage business.

Brokerage financials need to adhere to generally accepted accounting principles (GAAP) to maintain information from the past into the future.

The business income statement is a financial statement that reports the brokerage's financial performance over a specific accounting period.

Financial performance is assessed by giving a summary of how the business acquires its revenues and incurs its expenses through both operating and non-operating activities. It also shows the net profit achieved or loss incurred over a specific accounting period.

Operating activities—disclose information about revenues and expenses that are a direct result of regular brokerage operations.

Non-operating activities—disclose revenue and expense information about activities that are not directly tied to a brokerage's regular operations.

The balance sheet is a summary in time of the brokerage's assets and liabilities and the broker's equity position.

The balance sheet is used to analyze trends in assets and debts. It follows this formula: Liabilities + Equity = Assets.

The balance sheet is a basic financial report because a brokerage must pay for all things it owns (assets) by borrowing money (liabilities) or by taking it from profit (equity).

Assets are anything of value owned by the brokerage and include things of short- and long-term value:

- *short-term assets*—can be converted to cash in one year or less:
  - cash and cash equivalents—Treasury bills, CDs, cash
  - marketable securities—stock market
  - accounts receivable—clients who owe commissions to the brokerage
  - inventory—employment agreements (e.g., listing and buyer representation agreements)
  - prepaid expenses—insurance, rent
- *long-term assets*—will take longer than a year to convert to cash:
  - long-term investments—brokerage office building

- fixed assets—land, equipment, buildings, and other capital assets
- intangible assets—intellectual property and goodwill

Liabilities are money the brokerage owes to outside parties and include short- and long-term debts:

- *short-term liabilities*—those debts or obligations that must be paid within a year
- *long-term liabilities*—those debts that are payables at any point after a year

Equity (net assets) represents the broker/owner's investment in the brokerage minus the broker's withdrawals from the brokerage plus the net income since the business began.

The cash-flow statement provides an overview of the brokerage's cash flows from operating activities.

A small, local, independent brokerage does not have much actual value, and so the broker can finance it and need very little working capital to operate.

A medium-sized brokerage is a brokerage that has one or only a few office locations and 10–20 license holders at each location. These brokerages are sold for several thousand dollars to several hundred thousand dollars, and their working capital is much greater than that of a mom-and-pop shop but not as much as that required by a megafirm.

The purchase of a large, multi-office megafirm could cost millions of dollars, and the monthly working capital could be in the hundreds of thousands of dollars.

Profit is the financial benefit that is realized when the amount of revenue gained from a business activity exceeds the expenses and taxes needed to sustain the activity.

Profit should be paid first.

The loan package a broker presents to a potential lender should include:
- contact information for the borrower
- completed application
- broker/owner's full credit report (usually ordered by lender)
- loan proposal letter
- full business plan
- separate executive summary
- all business financials
- business financial summary

- all personal financials
- personal financial summary
- amount, purpose, and collateral for loan
- purchase agreement, signed (if buyout)
- appraisal (if loan includes real property)

The broker's ability to repay must be proven in the loan package.

Collateral is anything of value that a lender could take to replace the loss of money in case of a default on a loan.

Credit rating is the overall credit score that the broker has personally obtained.

A lending institution will need to know that the broker is prepared for business before applying for a loan.

Equity is the difference between what is owed on a business and its actual worth.

The two main functions of a business plan are:

1. to give direction and purpose to an organization; and
2. to provide information to lenders and investors about the company's viability and vision.

The following questions need to be asked and answered by the broker:

- Can the business repay the loan?
- Can the broker repay the loan if the business fails?
- Does the business pay its bills?
- Are the owners committed to the business?
- Does the brokerage have a profitable operating history?
- Are sales growing?
- Does the broker control expenses?
- Is there any discretionary cash flow?
- What is the future of the real estate industry?
- Who is the competition, and what are the competition's strengths and weaknesses?
- Has the broker filed all income tax returns and paid all taxes?
- Does the business have a positive net worth?
- Is the brokerage carrying too much debt?
- Is the broker willing to personally guarantee a loan?
- Does the brokerage have qualified managers and advisors?

A proposal letter describes the need for the loan and the ability to pay the loan back.

The following are just a few alternative lenders:

- partners
- friends and family
- business associates
- currently sponsored real estate license holders
- competitive license holders
- title attorneys
- real estate attorneys
- real estate instructors
- real estate managers of competitive brokerages
- staff
- mortgage officers
- inspectors
- marketing company owners
- owners of mortgage companies
- appraisers
- structural engineers
- real estate investors
- owners of title companies
- escrow officers
- surveyors
- current and past clients of the brokerage
- providers of residential services
- repair and remodel professionals
- insurance salespeople and owners
- investment groups
- venture capitalists
- credit cards
- home equity loans
- Small Business Administration (SBA)

A general operating budget is a document set forth with projections of costs and income. These estimates are budgeted to provide enough money to make ends meet.

CHAPTER QUESTIONS

1. What is the best way for a real estate broker to determine how the brokerage is performing currently and how the brokerage should perform in the future?
   A. the number of license holders recruited
   B. the financials
   C. competition leaving the market area
   D. no good way to forecast the future

2. What is essentially everything a person owns of significance minus what the person owes in debts?
   A. assets
   B. cash flow
   C. account management
   D. net worth

3. What is the formula for a balance sheet?
   A. Liabilities + Equity = Assets
   B. Cash + Assets + Accounts Receivable = Short-Term Assets
   C. A + B = C; "A" is Assets, "B" is Bank Notes, and "C" is Cash Equivalents
   D. none of the answer choices

4. Generally, how much "working capital" does a mom-and-pop shop require?
   A. none (It does not take money to make money.)
   B. very little (Overhead is low.)
   C. quite a bit (Costs for office, staff, and marketing are high.)
   D. a handsome share. (These shops cannot make money, so large cash influxes are required monthly.)

5. What of value can a lender take to replace the money lost in a loan default?
   A. reserves
   B. certificate of deposit
   C. collateral
   D. a pledge

6. What is the difference between what is owed and what the brokerage is worth?
   A. debt
   B. liabilities
   C. assets
   D. equity

7. What type of letter describes the need for a loan and the ability to pay the loan back?
   A. loan letter
   B. recourse letter
   C. proposal letter
   D. summary letter

8. Which of the following would be a good person from whom to obtain a loan?
   A. currently sponsored license holder
   B. title attorney
   C. appraiser
   D. all of the answer choices

9. Which of the following questions would a lender possibly ask during the loan process?
   A. Can the business repay the loan?
   B. Does the broker control expenses?
   C. Is the brokerage carrying too much debt?
   D. All of the answer choices

10. When should profit be paid?
    A. first on the monthly budget
    B. last on the monthly budget
    C. after all expenses have been paid for the month
    D. at year – end after audit of bank reconciliations

CHAPTER 7

Negotiating a Commercial Lease

Negotiating a commercial lease is a much more detailed process than negotiating a residential lease and involves many more factors. The good news is that commercial leases are more about business and as such less about personal emotions and bias. If the lease makes sense, then it makes sense and the lease will be consummated.

Buying Versus Renting

When opening a real estate office, should the broker/owner go to the expense of buying a building, or should he/she simply rent a space and operate the business from there? This is an important question that needs analysis before operations begin. It is much more difficult to move the brokerage after it has opened its doors. The logistics of transferring one office to another is a nightmare, and the brokerage may be nonfunctioning for several days and perhaps not up to normal business levels for months. All this equates to loss of income. The broker therefore needs to spend a considerable amount of time choosing an office space so that moving offices will not become an issue.

Buying

The decision to buy a building to operate a real estate brokerage is one that should not be taken lightly. Some brokers open a real estate brokerage because they have just bought an office building as an investment and no other business is eager to move into the space. This is the wrong reason to establish a real estate company. Other brokers transfer their current (profitable) real estate company from one location to the new building they have bought because they need the building rented. Again, not smart. The broker should only buy a building to house a real estate company if doing so makes logical economic sense. Some logical reasons include the following:

1. *rent replacement.* Rent replacement is transferring from paying rent to paying principal. Suppose the real estate office is currently paying $850 per month in renting a small office space. If the company could find a place to buy where the monthly payments total $1,000 per month, the bank would consider the amount an increase of only $150 per month because the $850 would count as rent replacement.
2. *area recognition.* Area recognition is when the community knows the brokerage and where it is located. Area recognition is higher if the broker buys rather than rents. Everyone knows where the Acme Real Estate Company is located, for example, because it is visible, and the best way to become visible is to purchase a building. The community respects business owners with permanent stakes in the community more than "the passersby," who are just renting. A further advantage is that the signage can be exactly what the broker wants, without restrictions imposed by a landlord. Also, taxing authorities know the name of the real estate brokerage.
3. *cost savings.* Once a real estate company begins operations in a facility that is owned, certain costs savings can begin. The owner can better negotiate utilities, maintenance, landscaping, and any other services that are required for a building. A landlord, in contrast, may not be interested in cutting the best deal on such services because the tenants have to pay for them anyway. Any interest that is paid on an owned building is a tax savings, whereas none of a rent payment would be. As with any tax advice, the broker should consult an accountant to be sure to take advantage of any possible tax savings.
4. *long-term investment.* Before making the decision to buy a building for a real estate office, the broker should make sure the decision is based on logic and not emotion. To own a building on the town's Main Street is prestigious, but if the cost of the location bankrupts the brokerage, it is not a wise decision. Buying a building to house a real estate brokerage is a choice engendering effects that could last 60 years or longer, so the broker needs to be sure. Over the long term, however, buying is probably the better investment.

Leasehold

A leasehold estate (which is a less-than-freehold estate) is a leased or rented property with the tenant gaining the right of possession. When the tenant leases the property, the tenant has rights and obligations under that lease. A lease can last from a single day to 999 years. Longer term leases of more than 40 years are another class of leasehold estates typically reserved for commercial transactions and apartments in major metropolitan cities.

Types of Leases

A lease is a contract between an owner of real estate (i.e., the landlord, also known as the lessor) and a non-owner of the real estate (i.e., the tenant, or lessee). The owner has all the key rights of ownership:

- ✓ D—Disposition: the right to sell or give away a property
- ✓ E—Enjoyment: the right to peacefully enjoy a property
- ✓ E—Exclusion: the right to keep others off a property
- ✓ P—Possession: the right to occupy and use a property
- ✓ C—Control: the right to control what happens on or to a property

With a lease, by accepting rent money the owner sells the right of possession. Once the right of possession is sold to the tenant, the tenant gains rights and obligations of possession of the property with certain exclusions defined in the lease agreement. There are several types of lease agreements:

- *estate for years*. An estate for years (also called tenancy for years or estate for term) is a leasehold estate that continues for a specific period and then ends, at which time the tenant must surrender the premises back to the landlord. No notice is required by either party to end the estate for years; it just ends. In Texas, a 30-day notice is required by the Texas Property Code.
- *estate from period to period*. An estate from period to period (also called periodic tenancy) is a leasehold estate that continues for a nonspecific period of time. The tenancy continues until proper notice is given by either party. Generally, these start out with a specific period of time (estate for years) and then move into an estate from period to period. Suppose that a tenant has a six-month

lease (estate for years) and at the end of the lease does not move out, but neither does the landlord tell the tenant that he/she must move out. This lease then continues as an estate from period to period.
- *estate at will.* An estate at will (also called tenancy at will) is a leasehold estate that continues for a nonspecific period of time. The difference between an estate from period to period and an estate at will is that here the lease can be terminated at ANY time by either party with proper notice.
- *estate at sufferance.* An estate at sufferance (also called tenancy at sufferance or holdover tenancy) is not actually a leasehold estate because in an estate at sufferance, the tenant should have moved out of the premises but did not. This type of tenancy usually ends up in court.

Each of these lease types applies to commercial lease arrangements as well. A broker should consider each type to determine which is the best for the brokerage. The broker may want to consult a commercial real estate attorney before signing a lease because of all the lease clauses that a typical commercial lease contains.

Typical Lease Clauses

The Texas Real Estate Commission does not promulgate a specific commercial lease. However, the Texas Association of REALTORS® does have a commercial lease that is frequently used. An owner/landlord or tenant may have a lease agreement drawn up by an attorney, and all types are legal. Before leasing a space, the broker should examine the proposed commercial lease to analyze several factors:

Actual Rent

The actual rent a broker will pay to operate a real estate brokerage company is an extremely important factor; however, it may not be the most important factor in choosing a site. For example, the cheapest rent in town may well be for a propreaty in the most dangerous part of town and therefore not a good place to meet potential clients. Actual rent is based on supply and demand. If the broker is looking to put a real estate office in an area in high demand, the broker should expect to pay a greater monthly rent than for an office in a less desireable area. The good thing about placing a real estate office is that the brokerage does not need to be located in the highest traffic areas. People will seek the brokerage out provided that they know where the brokerage is located.

Some questions to ask when considering arranging a rental:

- How much is the rent rate?
- Is it comparable to the area?
- Is the area increasing in stature or in a declining state?
- Where is the rental space located?
- Will the location draw drive-by traffic?

All these factors affect the amount of rent that should be paid.

Term of Rent

The term of rent is the length of time the rental agreement is in effect. Usually the term of rent is in accordance with the needs of the parties. A landlord may want a long-term lease to ensure that the property will have a tenant for a long period of time. On the other hand, a landlord may want a short-term lease if he/she believes rental rates for the area will be escalating. The tenant may want to have a long-term lease to be sure to lock in the current rental rate and to be able to establish the company on that spot. The tenant may, however, want a short-term lease if he/she expects to move in a short period of time. All these factors must be negotiated in the lease.

A real estate broker should not operate with a short-term lease unless he/she plans to be in the location for under six months. Operating under a "handshake" agreement may expose the broker to major trouble. Suppose that a broker wants to open up a real estate company and knows a friend with a rental spot that would be perfect. They consummate the transaction with a handshake. The real estate company spends thousands of dollars in marketing to let the public know the company is now in business and where they are located. A year later, the two "friends" get into a dispute, and the owner of the location tells the other to vacate in 30 days. The broker has no recourse because a long-term agreement had not been signed. Brokers should not allow this to happen. Brokers need to be sure that once they have found the location they desire, they also have a long-term agreement of at least five years with options to renew at the end of the lease.

Timing of Payment

When is the monthly rental payment due? Timing can have a major effect on how easily the payment can be made. Real estate transactions tend to close at the end of a month; so if the rental payment is also at the end of the month, it may be difficult to pay if the closings are delayed. The ideal payment date would be near the fifth of the month. Owners also tend to want the payment at some time other than the first of the month because it looks bad if two or three tenants are moving at one time. The broker should be able to negotiate the timing of the rent payment to meet the brokerage schedule.

Penalties

Will there be any penalty for late payments? If so, how much? Will there be any penalties for additional salespersons, additional parking spaces? Will there be any penalty for working after normal working hours?

The broker should be careful to understand all the potential penalties and whether they could be a burden. Some landlords create penalties to create an additional income stream. They bury the penalties deep in the contracts knowing the broker is excited and will agree to almost anything. Then the broker moves in and starts incurring penalties every month, penalties that the broker never dreamed would occur. The broker has signed a long-term contract and is bound by the contract. The best protection is to have an attorney examine the contract and detail any penalties the brokerage may incur.

Assignment

Assignment of a contract is the changing of principals to the contract. The new principal has all the same rights and obligations as the previous principal. If the broker has the right to assign a contract, the broker has the right to find another tenant and assign the lease agreement to the new tenant without interference from the landlord. The new tenant now rents the space from the landlord under the same lease agreement the broker established in the beginning.

Can the rental agreement be assigned to another person? If the broker has plans to sell the brokerage, the broker will want to get this consideration written into the lease. If the brokerage enterprise is undercapitalized, the broker will want this right just in case the real estate business does not make the money anticipated and the broker needs out of the lease. Everyone hopes this is not the case, of course, but good brokers always think of the best-case scenarios and strive to achieve them, and they think of the worst-case scenarios and determine how to avoid them.

Factors in Selecting a Facility

When a broker is selecting a facility in which to operate a real estate brokerage, the broker must consider multiple factors. These factors will eliminate certain facilities from being considered. The broker must weigh how important the factors will be to the brokerage's success.

Common Areas

Common areas are the spaces that all leases share in both use and cost. Are there common areas associated with the lease? These can be either beneficial or negative. The benefits would be such things as a common break area, restrooms, and even secretarial staff. If the space provides these services to all the tenants, the cost is divided and as such is reduced for each individual. The broker/owner will not pay totally for the space used. The negative consequence of common areas is that the broker/owner may end up paying for spaces and services that are not important to the operation of the business. One broker, for instance, was paying several hundred dollars per month for a huge entryway complete with flowers, trees, and a waterfall, none of which was necessary to complete real estate sales.

Total Space

Total space is the entire amount of space rented. It does not include common areas. What is the total space offered, and what is the total space needed? The biggest waste possible in a lease is paying for unused space. The broker should negotiate in the lease the possibility to expand the amount of space but not pay for it until it is needed. A small real estate brokerage had an office where everyone seemed to be getting things done, whereas a huge real estate office seemed dead. Both offices had the same number of license holders. The only difference was the size of the office. The first office had the perfect size; it was big enough to get things done and yet small enough to seem active. The second office was too big for the number of license holders the brokerage was carrying, and as such it looked empty. To avoid creating such a bad impression, it is better to start with a smaller office and negotiate for more space in the lease or to look for a different location altogether.

Operational Hours

Operational hours are the hours the business is open to the public. Some leases will limit the operational hours of the tenants. Real estate is a 24-hours-per-day, seven-days-per-week business. If the landlord will allow access only Monday to Friday from 8 a.m. to 5 p.m., the property may not be the proper lease for the brokerage.

Most real estate offices never close. If a license holder wants to unlock the doors for a client, then so be it. If the license holder wants to open up on Christmas Day, that is his/her choice. The broker does not have to be there and neither does the staff, but the office is technically never closed.

The counter argument to remaining open 24/7 is control. Never closing a brokerage office means that license holders can go to the office at all hours, and the broker has no idea what they are doing. The broker hopes and believes that they are engaged in brokerage business, but if activities the broker would not approve of are occurring, the broker should know. In one instance, one evening far past normal business hours a broker walked into the brokerage office because the lights were on, and the broker noticed that a low-producing salesperson was inside making copies. She was making hundreds and hundreds of copies. She was copying booklets for her church. Each booklet had hundreds of pages, and there were hundreds of booklets. When questioned, she retorted that it was for a good cause. The broker did not believe that her church would approve of her "stealing" the brokerage's paper and ink and fired her. This type of theft would never have occurred during the day, when someone else would be around.

Finish Out

Most spaces will need to be designed and remodeled (i.e., finished out) for the broker as a new tenant. Open work areas (i.e., bullpens) will need to be set up; a reception area with a desk and any special accommodations the particular office will need should be negotiated. Telephone systems must be installed. Arranging these things is easier and much less disruptive if completed before the brokerage begins moving the business furniture and equipment into the space. Whether the brokerage firm will pay for all, part, or none of the design and remodel, the finish out is part of the negotiations in the lease. The longer the lease term, the more finish out the landlord will be willing to complete.

The finish out for startup or small real estate operations is rather ordinary and not expensive. The larger the office operations, the more complex and intense the finish out can be. Large offices have been known to buy the services of an interior designer specializing in office space management and functionality.

Signage

A real estate office should have some sort of outside signage. Signage allows the general public to know where the brokerage is and what service is provided. The outside sign should be elevated on a pole or rooftop. The best and most expensive signs are lighted. The sign should be visible from both directions and kept simple, without too much information that could obscure the key message. The broker should pay close attention to be sure no tree branches block the view of the sign. Once the sign begins to wear and fade in color, the broker needs to replace it no matter the cost. The only thing worse than no sign is a sign in disrepair, indicating that the brokerage is unsuccessful or that the broker simply does not care. The front door should have signage to indicate the brokerages business hours. This can be simple lettering or a professionally prepared, separate sign.

Building Types

There are many building types within which a broker can choose to operate a real estate brokerage. Some are more practical and some more exciting. Some are more expensive and some are less. The choices are many, and the decision is critical.

Stand-alone

A stand-alone building is not attached to any other building. It is usually a building containing one business rather than a row of stores or businesses with a common roof and sidewalls. This is the typical real estate office. Such offices are typically near residential neighborhoods. Some are very fancy white stone palaces with marble entries and massive stained-glass double-entry doors. Some are metal buildings with brick- or wood-front elevations. Some are converted residential houses that have been rezoned for commercial use. The public can easily recognize the brokerage operation with this type of building. The disadvantages usually include high utility and maintenance costs.

House

As previously mentioned, operating a real estate business out of a house is a popular idea. Buyers want to buy a house, so what is better than settling that transaction in the comfort of a home? The bedrooms are converted into offices, and the living room serves as a conference room. The kitchen and bathrooms stay the same. The renovation to convert a house to a real estate office is remarkably simple.

The downside to having a house as a real estate office is that even though older homes are the best for looks, they do not make the best real estate offices. The house is usually chopped up so that there is no open work area. The best and most effective real estate offices have huge bullpens where a majority of salespersons operate. The synergy that comes from working in a bullpen should never be underestimated. Other disadvantages include the fact that the overall floor plan will not be fit for a real estate office without major construction expense.

Bricks-and-Mortar

A bricks-and-mortar building is the standard commercial building. The cost savings are great, but the uniqueness is limited. The term "bricks-and-mortar" refers to the construction method rather than to an actual building. These buildings can be constructed in any shape or size, but the more differentiated the broker intends to make the building, the greater the cost the broker will incur.

Bricks-and-mortar buildings are very strong and sturdy. They can take varied weather conditions and will still look good. Expanding a

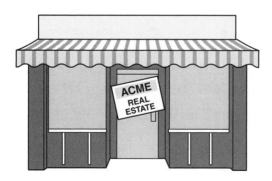

bricks-and-mortar building tends to be more difficult than expanding a wood-constructed building.

Strip Center
A strip center is a business center with outside entrances to each tenant unit for the tenants and their clients. Frequently, a real estate office will set up in a strip center to locate close to the market in which the brokerage specializes. The business center is not a shopping center, however. A business center attracts business clients, whereas a shopping center attracts shoppers. Brokers who do not know the difference could well write their bankruptcy papers.

Office space in a strip center tenant unit can range from a few hundred square feet to several thousand square feet. The leases, rights, and obligations must be spelled out in writing and reviewed by an attorney. Whether to lease in a strip center is a long-term decision and should never be taken lightly.

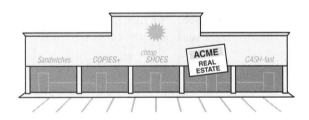

Office Building
An office building is a less frequently used real estate office because most office buildings are located in commercial areas that are not convenient to residential real estate. On the other hand, office buildings are ideal for commercial real estate brokerage companies. If a residential real estate brokerage is large enough to have business headquarters separate from an actual real estate office, then the headquarters could be located in an office building.

Virtual Office Versus Physical Office

A virtual office is not a traditional office at all. It can be mobile, at a license holder's house or even at a coffee shop. A virtual brokerage gives license holders and consumers the same experience as a bricks-and-mortar establishment but without the bricks and mortar. Creating the identical experience—providing services, technology, performance, communication, training, and supervision—is much the same in the nontraditional (virtual) and the traditional (bricks-and-mortar) brokerages. Technology has changed many aspects of the real estate business. Computers first started the possibility of a mobile real estate agent.

The internet is often the first place most home buyers start their search. Because of the internet, customers may have more information about a specific real estate property than most real estate license holders. The license holder now has to show value to attract the consumer. Information is no longer the key.

Potential clients accept and expect the use of technology by the real estate industry. The consumer demands that a real estate professional has greater access to the real estate market but at a faster response time than in the past.

Once laptop computers and smartphones became readily available, the virtual office became a reality. Real estate license holders can now work from home or on the road. There is an application (app) for everything imaginable. Communication is virtually instant. Real estate training can be conducted remotely. The broker can monitor all of a sponsored license holder's activities, transactions, and overall production online. With all this technology, the office can now disappear and the brokerage can become virtual. No more staff and those wages. Overhead has dropped drastically. The broker can add more sponsored license holders without increasing costs. The broker can expand virtually anywhere without adding huge amounts of debt. Laws of states may change, but the virtual office can go anywhere.

The costs of a virtual office are typically upfront costs. There will be a cost to purchase the latest in technology to stay on the cutting edge. There are also other costs: the cost to upgrade these systems on a regular basis, the cost in time to research the latest in technology, the cost of maintenance and repair of all these systems, and finally the cost of educating the sponsored license holders to understand how to use the technology.

Executive office space is another trend that is extremely compatible with a virtual office and/or a brand-new brokerage because it appears more professional than a home office but can still be limited as to how much startup capital is required. How? In this type of situation, many small companies—each with just a few people—join together to rent or lease office space (whatever size they jointly desire) in a professional office building. The advantages are these:

- *shared costs*—The cost of the utilities, maintenance, and (usually) parking are shared; the fee is usually prorated on the square footage of the office space the individual company holds.
- *receptionist*—A receptionist and phone system are provided. When a call comes in to the office, the receptionist can identify whom the call is for and can greet the caller with that company's name. When clients, customers, or other persons come into the office, they are greeted by the receptionist, just as in a larger, professional office. The image created is that of a highly professional and successful company.
- *minimal costs*—Sharing space offers a great way to get started on a minimal budget. The broker has the ability to rent month to month or to lease for the length of time that feels comfortable, given the broker's finances. The broker generally has a choice of exactly how much or how little office space he/she will need. The broker can start out small and expand as time goes on. The rent is reasonable to the situation, and smaller office equipment is usually provided to the individual company.
- *other office equipment*—There is usually a room with larger office equipment such as copiers, collating and binding equipment, and photo printers. These are paid for on an "as-used" basis. There is usually a breakroom with a microwave, refrigerator, coffee machine, vending machines, and, of course, nice, clean restrooms. After-hours voice messaging may be optional.

Facilities Management

Day-to-Day Operations

Day-to-day operations are those tasks that have to be completed by the broker or assigned to another competent person. These tasks must be completed each day. Neglecting the accomplishment of day-to-day operations spells doom for many a brokerage. Here are a few day-to-day operational tasks that must be performed by the broker:

- review office budget
- monitor utilities
- meet with sponsored license holders
- check/respond to mail, email, voice mail, etc.
- work on acquisitions
- review office marketing

- work on recruiting
- review any new purchase agreements
- monitor/order office supplies
- determine the cleanliness of the office
- observe landscaping
- determine if office maintenance is required

These are some of the day-to-day tasks a broker must perform. There may be others depending upon the broker's situation. Some tasks are weekly tasks, some are monthly, and some take over a year to complete.

Utilities

Utilities are necessary for every real estate office. Utilities include electric, water, garbage, telephone, and gas (natural and/or propane). Real estate brokers, owners, and/or managers should monitor all these expenses to be sure they can save as much money as possible. The broker needs to look at expense trends to detect any drastic fluctuations in utility cost. These fluctuations could be a sign of problems. If the average gas bill is $120 per month and it escalates to over $200, it may mean there is a leak in the gas lines somewhere, and the gas company needs to be alerted. In one real estate office, the water bill was much greater than it should have been. The water company determined that the usage was occurring early in the morning. The broker spied on his office and found that the person next door was tapping the water spigot and watering his yard with the broker's water. Needless to say, that usage was stopped, but it would never have been corrected had the broker not been so thorough.

All thermostats should be programmable only by secure access. Telephone service should be investigated to find the best prices and deals. Also, perhaps the company in the office next door could share in the garbage collection and cost.

Office Cleaning

Should the broker/owner of a small real estate office have to clean the office himself/herself or have it cleaned professionally? (Generally, large offices must be cleaned by professionals.) The broker should not expect the salespersons to clean the office. At best they will pick up after themselves, and most will not do even that. If the owner cleans the office, it may save some money, but is that the best use of his/her time? If a cleaning service is hired, the broker needs to be sure the company is bonded and has references. The broker is trusting the cleaning service with access to the office after hours. When negotiating with a cleaning company, the broker should be sure of what is wanted and what is needed. Some questions a broker may want to ask include these:

- Does the broker want to save a little money and let a relative of one of the salespersons clean the office, or should the broker pay a great deal more to have professionals do the job?
- Does the office need to be cleaned every day?
- Could the office trash be picked up once a week and a thorough cleaning done only once per month?
- Should the cleaning company clean the salespersons' desks?
- Do the windows need cleaning, and if so, how often?
- Should the cleaning company stock bathroom supplies?
- Should the cleaning company have its own cleaning equipment, or should the broker provide it in return for a discount?

All these questions should be answered before the broker selects a cleaning company.

Landscaping

Landscaping ranges from planting a new bush, to putting flowers in a pot, to mowing and trimming the lawn. If the proprietor of the property the broker is buying or leasing has neglected the landscaping, the broker may have to compensate. Landscaping may be the first impression a potential client will receive. If the landscaping is impressive, the brokerage is impressive. If that impression is dead, so is the brokerage. The broker should regularly stroll around the property and take along a checklist to make notes on additions or subtractions the broker should make to the exterior landscaping. This is a task easily overlooked and neglected.

As with office cleaning, the broker needs to make sure he/she trusts the company hired. When negotiating with a landscaping company, the broker should be sure of what is wanted versus what is needed. Some questions a broker may want to ask include these:

- Does the broker want to save a little money and let a relative of one of the salespersons mow the grass, or should the broker pay more to have professionals do the job?

- Does the property need to be maintained weekly, or is once per month adequate?
- Do the trimmings need to be picked up?
- Should the landscaping company have its own equipment, or should the broker provide it in return for a discount?

All these questions should be answered before the broker selects a landscaping company.

Maintenance

Office maintenance involves the repairs and remodeling that occur in all offices. A window gets broken. The carpet gets worn. All these things occur in offices all the time. Large, multi-office companies usually have their own maintenance person or persons. Smaller companies without their own maintenance crew must hire from the outside. As with all who are hired to perform services for your company, maintenance workers need to have acceptable credentials and be bonded.

Office in General

There are many ways a brokerage can be developed. Choosing the correct way should be a long and well-thought-out process. There is no one correct answer to the all-important question of how to develop the brokerage, but it is necessary to keep in mind that developing a brokerage that matches the broker's philosophy and business goals has a huge impact on the brokerage's productivity. The broker needs to consider several questions before selecting the way to operate. Here are just a few to consider:

1. Does the broker have the funds to operate a real estate office? To buy the infrastructure needed to start up a real estate enterprise? Does the brokerage have reserve funds necessary to continue operations for at least six months?
2. Does the broker have the expertise to manage a real estate office? The broker needs to be honest with this one.
3. Does the broker want to operate a single office or develop into a multi-office enterprise?
4. What type of real estate does the broker want to concentrate on? Residential? Commercial? High-end?
5. In which geographic areas does the broker want to specialize?
6. What does the broker predict the office market share will be? And the profitability?

7. What is the maximum number of salespersons the broker wants in the office?
8. What are the office policies to be? Will the broker be strict or flexible?
9. Does the broker believe in a family atmosphere or a corporate structure? What type of reputation does the broker want to project?
10. What are the broker's growth strategies for the business? Expansion? Franchise affiliation? Merger?
11. What type of training does the broker plan to provide?
12. Is the broker concerned about name recognition in the market? What will the broker do to address this issue?
13. Will the brokerage offer ancillary services? Will the broker charge for these services?
14. Does the broker plan on being technology proficient or doing things the old-fashioned way? How much is the broker willing to pay for technology?
15. Should the broker buy an existing real estate company, or should the broker open a start-up brokerage?
16. Should the broker buy or lease a location?
17. What business equipment should the broker purchase?

All these questions and many more must be answered before the correct decision can be made.

Office Identity

Based on these preceding questions, the broker should be able to form an office identity. The office identity must be consistent throughout the organization. Lack of consistency in the brokerage's message will dilute the broker's recruiting effectiveness. Say, for example, that a broker decides to project an office image in which the salespersons are empowered to make decisions on their own and have a great deal of autonomy, but in action the broker rules with an iron fist. The broker is now sending mixed messages to his/her sponsored salespersons and the real estate community.

Office Philosophy

The philosophy of an office is how the broker wants the office to be seen and operated. The philosophy of an office has a critical effect on the types of real estate license holders a broker can recruit. If an office is seen as cutthroat, that is the only type of license holder the broker will be able to recruit. The same goes with a "nonproducing" office, a "community service" office, a "100%" office, and so on. Ultimately the broker will determine the philosophy of the office. The philosophy is the broker's beliefs. If a broker decides to have a team-oriented office, one where all sponsored license holders work together as a team, but then lets a cutthroat salesperson stay, the synergy of the office is ruined.

In one real estate office, the broker was more concerned about partying than doing business. That office was fun—but no one made any money. Eventually, the salespersons began to leave because not having any income stopped being fun. The broker, in desperation, began recruiting experienced salespersons from other companies, to no avail. No real estate salesperson wanted to be associated with the "party" office. The office closed its doors permanently only six months after this philosophy was put in place.

Office Supplies

To operate an office, the broker will need office supplies such as staples, paper clips, and writing instruments. The broker will also need space to store all that is needed and some type of inventory tracking to be sure the brokerage does not run out of needed supplies. There is no worse feeling than having to run to an office supply to pick up one item, even a very important item, because the brokerage has run out. The broker does not want too much inventory either. Too much inventory takes up too much valuable space. A broker need to decide which he/she would rather have: a room full of paper clips or a room full of productive salespersons? Keeping the inventory in line also keeps the salespersons in line: If the brokerage has a sufficient amount of supplies instead of a room full, the salespersons will be less likely to take supplies home.

Office Layout

The layout of the office—where things are located in the office space—is of utmost importance. Good office layout can help the office function smoothly. If the office space does not flow, however, the day-to-day operations suffer. Some brokerages, for example, have office machines located all over the office, which creates clutter and obstacles. The breakroom may also be the conference room, and the bathroom may be adjacent to the front desk. Some things cannot be changed, but those that can should.

Reception Area

The reception area is where customers wait for service. Often it is the customer's first impression of the brokerage. Therefore the reception area should be comfortable and inviting, its colors neutral and warm. It should be separated from the workings of the office to reduce noise. A video screen should show a buyer happily enjoying the purchase process. The reception desk should be large enough to hide all the papers, files, and equipment there but should not be some type of fortress. The broker should provide a standing entry sign that welcomes each new client who has an appointment by name.

It is important to emphasize that real estate recruits as well as potential new clients get their first impression of the brokerage office as they wait in the reception area. If the reception area is clean and bright, so will their thoughts be about the broker. If the reception area is neglected, they might think, "Is this how I will be treated?" Keeping first impressions in mind, the broker should spend a little more time and money on the design and layout of the reception area.

Conference Rooms

A conference room is where agents meet their clients. Conference rooms should be provided in each office. Some broker/owners believe their real estate salespersons can take clients to their personal desks to conduct business there. Such a policy is less than professional, however. If the broker does not have a conference room, the broker should wall in a space to provide one. The conference room should have a table that is big enough for at least four people. If the space permits the luxury of two conference rooms, one should be large enough to hold eight people. The conference room should be equipped with a telephone and computer system with access to the internet.

The conference room should be given the same care that the reception area receives. The broker should not just throw in old chairs and a kitchen table salvaged from his/her garage; rather, the broker needs to take the time to do it right.

Bathrooms

The brokerage's bathrooms should be nicely decorated and adequately supplied. The broker should be quick to clean them even if it is the broker who must clean them himself/herself. Also, there needs to be air freshener handy.

Bathrooms should be located between the public space and the license holder area so that both the public and the license holders have access to them. Bathrooms should not be located such that a guest would have to walk through the license holder work area to get to them. Correctly situating bathrooms may require the broker to redesign the layout of the entire office if necessary or even consider moving to another space. It is that important. Real estate companies that are large enough tend to have separate bathrooms for clients and for license holders.

Bullpen
A bullpen is an open area with several desks or work areas close together and half-walls that separate the spaces. License holders tend not to like the bullpen because, they will say, they work better without the distractions. In a bullpen, however, if one person is working, that is contagious and breeds activity for all the people around. Also, the feedback is immediate. If a rookie license holder needs help, it is usually right around the corner. If an office has both a bullpen and private offices, the bullpen is usually then reserved for the new license holder or the lower producing license holders.

Semiprivate Offices
Semiprivate offices are large offices that have two or more desks and license holders at each desk. Most of the time these offices seem private because it is rare to have all the sponsored license holders in the office at one time. These offices are a hybrid between the bullpen and private offices. Sometimes a broker uses these as a type of promotion out of the bullpen.

Brokers are always concerned with the number of salespersons they can house in their offices. Some have analysis performed to compare the square feet of the building to the dollar-profit earned. With those data they can, for example, determine that they need 22 real estate salespersons per office. Needless to say, the salespersons do not agree. By overcrowding a single office, the broker creates disgruntled, disaffected, and ultimately disinterested license holders.

Private Offices
Private offices are usually reserved for the top-producing salespersons and the brokers and managers. The total office space needs to

be midsize or larger because of the space these private offices use. Frequently, a broker will charge a fee to the salespersons who occupy the private offices. Private offices might be prestigious, but they can also take away from office synergies because the salespersons do not have an opportunity to interact.

Equipment Room
The equipment room houses the office equipment to help run a real estate office. This equipment includes the license holder computer, copiers, and central printers. The equipment room needs adequate space to allow several people in the room operating different office machines. This room should be closed and locked to protect the machines after hours. The location should be in the back of the office near the bullpen.

Storage
Storage is mandatory in a real estate office. There are two types of things that need to be stored. One is items that are infrequently needed, and the other is past client files. The item storage should be in the office. The client-file storage could be in a separate location because although a file that is three years old is never looked at, it must be kept in case of a dispute. Conversion of files into digital is the best way to store documents.

Operations Office
The administrative staff uses the operations office to perform their duties. In small offices, the broker might provide all these administrative services. In larger brokerages, one office or diverse offices might house accounting, finance, marketing, administrative, or processing operations. Some real estate brokerages are so large that their operational offices are in a separate building altogether.

The operations office should have office equipment to make the administrative staff more efficient. Equipment they may need includes computers and a small desk-type copier. The better the equipment, the better the production the staff should provide. They should not be hindered by inadequate equipment. These machines are for administrative use and not for the license holders. Because the administrative staff have confidential information and use valuable equipment, these rooms should be larger than others and have a locking system to prevent access.

Breakroom

The breakroom can be a simple area with a table and two chairs outside under an awning. It can be as complex as a large cafeteria with several tables and all the appliances to cook a feast. Most breakrooms, though, have just a table or two with a refrigerator and a microwave. Some have vending machines that can be a revenue source if a broker so chooses. Without this area, salespersons will most probably eat at their desks, which creates the possibility of seeing and smelling all kinds of leftover food that should not permeate a work area. A break area allows the license holders and staff to enjoy some time together without the pressures of work.

Buying Office Equipment

The broker is now at the point where the brokerage needs office equipment. This can be a daunting and expensive experience, but there are a variety of things the broker can do to accommodate the brokerage's needs.

The suppliers and lenders the broker chooses at the startup of the brokerage can prove to be multifunctional and beneficial. These are businesspeople, and so they understand the difficulties of opening a business. These suppliers and lenders will more than likely take a risk and help carry a brokerage if the future looks bright.

Suppliers have multiple ways of financing the sale of their equipment. Many will offer a lease/purchase agreement. Some will finance the purchase themselves, but the broker needs to be careful of the interest rates charged. It is a good idea for the broker to look at what financial institutions can do and make a comparison between them and the supplier. It is not always wise to go with the first offer the broker receives.

Another tremendous resource for office equipment is the internet, eBay, or some other resource with ads selling used office equipment. Cinching in the purse strings in the very beginning can reap huge rewards at the end. Many failed or expanding businesses sell their used furniture and equipment online, at discount centers, or at an auction.

Office equipment should help the real estate office become more efficient. The wrong equipment is a waste of money and office space. Some brokers order the largest and most expensive copier money can buy, just to have no one understand how to use it.

One consideration is whether to lease the office equipment or to purchase. Some factors to consider are cost and repairs. To lease the equipment is a lower upfront cost but over the years a great deal more expensive. Some vendors offer maintenance contracts that provide any necessary repairs and maintenance; if the equipment breaks down, it will be repaired or replaced at no cost to the broker. Some leases even provide printer cartridges with limits on the copies made.

Computers seem to change daily. The best computer today will seem a dinosaur in a few months. Leasing provides the ability to upgrade with a lot less capital expense. The broker should be careful with leases, though, because lease contracts are binding; this means that if the broker is short of funds, the lease still needs to be paid.

Facsimile Machines

Facsimile machines, or fax machines, are still around in real estate offices but rarely used.

Printers

Printers are used to print out information and pictures from the computer. Printers have a wide range of functions and quality. Some can print brochures that look as professional as anything on the market. Most real estate companies cannot afford the cost of such machines, however, and have instead the standard black-and-white or color printers off the shelf, which are sufficient for most of the work a real estate license holder needs. All other printing needs can be satisfied by professional printers.

Some real estate companies spend money on one really good printer and network all computers in an office to that printer. The only problem with this approach is that when someone has a big project, it could back up the print jobs.

Copier

A generic copier makes reproductions of what is placed on the copier's glass plate. Some copiers have collators, sorters, staplers; they can make enlargements; and they have multiside and multisize functions. All these features are great, but the broker/owner should perform a needs analysis to determine what the brokerage really requires. A copier salesperson is paid to get the broker to buy all the add-ons, but the broker should not buy them if they are not needed.

A typical real estate office should have one main copier for all the heavy workloads and a few smaller units for convenience. The main copier should collate and staple mass quantities of paper. There are forms and contracts that will require copies, so the main copier needs to handle that production. It should have the capability to print in color for marketing pieces.

A copier can be linked to several computer terminals. This allows access to a top-of-the-line copier from the license holder's desk so that he/she can print color documents directly to the main copier, eliminating the need for color printers at every desk.

Desks

Somewhat surprising is the emphasis real estate salespersons place on having their own desks. A desk should be a place to work, but some feel having one is a status symbol. The larger the desk, the more productive the real estate salesperson feels. Having larger desks is actually counterproductive to the goals of the broker/owner because the larger the desks, the fewer salespersons an office can hold. Having more real estate salespersons does not correlate to the profitability of the office, of course, but it usually does not hurt to have more.

Some offices have desks that are shared among several real estate license holders. In these offices, a salesperson who needs a desk goes to one of the community desks to work. Once the salesperson is finished, he/she vacates the desk and takes along the paperwork too. These community desks are perfect for larger offices, where license holders must produce to get desks of their own.

Chairs

Chairs are another of those "mine" items that real estate salespersons in an office claim. They will fight over the best chairs in an office. If someone leaves the company and leaves behind a special chair, one of the remaining salespersons will quickly take it. The chairs should have rollers to move around and should be comfortable, but they do not need to be top of the line or ergonomically constructed. It does look more professional if they all match.

File Cabinets

File cabinets are an evil necessity: evil because they are typically ugly and always in the way; necessary because they are absolutely required in a professional real estate office. Files should be kept on listing agreements, buyer representation agreements, current pending sales, and past sales. Files should be kept for at least four years. Some brokers will keep files for 10 years because they believe it is better to be safe than sorry, especially when it comes to documentation.

Art

Art should be displayed throughout a real estate office but at the very least in the main reception area and conference rooms. The art should be tasteful and conservative. It can be in the form of paintings, vases, tapestries, and floral arrangements. If the broker has display cases for awards the office has received, the broker should be sure the display is attractive and up-to-date. All the art should be maintained and cleaned. The art does not have to be extremely expensive, but it should definitely not be cheap, as that would send a very bad message.

Before the broker ventures out into the real world of setting up a brokerage office, there is more planning to be done. The broker should sit down to make a basic plan of what should be the makeup of the office. How many agents does the broker intend to employ in the beginning? Will any of the sponsored license holders be working out of their homes? What kind of office does the broker have in mind? Is it a formal office or a relaxed office? How large of an administrative staff does the broker intend to have, if any?

After the broker has answered these questions, the broker can begin to understand what it is that will be needed to get his/her dreams under way. Some additional items to consider in this regard are the following:

- dividers for agents' stations
- reception area desk and chair
- several waiting area chairs
- phone system and phone lines
- a 1-800 number
- computers and printers
- computer desks, as needed
- internet service
- digital camera
- lamps, as needed
- decorating touches (pictures, mirrors, plants, silk or real flowers)
- breakroom appliances and furnishings (microwave, refrigerator, coffee machine, table, chairs, etc.)
- signage for the door and exterior

Communications and Information Systems

Telephone Systems
One of the largest expenses of a startup real estate company is the investment in a telephone system. Depending on the number and volume of calls, the number of telephones needed and the number of lines all add to the cost of a system. The broker should beware of spending the most money for the latest technological innovations because they could be beyond the brokerage's needs or the salespersons' and staff's understanding.

Personal Computers
Personal computers should be provided to the real estate license holders—not a computer per license holder but a few for all to use. There should be computers located in the computer room and the conference rooms. The computers should have a passcode to eliminate any trespassers. The computers should have a way to track which websites the operators are viewing. The computers should also restrict what information can be downloaded.

Computer networks are used in virtually every real estate company. The networks allow several individuals to work on the same project throughout the network. Software is extremely expensive, and a network allows multiple individuals to access the programs. With a normal computer system, one that is not networked, the broker would have to buy software for every computer terminal, and the information would be more difficult to share.

There is nothing worse than having a computer go down and not knowing how to fix it. The next worst thing is not having anyone else conveniently available who knows how to fix it. Real estate professionals rely on computers for so many things, and computers have literally become such an extension of agents' arms (and brains) that it is hard for an agent to think about going without them. So when the computer goes down, *so does the agent*.

Real estate license holders are totally lost when they cannot access the internet, input important information, get email, or type letters or forms. Having an information technology (IT) person who is readily and easily available is mandatory. This is the person who understands not only the physical workings of the computer (Does the computer need a new chip? Is the computer just too old? Does the computer need a new fan?) but also all the keystrokes and what they do (Did a license holder hit a wrong key and screw everything up? What was the license holder doing when everything failed?).

This IT person can be someone from a company that specializes in computer repair and maintenance, or it can be the secretary's computer-saavy teenage son. The person has to be not only good but also readily available to come right away when the broker calls for assistance, even if it is after hours. The broker does not want to have to wait for even a half-day to get the brokerage's production going again.

CHAPTER SUMMARY

Logical reasons to buy a building to house a real estate brokerage are these:
- **Rent replacement** is transferring from paying rent to paying principal.
- **Area recognition** is when the community knows the brokerage and where it is located.
- **Cost savings** occur when the broker/owner can better negotiate utilities, maintenance, landscaping, and any other services that are required for a building.
- **Long-term investment** means buying for the long term, which should be better than buying for the short term.

A leasehold estate (which is a less-than-freehold estate) is a lease or rental of a property with the tenant gaining the right of possession.

A lease, which can last from a single day to 999 years, is a contract between an owner of real estate (the landlord, or lessor) and a non-owner of the real estate (the tenant, or lessee).

In a lease arrangement, the real estate owner enjoys all the main rights of ownership:

- ✓ D—Disposition: the right to sell or give away a property
- ✓ E—Enjoyment: the right to peacefully enjoy a property
- ✓ E—Exclusion: the right to keep others off a property
- ✓ P—Possession: the right to occupy and use a property
- ✓ C—Control: the right to control what happens on or to a property

With a lease the owner sells the right of possession by accepting rent money. There are several lease types:

- An **estate for years** (also called tenancy for years or estate for term) is a leasehold estate that continues for a specific time period and then ends.
- An **estate from period to period** (also called periodic tenancy) is a leasehold estate that continues for a nonspecific period of time.
- An **estate at will** (also called tenancy at will) is a leasehold estate that continues for a nonspecific period of time. Unlike the other types of leases, an estate at will can be terminated at ANY time by either party with proper notice.
- An **estate at sufferance** (also called tenancy at sufferance or holdover tenancy) is not actually a leasehold estate because with an estate at sufferance the tenant should have moved out and did not.

The Texas Real Estate Commission does not promulgate a commercial lease, whereas the Texas Association of REALTORS® has a commercial lease that is frequently used. Also, an owner/landlord or tenant may have a commercial lease drawn up by an attorney—and all these leases are legal.

Before leasing a space, the broker should examine the commercial lease that will be used and will need to analyze several factors:

- **actual rent:** the rent paid
- **term of rent:** the length of time the rental agreement is in effect
- **timing of rent payment:** the rent due date

- **penalties charged:** all penalties and amounts
- **assignment of a contract**: the changing of principals to the contract

When selecting a facility to operate a real estate brokerage, the broker must consider multiple factors, including the following:

- **Common areas** are areas that all leases share both in use and cost.
- **Total space** is the entire amount of space rented.
- **Operational hours** are the hours the business is open to the public.
- **Finish out** refers to the redesign and remodel of office space as needed.
- **Signage** is the advertising a real estate brokerage should have outside the office.

Building types:
- A **stand-alone building** is not attached to any other building.
- A **house** can be used to operate a real estate business.
- A **bricks-and-mortar building** is the standard commercial building unit for tenants and their clients.
- An **office building** is frequently used by a commercial real estate office.

A virtual office is not a traditional office at all. It can be mobile, at a license holders house, or even at a coffee shop.

- The internet is the first place most home buyers start their search.
- Potential clients accept and expect the use of technology by the real estate industry.
- With technology, communication is virtually instant.

Executive office space comprises many small companies—each with just a few people—that join together to rent or lease office space (whatever size they desire) in a professional office building.

Day-to-day operations involve tasks that have to be completed by the broker every day. These are:

- **monitoring utilities,** including electric, water, garbage, telephone, and natural and/or propane gas
- **cleaning** the office regularly
- **landscaping,** ranging from planting new bushes, to putting out flowers, to mowing and trimming the lawn

- **office maintenance,** involving the repair and remodeling that are needed in all offices

Other considerations for a broker:

- **office philosophy:** how the broker wants the office to be perceived and operated
- **office supplies:** items such as staples, paper clips, and writing instruments
- **office layout:** where things are located, which affects how the office functions
- **reception area:** where customers wait for service
- **conference rooms:** where agents meet their clients
- **bathrooms:** to be nicely decorated and adequately supplied
- **bullpen:** open area with several desks or work areas close together and half-walls separating the spaces
- **semiprivate offices:** large offices with two or more desks and license holders at each desk
- **private offices:** usually reserved for top-producing salespersons and for brokers and managers
- **equipment room:** housing the office equipment required to run a real estate office
- **storage:** mandatory in a real estate office for client files
- **operational offices:** used by administrative staff
- **breakroom:** simple area for agents to refresh themselves and eat

Office equipment needed includes:

- **facsimile machines,** or fax machines—still exist in real estate offices but are rarely used
- **printers**–to print out information and pictures from the computer
- **generic copier**–to reproduce what is placed on the copier's glass plate
- **desk and chairs**–for a place to work
- **file cabinets**–to store files
- **art**–to display throughout the real estate office
- **telephone systems**–one of the largest expenses of a startup
- **personal computers**–for use by the real estate license holders

CHAPTER QUESTIONS

1. Which of the following is a logical reason to buy instead of rent a building to house a real estate brokerage?
   A. rent replacement
   B. area recognition
   C. cost savings
   D. all of the answer choices

2. In what type of property rental does the tenant gain the right of possession?
   A. leasehold
   B. exclusive right to rent
   C. mortgage
   D. fee simple

3. What ownership right allows the owner to give away the property?
   A. enjoyment
   B. exclusion
   C. disposition
   D. control

4. What type of lease continues for a specific time and then ends?
   A. estate for years
   B. estate from period to period
   C. estate at will
   D. estate at sufferance

5. Which of the following could cause a landlord to charge a penalty?
   A. late payments
   B. additional salespersons
   C. additional parking spaces
   D. all of the answer choices

6. What is the term used when the principals in a contract change?
   A. reverse stipulation
   B. assignment
   C. term at will
   D. disposition

7. What type of building is not attached to any other building?
   A. stand-alone
   B. strip center
   C. office space
   D. none of the answer choices

8. What is an open area with several desks or work areas close together and half-walls that separate the spaces?
   A. lock-in area
   B. semi-open sales room
   C. bullpen
   D. rookie room

9. What office equipment should a broker consider?
   A. printers
   B. copiers
   C. computers
   D. all of the answer choices

10. What is an IT person at a brokerage office?
    A. intelligence trainer
    B. information technology
    C. interested-to-buy/sell
    D. none of the answer choices

CHAPTER 8
The Marketing Plan

The services offered to the public need to be carefully analyzed to determine if they meet the company's mission, vision, and culture statements. Choosing the wrong services to offer will cause confusion and frustration, which lead to failure. These services need to be viewed in terms of how they affect the public and the bottom line.

Marketing is the overall concept of offering a property for sale to the general public. The brokerage firm wants to market the office and its inventory of properties. The more people know about a real estate office, the better chance that broker will have to recruit new license holders. The more people know that a property is available, the better chance it has to sell for the most money in the fastest time. Marketing per se does not sell an overpriced property, but good marketing will help sell the properties that are priced correctly. Advertising is only one aspect of marketing but probably the most recognizable.

Each real estate company will market its listing inventory in the way it feels is best for its clients, given the resources the company can apply. Real estate companies can market a property many different ways, but in the modern era online advertising is the most widely known and used. Most companies place listings on a rotating basis depending on the number of listings in their inventory and the advertising space available. A rotating basis simply means that if the real estate company has slots on a webpage for advertising 10 properties each week and is carrying 100 properties, each property will be in the advertisement every 10 weeks.

Marketing the broker and the brokerage correctly can promote image, credibility, and recognition in the marketplace. The more money the brokerage spends getting its name and logo out to the public, the more recognition the brokerage will have.

The marketing should be appealing to customers and for their benefit, and it should be consistent. If the broker uses the same phrase or logo over and over, it will become more and more familiar to the public and will create a higher level of recognition and then trust. The broker should determine the target markets and design the brokerage marketing program for these selected populations.

To begin with, the broker needs to identify the brokerage sphere of influence. The broker should think about where the brokerage is generating the most clients. That is probably the sphere of influence that is best for the brokerage, and it should be the top market to focus on. That is the place where the broker should concentrate the brokerage dollars and efforts.

Company Marketing Strategies

A marketing strategy is a brokerage firm's overall marketing direction. It should guide the broker in the decision-making process for spending money and spending time. The marketing strategy should include projections for what the broker wants to accomplish through marketing. It should detail the philosophies and concepts the broker will employ. It should be mostly in written form, with very few numbers and finite dates. These latter items will be in the company's marketing plan.

McDonald's dominates the fast-food burger market. It discovered that the most vocal group when it comes to choosing where to eat is usually the children. McDonald's strategy was to specialize in what the decision makers want most, and in the case of children, it is a hamburger, French fries, and soda. McDonald's targets the advertising to children, and it works. Likewise, the broker needs to determine the decision makers for the brokerage services and then give them what they want.

The brokerage marketing strategy is the reason behind marketing for the brokerage. What is the broker trying to accomplish? What are the short-term goals? What are the long-term goals? The marketing strategy is not specific but written in general terms. The broker can have multiple marketing strategies, of course, but this is not recommended. Multiple marketing strategies divide the loyalties and double the expenses. The broker should therefore limit marketing strategies to one main area of marketing but then do business with all comers. The brokerage can help all clients with their real estate needs, not just those from the target market.

The marketing strategy is used to monitor all the marketing ideas. Before spending a cent on marketing, the broker must ask, "Is this in alignment with the marketing strategy?" The marketing strategy can be as simple as this: "The main focus for marketing is first-time home buyers in the Garland area for properties between $100,000 and $350,000." So the broker would refuse to pay for advertising in *Elite Homes* magazine, which offers properties of $500,000 or more.

Brokerage Marketing Plan

The brokerage marketing plan should put forth in an orderly manner the company marketing strategy that has already been developed. It should have each step detailed with exacting standards. Each step should have a beginning date and an end date. Each step should be analyzed to determine its purpose and whether it aligns itself with the marketing strategy. The costs of each step need to be analyzed to determine the best approach. All contact people should be addressed. If the broker is directly involved in any step, the broker's time needs to be analyzed. Finally, the entire marketing plan needs to be compared to the brokerage's competition. A complete stranger should be able to pick up the brokerage's marketing plan and understand all aspects of it.

All types of promotion, marketing, and advertising should be included in the company marketing plan. All planned promotional events, direct mail campaigns, or advertising on the internet needs to be included. If the brokerage does advertise, the broker will need to separate name recognition advertising from prospect-generating advertising.

Name Recognition Advertising

Name recognition advertising gets people to know the brokerage name and what services are offered. Name recognition advertising is used to create a name that the public will know and will want to do business with. It is not used to make the prospect call on the telephone; that is prospect-generating advertising. These two are often mistaken. If a billboard ad reads, "Call me at 817-555-1212," most people think that is prospect-generating advertising. It is not, even though someone might call. The broker's pretty face plastered on a billboard is just to get people to know that face, the name, and the services offered. Name recognition advertising is critical to make the sales job easier, but it is expensive and takes a long time to work. Most national real estate companies spend millions per year on name recognition advertising. Examples of name recognition advertising include, but are not limited to, television advertising, radio advertising, advertising on bus-stop benches, airplane trailer banners, personal brochures, shopping cart cards, name badges, career apparel, and car signs. This type of advertising is extremely expensive because of the variety of media and the frequency of advertising required. Companies like McDonald's, IBM, Home Depot, and General Motors spend millions so that the public can recognize their names. A broker can therefore expect to spend a great deal of money to achieve viable name recognition.

Prospect-Generating Advertising

Prospect-generating advertising makes the telephone ring, webpage click, or email post. Ads showing houses for sale on the internet should generate an enquiry. If the broker is on a limited budget, the broker should concentrate on prospect-generating advertising to get the most for the brokerage's buck and let the competition worry about name recognition advertising. Examples of prospect-generating advertising include online marketing, social networking, direct mail, yard "For Sale" signs, and business cards, to name a few. Determining which type of advertising is right for the brokerage will be part of the company marketing strategy.

Every dollar spent in prospect-generating advertising is meant to generate business. A picture of a house is advertised to get a potential buyer interested enough to take action. In fact, real estate license holders spend most of their marketing budget in this area.

Marketing Properties

Residential

Most real estate companies are residential in nature. The larger the city, the more specialized the office will become. In metropolitan areas, real estate offices tend to concentrate on a narrow range of clients, such as a particular community. In more rural areas, real estate offices may have more diverse offerings such as residential, commercial, and farm and ranch properties.

Residential real estate companies handle the sale of homes for their clients. They also handle the purchase of homes by their clients. Residential real estate salespersons must be better at relationships than their commercial counterparts. Brokers of residential real estate company must be aware of the relationship aspect of this industry and coach their salespersons to achieve greater success. A few of the marketing techniques used frequently for residential properties follow.

Yard Signs

Independent brokers must decide the type, size, and layout of the yard signs they provide. There are two basic types:

1. *post*—large wood or composite material post in an upside-down "L" shape with the sign panel made of steel and hanging from the arm of the post. The advantage of these signs is their size because they make a statement and can be seen from several blocks away. The downside is that the initial cost is greater, and they are so difficult to install that a sign company is needed to take care of the installation. The sign company charges a

fee for each sign placed on a property. Additional charges from the sign company occur if the signs get damaged or the sign company has to drive out of the city. The real estate company usually pays for the metal panels, and then the salesperson pays the sign company to put them up.

2. *stake*—usually all steel or aluminum and smaller in size than its post counterpart. Because of the stake's smaller size, most real estate salespersons can place the stakes in their cars and install them without the need for professionals. The cost of a stake sign is usually less than purchasing a post sign. The real estate company ordinarily buys the stake signs, and the real estate salespersons will check out one at a time to place on each of their listings. Some real estate companies use both the stake and the post signs. The stake sign is used for lower-priced properties and those on the outskirts of the city. The post sign would be reserved for all other types of listings.

Sign Riders

Sign riders are the metal information attachments that are placed on yard signs. These can be used to identify a specific number to call, identify the listing agent, advertise a special feature of the property, or announce the status of the property and showing instructions. The riders give additional valuable information to any potential buyer who may be driving by. Riders make the real estate sign more interesting and relate information for that specific property.

Usually the information riders ("lakefront, 4 bedrooms, and pool," for example) are purchased and provided by the broker. The riders that identify the salesperson and his/her telephone numbers are provided by the salesperson.

Buyers who drive by will tend to have more interest in calling about a property if the rider identifies a feature that is of interest to them. Having riders available is another investment the brokerage office should make as soon as possible. Then the broker needs to make sure they are put up.

Information Boxes
Information boxes or tubes are also attached to the yard signs. Inside the box or tube are information sheets that offer consumer data on the particular property and usually a picture of the property on a high-quality paper. These sheets are protected from the weather by the box or tube. Most real estate offices require their salespersons to buy these boxes if the salesperson so desires.

Key Boxes
Key boxes (also called lockboxes) are usually placed on the outside of the front door of a listing providing a key to real estate salespersons with the authorized access codes. The key box is a necessity in marketing a property for sale because a competing real estate license holder is not willing to travel to each office to get a key. A lockbox provides access without the hassle.

A broker should go to any crafts store to purchase ⅛-inch rubber foam board. The broker then cuts the board out to match the width of the key boxes. The broker should allow several additional inches above the key box and several below the key box. The broker can now use this extra space to market the brokerage. Above the key box the broker should have the words "Professionally marketed by Acme Real Estate." Below the box should be written the office contact information. The license holders can tell the sellers that the foam backing is to protect their door from scratches. A broker should never miss an opportunity to market the brokerage company. The salespersons can do this, but most will not.

These lockboxes come in two basic styles:
- *electronic*—key boxes that allow access by means of an electronic key card. The advantage of this type of key box is that it keeps electronic records of all who have gained access and of all the properties that have been accessed. Both records provide immense protection in case of a break-in or fair housing accusation.

- *combination*—key boxes that allow access by means of a combination of either numbers or letters. These are like the traditional "locker" type of lock where a person turns the dial to unlock it with the right sequence of letters or numbers. The advantage of this type of key box is that everyone a salesperson allows can get access. The disadvantage is that there is no record of how many times access was given or that someone could have gained access by illegally obtaining the passcode.

Some sellers are apprehensive about placing a key outside their door.

> CASE IN POINT—One broker had a seller who refused to allow a key box on his door. The broker went to his car and got out a key box and brought it back inside (anything that MAY be needed on a listing appointment should be in the agent's car). The broker handed it to the seller and told him that if he could get the key out in less than a minute, the broker would give him $10. The seller struggled, pried, banged, and pounded the key box for a while. The broker turned to his wife and casually asked her, "If you were a burglar, wouldn't it have been faster just to break the window?" She laughed, and the husband allowed the key box to be placed on the door.

Brokers may purchase a few key boxes for emergency use for their salespersons, but most brokers make their salespersons provide their own key boxes. Salespersons who own the key boxes seem to take better care of them.

Multiple Listing Service

A multiple listing service (MLS) allows a property to have worldwide exposure. Buyers transferring from out of state can find houses that are currently for sale on an MLS. Some services are more protective than others and allow only members on the site. Other services allow limited consumer use online. A majority of real estate sales result from MLSs, and almost every residential real estate company is part of a local MLS.

Posting on an MLS is the best possible way to market listings. More than 70% of property sold is sold through an MLS. Most real estate brokers take for granted the power of an MLS to market their brokerage. If a real estate brokerage inputs the listing data into the MLS for their salespersons, this brokerage should make comments in the "Remarks" section to help market the brokerage. Such comments as the following are appropriate:

- "Acme Real Estate professionally offers this property for sale."
- "For a personal tour, please call Acme Real Estate."
- "For additional information on this property, please call Acme Real Estate."
- "For information on similar properties, please call Acme Real Estate."

Any way the broker can mention the brokerage is helpful in marketing.

Almost all real estate companies are members of their local MLS, but very few pay for the access fees for their salespersons.

Residential Service Contract (Home Warranty)
Residential service contracts (also called home warranties) are basic insurance policies that protect buyers for one year after the purchase of a home, though the time the contract is valid can be extended. The primary fear of any buyer is that of having purchased a lemon. Most real estate lawsuits result from a buyer's feeling he/she was lied to about the property condition. A residential service contract can remove many of these problems, given that these contracts cover most mechanical items in the home. Brokers should check each policy for terms or, better yet, provide buyers with several policy options so that they can choose the residential service company that best suits them.

The broker should establish an office policy that requires each sponsored salesperson to offer a residential service contract to both the sellers and the buyers in a transaction. If the clients refuse to purchase a contract, they should sign a disclosure statement asserting that they were offered the service. A residential service contract can save the brokerage company from being tied up in a long court battle when a property condition problem occurs.

Commercial
Offices that specialize in commercial real estate will need to choose their niche. Commercial real estate sales include small retail, big box, office, industrial, business, and high-rise real estate, to describe a few. Brokers will concentrate their efforts on one or only a few of these types of commercial brokerages.

Commercial brokers deal with clients more formally, in a businesslike manner, than do their residential counterparts. Commercial brokers rarely work weekends or after normal business hours. The commercial broker deals with little emotion and mostly facts. A few ways to help commercial brokers market properties include using billboards and attending trade shows.

Billboards

Some real estate commercial brokers have used billboards with great success, but most cannot afford the enormous expense to make this type of marketing work. One real estate professional has had the same billboard in her market area for over 10 years. She has said that she has not received much business from the sign but that people do recognize her at appointments, and that recognition does help her convert the appointment into a commercial listing. She has spent thousands and thousands of dollars to get that recognition. If she canceled that billboard, she would lose that benefit within a few months.

Trade Shows

Trade shows are gatherings of vendors and tradespeople to offer their products and services from a central location. Usually they feature industry updates in a stadium-like locale and skills training in break-out sessions. Some trade shows combine with conventions to draw individuals from the convention. Trade shows having anything to do with real estate are worth attending.

A broker may want to become a vendor to promote his/her commercial brokerage to potential clients and recruits. Most of these shows provide vendors with a table and very little else. The commercial broker should therefore become self-sufficient. The first thing the broker should develop is a trade show checklist. The checklist should identify everything needed to take to these shows and will save the broker from forgetting an item that may desperately be needed at a show.

The broker needs a tablecloth to put over the presentation table. The tablecloth should have the brokerage logo in the middle front so that people can see the brokerage name from across the room. The broker should develop some type of backdrop to display items that are important to the people who will be passing by. The broker needs to bring lots of giveaways and print material. Most important, the broker should have some type of sign-up sheet for customers and potential recruits.

Property Management

Property management occurs when a property owner who is renting property no longer wants the duties associated with being an active landlord. The duties a property manager performs on behalf of an owner include:

- leasing
- contract negotiation
- rent collection
- reporting
- marketing

The property manager and the owner typically have a general agency relationship that allows the property manager the right to bind the owner to lease agreements with tenants. Some marketing ideas that property managers use include advertising on radio, television, and the internet and developing a company website.

Radio

Real estate brokers rarely use radio advertising for recruiting or advertising specific properties. When used, radio is best for advertising multiple tenant or multiple property sales. Radio is frequently used to advertise newly built apartment complexes desiring a significant number of tenants immediately. Radio is also used for builders who have just opened a new subdivision.

One way a real estate broker can get on the radio without the cost would be to volunteer for a real estate information radio show. Usually these shows are promoted and paid for by the participants, but it is worth investigating because of the immense credibility the broker will receive from doing radio.

Television

Television is very impressive but rather expensive. National television is reserved for national real estate companies that are promoting name recognition. Local television can be an avenue for real estate brokers as long as the costs align with the marketing budget. Television can show how the lease property will look to a prospective tenant.

The Internet

The internet is the most used real estate medium for residential, commercial, and property management. Real estate-related advertisers are one of the internet's largest advertising segments, with local real estate companies being the most active advertisers with the purchase of local search phrases. Web-based companies and individual brokers make up most of these real estate advertisers, with "For Sale by Owners" (FSBOs) trailing far behind. The internet is where almost all buyers begin their research for their next home. The most important reasons for a consumer to use the internet include ease of access, ability to search by criteria, personalized searches, and availability of online preliminary qualifications.

A real estate broker should not think the internet is a savior to all real estate office problems, however. Some real estate brokers pay thousands of dollars per month for websites that no one sees.

The real estate broker should also be keenly aware that real estate license holders from competing companies are watching the brokerage's presence on the web. An incredible site may be enough to get a call or email. Those individuals who are considering a career in real estate generally search the web first before calling a real estate company to seek employment.

Company Website

The brokerage must have a website. The reason is simple: If a consumer goes online to look up the brokerage but does not find a website, that consumer will not trust that the brokerage is a sound business and will look elsewhere. Although a website should give the brokerage some business, the main reason for having one is to establish credibility.

The company website does not need to have all the bells and whistles, but it should at least have:

- the ability to allow consumers to search for available properties
- a mortgage calculator

- contact information for sponsored license holders
- a question-and-answer section
- a section on the procedure to buy or sell a house
- a section on the loan process
- a featured home
- a featured sponsored license holder
- a mapping feature to locate available properties for drive- by
- an initial setup for consumers to begin to obtain a loan
- pictures of the office
- pictures of the sponsored license holders
- pictures of available properties

There can be a great deal of information on a website. The broker should be careful to avoid giving too much because if the consumer does not need the broker, then no contact will be made. When no contact is made, no commission is earned. The website becomes a waste of potential income.

Direct Marketing

Direct marketing entails the mailing of ads and information to the home market in hopes that property owners may want to buy or sell real estate in the not too distant future. Direct marketing is still effective, but consumers have been opposed to mass mailings for decades. A wise broker is extremely careful when attempting direct marketing because of the negative response from consumers.

Direct Marketing Companies

A broker with the right equipment, such as a high-capacity professional grade printer, and the capability to use it can engage in direct marketing without any outside help. Direct marketing can be very labor intensive. The area to direct market will need to be determined. The contact information for each homeowner in the area must be obtained. A direct marketing campaign needs to be developed. The marketing piece needs to be designed, laid out, and proofed. The marketing piece requires the contact information to be individually placed on the marketing piece. The marketing piece also needs to be properly postmarked and then taken to the postal facility. Finally, the piece needs to be tracked to determine the direct marketing campaign's effectiveness.

There are a multitude of direct marketing companies (DMCs) in every area of the globe. A broker who wants to hire one to design a professional direct marketing campaign can choose from several viable companies. These DMCs range in cost from very expensive to very reasonable. Some DMCs can handle all the phases, from setup, production, postage, mail-out, and follow-up to reporting; others just specialize in one of these tasks. The broker has to understand which tasks he/she is or is not willing to perform and which will need an investment of money.

Postcards

Postcards are one of the most used direct marketing pieces. Postcards are easy to handle and inexpensive to send. Postcards are a quick reminder to the public about the brokerage and should offer a bit of information to help the consumer. The help could be any of the following:

Market Data. This postcard not only informs local residents but proves that the broker is a knowledgeable real estate practitioner. The data simply come from the local MLS.

Recipes. This postcard is still a favorite. Millions of recipes can be found on online, but it is still nice to get one in the mail that someone recommends. If the broker chooses this one, before sending the postcard the broker must be able to make the recipe and ensure that it turns out well.

Local Events. This postcard is a promotion of local events to the consumer. The events could be the Octoberfest at the park, the opening of the high school play, or a host of other events that area residents may find interesting and want to be involved in.

Announcements. This postcard is an announcement to the consumer about a win for the local football team, a promotion in a civic organization, or anything that can be announced to a broad range of consumers. Brokers should insist that sponsored real estate license holders always send out "Just listed"/"Just sold" postcards that announce this real estate activity.

Notices. This postcard reminds the consumer to file for homestead exemption, to register to vote, or to complete any number of things the consumer may forget during a busy lifestyle.

Company Brochures

Company brochures are usually trifold letters that introduce the brokerage company and tell about the office accomplishments. Like the personal brochures that license holders use to market themselves, these brochures are to be used to market the brokerage to other competing license holders to get them to join the brokerage. These are to be used sparingly. Their cost prohibits mass mailings. The broker should send them to any potential recruits the broker may have. The broker should leave the brochures with anyone the broker talks to about a real estate career. The difference between these and business cards is that everyone is given a business card, but company brochures are to be given only to serious prospects.

A broker can use a personal computer to compose and print company brochures if the computer has this capability. If the broker does make the brochures, the broker should be sure that they are done well. A cheap brochure means a cheap real estate brokerage. Of course, there are printing companies that can produce company brochures, but the cost is high.

Property Brochures

A property brochure is a pamphlet that tells of a specific property. The brochure is a minimum of four pages and is usually in color on high-quality paper. The cost of a property brochure usually prohibits its use except for fine homes and estates. Because property brochures market one specific property, most real estate companies require their salespersons themselves to publish these for their clients.

Property Profile Sheets

Property profile sheets are also called "property graphics." The property profile sheet is usually a single sheet of paper that describes the real estate property and has a picture of it. Property profile sheets are much less expensive than property brochures and should be used on almost all the brokerage's listings.

The profile sheet contains information about the numbers and sizes of rooms. It should list all the best amenities of the property and provide information about schools and taxes, as well as information about the brokerage and how to get in touch with the listing salesperson for a showing.

Graphics should be professionally composed and of high quality. If the brokerage has the print capability to provide these, it is a cost savings. There are several printing companies that will print these for the brokerage for a fee. The fee is usually reasonable. The broker should have the printer provide two sets of flyers for the listing agents: one set in full color and another set in black and white. The colored ones are to be passed out by the salespersons to potential clients. The salespersons will want to place some of the colored ones on the kitchen table at the property. The black-and-white ones should be used to fill up the information box on the yard sign. These are for those who pass by and grab a flyer. The brokerage will lose many of the profile sheets out front, which is why they should be black and white. If the broker is really clever, he/she will teach the listing agents to have the sheets mailed directly to the seller and have the seller put out only a few in the information box. The seller then monitors the box and fills it up when necessary. Sellers are glad to help. Whether the broker provides these property profile sheets for the sponsored salespersons or they provide them on their own, the broker should be sure they are of top quality.

Flyers

Flyers are photocopies with information about careers in real estate and usually with a picture of the office. The flyers may also be used as advertisements for specific properties. The flyers are distributed in an area where the real estate company wants to generate business. These flyers should be inexpensive so they can be passed out to everyone in an area. The best way to distribute them is door to door. Here is a typical flyer wording:

> *"Have you ever thought about real estate as a career? Currently, a local real estate company is looking for self-starting individuals interested in making a difference in their lives as well as the lives of others. The income is limited only by the effort of the person. No experience necessary; all training is provided. Call today!"*

One broker would combine duties to get more done in less time. Instead of working out and then hiring someone to pass out flyers, this broker did both at the same time. The broker would start in the morning in his running outfit clothes and run from house to house in the area distributing flyers. He would not talk with the owners because he was all sweaty. But he distributed a lot of flyers and also got a decent workout.

Mail-Outs

Mail-outs are a great way to prospect. The brokerage office should buy custom envelopes and letterhead with the brokerage's name and contact information. Any correspondence should use this custom stationery.

Business Cards

If the brokerage's salespersons are not carrying their business cards, they are out of business. A broker should be sure to train the salespersons to always have on hand more than they will ever need (the cards are cheap) and then have the salespersons make every effort to pass them all out immediately. The broker should teach the salespersons that they should never shake a hand without offering a business card. The license holders should place their business card in any of their outgoing mail—even bill payments—no matter to whom the mail is sent. That piece of mail has now become a marketing piece.

Here is one thing a broker can do: Have a broker card with the question, "Have you or someone you know thought about a career in real estate?" The broker should then develop the policy of handing out at least 10 of these business cards per day. The rules are that the broker must actually hand out the card. The broker cannot leave a stack on some office table and think that is good enough. The broker must give the business card to someone new every day. The first day it is no problem. The first week, it is still no problem. After the first month, it begins to get tough. The second month, the broker is scrambling to find anyone to take his/her business card. Soon the broker will be dreaming of people to give the business card to. The broker will hand one to the neighbor he/she has known for 10 years. The broker will give one to his/her daughter's teacher. The broker's mind is now changing. The broker is now desperately seeking anyone to give the business card to. This is a moneymaking mindset. Now that the broker has this down, the broker must teach this approach to all the sponsored salespersons!

Marketing Budget

The marketing budget spells out the money to be spent in the marketing plan. The plan should budget the money for marketing for an entire year. The marketing budget needs to be an act of self-discipline. If the money is not there, the broker should not spend it. The budget should analyze the money in the bank and the anticipated income for the year. If a great marketing idea is presented but will wreck the budget, the broker cannot pursue it until there is money in the budget. Too many good brokers have failed because they banked on a marketing campaign and then the marketing did not work, but there was no more money to do anything different. The broker needs to put 10% of all that is earned in the brokerage into the marketing budget.

A marketing budget is easy to compose. The broker will need a simple spreadsheet and then develop categories that are specific to the brokerage. The budget can have simple line-item categories, or the broker can break each main category down into subcategories for a more precise marketing budget. For example:

- *marketing campaigns.* This budget category is for all anticipated listings the brokerage will take during the year. This could be a large part of the total marketing budget.
- *marketing the brokerage.* This is a generic category for any type of marketing done on behalf of the brokerage. This involves name recognition advertising, sponsorships, and many other approaches. This category can be broken into subcategories for these types of items.
- *marketing for recruits.* This category is used for obtaining recruits for the brokerage. This might be advertising, entertainment, or attendance at real estate license holder events.
- *marketing supplies.* Marketing has the need for supplies.
- *marketing materials.* This category includes any printing, purchasing, or customizing of marketing materials.
- *marketing expenses.* Costs could include the temporary hiring of marketing experts, consulting fees, and similar expenses.

These expense categories should have 13 columns, one for each month and one a carry-over month into a new budgeting year. Each column should have the total amount of money allocated for each expenditure for each month. Some items may have a larger amount allocated at certain times of the year. Suppose that there is a subcategory for high school football schedules. This category may have a large amount of money allocated to it in June when the high school announces its schedule for the upcoming year. The broker then could pay for the schedules to be printed. This same category may not have anything allocated to it for the rest of the year.

A marketing budget should be designed to provide the needed funds to marketing but not allow marketing to get out of hand and lose the brokerage money. A marketing budget should not be so restrictive that the broker and/or marketing team cannot operate. Without a marketing budget a brokerage will spend too much money for the return of business. Money for marketing can easily result in a loss if it is spent without regulation and forethought. Without a marketing budget some brokers will not spend a dime on marketing, and that will not build a brokerage the way it should with proper marketing spending. A proper marketing budget should free up that money to develop the brokerage.

Marketing Campaign

A marketing campaign involves the marketing of individual properties in alignment with the marketing strategy, marketing plan, and marketing budget. Campaigns are ongoing and continuous. The broker should have several operating at one time. One marketing campaign might be to get the listing on 2345 Montgomery Street sold. The broker can also have a marketing campaign to recruit three new salespersons from the Summerfield area.

There are several benefits to a good marketing campaign. The word "campaign" refers to the fact that there is a continuous effort until the property is sold. One of the major reasons to market a property is to increase the number of people who know the property is available. Everyone learned back in Economics 101 that the more exposure a product receives, the faster the product will sell. Sellers expect that real estate professionals can use expert marketing skills to get them more money than they could get themselves. This simply is not true. Through marketing, real estate professionals can expose a well-priced property to the market and get it sold faster than a seller can. But what marketing will not do is get a property more money than the open market will offer. The following sections present a few interesting ideas that a broker could add to a marketing campaign.

Bus Benches
The benches that a person sits on to wait for the bus have advertising on them. The benches could be utilized in one specific location and for one specific marketing campaign. This is strictly name recognition advertising, and for the real estate industry bus benches may not be the best place to use the money in the marketing budget.

Grocery Store Place-Card Boards
Place-card boards, usually posted on a wall at the front of a store, hold place cards with advertising on them, but the public rarely scrutinizes these. Place cards can be used in a property-marketing campaign for one specific property and changed out once that property is sold. Generally, people going into a grocery store want groceries, not real estate brokers.

Shopping Carts
Shopping carts have an advertising spot on the front that a real estate broker can purchase. Like place cards, these can be used in a property-marketing campaign for one specific property and changed out once that property is sold. This is merely name recognition advertising, and there are better places to be if the broker wants the brokerage's name out to the public.

Movie Screens
Movie theaters sell a few seconds of advertising in front of a captive audience. The people waiting to see the feature film will watch the advertisements pass in front of them. The broker could run an advertisement on select high-end properties to add to a marketing campaign. This is also strictly name recognition advertising. Again, real estate brokers seldom use this type of advertising.

Bathroom Ad Cards
Advertising in bathrooms is an approach that is difficult to believe. When a person goes to many public restrooms, he/she may see ad cards on the wall or inside the stall doors. Not the place most brokers want to be thought about!

Moving Trucks
Some brokerages have bought a box truck and allow their clients to borrow the truck to help them move. A broker should be careful about

liability on this one, and the broker should be sure to have insurance protecting the company. The company can then advertise that "We really help you move!" These trucks become moving billboards on the outside of the trucks—a really neat idea but relatively expensive to buy, customize, and maintain. The marketing campaign would need the long-term funds to effectively use this marketing idea.

Giveaways

Giveaways are small items with the brokerage name and contact information on them. A listed house could have certain items that specifically market that property, such as squeeze balls, breath mints, pens, pads, business card holders, and the like. The listing agent should give these away to any potential buyer. Here are some additional helpful ideas:

- *calendars.* Many real estate professionals provide calendars as one of their giveaways. The picture of the month on the calendar could be a listed house the brokerage sold in the past year. The good thing about calendars is that the brokerage's name is in front of potential recruits and clients every day for an entire year. The bad thing is that the broker must provide these every year if they are to work. If the broker provides these every year, people will begin to look forward to receiving them. If the broker provides these once and never again, the enterprise was a waste of money.
- *sports schedules.* The broker can print high school, college, or professional game schedules on a small card. The broker has the brokerage name and contact information on the back. The schedule could also note a specific house that the broker is featuring at that time. This should be in alignment with the marketing campaign for the featured listing. The broker should be sure to have the authorization to publish this information.

- *flying discs.* The broker can get the brokerage name and contact information printed on the back of a flying disc. The broker can give these discs to youth groups to use and keep. The broker can also give them to high school cheerleaders to throw at football games (small plastic footballs are good too).

These are just a few ideas—the broker can put the company name and contact information on about anything. The broker should be creative here. The broker should think about the brokerage's objectives and use them as the guide to giveaways.

HomeBuyer Seminars

Home buyer seminars are presented to attract members of the public who are in the market to purchase a home. The broker will also find that there will be people in attendance who want to make real estate their career but do not know where to start. During the seminar, the broker demonstrates the process of purchasing a home. The broker should give good and helpful information—that is what was promised. This does not limit the possibility to emphasize the benefits of using the broker to help potential home buyers in the purchase of their next home, nor does it prevent the broker from demonstrating the benefits of real estate sales as a business.

The seminar should be scheduled once per month. It should be as good and as simple as possible. The broker should develop a notebook of approximately 25 pages for each participant to have the information to take home. The broker's name, office name, and contact information should be in every manual. It would be best to have the important points written up in a computer presentation to project onto the wall or projection screen from a data projector. Then the broker should market this seminar through whatever means the broker feels are appropriate. Different marketing will bring different clientele.

The broker should do all the speaking. There is no need to bring in any experts. There are two reasons for this: First, the broker should be the expert. The broker can have some of the sponsored salespersons there to work with those attendees who want to buy real estate. Second, it is very embarrassing to have three or four experts in real estate show up to speak when only two couples show up to participate. On the positive side, the broker now has two couples of potential clients he/she did not have before the seminar; this, however, is diminished by the humiliation at having more speakers than participants. If the broker is the only speaker and just two couples show up, the broker can sit down with them and make the presentation more of a question-and-answer session.

The broker should charge the participants a fee for attending. Most brokers believe that if the seminar is free, more people will attend. Actually, the opposite is true. Consumers often believe that if a seminar is free, no useful information will be given out, and the whole thing is just a hoax to sell to them. Conversely, people feel that if they have to pay for something, it must be worth something. The broker could say the cost is $15 per person or $25 per couple. People can get discount or even free tickets at a mortgage company that is helping with the cost of the seminar. The broker could work with local real estate schools to offer the same discount tickets.

The broker should hold these discount tickets in the brokerage office if at all feasible because of the cost. The broker should hand out a seminar manual with important topics summarized but not much else. The broker does not need to cater these events. The broker could offer refreshments, but they should be kept to a minimum.

When the participants enter the room, there should be music playing or an introductory presentation playing from the data projector on a continuous loop.

Before the attendees are dismissed, the broker should ask for the opportunity to represent the attendees in the purchase of their next home. If they are interested in real estate as a career, the broker should set up a time for a more formal interview. The broker is expected to ask for the business.

Home Seller Seminars

Home seller seminars are exactly the same as home buyer seminars except that instead of helping the buyer buy a home, the broker will help a home seller sell a home. The preparations are the same. There should be a seminar manual to pass out, and the broker should make the presentation using a computer and a data projector. Not everyone there will have real estate to sell; some individuals may be looking to better their lives through the profession of real estate sales.

Advertising

Advertising is the most common and widely used forms of marketing. Advertising is a passive way to market a property because a brokerage runs an ad and then waits until a prospect contacts the brokerage. Advertising can be extremely expensive. Running a full-page ad in the *Wall Street Journal* could cost $30,000 per issue, which would not be smart on a $60,000 house. Advertising does not need to be expensive, so the broker should be careful before spending.

Writing Effective Advertising

When preparing ad copy, the broker should first determine the purpose of the advertisement. Is the advertisement to promote the real estate company or to sell a real estate property to benefit a client? The broker should analyze the property or the brokerage firm and decide on the advantages and benefits. The broker needs to decide which potential client (buyer, seller, landlord, or tenant) the broker is trying to attract. The broker should add a personal call to action to the ad copy because such a call is critical to success.

Every classified ad should carry the reader through four selling steps. In the advertising community, the four steps compose the acronym AIDA:

1. *Attract attention:* To attract attention, for example, a broker could use a catchy headline. The headline is probably the most important part in writing an ad. The broker needs to catch the prospects' attention within the first few words; otherwise, the ad will lose them forever. The broker should always document the results to determine the best use of the brokerage's money. The broker should use a lot of white space (i.e., that space where nothing is printed). White space in print advertising attracts attention. The broker could occasionally ask questions in the ad. People have a natural tendency to be attracted to questions.
2. *Arouse interest:* To arouse interest, the broker should tie the body copy into the heading. The broker must create interest and desire by listing features and detailing the benefits of these features to the clients. The interest stage is the broker's opportunity to get the consumer to want to read further. If the ad does not create interest, the prospect stops reading and moves on to the next ad.
3. *Create desire:* To create desire, the broker should list only the best features and benefits. The desire stage creates that intense desire to have the services promised. Writing skill is necessary here to create the right atmosphere for the prospects. The prospects should be able to see themselves living in that house

or becoming a sponsored salesperson at the brokerage office. Anything less and the brokerage will not receive a phone call.
4. *call for action:* The call for action is a must for advertising. It tells prospects what to do, such as "better hurry" and "call now." An ad that does not direct the consumer to take action will not get the results desired. An ad will receive a greater response if it closes with a request to call the broker, using the brokerage name. Using the word "please" softens the closing and results in a greater response. Ask and thou shalt receive!

If the ad copy tells all the essential facts clearly, holds the reader's attention from start to finish, and makes a specific call to action, it will be successful. The following is a checklist for writing the ad:

- The ad must organize all the facts from the viewpoint of the reader.
- The ad must appeal to emotions, such as love of comfort, status, family responsibility, and so forth.
- The ad must "keep it simple and short" (KISS). The ad should not have long, windy sentences; however, the ad should not have abbreviations. If information is important enough to put in an ad, it is important enough to spell out. Sometimes brokers get so close to real estate that they forget what it is like to be a consumer.

CASE IN POINT—A person once wanted to buy a mini pickup truck. He would read ads in the newspaper that would have the word "OBO" at the end. Now what does a musical instrument have to do with buying a truck? Okay, so he knew they were not talking about a musical instrument, but he really did not know what the letters "OBO" meant. He never called in response to those ads. It could have been a great truck, but he would not call and be embarrassed by his lack of knowledge. He has a friend who owns a used-car lot, and he asked him what "OBO" meant. After a laugh, his friend said it is "Or Best Offer." The point is that a broker should not eliminate a potential client by using cute abbreviations, because someone might not know their meaning.

- Every ad should have meaningful words that stir emotion. If the broker is recruiting, the broker should make readers "wade through the money they will make at the brokerage office," or if the broker is marketing a property, the ad needs to let them feel

the "cool" water across their skin when they jump into their new swimming pool.
- The ad should inspire confidence. The broker should not use exaggerated descriptions that are not believable.
- The broker should write copy just long enough to tell the whole story. Flowery expressions and literary gymnastics will not hold the reader's interest.
- The broker should avoid clichés and overused words such as "super" and "great."
- Clients buy houses and real estate; salespersons buy brokers. For effective marketing in real estate, the broker should not mix marketing strategies. Advertise for one or the other but not both in the same advertisement.
- The broker must stick to the truth. Misleading advertising is illegal and unethical.
- If the broker wants to use a slogan, it should be seven words or fewer; otherwise, it becomes counterproductive. For even better results, the slogan should have three words or fewer.
- The broker should keep in mind that the average person retains just 1% of what he/she sees each day and that the average person inherently mistrusts and sometimes fears things and people that are unfamiliar.
- Advertising campaigns should be no less than weekly for a minimum of three months.
- The more meaningful the message, the more it is received.
- There is an inverse relationship between the number of messages in any given ad and the effectiveness of its results.

Here are some other questions the broker should ask:

- Do people like a particular ad?
- Is a particular ad memorable?
- Does a particular ad give the broker personality?
- Does a particular ad provide a simple message?

Once an ad has been run, the broker should:

- change the ad layout and words each time

- experiment with features of the ad (If the ad isn't working, the broker should change it!)
- document the calls received with each change (This tracks the correct changes and the ones that did not work. The broker should not make the same mistakes twice.)

Most brokers have the following policies about advertising:

- If the real estate brokerage pays for the advertising, the broker makes a determination about which publication to use and then specifies which brokerage properties to advertise. If the brokerage company has a marketing director, this would be his/her job.
- If the salesperson pays for specific advertising, the salesperson makes the determination about which publication to use and then specifies which of his/her own personal listings to advertise.
- All advertisements must be reviewed and approved by the broker for compliance.

Texas Real Estate Commission Rules on Advertising

The Texas Real Estate Commission (TREC) has established the following rules related to real estate advertising:

> TREC Rules §535.2 (g) A broker is responsible to ensure that a sponsored salesperson's advertising complies with the Texas Real Estate License Act (Act). An "advertisement" is a written or oral communication by a license holder which induces a member of the public to use the services of the license holder. The term "advertisement" includes all publications, radio or television broadcasts, all electronic media including email, text messages, social networking websites, and the Internet, business stationery, business cards, signs and billboards.

The following information is not considered advertising:

- a communication from a license holder to a member of the public who has agreed to work with the license holder
- real estate information available to the public on a license holder's website that is behind filtering software that requires registration to access

An advertisement must clearly and conspicuously contain the name of the broker, either a business entity or an individual. A salesperson sponsored by the broker may use the broker's assumed name, instead of the name in which the broker is licensed, if the assumed name is registered with the Commission.

According to the TREC, deceptive advertising includes any advertising that:

- misrepresents any property, terms, values, services, or policies;
- advertises a property that is subject to an exclusive listing agreement without the permission of the listing broker and without disclosing the name of the listing broker;
- is not removed within a reasonable time after closing or termination of the listing agreement it advertises;
- identifies as a broker the salesperson who sponsored the advertising; or
- creates a reasonable likelihood of confusion regarding the permitted use of the property.

An advertisement placed by a license holder must include a designation such as "agent," "broker," or a trade association name that serves clearly to identify the advertiser as a real estate agent.

A broker or salesperson may not place an advertisement that in any way:

- implies that a salesperson is the person responsible for the operation of a brokerage; or
- causes a member of the public to believe that a person not authorized to conduct real estate brokerage is personally engaged in real estate brokerage.

A real estate license holder placing an ad online must include on each page on which the license holder's advertisement appears the identification of the broker or brokerage with whom the license holder is affiliated and the completed Information About Brokerage Services (IABS) form. The IABS form identifies for consumers the types of brokerages and the aspects of each.

A real estate license holder placing an ad by using electronic communication, including but not limited to email and email discussion groups, text messages, and social networking websites, must include in the communication and in any attachment that is an ad the identification of the broker or brokerage and the completed IABS.

An advertisement containing an offer of a rebate must disclose that payment of the rebate is subject to the consent of the party the license holder represents in the transaction.

Frequency

Frequency refers to the number of ad exposures and the amount of time between exposures. Frequency is both positive and negative. The positive side of frequency is that the more exposures there are to the open market, the more the chance that the right buyer will see the property. The negative aspect is that the more exposures there are to the open market, the higher cost to the broker. The broker must weigh the positives and negatives of frequency before agreeing to an advertising contract. Real estate brokers should market all their inventory of properties through a variety of media and with the appropriate frequency.

Types of Advertising

There are many types of advertising a broker could choose. The broker must be aware of all types of advertising and choose the best type for the goals of the brokerage. If the advertising is not in the correct medium or lacks an appropriate frequency at the best price, the brokerage will waste precious money from the marketing budget.

Print

Print advertising is running an ad in any print medium. The mainstay for the real estate industry has been the print media, but print is now used only by small brokerages in small communities. Print media should be used only to generate buyers. If the local buyer no longer looks to print media, then the broker should avoid it. At one time, every broker needed to set aside a large portion of the marketing budget to pay for print media; this is no longer true. Most print media outlets are now begging the real estate community to use their services for advertising. The best choice for the modern broker is to buy an advertising package from the ad company that mixes print with online ads, thereby obtaining the best of both worlds. The print media include newspapers (international, national, local, and community), magazines, and any homes guides.

Newspapers

Newspapers sell themselves to readers by printing interesting and newsworthy stories. The way the newspaper makes its money is by

selling ad space. The better the location within the paper and the larger the ad, the more it will cost to run. If the broker wants the front page, the broker will have to pay dearly for it because that is the space most consumers see first. If the broker is willing to have the ad buried in the middle of the newspaper, the broker will pay less but there will be less viewership. These are the considerations the broker must make before running a newspaper ad.

International International newspapers are newspapers from other countries or that reach global markets. Both types are probably too expensive for most brokers and not conducive to real estate sales in a local market area. The only exception is if the broker knows that a business from a foreign country is moving to the local area. In this case, the broker could put an ad in the local newspaper to market the company to local area people from that area who might be affected.

National National newspapers reach throughout the entire nation. These are newspapers such as the *Wall Street Journal, Chicago Times, New York Times*, and *USA Today*, to name a few. Again, putting ads in these newspapers is too expensive for most brokers and not conducive to real estate sales in a local market area. The only reason a broker might want to use a national newspaper is if his/her brokerage is marketing a very high-dollar estate, and the broker wants to reach top executives across the nation. The broker should be careful with the marketing budget on this one. Here is a thought: If the seller demands that the broker advertise in a national newspaper, the broker should tell the seller that the brokerage must have an upfront "marketing fee" and specify the amount. The fee could be taken off the real estate commission when and if the property sells. This is a brave statement, but it will either cause the seller to back off or get the brokerage money for a solid advertising campaign for that specific property without breaking the marketing budget.

Local Local newspapers typically reach a local area or region. For example, in Fort Worth, Texas, the major local newspaper is the *Fort Worth Star-Telegram*. A real estate company will spend most of its print advertising budget dollars in local advertising. This type of advertising not only gets properties sold but also makes a good and active name for your real estate company. Print advertising is dwindling because of online advertising, but at the current time print remains very popular.

Community Community newspapers are distributed to a limited local area, usually a small community or neighborhood. In Azle, Texas, the major local newspaper would be the *Fort Worth Star-Telegram*, but the community newspaper would be the *Azle News*. Local independent real estate companies use community newspapers quite effectively. These companies want to create a name for themselves within the community, and the community newspaper is a great place to do that.

Community newspapers tend to be less expensive than local newspapers because their circulation is smaller than that of the local papers. The cost of a full-page advertisement in a community newspaper would get only a small block ad in the local newspaper, which makes community newspapers a cost-effective advertising venue for real estate brokers.

The community newspapers have a more specialized kind of advertising than generic newspapers. These newspapers are more like a family newsletter than a newspaper. They carry ads for small dollar items such as lawnmowers, bicycles, and furniture. These community newspapers specialize in selling cars and real estate.

Magazines

Actual special-interest magazines are different from newspapers because issues come out less frequently and the content focuses on only a few key topics. Real estate is not best promoted in a magazine; it tends to be more fluid than magazines allow. A magazine may take several months from idea to issue, so it would be an incredible waste of money to advertise a property that sold before the issue hit the stands. The brokerage may receive calls based on a magazine ad, but the callers may get frustrated calling on properties that are no longer for sale. Magazine ads are usually placed by national real estate companies that are advertising for name recognition, not for property sales.

Real Estate Magazines Real estate magazines are dedicated solely to advertising currently active properties for sale. They usually feature pictures of the houses with a small amount of information on the property. These magazines are frequently distributed to airports, grocery stores, and convenience stores. They contain some of the best print advertising space available. People who pick these up are serious about buying a property. The broker is directly marketing to the target group—namely, those interested in buying real estate. The best places in the magazine are the inside front cover and the back cover, and these spots are also the most expensive.

Car Signs

Car signs feature the real estate company name and/or logo on magnetic signs that are placed on car door panels or the back of the car. These should be purchased as soon as possible. The car signs are marketing the brokerage whenever sponsored license holders are driving around town. These car signs are another form of name recognition marketing, so the broker should not expect to get any direct business from them. However, it could happen. One broker was driving really slowly, looking for investment properties. In his rearview mirror he saw a man running after him. It turns out that the man needed to sell his house, and he had seen the car signs. Because of that one sale, those signs paid for themselves 10 times over! The broker can also paint or use vinyl lettering to have the brokerage name permanently displayed on business vehicles. The broker needs to formulate an office policy regarding car signs. Will the brokerage buy them for the sponsored license holders, or will they have to buy their own? License holders who do not take care of car signs properly can lose them easily.

Name Tags/Name Badges

Sponsored license holders should wear their professional real estate name tag at all times. A name tag is usually plastic or vinyl and has the license holder's name across it and the name of his/her brokerage. The name tags come in a wide variety of shapes, colors, styles, and customized options. The broker should not overlook attachments such as award pins and ribbons—they are a great way for the broker to recognize a real estate salesperson who has achieved something beneficial for the company and at the same time encourage salespersons to wear their name tags. The name tag is not a silent salesperson. If a license holder somehow fails to introduce himself/herself, the name tag will do the talking.

License holders should wear the name tag on the right side of the chest so that it can be read when they shake hands in a greeting. Some brokers will buy new real estate salespersons their first name tag for them. The broker should be sure to pay a little extra to get the sponsored license holders professional name tags to demonstrate their professional image.

Public Relations

Public relations encompasses all aspects of letting the public know that the brokerage is in the real estate industry. Public relations includes writing editorial pieces for print media or real estate blogs, commenting on other real estate blogs, speaking at public engagements, and issuing press releases.

Engaging "public relations" means getting the media to notice a business in a positive light. This should be achieved at least once a month. When a newspaper publishes an article about one of the brokerage's achievements, that news becomes truth to the reader, whereas the same reader might discount an advertisement because it is a paid ad. The same goes for blogs or any other online "expert analysis" or "subject matter expert." The internet is free (with exceptions) and exposes the broker to countless potential buyers, sellers, landlords, and tenants.

A broker should submit public relations stories to the newspaper every week. The worst that could happen is that the article is not used. Newspapers need to fill in sections in their newspaper with stories. If the broker has stories handy for them, they might use a brokerage story to complete the newspaper.

A broker should submit public relations stories on virtually any subject. For instance, one broker once submitted a story about how the real estate office rescued a trapped kitten. It made the front-page news complete with pictures, and the brokerage received many calls thanking the broker for the kindness and concern.

A broker never knows what will be accepted or rejected; the broker's job is to submit. The broker must engage in newsworthy activities; however, almost anything is newsworthy if worded correctly. Has the brokerage helped at a charity event? Has the brokerage won an office production award? Was the broker selected as the real estate broker of the month? All these could be advertised as press releases. Here are some suggestions for public relations stories:

- new associate
- top-listing salesperson
- high-dollar listing
- any charity event
- any award or recognition

The broker should encourage the sponsored license holders to submit their press releases too. When their names are mentioned, the office name is mentioned as well. The best way to ensure that these press releases go out on a regular basis is to assign this task to one of the office staff.

Conventions

Real estate companies love to have their conventions. Each real estate professional expects some sort of award for his/her contribution to the business. Almost every major real estate franchise has at least one award convention in which it presents production awards to its salespersons. There are conventions for the National Association of REALTORS® (NAR) as well as all the state and local associations.

When the broker attends these conventions, the broker should be prepared to press a lot of palms and pass out hundreds of business cards. The broker could pass out company brochures when talking with people attending the convention.

Home Improvement Shows

Home improvement shows feature the latest in amenities for the home, from windows to bathroom fixtures and oak flooring. The shows also have vendors who promote home improvement items, such as gazebos, spas, gardens, and decking, to name a few. Sellers may want to improve their property before they actually put their home on the market to sell. These shows are a great way to meet these sellers before they call the broker's competition.

Career Days/Career Fairs

Colleges and universities have career days for their students. The broker should have a booth at these events. The broker can ask to be added to a mailing list to receive invitations to these events. Some events impose nominal fees, whereas others are free. These career days can yield 20 or more potential recruits. Most do not pan out, but the effort is well worth it.

Most brokers do not go to high school events simply because most high school students lack the maturity for a career; they are simply looking for a job. Brokers love young people, but recent high school graduates do not seem to work out in this business.

Colleges and universities usually will also allow a broker to post job listings, accept resume submissions, and hold on-campus interviews. The broker should be sure to go through the Career Center or Placement Office before entering campus to recruit. Most colleges will not allow any business to recruit for sales positions, but a wise broker can instead recruit for management positions. Every real estate company needs to be recruiting for better managers. If the broker is the manager, the broker should recruit to replace himself/herself so that the broker can proceed to bigger and better things. No manager without previous real estate sales experience should be considered. The broker may be hiring for managers, but they must start working as salespersons.

Some colleges will allow a business to hold an information session or information luncheons with their students. The information session is to inform the students about the brokerage and what real estate is about. Although the college wants a potential employer to educate rather than to recruit openly, they know and expect the broker to recruit afterward. The broker should provide the students with take-home material and use visual aids to facilitate the presentation. After the presentation, students will wander up to the front to ask specific questions. This is a great time for the broker to recruit, so the broker should have a registration form handy.

Word of Mouth

The broker should tell everyone that he/she is a real estate broker. The more people the broker tells, the more they tell, and so on and so on. Word of mouth is one of the best forms of marketing and by far the least expensive. Here are some examples of opportunities to use word-of-mouth marketing:

- *local Association of REALTORS® meeting.* The broker pays money to belong to the local Association. The broker should become well known in that Association. This is a natural way to promote the brokerage. The Association will also give the broker access to many real estate professionals from surrounding areas and perhaps

regions. Affiliates of the real estate industry, such as title and mortgage companies, make good recruits. The best way to get to know the affiliates is through the Association.
- *networking groups.* There are professional networking groups in all areas that meet and discuss current topics, but the major emphasis is on building referral business. The broker needs to be active in marketing the brokerage to these groups. This gives the brokerage exposure to a wide range of potential sales and recruits.
- *sphere of influence.* The broker's sphere of influence is the group of people who know the broker and his/her business. The broker wants to help friends, and they want to help the broker. As the broker, you must let this group know that you are in the real estate profession and are looking for potential recruits. Do not tell them once and expect them to remember. The broker must be in contact with his/her sphere of influence monthly so that the broker will immediately come to mind if anyone talks buying, selling, or starting a real estate career.
- *referral networks.* A referral network is a way for a brokerage firm to encourage individuals to earn referral fees from the real estate business without actually practicing real estate. Some real estate license holders do not make a career of the real estate business. For one reason or another, they give up selling and just let their real estate licenses expire. This is a tragedy because these people can help a brokerage business. The broker should develop a referral network. The members of the network do not sell real estate, but they have an active real estate license. Any time they hear of a buyer or seller of real estate, they call the lead coordinator or broker and pass along the referral. The lead coordinator will assign the lead to a sponsored, active license holder. Once the property closes, the referral license holder will receive a portion of the commission. By forming a referral network, the broker can have the benefit of additional real estate sales.

The broker can search the state real estate commission's website or subscribe to a list of "sent back" licensees. The broker should call them, write them a letter, or email them. If the broker intends to call them, the broker could use the following script:

Broker: "Mr. Jones?"
Jones: "This is Mr. Jones."

Broker: "Mr. Jones, this is Dan Hamilton with Acme Real Estate. I noticed you have turned your license back to the state real estate commission. May I ask why?"
Jones: "I have another job."
Broker: "I see. That is a shame to have earned the license and now have it be useless to you. Let me ask you, can I show you a way that the license could still make you some money without your ever having to actually sell real estate?"
Jones: "What do you mean?"
Broker: "We have a referral network you could join. The referral network would allow you to refer your friends and relatives to us for their real estate needs, and once the transaction has closed, you will receive a referral fee. Does this make sense?"
Jones: "That's great!"
Broker: "Why don't you come to my office, and we can take care of the transfer."

Rules of the Referral Network

Upon forming a referral network, the broker should follow some simple rules regarding the individuals who make referrals. The referral person:

- does not sell any real estate at any time for any one (This is a must, and the person should sign an affidavit to this fact. The broker cannot tolerate a person who does not follow rules.)
- must keep his/her license active
- refers only to the brokerage referral network
- receives money from real estate business only through his/her designated broker
- acts with the utmost in professionalism when representing the company

The referral network can grow to have several hundred licensees working within it. The broker should take this slowly. Some brokers establish the entire network under a different broker's license to avoid additional fees associated with the real estate industry. The broker should be sure to check with state and local laws and regulations for this type of business.

Affiliates

Affiliates are people who do business related to the real estate industry but outside of sales. These businesses need the brokerage's ability to generate clientele. If the broker helps these affiliates with their businesses, they should in turn help the broker. Affiliates send potential business and recruits to the broker. Some of the following are affiliates that fall into this category:

- *Inspectors*—These people take a look at real property and give their expert advice on the condition of that property. They are absolutely necessary to limit the real estate license holder's liability in a real estate transaction. The buyers should select the inspector. The buyers do want advice to help them choose an inspector, and there should be a brokerage office policy on this matter. The license holder may recommend a qualified inspector. First, the license holder should know the inspector and be certain that he/she has the expertise and integrity to do a good job. The inspector should have a license number from the state in which he/she does business. Second, the inspector should be bonded and have errors and omissions (E&O) insurance. Both of these will protect the buyer and license holder just in case the inspector will not.
- *Title Companies*—These companies provide the owner's policy of title insurance for the buyer of real property to protect the buyer from claims against the property that were undiscovered. A title policy should be issued for every real estate transaction the company is involved in. As a result, the brokerage can direct a great deal of business to a title company. Regulations prohibit referring business to companies expecting to receive a monetary return, but nothing prohibits the broker from marketing services in conjunction with these title companies. Occasionally, these title officers will hear of an unhappy real estate salesperson. They should call the broker and give the broker the information.
- *Mortgage Companies*—These companies provide the funds necessary for the buyer to purchase real property. When buyers begin the process of finding a home to purchase, they look to a real estate professional to help. As a result, license holders can send business to the mortgage company that provides the buyers with the best options. License holders should get business back from the mortgage company because that would be a fair trade.
- *Appraisers*—These individuals are professional property evaluators. Their job is to determine the worth of a real estate investment. Generally, their role is to protect the mortgage company from lending money on an inadequate property. Appraisers can work

as staff appraisers, meaning they work directly for that particular mortgage company and are usually on salary with that mortgage company. However, some work as fee appraisers or with appraisal management companies, meaning they work independently of a particular mortgage company and are paid in fees from their clients. The broker's recommendations of a particular appraiser can be very valuable to that appraiser. The same appraiser should recommend the brokerage when a client asks him/her about the real estate profession. The broker must let the appraisers know that he/she will appreciate their recommendations and have a system to market to each appraiser with whom the brokerage does business.
- *Structural Engineers*—These engineers evaluate the property's structure to determine its soundness. Most structural engineers cherish recommendations from real estate professionals. The broker should market to these engineers because sometimes owners will seek out a structural engineer before putting their homes on the market.

Speaking

Most people are afraid of public speaking, but those who practice it garner a great deal of respect. Speaking for groups on the subject of real estate allows a person (and company) to demonstrate expertise. A speaker does not need to know all about the subject but should be able to find the answers to participants' questions and follow up with them after the event. A script for fielding a difficult question would go something like this:

Speaker: "That is an excellent question, and I want you to have the best answer, so let's do this: I will research it and follow up with you after this event to discuss the solution. Will you please leave me some way to get back in touch with you?"

This script is a helpful way to defer a question. Another way to diffuse a question is to solicit responses from the audience. For example:

Participant: "What is the most popular loan program available right now?"

Speaker: "All right, let's find out from the rest of you what types of loan programs you are using currently or have used in the past."

A speaker can buy time and perhaps avoid sole responsibility for answering the question. This all depends on the responsiveness of the audience. The fastest way a speaker can lose respect and credibility is to answer a question incorrectly. The speaker should not act as if he/she knows everything.

This is not a speech-coaching course. However, a broker should know how to be an effective a speaker.

Here are a few places where a broker might want to speak and groups a broker might want to speak to:

- *house of worship*—Local places of worship want informative speeches for their congregations. It is usually difficult for them to book talent because most want to be paid, and these places generally will not pay for talent.
- *civic groups*—Civic groups tend to specialize in certain groups of people with similar interests.
- *schools*—Sometimes high schools and colleges will want a broker to speak on career nights. These are different than recruiting events. During the speech, the broker should explain to the students the benefits of being in the real estate business. This service will land the broker in good favor with the campus counselors and other faculty, as well as the parents of the students, all of whom could be potential clients. The broker should be sure to market to these people when appropriate.

Speaking to a quilting group would be quite different from speaking to a group of handymen. The broker should be prepared to handle the different types of groups. The broker should ask plenty of questions before accepting a speaking engagement. The broker will want to know the following details:

- exact subject matter
- length of time for speech
- number of people in attendance
- seating arrangement and speaker platform
- sound and lights if provided

Community Service

Community service is working with worthy causes for the benefit of all. The broker should market the brokerage by being active in the charities the broker chooses. People want to help those who contribute. The broker should not be involved with these groups just to market to them; the broker should be working because he/she wants to give back.

Shopping Mall Kiosks

Indoor regional malls offer small kiosks (i.e., booths) that the brokerage can rent to provide real estate services to passers by. This unique idea provides a lot of exposure but very little actual business. The benefits are simple: The more people a brokerage can get in front of, the greater chance the brokerage will have of finding someone who wants to buy or sell real estate. However, not too many people seeking a real estate professional would head to the mall. The disadvantages are the expense of rental, the length of the rental term, and the time it takes to work at one of the kiosks. A better idea would be to see if the mall management would allow the brokerage to rent a kiosk just once per month. They will probably not, but it does not hurt to ask.

Closing Gifts

Closing gifts are things license holders give to their clients at the closing of their transactions. Closing is a happy time, and a gift just adds to the joy. Closing gifts are a lovely way for license holders to say "thank you" to their clients by purchasing them a gift, but they are also marketing tool. License holders should not give gifts that are disposable, can be used up, or could potentially die, because if the client gets rid of the gift, he/she gets rid of all the contact information.

The job of the broker is to ensure that the sponsored license holders are presenting gifts to their clients. Some real estate brokerages buy the gifts to make sure that they are given. These brokers keep a supply of the gifts in the office. The following are examples of some closing gifts:

- *brass doorknocker with engraved name.* The doorknocker should have "Presented by _____," with the brokerage name and contact information engraved in small letters below the buyer's name. These doorknockers are great because they will remind the owners of

the brokerage every time they open their front door. The broker might hire someone to deliver the gift and actually install it, because otherwise the buyers might never get around to doing so.
- *leather binder to hold important papers.* The buyers, now owners, will have many important papers they will need to be able to retrieve at a moment's notice, including closing papers, deed, purchase agreement, insurance papers, note and mortgage, title policy, and many others. The brokerage could provide the buyers with a leather binder to hold all these papers. The binder should look highly professional and should have the brokerage's name and contact information embossed on the inside so that if the buyers ever want to sell, they will know whom to call. These binders can be bought or constructed. The broker should be sure the gift looks professional because it is a reflection of the brokerage.

Referral Gifts

A major portion of brokerage business should come from referrals. Referrals occur when people the license holders have worked with recommend the brokerage to their sphere of influence. This is the easiest and best business. With these people there is no competition. The license holder is the only real estate professional the clients interview. The client will think, "If my friend believes your salesperson can do the job, I believe the same."

These referrals do not just happen; the broker must market to get referrals. The best way to get referrals is to encourage the sponsored license holders do an excellent job for the referral and then give a gift to the person who provided the referral. By cultivating the relationship with this person, the broker will ensure that the person will continue to give referrals.

Sports Team Sponsorship

Local youth sports teams are always seeking sponsors. By sponsoring one or more of these teams, the broker can market the brokerage to the coaches and to the players' parents. The brokerage can simply donate money, or the broker can go as far as sponsoring uniforms with the brokerage name and contact information on the back.

School Programs

Educational institutions, from elementary schools through colleges, have events they want to print programs for so that the participants and audience know the players and the schedule of events. By paying to have these programs printed, the broker can be sure to include (with the school's permission) the brokerage's name and contact information.

Rarely will these programs be thrown away, because the parents want to keep the mementos of their children playing in a sporting or scholastic event. The following are a few examples of events that might require a program:

- *football game*—Football programs list all the players and coaches, the cheerleaders, the opposing team, and any additional information that might be of interest.
- *graduation ceremony*—Graduation programs list all the students who are graduating and identify the faculty who are important to the school.
- *concerts*—Music programs list all the participating students, the instruments they play, and the music they sing. They also list all the music teachers and staff and parents who helped put the program together.
- *plays and performances*—Program for school theatrical productions list all the student actors, the acts, the director, and all the people who helped to put on the performance.

Event Sponsorship

The broker should select some type of community event to sponsor at least once each year. This type of marketing can be expensive, but it can also make a positive name for the brokerage in the community. The event does not have to be huge, just memorable. Here are a few:

- *cheerleading championships*—Many cheerleaders cannot afford to go to national championships, so the broker could hold local championships. The broker should invite all the local cheerleader groups to participate. The broker should provide necessary items like water, trophies, and stipends for judges. The broker, office personnel, and sponsored license holders will need to plan this one out ensure a quality event. The broker should have the local media on hand for the awards. As with all events, the broker should be the coordinator, but the broker should not do everything.
- *parades*—A brokerage should be involved in the local town's annual parade. Almost every town will have a parade at least once per year. The broker could sponsor a float, ride on a float, or be a director. Working on the parade committee puts the broker in touch with very influential people. The broker should use these events

for marketing purposes. For example, the sponsored license holders can throw out bags of candy with a business card attached. The broker can have banners with the brokerage company's name and contact information along the side of the float. The broker can also sponsor part of the program and then have company banners along the parade route. The broker should always be thinking of ways to market.

- *Easter egg hunt*—One broker decided one year to hold an Easter egg hunt for people in the neighborhoods surrounding the office. Office license holders marketed the event by posting flyers throughout the area. The brokerage designed a registration form to be filled out in advance or at the event. The form gave the brokerage names, addresses, and telephone numbers to continue marketing after the event. The broker purchased an Easter Bunny outfit, and the license holders from the brokerage office bought plastic eggs, candy, and small toys. The brokerage then had a party and stuffed all the plastic eggs. The brokerage expected 400 people, but 800 showed up. License holders madly ran to the store to buy more eggs. In the end, everyone was very happy and appreciative.
- *flag distribution on Independence Day*—A favorite of real estate license holders is to distribute little plastic U.S. flags on wooden sticks with the license holder's business card attached. License holders go up and down the streets placing the flags in the yards of the houses by the edge of the street. This creates a great effect when a person drives down these streets—flags blowing in the wind all in a line. Impressive! Putting out flags on Independence Day is so popular that a brokerage might want to think of placing the flags out on September 11. Being different in marketing sets a brokerage apart.
- *pumpkins on Halloween*—Another great idea that is often used is placing pumpkins with the brokerage's business card on owners' front porches and doorsteps. The broker should make an attempt to find a seller of pumpkins with an oversupply and make a deal to buy all of them. The broker can buy these for the sponsored license holders willing to put them out or can leave the purchasing up to them.
- *Boy or Girl Scout campout*—A broker could find the local Boy Scout or Girl Scout troop in the brokerage area and offer to sponsor its next camping trip. The brokerage will provide the money for food and maybe even buy some piece of outdoor equipment with the brokerage's name and contact information on it to give it to each scout. A broker does not need to have a son or daughter in Scouts to sponsor a campout.

Membership in Civic Groups

The broker should be a member of at least one civic group and actively participate. Civic groups allow the broker to give back. As always with community service, the broker should be a member for the right reasons, not just as a marketing strategy. However, civic participation can be a good vehicle for earning respect in the brokerage's community, and it is therefore one of the best types of marketing. Some groups to consider:

- *local homeowners associations*—Generally, homeowners association leaders get little respect. Association members often think they do not do enough, but the leaders' spouses think they do too much. These people are seldom paid and often berated. A broker should call up the nearby homeowners associations and ask to be an honorary member or an affiliate. The president will be surprised yet pleased to have a respected member of the real estate profession interested in the association. The broker now can market the brokerage directly to all the homeowners. The broker could volunteer to maintain the association's roster and mail out the monthly newsletter. No doubt the president will be so glad a professional is now handling the newsletter that he/she will let the broker put a business card–size note in the corner of the page. The note could read:

    > *Have you ever thought about selling your current residence or possibly pursuing a career in real estate? If you have, please contact the editor of this newsletter at:*
    > *Dan Hamilton*
    > *Broker/Owner, Acme Real Estate*
    > *817-555-1212*

    If the group does not have a newsletter, the broker should volunteer to publish one. The best would be an electronic newsletter rather than a print newsletter sent through the postal service. Homeowners will come to the broker if they want something in the newsletter, and the broker will also have the roster of everyone in the association.

- *school parent-teacher associations*—School parent-teacher associations (PTAs) are always in need of a helping hand. A broker could volunteer to collect money for new textbooks or make arrangements to have the brokerage purchase them. This may be very expensive, but think how long a school will keep the books that are bought.

- *clubs*—Civic clubs such as the Lions Club, chess clubs, and sewing clubs usually have a theme, and if the broker enjoys their theme, the broker will also probably enjoy the company of the other club members. Marketing to these people is best accomplished by word of mouth.

Open House for the Public

Open houses attract people interested in buying in that particular area. They also attract people who live in the area who may want to sell. The best part for a broker is that an open house can also attract recruits who are considering real estate as a career. The more marketing flash and publicity the license holders put on at an open house, the more potential clients it will attract. Banners, flags, and signs should be displayed at the house on the open house day. The salespersons should put open house placards giving directional signs at the corners of all major traffic intersections in the area. The broker should be sure to check local laws for sign placement. If a sign is to be placed at a corner of someone's yard, the broker should be sure to ask permission.

The license holders should market at least two open houses per week. Yes, this is work, but isn't that what they are supposed to be doing? Open houses are traditionally held on Saturday and Sunday–both great days for buyers to be out and looking for property. The broker could hold an open house during the week to seek out the buyers and sellers who may not have the ability to go on the weekends. The broker could also hold the weekday open houses in the evening or perhaps provide a light lunch to get the working crowd. If the salespersons do not have any listings or have too few to hold an open house every week, they could ask real estate professionals in the office if they could hold one of their houses open. The license holders could contact a builder of new houses to see if they could hold one of their newly built houses open. Salespersons could even call an FSBO and offer to hold the house open. This helps the salespersons in two ways: First, they get all the leads into that FSBO during the open house time; and second, they build a rapport and respect in the FSBO's eyes.

Broker's Open House

A broker's open house is marketing a property and the brokerage to other professional real estate salespersons. A sponsored salesperson in the brokerage office uses one of his/her new listings on the market and provides lunch for all who come to look at that property. The license holder markets this exclusively to real estate professionals—no outside marketing to the public. The license holder does not put up yard signs. The license holder markets the broker's open house with flyers to the local real estate offices. These flyers can be hand delivered, faxed, or emailed, although these last two methods are less effective, and the licensee must check the do-not-fax and antispam laws in the local area.

The more talented the salespersons are at preparing a meal, the better the broker's open house will be. Some real estate salespersons have special items they can prepare that are hits and always bring a crowd. Some offer drawings for free stuff to add attendance.

The broker could organize a group of salespersons with listings in close proximity and hold the broker's open house together. This cuts down on the marketing and increases the attendance. Appetizers could be offered at the first house, the main course at the second house, and dessert at the third house. At the fourth house the broker could hold a drawing for prizes for those who visited all four houses.

At the broker's open house, the broker's function is to greet the real estate salespersons from other offices. Here the broker is at one of his/her salesperson's broker's open houses, shaking hands. The other competing salesperson thinks that his/her broker would never do that. If that salesperson is unhappy, he/she might seek out the broker because of the support shown for his/her people. By the way, the broker's second function is to retain the currently sponsored salespersons by supporting their efforts to generate sales.

Office Tour (Caravan)

A very effective way to market the brokerage and to retain salespersons is to take them to see the new listings acquired over the past week. In most offices, this is a scheduled time to preview the new listings. The broker should be sure to set time aside to go on these caravan tours. It allows the broker the opportunity to see the inventory the office is carrying, and it also shows the broker's dedication to and support of the people in the office.

The listing salespersons should give everyone a card with a few questions on it to answer as they view each listing, such as these:

- What was your overall opinion of the house?
- How did you feel about the price?
- What improvements could be made to help the salability?
- Any additional comments?

The salesperson should keep the questions to a minimum and leave enough space for the real estate people to write their comments. The license holder should use these cards as information on the marketability of the property. When the seller insists on overpricing the house, these cards could indicate that all the other real estate professionals agree that the price should be lowered to get the property sold. It also shows the seller that the brokerage is professional.

Some real estate brokers use virtual tours of the properties instead of actually touring them. This is a great idea to save time and money. Each listing agent submits a short video or slide show of the properties instead of leaving to view them.

The local Association of REALTORS® typically offers property tours for its members. These are similar to office tours, except that the entire association is invited. The broker should participate in these if the broker is a member. This is a spectacular way to market the brokerage and actively recruit other license holders. The broker would have uninterrupted time to talk with other competing salespersons and invite them to a one-on-one lunch to discuss their future. If the broker does go, the broker may be the only other broker to attend. That sends a tremendous message about the broker's dedication to this business.

Career Apparel

Career apparel simply means that the clothes a person wears have identification indicating that the wearer is in the real estate industry and proud of it. The broker should always wear his/her name badge as a silent and constant marketing item. The broker should dress professionally with career insignia on the left-hand side, and the broker should encourage all the sponsored salespersons to do the same. Some brokers press their salespersons to always wear their name tag without wearing one themselves. Brokers should not send such mixed messages; instead, brokers should wear their name tags first, and others will follow their example.

Radio Broadcasting Station

Certain companies produce a small briefcase-size radio broadcasting station. It can broadcast approximately 400 feet in every direction. The radio station runs on a digital continuous loop of about four minutes of information. The broker can record a message about a particular house and broadcast it from that house. On the yard sign, a rider can indicate which frequency the message is on. The broker could put these notices in the brokerage window and also broadcast information about the next real estate career seminar.

Recorded Messages About Properties

Some offices offer recorded messages about properties through a toll-free telephone number. The prospect can call into the number and then dial in the property code and listen to the information. The number is marketed by posting a name rider on the yard sign. Another way to market the number is by posting graphic in the window of the real estate office. Passersby can stop and look at the graphics, and if they want more information they can call the toll-free number. The broker should be sure that the recording also offers advice about how to start a real estate career.

Protecting the Company's Image

The broker should be very cautious about the company's image. One of the best ways to protect the company's image is by controlling what marketing is being attempted by the sponsored license holders. A broker needs to be aware that the company's image may be tarnished by one bad marketing piece, and if really bad it may end the brokerage. The broker needs to be sure that all marketing pieces abide by:

- *TREC rules and regulations.* TREC has set up advertising rules and regulations, and it is the broker's responsibility to be sure all advertising that leaves the brokerage office is in compliance.
- *fair housing laws.* The federal government has long established that advertising must comply with the federal fair housing laws. It is the broker's responsibility to be sure that all advertising is in accordance with the law.
- *Regulation Z.* Regulation Z under the Truth-in-Lending Act has set up strict rules on advertising involving financing terms that a broker must be certain are followed with all brokerage marketing.
- *NAR guidelines.* The NAR publishes the Code of Ethics, which makes it a violation to discriminate in advertising or to mislead the public in advertising.
- *the brokerage's policies and procedures manual.* The brokerage has set up a policies and procedures manual to protect the brokerage and its image, and the broker must insist that the manual is followed.

The broker should never want a bad public image, and so double-checking the standards of outgoing marketing pieces is the best place to start.

"Coming Soon"

A trend in the industry that could create a bad image to a brokerage is to use the words "coming soon" and creating a pocket listing. A pocket listing is when the listing agent does not openly market the property in an effort to find the buyer and get both sides of the commission. This is not in the best interest of the client (the property owner) because the market is limited to only the listing agent's marketing ability and to the marketing power of the MLS and other professional license holders. If it is not in the best interest of the client, then the broker and listing agent could be exposed to a breach of their fiduciary duties to their client.

The real estate system works for the public as well as the license holders because of the necessity for both groups to cooperate. A pocket listing is noncooperative. While there may be legitimate reasons for the use of this marketing method, license holders should be aware that selling property using this method may, under certain circumstances, result in a complaint with the Commission and finding that the license holder has violated TREC laws and rules.

Some common characteristics of this dangerous practice are that a license holder has a listing on a property and advertises it as "coming soon" or does not advertise it at all outside of his/her own brokerage (i.e., a pocket listing); that the property is not entered into the local MLS system or other online property listings such as Realtor.com; that the property is not available for showings from competing brokers. Although the TREC does not restrict how a property can be marketed, license holders must nonetheless comply with their required fiduciary duties.

Under §531.1 of the TREC Rules, a license holder cannot put his/her self-interest above that of his/her client. So the motivation for and disclosure of the effect of an off-market listing are key factors that the TREC will consider when investigating a "coming soon" listing complaint. If the property is being marketed as "coming soon" because the seller is still preparing the property for sale, that is a legitimate use of this method. If, however, the property is being marketed as "coming soon" so that the listing broker can try to acquire a buyer before it is exposed to other agents, then it appears that the listing broker may be putting the broker's own financial interest ahead of the client's interest.

To counter this complaint and potential finding, a broker should fully inform the seller as to the potentially negative effect of any limited exposure to the market and obtain the seller's clear and unambiguous consent—in writing—to the use of any limited exposure marketing method.

CHAPTER SUMMARY

Marketing is the overall concept of offering a property for sale to the general public. The more people know that a property is available, the better chance it has to sell for the most money at the fastest time.

A marketing strategy is a brokerage firm's overall marketing direction and should guide the broker in deciding how to spend money and time in the best interest of the brokerage.

The brokerage marketing plan should have each step detailed with exacting standards and have a beginning date and an end date.

Name recognition advertising gets people to know the brokerage name and what services are offered.

Prospect-generating advertising makes the telephone ring, webpage click, or email post.

A post sign is a large wood or composite material post in an upside-down "L" shape with the sign panel made of steel and hanging from the arm of the post.

A stake sign is usually all steel or aluminum and smaller in size than its post counterpart.

Sign riders are the metal information attachments that are placed on yard signs.

Information boxes or tubes are attached to the yard signs, and inside are information sheets that offer data on the particular property and usually a picture of the property on high-quality paper.

Key boxes (also called lockboxes) are usually placed on the outside of the front door of a listing to provide a key to real estate salespersons with the authorized access codes, and they come in two basic styles:

1. Electronic key boxes allow access by means of an electronic key card.
2. Combination key boxes allow access by means of a combination of either numbers or letters.

A multiple listing service (MLS) allows a property to have worldwide exposure.

Residential service contracts are basic insurance policies that protect buyers for one year (which can be extended) after the purchase of a home for most mechanical items in the home.

Commercial real estate sales include small retail, big box, office, industrial, business, and high-rise real estate, to name a few.

Billboards are another form of name recognition advertising.

Trade shows are gatherings of vendors and tradespeople to offer their products and services from a central location.

Property management occurs when a property owner who is renting property no longer wants the duties associated with being an active landlord, which include:

- leasing
- contract negotiation
- rent collection
- reporting
- marketing

Radio is frequently used to advertise newly built apartment complexes desiring a significant number of tenants immediately. Radio is also used for builders who have just opened a new subdivision.

Television can show how the lease property will look to a prospective tenant.

The internet is the medium that is used most often for residential, commercial, and property management. The internet is where almost all buyers begin their research for their next home.

Direct marketing entails the mailing of ads or sending other direct communication to the home market in hopes that property owners may want to buy or sell real estate in the not too distant future.

Postcards are one of the most used direct marketing pieces.

Company brochures are usually trifold letters that introduce the brokerage company and tell about the office's accomplishments.

A property brochure is a pamphlet that tells of a specific property.

The property profile sheet is usually a single sheet of paper that describes the property and has a picture of it.

The marketing budget spells out the money to be spent in the marketing plan.

The budget can have simple line-item categories or the broker can break each main category down into subcategories for a more precise marketing budget. For example:

- *marketing campaigns*—This budget category is for all anticipated listing the brokerage will take during the year.
- *marketing the brokerage*—This is a generic category for any type of marketing done on behalf of the brokerage.
- *marketing for recruits*—This category is used for obtaining recruits for the brokerage.
- *marketing supplies*—Marketing needs supplies.
- *marketing materials*—This category includes any printing, purchasing, or customizing of marketing materials.
- *marketing expenses*—Costs could include the temporary hiring of marketing experts, consulting fees, and similar expenses.

A marketing campaign involves the marketing of individual properties in alignment with the marketing strategy, marketing plan, and marketing budget.

The benches that a person sits on to wait for a bus have advertising on them.

Place-card boards, usually posted on a wall at the front of the store, hold place cards with advertising on them.

Shopping carts have an advertising spot on the front that a real estate broker can purchase.

Movie theaters sell a few seconds of advertising in front of a captive audience.

Some brokerages have bought a box truck and allow their clients to borrow the truck to help them move.

Giveaways are small items with the brokerage name and contact information on them, such as:

- calendars
- sports schedules
- flying discs

Homebuyer seminars are presented to attract members of the public who are in the market to purchase a home.

Home-seller seminars will help a home seller sell a home.

Advertising is the most common and widely used forms of marketing.

Every classified ad should carry the reader through four selling steps, which are:

- **A**ttract attention
- **A**rouse interest

- Create desire
- Call for action

An advertisement is a written or oral communication by a license holder that induces a member of the public to use the services of the license holder.

The term "advertisement" includes all print publications; radio and television broadcasts; all electronic media, including email, text messages, blogs, posts on social networking websites, and internet publications; business stationery and cards; and signs and billboards.

The following information is not considered advertising:

- a communication from a license holder to a member of the public who has agreed to work with the license holder
- real estate information available to the public on a license holder's website that is behind a filtering software that requires registration to access

An advertisement must clearly and conspicuously contain the name of the broker, either a business entity or an individual.

A salesperson sponsored by the broker may use the broker's assumed name instead of the name in which the broker is licensed, if the assumed name is registered with the TREC.

An advertisement placed by a license holder must include a designation such as "agent" or "broker" or a trade association name that serves clearly to identify the advertiser as a real estate agent.

A broker or salesperson may not place an advertisement that in any way:

- implies that a salesperson is the person responsible for the operation of a brokerage; or
- causes a member of the public to believe that a person not authorized to conduct real estate brokerage is personally engaged in real estate brokerage.

A real estate license holder placing an ad online must include on each page on which the license holder's advertisement appears the identification of the broker or brokerage with whom the license holder is affiliated and the completed Information About Brokerage Services (IABS) form, which identifies for consumers the types of brokerages and the aspects of each.

A real estate license holder placing an ad by using an electronic communication, including but not limited to email and email discussion groups, text messages, and social networking websites, must include in the communication and in any attachment that is an ad the identification of the broker or brokerage and the completed IABS.

An advertisement containing an offer of a rebate must disclose that payment of the rebate is subject to the consent of the party the license holder represents in the transaction.

Frequency refers to the number of ad exposures and the amount of time between exposures.

Print advertising is running an ad in any print medium.

Newspapers sell themselves to readers by printing interesting and newsworthy stories.

International newspapers are newspapers from other countries or that reach global markets.

National newspapers reach throughout the entire nation.

Local newspapers typically reach a local area or region.

Community newspapers are distributed to a limited area, usually a small community or neighborhood.

Actual special-interest magazines are different from newspapers because issues come out less frequently and the content focuses only a few key topics.

Real estate magazines are dedicated solely to advertising currently active properties for sale.

Car signs feature the real estate company name and/or logo on magnetic signs that are placed on car door panels or the back of the car.

A name tag is usually plastic or vinyl and has the license holder's name across it with a note indicating that the license holder is in real estate.

Public relations encompasses all aspects of letting the public know the brokerage is in the real estate industry.

Home improvement shows feature the latest in amenities for the home.

The broker should tell everyone that he/she is a real estate broker through:

- local Association of REALTORS® meetings
- networking groups
- spheres of influence
- referral networks

Affiliates are people who do business related to the real estate industry but outside of sales and include:

- inspectors
- title companies
- mortgage companies
- appraisers
- structural engineers

Community service is working with worthy causes for the benefit of all.

Indoor regional malls offer small kiosks (i.e., booths) that the brokerage can rent to provide real estate services to passers by.

Closing gifts are things license holders give to their clients at the closing of the transaction.

Open houses attract people interested in buying in that particular area.

A broker's open house is marketing a property and the brokerage to other professional real estate salespersons.

Career apparel simply means that the clothes a person wears have identification indicating that the wearer is in the real estate industry and proud of it.

The broker should be very cautious about the company's image.

A pocket listing is when the listing agent does not openly market the property in an effort to find the buyer and get both sides of the commission.

CHAPTER QUESTIONS

1. What is the overall concept of offering a property for sale to the general public?
   A. marketing
   B. sales
   C. listing
   D. offer to sell

2. What is the brokerage firm's overall marketing direction?
   A. marketing direction
   B. marketing strategy
   C. marketing position
   D. marketing fundamentals

3. What type of advertising is used primarily to create public image?
   A. niche advertising
   B. prospect-generating advertising
   C. name recognition advertising
   D. buyer advertising

4. A sign made of a large piece of wood with an upside-down "L" shape and a steel sign panel hanging from the arm is a(n):
   A. stake
   B. post
   C. panel
   D. inverted "L"

5. What are the two types of lockboxes?
   A. electronic and key insert
   B. key insert and touchpad
   C. digital and remote sensor
   D. combination and electronic

6. Every classified ad should carry the reader through four selling steps, which include all of the following except:
   A. attract attention
   B. include price
   C. create desire
   D. call for action

7. What is it called when a listing agent does not openly market a listing in an effort to find the buyer and get both sides of the commission?
   A. marketing
   B. dual agent
   C. pocket listing
   D. exclusive right to sell

8. Which of the following is not considered affiliated with the real estate business but not in sales?
   A. inspectors
   B. title companies
   C. appraisers
   D. all of the answer choices

9. An ad containing an offer of a rebate must disclose that the rebate payment:
   A. requires consent of the party the license holder represents
   B. is subject to TREC approval
   C. must be paid to a disinterested third party.
   D. should be advertised through multimedia channels

10. A trifold letter introducing the brokerage company and telling about its accomplishments is a(n):
    A. introductory email
    B. introductory meeting
    C. company brochure
    D. informational postcard

CHAPTER 9

Management Style and Structure

Management style has to do with the characteristic way someone makes decisions and relates to those who work for him/her. Management structure in a real estate office has to do with the broker's organization of the roles and responsibilities in the brokerage. Management is getting the best out of those around the manager. Some believe that the best way to achieve success as a manager is to yell, scream, and threaten all those around. Others believe that the best managers do not interfere with their sponsored license holders and just let the license holders work (or not work) as they please. There is plenty of ground between these extremes, and exploring various management styles and structures is the basis of this chapter.

Scope of Activities and Authorization

The Texas Real Estate Commission (TREC) has established rules defining the scope of activities that real estate brokers and salespersons are permitted to perform.

> (a) *A broker is required to notify a sponsored salesperson in writing of the scope of the salesperson's authorized activities under the Act. Unless such scope is limited or revoked in writing, a broker is responsible for the authorized acts of the broker's salespersons, but the broker is not required to supervise the salespersons directly. If a broker permits a sponsored salesperson to conduct activities beyond the scope explicitly authorized by the broker, those are acts for which the broker is responsible. [...]*
>
> (i) *A broker shall maintain, on a current basis, written policies and procedures to ensure that each sponsored salesperson is advised of the scope of the salesperson's authorized activities subject to the Act and is competent to conduct such activities. (TREC Rule §535.2)*

Real estate industry terms are explained in the Texas Real Estate License Act (TRELA). TRELA §1101.002 defines the following:

Person: *individual, partnership, corporation, or other legal entity*

Real estate: *any interest in real property, including a leasehold, located inside or outside Texas*

Sales agent: *a person who is associated with a licensed broker for the purpose of performing real estate brokerage*

Real estate broker: *a person who, for another person and for valuable consideration:*

- *sells, exchanges, purchases, or leases real estate*
- *offers to sell, exchange, purchase, or lease real estate*
- *negotiates or attempts to negotiate the listing, sale, exchange, purchase, or lease of real estate*
- *lists or offers, attempts, or agrees to list real estate for sale, lease, or exchange*
- *auctions or offers, attempts or agrees to auction real estate*
- *deals in options on real estate, including buying, selling, or offering to buy or sell options on real estate*
- *aids, offers, or attempts to aid in locating or obtaining real estate for purchase or lease*
- *procures or assists in procuring a prospect to effect the sale, exchange, or lease of real estate*
- *controls the acceptance or deposit of rent from a resident of a single-family residential real property unit*
- *provides a written analysis, opinion, or conclusion relating to the estimated price of real property if the analysis, opinion, or conclusion is:*
  - *not referred to as an appraisal*
  - *provided in the ordinary course of the person's business*
  - *related to the actual or potential management, acquisition, disposition, or encumbrance of an interest in real property*

[The term "real estate broker"] also includes a person who is employed by or for an owner of real estate to sell any portion of the real estate or is engaged in the business of charging an advance fee or contracting to collect a fee under a contract that requires the person primarily to promote the sale of real estate by:
- *listing the real estate in a publication primarily used for listing real estate*
- *referring information about the real estate to brokers*

A broker is required not only to explicitly tell a sales agent which brokerage activities a sales agent can perform while under the broker's supervision but also to have in place policies and procedures to ensure that the sales agent is competent to conduct any such real estate acts.

TREC may discipline brokers who fail to define the scope of authorized acts or fail to properly train their sales agents before authorizing them to conduct such acts. If an act is performed for the license holder's own account, that action does not fall under the definition of brokerage. However, under certain circumstances TREC may discipline license holders who buy, sell, or lease property for their own account.

Leadership

"Leadership" is a word that is used so frequently that it has many definitions. Leadership means to guide a path to success. Some leaders do this through their charisma. Others do this with their ability to influence the direction of entire companies.

Brokers Need to Lead by Example

Brokers need to do the things that they require of their sponsored license holders to maintain the credibility needed. If brokers require their salespersons to prospect for listings, the brokers should prospect for recruits. If brokers require additional education for their salespersons, the brokers themselves should continue their education. If brokers require their salespersons to dress properly, they must do the same. Too many real estate salespersons believe that if they could only become brokers, their lives would be so much easier. No more problems with sellers. No more late nights babysitting a troublesome transaction. No more pressure to continually prospect. Not so! All these problems increase, not diminish, when a salesperson becomes a designated broker. Everyone is watching the broker—everyone from the staff to the new salesperson—will be watching the broker's every move. Everyone from the real estate commission to the broker's competition will be watching to see if the broker falters.

> CASE IN POINT—A broker was once at a real estate conference and bought a REALTOR® doormat. About a month later the same broker received the same type of doormat in the mail. Obviously, the doormat company made a mistake and sent one even though the broker already had one. The receptionist said, "Great! We need one for the back door!" That broker said, "No, box it up and send it back." Now, in the worldly scheme of things, did that doormat matter? No. But the broker's integrity did. Imagine that later on, that same receptionist felt she was cheated on her salary check. She would not trust that broker because of what she had witnessed, even though it was she who suggested keeping the mat. Everyone is always watching.

Leader or Manager

Many people have used the terms "leader" and "manager" interchangeably, but they are in reality very different. Is the broker a manager or a leader? By learning whether to be more of a leader or more of a manager, the broker will gain the insight and self-confidence that comes with knowing more about himself/herself. The result is greater impact and effectiveness when dealing with others and running the brokerage business.

The Differences Between Managers and Leaders

There are some general differences between a manager and a leader. A manager will look at business differently than a leader. A manager is most effective in certain business systems and situations, and a leader is better in others. A broker must figure out which is best suited for the brokerage company.

Managers—Emphasizing rationality and control, managers are problem solvers by nature. They focus on goals, handling resources, management structures, and people. They are diligent in getting their job done. They are tough-minded, hardworking, smart, and tolerant. Managers are good at following the direction of a leader and are excellent in a real estate corporate environment. Managers need to be held accountable by someone of higher authority.

Managers understand goals but would rather just get done what they are told. Managers are therefore deeply tied to their organization's culture and tend to be reactive because they focus on current information. They accomplish the goals the company sets, but rarely do they exceed those goals.

Leaders—Perceived as brilliant, leaders achieve control of themselves before they try to control others. They can visualize a purpose and generate value in work. They are imaginative, passionate, and nonconforming and are risk takers. Leaders do not want to be micromanaged. They are self-starters. They lead by example and tend to work long hours.

Leaders tend to be active because they envision and promote their ideas instead of reacting to current situations. Leaders shape ideas instead of responding to them. They have a personal orientation toward goals and provide a vision that alters the way people think about what is desirable, possible, and necessary. Once they achieve the goals they have set, they are quick to expand those goals to new levels. Accomplishing their goals is extremely important to true leaders.

Differences in Conceptions of Work

Managers—Viewing work as a process, managers are good at reaching compromises and mediating conflicts between opposing values and perspectives. Managers enjoy practical, mundane work because of a strong survival instinct that makes them risk averse. They will do what is expected of them but are not that interested in doing more. They want the real estate office to run smoothly and are good at delegating.

Leaders—Leaders develop new approaches to long-standing problems and open issues to new options. First, they use their vision to excite people, and only then do they develop choices that give those images substance. They focus people on shared ideals and raise their expectations of the possibilities. Leaders work from high-risk positions because of a strong dislike of mundane work. They are frustrated with others who will not work all the time. They believe that only they can do the job well, and because of that they tend to be poor at delegating.

Relationships with Others

Managers—Preferring to work with others, managers report that solitary activity makes them anxious. Managers are typically collaborative and maintain a low level of emotional involvement in relationships. Managers relate to people according to the role they play in a sequence of events or in a decision-making process. Managers focus on how things get done. They maintain controlled, rational, and equitable structures and may be viewed by others as inscrutable, detached, and manipulative.

Leaders—Maintaining an inner perceptiveness that they can use in their relationships with others, leaders relate to people in an intuitive, empathetic way. Leaders focus on what events and decisions mean to participants. They create situations where human relationships may be turbulent and intense.

Differences in Self-Image

Managers—Managers report that their adjustments to life have been straightforward and that their lives have been more or less peaceful. They tend to have a sense of self as a guide to conduct an attitude derived from a feeling of being at home and in harmony with their environment. Managers see themselves as regulators of an existing order of affairs with which they personally identify and from which they gain rewards. They report that their role harmonizes with their ideals of responsibility and duty. Managers perpetuate and strengthen existing institutions and display a life-development process that focuses on socialization. This socialization process prepares them to guide the real estate office and to maintain the existing balance of social relations.

Leaders—Leaders do not take things for granted and are not satisfied with the status quo. Leaders may work in organizations, but they never belong to them. Leaders report that their sense of self is independent of work roles, memberships, or other indicators of social identity. They seek opportunities for change (i.e., technological, political, or ideological) and support it; find their purpose is to profoundly alter human, economic, and political relationships; and display a life-development process that focuses on personal mastery and impels them to strive for psychological and social change.

Development of Leadership

Managers and leaders are very different. It is important to remember that there are definite strengths and weaknesses that characterize both types of individuals. Managers are very good at maintaining the status quo and adding stability and order to the brokerage culture. However, they may not be as good at instigating change and envisioning the future.

Leaders are adept at stirring people's emotions, raising their expectations, and taking them in new directions, both good and bad. However, like artists and other gifted people, leaders often have a tendency toward self-absorption and preoccupation.

Throughout history, it has been shown again and again that leaders have needed strong one-to-one relationships with teachers and/or mentors whose strengths lie in cultivating talent to enable individuals to reach their full potential. If a license holder thinks he/she is a leader at heart, that person needs to find a teacher/mentor whom the license holder admires and connects with, someone who can help the license holder develop natural skills, talents, and interests.

Managing People

The TREC requirement for a designated broker to be in good standing is specified in TREC Rule §535.53 (b) DESIGNATED BROKER as follows:

1. *A real estate business entity must designate an individual holding an active Texas real estate broker license in good standing with the Commission to act for the entity.*
2. *An individual licensed broker is not in good standing with the Commission if:*
   (a) the broker's license is revoked or suspended
   (b) a business entity licensed by the Commission while the broker was the designated broker for that business entity had its license revoked or suspended in the past two years
   (c) the broker has any unpaid monetary obligations to the Commission
   (d) a business entity licensed by the Commission has any unpaid monetary obligations to the Commission that were incurred while the broker was the designated broker for the entity

A manager is usually someone other than the designated broker, broker of record, or owner in larger brokerages. In multi-office systems, a manager is hired to manage an office for the owner. Hiring of the manager is critical.

Most people feel that a manager should not compete with his/her sponsored license holders. Competing involves listing and selling real estate along with managing an office. Competition from a manager can cause a conflict of interest. If a broker/owner does not want managers competing, that broker/owner will have to pay the managers a great deal of money so they can manage and not have to worry about personal sales to survive. Other broker/owners offer managers a small salary and then bonuses when the office is in the black. Some broker/owners cannot afford to offer a full salary, so they opt instead for a combination of salary plus commissions. The commission-split is highly favorable to managers, but it nonetheless distracts from managerial duties. However, it does keep the manager active and therefore up-to-date on the current market.

Delegated Licensed Supervisor
TREC Rule §535.2 states:

(e) A broker may delegate to another license holder the responsibility to assist in administering compliance with the Act and Rules, but the broker may not relinquish overall responsibility for the supervision of license holders sponsored by the broker. Any such delegation must be in writing. A broker shall provide the name of each delegated supervisor to the commission on a form or through the online process approved by the Commission within 30 days of any such delegation that has lasted or is anticipated to last more than six months.

Business Entity Requirements

TREC Rules §535.2 states, "When the broker is a business entity, the designated broker is the person responsible for the broker responsibilities under the Texas Real Estate License Act."

The primary benefits of business entities commonly selected by license holders are liability protection of the individual license holder and pass-through tax status (i.e., no double taxation). The selection of the appropriate entity for a particular license holder should be made after careful consideration and consultation with legal and accounting advisors.

If a license holder establishes a business entity, to be paid commissions the entity must be licensed.

The legal entity must designate an individual broker who will be responsible for the actions of the licensed business entity. The designated broker must be:

- an officer of the corporation
- a manager of the limited liability company
- a general partner of the partnership

If the designated broker owns less than 10% of the business entity, the business entity must obtain and maintain E&O insurance of at least $1 million.

Assumed Name A business entity may have one legal name and do business under another assumed name. If a business entity elects to conduct business under an assumed name, the assumed name should be filed with the secretary of state and the local county clerk. Rules require license holders using an assumed name to notify TREC in writing within 30 days of starting to use the assumed name. A license holder may use form TREC DBA-2 "Notice of DBA or Assumed Name for a Broker's License" to notify TREC.

Sources for Managers

Future managers can be culled from currently sponsored license holders or hired from the outside. Here are some ideas on where to look for the next real estate office manager.

Experienced License Holders

Employing experienced currently sponsored license holders from the brokerage is the easiest way to fill a manager's position. The designated broker has seen these salespersons handle real estate transactions and potentially difficult situations, and the broker has determined that they are ready for management. These manager recruits are not necessarily the top producers.

Some real estate companies believe it is best to promote the top producer of an office to the manager of that office when a management position opens up, but doing this can create a lot of problems for the office. First, the broker has taken the top producer out of production, and so a drop in the office's overall production is bound to follow. Second, the broker has taken a salesperson with no management experience and promoted him/her to a position for which the license holder is also untrained. In one real estate office, the manager quit and the top producer was promoted to manager. She had no idea how to manage an office. The office lost the income that she had been bringing in as top producer because she had been taken away from production. Within a few months, the office doors closed, and the manager went to another real estate company and got back into production. The end result was the collapse of a viable real estate company and the destruction of a potentially great career (the top producer's productivity never returned to the level she enjoyed before the promotion). The theory behind promoting top producers is understandable because the company wants to reward its producers, but is being a manager truly a reward?

This problem can be resolved if the broker has a Management Development Program (MDP) for sponsored license holders who want to manage. The program will allow them can find out if they enjoy and are good at management without their making the commitment and the brokerage suffering a loss of production. The MDP will be discussed in detail next.

Competitors

A broker should pay attention to up-and-coming real estate license holders from other real estate offices. These salespersons may make good candidates for the brokerage's MDP. The program is designed to train individuals to become managers of a real estate office. You will find that the MDP is a great way to eliminate managers. Most real estate license holders think about managing or owning a real estate office themselves. One broker interviewed all his salespersons about this topic, and over 60% said they had thought about managing/owning a brokerage. A broker does not want to tell them, "No, you would make a terrible manager!" even if it is true, because they may get angry and go to the competitor. The broker's new script is, "Great, you can start in the Management Development Program immediately." Once in the program, the sponsored license holders figure out on their own that they are not cut out to be managers and fade back into real estate sales. No harm, no foul. If the interviewee is a salesperson from one of the brokerage's competitors and he/she does not work out in the MDP, the brokerage still has a new salesperson for production.

Compatible Businesses

Other businesses, such as banks, retail stores, insurance agencies, and especially the sales professions, make great places to look for management recruits. These people already have some management experience; however, they lack real estate experience. Each of these management candidates must go through MDP training to learn about real estate. It is difficult to believe that anyone outside the real estate industry would have the respect of their sales agents without first knowing about the real estate business from the position of a productive real estate salesperson.

Management Students

Most areas have a local college or university. If these educational facilities offer management degrees, brokers can look to them to provide management candidates. Colleges and universities want to place their students into fields that relate to their course objectives, and they usually have career days during which businesses that are recruiting put up information booths for students. Generally, sales companies are not permitted to attend. But brokers are not there to hire sales agents, at least not ostensibly; they are there to recruit for the MDP. Yet to be eligible for the MDP, one must have a real estate license and currently be selling real estate for a career. Interested students must therefore obtain a real estate license and join one of the brokerage offices. Once students begin selling, they can enter the program.

Manager Development Program

This model is an overview of the MDP levels of instruction. These levels can be modified according to a broker's wants and needs.

Tier 1—Manager Candidate

- monthly performance reviews with branch manager
- main objective to recruit new license holders
- assist in training newly sponsored license holders
- compensation:
  - full-time real estate salesperson
  - recruiting bonus for each new sponsored recruit (paid out over the first three closings of the recruit)

Tier 1—Manager Candidate—Office Recruiter and Training Coordinator

At the Tier 1 stage in the MDP, the management candidate will learn the basics of managing a real estate office. Very little time will be spent learning the back-office workings; instead, most of the time will be spent on learning how to recruit new license holders to the office. The second most important thing the manager candidate will learn is how to retain the license holders already in the office.

Here are the limited duties of the Tier 1 manager candidate:

- *continue to produce real estate sales.* Manager candidate must continue to produce real estate sales to survive. Few trainees can make a living only on recruiting bonuses. The more experience in the

actual practice of real estate sales, the better real estate managers they will be.
- *recruit real estate license holders.* The manager candidate starts out learning about recruiting because it is the most important factor in being a successful real estate branch manager. Nothing else comes close. If a branch manager cannot recruit, the manager cannot survive as a manager—it is as simple as that. Some managers and brokers hire recruiters to help in this endeavor. Perhaps that will work, but more often than not the manager must get involved in recruiting for the process to work effectively. If the manager does not recruit—and recruiting is all about relationship building—how can the manager establish a relationship with the person who will be making the brokerage money in the future? It is here the designated broker will find that most manager candidates will fall out because they had not realized that a branch manager actually has to work as a manager. Because of the fear of rejection, most individuals are poor recruiters.
- *assist in retention of sponsored license holders by assisting in training.* The second important training aspect of Tier 1 focuses on retention of sponsored license holders. The best way to retain a sponsored license holder is to make sure that he/she has the proper training for real estate success. Some people fear getting up in front of others and speaking. This is important information for the designated broker to know because public speaking is an integral part of managing. A salesperson can avoid public speaking in real estate sales but not in management. The branch manager is expected to lead training classes, hold sales meetings, and speak in front of hundreds if asked.

The branch manager of a real estate office should be training salespersons almost all the time. He/she should conduct just-in-time training when a salesperson needs a boost. Branch managers should also conduct weekly new-salesperson training, and they should be able to "field" train on a real listing appointment. These are just a few training opportunities.

Any training conducted by the manager candidate must be reviewed and approved by the acting branch manager. Some people are born trainers, but other people need training to become good at training, and some will never improve. The MDP provides a good way to weed out those who cannot or will not train.

Compensation

The manager candidate deserves some kind of additional bonus for recruiting. Generally, the bonus is based on the recruit's production. Once the recruit closes a transaction and the company is paid, the manager candidate might receive a set amount of cash. For example, the manager candidate may receive cash bonuses for the first three closings and then nothing more. The manager candidate is an independent contractor during his/her entire time as a Tier 1 management candidate. The bonuses give the manager candidate an incentive to recruit as many salespersons as possible.

Monthly Performance Reviews with the Branch Manager or the Designated Broker

As long as a manager candidate remains in the MDP, he/she should undergo a monthly performance review from the current branch manager or the designated broker. This performance review could be short or long, depending on whether additional training for the manager candidate is needed. The performance review is also the time to weed out the manager candidates who have little or no potential to make a great real estate branch manager. And finally, the performance review is the time to promote the best manager candidates to office manager trainees if a position is available for that promotion.

Tier 2—Manager Trainee

- monthly performance reviews with branch manager
- continued recruiting (paid flat fee per hired recruit)
- review all contracts (buyer rep, listing, purchase, lease, etc.)

- attend management meetings (if the company has management meetings)
- learn office systems (accounting, payroll, etc.)
- specific sponsored license holder coaching with branch manager supervision and guidance
- assist branch manager with inner-office management tasks
- attend interviews with potential recruits
- compensation:
  - part-time real estate salesperson
  - recruiting bonus for each new sponsored recruit (paid out over the first three closings of the recruit)
  - small management bonus (not enough to survive but enough to make up for the time spent managing)

Tier 2—Manager Trainee—Additional Duties

The office manager trainee must continue to perform the duties assigned during Tier 1 as well as perform these additional duties:

- *recruit real estate license holders.* Recruiting is the most important criterion of a great manager. The manager trainees must continue to recruit real estate licensees to prove that they have the ability to succeed as a branch manager. A manager who cannot recruit will have to be replaced.
- *retain sponsored license holders.* The second important criteria defining a great manager is retention of sponsored license holders. Retention means:
  - handholding new sponsored license holders by making sure that they know what they should be doing every day
  - supporting "middle" sponsored license holders—those who produce in the middle of the pack but are not new so that they require handholding (Middle producers need to know the manager cares for and notices them.)
  - having one-on-one time with top producers (Generally, this is time to expand the top producers' business, and no one else but the manager will suffice for this task.)

If a manager cannot retain the sponsored license holders, the manager will have to be replaced.

- *review contracts.* The office manager trainee will begin to review purchase agreements and employment contracts completed by the sponsored license holders to discover any mistakes in the contracts and to correct them, through licensee training, before any damage

can be done. This is a very important responsibility, and the person assigned to complete the task must be very trustworthy. The manager of record (i.e., designated broker) must be sure the candidate has been trained well.
- *attend management meetings.* The manager trainee should attend company management meetings, conference calls, or training sessions. These may vary by the size of the organization. If the company has only two offices and the training is for the manager of the other office, most likely no management meetings will be held. If the training is for the manager of a multi-office company, then management meetings are much more likely. The company may be part of a real estate franchise or group of real estate brokers in an area. These people meet frequently, and the manager trainee should attend their meetings. In addition, real estate management training is sometimes offered at local colleges or by nationally recognized speakers, and in such cases the manager trainee should attend this specialized training.
- *learn to manage office systems.* The office manager trainee should begin learning office systems and how to manage them effectively. These tasks include accounting, billing, collecting, recordkeeping, charting, reporting, inventory management, advertising, public relations, and all the other office systems that are relevant to the responsibilities that managers will have. If the office has departments and sophisticated systems, the manager trainee does not need to perform the tasks but should understand how they work and how to manage them in case of turmoil.
- *assist current manager with management tasks.* The time will come to let the manager trainee walk in the shoes of a real branch manager. The latter should be sure that the manager trainee is ready for his/her new role. A branch manager or a designated broker should NEVER take advantage of manager trainees to get them to do all the branch manager's dirty work. The manager trainee should be assisting with valuable and important work.
- *attend interviews with potential recruits.* The manager trainee should attend as many interviews with potential recruits as possible. This experience will be highly valuable later when the manager trainee will be handling these interviews himself/herself. The manager trainee should not be involved in the interview but should watch and take notes on the interaction. In addition, the manager trainee should be involved in the planning and execution of any recruiting events, such as career nights.

Compensation

Typically, the compensation for a manager trainee comprises the recruiting bonuses and a small monthly bonus for the additionally performed services. Because the services are recompensed as a bonus, the broker may be able to retain the manager trainees as independent contractors (in this instance, he/she would need to consult an employment attorney). The designated broker may want to begin to pay these manager trainees a little better and make theirs a salaried position. If they are good, they are worth it. If they are not good, the designated broker should eliminate them from the program. A designated broker who does not pay the trainees well invites the competition to pay them better.

Monthly Performance Reviews with Branch Manager or Designated Broker

The monthly performance reviews will continue throughout the MDP training. The performance review ends with termination from the program, a continuation at the manager trainee tier, or promotion to assistant manager. Promotions can be made only if a position is open.

Tier 3—Assistant Manager

Duties added to Tiers 1 and 2:

- oversee office administrative staff
- oversee office physical plant
- assist branch manager in transaction issues
- assist branch manager where needed
- compensation:
  - occasional real estate transactions performed (referral generated)
  - recruiting bonus for each new sponsored recruit (paid out over the first three closings of the recruit)
  - large management bonus (enough to survive but not enough to only manage)
  - employee benefits

NOTE: An assistant manager does not always move up to branch manager. Also, the person should never manage an office where he/she was assistant manager.

Tier 3—Assistant Manager—Additional Duties

The assistant manager must continue to perform the duties assigned during Tier 2 as well as perform these additional duties:

- *recruit real estate license holders.* The assistant manager must continue recruiting. Recruiting is never-ending. If a manager believes he/she has recruited enough, that same manager will be out of business in a short period of time. Recruiting is the lifeblood of a brokerage and must be worked on every day.
- *retain sponsored license holders.* The assistant manager must continue to retain sponsored license holders. There is nothing less productive than to recruit license holders and then see them switch to a competing real estate office within a year. A manager who believes his/her license holders are so happy that they will never leave will be lonely soon after that thought. If a manager's license holders are not being recruited by competing brokerages, that may be because the license holders are not worth recruiting.
- *manage office administrative staff.* The assistant manager now begins the real tasks of managing: overseeing office administrative staff and managing their performance. The assistant manager should be familiar with the duties of the staff based on his/her experience as a manager trainee. The assistant manager does not hire or fire staff but should be fully involved in the decision-making process.
- *manage the office appearance.* The assistant manager should take over the task of making sure the office appearance meets the public's expectations. This includes everything from having enough office supplies on hand to having the lawn trimmed and the parking lot swept. The assistant manager should make the rounds every few hours to check the office appearance and should pay close attention to sponsored license holder' desks, conference rooms, breakrooms, and bathrooms.
- *conduct potential recruit interviews.* During the manager trainee experience, the assistant manager should have learned to conduct an interview with a potential recruit and to get that recruit to commit to working with the brokerage. The branch manager should monitor these interviews closely because if the assistant manager does a poor job, the brokerage could lose a good recruit.
- *assist branch manager in transaction issues.* The assistant manager should be present during discussions with sponsored license holders on transaction issues. These discussions can become heated, and the assistant manager should learn how to handle these tense situations. It is important for the assistant manager not to get involved but to be an observer. The assistant manager can handle less difficult tasks with the branch manager's guidance and direction.

Compensation

At this point in MDP training, it may become necessary to have all assistant managers on a salary. Their production in real estate sales has probably dropped off because of all their duties as assistant manager are taking up a majority of their time.

Monthly Performance Reviews with Branch Manager or the Designated Broker

The monthly performance reviews will continue throughout MDP training. The performance review ends with termination from the program, continuation of the assistant manager stage, or promotion to branch manager. A promotion can be made only if a position is open, and promotions are never made to an office where the candidate has served as assistant manager.

Tier 4—Branch Manager

Duties added to Tiers 1, 2, and 3:

- provide production counseling
- recruit staff and license holders
- upgrade staff and sponsored license holders
- retain staff and sponsored license holders
- terminate staff and sponsored license holders
- engage in coaching
- maintain office direction
- manage net profit of the specific real estate office

Compensation

The Tier 4 branch manager receives a base salary that is enough for the branch manager to live on comfortably. In addition, the branch manager receives an incentive compensation based on net profit production; this income is paid monthly. *(This incentive-type compensation is called an "override.")*

Tier 4—Branch Manager—Additional Duties

The branch manager must continue to perform the duties assigned during Tier 3 (except that branch managers are not expected to conduct real estate sales) as well as perform these additional duties:

- *recruit real estate license holders.* Recruiting is still the most important aspect of being a great manager. The biggest mistake a branch manager can make is to delegate recruiting. The most effective recruiting comes directly from the branch manager.
- *retain sponsored license holders.* Retention of sponsored license holders who are currently working with the branch manager's brokerage office is the second most important responsibility of any manager. Most designated brokers want a branch manager who is a great recruiter of license holders and a great retainer of those license holders who are already sponsored. These go-getter branch managers are worth their weight in gold. There are many factors to retention, but the main one is caring. Most sponsored license holders leave one real estate office for another because of management, not because of money. The license holders who feel management does not care about their situation leave. Branch managers should care to have the proper office structure, training, and so forth, to aid in real estate sales. They should also monitor the activities of competing real estate companies to be sure they are not providing something the branch's sponsored license holders may want badly enough to leave.
- *engage in coaching.* The branch manager becomes a coach to experienced salespersons. These salespersons tend not to need typical training because they are already experienced in real estate sales. What they need in a coach is someone to make them accountable for their goals and to help them with unique problems at work and in their personal lives.
- *hire, fire, and upgrade staff and sponsored license holders.* The branch manager is typically responsible for hiring and firing of staff members and sponsored license holders in the specific branch office. The hiring is easy; the firing is not. Many nonproductive staff members are kept around simply because the branch manager did not have the fortitude to terminate them. These staff members become an infection, and the production of the entire staff team drops.

CASE IN POINT—A broker bought an office that had five staff members. The broker and all the staff members had a "get acquainted" meeting in which the broker fired the first two individuals she talked with (both were deemed nonproductive). The next person in line said, "Well, if you fire them, then I will quit!" The broker said, "DONE!" The broker looked at the other two staff members still left and said, "How about you two?" Both said they wanted to stay. The broker must have control. If a broker lets the staff manipulate the broker, the broker loses control. The broker should be the last person out that office door (figuratively), and the broker should rather lock it for good than lose control. To finish that story, the production of the two remaining staff members skyrocketed, and they handled the workload of all five of the previous staff, saving the company thousands of dollars.

A good branch manager is never satisfied with the talent in the office but is constantly on the lookout for the next superstar salesperson or assistant manager. The branch manager is also looking to eliminate any "dead wood" in the office—those who make themselves look good through the work of others but do not really produce anything themselves. Only the branch manager should terminate staff or salespersons.

- *maintain office direction.* The branch manager is also responsible for the office direction, philosophy, and culture. If the office is part of a larger company, the branch manager must be sure that his/her office direction, philosophy, and culture are aligned with the main brokerage's direction, philosophy, and culture. However, a branch manager has a great deal of influence on his/her specific office. Branch managers who believe in providing the best in service will tend to hire the same types of salespersons. Branch managers who believe in having fun while getting the business done, for example, will tend to hire those salespersons who like having fun while getting work accomplished.
- *manage net profit of the specific real estate office.* The branch manager needs to know all the financial numbers of his/her specific office. The branch manager also needs to know how the numbers compare to other specific offices as well as to the financial numbers for the entire company. These numbers will tell the branch manager how successfully his/her specific office is performing. The branch manager must pay close attention to income and expenses because these are the key factors in net profit.
- *participate in community activities.* The branch manager is the face of the specific brokerage office. As such, the branch manager needs to be involved in the community and at the local Association of

REALTORS®. The branch manager should participate in networking groups, social clubs, and any number of other community-involved activities. In short, the branch manager needs to see and be seen. Branch managers should spend their time in the following areas:

- 25% of the week in recruiting: prospecting, interviewing, hiring
- 25% of the week in retention: production counseling and training
- 25% of the week in office management tasks: charts, financials, management meetings, etc.
- 25% of the week in community activities: community groups, boards, broker council, etc.
- 75% of each day in their office and available

Compensation

All branch managers are full salary with company benefits. Branch managers should not be in production. If someone he/she knows wants to buy or sell real estate, the branch manager should refer that transaction to a sponsored license holder. The branch manager should receive an override for any excess in net profit the managed office produces.

Monthly Performance Reviews with the Branch Designated Broker/Owner

The monthly performance reviews will continue, but now they will be with the designated broker or the owner (of course, these may be the same person). The performance review ends with termination or continuation of the branch manager position.

Management Styles

There are many approaches to or styles of management; the broker needs to choose the best fit between his/her goals and the sponsored license holder's goals. The broker can read up on the numerous techniques, but here are a select few. These techniques are listed in no particular order of importance.

- The Commander
- The Peacemaker
- The Collaborator
- The Controller

Management Style and Structure

The Commander

The Commander approach to management believes it is "my way or the highway." These brokers will fire any sponsored license holder who gets just a smidgen out of line. The office meetings of Commanders are strictly authoritarian. Their training style is directive. Commanders tend to be competitive and not as sociable as any other of the management types, preferring to get right to the point.

Advantages

The staff and license holders of Commanders know what to expect. The license holders work just as the Commander broker expects, and the license holder gets no flack. As long as the broker does not run everyone off, the office will tend to get things done and make a profit. The office expenses will be accurate. There will be no waste. Smart brokers who understand and use this style will hire assistant managers to counterbalance their actions.

> CASE IN POINT—The Commander broker would be sure everyone was selling real estate, and if not, he would be quick to address the issue. The assistant manager would be all bubbly and make everyone feel happy. Together they appealed to almost all their salespersons. When the sponsored license holders needed to get something done or a decision made, they would go to the Commander broker and the decision was made. The Commander broker never even thought to consult with the assistant manager. When the license holders needed a break from the hectic pace of real estate or a break from the Commander broker, they would turn to the assistant manager. No one was told to do so; the license holder just knew. Either one of these managers working alone would not have been as effective as they are together.

Disadvantages

Commanders tend to wear out their salespersons. Most people did not get into this business to be told what to do. Funny thing though, without being told what to do, the average real estate salesperson will not do much or be as productive as when given strict direction. Real estate salespersons need some guidance, but when that guidance is relentless, it is too much pressure. In one instance all the sponsored license holders told the owner of the company that if the Commander broker was not replaced, there would be a mass walkout. Consequently, the owner let the Commander broker go. Funny thing again, production dropped but the morale of the office went up and eventually the production went up also. Without some type of temperance, as shown in the Case in Point, these brokers will tend to run salespersons away.

The Peacemaker

The Peacemaker is the broker who wants to make everyone happy. This broker does not like conflict and will avoid it at all costs. Peacemakers typically hire other Peacemakers as sponsored license holders to make the culture beneficial to all involved. Peacemakers may be the most sociable of all types of managers and sometimes may need help to stay on task.

Advantages

Everybody loves the Peacemaker. The office atmosphere is calm and serene. The salespersons tend to stay with this company for many years. The office maintains its position in the market, and its clients are loyal.

> CASE IN POINT—One Peacemaker broker owns her brokerage in a small Texas town. She arrives in the office early and has the coffee made for those who show up after. She always has a kind word to say to all she comes in contact. Her sponsored license holders love her and would never leave. Some have been with her for decades. The Peacemaker's office will never set any production records, but everybody is okay with that. The clients who buy and sell real estate with the brokerage have also been clients for decades. The parents bought homes, and now the kids are buying homes. These people would never consider dealing with any other brokerage.

Disadvantages

One bad apple hired can spoil the whole bunch. If the broker hires someone who looks pleasant and calm but ends up being a tyrant, the Peacemaker broker will have a hard time deciding whether to fire the tyrant. Also, this office tends not to live up its potential because the Peacemaker broker does not drive the organization to perform better. The office listed in the preceding Case in Point is not and will not ever be a highly productive office, and everyone there is okay with that. The actual office location is in an area that is experiencing extreme growth, but the salespersons are not interested in aggressively going after new business. The potential profit that brokerage could experience with a better manager would be astronomical.

The Collaborator

The Collaborator wants everyone's opinion before making a decision. Collaborators differ from the Peacemakers in that they will not back down from confrontation but will want to have agreement on major decisions. These brokers will organize office committees on any number of projects. All the office salespersons will vote on any decision to benefit the office; everything must be agreed to. Things such as purchasing new computers to advertising to selecting a brand of coffee all require discussion and a vote. Generally, Collaborators are sociable, enthusiastic, and visionary. Because Collaborators often neglect the details, they need to hire support staff who can fill in where they themselves are weak. Similarly, brokers looking to hire staff members can look for people with complementary behavioral styles. The Commander gives orders, but the Collaborator gives direction. The Collaborator makes every effort to find a place for everyone and then guide everyone's career.

Advantages

The salespersons feel that they have input on the decision-making process. This system works well for the producers who also want a voice in how the office is run. Frequently, sponsored license holders complain that they left the corporate world to have more of a say in their career. With Collaborator brokers, these license holders have that voice.

Disadvantages

No leadership. The salespersons begin to ignore the broker because the broker leads by committee. Salespersons will begin to form alliances and vote together in blocks to get their position voted for, perhaps to the detriment of the office in general.

> CASE IN POINT—In a Colleyville, Texas, real estate office, the Collaborative broker made all the decisions by votes from the sponsored license holders. The license holders were charged a desk fee to be part of this office. The office was the largest and highest-producing office in the state. Within two years, however, the company was bankrupt. Why? Because different salespersons want different things. One group of license holders was worried about the rising monthly desk fee. Others were concerned about more services provided by the company. Votes went the way of services. The sponsored license holders would form alliances and vote in another receptionist, remodeling of the entryway, free bottled water, five new state-of-the-art computers, and a top-of-the-line, high-speed, high-capacity printer. Each service or capital expense increased the desk fee until only a few could afford the costs and the company folded. The lesson: The leader MUST make the ultimate decisions, or the company is led by alliances only out for their own good.

The Controller

The Controller broker must know and control all aspects of the brokerage company. Controllers differ from Commanders in that they do not demand respect but must have their hands in all operations. A controller is a perfectionist and expects others to be the same. These are detail people, and they focus on objectives. Controllers are cerebral and do well at structured tasks, making them good at back-office functions such as accounting and technology support. They may not make the strongest brokers/managers, but they could be outstanding if they learned to be more assertive and make decisions more quickly. They may not always mix well with Collaborators.

Advantages

The office is run perfectly with every single detail being performed flawlessly. Some salespersons love this system and thrive under it. However, most salespersons in general are less restrictive in nature. This type of company is rarely involved in court cases because all the paperwork is filled out and filed accordingly. The office is highly efficient. Controllers monitor the office supplies and distribute them only by request. They have counters on the copiers, faxes, and telephones to control the costs.

Disadvantages

The Controller has a hard time making money in the real estate business because he/she is so busy with detail work that there is never time to prospect for clients. It is very difficult for Controllers to delegate because no one else can do as good a job as they can, or so they believe. Some Controllers are so restrictive that they read all their salespersons' email and post mail, and they will listen in on conversations in the office. If they were to delegate a project, they would follow every detail and take as much time or more than if they did it themselves. Because Controllers are perfectionists, they believe that nothing is ever correct, and they keep working at perfection well past the point of diminishing returns.

> CASE IN POINT—In a brokerage in Azle, Texas, a Controller broker would monitor and have his secretary monitor every expense to the penny. He had charts to check the number of light bulbs used per month, the sheets of copy paper used per month, and even the average use of toilet paper per month. He would count the ink pens in the front desk, and if one was missing, he would start an investigation until some sponsored license holder just gave him one of theirs to make him stop the witch hunt. This broker lost his brokerage because he was so worried about each cent that he did not see the dollars—the salespersons who produced for the brokerage—walking out his front door.

The best brokers and managers use aspects of each type. This blend or hybrid brings in more of the advantages and fewer of the disadvantages. Salespersons like certain things to be very strict, very controlled, and yet they like some input and direction in a fun an enjoyable real estate office. Sometimes a broker must be all things to all people and still accomplish the brokerage goals—this is called leadership. A broker should be aware of his/her style because this awareness will help the broker understand his/her own weaknesses and strengths.

Management Structure

Management structure in a real estate office has to do with the broker's organization of the roles and responsibilities in the brokerage—how it will operate. The types of organizations include horizontal and vertical management structures. The selection of the management structure is of great importance and should be accomplished through diligent research and consultation.

Horizontal management structure is typically characteristic of small sole-proprietorship brokerages. Vertical management structure is typically characteristic of a large corporation with multiple levels of management.

Horizontal management–structured offices are not sophisticated in their structure. A sole proprietorship may have only the broker working the business and no one else. This setup is the simplest management structure possible. The broker manages only himself/herself and no other license holder. This single-broker-only scenario is one of the most common types of management structures.

LEVEL 1   BROKER

A mom-and-pop shop may add one or two other license holders but no others. In this case, the broker is the leader and no one else is part of the management structure. These mom-and-pop shops may grow to have a multitude of sponsored license holders, but the broker remains the only one on the actual management level. The broker may even add staff such as a secretary or receptionist. These staff positions carry no decision-making ability and are not considered management. This arrangement may look something like this:

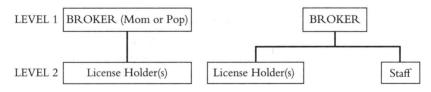

A sole-proprietorship brokerage could be a partnership, in which case there may be two or more persons involved in management. Partnerships are the forming of a company by two or more individuals or entities. These partnerships are usually composed of two real estate associate brokers who believe they can do a better job at real estate brokerage together than where they are currently associated. They talk themselves into opening their own business but want to do so as partners. "Split all the costs and profits!" they say.

There are several types of partnerships that could be formed to operate a real estate company. Tenancy in common is the typical way a partnership is drawn up. Given the intricacies of real estate partnerships, an attorney should draw up all types of partnerships.

Tenancy in Common

Tenancy in common is a way for two or more people to own a real estate brokerage business together. In this arrangement, upon death each can leave his/her interest to the beneficiaries of his/her choosing. Each tenant has a separate share of the business, and these shares do not need to be equal. Each co-owner may deal with his/her interest (share) as he/she pleases. This type of partnership is noted for the ease of transferability of ownership. Anyone who is invited into the partnership can join and leave any time he/she wants. The company's direction is guided by those who own the most shares of the tenancy.

Joint Tenants with Rights of Survivorship

Joint tenants with rights of survivorship is a partnership structure characterized by four unities:

1. Unity of interest—Each joint tenant must have an equal interest, including equality of duration and extent.
2. Unity of title—The interests must arise from the same document.
3. Unity of possession—Each joint tenant must have an equal right to occupy the entire property.
4. Unity of time—The interests of the joint tenants must arise at the same time.

These unities are required for a joint tenancy to be considered valid.

The ownership is vested in a group of individuals. Any single individual cannot claim any separate ownership of the real estate business. The group can collectively dispose of the joint real estate business but only with the entire group's consent. An individual can act on behalf of the group and bind the group to an agreement. Each member has an "undivided" interest in the real estate business. An *undivided interest* means that a division of the business cannot be separated from the rest. Each tenant has rights to the entirety.

The central characteristic of joint tenancy is the right of survivorship. Until the group is reduced to one person, ownership remains in the group. The tenants have no separate ownership of the real estate business and cannot leave any rights in their will. If one of the members dies, the group gains the interest of the deceased. The ownership is still vested in the group. If all the members die, the last remaining member will own the business in severalty, the rights of all others having been severed away.

> CASE IN POINT—A broker opened a real estate office with a real estate–sponsored license holder who had been loyal to the broker for years. She was talented and trustworthy. Her husband, however, was not; furthermore, he was not in the real estate industry and knew nothing about it. The salesperson and the broker formed a joint tenancy because if she died, the broker did not want her husband to be his partner. The broker would have done all the work, and he would have taken half the profits. The problem was, the broker's family would be exposed if the broker died. So, the company paid for "key man" insurance in case of either partner's death. In such a circumstance, the remaining spouse would receive several hundred thousand dollars of insurance—a considerable amount more than the real estate brokerage was worth.

General Partnerships
A *general partnership* is an association of two or more individuals conducting a real estate business. The partnership agreement has very little formality. For the most part, the partners own the business assets together and are personally liable for business debts.

Limited Partnerships
In a limited partnership, one or more *general* partners manage the real estate brokerage business, whereas *limited* partners contribute capital and share in the profits but take no part in running the business. General partners remain personally liable for the partnership's debts, whereas limited partners incur no liability with respect to partnership obligations beyond their capital contributions. The purpose of this form of business is to encourage investors to invest without risking more than the capital they have contributed.

Joint Ventures

Joint ventures are a special type of partnership that exists only as long as the venture lasts. Once the venture is completed, the partnership is dissolved. Quite frequently a builder will form a joint venture to get the capital to build a subdivision of houses. The builder will gather some wealthy investors together and form the joint venture. Once the subdivision is completed and the investors are paid, the venture is dissolved.

Most partnerships in the real estate industry are general partnerships and look like this:

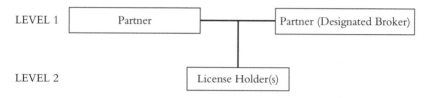

Notice that this is horizontal, but it is only one-level vertical. As brokerages grow, the management structure tends to be more vertical. Suppose that a mom-and-pop shop adds a branch manager and several license holders. The brokerage is now no longer a mom-and-pop shop but has become a medium-sized brokerage and would look like this:

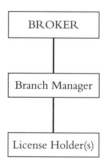

As the real estate brokerage grows, more levels develop. Assistant managers will create a level. A president will create a level. Vice presidents will create a level until the management structure becomes primarily vertical. The dangers of a vertical brokerage are evident. Each level creates costs (e.g., salaries, benefits) without the direct source of income. The second danger of a truly vertical real estate brokerage business is that the upper levels begin to lose touch with their assets—namely, the sponsored license holders.

CHAPTER SUMMARY

Brokers must notify their sponsored salespersons in writing of the scope of the salespersons' TREC-authorized activities.

Real estate: any interest in real property, including a leasehold, located inside or outside Texas

Sales agent: person associated with a licensed broker for the purpose of performing real estate brokerage

Real estate broker: person who, for another person and for valuable consideration:

- sells, exchanges, purchases, or leases real estate
- offers to sell, exchange, purchase, or lease real estate
- negotiates or attempts to negotiate the listing, sale, exchange, purchase, or lease of real estate
- lists or offers, attempts, or agrees to list real estate for sale, lease, or exchange; auctions or offers, attempts or agrees to auction real estate
- deals in options on real estate, including buying, selling, or offering to buy or sell options on real estate
- aids, offers, or attempts to aid in locating or obtaining real estate for purchase or lease
- procures or assists in procuring a prospect to effect the sale, exchange, or lease of real estate
- controls the acceptance or deposit of rent from a resident of a single-family residential unit
- provides a written analysis, opinion, or conclusion relating to the estimated price of real property if the analysis, opinion, or conclusion is:
  - not referred to as an appraisal
  - provided in the ordinary course of the person's business
  - related to the actual or potential management, acquisition, disposition, or encumbrance of an interest in real property.

Leadership means to guide a path to success. Brokers need to do the things that they require of their sponsored license holders to maintain credibility. Here is what TREC Rules has to say about it:

A broker may delegate to another license holder the responsibility to assist in administering compliance with the Act and Rules, but the broker may not relinquish overall responsibility for the supervision of license holders sponsored by the broker. Any such delegation must be in writing. A broker shall provide the name of each delegated supervisor to the commission on a form or through the online process approved by the Commission within 30 days of any such delegation that has lasted or is anticipated to last more than six months.

A real estate business entity must designate an individual holding an active Texas real estate broker license in good standing with the Commission to act for it.

When the broker is a business entity, the designated broker is the person responsible for the broker responsibilities under the Texas Real Estate License Act (TRELA).

The primary benefits of business entities commonly selected by license holders are liability protection of the individual license holder and pass-through tax status (i.e., no double taxation). The selection of the appropriate entity for a particular license holder should be made after careful consideration and consultation with legal and accounting advisors.

The legal entity must designate an individual broker who will be responsible for the actions of the licensed business entity. The designated broker must be:

- an officer of the corporation
- a manager of the limited liability company
- a general partner of the partnership

If the designated broker owns less that 10% of the business entity, the business entity must obtain and maintain E&O insurance of at least $1 million.

Assumed Name A business entity may have one legal name and do business under another assumed name. If a business entity elects to conduct business under an assumed name, the assumed name should be filed with the secretary of state and the local county clerk. Rules require license holders using an assumed name to notify TREC in writing within 30 days of starting to use the assumed name. A license holder may use form TREC DBA-2 "Notice of DBA or Assumed Name for a Broker's License" to notify TREC.

A competing manager is one who lists and sells real estate along with managing an office.

A real estate office manager can come from:

- experienced salespersons
- competitors
- compatible businesses
- management students

Tier 1—Manager Candidate

- monthly performance reviews with branch manager
- main objective is to recruit new license holders
- assist in training newly sponsored license holders
- compensation:
  - full-time real estate salesperson
  - recruiting bonus for each new sponsored recruit (paid out over the first three closings of the recruit)

Tier 2—Manager Trainee

- monthly performance reviews with branch manager
- continued recruiting (paid flat fee per hired recruit)
- review all contracts (buyer rep, listing, purchase, lease, etc.)
- attend management meetings (if the company has management meetings)
- learn office systems (accounting, payroll, etc.)
- specific sponsored license holder coaching with branch manager supervision and guidance
- assist branch manager with inner-office management tasks
- attend interviews with potential recruits
- compensation:
  - part-time real estate salesperson
  - recruiting bonus for each new sponsored recruit (paid out over the first three closings of the recruit)
  - small management bonus (not enough to survive but enough to make up for the time spent managing)

Tier 3—Assistant Manager
Duties added to Tiers 1 and 2:

- oversee office administrative staff
- oversee office physical plant
- assist branch manager in transaction issues
- assist branch manager where needed
- compensation:
  - occasional real estate transactions performed (referral generated)
  - recruiting bonus for each new sponsored recruit (paid out over the first three closings of the recruit)
  - large management bonus (enough to survive but not enough to only manage)
  - employee benefits

NOTE: An assistant manager does not always move up to branch manager. Also, the person should never manage an office where he/she was assistant manager.

Tier 4—Branch Manager
Duties added to Tiers 1, 2, and 3:

- provide production counseling
- recruit staff and license holders
- upgrade staff and sponsored license holders
- retain staff and sponsored license holders
- terminate staff and sponsored license holders
- engage in coaching
- maintain office direction
- manage net profit of the specific real estate office

Compensation
The Tier 4 branch manager receives a base salary that is enough for the branch manager to live on comfortably. In addition, the branch manager receives an incentive compensation based on net profit production; this income is paid monthly (override).

Management Styles
The broker needs to choose the best fit between his/her goals and the sponsored license holder's goals.

The Commander approach to management believes it is "my way or the highway":

- Commander brokers will fire any sponsored license holder who gets just a smidgen out of line.
- Commander brokers' office meetings are strictly authoritarian.
- Commander brokers' training style is very directive.
- Commander brokers tend to be competitive and not as sociable as any other of the approaches, preferring to get right to the point.

The Peacemaker is the broker who wants to make everyone happy:

- Peacemaker brokers do not like conflict and will avoid it at all costs.
- Peacemaker brokers typically hire other Peacemakers as sponsored license holders to make the culture beneficial to all involved.
- Peacemaker brokers may be the most sociable of all types of managers.
- Peacemaker brokers may need help to stay on task.

The Collaborator broker wants everyone's opinion before making a decision:

- Collaborator brokers will not back down from confrontation.
- Collaborator brokers will want to have agreement on major decisions.
- Collaborator brokers will organize office committees on any number of projects.
- Collaborator brokers are sociable, enthusiastic, and visionary.
- Collaborator brokers give direction.
- Collaborator brokers make every effort to find a place for everyone.
- Collaborator brokers guide his/her sponsored license holder's career.

The Controller broker must know and control all aspects of the brokerage company:

- Controller brokers must have their hands in all operations.
- Controller brokers are perfectionists and expects others to be the same.
- Controller brokers are detail people who focus on objectives.
- Controller brokers are cerebral and do well at structured tasks.

Management structure is divided into two main categories: horizontal and vertical.

1. Horizontal management structure is typically characteristic of small sole-proprietorship brokerages that have few levels of management.
2. Vertical management structure is typically characteristic of larger, corporate-type brokerages that have many levels of management.

Tenancy in common is a way for two or more people to own a real estate brokerage business together. Upon death, each can leave his/her interest to the beneficiaries of his/her choosing. Each tenant has a separate share of the business, and those shares do not need to be equal.

Joint tenants with rights of survivorship is a partnership structure characterized by four unities, all of which are required for a joint tenancy to be valid:

1. Unity of interest—Each joint tenant must have an equal interest, including equality of duration and extent.
2. Unity of title—The interests must arise from the same document.
3. Unity of possession—Each joint tenant must have an equal right to occupy the entire property.
4. Unity of time—The interests of the joint tenants must arise at the same time.

A *general partnership* is an association of two or more individuals conducting a real estate business. The partners own the business assets together and are personally liable for business debts.

In a limited partnership, one or more *general* partners manage the real estate brokerage business, whereas *limited* partners contribute capital and share in the profits but take no part in running the business. General partners remain personally liable for the partnership debts, whereas limited partners incur no liability with respect to partnership obligations beyond their capital contributions.

Joint ventures exist only as long as the venture lasts. Once the venture is completed, the partnership is dissolved.

CHAPTER QUESTIONS

1. What is defined by TREC as any interest in real property, including a leasehold, located inside or outside of Texas?
   A. a lease
   B. a potential seller
   C. real estate
   D. a potential buyer

2. Which of the following is true about a real estate business entity?
   A. Real estate business entities must have 25% or more of their income derived from residential sales.
   B. Real estate business entities must designate an individual holding an active Texas real estate broker license in good standing with TREC to act for it.
   C. Real estate business entities are required to keep all records for a minimum of seven years from the date the transaction closed.
   D. All of the answer choices are true.

3. A "competing" manager is:
   A. listing and selling real estate along with managing an office
   B. interviewing with a competing brokerage while currently managing a brokerage
   C. competing for a state or national recognition award
   D. actively pursuing an advancement to become a regional manager

4. How long does a broker have to provide the name of a delegated supervisor to the TREC?
   A. 30 days
   B. 60 days
   C. 90 days
   D. 180 days

5. Which of the following is a good source of potential real estate manager candidates?
   A. experienced salespersons
   B. competitors
   C. compatible businesses
   D. all of the answer choices

6. What is the final tier (Tier 4) in the Manager Development Program?
   A. manager trainee
   B. assistant manager
   C. branch manager
   D. manager candidate

7. Which of the following is NOT a management style?
   A. commander
   B. collaborator
   C. peacemaker
   D. negotiator

8. What type of broker has the management style that seeks to have agreement on major decisions?
   A. commander
   B. collaborator
   C. peacemaker
   D. controller

9. What type of broker will fire any sponsored license holder who gets just a smidgen out of line?
   A. commander
   B. collaborator
   C. peacemaker
   D. controller

10. What are the two main categories under the management structure?
    A. over and under
    B. front of the house and back of the house
    C. horizontal and vertical
    D. first tier and second tier

CHAPTER 10

Employment Law and Compensation Management

Employment law refers to all the laws, rules, relationships, and regulations that are involved with the employment of staff and sponsored license holders. Employment law is very daunting for the average broker. There are so many laws with pages and pages of words constructed in a manner that only a trained legal mind can understand. The effort in this chapter is not to practice law but to introduce some of the laws that relate closely to real estate in an effort to demonstrate the need for legal consultation on employment law.

Compensation management refers to the compensation method for sponsored license holders. Compensation can be constructed in a multitude of ways depending on the needs of the sponsored license holders and the brokerage. The more personalized the compensation method, the better the retention value for the sponsored license holders. However, this has to be weighed against the need of the brokerage to make a profit.

Employment Relations

"Employment relations" refers to the care that needs to be taken when hiring and firing both license holders and staff. Violation of employment laws and regulations can result in severe financial loss. Consulting with an employment law attorney instead of steaming ahead could save the brokerage a great deal of money. Here are a few questions that should be asked of potential managers; some of these questions could be asked of potential staff members as well:

1. How often were you supervised in your previous job?
2. Do you prefer working alone or in groups?
3. Can you give me an example of your ability to manage or supervise others?
4. What are some things you would like to avoid in a job? Why?
5. In your previous job, what kinds of pressures did you encounter?
6. What would you say is the most important thing you are looking for in a job?
7. What were some of the things about your last job that you found most difficult to do?
8. What are some of the problems you encounter in doing your job? Which one frustrates you the most? What do you usually do about it?
9. What are some things you particularly liked about your last job?
10. How do you feel about the way you and others in the department were managed by your supervisor?

11. If I were to ask your present employer about your ability as a receptionist (accountant, secretary, lead coordinator, etc.), what would he/she say?
12. What is your long-term employment or career objective? What kind of job do you see yourself holding five years from now?
13. How does this job fit in with your overall career goals?
14. Who or what in your life would you say influenced you most with your career objectives?
15. What would you most like to accomplish if you had this job?
16. What might make you leave this job?
17. What things do you feel most confident in doing?
18. How would you describe yourself as a person?
19. Do you consider yourself a self-starter? If so, explain why (and give examples).
20. What things give you the greatest satisfaction at work?
21. What things frustrate you the most? How do you usually cope with them?
22. In your work experience, what have you done that you consider truly creative?
23. Do you consider yourself to be thoughtful or analytical, or do you usually make up your mind fast? Give an example.
24. How do you go about making an important decision affecting your career?
25. What organizations do you belong to?
26. Tell me specifically what you do in the civic activities in which you participate.
27. How do you keep up with what's going on in your company? Your industry? Your profession?
28. Describe how you determine what constitutes top priorities in the performance of your job.
29. In your position, how would you define doing a good job? On what basis is your definition determined?
30. What approach do you take in getting your people to accept your ideas or department goals?
31. What specifically do you do to set an example for your coworkers?
32. How frequently do you meet with your immediate supervisor?
33. If you have little time for your meeting and your supervisor holds seriously differing views to yours, what would be your approach?
34. How would you describe your basic personality style?

35. Have you ever done any public or group speaking? Recently? Why? How did it go?
36. What kinds of books and other publications do you read?

Asking these questions and more can help a broker separate the true professionals from those who just need a temporary job. Hiring managers and staff is an expensive proposition and one that should not be taken lightly. It is better to be understaffed than to have a large amount of turnover. The only way a broker has a chance at low turnover is to be prepared before hiring.

Federal Employment Guidelines

Federal employment law establishes guidelines in hiring, managing, and firing employees and independent contractors. These laws and guidelines can be complex, and to understand them would require more education and knowledge than a broker has typically obtained. An unprepared broker could end up in a situation from which the broker may not be able to recover. A mistake in hiring and firing procedures could be devastating to a brokerage. A broker would therefore be wise to hire an attorney to define the role of the broker in such matters and develop an employment system that coincides with the current, applicable law.

Employment Law

Employment law consists of thousands of federal statutes, administrative regulations, and judicial decisions. A broker must be informed about federal laws and regulations to perform in a legal manner. The broker should check with human resources departments and the workforce commissions or departments of labor. These entities exist to help small businesses understand employer rights and employee rights. A broker could seek education through the college system, but taking courses takes a great deal of time, money, and effort. Some things should be delegated to legal counsel, and employment law is one of them. The federal government has a multitude of employment laws that could affect the real estate brokerage business. Here are a few.

The Fair Labor Standards Act

The Fair Labor Standards Act (FLSA) establishes minimum wage, overtime pay, recordkeeping, and youth employment standards affecting employees in the private sector and in federal, state, and local governments. The FLSA basic requirements are:

- payment of the minimum wage;
- overtime pay for time worked over 40 hours in a workweek;
- restrictions on the employment of children; and
- recordkeeping.

The Family and Medical Leave Act (FMLA)

The Family and Medical Leave Act (FMLA) entitles eligible employees of covered employers to take unpaid, job-protected leave for specified reasons with continuation of group health insurance coverage under the same terms and conditions as if they had not taken leave. Eligible employees of covered employers are entitled to FMLA leave for:

- the birth of a child and to care for the newborn child;
- the placement of a child for adoption or foster care and to care for the newly placed child within one year of placement;
- care for a family member with a serious health condition;
- the employee's own serious health condition that makes the employee unable to perform the functions of his/her job; and
- certain reasons related to the military service of the employee's family member (e.g., qualifying exigency and military caregiver leave).

Brokers must be aware of all federal employment laws, not just the laws that are most frequently referenced. Minor laws are not covered in this material, but brokers are required to know and understand all employment laws. Brokers should seek legal advice when addressing employment laws and should have a written policy that is acknowledged by an employment attorney.

State Employment Guidelines

All states have certain employment laws and guidelines that pertain only to that state. These are important laws that a broker must follow to avoid placing the brokerage in financial danger. Most state laws mirror federal laws, with a few exceptions. Here are a few of the Texas state employment laws that most often affect real estate brokerages.

Labor Code—Title 2. Subtitle A Chapter 21—Employment Discrimination
Sec. 21.001. Purposes. "The general purposes of [Title 2. Subtitle A Chapter 21] is to secure for persons in this state, including persons

with disabilities, freedom from discrimination in certain employment transactions, in order to protect their personal dignity."

Sec. 21.051. Discrimination by Employer. "An employer commits an unlawful employment practice if because of race, color, disability, religion, sex, national origin, or age of the employee [the employer]:

1. refuses to hire an individual, discharges an individual, or discriminates in any other manner against an individual in connection with compensation or the conditions of employment; or
2. limits an employee for employment in a manner that would deprive an individual of any employment opportunity or adversely affect in any other manner the status of an employee."

Texas Payday Law
Texas Payday Law covers all Texas business entities regardless of size. All persons who perform a service for compensation are considered employees, except for close relatives and independent contractors. Both employees and employers should be aware of the law so that they know their rights and responsibilities.

Wages
Wages in U.S. currency must be delivered to the employee not later than payday by any reasonable means. The Payday Law requires that employees be paid for all time worked. Compensable time is normally defined as "all the time during which an employee is necessarily required to be on the employer's premises, on duty or at a prescribed work place."

Breaks
If rest breaks of 20 minutes or less are given, they must be paid because they are considered to be beneficial to the employer, given that they generally promote productivity and efficiency on the part of the employee. Lunch breaks, defined as a break of 30 minutes or longer for the purpose of eating a meal, where the employee is fully relieved of duties (i.e., performing no work), do not have to be paid.

Pay Periods
Each employee who is exempt from the overtime provisions of the FLSA must be paid at least once per month; others must be paid at least twice per month.

Collections

If the Texas Workforce Commission (TWC) determines that the employer must pay back wages, the employer pays those wages to the TWC, and then TWC pays the person owed the wages. If necessary to collect the wages due, TWC may impose administrative liens and bank levies.

Penalties

If the TWC determines that an employer acted in bad faith by not paying wages as required by law, the TWC may assess an administrative penalty against the employer equal to the wages claimed or $1,000, whichever is less.

Texas Minimum Wage Act

The Texas Minimum Wage Act establishes a minimum wage for non-exempt employees. The current provisions require covered employers to provide each employee with a written earnings statement containing certain information about the employee's pay. The Act:

- establishes a minimum wage for non-exempt employees
- designates the TWC as the agency responsible for disseminating information about state minimum-wage requirements
- exempts a variety of employers from its coverage
- provides civil remedies for its violation

Texas Real Estate Commission—Independent Contractor Status

The Texas Real Estate Commission (TREC) has established rules defining independent contractor status, as follows:

> **TREC Rule §535.2.** *This is not meant to require an employer/employee relationship between a broker and a sponsored salesperson.*
> **Texas Labor Code §201.072.** *Employment does not include service performed by an individual as a real estate salesperson if:*
> - *the individual engages in activity described by the definition of "salesperson" in the Texas Real Estate License Act (TRELA)*
> - *the individual is licensed as a salesperson by TREC*
> - *substantially all remuneration for the service is directly related to sales not to the number of hours worked*
> - *the service is performed under a written contract between the individual and the person for whom the service is performed, and the contract provides that the individual is not treated as an employee with respect to the service for federal tax purposes*

Independent Contractor Challenges

The independent contractor status for real estate licensees is frequently challenged in the courts, but the end result is that real estate licensees are independent contractors. Although this is an Internal Revenue Service (IRS) issue and not necessarily a TREC issue, it is important that brokers be sure they understand the choices and ramifications. Brokers may choose for their license holders to be employees or independent contractors. TREC recommends seeking advice of competent legal counsel and a competent certified public accountant when making these choices.

Brokers who use the independent contractor status for federal tax purposes need to be certain they have obtained a written independent contractor agreement and a memorandum of understanding for every license holder associated with their brokerage. These documents should be drawn up by an attorney (the Texas Association of REALTORS® also has forms). The memorandum of understanding should be renewed annually and retained in the broker's records. Failure to procure these documents could cause the broker to be liable for federal taxes on commissions paid to license holders.

The federal government in the Affordable Care Act has recognized that "qualified real estate agents" will be statutory non-employees under the IRS code and thus non-employees for the purposes of the "Shared Responsibility for Employers." This clearly states that the federal government acknowledges the independent contractor relationship between sponsoring brokers and their license holders.

Independent Contractor Versus Employee

An independent contractor is someone who is contracted to complete a task but is not hired for a job. An employee is hired to fill a job position. The difference is how they are handled. An independent contractor:

- should have a written independent contractor agreement
- can be told what the task is but not how to do it
- must pay his/her own income and Social Security taxes
- cannot receive any company benefits

Consequences of Treating an Employee as an Independent Contractor

If a broker classifies a staff member as an independent contractor and the broker has no reasonable basis for doing so, a broker may be held liable for income taxes, Social Security and Medicare taxes, and unemployment tax on wages that should have been paid. The broker does not generally have to withhold or pay any taxes on payments to independent contractors.

Relief Provisions
If a broker has a reasonable basis for not treating a sponsored license holder as an employee, the broker may be relieved from having to pay employment taxes for that license holder. To get this relief, the broker must file all required federal information returns on a basis consistent with the treatment of the license holder.

Managing Independent Contractors
The real estate broker/owner must determine how to manage sponsored real estate licensees. Some brokers believe that salespersons should receive a draw and also commission money. A "draw" is a small amount of money fronted to an independent contractor under the agreement that this would be paid back to the company once commissions were being earned. This arrangement allows a new real estate salesperson the ability to survive in the beginning. Once established, the salesperson will no longer need a draw. A broker needs to be wary of this arrangement, though, because the broker loses if the salesperson never produces. A broker could, under the circumstances, sue the nonproductive salesperson, but brokers do not like to sue. Also, that salesperson likely has no money; otherwise the salesperson would not have needed the draw. One broker filed an "unpaid debt" against the nonproductive salesperson with an unpaid draw and kept it on the salesperson's credit report for years. Needless to say, this broker did not have a good reputation in the real estate community.

If the real estate salesperson were considered an employee, the broker/manager would have much more control over the salesperson's activities. The broker could demand that the employee make prospecting calls and see a quota of people each day. The real estate business is about being independent from the "boss," however. Real estate salespersons who are employees see themselves as right back in the corporate world, and that is not conducive to success in the real estate world. Having salespersons as employees has been tried in real estate, but the arrangement has not succeeded. Real estate salespersons who make the most money generate their own leads and as such perform better as commission based without a safety net that a small salary, or draw, would provide. Most brokers require their salespersons to be independent contractors, and then they are paid only what they earn. This decision must be made before any real estate salespersons are brought on board because of the difficulty of changing hiring policies once brokerage operations have begun.

Compensation Management

The compensation structure is a critical part of recruiting and retaining real estate salespersons. If brokers pay the sponsored license holders too much money, the brokerage will go broke. If brokers pay themselves too much, the salespersons will leave. If salespersons leave, the brokerage will go broke. The broker should not blame the compensation structure for all the sponsored license holders leaving, however; studies show that the main reason salespersons leave a brokerage is lack of management guidance.

Sherman Antitrust Act

The Sherman Antitrust Act prohibits any agreement between brokerages to charge the same commissions or fees. The section on compensation management is only for discussion purposes. A broker should not assume that any of the following is a recommendation or an agreement to violate the Sherman Antitrust Act.

Multiple Plans

Hoping to strike a deal that is best for both parties, some real estate brokerages will offer their salespersons multiple plans. These plans can range from 100% to a variable split of the commission between the broker and the salesperson, with some or all expenses of the sale paid by the broker. The brokerage company that offers multiple plans to its salespersons is basically telling its salespersons, "We want you working here, so let's work a mutually beneficial system where you can make the money you deserve, and the real estate company can survive and thrive."

Single Plans

Some real estate brokerages offer only a single plan. Because the single plan does not work for all sponsored license holders, usually the broker will customize certain aspects of the plan to fit a particular salesperson—which results in the single plan now resembling a multiple-plan system. Single plans are quickly fading as a brokerage strategy. When a salesperson is offered multiple plans, any of which would be better than the single plan his/her current broker is offering, that salesperson may leave.

The reason brokers are hesitant to offer multiple plans is usually that they do not understand them, and they fear the unknown. A broker thinks, "What if I offer a plan that makes me go bankrupt?" The broker should analyze the brokerage office and its expenses, including profit as an expense item, and then the broker should develop plans to offset the expenses and provide for a reserve account. With this mindset, brokers can offer many plans. The broker could offer the salesperson 100% commission if that same salesperson paid a monthly fee to offset the expenses the office incurs. A broker could pay for everything for a salesperson if that salesperson would allow the broker to keep most of the commission to offset the expenses the brokerage has incurred.

Splits
The most common way to compensate sponsored real estate license holders is the "split," which involves the dividing of a commission between a sponsored real estate license holder and the broker. Most commission-splits start with the 50/50 split, which means the salesperson receives 50% of the commission and the broker the other half. Generally the salesperson's split is mentioned first. As the salesperson's production increases, so does the salesperson's split. The reason for this is twofold: First, as the salesperson conducts more and more transactions, the salesperson learns the business more and more. The more the salesperson learns, the less the salesperson needs the broker/manager. The broker now has more time to devote to other lower-split license holders. The license holders who increase their production deserve more of the commission. Second, the salesperson deserves more of the commission because that salesperson is the one putting yard signs up on each listing obtained. The best advertising a brokerage can get is yard signs. The more a salesperson lists, the more advertising the brokerage has, so the salesperson is in essence being compensated for that advertising.

Rollback Generally, a sponsored real estate license holder on a split will be "rolled back" at the end of a calendar year. If a salesperson has earned the position of 80/20 (i.e., 80% commission for the salesperson and 20% for the broker) and December 31 hits, he/she will be rolled back to 50/50 (i.e., 50% each for the salesperson and the broker) at the beginning of the year. This is dangerous for the brokerage because the broker is in essence telling the sponsored license holders not only to leave the brokerage but also *when* to leave the brokerage. The brokerage's competition will heavily recruit the brokerage's salespersons near the rollback time by promising them a fairer compensation agreement. If this particular broker does not roll back the sponsored license holders, the brokerage could go broke. Without rollbacks, a real estate salesperson could do really well one year and then coast from there. Unfortunately, the brokerage company would then have a great number of high-split, low-producing salespersons and would eventually go broke.

Rolling Rollback Many brokerages are now implementing the "rolling rollback." The rolling rollback is evaluated each month through a review of the previous 12 months. Basically, this calls for looking at a 12-month period at the beginning of each month and then determining the split based on those 12 months. The following month, the salesperson is reevaluated and by doing so adds the previous month and drops off the 13th month.

Suppose a salesperson starts out on a 50/50 split and has increasing production (the number represented is the salesperson's percentage):

Jan	Feb	Mar	Apr	May	Jun	Jul	Aug	Sep	Oct	Nov	Dec	Jan
50%	50%	50%	50%	50%	50%	50%	55%	55%	55%	60%	60%	60%

With a typical rollback, this salesperson would be rolled back to 50% because the year ended, not because the production dropped. It is this automatic rollback that frustrates producing sponsored license holders. If the salesperson should be on a 50/50 split one month and then produces really well the next month, his/her split could go up. This means the salesperson's commission could be increased if his/her production increases, rolled back if the production drops) or simply stay the same if he/she maintains production. With a rolling rollback, the January split for the salesperson is 60%. Now suppose the production of the salesperson begins to drop in January. It would look like this:

Jan	Feb	Mar	Apr	May	Jun	Jul	Aug	Sep	Oct	Nov	Dec	Jan	Feb	Mar	Apr	May	Jun
50%	50%	50%	50%	50%	50%	50%	55%	55%	55%	60%	60%	60%	60%	60%	60%	55%	55%

Notice in this scenario that the salesperson's commission-split did not immediately drop just because his/her production dropped in one month. It did eventually drop because the salesperson did not increase production. This arrangement is probably the fairest and most motivating of any split system because the split is based on the previous 12 months and not just the current month or year end.

Table 10–1 is a rough look at a split system. It is provided only by way of example. A broker should not use this system for a brokerage office until the broker knows the brokerage's break-even numbers and how much is needed to earn a profit.

Table 10–1 Example of a Split System

Stage	Commission Earned	Split for Stage
1	$0–$20,000	50%
2	$20,001–$25,000	55%
3	$25,001–$35,000	60%
4	$35,001–$50,000	65%
5	$50,001–$70,000	70%
6	$70,001–Unlimited	75%

A salesperson can start on a higher split, but to reach the next stage, he/she must qualify at a higher amount. For example, a salesperson may desire a 60% split. The broker could start the salesperson out on 60%, with the first stage being $50,000 before he/she moves up. The salesperson gets a higher starting split, but moving up takes longer. With this system, a salesperson can attain any stage he/she desires. A salesperson who wants a higher split can also compensate the broker by paying a desk fee.

Desk Fee

A "desk fee" is the costs of the office (including a brokerage profit) divided by the total number of desks the office holds. If the broker can get a fee per desk, then he/she can make a profit. The desk fee can be a prorated amount depending on the split the salesperson is willing to take. With the compensating desk fee, a 100% commission can be obtained. The desk fee can be an upfront yearly fee or a prorated monthly amount.

100%
The 100% concept is just that—a concept. In reality, no real estate office could offer all its salespersons 100% of their commissions and stay in business. The concept is basically that the sponsored license holder keeps all the commission and pays the broker a fee to do business. This concept works well for the trained, experienced, and independent real estate salesperson. It is not the best avenue for the real estate neophyte who needs broker support.

> CASE IN POINT—A broker was once at a real estate conference where he heard the keynote speaker talking individually to attendees. One person told the speaker that he was new and hired at a 100% office. The speaker advised him to find another broker. This was not what the new person wanted to hear, but the speaker was correct because at a true 100% concept office, the salesperson will get very little help or training. The alluring chance to make more money and to run one's own business with limited management interference is the draw for the 100% office.

The 100% concept works well for the experienced real estate license holder who has an established real estate business and does not need additional training from the broker. The downside for the license holder is that he/she must pay for almost all expenses related to the real estate sales business. The 100% salesperson is basically operating his/her own real estate company under the name of the broker.

The 100% concept works well for salespersons who are tired of showing rookies how to scan and email contracts, helping them handle sellers who are obstreperous, or assisting them with any number of other day-to-day situations that come up in the real estate business. Experienced salespersons are busy with their own real estate business and do not want to babysit others. A broker needs to be cautious, though, because this concept can get out of hand quickly; a broker can lose control of the 100% salespersons because they will threaten to leave if they do not get their own way.

Modified 100% Concept   In the 100% concept offices, a new salesperson can be hired at a traditional commission-split and then move to a 100% split when he/she is capable of handling it. In the beginning, the salesperson needs a great deal of the broker/manager's time. As the salesperson improves, he/she needs less and less of that time and eventually becomes completely independent and capable to be at 100%. This type of brokerage is called a "modified 100% concept."

Profit Sharing (Recruiting Bonus)

Some real estate brokerage firms offer a type of profit sharing. However, the brokerage firm has to make money somehow, and a majority of the new concepts are just another way of dressing up the same old concepts.

Profit sharing generally works more like a recruiting bonus than true profit sharing. For example, a currently sponsored license holder recruits a new license holder to the office. The recruiting salesperson will receive a portion of the new salesperson's commissions: This is profit sharing. The downside for the recruiting salesperson is that the office must be in profit before the salesperson can receive any profit. If the brokerage is at the break-even point or losing money, the recruiting salesperson receives nothing. Thus, most real estate companies offer a bonus for recruiting a new, productive salesperson and will pay with no requirement of the brokerage being profitable.

Teams

Real estate salespersons sometimes want to work together and form a team. Teams are a great concept, except that, like Marxism, in actual practice the concept is not so great. The best real estate license holders are independent in nature, which works against teams. However, teams will always exist in the real estate industry, and a broker must account for them. When planning compensation plans, for example, the broker must include the team concept or else he/she might be taken for a loss. A real estate salesperson earns his/her way up to a high split and then forms a team that operates under him/her. All production goes under the salesperson with the higher split, and the only loser is the broker. The broker bears the expense of the team; but instead of each salesperson being on a different, lower split, they are all paid based on the team leader's high split.

The brokerage must be paid first, after which the brokerage pays every sponsored license holder on the team. By requiring this procedure, the brokerage protects its profitability.

Home Office
Another way a real estate salesperson can get a higher split is to work from his/her home. Without the cost of the desk, the broker can offer higher splits. Some salespersons have a problem being disciplined to work from home. An additional problem is the disconnect that might develop between the broker and the salesperson. A broker needs to connect with his/her sponsored license holders or potentially lose them to a competing broker who will connect with them. Without the aid of the broker, a salesperson must be independently knowledgeable and responsible.

Virtual Brokerage
Some brokerages are virtual offices where all the license holders work from home. The brokerage has no building. If the brokerage wants to hold meetings, the broker will rent a conference room at a hotel. All documentation and required paperwork are completed using the internet.

Employee
A few real estate companies offer their salespersons the position of employee instead of independent contractor. They pay their employees a salary instead of commission-splits. Very few real estate companies actually do this. The upfront costs for a real estate brokerage make paying salaries almost prohibitive.

Bonuses
A bonus is an extra incentive to sell a particularly difficult property, such as those with foundation problems, fire damage to part of the structure, failure to fit in with the surrounding area, location near industry or busy streets. All latent structural defects are to be disclosed, and the issue cannot be a fair housing violation. The property could have a so-called psychological stigma associated with it, as happens when an event occurs on a property that creates a positive or negative feeling about the property that has no basis in actual condition. For example, if someone had been murdered on a property, the murder

should be disclosed to any potential buyer because it could hinder the sale. Many buyers will shy away from viewing a property with such a psychological stigma associated with it. Any of these reasons could make a property difficult to sell. Some brokers will offer a bonus to the selling salesperson who can find a buyer. Most bonuses range from a few hundred dollars to paid vacations. Once a brand-new cherry red Ferrari was given away as a bonus!

The discussion here is whether the broker should take these bonuses or allow the salesperson to receive them. All monies earned in a real estate transaction must be paid through the broker, but the broker can pass the money on to the sponsored license holder involved in the transaction. Some brokers allow the salesperson to receive all of any bonuses paid. This money does not apply to dollars earned for calculating a change in a commission-split. The problem with allowing a salesperson to receive bonuses is that an unscrupulous salesperson might rig a portion of his/her transactions to be paid as a bonus. The downside of splitting the bonus according to the salesperson's agreed split is ill will and recruiting opportunities for competing brokerages. Most real estate companies allow bonuses to be paid to the salesperson, but they are monitored closely to avoid abuse.

Salespersons

Salespersons should be the lifeblood of a real estate company, but the wrong salespersons can be the death of the same organization. The only way to prevent the wrong ones from infecting the entire company is to eliminate them, and the only way to be comfortable that you can eliminate the bad ones is to have a continuous recruiting policy. There are several types of salespersons, discussed below.

Top Producers
Brokers will sometimes open a real estate office with three or four top producers, believing that is all they need to dominate a market. Top producers can be very good to have, but they can also hold the broker prisoner. Top producers can threaten to leave, and if the broker does not meet their demands, the brokerage folds. A broker should treat top producers with respect, but a broker should not let them take control. The maximum proportion of top producers in any office should be 10% to 20%; any more than that, and they can take control.

Middle Producers

Middle producers generally do not become the headaches that top producers can become, and they do not need the broker to hold their hand, as new people do. The middle producer may never become a top producer, but he/she will consistently produce respectable numbers in the middle. A broker can make a fair share from their production, and they appreciate the opportunity. Middle producers should make up 40% to 60% of any brokerage.

Bottom Producers: Zero Agents

Bottom producers must be on an accountability schedule or be terminated. They are not doing themselves any good, and they certainly are not doing the brokerage any good. As a broker/manager, it may be difficult to fire a bottom producer. The broker may think doing so seems cruel. The broker may fear that if the bottom producer is fired, he/she may go to a competing brokerage to becomes a top producer there. The broker cannot operate from fear. The rest of the office will take notice that the broker will no longer tolerate bottom producers. Brokerages made up of 60% bottom producers tend to fail, whereas brokerages with just a few good producers (both middle and top) make a fortune. A brokerage should never be made up of more than 10% bottom producers and preferably have none.

New Sponsored Licensees

A brokerage must have new license holders or it will eventually die because of attrition. All brokerages lose salespersons. Some brokers do not like to face facts. The salespersons in any brokerage move away, retire, or find what they consider a better deal from the competition. The broker must bring in new salespersons to survive. New sponsored license holders should make up 20% to 30% of the brokerage.

The Perfect Office

The perfect office is one that looks like an overstuffed sandwich, with the bread on top being the top producers, the bread on the bottom being the new sponsored license holders, and the filling being the people in the middle—yes, the middle producers. This is where the meat of any office is located, and it should be thick and hearty!

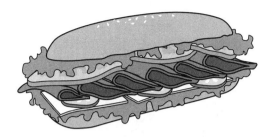

Top producers = 20%
Middle producers = 60%
New license holders = 20%
Bottom producers = 0%

Shooting Stars

A shooting star is the real estate salesperson who just blows the doors off the place. This salesperson lists everything in sight. He/she is constantly showing buyers. The shooting star produces more than any other salesperson within his/her first few months. This continues for maybe a year, but then these stars fade away and are out of the business within two years. What happened? Some people are very good at starting projects but very bad at finishing them. The manager must keep challenging shooting stars with new projects and avenues, or the company will lose them.

Other shooting stars are burnout victims. They work so hard that they leave nothing in the gas tank and simply burn out. The manager must be aware of the potential burnout victim, because burning out can be prevented. Sometimes the manager must force a shooting star to take time off and eventually even take a vacation. The manager should teach salespersons time management techniques that may free up time for relaxation.

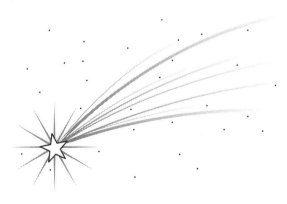

Searchers

Searchers are real estate license holders who are never happy with the real estate company at which they are currently working. They are always looking for a bigger, better deal. They spend their time talking about how good other real estate offices are to other sponsored license holders of the current brokerage. They never blame themselves for their own failures. They are called searchers because they transfer their license from broker to broker to search for that sanctuary where all is good and money falls from the sky. Of course, they never find that place, but they make everyone miserable while they are around. They will say things such as:

- "If the broker advertised more . . ."
- "If we had a better looking office . . ."
- "If we had more help . . ."

One searcher literally went to every single office in a small town and still did not find happiness. A license holder once had a real problem with a broker he was working with, so he called his mentor, who was with a different company. He told the mentor of his troubles, and the mentor quickly shot back that the license holder could move and then move again because there is no perfect office and that until the license holder figured out that it was up to him, not others, he would never make it. Now that is what is called dead-on advice. Searchers find fault with everyone but themselves.

Kennel Dogs

Go to any dog kennel, and in one of the back cages there is this little mutt that no one adopts, but the kennel keepers cannot get rid of the dog because they have fallen in love with the mutt. The dog has no real use or productive value, but there it sits year after year. Brokerages also have "kennel dogs." They are in any real estate office. The kennel dog license holder is the one who is in the office first to make the coffee. The kennel dog will answer any question that a newbie will ask and will  probably know the answer because he/she has been there so long. The kennel dog will always have a kind word and would do anything for another. The problem is, the kennel dog does not sell any real estate. The broker/manager should fire this licensee, but who could get rid of the kennel dog? This person is so nice. The broker should realize that the kennel dog is taking up space a productive agent could use.

Warning! Kennel dogs will gather together. If the broker is known to keep kennel dogs around, the broker will get more of them. Does the broker want an office full of kennel dogs and no producers? If the broker has the courage to fire the kennel dog, the other sponsored license holders will respect the fact the broker is serious about the real estate business.

Prima Donnas

Prima donnas start out as the "nobody" real estate license holder, but they do everything they are supposed to do. By doing all the things the license holder should be doing, he/she begins to become successful. Now two things can happen: Either they respect where they came from and help others who are trying to make it, or they become prima donnas. The prima donna license holder feels that he/she is now better than anyone else, including the broker. Prima donnas will not participate in any office functions because

they do not want to be seen with the little people. If any new salesperson starts to outproduce them, prima donnas will sabotage the new salesperson's efforts. In one office a prima donna went after a new salesperson and just to get rid of her accused her of stealing leads. Nothing was ever proven, but the manager had to get rid of the new salesperson just to make the prima donna happy. The new salesperson went on to become one of the better producers of her next company, and the prima donna went on to destroy her current office. Prima donnas cause brokers many sleepless nights. The broker wants to fire this troublemaker, but the troublemaker is usually the broker's best producer.

> CASE IN POINT—A broker once fired his top three producers because they all had become prima donnas. They would sit around and devise schemes against all the other licensees. The broker had finally had enough and fired all three. They screamed that they would ruin the broker and went out to form their own office. The profitability of the broker's office went up after they were gone because the prima donnas had been scaring away any other real estate salesperson the broker had from showing up at the office, and the prima donnas were then taking all the office leads. Now the new real estate salespersons received some incoming leads, and they were on a more favorable split with the office. The brokerage's total production numbers went down without the prima donnas, but profitability went up. One further note: The prima donnas' office held together for only three months before the prima donnas tore each other apart and shut the business down.

Nesters

Nesters are the sponsored real estate license holders who would rather "nest" (i.e., do nothing productive) than find business. As a matter of fact, business could actually get in their way. Nesters are to be found in any brokerage office. A person just needs to walk through the office to notice the workspace that has a wall full of awards. Then read the dates on those awards. Those plaques will have dates on them from 10–15 years ago. What have these license holders been doing for the past 10 years? Answer: They have been nesting. They sit around and admire their past work instead of finding new work. Nesting is a contagious disease. A broker needs to correct it or eliminate it; otherwise the brokerage will lose production.

Dead Wood

License holders who are dead wood are a lot like nesters, except that they may or may not be in the office. Dead wood has never had the production level of the nesters and never will. These licensees are dead wood and must be cut before they drop the morale of the entire brokerage.

Sponge

Sponges are the sponsored license holders who never produce any business from their efforts but instead "sponge" off the brokerage's business. Sponges are the first to take any brokerage leads. They sit on floor time. They are always available to take the internet leads. If someone does not want to show a property, sponges will show the

property just in the hope of getting business. The broker needs to be cautious of sponges because it becomes easy to give them business, but doing so may cause bad feelings among the actual producers of a brokerage.

Employment Process

The employment process includes many different aspects of the onboarding and initial startup of employees and sponsored license holders. Each of these groups must be handled in a different way. Employees must understand what is expected of them and how their salary and employment status will be affected by their performance. Likewise, the sponsored license holders need to know what is expected of them, but they also need to know that if they do not perform, they will not have any income. The first thing that license holders must understand is how their actions can cause their license to be suspended or revoked.

Grounds for Suspension or Revocation of License
Texas Occupations Code (OCC) § 1101.652 states:

> *(b) The commission may suspend or revoke a license or take other disciplinary action if the license holder, while acting as a broker or salesperson:*
> 1. *acts negligently or incompetently*
> 2. *engages in conduct that is dishonest or in bad faith or that demonstrates untrustworthiness*
> 3. *makes a material misrepresentation to a potential buyer concerning a significant defect, including a latent structural defect, known to the license holder that would be a significant factor to a reasonable and prudent buyer in making a decision to purchase real property*
> 4. *fails to disclose to a potential buyer a defect that is known to the license holder*
> 5. *makes a false promise that is likely to influence a person to enter into an agreement when the license holder is unable or does not intend to keep the promise*
> 6. *pursues a continued and flagrant course of misrepresentation or makes false promises through an agent or salesperson, through advertising, or otherwise*
> 7. *fails to make clear to all parties to a real estate transaction the party for whom the license holder is acting*
> 8. *receives compensation from more than one party to a real estate transaction without the full knowledge and consent of all parties to the transaction*
> 9. *fails within a reasonable time to properly account for or remit money that is received by the license holder and that belongs to another person*
> 10. *commingles money that belongs to another person with the license holder's own money*
> 11. *pays a commission or a fee to or divides a commission or a fee with a person other than a license holder or a real estate broker or salesperson licensed in another state for compensation for services as a real estate agent*

12. fails to specify a definite termination date that is not subject to prior notice in a contract, other than a contract to perform property management services, in which the license holder agrees to perform services for which a license is required under the Texas Real Estate License Act
13. accepts, receives, or charges an undisclosed commission, rebate, or direct profit on an expenditure made for a principal
14. solicits, sells, or offers for sale real property by means of a lottery
15. solicits, sells, or offers for sale real property by means of a deceptive practice
16. acts in a dual capacity as broker and undisclosed principal in a real estate transaction
17. guarantees or authorizes or permits a person to guarantee that future profits will result from a resale of real property
18. places a sign on real property offering the real property for sale or lease without obtaining the written consent of the owner of the real property or the owner's authorized agent
19. offers to sell or lease real property without the knowledge and consent of the owner of the real property or the owner's authorized agent
20. offers to sell or lease real property on terms other than those authorized by the owner of the real property or the owner's authorized agent
21. induces or attempts to induce a party to a contract of sale or lease to break the contract for the purpose of substituting a new contract
22. negotiates or attempts to negotiate the sale, exchange, or lease of real property with an owner, landlord, buyer, or tenant with knowledge that that person is a party to an outstanding written contract that grants exclusive agency to another broker in connection with the transaction
23. publishes or causes to be published an advertisement, including an advertisement by newspaper, radio, television, the Internet, or display, that misleads or is likely to deceive the public, tends to create a misleading impression, or fails to identify the person causing the advertisement to be published as a licensed broker or agent
24. withholds from or inserts into a statement of account or invoice a statement that the license holder knows makes the statement of account or invoice inaccurate in a material way
25. publishes or circulates an unjustified or unwarranted threat of a legal proceeding or other action
26. establishes an association by employment or otherwise with a person other than a license holder if the person is expected or required to act as a license holder
27. aids, abets, or conspires with another person to circumvent the Texas Real Estate License Act

28. *fails or refuses to provide, on request, a copy of a document relating to a real estate transaction to a person who signed the document*
29. *fails to advise a buyer in writing before the closing of a real estate transaction that the buyer should:*
    (a) have the abstract covering the real estate that is the subject of the contract examined by an attorney chosen by the buyer
    (b) be provided with or obtain a title insurance policy
30. *fails to deposit, within a reasonable time, money the license holder receives as escrow agent in a real estate transaction:*
    (a) in trust with a title company authorized to do business in Texas
    (b) in a custodial, trust, or escrow account maintained for that purpose in a banking institution authorized to do business in the GREAT STATE OF TEXAS
31. *disburses money deposited in a custodial, trust, or escrow account before the completion or termination of the real estate transaction*
32. *discriminates against an owner, potential buyer, landlord, or potential tenant on the basis of race, color, religion, sex, disability, familial status, national origin, or ancestry, including directing a prospective buyer or tenant interested in equivalent properties to a different area based on the race, color, religion, sex, disability, familial status, national origin, or ancestry of the potential owner or tenant*
33. *disregards or violates the Texas Real Estate License Act*

The sponsored license holder must also know how to perform within the guidelines of the brokerage. Some brokers are residential brokers only, and the sponsored license holder cannot practice commercial, farm and ranch, or property management. If the license holder demands to perform any function outside of residential sales, that license holder would have to quit and work with another broker who would allow those actions.

The sponsored license holder and all employees must know office procedures, from how to process a listing, to proper answering of the telephone, to ensuring that a commission will be paid in a timely manner. The license holder and all employees should know how all office equipment works and any passcodes needed for operation. All these issues take time to learn, and the process should be organized.

Here are a few things that new employees and sponsored license holders should know:

- how to use the printer and necessary passcodes
- how to use any office-provided computers and necessary passcodes
- where to find office supplies and how to pay for them if necessary

- how to handle office equipment failures
- how to process a listing
- how to process a sale
- how to obtain a commission disbursement authorization
- what desk space is available if any
- when and how to file for a paycheck
- what is the smoking policy
- what is the handgun policy
- what are the office hours
- what is the dress code
- what are the safety procedures
- what is the fair housing policy
- how violations are handled

These are just a few ideas. More topics should be addressed to cover possible questions from the new employee or license holder. The fewer the questions employees and licensees have, the better they feel the office has taken care of them. The onboarding process should be organized for every employee position and the position of a sponsored license holder. This process should be in writing, included in the office's policies and procedures manual, and updated frequently to meet the concerns of the changing real estate industry.

CHAPTER SUMMARY

The FLSA establishes minimum wage, overtime pay, recordkeeping, and youth employment standards affecting employees in the private sector and in federal, state, and local governments. The FLSA basic requirements are:

- payment of the minimum wage;
- overtime pay for time worked over 40 hours in a workweek;
- restrictions on the employment of children; and
- recordkeeping.

The Family and Medical Leave Act (FMLA) entitles eligible employees of covered employers to take unpaid, job-protected leave for specified reasons with continuation of group health insurance coverage. Eligible employees of covered employers are entitled to FMLA leave for:

- the birth/care for a newborn child;
- the placement of a child for adoption or foster care;

- care for a family member with a serious health condition;
- the employee's own serious health condition that makes the employee unable to perform the functions of his/her job; and
- certain reasons related to the military service of the employee's family member.

Labor code rules to prevent employment discrimination are as follows:

§21.051. Discrimination by Employer. An employer commits an unlawful employment practice if because of race, color, disability, religion, sex, national origin, or age of the employee [the employer]:

1. discriminates in any manner against an individual in connection with the conditions of employment; or
2. deprives an individual of any employment opportunity.

Texas Payday Law covers all Texas business entities. All persons who perform a service for compensation are considered employees, except for close relatives and independent contractors.

- Wages in U.S. currency must be delivered to the employee not later than payday by any reasonable means. The Payday Law requires that employees be paid for all time worked. Compensable time is normally defined as "all the time during which an employee is necessarily required to be on the employer's premises, on duty or at a prescribed work place."
- Breaks of under 20 minutes must be paid.
- Breaks of more than 30 minutes do not have to be paid.
- Each employee who is exempt from the overtime provisions of the FLSA must be paid at least once per month; others must be paid at least twice per month.
- If the TWC determines that the employer must pay wages, the employer pays those wages to the TWC, and then the TWC pays the person owed the wages. If necessary to collect the wages due, the TWC may impose administrative liens and bank levies.
- If the TWC determines that an employer acted in bad faith by not paying wages as required by law, the TWC may assess an administrative penalty against the employer equal to the wages claimed or $1,000, whichever is less.

The Texas Minimum Wage Act establishes a minimum wage for non-exempt employees. The current provisions require covered employers to provide each employee with a written earnings statement containing certain information about the employee's pay. The Act:

- establishes a minimum wage for non-exempt employees
- designates the TWC as the agency responsible for disseminating information about state minimum wage requirements
- exempts a variety of employers from its coverage
- provides civil remedies for its violation

Texas Labor Code §201.072. Employment does not include service performed by an individual as a real estate salesperson if:

- the individual engages in activity described by the definition of "salesperson" in TRELA.
- the individual is licensed as a salesperson by TREC.
- substantially all remuneration for the service is directly related to sales not to the number of hours worked.
- the service is performed under a written contract between the individual and the person for whom the service is performed

An independent contractor is someone who is contracted to complete a task but is not hired for a job. An employee is hired to fill a job position. An independent contractor:

- should have a written independent contractor agreement
- can be told what the task is but not how to do a task
- must pay his/her own income and Social Security taxes
- cannot receive any company benefits

A draw is a small amount of money fronted to an independent contractor under the agreement that this would be paid back to the company once commissions were being earned.

The Sherman Antitrust Act prohibits any agreement between brokerages to charge the same commissions or fees.

A "split" involves the dividing of a commission between a sponsored real estate license holder and the broker.

A "rollback" is when a sponsored real estate license holder on a split will be rolled back at the end of a calendar year.

The "rolling rollback" calls for looking at a 12-month period at the beginning of each month and then determining the split based on those 12 months. The following month, the salesperson is reevaluated, and by doing so adds the previous month and drops off the 13th month.

A desk fee is the costs of the office (including a brokerage profit) divided by the total number of desks the office holds.

With the 100% concept, the sponsored license holder keeps all the commission and pays the broker a fee to do real estate business.

Profit sharing is when a recruiting salesperson will receive a portion of the new salesperson's commissions.

Some brokerages are virtual offices where all the license holders work from home.

A bonus is an extra incentive to sell a particularly difficult property.

A shooting star is the real estate salesperson who produces a great deal in the beginning but then fades away and is out of the business within two years.

The maximum proportion of top producers in any office should be 10% to 20%.

Middle producers should make up 40% to 60% of any brokerage.

The broker should never have a brokerage made up of more than 10% bottom producers and preferably none.

New sponsored license holders should make up 20% to 30% of the brokerage.

Searchers transfer their license from broker to broker to search for that sanctuary where all is good and everyone makes money.

The kennel dog licensee does not sell any real estate but is too nice to fire.

The prima donna license holder feels that he/she is better than anyone else, including the broker, and lets everyone know it.

Nesters are the sponsored real estate license holders who would rather "nest" (i.e., do nothing productive) than make money.

Sponges are the sponsored license holders who never produce any business from their efforts but instead "sponge" off the brokerage's business.

The perfect office is one that looks like an overstuffed sandwich, with the bread on top being the top producers, the bread on the bottom being the new sponsored license holders, and the filling being the people in the middle, the middle producers.

> The TREC may suspend or revoke a license or take other disciplinary action if the license holder, while acting as a broker or salesperson:
> 1. acts negligently or incompetently
> 2. engages in conduct that is dishonest or in bad faith or that demonstrates untrustworthiness

3. makes a material misrepresentation to a potential buyer concerning a significant defect, including a latent structural defect, known to the license holder that would be a significant factor to a reasonable and prudent buyer in making a decision to purchase real property
4. fails to disclose to a potential buyer a defect that is known to the license holder
5. makes a false promise that is likely to influence a person to enter into an agreement when the license holder is unable or does not intend to keep the promise
6. pursues a continued and flagrant course of misrepresentation or makes false promises through an agent or salesperson, through advertising, or otherwise
7. fails to make clear to all parties to a real estate transaction the party for whom the license holder is acting
8. receives compensation from more than one party to a real estate transaction without the full knowledge and consent of all parties to the transaction
9. fails within a reasonable time to properly account for or remit money that is received by the license holder and that belongs to another person
10. commingles money that belongs to another person with the license holder's own money
11. pays a commission or a fee to or divides a commission or a fee with a person other than a license holder or a real estate broker or salesperson licensed in another state for compensation for services as a real estate agent
12. fails to specify a definite termination date that is not subject to prior notice in a contract, other than a contract to perform property management services, in which the license holder agrees to perform services for which a license is required under the Texas Real Estate License Act
13. accepts, receives, or charges an undisclosed commission, rebate, or direct profit on an expenditure made for a principal
14. solicits, sells, or offers for sale real property by means of a lottery
15. solicits, sells, or offers for sale real property by means of a deceptive practice
16. acts in a dual capacity as broker and undisclosed principal in a real estate transaction
17. guarantees or authorizes or permits a person to guarantee that future profits will result from a resale of real property
18. places a sign on real property offering the real property for sale or lease without obtaining the written consent of the owner of the real property or the owner's authorized agent
19. offers to sell or lease real property without the knowledge and consent of the owner of the real property or the owner's authorized agent
20. offers to sell or lease real property on terms other than those authorized by the owner of the real property or the owner's authorized agent

21. induces or attempts to induce a party to a contract of sale or lease to break the contract for the purpose of substituting a new contract
22. negotiates or attempts to negotiate the sale, exchange, or lease of real property with an owner, landlord, buyer, or tenant with knowledge that that person is a party to an outstanding written contract that grants exclusive agency to another broker in connection with the transaction
23. publishes or causes to be published an advertisement, including an advertisement by newspaper, radio, television, the Internet, or display, that misleads or is likely to deceive the public, tends to create a misleading impression, or fails to identify the person causing the advertisement to be published as a licensed broker or agent
24. withholds from or inserts into a statement of account or invoice a statement that the license holder knows makes the statement of account or invoice inaccurate in a material way
25. publishes or circulates an unjustified or unwarranted threat of a legal proceeding or other action
26. establishes an association by employment or otherwise with a person other than a license holder if the person is expected or required to act as a license holder
27. aids, abets, or conspires with another person to circumvent TRELA
28. fails or refuses to provide, on request, a copy of a document relating to a real estate transaction to a person who signed the document
29. fails to advise a buyer in writing before the closing of a real estate transaction that the buyer should:
    (a) have the abstract covering the real estate that is the subject of the contract examined by an attorney chosen by the buyer
    (b) be provided with or obtain a title insurance policy
30. fails to deposit, within a reasonable time, money the license holder receives as escrow agent in a real estate transaction:
    (a) in trust with a title company authorized to do business in Texas
    (b) in a custodial, trust, or escrow account maintained for that purpose in a banking institution authorized to do business in Texas
31. disburses money deposited in a custodial, trust, or escrow account before the completion or termination of the real estate transaction
32. discriminates against an owner, potential buyer, landlord, or potential tenant on the basis of race, color, religion, sex, disability, familial status, national origin, or ancestry, including directing a prospective buyer or tenant interested in equivalent properties to a different area based on the race, color, religion, sex, disability, familial status, national origin, or ancestry of the potential owner or tenant
33. disregards or violates TRELA

CHAPTER QUESTIONS

1. What law establishes minimum wage, overtime pay, record-keeping, and youth employment standards?
   A. Texas Real Estate License Act (TRELA)
   B. Fair Labor Standards Act (FLSA)
   C. Fair Housing Act
   D. Employment Actions and Prohibitions Act of 1978 (EAPA)

2. What law entitles eligible employees of covered employers to take unpaid, job-protected leave for specified reasons with continuation of group health insurance coverage?
   A. Settlement Procedures Act (SPA)
   B. Unreasonable Termination Act (UTA)
   C. Family and Medical Leave Act (FMLA)
   D. Conrad Amendment to the Federal Health Act (FHA)

3. Which of the following is NOT a protected class under the Labor Code–Employment Discrimination?
   A. color
   B. sex
   C. family status
   D. age of the employee

4. What is defined as "all the time during which an employee is necessarily required to be on the employer's premises"?
   A. quality time
   B. compensable time
   C. statutory time
   D. ancillary time

5. Which of the following is true about the Texas Minimum Wage Act?
   A. establishes a minimum wage
   B. exempts a variety of employers from its coverage
   C. provides civil remedies for its violation
   D. all of the answer choices

6. Who is someone that is contracted to complete a task but is not hired for a job?
   A. government employee
   B. office manager
   C. independent contractor
   D. all of the answer choices

7. An independent contractor:
   A. should have a written independent contractor agreement
   B. can be told how to do a task but not what to do
   C. cannot pay for his/her own Social Security taxes
   D. must receive any typical company benefits

8. What is a small amount of money fronted to an independent contractor under the agreement that this would be paid back to the company once commissions were being earned?
   A. preliminary salary
   B. draw
   C. frontage fee
   D. inducement

9. What law prohibits any agreement among brokerages to charge the same commissions?
   A. Real Estate Settlement Procedures Act
   B. Regulation Z
   C. Sherman Antitrust Act
   D. Consumer Financial Protection Bureau

10. What is it called when a sponsored real estate license holder on a split is moved back to a 50/50 split at the end of the year?
    A. point of beginning
    B. return on investment
    C. renewal
    D. rollback

CHAPTER 11
Recruiting Sales Agents

Recruiting is the most important function a broker must be able to perform. The second most important function is retaining those who are hired. If a broker cannot perform these two seemingly easy tasks, the broker will fail. This is not to say that only some brokers will fail—all brokers will fail. Brokerage is not like ordinary real estate sales in that if a license holder does not prospect, that license holder may not have any business or make any money but could still remain a "license holder." A broker has overhead, perhaps even thousands of dollars per month of overhead. The broker must have income, and that income must come from productive sponsored license holders. If the broker is making all his/her money from direct sales, that broker should give up brokerage and go back to sales full time because brokerage is taking away from that broker's obviously first and best talent—sales.

Recruiting in the real estate brokerage business is the same as prospecting in the real estate sales business. Without constant recruiting efforts, a real estate brokerage business is destined to fail because of attrition. Real estate salespersons are always changing. Some leave the business because they are tired of it or make no money at it. Some leave because of a spouse's job transfer. Some leave because of retirement. No matter what the reason, turnover happens. A real estate company that is fully staffed today may be badly behind in a year.

> *The salesperson who will make the brokerage the most money in five years is not in the real estate business today.*

The real estate business has changed drastically in the past decade. Current growth plans of real estate companies of all types will ignite the need for license holders who can effectively sell more real estate. This demand will drive up the value of those license holders who are experienced and productive. Because of this demand, the real estate broker should always be recruiting "agents with other companies," or AWOCs, and spend a great deal of time and effort in retaining currently sponsored license holders. To continue adding sponsored license holders, a broker must also consider hiring and training people with no formal sales experience or real estate knowledge.

The rules of real estate sales have changed in the past few decades. Previously, the real estate salesperson's role was centered on polished canned presentations and the ability to access the multiple listing service (MLS). That real estate professional had access to all the information about available properties, and consumers knew it.

Consumers now have the same access to available properties as any license holder. The same license holder must function as a valued and trusted advisor and be a source of a competitive advantage, not just an information provider. If the license holder fails as an advisor, the consumer will move on to any other real estate license holder who will advise and not just provide information. The professional real estate salesperson must be able to understand the problems customers face and sort through all the available alternatives to provide quality advice.

Selecting Potential Recruits

One of the most important aspects of recruiting is selecting the right talent. The wrong talent will deplete the broker's resources and drain the broker's energy. The broker must spend a great deal of time with each recruit who is new to the real estate brokerage business because of the recruit's lack of knowledge. The broker should not risk an unqualified sponsored license holder practicing real estate without guidance and supervision.

Selecting potential recruits involves the right marketing plan to get to that particular person who is interested in real estate as a career. The proper interviewing process eliminates the undesirable prospect, and the follow-up procedures ensure that the prospect stays with the brokerage. The following sections look at the types of real estate license holders who can be recruited.

Prelicensed Prospects

A prelicensed prospect is a person off the street. He/she may be interested in the real estate profession or may have no interest at all at this time. However, with the right push, these prospects may be the best real estate salespersons in the future. The recruiting process for these individuals is like a "shotgun approach." A shotgun approach is to shoot a bunch and put a lot of lead in the air. Prelicensed people are individuals found anywhere and everywhere. All that is needed to be considered a recruit is that he/she shows a little interest in the real estate business as a career and can pass the Texas Real Estate Exam.

New Licensees
New license holders have just been licensed. They know a great deal about real estate matters that helped them pass a state exam, but that knowledge will not make them money. The best thing about new license holders is that they are trainable. They are excited to be in the real estate business as a career and are willing to do what it takes to become a success. Without proper guidance, these new license holders will tend to fade into obscurity. With the proper guidance, however, they can go on to become the top producers of the office.

Experienced License Holders
Experienced license holders are licensed real estate salespersons who have been in the business for at least two years. The experienced license holders a broker may want recruit are currently with competing real estate offices. Experience does not equal production, though. There are real estate salespersons who have been in the business for 20 years and still produce on the poverty level. Some license holders will never have the drive and motivation to become a success, and so the broker should be careful in selecting experienced license holders.

License-Returned People (Expired)
License-returned people have had their licenses and for some reason have sent them back to the Texas Real Estate Commission (TREC). These individuals no longer practice real estate but could be a huge resource of referral business. If they keep their licenses active and then send the brokerage referrals, the brokerage can still pay them for the referrals. If their licenses expire, they can no longer receive those monies. A brokerage can have several hundred of these "held" licensees and get business from them. The major rule is that these "held" licensees cannot sell; all they can do is refer, no matter how tempting a sale may be.

Top Reasons License Holders Choose a Broker

Real estate license holders are an interesting lot. They can be energetic or lethargic. They can be organized or unorganized. They can see the glass half-full or half-empty. A talented broker must make every effort to understand why and how the typical license holder chooses a broker to work with on a day-to-day basis. The following are a few of the reasons real estate license holders have chosen their broker:

- company reputation
- broker reputation
- proximity to personal residence
- successful office
- professional office appearance
- education and training
- experienced management
- skilled and helpful staff
- autonomy to do their own business
- name recognition

Some of these reasons make a great deal of sense. A license holder should want a broker with an extremely good reputation in the community and the real estate industry. Without that quality reputation, a broker cannot inspire license holders, who may have difficulty following the broker's lead. However, close proximity to personal residence is not a good reason to choose a brokerage, and yet it happens frequently. It is critical to a license holder's success to choose the correct brokerage from day one.

The following are reasons that a salesperson leaves an office:

- high office expenses
- too much bureaucracy and company control
- size of commission
- too many mandatory meetings
- too many fees and charges related to transactions

A broker should notice that the reasons for joining a brokerage all have to do with management and not commissions, yet the reasons for leaving have to do with commissions, expenses, and wasting the license holder's time. The underlying factor is the difference between cost and value. If the real estate license holder recognizes the value of the brokerage, he/she will concentrate less on costs. A broker should spend time selling the expertise of the management team and should not compete or adjust a fair compensation structure.

Brokers Should Recruit the Best Salespersons

Before a broker begins recruiting any salespersons for the brokerage, the broker should consider what type of salesperson is wanted and, more important, needed. The broker can choose the type of license holder wanted as long as the choice is not based on certain protected classes as specified by employment law. Does the broker want an aggressive salesperson? Does the broker want a technology-savvy salesperson? Does the broker want the fun people? A broker should think about all the things wanted in the perfect real estate salesperson and begin to put a list together of the required characteristics. This list becomes the "Characteristics Profile." Some of the characteristics a broker may consider important could include the following:

well educated	financially secure	full-time worker
logical	honest	competitive
trustworthy	quick witted	experienced in sales
intense	aggressive	technology savvy
business savvy	team player	mild mannered
family oriented	ethical	psychologically mature
well spoken	punctual	humorous
hungry	willing to learn	fun loving
professional	well dressed	intelligent
spiritually balanced	charismatic	has a great work ethic
energetic	talented presenter	goal oriented
organized	emotionally stable	enthusiastic
self-disciplined	risk taker	persistent
practical	decisive	well adjusted
optimistic	energetic	poised
socially interactive	focused	discerning
communicates well	opportunistic	good problem solver
has a great memory	detail oriented	patient

The broker will then need to determine how to measure these characteristics in a potential recruit. Can the broker observe the important characteristics in an interview, or should the broker ask certain questions to get the answers? Will the candidate's background reveal the answers? Whatever the method, the characteristics must be measurable; otherwise they should not be used.

Next, the broker will need to pick the top 10 measurable characteristics. The broker should limit the number to only 10 because too many items could confuse the broker and then pressure the broker to reject a potentially good recruit who met 12 of 50 characteristics but nowhere near the 50 potentially needed. That same recruit, however, may have met nine of the 10 MOST IMPORTANT criteria and on this basis can be hired.

Take the 10 characteristics and put them in rank order from the most important to the least important. The most important should get the highest value and the least important a lesser value. If there are three very important characteristics, the broker should give them each a value of 20 and put the rest in order. No matter how the broker determines the points, the values should total 100. Now, the broker should put these characteristics and point values on a paper and use this paper to evaluate the recruit. The value number is the total number the recruit actually displays. The scale is from 1 to 10, with 10 meaning that for the specified characteristic the recruit has a perfect value score. The broker should then multiply the value number with the scale number to determine the recruit's total points. The recruit should attain at least 700 total points to be hired. Otherwise, the recruit may not fit well into brokerage system.

The Characteristics Profile could look like this:

Characteristics Profile for a Real Estate Professional

Characteristic	Source	Value	Scale	Total
1. Integrity	References	20	5	100
2. Enthusiasm	Appearance	20	10	200
3. Persistence	Interview	20	8	160
4. Willingness to learn	Interview	12	10	120
5. Competitiveness	Interview	8	7	56
6. Family oriented	References	5	10	50
7. Communicates well	Interview	5	8	40
8. Psychologically mature	Interview	4	10	40
9. Goal oriented	Interview	4	8	32
10. Well educated	Credentials	2	8	10
TOTAL		**100**		**814**

This recruit has a score of 814 and, all things considered, should be hired. Using this scoring approach, the broker should be able to avoid the hassles of recruiting a misfit to the organization. NOTE: There is a blank Characteristics Profile located in the appendix to this book.

Recruiting Actions

The broker must take action to get recruits. Some brokers sit around the real estate office and wait for recruits to come to them. It will happen occasionally, but the broker will never have a fully functional brokerage unless the broker actively recruits.

The Best Source of Recruiting Leads

The best source of recruiting leads is by far the existing sponsored license holders. They are constantly in contact with other real estate license holders in an unobtrusive way. The currently sponsored license holders meet other real estate salespersons at various events, during open houses, or in everyday business. The broker's salespersons believe in their current brokerage system and could be active ambassadors for the brokerage if the broker would simply ask them to do so.

A broker should develop some kind of incentive to encourage the currently sponsored license holders to recruit. This could be based on the new salesperson's production. The bonus could be a few hundred dollars on the new salesperson's first closing and a few hundred more on the second. The broker could pay a long-term bonus for recruits, such as a small percentage of the sales of the new recruit for life. Most brokers will want to wait until the new recruit actually produces before a bonus is paid.

The broker should develop a system to contact every one of the current salespersons per month just to persuade each to recruit. The meeting could be short, or it could be a training session for those who need it. If the salespersons feel weird about recruiting for the broker, the broker should encourage them to name real estate salespersons from competing firms whom they would enjoy working with; then the broker can take steps to recruit these named salespersons. Whatever the broker does, the broker should not let another month go by without developing the best source of recruiting leads—the brokerage's current salespersons!

Telemarketing

In the real estate sales business, brokers train their salespersons to do telemarketing—"cold-calling"—for buyers and sellers. The same should be said for brokers in the brokerage business. Brokers can call certain neighborhoods from which they want to solicit real estate salespersons. Brokers can call those in their sphere of influence (i.e., those who know the brokers and what they do). Brokers can call around a recent listing or sale.

Be sure to follow the "National Do Not Call" rules.

Telemarketing (also called warm-calls and cold-calls) is the random calling of homeowners to see if there is any interest in selling real estate as a career. This is the best type of prospecting for new real estate brokers because of the following factors:

- Finding recruits from cold-calling is easy.
- More contacts are made in less time than by other means of prospecting.
- Unlimited markets exist because almost everyone is interested in real estate.
- No competition comes from other real estate brokers who do not cold-call.
- The broker can prove that he/she can always get recruits.
- When brokers perfect cold-calling, they gain confidence.

Telemarketing Procedure

When prospecting by telephone, the broker should call from the office. There are several reasons for this, but the main one is the broker's connection with the business environment. The broker is physically near the brokerage's real estate sponsored license holders demonstrating how to cold–call and proving that they will do what they are being asked to do.

Here are the actual steps in telemarketing:

1. **choose an area**—The broker should quickly choose an area from which the broker wants salespersons.
2. **call anytime**—The broker should be sure to follow local and national "Do Not Call" laws.
3. **call the individual**
4. **be professional**—The broker should sound businesslike and in control, not desperate. The broker is offering an opportunity for a career.
5. **set up an interview**

6. **meet the recruit**—The interview should take place in the broker's office. The broker should be professional but not intimidating. The broker needs to ask the recruit lots of questions. The actual interview process will be discussed later in the book.
7. **contact recruits at least once per month**—All the broker's efforts are wasted if the broker does not follow up at least once per month. Following up with these recruits is essential. They have many things in their lives pulling them in every direction. Were it the perfect time for them to work real estate, they would have called the broker themselves.

Telemarketing Scripts

Brokers can use two possible approaches to telemarketing: the general approach and the specific-property approach. Here are sample scripts for each approach.

General Approach

Broker: "Hello, is this Mr. or Mrs. _____? (Pause, wait for answer.) My name is Dan Hamilton. I'm a broker with Acme Realty. Have you ever thought about real estate as a career?"

Homeowner: ("No.")

Broker: "Okay. Well, thank you. Bye."

Homeowner: ("Yes.")

Broker: "Great! The reason I asked is that we are looking for a real estate professional in your area. Do you have a second to tell me a little about yourself and what interests you about real estate?"

Specific-Property Approach

Broker: "Hello. Is this Mrs. _____? (Pause, wait for answer.) My name is Dan Hamilton. I'm the broker at Acme Realty. I am calling to see if you have considered selling real estate as a career. Have you?"

Homeowner: ("No.")

Broker: "The reason I ask is, we recently listed/sold a house near yours at _____. As a result of our extensive advertising, we have generated quite a bit of interest

	for homes in this area, and we need more real estate salespersons to handle the interest. Do you know anyone who may be interested? How about yourself?"
Homeowner:	("Yes.")
Broker:	"Do you have a second to tell me a little about your situation and maybe when you could begin your career?"

The general approach can be used at any time for any potential recruit. Notice how fast the broker gets to the main question—the first question. This is important, because most people do not want to talk to a broker because they think the broker is selling something. Being a broker is proud work. The point is to get to the question and get off the telephone. People will not be angry if the broker does not waste their time. So, the faster the broker gets off the telephone with an uninterested person, the faster the broker can find someone who is interested. If an answering machine picks up, the broker should leave a message with the same script given above. The broker should be sure to leave a telephone number and email address.

"Do you have a second to tell me a little about yourself and what interests you about real estate?" is a great question for many reasons. When individuals are called from out of the blue and asked if they have ever thought of selling real estate, they are usually a little skeptical of the caller's motives, whereas the broker may be a little nervous talking with a live prospect. The question relieves the tension of both parties. First, because respondents who are willing to talk about themselves relax as they tell the broker in detail about their situation. Second, because once the individual is talking, the broker has time to gather together his/her thoughts and arrange the interview appointment.

The broker should be consistent in telemarketing. The broker should not call one day and then do nothing for the rest of the month. Consistent recruiting is always more effective than taking a haphazard approach to finding new salespersons for the brokerage.

Tips for Speaking with a Recruit

Here are some suggestions for speaking with a recruit once the broker gets him/her on the telephone:
- *stand*—Standing gives the broker more energy. The broker should not get comfortable and relaxed because that is how the

broker will sound on the telephone. When standing, the broker sounds energized.
- *smile*—People can "see" a person smiling over the telephone. As with standing, the broker needs to show that he/she is having a good time and that he/she believes in real estate as a career. The broker should check himself/herself by facing a mirror when making calls.
- *establish rapport*—The best way to accomplish rapport is to ask the respondents lots of questions. The more questions the broker asks, the more they believe the broker really cares. The broker cannot hire new recruits until they believe the broker cares for them.
- *give a reason for calling*—The broker is calling to announce the need for real estate salespersons in the respondents' immediate area. Because the brokerage does not have a salesperson in the direct area, it creates an opportunity for someone who does want to sell in the area.
- *qualify their interest in the real estate business*—This is where the broker builds the sense of urgency. Recruits should not wait until their children graduate from high school. They should not wait until their spouses retire. They should take this opportunity now and make their move toward their future.
- *gain the recruit's confidence*—The broker should make recruits believe in the broker and what the broker does. The broker should show his/her knowledge of the real estate business by indicating how the recruit fits into this opportunity. The broker should ask the recruits questions to find out what their "hot buttons" are and then use these areas of interest to gain an interview.
- *close for the appointment*—The broker should ask the recruits for an interview. Once the broker has gained their interest, the broker must ask for an interview or offer a career night to them. The broker should not skip this part. All the effort is wasted if the broker does not close for the appointment.

Telemarketing is a numbers game: The more the broker plays, the greater is the chance of winning. The more calls the broker makes, the more recruiting appointments the broker should arrange. The broker should block out time in his/her day for prospecting.

Recruiting Door to Door

Recruiting door to door is "door-knocking." Recruiting door to door puts the broker face to face with potential recruits. With all the do-not-call, antispam, and do-not-fax laws and more to come in the future, door-knocking may be the preferred choice of generic prospecting. There are two basic approaches to recruiting door to door:

- *territory canvassing*—This is getting out in a neighborhood in which the broker wants to recruit salespersons for work and door-knocking for leads.
- *the warm-canvass door*—The broker has no real reason to be in the area, but the neighborhood is nice, and the broker is going to spend a day there to try to discover someone with an interest in selling real estate.

Basics of Recruiting Door to Door
Brokers should take the following steps when calling door to door:

1. after ringing the doorbell, back up a minimum of 2 feet
2. do not stare at the door but instead turn to look away up the street
3. do not turn toward whoever opens the door until he/she speaks
4. turn with a welcoming smile (The broker must have on a real estate name tag.)
5. use this phrasing:

Broker: "Good afternoon. My name is Dan Hamilton. I'm the broker at Acme Realty. There has been a tremendous amount of real estate activity in this area. I was wondering if you'd thought of selling real estate as a career. Do you know of anyone in the neighborhood who might be interested in a new career?"

This type of approach can lead to a discussion during which the broker will learn more about the community and its residents and the community learns more about the broker and his/her brokerage office. The broker's new acquaintance may know of some neighbor who intends to change careers later on and will tell the broker about him/her.

If there is no answer at the door, the broker should leave a door hanger with information about the brokerage and opportunities in the real estate profession.

Categories of Recruits

There are certain categories of recruits to be aware of:

- *not interested*—No prospect—The broker should not follow up with these people. If they are not interested, the broker should not

waste time tracking them. The broker should spend time calling other people.
- *not interested now but perhaps in less than two years*—Lead Prospect–The broker should follow up with these individuals. Two years in the real estate industry is no time at all. The broker should develop some type of database management system on the computer. The broker can buy elaborate software or use the software that is installed on the computer when it was purchased. With this technique, the broker is building a pipeline of future recruits.
- *interested soon but not now*—Possible Prospect–These prospects could be good, but the broker will need to create a sense of urgency. Perhaps they want to enter the business when their children graduate from high school. They may want to get in real estate after their spouses retire. Whatever the reason to wait, the broker needs to create the urgency or else they will simply wait.
- *interested now*—Grand Prospect–This is a winner! The prospect starts real estate school right after hanging up with the broker. He/she is making money six months later. The broker should be sure to follow up with these recruits weekly to make them feel supported.

Forms of Follow-up Contact

The broker can stay in touch through a variety of methods. The broker should change the contact method frequently unless the prospect requests a specific method. The broker can use the telephone, mailouts, and emails or knock on the prospect's door. Here are some suggestions:

- *telephone calls*—Just to let prospects know the broker is there for any questions.
- *monthly mail-out cards*—The broker can get cards printed to mail out to prospective recruits. These cards are a great way to disseminate small amounts of information to recruits.
- *monthly email letters*—Email is probably the most effective way to communicate with recruits if the broker has their permission and follows all laws. Email is virtually free. The only cost is the time it takes to email. Email is also less work than regular mail. The broker can draft one letter and email it to all recruits.
- *knocking on the prospect's door*—The broker should rarely do this, but if he/she is in the area touring property, the broker could stop by

and invite the prospect to go along. The prospect probably will not do so, but he/she will remember that the broker thought to ask.

Agent with Other Company

The "agent with other company" (AWOC) is an individual who is currently licensed with a competing real estate company who believes himself/herself to be happy with his/her current real estate broker. Who would not want to stay with a current broker if moving to a new company would cost thousands of dollars in expenses and lost income? The broker's job is to prove to this satisfied salesperson that moving would be worth the cost.

One important advantage is that the AWOC is obviously interested in selling real estate. AWOCs believe that they can sell real estate effectively with their current real estate company, and if a competing broker tries to tell them they cannot, then the AWOCs typically get irritated. Most AWOCs, however, struggle to obtain listings and sales, which struggle creates resentment against their brokerage and desperation to find a better way. Eventually they get the idea that they need help with marketing and selling skills. Now they begin to take notice on the outside. "Why are others succeeding but not me?" What a good broker needs to do is be there in their thoughts when they decide to consider a change.

Recruits are always at competitors' offices. Some brokers claim, "I don't want to recruit other real estate salespersons because I wouldn't want other brokers recruiting mine." NEWSFLASH! They are recruiting, but that broker just does not want to face the fact. A broker needs to remember way back to when he/she was a real estate salesperson and remember the times he/she was recruited.

Keys to Working with AWOCs

There are specific attitudes a broker should have and specific actions he/she should take to work successfully with AWOCs. Working with AWOCs requires the broker to:

- *meet AWOCs face to face, or else the broker has nothing*—The broker should not believe he/she has an AWOC recruiting campaign until the broker has actually met these recruits face to face. The broker could meet them for a lunch, invite them to a motivational

seminar, or meet them at the brokerage office (meeting AWOCs at the office can be intimidating, so the broker should be careful). The broker should not believe that sending mailouts is a recruiting campaign; it is not—it is a marketing campaign.
- *behave as a professional, not just as a broker*—Sometimes brokers think themselves as somewhat better than the common folk because brokers have a license and are owners of a real estate company. Brokers are not better, however, and brokers should not project some sense of superiority. Brokers should instead act professionally. A broker should not meet a recruit at a bar—it is not professional. A broker should not wear shorts and a T-shirt when meeting a recruit. All this is a major turn-off to the AWOCs the broker wants to recruit. The broker will be their broker, not their buddy. The broker should not embarrass recruits by making a spectacle out of their being in the office. All these actions could spell the end of the recruiting effort.
- *have personal appeal*—The broker's charisma is key to the recruit's decision to join a firm. The broker should ask, "Would I work for me?" The broker is constantly in the limelight and needs to accept this. Do I listen well? Can I show empathy? Answering such questions, the broker should determine his/her own weaknesses as well as his/her own strengths because these are the basis of becoming a powerful broker.
- *be committed to this program for at least 12 months or else not even start*—If a broker makes a concerted effort to recruit AWOCs for two months and then quits, the broker will see very few results. These recruits may not believe they want to leave their current office. What happens is that their current broker has angered the recruit, and then the recruiting broker has a shot at them. The problem is that there is no way to determine when the current broker will anger the potential recruit. It could happen at any time. That is why the recruiting broker should ensure that he/she is always on the mind of the recruit by following up continually.
- *follow up, follow up, and follow up again*—The importance of following up cannot be stressed enough.

AWOC Action Plan

The AWOC action plan requires the broker to take the following steps:

- *call the AWOC*—The broker should call the AWOC's cellular telephone number, not his/her real estate office telephone number. If the broker does not have the potential recruit's cell number, the broker should call the office and ask for it. The broker should talk with an AWOC at his/her office only as a last resort.
- *set up an interview with the recruit*—The broker should determine the best time for the interview. The broker needs to realize the AWOC's time is money. The broker should be sure he/she is not interrupted during the meeting.
- *meet the recruit*—The interview should take place in the broker's office. The broker should be professional but not intimidating. If the AWOC is apprehensive about meeting at the brokerage office, the broker can meet the AWOC at a nice restaurant (but not during the lunch rush). Also, the meeting should not be for dinner because a dinner meeting could be misunderstood. During the meeting, the broker should ask the AWOC lots of questions.
- *contact the recruit at least once per month*—The broker's efforts are wasted if he/she does not follow up at least once per month. Whether the broker contacts an AWOC more than once per month depends on the recruit's motivation. If the AWOC has no interest at this point, the broker can contact once per month and that is sufficient. If the AWOC is close to a decision, the broker may want to call him/her a few times per week.
- *follow up for 12 months*—This is a reasonable period of time for most brokers.
- *follow up, follow up, and follow up again*—Follow-up is the theme of recruiting AWOCs.

Calling on an AWOC

Here is a sample dialogue illustrating a conversation between the broker and a recruit.

Broker: "I am calling for Bob Vinson."
AWOC: "This is Bob."
Broker: "Bob, my name is Dan Hamilton, and I am the broker at Acme Realty. I have been tracking your performance, and I was wondering if you have thought about looking into the advantages of working with our company."
AWOC: "No, I am happy where I am, but thanks for calling."

Broker: "I am glad to hear that. One more thing: Our company is offering an invitation-only real estate seminar on the morning of the 16th describing how to increase your real estate business, and I was wondering if you would be my guest to that event."

The first thing the broker should say is to urge the AWOC to switch companies. Some people may think this is too early to bring up the topic. Brokers teach their salespersons that they must ask for business, so the brokers had better do the same. The broker should ask again but this time disguise the request by offering a seminar. If AWOCs are really that happy, they will say "no" to the offer of education, but if they are not getting the training and education they feel they need, they will say "yes."

Now, about that seminar: The broker should be offering real estate–training classes in the brokerage office at least once per week. If the brokerage is not offering education, the broker needs to remember that other brokers are reading this book, and these brokers will be recruiting his/her salespersons and offering THEM training and education. The broker is simply asking the AWOCs to attend a training session. Once there, they will see that the broker provides services to his/her salespersons that their current broker does not. After the seminar, the broker should ask the AWOCs to take a look at the brokerage office. The broker should plan to have the tour end at his/her office door, and then the broker can ask the AWOCs to take a seat. Now the broker follows the interview process and ends the interview with a "close" to get them to change brokerages.

Response
If the AWOC resists the broker's overtures to change brokerage affiliations, the broker could try this:

Broker: "Is it the interruption of your business that is keeping you from simply talking with me about your future?"

If they respond "no," probe further; if they respond "yes," continue:

Broker: "Well, would you mind if I sent some information that might help you build your real estate business?"

Whatever the answer:

Broker: "I'm sure you have thoughts about your future; before you make any changes, will you at least talk with me?"

This script is designed to get an interview and build goodwill. This is only the first step in the recruiting process.

Alternate Response
Alternatively, the broker could respond thus:

Broker: "I believe in the real estate business, and I believe we should all work together. When you get a new listing, please email an information graphic sheet to me, and I will distribute it to my salespersons to help you get your listings sold.

If the AWOC responds:

AWOC: "I am on a high split that you couldn't match."
Broker: "Great, that must mean you are a top producer. When would you like to sit down and discuss how we can make you even more money?"
AWOC: "Not right now, maybe by the end of the year."

Whatever timeframe the AWOC gives, the broker should call back every month to verify that the AWOC's situation has not changed. AWOCs can get angry at a moment's notice. The recruiting broker might be the only real estate broker who has kept up with them and cared about their situation, so they might end up leaving their current situation to join the recruiting broker. Once the broker has the AWOC interview, the broker should send the AWOC a card reminding him/her of the appointment.

AWOC Fair Deal
The dialogue with the AWOC is one of a fair deal. As the words "fair deal" indicate, it is a deal of valuable items. What the real estate broker wants is a recruiting interview. What the AWOC might need is any number of services, and the broker has to find which service will trigger the AWOC to act. The services the broker has to offer include:

Table funding	National	Production awards
Professional ad writing	company	Great location
Marketing assistance	Administrative	Management
Family culture	help	expertise
Unparalleled training	Advantageous	Private office
Relocation business	compensation	Top-block
Ancillary business	Team atmosphere	service
Community service	Noncompetitive	Social events
Management	managers	Accounting
advancement	Career planning	functions

. . . and any number of other services the broker may offer. Of course these are simply examples; if the brokerage company does not offer some of these services, the broker should delete them from his/her list and add the brokerage's advantages. What the broker offers as a fair deal is extremely important. This is the beginning of the brokerage's value package.

Each time the broker calls an AWOC, the broker should begin with some small talk such as "How is your business going?" or "Did you have a successful weekend?" An AWOC's responses to these types of questions are always the same: The AWOC did great, even if nothing really happened. AWOCs respond in this way because they want to look good. After the small talk, the broker needs to offer a fair deal.

Additional Items the Brokerage Could Offer

Sometimes the broker must offer the top producers just a little more to help convince them to make the move. These items range from simple gifts to monetary contributions to the AWOC's bottom line; of course, the broker would offer such perks only if the brokerage actually provided the service or gift. Thus, the broker could:

- offer to have the company pay for the first set of personal marketing materials
- offer to have the company pay for announcements sent to the AWOC's service area and clients
- send flowers, books, gift certificates, or dinner certificates
- send a letter of appreciation as soon as the interview is over
- offer the recruit a private office if there is one available
- give a recruiting bonus for any real estate salesperson the recruit brings

If the brokerage has several different real estate offices and a corporate headquarters, the broker should arrange to have the recruit visit and have a tour of the place.

The Broker Should Watch for Events

Events taking place in any competitor's real estate office are some of the best leads to find possible recruits. Every dispute, policy alteration, promotion, demotion, arrival, and departure—that is, every change—can develop into an opportunity.

Additional Ways to Improve Recruiting Efforts

There are a number of additional ways a broker can improve his/her recruiting efforts. Here are some of them:

- *The broker MUST terminate unproductive sponsored license holders*— Terminating unproductive salespersons will not only give the office a lift but may help in recruiting additional license holders. No true professional real estate salesperson wants to work with those who are not serious. The broker should give competitors his/her problems and attract their solutions. A broker should immediately target offices that hire unproductive salespersons.
- *The broker should respond when competition offers his/her salespersons a great package*—When competitors are recruiting one of the broker's salespersons, the broker should see how what they offer is different from what they offer their existing salespersons. If the broker finds out they are offering a special package not offered to their

own salespersons, the broker should call and ask the brokerage's sponsored license holders, "What's going on?" The only way for a broker to find this information out is through open communication with his/her salespersons.

- *The broker should respond if the competition alters their current compensation to keep salespersons*—Many brokerages will arbitrarily raise a salesperson's commission to keep him or her. The broker should inform that individual's fellow salespersons who had earned more and are on the same commission-split about this arbitrary raise.
- *The broker should respond when competitors send letters to his/her salespersons*—When competitive brokers send recruiting letters to the brokerage's salespersons, the broker should use this as an opportunity to praise. The broker should tell his/her salespersons that they must be doing a good job because others want them and emphasize that they are appreciated by the brokerage where they are currently working. The broker should have the salespersons take the letters to listing appointments and use the following script:

   Salesperson: "Mr. and Mrs. Seller, I appreciate the fact that you are going to interview with Nosale Real Estate Company, and as a matter of fact I have been offered work with them (show letter). Instead, I have chosen to work with the best company, my company—shouldn't you?"

- *The broker should respond when one of his/her salespersons is recruited*—The broker should send a thank-you note to the competing real estate brokerage addressing the fact that the brokerage wants his/her salespersons because these salespersons are obviously good. This action will tend to stop further recruitment because the other broker now knows that the broker is aware of what is happening.
- *The broker should respond if a competitor's salesperson appears in the newspaper or is featured on a website*—The broker should send flowers and a note to the salesperson at the other office saying, "Congratulations!" Then the broker should call a few days later. The salesperson's current broker probably did not say a thing to him/her.

Advertising for Recruits

The easiest and most frequently used form of recruiting is print advertising. Many brokers have enjoyed success with the use of simple classified ads. The ads are designed to make the telephone ring with inquiries of interest. The ads should be aimed at new licensees; very few experienced real estate licensees will answer an advertisement.

Recruiting ads do not need to be wordy. They need to catch the eye of the reader, create enough interest to cause the reader to take a desired action, and direct that action. Before preparing the ad copy, the broker should analyze the types of prospects the broker wants in the brokerage office and identify their traits and characteristics. The broker needs to decide who the target recruit might be.

Every classified ad should carry the reader through four selling steps. These steps are attention, interest, desire, and action, or AIDA, as they are known through the advertising community.

1. *attract attention*—The broker needs to catch the prospects' attention with the first few words of the ad, or else he/she will lose them forever. A catchy headline may do the trick. In fact, the headline is probably the most important part of an ad. Other tips for attracting attention in the ad include:
   - using sincerity and not clichés
   - describing the ability to control personal time (Real estate salespersons can make their own schedules and work when they choose. People want to control their own time. The broker should always document the results to determine the best use of the brokerage's money.)
   - using lots of white space, which is that space where nothing is written
   - occasionally asking questions in the ad (People have a natural tendency to be attracted to questions.)
2. *arouse interest*—Once the broker has a reader's attention, the broker should use the interest stage to pull him/her in for further reading. Otherwise, the prospect will stop reading and move on to the next ad. The broker needs to create interest and desire with the features the brokerage offers to real estate salespersons and the benefits these features deliver.
3. *create desire*—This stage creates the desire to be part of the brokerage. Writing skill is necessary here to create the right atmosphere for the prospect. If space is available, the broker should list the brokerage's most desirable features.
4. *call for action*—To get the interview, the broker must ask for the interview. Research has found that:

- the broker will receive a greater response if the ad closes with a request to call. The broker should tell readers, "Call now!"
- the broker should use the word "please" because it softens the close, resulting in a greater response.
- if the ad copy tells all the essential facts clearly, holds the reader's attention from start to finish, and makes a specific call to action, it will be successful. The following is a checklist for writing the ad:
    - All facts are organized from the reader's viewpoint. Potential real estate salespersons are looking for a brokerage they feel meets all their needs.
    - There is an appeal to emotions such as love of success, status, and family responsibility.
    - Wording is concise, following the "Keep it simple and short," or KISS, guidelines. The ad avoids long-winded sentences but does not abbreviate or use real estate jargon.
    - Meaningful words that stir emotion are included. Readers need to "feel" the money pouring in. The ad has them touch the cash.
    - The ad inspires confidence. There are no unbelievable, exaggerated descriptions.
    - The target audience is clear. The broker has differentiated marketing and advertised in different types of print media.

Ads have the potential to yield large numbers of telephone inquiries. It is important for the broker/recruiter to have a system in place in the company to handle these inquiries. Brokers should consider the following tips:

- The broker/recruiter should NEVER take these incoming calls directly. The broker should want to control the conversation. The receptionist should be trained to field these calls and solicit the information the broker needs for an appropriate callback. This allows the broker greater control of time and positions the broker to structure the phone conversation.
- Individuals calling into the office should be invited to a "career event" held on a regular basis in the conference room at the real estate office. The broker should avoid the temptation to "sell" over the phone. Recruiting is a process. Answering this call is only a part of the process. It is the first step.

Examples of Advertisements

The following are examples of advertisements that could be run to get real estate recruits to call the recruiting broker's company:

> ***NEED A "JOB"?*** *Then don't call me; I am looking for the person who is pursuing a career. I can offer you the opportunity to make a living and a life for yourself. Call today for a career event date. Dan Hamilton **817-555-1212.***
>
> ***DON'T QUIT JUST YET!!!*** *Before you leave your present job, let us show you how you can increase your income. No experience necessary. We will train you. Once trained, you can quit your job and pursue a rewarding career in real estate. For the next career event date, call Dan Hamilton **817-555-1212.***
>
> ***JOB SECURITY!!!*** *A career in real estate offers you job security. Never worry about layoffs or terminations. Once you learn the real estate business, you can control your destiny. We will train you. All you need is the willingness to work, to be trained, to work flexible hours. For more information on the next career event, call Dan Hamilton **817-555-1212.***
>
> ***YOU DETERMINE YOUR WAGES!!!*** *You work and you earn. No one can stop you except yourself. Call today and learn when the next real estate career event is to be held in your area. Dan Hamilton **817-555-1212.***

Message for Voice Mail

The broker can leave a clear, professional message for voice mail callers. For example:

"Thank you for calling Acme Real Estate Company. Your call is very important, and answering your questions about a career in real estate is our greatest priority. If you will leave your name and a number where you can be reached between four o'clock and six o'clock this afternoon, our career development director will contact you. Again, thank you for calling, and we look forward to our discussion later today."

Recruiter Call-Back Script

Here is a sample script for calling back a potential recruit interested in becoming a real estate salesperson:

Recruiter:	"Hello. May I speak with Mr. Smith?"
Mr. Smith:	"This is Mr. Smith."
Recruiter:	"This is Dan Hamilton, Career Development Director of Acme Real Estate Company, returning a career inquiry call from you. How long have you thought about real estate as a possible career?"
Mr. Smith:	"Well, I haven't really. Your ad just sparked my interest."
Recruiter:	"Great. What I would like to offer you is a career event where I discuss all the information necessary for you to make an intelligent decision if real estate is right for you. Could I register you for an upcoming career event?"
Mr. Smith:	"Sure."
Recruiter:	"Great, I look forward to meeting you."

Once the broker/recruiter has set an appointment with a recruit, the broker must send a reminder card to help to be sure the person will show up. The broker can provide any additional information on the reminder card that is desired.

Potential Recruiting Opportunities

The Local Association of REALTORS®

The local Association of REALTORS® is a great way to promote a brokerage. Every time the Association has meetings, brokers can talk with real estate professionals from competing firms. The broker may be surprised to hear of real estate salespersons who are unhappy and looking for another place to work. With this knowledge the broker can now target a marketing campaign to these specific salespersons. The broker can bring company brochures to the meetings and pass them out; however, the broker will want to clear this activity with the Association first because members may get a little upset if the broker does not consult them first.

Networking

The broker should join a networking group. These groups usually meet once per month and talk about how each member can help the others by referring business. Networking groups can draw several hundred members and put the broker in contact with influential businesspeople.

It is also a great way to find a mentor. A professional broker should not miss out on the power of networking.

Roundtables

Similar to networking are roundtables, which are informal group discussions among professionals who voluntarily serve as information and support resources for one another. Participants meet regularly and learn from each other's experiences. With time, professional relationships develop and participants become familiar with one another's businesses. Roundtables are limited to the same select few businesspeople, however, so the broker should choose them carefully. The most common roundtable discussions are online newsgroups. Newsgroups are like bulletin boards where discussions can occur and be reviewed at the participants' convenience.

Recruit Interview

The broker has accomplished a worthwhile goal—that of getting an interview with a real estate recruit. That success will quickly be dashed if the broker stinks at interviewing. The new recruit and the AWOC must be treated differently. The first thing the broker should do is introduce the new recruit to real estate as a business.

Introductory Discussion

When recruiting a person considering a career in real estate, the broker should make the person aware that real estate sales is a unique business for the following reasons:

- Real estate sales involve complex and intense transactions, including written contracts, spaced negotiations (i.e., the buyer and seller do not negotiate directly), marketing, and finances.
- From the first meeting with a client to the actual closing, real estate business can take a great deal of time, many things can go wrong, and tempers can flare. The recruit also needs to understand that the money is not received until the property is closed.
- There are numerous laws and regulations that the real estate license holder must follow.
- Real estate is usually the largest single purchase a buyer will ever make and the largest sale the seller will ever make.
- Residential real estate is a relationship business. The more people like and trust the license holder, the greater success the license holder will achieve.

Questioning Techniques

When interviewing recruits to work with the brokerage, the broker must use lots of questions. Questioning is by far the best way to communicate. The broker should ask questions to achieve the following goals:

- gain control
- isolate areas of interest
- get minor agreements
- arouse emotions
- show "we care"
- isolate objections
- answer objections

Questions can be placed in two major categories: the open-ended question and the closed-ended question.

The Open-Ended Question

The open-ended question solicits a discussion on the part of the recruit. The recruit can talk forever because of the question. The best open-ended questions paint a picture, and the recruit finishes that picture. Some examples follow:

Broker: "Without limitations, how much would you like to earn in the real estate business? And think about what you would do with that money"

Broker: "What are your concerns about changing real estate companies?"

Broker: "Describe your ideal work environment."

The Closed-Ended Question

The closed-ended question is meant to solicit a "yes" or "no" answer. It is used to direct the recruit, preventing the recruit from expanding on an answer. Some examples of closed-ended questions include:

Broker: "Do you want this room as your personal office space?"

Broker: "Can you make a decision today?"

There is another reason to ask questions instead of immediately responding with answers: A question engages the other person and helps create a more meaningful exchange and a better relationship. It shows that the broker is interested in what that person has to say. The broker cannot move forward in real estate recruiting with a reluctant prospect unless and until the broker manages to create a climate in which that person is talking and not just listening.

Wants-and-Needs Analysis Questions

1. Who else will your decision affect?
2. Do you need a private office?
3. Do you have any special needs that are a concern?
4. How soon would you consider joining our company?
5. Must you settle any matters before making the decision?
6. Do you currently have any listings? Pendings? If so, when will they close?
7. Are you familiar with the procedures for changing real estate companies?
8. Have you interviewed any other offices that you liked?
9. Did you make any written agreements?
10. Are there any other real estate agents who may want to change?
11. Why are you thinking of changing?
12. What do you like best about your present company?
13. What do you like least about your present company?
14. Do you have any special interests or hobbies?

General Interest Questions

1. What do you like most about being in real estate?
2. Do you prefer listings or buyers? Why is that?
3. Where do you see yourself in five years? In 10 years?
4. How do you feel about the market?
5. What is your most successful marketing idea? How do you plan marketing yourself?
6. What is most important to you in a real estate company?

AWOC Questions

1. May I ask why you joined (competitor's name)?
2. Have the reasons why you chose the company then and the reasons why you are with them today changed at all?
3. What do you think of the company's overall office policies?
4. Would you like to see any of those polices changed or improved?

Recruit Interview Hints

When an individual agrees to meet with the broker to let the broker present the advantages of real estate work and working with his/her brokerage, the broker should keep in mind the following:

- During the interview, the broker should write down anything the recruit says. If it is important enough for the recruit to say, it is important enough to write down.
- The broker should prepare in advance for surprises during the interview. Flexibility is the key.
- The broker cannot use the same presentations with proven producers that are used with new licensees.
- The interview should be held in a conference room, not in the broker's office. A broker's office is too much of a power place for a recruit. The broker should offer the recruit a soft drink, a notepad, and a writing instrument.

The Interview

The first interview is really a planned presentation. The broker should create visual aids that address the wants and needs of the real estate salesperson. This is the time to show off the company website.

The broker should list the features of the office, and then the broker should emphasize the benefits of using these systems. The broker should differentiate the brokerage from the competition. If the broker knows that the competition cannot offer something that the broker can, the broker should ask the recruit: "Have you ever seen anything like that before? Can you see how we can help you build your business better than any other brokerage company?" When finished with the interview, the broker should show the recruit through the office and introduce him/her to any real estate salespersons who are present.

Interview Objectives

The broker must have a preplanned series of objectives for the interview. Here are a few objectives the broker must incorporate into the recruiting interview:

- *build rapport*—The broker and the prospect should get to know each other. The broker should concentrate on the prospect and his/her life, not just real estate. No one will work with a broker unless he/she likes and trusts that broker.
- *ask lots of questions*—The broker should spend most of the time asking questions. Questions will allow the broker to control the interview process and gain information.
- *eliminate the competition*—The broker must eliminate any competition. The broker has competition from the recruit's current employment and from any other brokerages out there. The broker should not disparage the competition, but the broker must know what services they offer to real estate license holders and design ways of using this information to an advantage.
- *perform a wants-and-needs analysis*—The broker needs to conduct a wants-and-needs analysis during the interview to find out what motivates the recruit and how the brokerage can aid him/her in fulfilling that motivation. A wants-and-needs analysis is explained next.

Wants-and-Needs Analysis

A wants-and-needs analysis helps identify a potential recruit's real estate brokerage's wants and needs and helps the broker to match the recruit's and the broker's wants, needs, and motives to the specific services available for the real estate salesperson.

The wants-and-needs analysis will give the broker an opportunity to "read" the recruits better and paint a picture of their wants and needs. The most effective way for a broker to read the recruit is to listen. The broker should spend more time listening and less time talking. When the broker does speak, the best way is through probing questions or questions that have purpose.

In a wants-and-needs analysis, the rapport-building step should take place in the first few minutes of each new, important contact with a person. From a psychological viewpoint, rapport building is extremely vital to the outcome of the communications process. The significance of the rapport-building step becomes apparent when analyzed from a behavioral viewpoint. When individuals place trust in each other or feel comfortable with each other, they lower their defense mechanisms and become more open and agreeable to listening to ideas. The intensity of the defense barriers will vary with each individual and the specific situation.

It is the broker's responsibility as a professional to take action to reduce these defense barriers and relieve the tension that exists in all communication situations in the initial stages. It is important for the broker to recognize that this defensive reaction on the part of the other person is not a reaction to the broker personally. It is a reaction to the situation and is normal and natural. The specific techniques the broker utilizes to lower defense barriers will vary depending on the broker's natural behavior and personality. The important point is that the broker should recognize that defense barriers do exist and develop techniques to lower them and establish rapport.

A person's decision to choose a particular real estate office to join is often more emotional than practical. The broker needs to get a sense of the individual's lifestyle because understanding the lifestyle gives the broker better insight into the person's emotional needs. The broker should ask questions such as these:

- Why are you thinking of moving?
- What do you like best about your present company?
- What do you like least about your present company?
- Are you familiar with the procedures for changing real estate companies?
- Have you interviewed any other brokerage offices that you liked?
- Do you currently have any listings? Pendings? If so, when will they close?

- How soon would you consider joining our company?
- Who else will your decision affect?
- Must you settle any matters before making the decision?
- Do you have any special needs that are a concern?
- Are there any other real estate agents who may want to move?

Additional Recruit Interview Questions

The main thing a broker should concentrate on is asking the recruit meaningful questions. Questions allow the broker to control the interview as well as show concern for the recruit. Following are a few general interest questions the broker could ask new recruits as well as questions an office manager might ask of an AWOC:

General Interest Questions for New Recruits

- What do you (think you will) like most about being in real estate?
- Do you (think you will) prefer listings or buyers? Why is that?
- Where do you see yourself in five years? In 10 years?
- How do you feel about the real estate market?
- What is your most successful marketing idea from your previous occupation? or How do you plan on marketing yourself?
- What's most important to you in a real estate company?

Office Manager Questions for the AWOC

- May I ask why you joined "Competitor Realty"?
- Have the reasons why you chose the company then and the reasons why you are with them today changed at all?
- What do you think of the company's overall office policies?
- Would you like to see any of those polices changed or improved?
- Do you feel the broker/manager relates to you and understands your wants and needs?
- Have you achieved the success you thought you would?

The broker should discover what the recruit likes most and least about the owner, manager, company, and other salespersons in the office. Anything the recruit likes about his/her current situation the broker had better be able to duplicate. Anything he/she dislikes the broker should be able to rectify (with limitations). The broker now has an idea of the recruit's wants and needs. The next step is to show the recruit how the brokerage meets those wants and needs. The best way for a broker to handle the presentation part of the interview is to use a presentation manual.

Recruit Presentation

A recruit presentation manual, also called a "marketing book," is a manual showing the recruiting candidate the broker's value package for a sponsored license holder. The manual has traditionally been an actual book showing information and pictures. The print manual is still better than nothing. However, a broker should have all this information on his/her computer and use a data projector to display the information or have separate computers linked with the same information. This presentation material sends a consistent message over and over again. Because it is consistent, the material keeps the broker from straying to areas that might be construed as violations of the federal, state, and local employment laws. (This is probably not a problem, but the manual helps prevent any errors.) The presentation material serves two main purposes:

1. **It provides a visual presentation of the services offered.** A majority of people are visual in nature. This means recruits may gain a greater understanding of the brokerage by seeing it all projected before them rather than just being told about it. The presentation material accomplishes this goal.
2. **It establishes a track for the real estate broker to follow.** One of the biggest fears of a new real estate broker is the recruiting appointment. The broker just does not know what to do and what to say. The presentation material overcomes this dilemma.

Main Topics of a Recruiting Presentation

The following is a list of topics that should be covered in a recruiting interview and the order in which they should be presented:

1. rapport building
2. wants-and-needs analysis
3. broker's duties
4. company value package
5. compensation structure
6. asking to join

Recruiting Packet

A recruiting packet includes all the documents needed to sponsor a license holder. Most real estate brokerages will make up recruiting packets before setting up any recruiting interview. A complete recruiting packet should include at least the following documents:

- Independent Contractor Agreement
- Company Office Policy Manual or Supplement
- Advertisement Request Form
- Compensation Agreement
- Company Agency Manual with Authorization
- Yard Sign Installation Form
- Suggestion-for-Training Form
- Office Repair Form
- Commission Disbursement Authorization
- any additional forms required by law or the broker

The broker should keep several of these packets in his/her briefcase and automobile. The broker never knows when he/she might need a recruiting packet.

Costs of Recruiting

In setting up a recruiting campaign, the broker must know the costs. The following lists several items that could cost the broker money:

- print advertisements
- design, printing, and postage for recruiting brochures
- salary and benefits or fees for a staff recruiter
- career event:
    - advertising the event
    - printing costs for marketing the event
    - time it takes to hold the event
    - signs that market the event
    - room rental
    - refreshments for the participants
- recruiting contests to generate recruits from currently sponsored license holders
- bonuses for current license holders who bring in new salespersons
- branch manager's time spent recruiting (calculated using a percentage of salary and benefits)

- interview time
- new salesperson's aptitude or other profiling assessments
- company-paid costs associated with licensing
- cost of trainers, office space rental, and training materials
- start-up supplies such as signs, stationery, and business cards
- administrative time for processing new salespersons

First, the broker should add up all the previous costs incurred for a given year and divide that by the number of new salespersons who have joined the brokerage in the past 12 months. The broker will get the cost for recruiting each new salesperson.

Second, the broker should calculate the other costs of operating the office, excluding sales commissions, off-the-top franchise fees (if required), referral fees, MLS and National Association of REALTORS® costs reimbursed by salespersons, and management commission overrides but including all other fixed expenses. Divide total fixed expenses by the number of full-time salespersons the brokerage has on board. That number is the cost of retaining salespersons. Add the cost of recruiting to that of retention, and the broker will have a sense of what the brokerage is spending to acquire and support a newly sponsored license holder. The broker may also want to factor in how long it will take a new sponsored license holder to generate enough dollars to offset recruiting and start-up costs.

Objection-Handling Techniques

When a broker practices the art of recruiting real estate license holders, the broker will find that some of them will have concerns that they believe will hinder them from joining the brokerage. These are objections that can become roadblocks, so the broker must be able to handle objections. Here are some suggestions to help the broker be successful at recruiting license holders:

- The broker should develop powerful, preplanned responses for each potential objection.
- The broker should create a list of compensating benefits. The broker should get current license holders' input about what they like about the brokerage.
- The objections will change depending on the person being recruited, and so the broker should customize responses.
- The best way for a broker to prevent objections is to be prepared and keep the responses short.

Objection Versus Rejection

It is important for the broker not to read the resistance in an objection as a personal rejection. Almost all people fear rejection to varying degrees, and it is important to recognize that a broker may have a tendency to take an objection personally, especially if the broker has had a tough day. The broker needs to begin thinking of objections as questions with emotional content. This will help the broker deal in a more positive way with the substance of the objection and the person objecting.

Most objections are not as serious or formidable as they initially seem. Often what appears to be an objection is merely a request for more information. The main distinction between an objection and a question is that a question requires only information. An objection has some emotional content and often indicates resistance to an offer. In the latter case, the broker has to provide reassurance as well as information. Objections can help the broker if they mean that the recruit:

- is interested in what the broker is saying
- is listening attentively enough to have objections
- is thinking through the broker's solution
- is trying to resolve foreseeable difficulties
- wants more information about the broker's proposed solution

The absence of objections can be a warning that the recruit may not be interested or is not listening.

Tips for Addressing Objections

Here are three tips for addressing objections:

1. The broker should agree with the recruit and then modify the recruit's thinking.
2. The broker should direct the recruit to his/her final objection by asking minor questions.
3. Now that the broker knows the recruit's final objection, the broker should be able to handle it.

The usual final objection from an experienced real estate person deals with commission-splits or office fees, whereas the usual final objection from a new real estate salesperson is training and broker support. Direct the recruits to the areas of their concern by using closed-ended questions. For example:

Recruit: "I would like to think it over first."
Broker: "I understand that this is a complex decision. Let me ask, are you thinking about the size of our office?"
Recruit: "No, the size is fine."
Broker: "Is it the area where the office is located?"
Recruit: "No, I like the area."
Broker: "Is it me? Do you like and trust me?"
Recruit: "Of course, I like you."

Big pause, then slowly . . .

Broker: "Is it your proposed commission-split with us?"
Recruit: "Well, you know, it is less than I was hoping for."
Broker: "I remember. But let me ask you, if we could agree on a commission-split, would you join my company today?"
Recruit: "Yes . . . yes, I would."

The broker moved through a series of questions toward the final objection and then closed on that objection.

Handle Objections by Asking Questions

To handle objections, the broker must ask lots of questions. When the broker becomes great at asking questions, the broker will be great at handling objections. The questions must have a purpose—called "probing questions." Here are seven steps for handling objections or addressing concerns that almost always work in the broker's favor. These steps also work well in diffusing tense situations.

- **Step 1: The broker must hear them out.** When a recruit talks, the broker should be courteous and listen. The broker should not be quick to address every phrase uttered. The broker should give the person time. The broker should encourage the person to tell the whole story behind his/her concern. While listening, the broker should take notes on everything the recruit says. Doing so allows the broker time to analyze what is said and also gives the broker notes to reflect on at a later time. But most important, it shows the broker cares about the recruit.
- **Step 2: The broker should feed it back.** The broker should rephrase the recruit's concern. The broker is in effect asking for even more information. The broker should be certain the recruit has aired all his/her concerns so that none crops up after these are

handled. In doing this, the broker is asking the recruit to trust him/her. The broker should clarify any concern by probing to learn why the recruit feels that way. People sometimes need help expressing their feelings. This approach helps all parties understand the true nature of the concerns. The broker should begin probing questions as follows:

> "If I understand . . . ."
> "Are you saying . . . ?"
> "Will you tell me more . . . ?"
> "Will you explain further . . . ?"
> "What I think you are saying is . . . ."

When the concerns are cleared up, the broker moves on to the next step.

- **Step 3: The broker should question it.** This step is where subtlety and tact come into play. If the concern is that the recruit objects to not having a private office, the broker should not say, "What's wrong with that?" Instead, the broker should gently ask, "A shared office makes you uncomfortable?" If it does, the recruit will tell the broker why. Perhaps he/she does not want privacy. Perhaps sharing an office feels like a demotion. Now the broker can move forward to handle the objection. The broker cannot ask too many questions if the questions are from the heart and are meaningful.

- **Step 4: The broker should dignify it.** The broker should dignify the concern of the recruit by voicing genuine understanding of how the recruit is feeling. Noting that many other people in the same situation have felt the same way warms the other person to the broker's response. The broker can say:

> "I can appreciate that. Other candidates for our company have felt the same way."
> "I think I understand how you feel."
> "That's a reasonable point of view."
> "That's a good question."

- **Step 5: The broker should discuss it.** Once the broker is confident that he/she has the whole story behind a concern, the broker can discuss it by providing information that explains the advantages of the broker's perspective and reassures the other party. The broker can say:

"We have a large number of salespersons who take advantage of our . . . ."

"Market data show we are selling our inventory in 90 days or fewer. . . ."

"I could help you with . . . ."

- **Step 6: The broker should confirm the answer.** Once the broker has answered the objection, it is important that the broker confirm that the recruit heard and accepted the answer. If the broker does not complete this step, the recruit is very likely to raise the same objection again. If he/she agrees that the broker's comment addressed the concern, then the broker is one step closer to persuading the recruit. If he/she is not satisfied with the answer, now is the time to know, not later. The broker should confirm that the concern has been successfully addressed:

    "Will that be okay?"
    "Does that sound like a service you could use?"
    "Do you see the benefit of . . . . ?"

- **Step 7: The broker should lead on.** The broker should lead on to the next section of the presentation. The broker should take a conscious, purposeful step back into the presentation. The broker should take some sort of action that signals to the other person that the broker is forging ahead.

These seven steps, if the broker learns them and applies them properly, will take the broker a long way toward achieving the goal of recruiting license holders, even when the recruits raise objections or concerns.

Objection-Handling Worksheets

Objection-handling worksheets are used to prepare for all anticipated objections during an interview session. All objections cannot be overcome, but good interviews help recruits move closer to a decision to join the brokerage. The main key to handling objections successfully is identifying the specific nature of the objection. Any time an objection is resolved, the opportunity exists to move the recruit closer to making a change.

The basic steps in writing an objection-handling worksheet require the broker to list:

1. all potential objections anticipated during an interview;
2. all potential causes of those objections;
3. potential questions to identify the cause for the individual's objection; and
4. objection-handling techniques to use for each cause.

If the broker completes these objection-handling worksheets, the broker will find that he/she is prepared to handle almost any objection.

Closing Techniques

The first goal of a broker when he/she meets a new person is to build liking and trust. The following sections present techniques that can be used to help a recruit reach a decision to join the brokerage. Some of them are manipulative (they are given here only as techniques; brokers uncomfortable with any technique should not use it). Manipulative techniques benefit only the broker, not the recruit. The broker should be sure that his/her interest is always directed toward the recruit. If the broker chooses not to use a specific technique, fine; the broker should, though, now be able to recognize the technique when used on the broker himself/herself. NOTE: These techniques are presented in no specific order.

Trial Close
The trial close is used to take the temperature of the recruit. A trial close asks a question. If the recruit agrees, he/she is interested. If the answer is negative, the recruit is not ready to make a decision. The best trial closes are "tie-downs" and "if-then" closes. The following is an example of a trial close: "When do you want to take possession of your office?" If the recruit likes the brokerage, he/she will answer. If not, he/she will protest. Now the broker knows whether to move to the final close.

The Tie-Down Close
A tie-down is a question at the end of a sentence that demands a "yes" response. It is used to affirm a positive idea in which the recruit shows an interest. If the recruit responds with a "yes," he/she might be interested. If the recruit is apathetic regarding the tie-down, this is not right for the recruit, and the broker must change direction. Here are some examples of tie-downs a broker might use:

- "A reputation for professionalism is important, isn't it?"
- "It would be convenient to move as soon as possible, wouldn't it?"
- "The services we offer could make you money, don't you agree?"
- "In a well-recognized office in this area, you could serve your clients better, couldn't you?"
- "You are interested in your listings having complete exposure, aren't you?"

The question is not necessarily used to get an answer; just a nod of the head will do. The broker could use the tie-down in the beginning of the sentence. Here are further examples:

- "Wouldn't you agree that this an enjoyable working environment?"
- "Isn't it exciting the activities that can be accomplished with a large advertising budget?"

As with all the techniques, this one can be overused, so the broker needs to be careful.

Alternate-of-Choice Close

An alternate-of-choice close is a question with only two answers. Both responses are minor agreements leading toward major decisions. For example, the broker might say any of the following:

- "I have an opening now for an interview, or would later today be more convenient?"
- "I can be available at 2 p.m. or 4 p.m. Which time would better suit your schedule?"
- "I can clear my schedule for you on Saturday or Sunday. Which would you prefer?"
- "If everything goes according to your plan, about how soon would you like to move, in 60 days or 90 days?"

Assumptive Close

An assumptive close is a question that assumes the recruit agrees with the proposal or statement; if not, the recruit will stop the broker. For example, the broker might say:

- "Mary, I am on TREC's website; what is your license number for the transfer?"
- "We have our office meeting on Friday, do you want me to introduce you at that time, or shall I wait another week?"

Feedback Question Close

The feedback question close is taking a minor objection and warmly feeding it back in the form of a question. For example:

Recruit: "I don't want to jeopardize my current pendings."
Broker: "You don't want to lose your pendings? Will you elaborate on that?"
Recruit: "I don't want to make anyone mad at me."
Broker: "Oh, you don't want to make your previous broker angry? What makes you think he (or she) won't understand?"
Recruit: "Can you guarantee me that I will make more money than I am now?"
Broker: "Can I guarantee you more money? Does your current broker guarantee you money?"
Recruit: "Will you put a notice of my changing brokerages on your website?"
Broker: "Do you want me to place a notice of your changing brokerages on our website?"
Recruit: "Will you advertise my listings on your website without my approval?"
Broker: "Would you prefer that we call before we advertise any of your listings?"

Similar Situation Close

A similar situation close involves relating a true story about someone else who was in the same situation that the recruit is in now. For example:

Broker: "He was so hesitant, and then he went ahead with the changeover to our brokerage, and today he is a top producer."
Recruit: "I think it would be best to move at the end of the year."
Broker: "That certainly is true. The best time of the year to transfer to a new real estate brokerage is at the end of a year; however, it's a proven fact that few recruits are willing to wait to the end of a year to take advantage of the income potential of working with our company. In fact, it's possible that any positive that you would achieve by waiting would be offset by the loss in income you would see if you did wait. Have you ever changed real estate companies before? It can be a rude awakening. Awhile back I had a real estate

recruit who was determined to wait to the end of the year to make a change. Unfortunately, by waiting he lost thousands of dollars in increased commission income that he would have received by making the change early. He said that after he analyzed the differences, he wished he hadn't waited. This is the type of thing that bothers me about waiting to make the change, and I would hate to see the same situation happen to you."

Reduce-to-the-Ridiculous Close

The reduce-to-the-ridiculous close is when a salesperson takes a large sum (usually money) and breaks it down so far that it seems meaningless. There are all kinds of ways of describing the cost of something. If a person went to the Boeing Aircraft Company and asked what it costs to fly a 747 from coast to coast, nobody would state that it is $50,000. He/She would instead say that it is 11 cents per passenger mile. If the broker is working with a recruit who truly wants to change real estate brokerages but does not want to pay the costs of making a move, the broker could consider using the following script:

Broker: "How much do you think it will cost you to make the move?"

Recruit: "Well, once you consider that I will have to produce new personal brochures, business cards, and marketing materials, probably $5,000."

Broker: "I know $5,000 seems like a lot of money, but tell me, how long do you plan on selling real estate?"

Recruit: "The rest of my life."

Broker: "Well, I appreciate that, but let's say you sell real estate for only another 20 years. If you break down that $5,000 per year, you're only looking at (punch your calculator on your smartphone) $250 a year. If you look at the big picture, you get the advantages of dealing with our company, including the world-class website we have, for the price of a nice hotel room for one night!"

"Let's see what that works out to be (punch the calculator) per month. Twenty dollars, hmm . . . . What does it cost for you and your spouse to go to the movies?"

Recruit: "Well, I guess about eight dollars a person."

Broker: "Add popcorn and a drink, and you are well over the 20 dollars. And for that 20 dollars, you can get your own private office and access to a shared secretary!"

"I wonder what that is per day. (Punch the calculator.) Sixty-six cents per day! That is less than you would pay for a cup of coffee, and I am not talking designer coffee."

"Let's get serious. You want to make the change. We are sure the costs will be outweighed by the increased services you will receive. As a matter of fact (rummage through your pocket for three quarters and toss them on the table), let me pay for your first day.

"All I need you to do is authorize this paperwork, and I will make the transfer right now on the Commission's website. (Hand the recruit your pen.)"

Some explanation is necessary. First, not all techniques work all the time, but all of them work some of the time. Also, notice that the recruit wants to make a change. If the broker is pushing the recruit into a decision just to get another recruit, the broker is being manipulative. Brokers are professionals, not high-pressure salespersons. To use this technique properly, the broker should start big at an annual figure and work down to the daily amount.

One broker used this technique on an accountant. After the broker finished, the accountant said, "Your numbers are all wrong. Financing $5,000 is a lot different; plus there are tax consequences and the time value of money to consider. But I do want to join your company, so I will pay the $5,000." Now, the broker was not sure what happened, but the recruit joined the brokerage. Sometimes the recruit just needs a moment to reflect, and ANY technique would have allowed the time.

Puppy Dog Close

The puppy dog close allows a person to "pretend" as if he/she owns something for a short period of time. This close is just as it sounds, and

it came from pet shop owners. A family might walk into the pet shop and look at a cute puppy dog. The kids and the wife fall in love with the puppy. The husband also falls in love with the puppy but is hesitant to buy it. The pet shop owner says, "It's Friday. Take the puppy home with you over the weekend, and if on Monday you don't want it, just bring it on back." What happens? Of course the family never brings the puppy back.

This is a favorite technique of auto dealers. They offer to let a person take the car for a test drive, hoping the person will fall in love with it and will not be able to give it up. So how can brokers use this in real estate recruiting? The broker could have the recruit use a spare desk with a telephone and computer, or better yet the broker could have his/her space already prepared. The broker then offers the recruit the use of the desk while the broker answers a few critical emails. While using the desk, the recruit begins to feel part of the office.

Take-Away Close
The take-away close literally takes away the object that the consumer wants to buy. A person has a stronger sense of motivation when there is a potential to lose something than when something is to be gained. The take-away close is most famously used by car salespersons. They ask a potential buyer for the best offer, and whatever the buyer says, they reply, "What? I can't do that; I guess you will have to find another, less expensive car. Could I show you the . . . ?" But no other car will do for the buyer, so the buyer pays the greater amount. A broker can use this technique in real estate, but the broker should be very careful. This one is touchy because recruits can and will feel that the broker is manipulating them if a broker uses this technique dishonestly. For example, the broker might say:

> "Look, if you don't agree to join my company today, you will not be asked again."

This is not the best script for building rapport. Also, the broker must really mean it because any other action will cause the recruit not to believe the broker.

Appeal to the Higher Authority
Appealing to the higher authority is not taking responsibility for a rule. When a real estate broker is asked to do something that he/she does not

want to do, the broker is tempted to blame it on someone or something else. For example, a recruit asks a broker to raise commission-splits, and the broker responds, "That is against the company policy." The real estate broker, not some company policy, must be thought of as the higher authority. The broker must project that he/she can handle any decision and should be able to negotiate with the recruit for the best of both parties.

No matter what, the broker should not appeal to the higher authority. Here is better script:

> "I will not negotiate a commission-split for you that is better than that of current license holders in my office; it would not be fair to them, and you would not appreciate it if that were done to you. If you want to get a higher split than what I am offering, please join our brokerage and earn it."

If-Then Close

The if-then close is when a salesperson states, "If I were to . . . , then would you . . . ?" The if-then close should be a broker's favorite technique to use. It is the perfect trial close. For example:

Recruit: "Will I get relocation business?"

Most real estate brokers respond with:

Broker: "If we have some, you will be put on a rotation basis."

Or

Broker: "Sure."

There just is not anything there. No talent, no skill. The recruit is clearly interested in joining the brokerage because the recruit asked a question about the income he/she could make only if he/she joined the brokerage. If the broker really listened to the recruit, it would sound like this:

Recruit: "I really want to join your company. I want to change today if you can close me. If not, I will join another real estate company. Oh, by the way, if you offer relocation business, that would be great!"

This is what the recruit is TRULY saying. The broker needs to see how motivated he/she really is by closing.

Broker: "Mr./Mrs. Recruit, if I can guarantee you relocation business, then would you agree to join our brokerage?"

However the recruit responds, the broker now knows a whole lot more than he/she did 10 seconds before the question was asked. As with all techniques, the broker should not overuse this one.

CHAPTER SUMMARY

Recruiting is the most important function a broker must be able to perform.

The second most important function would be to retain those who are hired.

Real estate salespersons leave the business because they are tired of it or make no money at it. Some leave because of a spouse's job transfer or retirement.

The salesperson who makes the brokerage the most money in five years may not even be in the business today.

A prelicensed prospect is a person off the street, whereas new license holders have just been licensed.

Experienced licensed holders are licensed real estate salespersons who have been in the business for at least two years.

License-returned people have had their license and for some reason have sent it back to the Texas Real Estate Commission (TREC).

The following are a few of the reasons real estate license holders have chosen their broker:

- company reputation
- broker reputation
- proximity to personal residence
- successful office
- professional office appearance
- education and training
- experienced management
- skilled and helpful staff
- autonomy to do their own business
- name recognition

The following are reasons that a salesperson leaves an office:

- high office expenses
- too much bureaucracy and company control
- size of commission
- too many mandatory meetings
- too many fees and charges related to transactions

Some of the characteristics a broker may consider important could include the following:

well educated	financially secure	full-time worker
logical	honest	competitive
trustworthy	quick witted	experienced in sales
intense	aggressive	technology savvy
business savvy	team player	mild mannered
family oriented	ethical	psychologically mature
well spoken	punctual	humorous
hungry	willing to learn	fun loving
professional	well dressed	intelligent
spiritually balanced	charismatic	has a great work ethic
energetic	talented presenter	goal oriented
organized	emotionally stable	enthusiastic
self disciplined	risk taker	persistent
practical	decisive	well adjusted
optimistic	energetic	poised
socially interactive	focused	discerning
communicates well	opportunistic	good problem solver
has a great memory	detail oriented	patient

The best source of recruiting leads is by far the existing sponsored license holders.

Telemarketing (i.e., cold-calling, also called warm-calls and gold-calls) is the random calling of homeowners to see if there is any interest in selling real estate as a career. This is the best type of prospecting for new real estate brokers because of the following factors:

- Finding recruits from cold-calling is easy.
- More contacts are made in less time than by other means of prospecting.
- Unlimited markets exist because almost everyone is interested in real estate.

- No competition comes from other real estate brokers who do not cold-call.
- The broker can prove that he/she can always get recruits.
- When brokers perfect cold-calling, they gain confidence.

Here are the actual steps in telemarketing:

1. choose area
2. call anytime
3. call the individual
4. be professional
5. set up an interview
6. meet the recruit
7. contact at least once a month

Here are some suggestions for speaking with a recruit once the broker gets him/her on the telephone:

- stand
- smile
- establish rapport
- give a reason for calling
- qualify their interest in the real estate business
- gain the recruit's confidence
- close for the appointment

Telemarketing is a numbers game: The more the broker plays, the greater is the chance of winning.

Territory canvassing means getting out in a neighborhood in which the broker wants to recruit salespersons for work and door-knocking for leads.

The warm-canvass door is where the broker has no real reason to be, but it's a nice area, and the broker is going to spend a day there to try to discover someone with an interest in selling real estate. Brokers should take the following steps when calling door to door:

1. after ringing the doorbell, back up a minimum of 2 feet
2. do not stare at the door but instead turn to look away up the street
3. do not turn toward whoever opens the door until he/she speaks
4. turn with a welcoming smile (The broker must have on a real estate name tag.)

Recruiting Sales Agents

5. use this phrasing:
   "Good afternoon. My name is Dan Hamilton. I'm the broker at Acme Realty. There has been a tremendous amount of real estate activity in this area. I was wondering if you'd thought of selling real estate as a career? Do you know of anyone in the neighborhood who might be interested in a new career?"

There are certain categories of recruits. There are those who are:

- not interested;
- not interested now but may be in less than two years;
- interested soon, but not now; or
- interested now.

Here are some ways to communicate with recruits:

- telephone calls
- monthly mail-out cards
- monthly email letters
- knocking on the prospect's door

The "agent with other company" (AWOC) is an individual who is currently licensed with a competing real estate company who believes himself/herself to be happy with his/her current real estate broker. Working with AWOCs requires the broker to:

- meet AWOCs face to face, or else the broker has nothing
- behave as a professional, not just as a broker
- have personal appeal (often key to the recruit's decision to join a firm)
- be committed to this program for at least 12 months or else not even start
- follow up, follow up, and follow up again

The AWOC action plan requires the broker to take the following steps:

1. call the AWOC
2. set up an interview with the recruit
3. meet the recruit
4. contact the recruit at least once per month
5. follow up for 12 months
6. follow up, follow up, and follow up again (Follow-up is the theme of recruiting AWOCs.)

The services the broker has to offer an AWOC include:

Table funding	National company	Production awards
Professional ad writing	Administrative help	Great location
Marketing assistance	Advantageous	Management
Family culture	compensation	expertise
Unparalleled training	Team atmosphere	Private office
Relocation business	Noncompetitive	Top-block service
Ancillary business	managers	Social events
Community service	Career planning	Accounting
	Management	functions
	advancement	

Among the additional ways to improve recruiting efforts, the broker should:

- terminate unproductive sponsored license holders
- respond when the competition offers his/her salespersons a great package
- respond if the competitors alter their current compensation to keep salespersons
- respond when competitors send letters to his/her salespersons
- respond when one of his/her salespersons is recruited
- respond if a competitor's salesperson appears in the newspaper or is featured on a website

There are four selling steps for writing an advertisement:

1. attract attention
2. arouse interest
3. create desire
4. call for action

The local Association of REALTORS® is a great way to promote a brokerage.

Networking groups usually meet once per month and talk about how each member can help the others by referring business.

Roundtables are informal group discussions among professionals who voluntarily serve as information and support resources for one another.

When recruiting a person considering a career in real estate, the broker should make the person aware that real estate sales is a unique business for the following reasons:

- Real estate sales involve complex and intense transactions, including written contracts, spaced negotiations (i.e., the buyer and seller do not negotiate directly), marketing, and finances.
- From the first meeting with a client to the actual closing, the real estate business can take a great deal of time, many things can go wrong, and tempers can flare.
- There are numerous laws and regulations that the real estate license holder must follow.
- Real estate is usually the largest single purchase a buyer will ever make and the largest sale the seller will ever make.
- Residential real estate is a relationship business.

The broker should ask questions to achieve the following goals:

- gain control
- isolate areas of interest
- get minor agreements
- arouse emotions
- show "we care"
- isolate objections
- answer objections

The open-ended question solicits a discussion on the part of the recruit. The recruit can talk forever because of the question.

The closed-ended question is meant to solicit a "yes" or "no" answer.

To prepare for an interview, the broker should keep in mind the following:

- During the interview, the broker should write down anything the recruit says.
- The broker should prepare in advance for surprises during the interview.
- The broker cannot use the same presentations with proven producers that are used with new licensees.
- The interview should be held in a conference room, not in the broker's office.

Here are a few objectives the broker should incorporate into the recruit interview:

- build rapport
- ask lots of questions
- eliminate the competition
- perform a wants-and-needs analysis

The presentation material serves two main purposes:

1. It provides a visual presentation of the services offered.
2. It establishes a track for the real estate broker to follow.

The following is a list of topics that should be covered in a recruiting interview and the order in which they should be presented:

1. rapport building
2. wants-and-needs analysis
3. broker's duties
4. company value package
5. compensation structure
6. asking to join

A recruiting packet includes all the documents needed to sponsor a license holder.

A complete recruiting packet should include at least all the following documents:

- Independent Contractor Agreement
- Company Office Policy Manual or Supplement
- Advertisement Request Form
- Compensation Agreement
- Company Agency Manual with Authorization
- Yard Sign Installation Form
- Suggestion-for-Training Form
- Office Repair Form
- Commission Disbursement Authorization
- Any additional forms required by law or the broker

The following are several items that could cost the broker money when setting up a recruiting campaign:

- print advertisements
- design, printing, and postage for recruiting brochures
- salary and benefits or fees for a staff recruiter
- career event:
  - advertising the event
  - printing costs for marketing the event
  - time it takes to hold the event
  - signs that market the event
  - room rental
  - refreshments for the participants
- recruiting contests to generate recruits from currently sponsored license holders
- bonuses for current license holders who bring in new salespersons
- branch manager's time spent recruiting (calculated using a percentage of salary and benefits)
- interview time
- new salesperson's aptitude or other profiling assessments
- company-paid costs associated with licensing
- cost of trainers, office space rental, and training materials
- start-up supplies such as signs, stationery, and business cards
- administrative time for processing new salespersons

Here are some suggestions to help handle objections:

- The broker should develop powerful, preplanned responses for each potential objection.
- The broker should create a list of compensating benefits.
- The objections will change depending on the person being recruited, and so the broker should customize responses.
- The best way for a broker to prevent objections is to be prepared and keep the responses short.

Here are three tips for addressing objections:

1. The broker should agree with the recruit and then modify the recruit's thinking.
2. The broker should direct the recruit to his/her final objection by asking minor questions.
3. Now that the broker knows the recruit's final objection, the broker should be able to handle it.

These are the seven steps to take to handle objections:

Step 1: The broker must hear it out.
Step 2: The broker should feed it back.
Step 3: The broker should question it.
Step 4: The broker should dignify it.
Step 5: The broker should discuss it.
Step 6: The broker should confirm the answer.
Step 7: The broker should lead on.

Objection-handling worksheets are used to prepare for all anticipated objections during an interview session. The basic steps in writing an objection-handling worksheet require the broker to list:

1. all potential objections anticipated during an interview;
2. all potential causes of those objections;
3. potential questions to identify the cause for the individual's objection; and
4. objection-handling techniques to use for each cause.

A trial close asks a question. If the recruit agrees, he/she is interested. If the answer is negative, the recruit is not ready to make a decision.

A tie-down is a question at the end of a sentence that demands a "yes" response.

An alternate-of-choice close is a question with only two answers.

An assumptive close is a question that assumes the recruit agrees with the proposal or statement; if not, the recruit will stop the broker.

The feedback question close is taking a minor objection and warmly feeding it back in the form of a question.

A similar situation close involves relating a true story about someone else who was in the same situation that the recruit is in now.

CHAPTER QUESTIONS

1. What is the most important function a broker must be able to perform?
   A. teach real estate courses
   B. coach salespersons
   C. recruit salespersons
   D. greet guests

2. What is the best source of recruiting leads?
   a. existing sponsored license holders
   b. short-order cooks from the local diner
   c. high schools
   d. placing a newspaper ad

3. What is "cold-calling"?
   A. illegal trading in Texas
   B. an ethical violation of the Texas Association of REALTORS®
   C. engaging in telemarketing
   D. calling friends and family to drum up real estate business

4. Telemarketing:
   A. makes it easy to find recruits
   B. creates more contacts in less time
   C. taps an unlimited market
   D. all of the answer choices

5. What is it called when a broker wants to recruit salespersons for the brokerage from a particular neighborhood?
   A. steering
   B. territory canvassing
   C. situs
   D. blockbusting

6. What is an AWOC?
   A. assisted work/occupation compensation
   B. available with overhead compartment
   C. answered with one call
   D. agent with other company

7. Which is NOT one of the four selling steps for writing an advertisement?
   A. attract attention
   B. arouse interest
   C. create determination
   D. call for action

8. What type of question solicits a discussion on the part of the recruit?
   A. open ended
   B. closed ended
   C. wraparound
   D. retaining

9. What two purposes does presentation material serve?
   A. visually presents the services offered and provides a track for real estate brokers to follow
   B. proves that the broker knows real estate and allows the recruit to request a change from THE TREC
   C. provides a legal way for the recruit and a legal way for the broker to rescind the agreement
   D. provides an alternative to the "yellow pad" technique and shows up technologically uninformed brokers"

10. What closing technique allows a person to "pretend" as if he/she owns something for a short period of time?
    A. Appeal to the Higher Authority close
    B. Puppy Dog close
    C. Same Situation close
    D. If/Then close

CHAPTER 12

Professional Brokerage Competency and Associate License Holder Productivity

Professional brokerage competency relates to the actions of the broker while operating a real estate brokerage. The broker as well as his/her sponsored license holders must have competency in the real estate industry.

Texas Real Estate Commission (TREC) on Rule 531.3 Competency

It is the obligation of a real estate agent to be knowledgeable as a real estate brokerage practitioner. The agent should:

1. be informed on market conditions affecting the real estate business and pledged to continuing education in the intricacies involved in marketing real estate for others;
2. be informed on national, state, and local issues and developments in the real estate industry; and
3. exercise judgment and skill in the performance of the work.

License holder productivity is the basis of a brokerage. If the license holders are not productive, the brokerage cannot make a profit. If the brokerage does not make a profit then the brokerage fails. The broker must make every effort to provide the tools necessary for all the sponsored real estate license holders to be productive.

Managing Employees and Independent Contractors

Managing employees is different from managing independent contractors. The broker has a great deal more authority in managing employees than independent contractors. However, there are numerous laws protecting employees, with far fewer protecting independent contractors. The broker must have policies and procedures in place to handle both the employee and the independent contractor.

Managing New Real Estate License Holders

The broker needs to take great care when managing new sponsored license holders. The new license holder needs his/her hand held, but the broker cannot let that person become dependent on the broker. Training and accountability are musts for new license holders. More time should be spent with new license holders than with veteran (i.e., experienced) license holders.

The biggest fear for a new real estate salesperson is lack of knowledge about how to make money. This is where the broker, assistant manager, or trainer teaches the "newbies" how to perform. It is a joy to teach them because they do not challenge and they are so excited to do well. Not only that, they are usually "hungry" (and that is literally as well as figuratively) to make some money fast.

Managing Experienced Real Estate License Holders

Managing experienced real estate sponsored license holders requires more talent than managing a new license holder. A broker could get away with not knowing much with new license holders because they do not know any better, but not so with the veterans. A lot of brokers cannot retain the services of their veterans because they have nothing to offer them. Experienced salespersons do not need the broker's help or advice very often. They do not need the typical training offered by real estate offices. The best way to handle experienced salespersons is to put them on a schedule of individual business development (IBD) coaching meetings. During these meetings, the broker can access the needs of these experienced license holders and then offer the solutions necessary to fulfill their needs.

Tracking

Brokers need to be aware of where their company has been, how they are performing currently, and where they expect to be going. The only way to do this is to monitor what is being accomplished. The broker should track each license holder's production. The broker should include the salesperson's number of sales, number of listings and buyer brokerage contracts, closed dollar volume, commissions earned, and average sales price. The broker should then tally all this information together to get numbers for the office in general. All these data should be accumulated into one "readable" document.

The broker can now analyze the data and take steps forward to maintain or change course as necessary. Tracking can be accomplished with charts, graphs, and reports monitored, recorded, and finalized through off-site companies specializing in such reporting. These companies usually charge a great deal of money for their expertise. This very valuable information is also rather costly, so only major real estate companies can usually afford off-site consultants. The typical real estate company must do this monitoring and reporting in-house, which may be better because the data are actually usable. Too many unusable reports are a waste of time and money. The broker should make sure the reports are valuable and then take action in response to what the reports find.

One broker required reports on everything. He had weekly reports, progress reports, expense reports, and listing reports, to name a few. These reports took a great deal of time to produce, and once completed, few were actually helpful. The individuals who had to complete the reports were never told of their purpose and in the end felt their time was wasted. A broker should be sure to produce only reports that will be used.

License Holder Operations

The broker should be keenly aware of the license holder's actions. A broker's number one job is to take care of the sales staff. If a broker correctly understands the business, he/she will understand that the salesperson is the only asset. The copy machine is a necessity of a brokerage firm, but it will not earn the broker a dime—it is clearly an expense. A broker needs to be spending a great deal of time observing the sponsored license holders. A broker who is alert should watch for both burnout and slumps.

Burnout

A person who concentrates on one aspect of his/her life and thereby loses perspective and balance in all other aspects of life experiences burnout.

After a period of time, the person will disengage from all activity and will go into seclusion, either physically or mentally. Once this occurs, no amount of motivation can shake the person out of it; only time will help. During the period of burnout, the person resembles someone with severe depression. Many brilliant real estate careers have been ruined because of burnout. The problem is that a person heading for burnout will generally not recognize what is happening until it is too late.

Remember, salespersons will go through both burnout and slumps. The successful broker will pay close attention to both of these situations. If the broker detects a salesperson who is heading for burnout, the broker must require the salesperson to take time off from real estate. This sounds counter to what a broker would want, but not doing so would be like killing the "goose with the golden egg." The broker should not want to make a lot of money from a salesperson and then lose that person forever. The broker should want make steady income from a salesperson long term. Preventing burnout is best for both parties. Some brokers have had to take cell phones from their salespersons and demand not to see them for three days. It might drive the salespersons nuts to be away from the business for that long, but this approach is best. When they come back, these salespersons are surprised to realize that their business is still there. Now with the knowledge that they can take time for themselves they are re-energized to perform even better. The broker can arrange for two real estate people to watch each other's business when they each take time off.

> CASE IN POINT—Burnout almost cost one broker his career. He was new in real estate, and he had a family to support. The broker (a salesperson at that time) wanted to be a success so much that he devoted all his time to real estate. This salesperson had no balance. He did not spend time with his family. He did not go out and play. He did not spend time winding down. All this salesperson did was work on real estate matters. Because all his time was spent on real estate and generating real estate income, he became a real estate success quickly. The problem was, this salesperson's broker never spotted the train wreck that he was steaming toward. The broker was excited about this salesperson's production. Within his first year the salesperson became the top producer of the office and in the top 10 of the entire real estate community.
>
> Then one day this salesperson could not continue any longer. He was sitting in his office staring at the walls in a numb trance. He could not go home, and he could not conduct his real estate business. The problem with this is that he did not recognize his predicament. If this salesperson had been given guidance, he could have taken a vacation and recharged and got back to business. Instead this funk lasted almost eight months. His production fell to nil, and he lost all the contacts he had made previously.
>
> Once this salesperson realized what had happened (with help from a mentor, not his broker), he got back on track. This salesperson was so disillusioned by his broker that he went with a competitor and became their top producer—with time for family and himself. The first broker made a great deal of money from that salesperson quickly but lost the long-term income he could have made for her. The salesperson later estimated that his burnout cost him and the first broker over a half million dollars of income!

Vacation

Brokers can easily fall into the trap of burnout. The problem is that no one is around to help the broker recognize it. A saving grace can be for the broker to take at least one two-week vacation per year during which the broker has no contact with his/her brokerage. The broker should arrange for all his/her duties to be taken care of by the staff or by a license holder in manager's training. The broker must not neglect him/herself.

Slump

A slump occurs when a license holder no longer has the motivation to do what is necessary to accomplish his/her goals. The slump is triggered by a lack of success for actions taken. The salesperson is doing what he/she must to be successful and yet is not receiving the expected rewards. This lack of success leads to the reduced action, which leads to less and less chance of success until the salesperson no longer accomplishes anything.

When brokers realizes that a sponsored license holder has fallen into a slump, the broker's job is to encourage and motivate the license holder to continue activity until the license holder achieves the success he/she wants. Brokers need to analyze the license holder's business plan to see if the license holder's actions are in line with the plan. New salespersons who want to make a million dollars their first year will experience a slump within the first three months when they have not made a dime. Brokers need to work with these ambitious salespersons to help them make their goals more realistic. These salespersons also need to be encouraged that they can make a million dollars in their career—but perhaps not in their first year. Brokers need to reward these "slumpers" for the actions they have taken rather than for the results of their actions.

Action Awards

In most brokerages, brokers give few production awards for achievements such as top producer, top lister, top sales dollar volume, and

the like. The downside to this type of award scenario is that the same agents always win. A broker should therefore consider giving action awards instead of production awards. The broker could give awards for some of the following achievements.

Met Personal Goals

Recognition for meeting personal goals is a good award because not all people are on the same level in terms of total production. A license holder who has been in the business for years and has established numerous contacts may easily win the award for top producer—an award may not mean much to him/her because he/she would have produced that much anyway. Moreover, the award for top producer does not motivate new salespersons who realize they cannot compete with the veterans. In contrast, recognizing the achievement of personal goals that are not competitive with each other gives each person a legitimate way to win an award. The prize could be a certificate, a gift card, or some other tangible award. The prize is not as important as the recognition of the salesperson's effort.

New Contacts

The broker can set a goal for each salesperson to call 10 new contacts per week for 12 weeks. Anyone achieving that contact goal will win the award. The contacts can be geared to what the broker wants. If the broker wants his/her salespersons to contact more "For Sale by Owners" (FSBOs), the broker makes the award based on contacting FSBOs. The awards can be small trophies, gifts, or cash prizes. Again, all the salespersons can participate, and all have a legitimate way to win.

Small Things

The broker is to notice the small things license holders are doing to accomplish their production goals. If a broker sees the license holders wearing their name tags in public, announce it at the next sales meeting, and give them a small award. If the broker notices them calling homeowners to inform them that their listing agreement with another real estate company has expired, reward them. Some brokers walk around with lottery scratch tickets or actual cash to give to those who are doing the small things to build their business. The broker needs to be careful here, though, to reward only those actions the broker wants repeated. One broker kept gold dollar coins in his pockets at all times to recognize any small thing his salespersons did. He would flip them a gold dollar and say great job! The production in his office went up by one-third by just this one action. Of course, the broker should not reward someone for making the coffee instead of prospecting, because prospecting is a much more important task.

Performance Management

Performance management comprises the brokerage, staff, and license holder management. Performance management is about handling all business situations in the most profitable and efficient manner. Brokers should manage all aspects of the brokerage, from the liability, cost, and profit angles.

Day-to-Day Operations

Some brokers with little capitalization and income may have to conduct day-to-day operations. These brokers may have to handle accounting, budgeting, payroll, receivables, and taxes, as well as sell real estate and broker sales staff. The broker may have to be the receptionist, mediator, trainer, and janitor. As an entrepreneur, the broker has the freedom to do anything—and everything!

Review Listings and Purchase Agreements

Reviewing listings and purchase agreements is a simple but very important task. Brokers are responsible for every authorized act of their real estate sponsored license holders. The main problem occurs when a salesperson fills in a contract with incomplete or incorrect information, obligating one of the parties to perform some detail that was not intended. This could be construed to be the practice of law and as such a violation of the Texas Real Estate License Act (TRELA). If the broker had taken the time to review the contracts, he/she would have noticed the error and could have corrected the problem without any damage.

Tickler files—The broker should encourage license holders to build tickler files for both buyers and sellers. Tickler files are usually actual paper files. A better way is to have them in a contact management database. The database allows faster contact with less work.

Buyer files—The license holder should have three files for potential buyers:

1. *Hot Buyer*–totally qualified individuals who will buy. These buyers have the money or financing and will buy within the next 30 to 60 days. The license holder should not try to work with more than three to five at any given time because of time constraints. For any more than that, the license holder should refer them to another in-house license holder. Not responding to hot buyers in a timely manner will lose them and create a bad reputation for the brokerage.
2. *Medium Buyer*–individuals who will buy within the next six months. Medium buyers may have a home in closing or currently listed. They may be transferred or have a specific date they must move by. The license holder should keep up with these buyers, who will buy if the motivation hits.
3. *Cold Buyer*–individuals who have no real need to buy. If a good opportunity comes up, they might buy. The license holder should refer these out because they are typically a waste of time.

Seller files—The license holder should create at least four lead files for sellers:

1. *Canvassing Leads*–These leads are part of the license holder's geographic marketing area or a lead found by using any other prospecting methods.
2. *Presentation Leads*–These leads are people with whom the license holder has talked to about selling, but they are not yet ready to make a move. The license holder should not forget them, or else when they are ready to sell they will list with someone else.
3. *Past Buyers and Sellers*–The license holder must keep in touch with past clients because when they think of real estate, they should think of their license holder. The license holder will have the opportunity to resell many homes this way. If the

license holder keeps records on all past clients and their contact information, the license holder will be prepared to handle their real estate needs at any time.
4. *FSBO or Specialized Area Leads*—Whether the license holder specializes in FSBOs, expired listings, certain types of professions, or some other area, the license holder should keep these people in tickler files.

General file—This file notes everyone the license holder knows. These individuals should include but not be limited to friends, relatives, social contacts, and anyone the license holder meets.

Expense file and tax records—The license holder should keep all receipts and business expenses.

Capturing the Leads

A centralized lead management program provides a real estate firm with a number of specific advantages, including benefits to the firm as well as efficiencies. These advantages include the following:

- All company internet advertising can publish contact information that is consistent throughout the market.
- Restricting lead management to a central location means less hardware is needed at the branch offices.
- Managing this process is easy because all the information on calls, leads, and customer contacts is in one location. The instances of lost leads are thereby be appreciably reduced.
- Sponsored license holders have no access to the customer service representative (CSR) responsible for managing the lead capture process.
- Equipment costs are reduced because all necessary computer hardware and software are housed in the central location.
- Wages can be reduced because the branches will not need web maintenance and web marketing personnel at each branch. All internet input relating to the lead management process occurs at the central location.

The job of the CSR is to answer EVERY call that comes in to the company. Once the call is answered, the CSR is responsible for taking the following steps:

1. determine the source of the lead and log it into the database (The source of the lead is important because it is a factor in

determining which agent would be assigned the lead. It is also important in measuring internet advertising and marketing results.)
2. secure the name and phone number(s) of the prospect
3. assign the lead to the appropriate agent (The agent is paged with a special customer code that indicates a lead call. The agent is expected to call the office in the prescribed time to secure the name of the prospect. The lead is immediately reassigned if the agent does not respond within the predetermined time.)
4. follow up with the customer to ensure contact in a timely fashion
5. reassign a lead that is not actively pursued by the agent to whom it was assigned
6. begin the follow-up process until closing

Orientation Programs

Orientation programs need to be structured to allow a newly sponsored license holder the opportunity to fit in in a timely manner. Too many brokers work hard to recruit new salespersons by promising them a better way to sell real estate, but then there is no orientation program (i.e., onboarding). Without an orientation program, new license holders are left to fend for themselves. The current license holders find it frustrating to always be answering the new salesperson's questions because there is no other help available. It is critical for a broker who wants to succeed to have an orientation program.

The following items should be part of the orientation program:

Meeting of the staff—The broker or manager should walk the new license holder around and introduce each member of the staff and explain the staff member's function.

Current office—The broker needs to give the license holder access and security codes to the office. If there are office hours, the license holder needs to know them.

Parking—The broker should inform the license holder of any restrictions to parking.

Office locations—The broker should make the license holder aware of any additional locations and their contact information. If the license holder is allowed to access other office locations, that should be discussed also.

Office equipment—The broker should take the license holder around to show the office equipment that the license holder will need to operate his/her real estate business. The broker should allow the license holder to practice if necessary. The broker must provide the license holder access codes if any of the equipment requires them.

Conference rooms—The broker should show the license holder the conference rooms and how to reserve the rooms when needed.

Kitchen/break area—If the office has a kitchen or break room, the license holder needs to know the location and any rules of the house for the refrigerator, coffee, and cleanup.

Signs/lockboxes—The broker needs to inform the license holder about yard sign and lockbox policies and how to obtain/order them.

Desk—If the license holder will be assigned a desk, the broker should show where it is located and tell what accompanies the desk.

Email—The broker needs to give the license holder access to an email account as well as internet access. Webpage design and hosting, if offered, should be discussed.

The Expectation Letter

Studies have shown conclusively that people perform at a higher level if the expectations of their leader or their peer group are high. This is true in athletics, academics, and every profession or activity that includes competition. Selling is competitive. The expectation letter sets the bar and focuses the expectation.

A broker should consider using an expectation letter in the onboarding process. This letter states what is expected of every sponsored license holder. The expectation letter should be brief but thorough. The following list explains the components of the expectation letter.

Personal production goals: Each sponsored license holder is expected to set personal production goals and will be coached and managed toward achieving them. The goals process begins as a part of the recruiting interview and continues throughout the license holder's career with the brokerage. The license holder understands that he/she will be expected to earn a living through listing and selling real estate.

Involvement and participation: The expectation is that the license holder will participate in team events and career-enhancing events. These include, but are not limited to, office business meetings, board of REALTORS® functions, and real estate rallies and conventions.

Training: A statement of the training that is offered and/or required of the new license holder should be included. This training could include system courses as well as National Association of REALTORS® curriculum designed to secure designations. A time structure needs to be included in the training expectation.

Professionalism: Professional standards are expected of the license holder. These standards may include dress code, concealed-handgun rules, personal conduct issues, appropriate language, smoking policies, and the like. License holders should understand that there are personal behavior expectations. License holders need to acknowledge from the beginning that they are in an industry in which personal reputation can affect business. Professionalism also applies to the quality treatment of peers, staff, and the public.

Quality service: The expectation is that the license holder will perform his/her duties in such a way as to receive an acceptable rating on any customer evaluation survey. The license holder should know that quality service is a way of life in this brokerage.

Performance Appraisals

"Performance appraisals" are a fancy way to say employee and independent contractor reviews. The broker needs to monitor, correct, praise, and review the conduct of every staff member and every sponsored real estate licensee. Doing this requires a major commitment on the part of the broker because a broker could have 15 staff members and 50+ sponsored license holders. The broker could delegate some of this review process, but for the most part it is a broker responsibility.

Individual Business Development Meetings

The broker should conduct IBD meetings with each sponsored license holder. The IBD meeting is held with a sponsored license holder to review his/her current and future production. This activity, also called "coaching," can be delegated to managers if the broker hires managers. These IBD meetings allow one-on-one time with the broker. This type of meeting may take up a great deal of the broker's time, but these meetings must be held. The primary reason a real estate salesperson leaves a brokerage is not because of money but because he/she does not like or respect the broker. If the broker gives the salesperson one-on-one time, that salesperson will get to know and perhaps like the broker, or at least the broker can discuss difficulties before they escalate into real trouble. During the IBD meetings, the broker will analyze the salesperson's current production and discuss ways to increase that production. Some salespersons need to learn to reduce the stress and time spent in real estate. The IBD is a great way for a broker to coach this behavior. The discussions can cover anything from private obstacles to production. At the conclusion of the IBD meeting, the salesperson should walk away with several action steps to implement immediately. These IBD meetings should be held monthly or quarterly at minimum. Waiting until the end of the year may be too late.

Training Programs

Overall, the most important thing that real estate salespersons believe their broker should do for them is provide training. Lack of training is the catch-all reason that real estate salespersons do not succeed. Some of the best training available in the real estate business is produced with only a few in attendance. The same salespersons who fail to attend these training classes then complain that they are not productive and leave for another real estate company because they believe that the new company offers better training.

The broker must provide the best training possible, given the costs involved. There once was a person from the pharmaceutical business

who wanted to own a real estate brokerage. The biggest concern for him was that he could not train his license holders how best to handle this real estate business because the sponsored license holders had more experience in real estate than did the owner. He went ahead and bought a brokerage but had very little credibility with his sales force. Although he was smart enough to hire an in-house trainer, that brokerage never had the production it could have had if he had spent the time in practice in the business before buying a brokerage.

Proper training will help the most experienced salesperson make more sales and the least experienced to get a good start on this new career, and it will save any real estate salesperson from some of the education that is obtained through the school of hard knocks.

Larger firms usually offer more extensive programs than smaller firms. Most universities, colleges, and junior colleges offer courses in real estate. At some learning institutions, a student can earn an associate's or bachelor's degree with a major in real estate or even advanced degrees concentrating on the real estate industry. Many local real estate associations sponsor courses covering the real estate fundamentals, risk reduction, and legal aspects of the field. Advanced courses in mortgage financing, property exchanges, investment, and other subjects are offered infrequently.

Covering the Costs of Training

Should a broker/owner of a real estate office charge for training? There are many aspects that should be considered.

Cost to the real estate company No matter what type of training is offered, there will be costs associated with it, such as the printing or purchasing of materials, the rent for the facility to hold the training, and the talent fee for an instructor. Presentation equipment may need to be rented or purchased. All these items add to the broker's costs.

Smaller brokerages usually provide all the training in-house; the broker instructs the classes, which are provided, at no charge to the salespersons, to make the license holders better at the real estate business. Larger brokers provide training in-house but also frequently hire trainers from outside their offices to provide specialty training at extremely high costs.

Brokers should not get caught up in the line, "If I can get your real estate salespersons to sell just one more house, this training will more than pay for itself." This is a standard promise. Lured by this line, brokers could spend a fortune on real estate courses when a better approach to gaining those extra sales would be for the broker to motivate and monitor his/her salespersons better. A broker should never pay for a course that he/she could provide.

Salespersons' expectations   A real estate salesperson expects his/her broker to provide certain types of training classes, such as new-agent training to get the newly hired salespersons started, risk reduction training to keep sales staff safe, and current topics training to keep them up-to-date. Veteran salespersons expect too much from new salespersons. They seem to forget what it was like to be new. If a new salesperson makes a mistake or costs a veteran salesperson some extra time, the veterans will blame the lack of training as the culprit.

Training offered by the competition   A broker/owner will need to monitor what the competition is offering to its own currently sponsored license holders. If a competing brokerage offers its salespersons training as a benefit free of charge, the broker/owner needs to consider likewise offering some classes for free or otherwise risk losing salespersons. Brokers who charge no fees can lose money by providing a great deal of training.

Other benefits of training   In one real estate office the broker had his own real estate school approved by the state's real estate commission to offer certified prelicense and continuing education, meaning he could hold certified training classes for his salespersons. For example, he offered a marketing class for free to the sales staff, but if they wanted the credit hours for their license renewal, they had to pay a fee. He had the right to publish that he offered FREE marketing classes to his salespersons, and he also offered to get their education requirements met while in class. Everybody loved the idea and paid the fee. A loss center became a profit center overnight.

Just-in-Time Training
Just-in-time (JIT) training is the training provided right before a sales event occurs. Suppose that a new real estate licensee wants to hold an open house but does not know how. The real estate trainer (e.g., the broker) teaches him/her the basics of holding an open house at that time. A real estate salesperson cannot know everything about the real estate business, especially if he/she is relatively new to the business. Although JIT training does not replace weekly training, it does add to it. It allows the salesperson to move ahead with the belief that if he/she needs training, it will be provided just in time.

The broker or training director should be available to train JIT classes when the need arises. Nothing is more frustrating to a salesperson than needing training and being unable to get it. A broker who finds himself/herself in too many JIT training situations may quickly realize that actual courses conducted in classrooms are necessary.

Field Training

Field training is offered to newly sponsored real estate license holders to help them on their first one or two listing appointments. The trainer, broker, or manager will attend the appointments of new salespersons to help win listings for them and the company. The trainer should not negotiate the listing but should be there to help. The salesperson must be the presenter. If the trainer does the presenting, two unwanted results may follow: First, the seller might bond with the trainer rather than the salesperson; and second, the salesperson might come rely on the trainer to always attend the presentations. Instead, the salesperson should feel the action and understand the dynamics. The salesperson should be the focal point. The trainer is there to help if a problem occurs and to review the presentation with the salesperson after the appointment. The salesperson should begin to believe that he/she can present independently.

Right after the presentation, the trainer should go to, say, a local fast-food restaurant and there review the events that occurred during the presentation. The trainer should make notes during the presentation so as not to forget what to cover during the review. Each negative comment should be offset by one or two positives. The feedback should be honest but not cruel, and it should be immediate because any time lost means the feedback will rapidly lose its impact.

Office Meetings

A broker/manager should offer sponsored real estate license holder's specialized training at every office meeting. The training should be short and concise. Topics could include:

Contracts update	Telephone techniques	Fair housing review
Agency law review	Listing new construction	Latest technology
Legal case studies	Figuring seller net sheets	Best practices
Prospecting quick hits	Marketing ideas	Business planning
Tax implications	Staging property	Working with referrals

The training should be diversified, timely, interesting, and even exciting. This is the time the broker gives the sponsored license holders what the broker wants them to learn. The broker can take requests if license holders want training on a specific topic. However, this is the broker's training program. If the broker feels his/her license holders need a class on risk reduction, new changes in TRELA, or any number of other topics, the office meeting is the place to give such training. The broker should not let his/her sales staff dread the training portion. Instead, the broker should give them a reason to show up.

New Salesperson Training

New salesperson training should be offered weekly, depending on the number of new salespersons the brokerage is carrying. This training should continue for 10 or more weeks or until the new salesperson can operate independently. The training should cover basic prospecting, basic career planning, and seller and buyer presentations.

Instructors should be rotated as often as possible so that the new salespersons will get differing insights to the real estate business and be exposed to a variety of moneymaking ideas. Frequently, a salesperson will bond with one trainer over another. This is why it is crucial to have more than one trainer. The more marketing and prospecting ideas the new real estate salesperson learns, the better.

To further the new salesperson training, the trainer should make the students accountable for completing an assignment before each class. The assignments could range widely: The broker could ask the students to talk with loan officers about mortgage services, to call on a particular group of individuals for business, or to design a real estate business plan for themselves. The broker could require the students to have the assignments checked off as they complete them. By being accountable for their assignments, the students prove that they have been paying attention, and the training will result in greater real estate production. The broker should not let the new sales staff become full-time students and part-time salespersons. Requiring follow-up actions on the lessons learned will get the new salespersons into production as well as provide them with practical experience.

Education without application is worse than worthless. Here is a list of classes that should be offered at regular intervals but selected according to the brokerage's needs:

- Real Estate Professionalism
- Characteristics of Successful Salespersons
- Time Management and Planning
- Real Estate Law of Agency
- Prospecting for Seller Appointments
- Prospecting for Buyer Appointments
- Objection-Handling Techniques
- Referrals in the Real Estate Business
- Real Estate Negotiation
- The Closing and Funding Process
- Ethics in the Real Estate Business
- Technology Uses in the Real Estate Industry
- Psychology of Marketing and Promotion
- Alternative Representative Agreements
- Seller Listing Procedures
- Buyer Listing Procedures
- Client Follow-up
- Real Estate Contract Writing
- Activities after Contract Acceptance
- Real Estate Financing

The broker should provide these and any number of other real estate–related courses on a rotating basis. The training should be offered frequently for the sake of the newest sponsored license holders.

Experienced Salesperson Training

Experienced salesperson training is for license holders who have been in the real estate business long enough to know the basics of the real estate business. The training should cover new types of prospecting, new technology, and using a personal assistant.

Every brokerage should devise ways to help the experienced salesperson attain top producer status. These classes would be designed to teach the experienced salesperson and then make him/her accountable for putting the learned technique into production. The broker must monitor what is taught because if the broker does not monitor progress, there may be none and the education may be wasted.

Top Producer Training

Top producer training is for license holders who fall within the upper 5% of production. This type of training should focus on developing the salesperson's character and on topics such as conflict management, retirement planning, and personal marketing. Business planning is a must for the top producers. Top producers do not need prospecting techniques, closing techniques, or how to show buyers because they are experienced in all these areas. The broker should coach each top producer individually. This accomplishes two major objectives: First, it builds the top producers' business by making them accountable directly to the broker, and second, it gives the top producers specific times to spend with the broker and makes them feel important.

Special Situations and Legal Training
During the course of a year, national training experts hold seminars in the local area, and the broker/manager should be aware of these events. These events generate a great deal of excitement and motivation. The broker should not miss these opportunities to get his/her license holders involved. The sales staff should be aware of all the new laws and any changes to existing laws. The broker's salespersons may act as if this training is unexciting, but in the end they appreciate it, especially if the training is enlightening and may save them from some legal battle.

Personal Education and Development
People wanting to become brokers should remember to continually better themselves through their own education. Brokers want trained salespersons to work for them but then neglect their own education. There are numerous courses a broker can take on real estate brokerage. If the broker cannot find one on real estate brokerage, he/she can take a course on business culture, time management, or any other subject that will make the broker better at his/her profession. The broker should think of what his/her salespersons need to learn and then himself/herself go out to learn these very subjects. Now the broker knows and can teach the new information.

Education and self-improvement can also come from reading books. With the internet, people forget the value of a simple book. Books can help the broker learn about real estate, sales, and business management. Why should a broker go through life the hard way? The broker should learn from others' mistakes and their successes. The broker should set a goal to read at least one business book per month. This might be a lofty goal if the broker has not read a book since high school. The broker may feel his/her time is already taken up without adding reading to the list. Yet the broker will find time if the broker has the determination. The broker could read over lunch, read while waiting, or read before bedtime. A wise broker should take the time, take the class, read the book—any of these activities will make the broker and his/her salespersons more productive.

Brokers must learn to cultivate methods for staying abreast of developments in the real estate industry, and they must learn to ignore information that is not productive. Here are a few suggestions for staying informed:

- The broker should subscribe to industry or trade publications that focus on the real estate business.
- The broker should read any newspapers that specifically address issues in the real estate industry.
- The broker should visit the local library and read books on sales, management, and real estate.
- The broker should join a professional association, chamber of commerce, or network with other entrepreneurs in the real estate business.
- The broker should look for information on the internet and watch for opportunities to interact with business or industry experts in chat room interviews.
- The broker should subscribe to internet newsgroups that focus on the real estate industry.
- The broker should attend real estate seminars and be actively involved in the learning process.
- The broker should develop a group of consultants and advisors.
- The broker should cultivate curiosity and be unafraid to try new things. The most important skill the broker can develop is not the ability to remember information but the ability to seek out and find the information needed and when it is needed, and then the broker should use the information for the benefit of the brokerage.

Mentoring

"Mentoring" is a term used to describe a teacher-student relationship. In the business world, mentoring occurs when a more experienced professional (the mentor) gives significant career assistance to a less experienced professional (the protégé). Mentoring relationships are particularly helpful during a real estate broker's first few years as a leader. A mentoring program in the real estate business is one in which a veteran real estate salesperson is paired with a rookie salesperson. The veteran is required to take the rookie out to show him/her the real estate business firsthand. Training occurs through observation and explanation. The broker needs to be watchful here because sometimes the veteran will use the rookie to do all the dirty work and not actually teach him/her anything. Some real estate companies charge a fee or a percentage of sale for this mentoring.

A salesperson should not leave finding the right mentor to chance. The broker will sometimes choose the mentor for the salesperson. The broker needs to look for someone who has the real estate knowledge and business experience in areas the salesperson does not. Just pairing two people is not the best for either the mentor or the protégé. The broker needs to make sure the chosen mentor desires to be a mentor. A mentoring relationship requires consent by both parties. The broker needs to tell the salesperson to look for what he/she can offer the mentor to make the relationship mutually beneficial. The salesperson can learn so much from a qualified mentor, so the broker should make sure he/she finds a good one. Brokers may themselves need to be mentored to improve their own businesses and careers.

Business Meetings and Retreats

The broker needs to conduct business meetings for the staff, for the management, and for the license holders. Business meetings are a fundamental part of being a broker, and so a broker must be able to plan, promote, develop, conduct, and review numerous business meetings each month. The broker should also plan a brokerage retreat. The retreat's purpose is to review the current year, project the upcoming year, and build rapport across lines of management and offices. Doing this is critical with a multi-office brokerage.

Business Sales Meetings

Brokers should meet with all their managers, staff, and salespersons on a monthly basis. Brokers should have scheduled sales meetings in which they update their sales staff on the activities of the brokerage. Depending on the brokerage's needs, the broker may feel that weekly meetings are more appropriate.

If the brokerage employs managers, the broker should meet with them monthly to be sure everyone is on the same track and that they are meeting their specific goals. The broker may want to hold weekly conference calls to update managers. Waiting for the formal, in-person monthly meeting may be too long to wait to discuss important topics with them.

The broker should meet with each of his/her salespersons each month. The broker may be able to delegate these meetings either to managers or to assistant managers, but it is the broker's duty to make sure these meetings happen. These meetings can be informal, such as stopping by the salesperson's office and simply chatting, or they can be more formal conference-room discussions. The broker just needs to regularly make personal contact with all the sponsored license holders. As stressed in this chapter, one major reason salespersons leave a brokerage is that they feel their broker is not available and/or they have no established relationship with their broker. When the broker meets each salesperson every month, he/she can head off such problems.

Office Meetings

Brokers will have to conduct office meetings with all their salespersons. Usually these meetings occur every week. During the meetings, the broker conducts a review of any new laws, regulations, or activities in the office and also reviews any new listings brought in by the brokerage's salespersons. These office meetings should be no longer than an hour so that the broker can get his/her people back out selling. It is hard for a broker to make these meetings mandatory, but everyone should be strongly urged to attend. To increase attendance, the broker must provide some value. The meeting should never be a complaint session.

Meeting Agenda

The meeting agenda is a roadmap for the meeting. It lets participants know where they are headed so that they do not get off track. Most important, the agenda gives a sense of purpose and direction to the meeting.

The typical real estate office meeting should model the following agenda:

1. introduction to the meeting
2. welcoming of any guests, affiliates, and new salespersons

3. announcements
4. guest or affiliate presentations
5. entertainment
6. training
7. wants and needs
8. wrap-up

Introduction to the Meeting
In the introduction the broker covers the purpose of the meeting and tells all the attendees that he/she appreciates their presence. The broker should allow only a minute or two for the introduction.

Welcoming of Any Guests, Affiliates, and New Salespersons
After the introduction is a special time when the broker welcomes the honored attendees. The broker should welcome any guests. From time to time the broker will have executives from the corporate office in attendance; it may be that a guest speaker for the training session or simply someone's friend is in attendance. The broker should always welcome the new salespersons to their first sales meeting. Also, the broker should recognize any affiliates who are in attendance. Affiliates are the ancillary businesses that help the brokerage serve clients and customers. These affiliates include title companies, mortgage companies, and inspectors, to name a few. The broker should allow only a few minutes to welcome guests, affiliates, and new sales associates.

Announcements
Following the welcome is the time for the broker to make any needed announcements. The broker should not make this discussion lengthy. This is where the broker poses decisions to the group for their opinion. The broker should not allow a lot of cross talk and should speed up this process as much as possible because all announcements should be listed in the agenda. The broker should limit this section to no more than 10 minutes.

Guest or Affiliate Presentations
Any guest or affiliate who wants a moment to speak is permitted to do so after the announcements. Some brokers, however, do not allow anyone to speak in front of their salespersons. If this latter is the broker's philosophy, the broker should eliminate this section of the meeting. The broker should not allow anyone to present a commercial to

his/her salespersons. He/she should require that the presenters actually provide information to the attendees. The broker should review any information that someone else is presenting to his/her salespersons. If the broker does not review what is to be presented, the broker should be ready for any surprises. The broker should allow no more than two presentations for no longer than five minutes each.

Entertainment
"Gotta give 'em some fun, or lose 'em forever." It is amazing that the sillier the event, the more fun the grownups have. The entertainment section is limited only by the broker's imagination. The broker should have a "get involved" type of action. Engaging the license holders gets their blood flowing and makes them want to come back next week to see what the broker will do next. The broker must limit the entertainment section to 10 minutes. Here are some other thoughts for entertainment:

- *contest for prizes.* The broker could hold contests for prizes. Some brokers have used the "contract toss" for distance game, business roller chair races, and "knowledge tests" on some real estate topic. The broker could hold listing contests and use this time to update these contests. The broker could hold "spin-the-wheel" prize giveaway for those who had a listing or sale during the previous week. The broker should pay attention to other businesspeople and what they are doing. Again, this activity is limited only by the broker's imagination.
- *presentation of awards.* The sales meeting is a great time to pass out monthly office awards. The broker should honor the top listing salesperson of the month, the top salesperson per month, and the top-dollar closed for the month as a minimum. Some brokers give the "office team player" award, the "rookie of the month" award, and the "best service given" award. The broker should be sure to cheer these awards mightily. This activity should take no more than five minutes.
- *surprise giveaway.* The broker could surprise the salespersons by having a random drawing for a giveaway by collecting their business cards. The broker could put a red dot under one of the chairs, and whoever sits in that chair would win the surprise. These surprises do not do much to promote production, but they are great for increasing attendance at the meetings.

Training

During the training portion of the meeting, the broker should offer the sales staff valuable training. The salespersons may indicate that they do not want another training session on fair housing, but if it keeps them from a violation and the intense prosecution that would follow, they will appreciate the broker greatly. The broker can invite guest presenters if desired. This training should be kept to 15 minutes.

Wants and Needs

Real estate salespersons want the time to discuss their new listings or the listings that they are struggling to sell. Some salespersons may talk about their need to sell a listing, a price reduction, or the offer of a selling bonus. Other salespersons may describe properties their clients are seeking. The broker should encourage cross talk and questions. If only one salesperson makes a transaction because of this promotion, the broker will have that person as an attendee to the office meetings for life. The broker should limit the time spent on wants and needs to five minutes. If the broker finds this discussion takes more than the time allowed, the broker needs to encourage the attendees to shorten their talk time and put more into a handout.

Wrap-Up

The broker should wrap up with any final comments. The broker should briefly review important points that were covered during the meeting and thank the guests and affiliates. Then the broker should say a special "thank you" to all the other attendees and cordially invite them to the next office meeting. This should take only a minute or two.

The total time for an office meeting as described should be no more than an hour. This gives the broker sufficient time to cover important points, but it is short enough not to interfere with the salesperson's production time.

Real Estate Office Meeting Tips

The following are helpful tips to make the next office meeting successful, effective, and even fun. If the broker's office meetings are dull and boring, the broker will be very lonely in a short time. Give the salespersons a reason to attend, and they will. The broker should make the meetings fun, and the salespersons will come back.

Before the Meeting

The broker should take the following steps to prepare for the meeting:

1. *define the purpose of the meeting*—Every meeting should have a purpose; otherwise, the broker should not hold one. The broker should not hold a weekly meeting "just because." If the brokerage can afford to hold meetings only once a month, the broker needs to consider making that change.
2. *develop an agenda*—The broker should develop an agenda in cooperation with key participants, as discussed previously. If at all possible, he/she should put items of interest in a company newsletter. Doing this saves a tremendous amount of meeting time. The broker should not allow the meetings to become a series of quick hits that the sales staff will not remember.
3. *distribute the agenda*—The broker should distribute the agenda and along with it background material, lengthy documents, or articles before the meeting so the salespersons will be prepared and feel involved and up-to-date. This can also limit the discussion if decisions need to be made.
4. *choose an appropriate meeting time*—The broker should set a time limit and stick to it, if possible. The salespersons have other commitments, and they will be more likely to attend meetings if the meetings are productive, predictable, and as short as possible. The broker should not get in the habit of changing the time or date because it will cause a great deal of confusion.
5. *find the best room*—The broker should choose a room suitable to the group's size. A small room with too many people gets stuffy and creates tension. A larger room is more comfortable and encourages individual expression. Too much space for too few people makes the meeting look unattended and unimportant.
6. *arrange the room*—The broker should be sure the room is set up so that members face each other. The broker could put them all in a circle or semicircle. For large groups, it may be better to set the room up in U-shaped rows. These types of layouts encourage participation and are less threatening. The broker should want the meetings to be fun and not intimidating.
7. *prepare visual aids*—The broker should make the presentation exciting and visually stimulating. The broker could post a large

agenda up front to which the salespersons can refer. The presentation should use computer display projectors and a graphic slide show to add flair.

During the Meeting

When conducting the meeting the broker should endeavor to follow these steps:

1. *review the agenda and set priorities for the meeting*—This is simply being prepared. The worst thing a broker can do is hold an office meeting and appear unprepared. Once or twice of not being prepared will run off all the salespersons from attending the meeting. It is rude to the salespersons. The broker should spend the time necessary to make these meetings special and meaningful.
2. *greet each of the sponsored license holders*—It is important to make them feel welcome.
3. *serve light refreshments if possible*—Refreshments are good icebreakers and make the salespersons feel special and comfortable. The broker could ask the affiliates to help sponsor the food. The broker should be cognizant of those on a diet. The broker should have someone pick up the food five minutes before the meeting starts. This will encourage salespersons to show up to the meeting early. The broker should always offer coffee and water.
4. *start on time*—This is critical. If the broker does not regularly start on time, more salespersons will show up late, until they won't show up at all. If the broker starts on time, the broker will demonstrate promptness. Some salespersons will insist on being late. The broker needs to speak with these individuals separately and discuss the need for them to show up on time.
5. *stick to the agenda*—Any variation will cause confusion, and again the broker will look unprepared. If the broker wants to add something, the broker should make a note to himself/herself and add the topic to agenda of the next meeting.
6. *encourage group discussion to share all points of view and ideas*—The broker will make better decisions as well as have highly motivated salespersons because they will feel that attending meetings is worth their while. Some things the broker could

get agreement on include advertising campaigns, floor-time schedules, or the next office get-together. The broker should keep the conversation focused on the topic. The broker should ask for constructive and nonrepetitive comments only. The broker should tactfully end discussions when they are getting nowhere or becoming destructive or unproductive.
7. *keep minutes of the meeting for future reference in case a question or problem arises*—The broker should distribute these minutes to individuals who want them. The broker can delegate this duty to the administrative assistant.
8. *be a role model by listening and showing interest, appreciation, and confidence in one's salespersons*—The broker should celebrate their successes and help them through the challenges. This is the time for the broker to be a cheerleader.
9. *summarize any agreements reached*—The broker should then end the meeting on a unifying or positive note.
10. *end on time if possible*—The broker should respect the salespersons' valuable time by ending on time. If there are guest speakers, the broker may have to interrupt them if necessary to avoid overtime. The broker should practice the presentation to be sure the time is correct. The broker should also have available additional material to cover should the meeting go faster than anticipated. There should be convenient stopping points if the meeting looks to go overtime.

After the Meeting

There are three actions the broker should take after the meeting:

1. *write up and distribute minutes within a few days of the meeting date*—Quick action reinforces the importance of meeting and reduces errors of memory.
2. *put unfinished business on the agenda for the next meeting*—Important business may require further discussion.
3. *conduct a periodic evaluation of the meetings*—The broker should note any areas that can be analyzed and improved for more productive meetings.

When brokers hold effective meetings, all the salespersons will keep coming back!

Company Direction (Retreat)
The broker needs to be continually aware of the company direction. However, the broker needs to meet at least once a year with the key players of the brokerage firm to discuss the company direction and any changes the market requires. The key players could be any staff members, respected salespersons, managers, or outside counselors, accountants, bankers, and businesspeople. This type of meeting is sometimes called a company retreat. Preferably, the meeting will not be held at the real estate office. If this is not possible, the broker must be sure to hold all calls and avoid interruptions. This meeting occurs only once a year, so the broker should take it seriously.

This company retreat should address the current status of the real estate business. All the accounting reports should be readily available. The meeting should discuss any new directions to enable the brokerage to keep ahead of the market trends and competition. The meeting should include business planning to guide day-to-day operations. This will be a lengthy meeting, so the broker and all invitees should plan accordingly.

Personal Interaction

Personal interaction with every one of the sponsored license holders is crucial for the broker. This interaction keeps the relationship with each license holder active. License holders, like most people, like to feel important. Sometimes brokers just need to make themselves available to give advice to their licensees. This is important to real estate license holders; they like to feel that their broker is available. The broker should make a concerted effort to wander around the office for a few minutes every few hours. The broker should stop in each salesperson's office to chat for just a moment. The broker does not want to disrupt the license holders, only to let them know the broker is there for them. One broker does this every hour on the hour for 10 minutes only, and his sales staff love him for it.

A good broker maintains an open-door policy. The broker should promote this to his/her license holders. Then the broker must deliver. If a salesperson walks into the office, the broker must stop what he/she is doing and give 100% to the salesperson. Brokers are sometimes tempted to perform other routine business tasks while a salesperson is in their office. Brokers should never do this. Aside from the fact that the brokers may miss important information, what are they conveying to the salesperson? Exactly, that they do not care.

The broker should be available 24 hours a day, seven days a week, unless the broker has delegated broker responsibilities to another trusted license holder or a manager. That might sound like it is too much time. If the broker wants his/her salespersons working into the evenings and on weekends, the broker should also be available at those times. A license holder who is working may need advice. Although the real estate industry is on when normal laborers are off, brokers will not receive calls at three o'clock in the morning. Brokers nonetheless want to project the image that they will be available all the time. Brokers who are available at all times will find that they do not receive calls at weird times, but the brokers' availability offers a comfort to their sponsored license holders. The salespersons will respect the broker's time if the broker respects theirs.

Retention

Brokers should work hard to recruit new real estate salespersons, but they should not neglect their current sales staff. Retention is the second most important step in making a brokerage profitable. Here are some words a broker should live by:

- recruit the right talent
- hire the right talent
- develop the right talent
- retain the right talent

Retention of the current salespersons in a real estate office is a key component of being a successful broker. The sponsored license holders of a real estate office are constantly being wooed and recruited by other real estate brokerages, which use techniques that can be very aggressive. Brokers who believe that their salespersons are happy and would never leave are vulnerable to having their offices raided. Here are a few ideas that help with production and retention.

Call Nights

Brokers design call nights for prospecting so that their salespersons can obtain buyers and sellers. Call nights are great for the brokerage because the more listings a company has, the more money that brokerage will make. It also has the benefit of retention. Most real estate salespersons like to gather together because they are a sociable bunch. The broker should host events at least once a month to keep the brokerage "family" together. What kind of social event would be best for the brokerage to hold? A gathering at a local bar, where attendees drink until they cannot stand up and then have to drive home, or a call night where pizza and soft drinks are served and telemarketing calls are made to generate business? The latter, of course. The calls that are made can be cold-calls if the salespersons do not have prospects to call. Prospecting generates new business. Some salespersons avoid making telemarketing calls and may not show up for that reason. The broker should allow the salespersons to have their own list of calls that need to be made. This list can be their past-client list or sphere-of-influence (i.e., friends and family) list. Any prospecting call is a good call.

The key to making a call night successful is, first, to call the event a call night. Brokers should not want to misinform anyone about the reason for the event. Brokers want telemarketing calls made. The broker hosting a call night should make a general announcement to everyone so that no one is excluded, but the broker may also want to send a few personalized invitations to the core group of license holders who listen and will do what is asked of them. Once these people tell others of the fun they have had and the business they are getting from a call night, more individuals will begin to participate.

The event should start with a snack or dinner so those who arrive late will not miss out completely. Call nights provide time for bonding, so the broker should allow about a half hour for license holders to eat and talk. Next on the agenda is to have about 30 minutes of introduction and training. During this time, the broker should welcome any new members and go over some of the highlights of past call nights.

Next, the broker should train the participating salespersons using the latest prospecting scripts and telephone techniques; the broker should also explain any new regulations that apply. The broker should have new information each time a call night is held so that the veterans can look forward to learning something new each time they participate. The broker should provide handouts about what was taught so that the salespersons will have something to take with them to review. The broker should not teach everything at once because a call night should be a recurring event. The broker will have plenty of time to teach about telephone prospecting, for example. The broker should demonstrate the actual script for prospecting several times to make the salespersons feel comfortable with the routine. Then the broker needs to put them on the telephone so that they can call. The broker should assign them to telephones and give them lists of numbers to call (remembering, of course, to follow the national do-not-call regulations), tracking paper to monitor their calls, and the script they should use.

The broker's job now is to monitor and coach the salespersons as they call. The broker should record any situations that happen from which others can learn. The broker should walk around from person to person. He/She should lead the salespersons in cheering for successes but should coach in private. After approximately 45 minutes to an hour, the broker should call all participating license holders back to the training room.

Once everyone is back in the training room, the broker should have a summary session to recapitulate what occurred while prospect calling. The broker should make sure to address any negative feelings, but he/she should primarily concentrate on and celebrate the successes. This is where the broker teaches the entire group using examples of situations the broker observed and offering better ways to handle those situations. The broker should match each person with an accountability partner. The two partners can then continue prospecting during the next four weeks. Each should call the other and make him/her accountable for prospecting.

The broker should end with some simple game to play together to build unity. After the game, the broker should give everyone an assignment page (e.g., to continue prospecting or any other specific assignment the broker deems necessary), and the broker should tell each person individually that he/she is appreciated.

The event should be fun and exciting. The event is even better if the broker can design it around some kind of theme. No one should be calling from behind a closed door. When someone gets a prospect, everyone cheers! The broker can generate this excitement only by having interaction among salespersons. The broker must lead those cheers.

Company Events

At least twice a year a broker should invite the entire company to participate in some type of event. The event should be big but not necessarily expensive. For example, the broker could hold a family day picnic to which sales staff and their families bring a covered dish and some meat to grill. The brokerage provides the drinks and condiments. The broker could arrange some type of game or sporting event, or the attendees could simply enjoy each other's conversation. Other events could include:

Chili cook-off	Day at the movies
Night at the opera	Sporting events
Community work	Fund raising for a charity
Easter egg hunt	Christmas party
Thanksgiving feast	Awards rally

The types of events should be geared toward the common preferences of the company's employees. If the group likes to play bingo, for example, the broker could arrange an event night complete with a bag of goodies and bingo markers. If, on the other hand, the group is into athletics, the broker could sponsor a brokerage softball tournament with a trophy for the winners and fun for all.

Award Rally

Holding a brokerage award rally is so important that it deserves its own section. Most successful brokers believe that every real estate brokerage should have a year-end award rally for their office to reward those who have made the brokerage a success. A broker should not underestimate the power of awards. Many a top real estate salesperson has left one real estate brokerage for another simply because he/she felt unappreciated.

The awards can be simple or elaborate, depending on the type of award given. Award criteria should be posted throughout the year so that the salespersons will know what it takes to get one. The broker should not give an award for mediocre production. The award should make the salespersons strive to earn one. Giving an award to everyone so that no one feels left out is just rewarding poor production and diminishing the value to the genuine producers.

Some real estate companies hold this award rally at hotel convention rooms where everyone dresses in formals for dinner. Others have a breakfast ceremony, and still others have this event at the office. No matter the size or spectacle, this event must be held. Major awards that should be given include:

- top producer in sales volume
- top producer in dollars earned
- top listing agent (total number)
- top sales agent (total number)

The broker has an unlimited ability to reward behaviors the broker wants repeated. If the broker wants the brokerage to concentrate on listings, he/she should develop more listing awards, such as:

- most listings from FSBOs
- most listings from expired listings
- most listings from sphere of influence
- top number of listings in any month

The kinds of awards the broker can give are limitless. The broker should be cautious not to give an award away to anyone who did not really work to achieve it. If the broker gives the award for top number of listings in any month and one of the salespersons lists 50 lots that belong to her father, the broker may be awarding someone who does not deserve the recognition. The broker should have minimum requirements for the awards that include a minimum dollar amount and a minimum listing length. Only 10% of the listings can come from any one source, for example. These requirements will allow the broker to reward the behavior the broker wants to see again.

Resignation and Termination

Eventually, a broker has to deal with resignation and termination. Some real estate license holders will not make it in the real estate business. For whatever reason, they just do not work out. If a license holder does not make enough money (of course, how much is not enough is different for everyone), eventually the license holder must resign. The broker should be continually recruiting to fill this void.

The broker must have minimum standards set for the office and written into the brokerage's policies and procedures manual. These minimum standards are just that, the minimum for production. The broker does not want to set minimum standards so high that they are not achievable for most license holders, nor should it be so low that dead wood hangs around. A minimum standard sets a pride level. No real estate professional wants to work in an office that is not about business. A party brokerage can be fun but is usually not profitable. Business is business and entertainment is entertainment, but the two do not mix well.

A clearly stated minimum standard allows all license holders to understand that the brokerage is a business, and therefore the license holder needs to produce or else expect to be fired. Most license holders who fit this description will quit long before the need to fire them arises.

A broker should be flexible with newly sponsored license holders. It may take two years to reach acceptable production levels. The broker should work with this salesperson; if the salesperson is following the broker's lead, the salesperson will soon enough be in production.

The other issue is termination. Brokers do not like to terminate license holders, so they call termination "career adjustment." If a sponsored license holder is not meeting minimum standards for the brokerage, that license holder must be terminated. The broker has to eliminate the nonproducer because allowing this license holder to continue lowers the production level for the entire brokerage. A brokerage is getting better or it is getting worse. No brokerage ever remains constant. Brokers who allow nonproducers to remain in their brokerage will consequently attract nonproducers and lose producers.

Most brokers do not like to terminate salespersons performing below their minimum standard for a number of reasons. A broker may:

- not want to hurt the license holder's feelings
- not want to lose the nonproducer's friend who IS a producer
- hope the license holder will improve
- have an open desk and feel that there might as well be someone there
- fear that the license holder will go to another brokerage and become a star
- be too lazy or incompetent to notice
- not enforce the minimum standard, so the minimum standard is of little use

Not one of these reasons has to do with what is best for the brokerage. The broker knows it is best to fire the nonproducer but hesitates. Countless brokerages are burdened with license holders who are "zero agents." Zero agents are license holders who have had no listings and no sales—zero production. Indeed, some brokerages have as many as 40% zero agents. What does this situation convey to the rest of staff, the current productive license holders?

For the following reasons, a broker should terminate license holders who are not performing at a minimum standard:

- Termination raises the expectations of the other currently sponsored license holders and thus increases overall production.

- It tells the competition that this brokerage is operational and will be production oriented.
- It strikes fear in those performing at or below the minimum standard, and some salespersons are motivated by fear.
- It frees up spots to recruit new, productive salespersons.
- It frees up time for the broker to spend with current productive salespersons.
- It frees up resources to help the current productive salespersons be more productive.
- Not doing so puts the broker at great risk because a license holder performing below the minimum standard is not producing enough to learn the business and is therefore more likely to jeopardize a transaction.

Productivity Management

Productivity management involves the monitoring of overall productivity from the broker's perspective and, to some degree, from the license holder's perspective. The broker is responsible for all operations of a brokerage, including productivity. Productivity management from the broker's perspective involves a few items that must be performed by the broker and all members of the brokerage: setting the commission rate, showing responsiveness and respect, providing training and support, and establishing rapport. In addition, from the broker's perspective, the license holder must engage in prospecting, be mindful of contact management, have a business plan, pay attention to time, and delegate tasks when necessary. These facets of productivity management are discussed here.

Commission

The commission rate must be competitive with other local brokerages. All commissions are negotiable, but if a broker is struggling then the first thing the broker wants to adjust is the commission base downward. This action could be the destruction of the brokerage. First, the best real estate license holders will leave the brokerage for another that pays better. Once they leave, the production in the brokerage will drop again, and this may lead to the dismantling of the brokerage. If the brokerage does survive, the broker will be left with nonproducers who have no incentive to produce.

Commissions should not give away all profit, but commissions are a major source of production incentive. Typically, the more production a license holder generates, the greater percentage of the incoming commission the license holder will receive. This type of commission structure gives a great incentive for the license holder to produce.

Response

License holders expect their broker to respond to them. If the broker is responsive, his/her responsiveness creates the ability for the license holder to be productive. If the broker cannot be found and it takes days for the broker to respond, that alone could reduce production. The TREC also states the brokers and license holders must respond in a timely manner.

TREC Rule §535.2

A broker or supervisor delegated must respond to sponsored salespersons, clients, and license holders representing other parties in real estate transactions within three calendar days.

A sponsoring broker or supervisor delegated shall deliver mail and other correspondence from the Commission to his/her sponsored salespersons within 10 calendar days after receipt.

Informing and Responding to Clients' Duty to Respond

A supervising broker, perhaps more so than other license holders, has a duty to respond to parties in a transaction. A sponsoring broker must also promptly respond to a sponsored salesperson. Promptness will be judged on the nature of the request, the time of day, and the type of transaction. A supervising broker should be reasonably available to supervised salespersons to provide needed advice and counsel. Being responsible for the supervised salesperson, the supervising broker should be available during all normal business hours of the brokerage to provide experienced, informed advice and counsel to assist the salespersons and the brokerage's clients. The supervising broker should monitor transactions handled by salespersons.

Respect

License holders want and need respect from their broker. Feeling respected increases license holders' productivity through the power of honor. A license holder will perform better when he/she is respected by the broker. Likewise, clients respond more favorably to license holders who have respect for the client. Respect is earned through hard work.

Training

Clearly, training is in direct correlation with production. The more and better the quality of training, the more and better the quality of production the license holders produce. Training is the lifeblood of the real estate brokerage world.

Support

As noted earlier, brokers must make themselves available to give their sponsored license holders advice when they want and need it. It cannot be emphasized enough that lack of broker support may be the primary reason that a license holder leaves one brokerage for another. The broker must regularly contact every one of the brokerage's license holders to show support. Showing support should be such an easy thing for a broker to do.

Rapport

The broker needs to be approachable as well as likable. A broker who is always in a bad mood is just one bad mood away from losing a brokerage. No one likes being around a grouch, even the boss grouch. The broker needs to shake hands, make eye contact, and converse with everyone who is around the brokerage. A pleasant demeanor will go a long way to encouraging licensees to perform their best. Also, to establish good relationships, the broker should go out of his/her way to find a real estate sponsored license holder with whom he/she has not talked in a while.

As noted in the introduction to this section, productivity management from the broker's perspective includes a few tasks that must be performed by the license holders.

Prospecting

Prospecting for clients always comes first. For license holders, prospecting is the most productive activity imaginable. Prospecting should be a continuous endeavor. Too many license holders call three potential customers, and when all three say no, they become discouraged. Such limited prospecting does not work, and that discouraged license holder may never attempt prospecting again. Yet prospecting does work, but it is a numbers game. The license holder would have been a success had he/she called 30,000 customers! Even when a license holder cannot handle any other business, the license holder should still be prospecting.

Contact Relationship Management

Contact relationship management (CRM) is a way for the license holder to organize and control his/her entire real estate business. The CRM can:

- prioritize contacts
- integrate with social network platforms
- integrate with email platforms
- help with taking listings
- provide calendar functions
- become the virtual address book
- provide templates for contact response
- be stored in the cloud

Business Plan

One of the most productive activities a license holder can engage in is to develop a business plan. The plan provides a roadmap to the destination (i.e., goal) of the license holder. A business plan gives the license holder power and confidence.

Objective Versus Time

To be truly productive, a license holder must realize that there is an objective to be accomplished no matter how long it takes. The opposite is also true: When there is no objective, the real estate license holder is no longer working. A closing may go late into the evening on a Friday, or perhaps the license holder has accomplished all the day's objectives by noon that day and has decided to go play golf in the afternoon. Both scenarios are fine in real estate because in both, the licensee has accomplished the day's objectives based on the "to do" list and the day's appointments.

Delegation

The license holder needs to think about delegating tasks if he/she hopes to become more productive. A license holder will hit a certain level of production beyond which it will become extremely difficult to increase output without hiring an assistant to whom the licensee can delegate some tasks. The license holder can also delegate tasks to unpaid others (usually friends and family), but this is only a short-term fix.

Productivity management is a new twist on a long-term idea in the real estate business. Not many brokers called the process productivity management; they just "pushed" and "hand-held" their license holders into sound production numbers.

Agent Business Plan

Brokers should require every sponsored license holder to formulate a written business plan. In fact, a license holder's success is most often a direct result of the licensee's written business plan. Those license holders without a business plan struggle for direction. To guide them, brokers should help each license holder develop a business plan for the license holder's own use.

Starting a career in real estate is a challenge in itself. Yet many people looking for a change are jumping into the real estate business without first planning their new venture. For these people, the importance of planning cannot be overemphasized. New license holders must carefully plan their career goals and how to achieve them. By taking an unbiased look at the real estate business and at themselves, license holders can identify areas of weaknesses and strengths that they might otherwise overlook. Planning can mean the difference between success and failure.

The idea of a business plan is to help keep the license holder mentally focused. In a sense, it is like a goal. The license holder writes the plan, follows it, and makes changes and updates as needed. The business plan allows the license holder to keep everything in proper perspective. Without a step-by-step business plan, a license holder will have great difficulty keeping his/her real estate business running successfully.

Just by setting up an achievable business plan and implementing it, the license holder will be way ahead of most people in the world. The difference between a person's financial success and simply retiring flat broke, as do 95% of people, is planning and taking action according to the plan. Yet most people have excuses for not writing a business plan:

- We are lazy and just don't do it.
- We think it costs too much.
- We feel that our real estate business is too small to have a plan.
- We just simply forget about it.
- It's too hard to actually do it.
- That's not for me.

These are all reasons that lead to failure. Better to formulate a business plan and go for it!

How to Write a Business Plan

Several steps need to be taken to write a business plan. The broker should encourage his/her license holders to take their time in writing personal business plans because some of the benefit comes from the action itself. Through the process of writing a business plan, the license holder may figure out that real estate sales in a certain area may not yield the results required by the business plan. The license holder now understands that another area may need to be added to meet the business plan requirements. Without the plan the license holder would not have realized the lack of business in just one area, and that may have spelled a career-ending failure.

Here are the steps to writing a successful business plan for any real estate professional:

1. The salesperson should gather all the information necessary to write a business plan:
   a. The salesperson should determine expenses and income from last year's sales if an experienced salesperson. This may take a while if the information needed is not readily available. A broker should teach all the sponsored license holders to track all their real estate expenses and income throughout the year so that this process is much easier than it would otherwise be.
   b. The salesperson should anticipate expenses and income for the next year if a new salesperson. The new salesperson needs to be realistic.
   c. Total Income − Expenses = Net Income.
   d. The salesperson should analyze his/her present situation.
   e. The salesperson should consider an exit strategy (i.e., what is the best way to quit the real estate business). Developing exit strategies is critical contingency thinking. The only thing worse than leaving the real estate industry is not being prepared if it became necessary.

Here is a simple worksheet:

a. Number of productive hours per week
   I will devote to real estate   _____
b. Monthly earnings from real estate necessary
   to maintain my standard of living   _____
c. Extra money I want available each month
   for immediate enjoyment   _____
d. Extra money I want available each month
   for my future security   _____
e. My monthly earnings will be   _____
f. Average sale or listing commission earned
   in my office   _____
g. Earnings $_____ ÷ Average commission $_____ = $_____
        (Line e)   (Line f)   (No. of transactions)
h. To achieve _____ transactions, I will maintain an
   average of _____ listings per month

2. The salesperson should identify his/her objectives:
   a. What does the real estate salesperson want from the real estate industry?
   b. What will it take to meet that objective?
   c. Is the salesperson willing to do what it takes to achieve the objective?
   d. Are these objectives placed in the order of their importance?
   e. What is the timetable for completion of each objective?
3. The salesperson should begin to develop a plan by taking all the information, organizing it, and then beginning the writing:
   a. The salesperson should analyze each objective and list what it will take to accomplish each.
   b. The salesperson should review the plan for accuracy.
4. The salesperson should implement the plan immediately:
   a. The salesperson must start taking action.
   b. A plan without action is only a plan.
   c. The salesperson is now heading in the right direction.
5. The salesperson should review the plan on a regular basis:
   a. The salesperson should make changes as needed.
   b. The plan is a working document and as such is never finished.

The broker should require the license holder to include some actions in his/her personal business plan. Here is a sample action plan without the data details:

Week 1 Activities

☐ Complete and sign the independent contractor agreement
☐ Complete the sponsored license holder profile sheet
☐ Complete all other necessary paperwork
☐ IRS forms
☐ Broker/Agent commission agreement
☐ Business card application
☐ Order name badge
☐ Read and sign the expectation letter
☐ Work station assigned and set up
☐ Receive building key and security alarm code
☐ Understand the systems and receive assigned passwords/codes to:
- brokerage email system
- brokerage voicemail/mailbox
- brokerage telephone
- brokerage copier/fax machine

☐ Understand/file for "also insured" rider on auto insurance policy
☐ Complete multiple listing service (MLS) application forms and write check for MLS dues
☐ Take MLS form/check to Association and obtain a lockbox key/cradle
☐ Get supplies for desk
☐ Read the policy and procedures manual and sign notice when completed
☐ Get introduced to the staff members
☐ Get issued a telephone roster/extension sheet

Daily Activities

☐ Add two people to your sphere-of-influence list
☐ Give business cards to five individuals you have not given one before
☐ Call 25 homeowners and ask them if they want to sell
☐ Preview at least two properties and put the information on note cards
☐ Present a professional image in appearance and behavior
☐ Read or listen to a book or CD on real estate for at least 30 minutes

- ☐ Call two FSBOs and ask to meet
- ☐ Call all expired listings in your market area and set a listing appointment
- ☐ Send letters to five non-occupant owners
- ☐ Call one FSBO to ask, "Where are you moving?," and ask for a referral
- ☐ Mail or email at least 10 follow-ups or marketing pieces
- ☐ Send at least two thank-you notes
- ☐ Write in your "Business Diary" the real estate aspects of the day. A business diary is one that details the day's events in the real estate business only. No personal entries. This business diary will later show the license holder how far he/she has come in real estate knowledge and wisdom.

Personal Marketing Plan

A broker needs to encourage each sponsored license holder to have a personal marketing plan. The marketing plan should organize the license holder's marketing strategy. A complete stranger should be able to pick up the license holder's marketing plan and understand all aspects of it.

The license holder should detail each step of the plan with exacting standards. The license holder should analyze each step to determine its purpose and whether it aligns with the overall marketing strategy. The marketing strategy is the "big picture" of marketing, whereas the marketing plan is the detailed action plan to accomplish the marketing strategy. If the plan does not align with the marketing strategy, the license holder should delete it or rework it until it fits with the plan. The license holder should include beginning and ending dates with each step, as well as costs and contact people. If the license holder is directly involved in any step of the marketing plan, the license holder's time commitment needs to be analyzed.

The license holder should also include all types of promotion, marketing, and advertising in the personal marketing plan. These may be planned promotional events, direct mail campaigns, or advertising in the local newspaper. If the license holder does advertise, he/she will need to separate name recognition advertising from prospect-generating advertising.

This is how the license holder plans to personally market his/her real estate business. The license holder will need to explain:

- Who/where is the license holder's market?
- Who are the license holder's customers?
- What are the characteristics of license holder's average customer?
- Who is the license holder's direct competition?
- What competitive advantage does the license holder have over the competitors?
- What is the best way the license holder plans to sell the real estate service?
- How will the license holder's real estate business differ from his/her competitors'?
- How will the license holder promote and market real estate services?
- Where is the license holder going to advertise?
- How much is it going to cost to advertise?
- What promotions will the license holder arrange?

The Marketing Plan for Clients

Under the Personal Marketing Plan for license holders the broker should review and approve of the marketing plan the license holder will give to seller-clients that will help them get their property sold. Here are several items that should be on the Marketing Plan for clients:

Verify room measurements
Obtain seller's work number
Verify data on house for MLS input
Put an electronic lockbox on the door
Log listing in MLS computer
Call for post yard sign
Send data for posting to webmaster
Write/Place advertisement in newspaper
Follow up on all calls on property
Call seller for weekly update
Design/Order a property profile sheet

Obtain a key and security codes
Determine best method for showing
Walk through property with "property checklist"
Make up listing folder
Write listing on marketing board
Mail sellers copies of all listing documents
Place information on showing systems
Submit listing to sales staff for their buyers
Announce at office meeting
Write/Place ad for real estate magazine
Plan office tour of property

Obtain/Analyze feedback of office tour

Place information tube on sign w/ sheets

Schedule area broker tour and luncheon at property

Promote property at board meeting

Discuss need for price adjustment

Plan/Hold open house

Schedule formal review

Mail invitations to open house

Time Management Plan

A time management plan can range from a complex system of schemes to monitor and control each minute of a person's day to the simple "to do" list and everything between. A real estate broker must have a method for time management, or else the broker will certainly reach burnout. The broker needs to be cognizant of each of the sponsored license holders to be sure each is equipped with a time management plan. Why is time planning important? Time is money. Time planning prevents future problems.

> Twelve Words to Live By:
> I must do the most productive thing possible at every given moment.

Time is precious and priceless. Ask the coach whose team is behind in the final seconds of a game. Ask the businessman who is late for a once-in-a-lifetime-promotion meeting. Ask the person who just entered the security line at the airport and whose plane leaves in three minutes. Ask the cancer patient who has recently learned she has only two months left to live.

The notion of time management is an oxymoron. Time is beyond a person's control, and the clock keeps ticking regardless of what a person does or how that person uses up his/her time. A time management plan is the answer to maximizing the time a broker has allocated in each day. No one has the ability to create time, but with direction, a broker can make the most of the moments he/she has been given.

Time is more valuable than money because time is irreplaceable. A person does not really pay for things with money; a person pays for them with time. People exchange their time for dollars when they go to work, and then they trade their dollars for everything they purchase. In essence, all anyone possesses can be traced back to an investment of time.

Time and Purpose
People who use time wisely spend it on activities that advance their overall purpose in life. Consistently using time and energy to achieve their purpose enables people to most fully realize their potential. The two greatest days in a person's life are the day the person is born and the day the person discovers the purpose for his/her birth. Uncovering this purpose helps to build passion, focus efforts, and deepen commitments.

Time and Values
People who use time well embellish their values with the time they spend. By acting in accordance with their beliefs, they find fulfillment. Failure to identify values leads to a mundane existence in which a person drifts through life. Clearly defined values direct a person's life as feathers direct an arrow. In a brokerage, values and ethics inspire a sense of broader purpose. They make work worthwhile. If a vision statement is the head and a mission statement is the heart, then the value statement is the soul of a brokerage.

Time and Strengths
People who use time correctly play to their strengths. By doing so, they are most effective. If a broker's skill level is a 2 in public speaking, the broker should not pursue improving his/her public speaking skills because the broker will likely never grow beyond a 4. However, if the broker is a 7 in recruiting, the broker should put time and effort into further developing that skill because when he/she becomes a 9, he/she will have reached a rare level of expertise. A broker needs to discover his/her gifts and then use time wisely to develop those gifts.

Time and Fulfillment
People who use time well choose fulfillment by prioritizing relationships and achieving balance. Too many brokers work all day, every day and never have time for family, friends, and recreation. These brokers end up losing virtually everything. A time management plan must balance all of life's priorities.

Brokers cannot find more time; it is a finite and constantly diminishing resource. However, brokers can learn to spend time wisely.

Time Management Plan Hints

Time management has been around since, well, time. Everyone has an idea on how to handle time better. Each idea has its merits, but the bottom line is that no time management technique ever thought of works without being put to use. The broker needs to implement a single time management technique and embed that one in his/her thoughts and actions. Once the technique has been mastered, the broker should then take on another time management technique, but the broker should not try to implement the techniques all at once.

Here are some time management hints for any broker to begin:

1. **The broker must have a written and prioritized "to do" list.** Most brokers know this list is important for organizing one's time, but only a few actually write one every day. This list will be long, and that is why it must be prioritized.
2. **The "to do" list should be flexible yet thorough.** The "to do" list is simply that, a reminder to do certain things during the day. However, if a sponsored license holder needs the broker's help, the broker should not forego meeting with the licensee just to complete some small task on the list. Brokers must be available to their licensees and therefore should not be focused only on accomplishing all the tasks on the list.
3. **The broker must complete the first things on the "to do" list first.** The broker must take on item 1 on the list and complete it—that is a great day. It is easy to pick off a few tasks from the list just to act busy. But if the broker accomplishes only one task on the list but it was the first and most important task, the broker should be satisfied. The tasks that were not completed need to be moved to the next day's list or delegated.
4. **The broker should work at work and play at play, which is a corollary to the notion that work is work and home is home.** Too many brokers do not know how to separate home and work, and because of this their family thinks that they are never home and their license holders think they are never at work. The broker must provide a "Broker's Office Hour" notice weekly. This notice shows the hours the broker will be in the office available for counseling. This notice needs to be emailed to all sponsored license holders each week, and it needs to be posted on the broker's office door. The broker should likewise notify his/her family of the

family hours, when the broker is available to his/her family for family time.

A broker should not have his/her home number on his/her business card. The broker should protect the home as much or more than he/she protects the brokerage. Family members need to know they are important, and so the broker should not take calls at all during family time.

5. **The broker should waste time honestly.** If a broker chooses to waste time, the broker should do so honestly. What this simply means is that if the broker decides to waste time, the broker needs to sit in a chair and do nothing. This is wasting time honestly. It will not take long for the broker to figure out that "that ain't no fun" and will get back to work. What dishonest time wasters do is shuffle papers, clean their desk, and search the computer for random, insignificant information. All these activities make the broker look busy, but that broker is actually wasting time and may continue to do that all day without notice.

6. **The broker should have an assistant.** A broker who does not have an assistant is the assistant! Brokers need an assistant to delegate all the work that is not necessary for the broker to actually handle. This time-saving measure is such a plus. Brokers fear that employing an assistant is one more cost, which is true, but if the broker hires three more license holders because the broker now has more time to recruit, employing an assistant is beneficial.

7. **The broker should work only five and one-half days per week.** This sounds easier than it actually is in brokerage life. The one and one-half days off should mean off. No business calls (with exceptions), no office time, and no meetings. Off is off. The broker should have someone in the office—perhaps a manager or an assistant manager—who can handle the business for a day and a half. When the broker takes time off, the broker will experience less burnout.

8. **The broker should handle paperwork only once.** Complete it, delegate it or eliminate it. Too many brokers have a form that needs to be filled in and emailed. The form sits on the broker's desk. The broker picks up the form a half-dozen times each hour. This is wasting time. If the form is

important, the broker just needs to deal with it. Can filling out the form be delegated? Perhaps it is a form to apply for chairperson of the yearly float, but the broker has no time for that, and so the form should be eliminated (this can be done any number of ways).

9. **The broker should combine activities.** The broker leaves for the title company to drop off an agreement. On the way there he makes return calls in the car. The broker stops to get his oil changed in the car. While waiting, the broker reviews three new contracts that came in today. On the way back to the office the broker stops to pick up coffee for tomorrow's sales meeting; he also calls his wife to tell her that he loves her. The broker has combined several "to do" tasks in one trip.

10. **The broker should start the day early.** Early is when the real businesspeople work. The office is quiet, and the broker can achieve great things without interruptions. What a great way to start the day—with a feeling of accomplishment. A secondary benefit is that starting early sets a great example for the brokerage's sponsored license holders. If the broker is in early, the license holders should also be in early.

11. **The broker should never let the car gas tank go under half-full.** This is a time management issue, but it is also a safety issue. The broker is late for an important meeting (which should not happen when following a time management plan) and realizes that he/she is almost out of gas and will not make it to the meeting. In filling the gas tank, the broker then splashes gasoline all over his/her new clothes. The broker does not need this extra headache. What he/she needs to do is keep the gas tank no less than half-full. The safety issue is not running out of gas in the middle of nowhere.

12. **The broker should listen to educational CDs, MP3s, or other listening apps for the car.** The broker can get a college education from all the time he/she spends in a car. Most people listen to music, and that is fine if the person needs entertainment. However, the wise broker will make this time productive. One broker had on her bucket list a stipulation to read novels by well-known authors. The broker never had time to do this, she thought. However, the broker began listening on a paid download to her smartphone and has now

listened to several hundred novels. Doing that may not be real estate-related, but it does expand the mind. The broker should always have an educational book or a reader on his/her smartphone in case there is a delay that opens time to read.

13. **The broker should pay for services to free up the broker's personal time.** If the broker hates mowing the lawn, washing the car, or cleaning the house, the broker needs to pay to have these chores performed. The broker now uses the free time to prospect for recruits. Prospecting for recruits is a much better use of the broker's time. This is "opportunity cost." If a person is doing one thing it prevents the person from doing another.

14. **The broker must learn to say no.** This is a time management must. A broker wants people to like him/her. So, for example, the broker volunteers to handle a community project. The broker volunteers for another project and then another project and so on. Soon enough, the broker is performing only community work and not brokerage work. It is not bad to participate in community projects, but the broker must know when not to.

    A corollary to learning to say no is to refuse to do another person's job. Some brokers want to help out their salespersons so much that they begin to do their job for them. The broker must say no. If a salesperson needs more training to be able to complete a task, the wise broker offers to teach the salesperson, not perform the task. Completing the job for the salesperson teaches that salesperson only how to get out of work.

15. **The broker should promise a little, deliver a lot.** The broker should promise new salespersons to interfere as little as possible, contributing only the minimum but delivering the best. This action alone will propel the broker to greatness. If the broker overwhelms a new recruit by focusing only on the potential to make millions, the recruit may be disappointed once engaged in the real estate business. The broker should make clear that making money is going to be a struggle; so when the recruit actually makes money, the new recruit will thank the broker.

16. **The broker should review and preview.** The broker needs to review the day's agenda and preview the program planned for the next day. By reviewing, the broker can look at the entire day's work to determine if the brokerage had a successful business day or whether some adjustments need to be made. This is the time to write in the broker's business journal. The broker should then preview the next day's agenda and complete the prioritized "to do" list.
17. **The broker should track his/her time.** Once a year, the broker should track his/her time for an entire day (or if brave, for an entire week). This means every minute for 24 hours. The broker needs to list what he/she was doing, what was spent, and even what was eaten. At the end of this period, the broker may see glaring holes in the workday when time was wasted. The broker can also use this information for cost control and weight loss. Although this tracking is very difficult to keep up with for even one day, the information is eye-opening.

Allocating Time

Allocating time involves a simple exercise to see how much time a broker really has in a day for brokerage. The best measure is to complete the "time-tracking" exercise. To find the number of hours the broker has available for building the brokerage, he/she should complete the following chart:

	_____	hours sleeping
	_____	hours for personal hygiene
	_____	hours with family, friends
	_____	hours eating
	_____	hours driving
	_____	hours shopping
	_____	hours at leisure
	_____	hours at sports/extras
Total	_____	hours committed to personal time
Subtract	_____	from 24 hours available for the brokerage

CHAPTER SUMMARY

The Texas Real Estate Commission (TREC) on Rule 531.3 Competency: It is the obligation of a real estate agent to be knowledgeable as a real estate brokerage practitioner. The agent should:

1. be informed on market conditions;
2. pledge to continuing education;
3. be informed on developments in the real estate industry; and
4. exercise judgment and skill in the work.

Burnout is when a person concentrates on one aspect of his/her life and thereby loses perspective and balance.

A slump occurs when a licensee no longer has the motivation to do what is necessary to accomplish his/her goals.

Buyer Files
1. Hot Buyer—Totally qualified individuals who will buy
2. Medium Buyer—Individuals who will buy within the next six months
3. Cold Buyer—Individuals who have no real need to buy

Seller Files
Canvassing Leads—These leads are part of the license holder's geographic marketing area or a lead found by using any other prospecting methods.
Presentation Leads—These leads are people with whom the license holder has talked about selling, but they are not yet ready to make a move.
Past Buyers and Sellers—The license holder must keep in touch with past clients.
FSBO or Specialized Area Leads—Whether the license holder specializes in FSBOs, expired listings, certain types of professions, or some other area, the license holder should keep these people in tickler files.

General File—This file notes everyone the license holder knows, including but not limited to friends, relatives, social contacts, anyone the license holder meets.

Expense File and Tax Records—The license holder should keep all receipts and business expenses.

A centralized leads management program provides a real estate firm with a number of specific advantages, including benefits to the firm as well as efficiencies.

The job of the customer service representative (CSR) is to answer every call that comes in to the company.

Orientation programs (also called onboarding) need to be structured to allow a newly sponsored license holder the opportunity to fit in in a timely manner. The following items should be part of the orientation program:

- meeting of the staff
- current office issues
- parking
- office locations
- office equipment
- conference rooms
- kitchen/break area
- signs/lockboxes
- desk
- email

The expectation letter should states what is expected of every sponsored license holder and should include:

- personal production goals
- involvement and participation
- training
- professionalism
- quality service

Performance appraisals are employee and independent contractor reviews.

The individual business development (IBD) meeting is conducted with a sponsored license holder to review his/her current and future production.

Just-in-time (JIT) training is the training provided right before a sales event occurs.

Field training is offered to newly sponsored real estate license holders to help them on their first one or two listing appointments.

A broker/manager should offer sponsored real estate license holders specialized training at every office meeting. The broker/manager should keep in mind that education without application is worse than worthless.

Experienced salesperson training is for license holders who have been in the real estate business long enough to know the basics of the real estate business.

Top producer training is for license holders who fall within the upper 5% of production.

"Mentoring" is a term used to describe a teacher-student relationship. Mentoring occurs when a more experienced professional (the mentor) gives significant career assistance to a less experienced professional (the protégé).

The broker needs to conduct business meetings for the staff, for the management, and for the license holders.

The broker needs to meet at least once a year with the key players of the brokerage firm to discuss the company direction and any changes the market requires; this meeting is called a "retreat." The purpose of a brokerage retreat is to review the current year, project the upcoming year, and build rapport across lines of management and offices.

Brokers should have scheduled sales meetings in which they update the sales staff on the activities of the brokerage.

During the office meetings, the broker conducts a review of any new laws, regulations, or activities in the office and also reviews any new listings brought in by the brokerage's salespersons.

The meeting *agenda* gives a sense of purpose and direction to the meeting.

In the *introduction to the meeting* the broker covers the purpose of the meeting and tells all the attendees that he/she appreciates their presence.

The *welcoming of any guests, affiliates, and new salespersons* is a special time when the broker welcomes the honored attendees.

Announcements is the time when the broker makes any needed announcements.

Guest or affiliate presentation is the section of the meeting in which these invitees may be permitted a moment to speak.

Entertainment is the "fun time" section and should include a "get involved" type of action.

Training is the time in which the broker should offer the sales staff valuable training.

Wants and needs is when the sales staff discuss their new listings or the listings that they are struggling to sell.

The broker should *wrap up* the business meeting with any final comments.

Before the office meeting the broker should:

1. define the purpose of the meeting
2. develop an agenda
3. distribute the agenda
4. choose an appropriate meeting time
5. find the best room
6. arrange the room
7. prepare visual aids

During the office meeting the broker should:

1. review the agenda and set priorities for the meeting
2. greet each of the sponsored license holders
3. serve light refreshments if possible
4. start on time
5. stick to the agenda
6. encourage group discussion to share all points of view and ideas
7. keep minutes of the meeting for future reference in case a question or problem arises
8. be a role model by listening and showing interest, appreciation, and confidence in his/her salespersons
9. summarize any agreements reached and end the meeting on a unifying or positive note
10. end on time if possible

After the office meeting the broker should:

1. write up and distribute minutes within a few days of the meeting date
2. put unfinished business on the agenda for the next meeting
3. conduct a periodic evaluation of the meetings

Personal interaction with each sponsored license holders is crucial for the broker. To this end, a good broker maintains an open-door policy. The broker should be available 24 hours a day, seven days a week, unless the broker has delegated broker responsibilities to another trusted license holder or a manager.

Retention is the second most important step in making a brokerage profitable. Here are some words a broker should live by:

- recruit the right talent
- hire the right talent
- develop the right talent
- retain the right talent

Brokers design call nights for prospecting so that their salespersons can obtain buyers and sellers.

At least twice a year a broker should invite the entire company to participate in some type of event.

A year-end award rally is held to reward those who have made the brokerage a success. Major awards that should be given include:

- top producer in sales volume
- top producer in dollars earned
- top listing agent (total number)
- top sales agent (total number)

For the following reasons, a broker should terminate license holders who are not performing at a minimum standard:

- Termination raises the expectations of the other currently sponsored license holders and thus increases overall production.
- It tells the competition that this brokerage is operational and will be production oriented.
- It strikes fear in those performing at or below the minimum standard, and some salespersons are motivated by fear.
- It frees up spots to recruit new, productive salespersons.
- It frees up time for the broker to spend with current productive salespersons.
- It frees up resources to help the current productive salespersons be more productive.
- Not doing so puts the broker at great risk because the license holder performing below the minimum standard is not producing enough to learn the business and is therefore more likely to jeopardize a transaction.

Productivity management involves the monitoring of overall productivity from the broker's perspective and, to some degree, from the license holder's perspective and includes the following:

- The commission rate must be competitive with other local brokerages.
- License holders expect their broker to respond to them.
- License holders want and need respect from their broker.
- Brokers must make themselves available to give their sponsored license holders advice.
- Brokers need to be approachable as well as likable.
- Brokers need to insist that prospecting always comes first.
- For license holders, prospecting is the most productive activity imaginable.
- Brokers need to insist that prospecting be continuous.
- License holders should develop a business plan.
- License holders need to delegate tasks to become more productive.

Contact relationship management (CRM) is a way for the license holder to manage his/her entire real estate business.

Here are the steps to writing a successful business plan for any real estate professional:

1. The salesperson should gather all the information necessary to write a business plan:
   a. The salesperson should determine expenses and income from last year's sales if an experienced salesperson.
   b. The salesperson should anticipate expenses and income for the next year if a new salesperson.
   c. Total Income − Expenses = Net Income.
   d. The salesperson should analyze his/her present situation.
   e. The salesperson should consider an exit strategy.
2. The salesperson should identify his/her objectives:
   a. What does the real estate salesperson want from the real estate industry?
   b. What will it take to meet that objective?
   c. Is the salesperson willing to do what it takes to achieve the objective?
   d. Are these objectives placed in the order of their importance?
   e. What is the timetable for completion of each objective?
3. The salesperson should begin to develop a plan by taking all the information, organizing it, and then beginning the writing:
   a. The salesperson should analyze each objective and list what it will take to accomplish each.
   b. The salesperson should review the plan for accuracy.

4. The salesperson should implement the plan immediately:
   a. The salesperson must start taking action.
   b. A plan without action is only a plan.
   c. The salesperson is now heading in the right direction.
5. The salesperson should review the plan on a regular basis:
   a. The salesperson should make changes as needed.
   b. The plan is a working document and as such is never finished.

The marketing strategy is the "big picture" of marketing, whereas the marketing plan is the detailed action plan to accomplish the marketing strategy.

A time management plan can range from a complex system to monitor and control each minute of a person's day to the simple "to do" list and everything between.

Here are some time management hints for any broker to begin:

1. have a written and prioritized "to do" list
2. make sure the "to do" list is flexible yet thorough
3. complete the first things on the "to do" list first
4. work at work and play at play (a corollary to work is work and home is home)
5. waste time honestly
6. have an assistant
7. work only five and one-half days per week
8. handle paperwork only once
9. combine activities
10. start the day early
11. never let the car gas tank go under half-full
12. listen to educational CDs, MP3s, or other listening apps for the car
13. pay for services to free up the broker's personal time
14. learn to say no
15. promise a little, deliver a lot
16. review and preview
17. track time

CHAPTER QUESTIONS

1. What is it called when a person concentrates on one aspect of his/her life and loses perspective and balance on all other aspects?
   A. slump
   B. burnout
   C. concentration
   D. balance

2. What is the purpose of an orientation program?
   A. meet TREC regulations
   B. meet national employment guidelines
   C. make sure the newly sponsored license holder fits in
   D. none of the answer choices

3. What is the purpose of the expectation letter?
   A. It specifies what the brokerage requires of each sponsored license holders.
   B. It clarifies the expectations of the TREC.
   C. It details the expectations of the license holder.
   D. It is a letter that is sent to potential clients of the new license holder.

4. The IBD meeting is a:
   A. business meeting with the local development council
   B. meeting individually by the broker with a member of an ancillary business
   C. development meeting for the brokerage
   D. meeting with a sponsored license holder to review his/her current and future production

5. What type of training is provided right before a sales event occurs?
   A. event training
   B. just-in-time training
   C. last-minute training
   D. prior-to-event training

6. What type of training is offered to newly sponsored real estate license holders to help them on their first one or two listing appointments?
   A. just-in-time training
   B. new agent training
   C. field training
   D. primary listing training

7. What term is used to describe the teacher-student relationship?
   A. mentoring
   B. facilitating
   C. broker-agent
   D. primary

8. What is the yearly meeting with the key players of the brokerage firm to discuss the company direction?
   A. IBD meeting
   B. a retreat
   C. key man review meeting
   D. review-and-preview meeting

9. Which of the following is true?
   A. recruit the right talent
   B. develop the right talent
   C. retain the right talent
   D. all of the answer choices

10. What is a detailed action plan to accomplish the marketing strategy?
    A. marketing budget
    B. marketing plan
    C. marketing mission statement
    D. marketing objectives

CHAPTER 13

Evaluating the Real Estate Brokerage Business

A broker must constantly be evaluating the brokerage. The brokerage business is, at times, a very fast-paced enterprise. Trends change; what was once the current trend is no longer important. Markets change; what was once a seller's market is now a buyer's market because the naval base closed down.

> **Seller's market**—A seller's market occurs when there are a great many buyers in the market looking for very few homes for sale. The seller has most if not all of the negotiating power. Multiple offers are likely, and the prices are increasing.
>
> **Buyer's market**—A buyer's market occurs when there is a great deal of inventory in the market but there are very few buyers looking for homes. The buyer has most if not all of the negotiating power. An offer may not be seen by a seller for months, and the prices are decreasing.

Preferences change; what buyers once used to prefer is no longer in style. Finances change; once sellers used to sell their home and move up, but now sellers are updating their homes and staying. Areas change; a once popular area is now run down and an eyesore. Changes happen in the real estate industry, and sometimes those changes can happen rapidly. A broker must constantly evaluate his/her brokerage business to adapt in a quick and positive manner.

> CASE IN POINT—One broker had a multiple-office brokerage corporation. The market was changing. The economy was pointing to a slowdown. The economy was pointing to job losses and was possibly heading for a recession. The experts were advising real estate brokerages to retrench and cut back and not to expand operations for any real estate brokerage. This broker received all this advice and did not take heed. The broker enlarged offices to handle more real estate license holders. The broker acquired several more real estate offices. To operate the brokerage offices, the broker bought large-ticket equipment such as high-speed printers and computers with high-speed internet access.
>
> Then the market turned down. Jobs were lost, businesses were closing, and few people were buying real estate. The money market tightened up, and few real estate loans were being made even to the people who wanted a home. It was the dreaded

market crash. This broker suffered dearly, losing over $100,000 per month for several years. The broker now retrenched by closing brokerage offices and firing staff, which cost people and himself a great deal of money. Had the broker looked and listened, he would have had the time to assign those people different jobs and in doing so saved himself millions.

Financial Controls

Every broker/owner should have set up financial controls to help operate and evaluate the real estate brokerage business. Without using the proper evaluation methods, a broker will have no idea what the results of his/her efforts are and will not have the means to know when and how to make adjustments for the betterment of the brokerage.

General Operating Budget

The general operating budget (GOB) is a document that has projections of costs and income based on past data. These estimates are budgeted to allocate money to the appropriate places for the success of the brokerage. Here is a sample GOB on a simple spreadsheet:

General Operating Budget for Hamilton Real Estate Company

	2018 Budget	2017 Actual	2016 Actual
Income	$850,000	$789,400	$742,030
Expenses	$(700,000)	$(658,780)	$(618,520)
Difference	$150,000	$130,620	$123,510
Expenses (yearly)			
Office lease	$168,000	$168,000	$168,000
Office equipment rent	$58,000	$57,600	$57,600
Salaries	$325,000	$325,000	$325,000
Marketing	$75,000	$50,250	$29,340
Utilites	$25,000	$22,660	$12,665
Maintenance	$15,000	$12,625	$9,085
Supplies	$34,000	$22,645	$16,830
TOTAL	$700,000	$658,780	$618,520

Typically, the next year's budget (2018 in table) would be rounded to thousands or hundreds. The actuals (2017 and 2016 in table) would be rounded to the nearest dollar. This sample budget indicates that the brokerage is increasing its income by about 6% per year, with expenses following the same path. If the broker could continue the 6% increase but lower the expenses, the broker would show a much greater gain. Potentially, the broker could purchase additional office equipment instead of renting, and that would, over time, lower the yearly expenses. The broker could look to outsource the marketing, and that may lower marketing expenses or it may allow the broker to eliminate a salaried position. Perhaps the broker notices a large increase in expenses or a lowering of income. Either of these situations would require the broker to spend time analyzing the causes.

Controlling the Finances

Financial controls also include the protection of the finances. The broker should not allow the brokerage checkbook in the hands of just anyone. If the broker has a manager, the broker should require two signatures (manager AND broker) on any checks above a certain amount. The amount would be at the discretion of the broker.

The broker should pay for the brokerage expenses of any staff person. The person must account for every dollar and provide a receipt or document proving the expense. The broker would then reimburse the staff person for the expense. A broker needs to be careful with credit cards. A manager could charge personal items and then quit, leaving the brokerage to cover those personal expenses. The broker could go after the manager (if the manager could be found), but think of the cost in time and attorney fees.

The broker should in no way allow license holders to obligate expenses to the brokerage in any way. This sets a bad precedent and could leads to financial disaster. This category includes simple things such as office supplies and the birthday cake for one of the license holders. All expenses must be paid by the brokerage upfront with no reimbursements from the brokerage. If any expense needs to be reimbursed, a staff member approved for reimbursements should pay for the expense.

For a brokerage to survive, the broker needs to be extremely diligent in asserting financial controls. What does not seem like an issue today could be the financial ruin of a brokerage tomorrow if not monitored and controlled.

Monitoring the Business

As with the finances, the broker must monitor the brokerage business. The broker must monitor everything associated with the brokerage business. This task can be delegated, but the broker must then monitor those to whom the broker has delegated this monitoring task.

> CASE IN POINT—A broker trusted a manager to run one of the three brokerage offices the broker owned. In time, the office began dropping in production and, more important, in profit. Sponsored license holders began to leave that office. The broker would quiz the manager, who would say, "Oh, it will get better." It never did get better. After termination of the manager, the broker discovered that the manager regularly stole business that was supposed to go to the office's sponsored license holders and kept it for himself. That caused a drop in overall production in the office and a huge hit to profits. The manager was never around, which caused the sponsored license holders to leave. It took years for the broker just to reach the "break-even" point again.

The following sections identify other potential dangers in the real estate brokerage business, areas that if not monitored carefully by the broker can lead the business over the cliff (these are presented in no order of importance).

Office Staff

The broker must monitor office staff. As the above Case in Point clearly shows, even office managers need monitoring. The broker should trust but verify. The broker needs to be aware of the relationships the staff members have with the sponsored license holders.

> CASE IN POINT—One broker had acquired a brokerage company. The broker did not make radical changes for fear of disrupting the current business operations. Later on, the broker discovered that the relationship between the sponsored license holders and the receptionist was not a business relationship but a friendship relationship. The entire group would go out to have fun together. This in itself is not an issue, but it needs to be monitored by the broker carefully. It turns out that the receptionist was working against the broker/owner in favor of her "friends," the sponsored license holders. The receptionist would allow the sponsored license holders to bring alcohol into the brokerage office, creating extreme liability for the broker. The receptionist would allow the sponsored license holders to bring pets and children into the office and remain there all day. The brokerage is a business, not a day-care or pet-care center. There are health and safety issues. The receptionist would also allow license holders to run real estate advertisements benefiting only one license holder and expense it under the brokerage marketing budget. Once the broker discovered these and several other issues, the broker had to let the receptionist go and in her place hired an unbiased receptionist.

Office Supplies

The broker must monitor all offices supplies. The broker must particularly monitor the office supplies that are provided to the sponsored license holders and the staff.

CASE IN POINT—One kind broker was trusting of his licensees, so he did not feel the need for monitoring office supplies. He did not monitor expenses very well either. When he realized that he was spending a great deal of money on office supplies but the production numbers did not warrant those expenses, he began to investigate. He quickly discovered that the supply room was stocked with office supplies and then regularly raided by the sponsored license holders wanting items for their personal use. The sponsored license holders would take boxes of pens, reams of paper, ink cartridges, staplers and boxes of staples, writing pads, file folders, lightbulbs, and even toilet paper. To deal with this theft, the broker had to assign the receptionist the duty to monitor office supplies and provide them on a limited basis only for office use from a locked cabinet.

Bonuses and Gifts, Investor and Builder Business

The broker needs to monitor bonuses and gifts as well as investor and builder business because sponsored license holders can take advantage of these situations. The licensee may ask for bonuses that could be construed by the Texas Real Estate Commission (TREC) as not in the best interest of the public. There is no problem with bonuses, however, if freely given by the client. Some brokerages allow bonuses to be paid directly to the sponsored license holder, creating the incentive for the license holder to get more bonuses any way possible. The broker should monitor all bonuses to be sure that one licensee is not getting an excessive number of bonuses.

Gifts work the same way as bonuses, except these could be easier to hide. A gift could be as innocent as flowers, gift cards, vacations, cash, and merchandise. All these items must be vetted through the broker before the recipient may use or keep them. The broker and the sponsored license holder's agreement on how to handle gifts is negotiable.

CASE IN POINT—A builder was offering a bonus for selling one of the company's inventory houses. The bonus was a $500 gift card for a local department store. The builder told the license holders that the gift card was for them and said, "Don't tell your broker." If any license holder hears the words "Don't tell your

> broker," the first thing the license holder should do is run to tell the broker. All compensation—no matter what type—must be vetted by the broker. For the license holder to take the gift card and use it without the broker's knowledge is a TREC violation and could expose the license holder to suspension or revocation.

Investors and Builders

An unscrupulous license holder could negotiate any number of advantages with investors and builders that can cut out the broker—all of which cannot be allowed by the broker. The broker is responsible for all authorized real estate actions of his/her sponsored license holders. "Side" agreements between license holders and investors and builders can place the broker in a position of liability without his/her knowledge.

Complaints

The broker needs to be aware of complaints against sponsored license holders. Of course, TREC-filed complaints are the worst case, but usually an astute broker will see problems well before a TREC complaint is issued. The broker needs to know if a seller or buyer is complaining about an unresponsive license holder. This may indicate that the license holder is being lazy or perhaps even deceptive. Either one is not good for the brokerage. The broker must be aware of such complaints. Again, this issue of unresponsiveness needs to be monitored by the broker. The best time to handle a complaint is before it is filed.

Computer Software and Downloads

The broker needs to monitor all software used by the brokerage and all downloads to brokerage computers. The software installed on the brokerage computers can be tremendously expensive, and the broker would therefore not want sponsored license holders to be able to tamper with the software. Any changes may leave the software unusable or may cause losses of important data. The software should be locked in such a way that no matter what a license holder does, the license holder's actions will not affect the integrity of the software.

The broker needs to know what is being downloaded to the brokerage computers. Malware is always an issue, of course, as well as inappropriate material. In addition, breaches in proprietary information will always be a threat to brokerages.

The broker needs to be aware of each of his/her sponsored license holders and the things they post online. Inappropriate material or posts on social networking sites or on the individual license holder's website can lead to issues for the brokerage. The TREC requires that any information that is inaccurate about a particular property be taken down or updated in a timely manner. A broker concerned about how to handle such matters should seek legal counsel.

Paid Workers

Frequently, a broker will hire landscapers, remodelers, repair and maintenance workers, and others to work on projects in the brokerage. The broker could be liable for these workers because they are being paid for by the brokerage. The broker needs to see documentation to determine the trustworthiness of these individuals. The workers should be bonded—that is, they should have a security bond from an insurance company insuring their performance—and have professional liability insurance, also known as errors and omissions insurance.

Money

Brokers should never allow sponsored license holders to manage the money of others. All earnest-money checks should be taken to the designated title company or placed in the brokerage trust account. The sponsored license holders should never take cash for any reason. The broker needs to monitor any collection of cash for gifts or donations.

> CASE IN POINT—One broker's sponsored license holder went into the hospital for a health issue. The assistant manager suggested that everyone pitch in money to buy the hospitalized person a nice gift. The assistant manager was dutiful in collecting the money. The hospitalized license holder got out of the hospital and eventually came back to work at the brokerage. One day the broker stopped by her office and asked, "Did you enjoy what everyone did for you?" The agent, mystified, responded, "What do you mean?" The broker soon found out that the assistant had collected several hundred dollars and pocketed all the money. No one knows why the assistant felt she would not be caught.

Management of Information

The TREC requires brokers to manage any information that comes into their brokerage firm.

TREC Rules §535.2 states the following:

> *Except for records destroyed by an "act of God" such as a natural disaster or fire not intentionally caused by the broker, the broker must, at a minimum, maintain the following records in a format that is readily available to the Commission for at least four years from the date of closing, termination of the contract, or end of a real estate transaction:*
> - *disclosures;*
> - *commission agreements such as listing agreements, buyer representation agreements, or other written agreements relied upon to claim compensation;*
> - *work files;*
> - *contracts and related addenda;*
> - *receipts and disbursements of compensation for services subject to the Act;*
> - *property management contracts;*
> - *appraisals, broker price opinions, and comparative market analyses; and*
> - *sponsorship agreements between the broker and sponsored salespersons.*

Properly maintaining records in all real estate transactions is important for brokers. The above rule lists only those records that the TREC requires of brokers. There are other reasons that a broker should keep records longer than four years. For example, brokers should keep tax records for much longer than four years. Generally, tax records must be kept for seven years if not longer.

Brokers should have proper means for destroying files after their use has ended. This task should be handled by professionals if large amounts of information must be destroyed, or at least a shredder should be used for individual forms. Brokers should also keep a list of the files that have been destroyed.

Chapter 521, Unauthorized Use of Identifying Information, of the Texas Business and Commerce Code requires a business to have procedures to protect against the unlawful use or disclosure of sensitive personal information received in the regular course of business. It requires the business to destroy such records that are not required or needed for business operations. Sensitive personal information includes an individual's first name or first initial and last name in combination with any one or more of the following:

- Social Security number;
- driver's license number or government-issued identification number;
- account number or credit or debit card number in combination with any required security code, access code, or password that would permit access to an individual's financial account; or
- information that identifies an individual and relates to the physical or mental health or condition of the individual, the provision of health care to the individual, or payment for the provision of health care to the individual.

Maximizing Income

The broker must develop the discipline to always be searching for ways to maximize income from the brokerage business. The broker may want to seek outside counsel to help determine different scenarios to maximize income. "Greater income solves all matters" is a saying that is not too far off from the truth.

Recruiting

Recruiting is probably the best way to maximize income for a real estate brokerage. The broker who can recruit can continually increase income. "The more sponsored license holders, the more money" is not an absolute truth, but it is a reality if those license holders are productive.

Retention

Retention means "keeping" sponsored license holders and helping them become productive, which is the second best way to maximize income. Productive sponsored license holders make money, and when they make money, the brokerage makes money. Training is the foremost way to increase production from currently sponsored license holders. The training should be "sales training." This type of training is aimed solely at increasing production.

Acquisitions and Mergers

A broker who wants to maximize income in a large way needs to look for an acquisition. In an acquisition, the broker "buys out" a competitor and now has up to twice the production potential. The more production, the higher the maximization of income is obtained.

Ancillary Services

Ancillary services or businesses are those that are partially or fully dependent on real estate sales but do not directly make such sales. Ancillary businesses include appraisers, inspectors, lenders, title companies, moving companies, relocation services, residential service companies, and more; the list is endless. The broker should figure out a way to receive some monetary benefit from each of these ancillary businesses. The broker could own the ancillary service or some part of the business. The broker could form alliances with these companies. Any type of rebate, commission, or referral from an ancillary business should be reviewed for compliance with the Real Estate Settlement Procedures Act (RESPA) and the Texas Department of Insurance (TDI) Rule P-53.

Real Estate Settlement Procedures Act

RESPA is a consumer protection statute enacted in 1974. Its purpose is to clarify settlement costs and to eliminate "kickbacks" and fees that increase settlement costs. RESPA prohibits the payment of fees as part of a real estate settlement when no services are rendered to the consumer. This prohibition includes referral fees for such services as title searches, title insurance, mortgage loans, appraisals, credit reports, inspections, surveys, and legal services.

Business relationships and affiliations among real estate firms, mortgage brokers, title insurance firms, and other such companies that are involved in a transaction are permitted, provided the relationships are disclosed in writing to the consumer and the consumer is free to go elsewhere for the relevant services and the companies do not exchange fees for referrals.

Texas Department of Insurance Procedural Rule 53

The TDI implemented Procedural Rule 53 (P-53), which prohibits anyone in the title insurance business from directly or indirectly paying for or subsidizing advertisements or promotional materials for any real estate license holder in a position to make a referral to a title insurance business. P-53 regulates only the relationship between title companies and license holders.

Title insurance is regulated by TDI. Anyone who receives an unlawful rebate from an insurance provider commits an Insurance Code violation, which is a third-degree felony. If title companies are able to supply free goods and services to real estate license holders, TDI's concern is that the cost of these goods and services will be passed on to the consumer who is purchasing title insurance.

The penalties for noncompliance are serious. The commissioner may impose, after a hearing, a single penalty of not more than $10,000 for each act or violation and for each day of violation. The penalties can apply to both the title company and the real estate license holder.

Minimizing Expenses

Brokers must be keenly aware of their business-related expenses because no matter how successful a real estate brokerage has become, if it outspends what it takes in, it will end up a failure. Real estate brokerages are designed to be profit centers. Brokerages are designed to earn income ABOVE that of their expenses. Profit is defined as income less expenses. The following sections identify ways a broker can control expenses.

Monitoring the Business
An entire earlier section is devoted to this topic. Here are some additional ideas that are specifically used to minimize expenses.

Utilities
Every utility expense should be monitored for fluctuations. The electricity should be monitored. The trash pick-up should be monitored. The office cleaning crew should be monitored. The water should be monitored.

CASE IN POINT—One broker was diligent in monitoring his brokerage expenses. He noticed that one month during the summer that his water bill had escalated, almost doubling. This was troubling, but perhaps it was a glitch. It had been a particularly hot month. Next month the same extreme bill. The broker then called the water company, which verified that the bill was correct. He then asked the company to identify the period of time that a large amount of water was being used. The water company found that water was being used between the hours of 4 a.m. and 6 a.m. Now that was odd because no one is around the office at that time. The next day the broker went to the office at 5 a.m. He immediately noticed a hose hooked to his outside water spigot and going almost two full blocks to a house watering that owner's lawn. The broker placed a lock on the outdoor spigot.

Energy Efficiencies

The broker should evaluate his/her office for energy efficiencies. The amount of energy used in a real estate brokerage is vast; a wise broker could make minor adjustments and thereby save hundreds of dollars per month. The broker should think about the following cost-saving strategies, although some of these make sense only if the broker has a new brokerage building under construction or is tied to a very long lease.

Use compact fluorescent lamps (CFLs). These produce light by passing electricity through argon or neon gases. CFLs use 20% to 25% less electricity when compared with traditional incandescent light- bulbs of the same light intensity, and they last up to 15 times longer.

Choose office equipment that uses less energy. The broker should take energy use into consideration when purchasing office equipment. Saving $10 per month over several years turns into real money.

Reduce plug load. The broker should get outlet monitors that reduce the energy pull when plugged-in equipment is not in use.

Turn thermostats down or up. The broker should understand that each degree higher in cold weather or lower in hot weather eats up energy. If possible the broker should use programmable thermostats to regulate the temperature when people are in the office and at night when no one is around. The broker should also secure the thermostats so that sponsored license holders do not burn up the brokerage utility bill just for their comfort.

Reuse what can be reused. The broker should, for example, use refillable ink cartridges to cut expenses and look into refurbished office equipment instead of buying new.

Use geothermal heat pumps. Heat pumps that are geothermal remove heat from the water in the buried pipes, concentrate the heat, and then transfer that heat into the building. The process is reversed to cool the building. Sometimes they are used to provide domestic hot water. Owners can reduce their heating and cooling costs by 35% to 70%.

Invest in solar power. Photovoltaic cells convert the sun's energy into electricity, and the broker should look into the advantages of solar power.

Promote water conservation. The broker should monitor the use of water in the brokerage. The broker should make sure any leak is fixed as soon as possible to cut down on water being wasted.

Use water collection systems. The broker could collect rainwater and use it for irrigation.

Check insulation. The broker should have an expert check the insulation in the building and add insulation or replace it if needed.

Use tankless water heaters. The broker should consider using tankless water heaters, in which water is heated only when needed.

Create a "tight envelope." The broker should caulk or foam any air leaks because 20% to 30% of energy is lost through air leakage. The broker should check the roof, doors, windows, and walls.

Replace old windows. If the brokerage is new construction, the broker should invest in dual-pane or triple-glaze windows that seal two spaces between three panes of glass coated with low-emissivity (low-E) glaze that reflects radiant indoor heat, dramatically reducing heat loss.

The broker should have an energy audit performed annually to identify health and safety issues, building durability, and energy efficiency in the brokerage.

Staffing

Staffing is usually the largest expense of any real estate brokerage. The broker should therefore evaluate each member of staff to determine if that staff member's position remains relevant. To economize, the broker should consider outsourcing the job and eliminating the position. This may sound cruel, but situations do change annually. The broker may be able to reassign the employee to another area or assign additional responsibilities to make the position more valuable to the brokerage.

Office Equipment
The broker should annually evaluate every piece of office equipment to see if it is still needed. Fax machines have to go. Office computers for individual sponsored license holders should be eliminated or phased out. All this equipment costs the broker money to buy and maintain. Professional real estate license holders should fund this equipment on their own.

Meetings, Rallies, and Conferences
Brokers should hold meetings, rallies, and conferences to retain their salespersons but should also consider getting some or all of the expenses covered by sponsors. Ancillary businesses love to get a chance to speak at a real estate brokerage office event and are willing to pay money to be there. The broker should take advantage of these expense eliminators.

CHAPTER SUMMARY

Seller's Market—A seller's market occurs when there are a great many buyers in the market looking for very few homes for sale. The seller has most if not all of the negotiating power. Multiple offer situations are likely, and the prices are increasing.

Buyer's Market—A buyer's market occurs when there is a great deal of inventory in the market but there are very few buyers looking for homes. The buyer has most if not all of the negotiating power. An offer may not be seen by a seller for months, and the prices are decreasing.

The general operating budget (GOB) is a document that has projections of costs and income based on past data.

The broker needs to monitor all:

- office staff
- offices supplies
- bonuses and gifts, investor and builder business
- computer software on and downloads to brokerage computers
- workers being paid by the brokerage
- monies to and from the brokerage

The Texas Real Estate Commission (TREC) requires brokers to manage any information that comes into their brokerage firm.

TREC Rules §535.2 requires brokers to maintain the following records, at a minimum, in a format that is readily available to the Commission for at least four years from the date of closing, termination of the contract, or end of a real estate transaction:

- disclosures;
- commission agreements such as listing agreements, buyer representation agreements, or other written agreements relied upon to claim compensation;
- work files;
- contracts and related addenda;
- receipts and disbursements of compensation for services subject to the Act;
- property management contracts;
- appraisals, broker price opinions, and comparative market analyses; and
- sponsorship agreements between the broker and sponsored salespersons.

Brokers should keep tax records for much longer than four years, usually seven or more.

Brokers should have proper means for destroying files after their use has ended and should also keep a list of the files that have been destroyed.

Chapter 521 of the Texas Business and Commerce Code requires a business to:

- have procedures to protect against the unlawful use or disclosure of sensitive personal information received in the regular course of business
- destroy such records that are not required or needed for business operations

Sensitive personal information includes an individual's first name or first initial and last name in combination with any one or more of the following:

- Social Security number;
- driver's license number or government-issued identification number;

- account number or credit or debit card number in combination with any required security code, access code, or password that would permit access to an individual's financial account; or
- information that identifies an individual and relates to the physical or mental health or condition of the individual, the provision of health care to the individual, or payment for the provision of health care to the individual.

The following are ways for the broker to maximize income:

- Recruiting is probably the best way to maximize income for a real estate brokerage.
- Retention means keeping sponsored license holders and helping them become productive, which is the second best way to maximize income.
- Acquisitions are the answer when a broker wants to maximize income in a large way.
- Ancillary services, which are partially or fully dependent on real estate sales but do not directly make such sales, could be a source of additional revenue.

The purpose of the Real Estate Settlement Procedures Act (RESPA) is to clarify settlement costs and to eliminate "kickbacks" and fees that increase settlement costs.

TDI Procedural Rule 53 (P-53) prohibits anyone in the title insurance business from directly or indirectly paying for or subsidizing advertisements or promotional materials for any real estate license holder in a position to make a referral to a title insurance business.

The commissioner may impose a single penalty of $10,000 for each act or violation and for each day of violation of P-53.

A broker can control expenses by:

- monitoring business utilities and becoming more energy efficient by:
  - using CFLs
  - choose office equipment that uses less energy
  - reducing plug load
  - turning thermostats down or up
  - reusing what can be reused
  - using geothermal heat pumps

Evaluating the Real Estate Brokerage Business

- investing in solar power
- promoting water conservation
- using water collection systems
- checking insulation
- using tankless water heaters
- creating a "tight envelope"
- replacing old windows
- evaluating staffing to annually evaluate each staff member to determine if that person's position remains relevant
- reassessing office equipment to annually evaluate every piece of office equipment to see if it is still needed
- holding meetings, rallies, and conferences to retain salespeople but also getting some or all of the expenses covered by sponsors

CHAPTER QUESTIONS

1. What is a market called when there are a great many buyers looking for very few homes for sale?
   A. seller's market
   B. buyer's market
   C. open market
   D. balanced market

2. Which of the following is NOT a characteristic of a buyer's market?
   A. There is a large housing inventory.
   B. Buyers have most of the negotiating power.
   C. Prices are decreasing.
   D. All of the answer choices are correct.

3. What document has projections of costs and income based on past data?
   A. projection analysis form
   B. general operating budget
   C. costs and income document
   D. comprehensive revenue analysis sheet

4. Which of the following should a broker monitor?
   A. office staff
   B. all office supplies
   C. bonuses and gifts, investor and builder business
   D. all of the answer choices

5. According to the TREC, how long should a broker keep transaction records?
   A. two years
   B. four years
   C. five years
   D. forever

6. According to the TREC, what types of records should be kept?
   A. disclosures
   B. commission agreement
   C. work files
   D. all of the answer choices

7. Sensitive personal information includes an individual's first name, last name, and which of the following?
   A. Social Security number
   B. address
   C. date of birth
   D. all of the answer choices

8. What types of businesses are dependent on real estate sales but do not directly make real estate sales?
   A. former
   B. ancillary
   C. primary
   D. state regulated

9. What law's purpose is to clarify closing costs and to eliminate "kickbacks" and fees that increase closing costs to the consumer?
   A. Real Estate License Act
   B. Sherman Antitrust Act
   C. Real Estate Settlement Procedures Act
   D. Texas Department of Insurance Procedural Rule P-35

10. What law prohibits anyone in the title insurance business from paying for materials for any real estate license holder?
    A. Real Estate Title Act
    B. Insurance Act of 1968
    C. Real Estate Title Insurance Securities Act
    D. Texas Department of Insurance Procedural Rule P-53

CHAPTER 14
Growth Opportunities

Brokers should constantly be looking for growth opportunities. If a brokerage is not growing, it is shrinking. No brokerage stays the same for long. Growth allows a brokerage to become more secure in its future by continually moving forward. If a brokerage is declining, it will only be a short time until failure. A broker needs to be wise when considering growth, however, because unchecked growth is also dangerous.

Horizontal Expansion

Horizontal expansion is the act of integrating into the current brokerage other assets and/or entire real estate brokerages. The acquisition of these assets typically results in an expansion of existing operations rather than the establishment of entirely new operations. Horizontal expansion also includes expanding into other locations, adding more brokerages, and even enlarging the geographic reach of the brokerage. Horizontal expansion provides several benefits, including but not limited to:

- *economies of scale*—These allow a brokerage to purchase large amounts of office supplies, office furniture, and office equipment, all on negotiated discounts from the suppliers because of the bulk purchase.
- *vendor discounts*—These allow a broker to negotiate more favorable rates with vendors because of the volume of business the brokerage could provide.
- *better serving customers' needs*—By expanding, the broker can now hire specific staff members who can better serve the consumer. The broker could, for example, hire transaction coordinators to see transactions through from beginning to end. The broker could hire top-tier trainers to improve the skills of his/her sponsored licensees. The broker could also hire managers to better handle issues that arise.

Expanding by Adding Offices

Real estate brokers could expand their business by adding offices to work in cooperation with the original office. Brokers who show great success in their current office should think of expanding. These brokers could expand into new markets or expand operations in their current market area. These decisions greatly affect the success or failure of the expansion.

Add Offices in Adjacent Areas

Brokers could decide on opening additional offices in adjacent areas of the current office. The offices should be a significant distance apart to avoid oversaturating the market and yet near enough to get name recognition. The broker needs to perform a significant analysis to determine the ideal location for these additional offices because the location is often the one factor that can spell the success or failure of a brokerage.

Advantages There could be many advantages to adding offices in a brokerage's current market area, including:

- *name recognition*—The public begins to recognize a name only after numerous exposures to it. The more signs that a brokerage has in any one market area, the better. Each office added in the current market area will add several new license holders into the current area, increasing the visible exposure to the public. Name recognition gives the public a sense of security in the business, seeing it as a viable and perpetual enterprise.
- *synergies of distance*—When two or more brokerages are within a relatively small distance from each other, there is a synergy of distance. If one brokerage runs out of yard signs, a sponsored license holder can go to the nearest office and get a sign. Each office can share conference rooms and office supplies, and one office can have the latest, fastest and highest-capacity printer that all the local offices can share. Synergies of distance can save a brokerage a significant amount of money.

Disadvantages There could be many disadvantages to adding offices in a brokerage's current market area, including that doing so may split:

- *sponsored license* holders—Opening a new brokerage in a specific area within the current brokerage office's location can split the sponsored license holders between the offices. Suppose the current office has 40 sponsored license holders. The broker opens another office within the current market area. Half (i.e., 20) of those license holders move to the new office. The broker now has the same amount of production split between two offices, doubling the costs. A broker cannot stop a sponsored license holder from moving offices without causing resentment. The broker must therefore recruit to the new office before that brokerage opens its doors.
- *customers and clients*—A broker needs to be sure that the immediate area surrounding the new office can produce enough real estate sales business to make the new office worth the investment. To determine this, the broker must perform an analysis of the new area (even though it is still in the market area of the current office) and prove that the market can bear another real estate brokerage, and he/she should do this BEFORE opening the doors. If the area cannot sustain the new office, the broker can consider other ways of expanding the current brokerage.

Add Offices in Different Areas

Brokers could open additional offices in areas not near their current office. Brokers could open an office on the other side of the city, state, or country, for example. They could even go international, although this rarely happens. These offices can be so far apart that each may require a separate broker to run it, so brokers frequently take on partners to help them.

Advantages There could be many advantages to adding offices in different areas, including:

- *larger presence*—If the office is across the city from the current office, the new office could be operating in an entirely different market but should increase the total market presence of both offices. Consumers on one side of town recognize the office on the other side of town and believe that that brokerage has a presence throughout the area; it is "all over." This increased presence increases the credibility of the brokerage. Also, sponsored license holders can now sell across markets and use any of the offices.

- *referral of a client from one area to another*—If the offices are located a large distance from each other, the sponsored license holders could refer customers between the offices. If a license holder from Texas had a client who was moving to New York and the brokerage had an office in New York, it would be an easy referral between offices all under one brokerage.

Disadvantages There could be many disadvantages to adding offices in different areas, including that there is:

- *greater distance and greater loss of control*—A broker can generally control the operations of one office. When the broker adds another office, the loss of control more than doubles. The broker adds an office out of the market but thereby loses almost all control.
- *loss of market presence*—If the offices are nowhere near each other, the brokerage could lose all name recognition. The new office would operate as if it were an independent office without any connection to the original office.

Add Offices in Similar Market Segments

Market segmentation is the process by which submarkets within a larger market are identified and analyzed. Market segments could include houses with different structural characteristics, neighborhood amenities, or some combination of both. The broker could expand offices located within the same market segment as the current office. Suppose the current market segment comprises vintage and/or historic homes in a highly influential area of the city. The current office has specialized in this niche market and has made a name for itself. The broker could choose to expand to another area with a large number of vintage and/or historic homes and locate a new office (probably in a vintage, remodeled house) within that market area.

Advantages There could be many advantages to adding offices in similar market segments, including that doing so:

- *solidifies reputation*—The new office could benefit from the reputation of the current office, which is known as the office that specializes in the specific market segment. If the market segment is "Hamilton Estates," a planned unit development (PUD) with

several hundred homes, the new office could be known as the "Hickory Estates" brokerage, a neighboring PUD.
- *creates redundancies*—The new office would have the knowledge base to better market to the specific market segment and would already have the systems to better serve that market segment. Also, the new office could rely on the current office for market segment advice.

Disadvantages There could be many disadvantages to adding offices in similar market segments, including that doing so limits:

- *market expansion*—Because the current office is the well-known office, adding new market segments is exceedingly difficult. It would be difficult to break into the commercial market if the current brokerage is known as the brokerage that specializes in two-story Tudor homes.
- *out-of-market-segment sales*—If the brokerage specializes in one market segment and a client wants a type of real estate not in that market segment, the broker would lose that sale. Suppose that the broker specializes in lakefront property but a client wants to buy a commercial building. The broker would have to refer that business to a competing brokerage. The Texas Real Estate Commission (TREC) prohibits a broker from engaging in any segment of real estate brokerage in which the broker is not an expert. If a brokerage had one office that specialized in lakefront property and another office that specialized in commercial property, however, the broker could refer the client to the office that specializes in commercial property and thereby keep the individual as a client of the brokerage.

Add Offices in Different Market Segments

When a broker adds offices in different market segments, the broker must have or must obtain knowledge in those market segments or risk legal and financial pitfalls. The broker should not enter any type of real estate without taking classes, studying, and getting hands-on experience in that line of real estate.

Advantages There could be many advantages to adding offices in different market segments including that doing so expands:

- *market area*—By adding offices in different market segments, the broker expands the brokerage's market by now reaching additional sources of potential clients. The broker could add a market segment that cooperates well with another market segment, for example. This synergy would create business for both segments.
- *reach within the market area*—The broker would increase the reach the broker has within the market area. More visibility translates to more business. The more market segments the broker reaches, the better for the brokerage.

Disadvantages   There could be many disadvantages to adding offices in similar market segments, including:

- *lack of specialization*—Once a broker adds too many market segments, the broker loses the uniqueness of being known as a particular boutique brokerage. Now the broker must compete with the largest national brokers.
- *unfamiliar markets*—If a broker is not familiar with properties in any market segment and then sells in that segment, he/she could create a breach of fiduciary duty to his/her client. Brokers must place the interest of the client above their own interests.

Vertical Expansion

Vertical expansion is the act of expanding into new operations for the purpose of decreasing a brokerage's reliance on outside ancillary businesses. By adding the new operations, the brokerage has more control over the services it offers and has the opportunity to add to the bottom-line revenue statement. Some of the new operations would take little for a broker to incorporate, and others may not be economically feasible.

Ancillary Businesses

Ancillary businesses are those that make their money through real estate sales but are not directly involved in the actual transactions. Ancillary businesses include notary functions, property insurance, property inspections, property appraisals, title insurance, mortgage lending, and property repair and remodeling, all the way to telephone service and discounts on travel. A broker could begin to add these ancillary businesses to the current brokerage business as a way to expand vertically.

Consumers want the real estate brokerage to be a one-stop shop where everything is provided without their having to shop around themselves. The more of these "concierge" services a real estate company provides, the more valuable that brokerage is to consumers. In some real estate offices, the ancillary business is a huge revenue source.

A broker who does not want to own these ancillary businesses but wants to offer the services they provide could charge a fee to the ancillary business owners who will provide the services for him/her. These ancillary business owners are willing to pay the broker to be able to contact his/her sponsored licensees to ask for referral business. The broker needs to be careful, however, and consult an attorney, because participating in this type of cooperative business practice could violate the Real Estate Settlement Act or state regulations if not handled properly.

Notary Functions
A broker could offer notary services as a convenience to clients and as a service intended for the general public. A notary must keep a sequential journal of notary acts and be certain that the individual whose signature on a document is to be acknowledged personally appears before the notary and provides acceptable forms of identification. The question is, "Should the broker charge for this service?" Most brokers do not offer this service because title companies often have a notary on staff.

Property Insurance
Most property insurance is sold through insurance companies. It is common, nevertheless, for the larger real estate brokerage offices to offer insurance policies. Generally these real estate companies represent insurance companies, but some actually purchase the insurance company and roll the company under their real estate umbrella of services. Insurance is a natural feeder business and an extra source of income for the real estate broker who already has real estate sales transactions originating in the broker's office.

A real estate broker who also acts in the capacity of an insurance salesperson is acting as the agent of the insurance underwriter and is governed by the carrier's instructions. A real estate broker could suggest that the client purchase the insurance offered by the brokerage, but of course the client should always have the opportunity to select his/her own source of insurance.

Property Inspections

Property inspections should be ordered on all residential real estate sales. The types of inspections include pest inspections, house inspections, foundation inspections, roof inspections, and structural inspections. Each of these the broker could operate if the broker hires the professional who has the required license(s). The professional would have continual business, and the broker would add another source of income.

Property Appraisal

Certified appraisals are required on almost all sales that involve financing of any type. Certified appraisers generally work for appraisal companies, but the broker could form an appraisal company subsumed under the brokerage. As in all cases, consumers would have to know that they could choose any appraiser they want, but with the right disclosures the broker could create another source of income by offering appraisal services.

Title Insurance

Title insurance is regulated by the Texas Department of Insurance (TDI) and not the TREC. These are different licensing entities and do not have the same regulations. To ensure compliance with state regulations, a broker wanting to own a title insurance company should work through an attorney with experience in this type of legal organization. Once created, it could be a valuable source of revenue for the brokerage.

Mortgage Lending

Mortgage lending is regulated by the Texas Department of Savings and Mortgage Lending. The broker would have to register and receive a license to originate loans. Frequently a broker will form a business alliance with a mortgage lender who is already licensed to operate the mortgage side of the overall brokerage business. The broker should work through an experienced attorney to comply with all the regulations of business alliances and/or affiliated business arrangements.

Property Repair and Remodeling

The brokerage could easily operate a property repair and remodeling company along with the real estate brokerage. Both would help each other with referrals and business operations. The broker must disclose in writing to the consumers that the brokerage owns both businesses, and the consumers are free to hire anyone they please. This business alliance could generate a fine source of additional income for the brokerage.

Organic Growth

Organic growth is the process of business expansion through increased production, adding to the customer base, or the addition of new real estate services. The broker should always conceive of ways to increase the production of the brokerage by expanding the processes. The more production the broker can derive from current sources, the more successful the broker becomes.

Land Development

A real estate broker might choose to add land development to the repertoire of services offered to the public. Land development is the taking of "raw" land and converting it into higher priced land by adding roads, sewage and water mains, and utilities to suit the needs of builders. The broker/developer may construct dwellings or commercial buildings on the subdivided land or even develop an entire community. Once these buildings have been completed, the broker/developer may then proceed to market them through other real estate licensees or through the broker's own organization. For this specialization in real estate, the broker must have a suitable contractor's license or work with or for a licensed contractor and comply with subdivision laws.

Real Estate Business Development

The business development/relocation business is an incredible source of revenue for the real estate brokerage office. However, in the day-to-day operation of a real estate business, brokers tend to overlook the relocation business. Relocation business ranges from the moving of a sole transferee to the relocation of an entire organization. The larger the move, the more detailed and technical the move becomes, requiring additional personnel to effect the move.

In many markets, bottom-line revenue from relocation activities may be as high as one-fourth of the office's total income. Corporate relocation business exists in good times and bad. When the economy is good, corporations tend to expand. When the economy is bad, corporations downsize or transfer employees to other areas of service. Mergers and acquisitions frequently take place, resulting in the movement of personnel.

Transferees have a high degree of motivation. The increasing practice is for corporations to offer bonuses for employees who sell their home themselves rather than depend on the corporation to sell their home for them. This often eliminates the necessity of the company purchasing the home, which means corporate dollars may be saved. Transferees are under a time crunch, however, given that living expenses in the new location may be paid by the company only for a limited time. For many transferees, the move to the new location is not optional.

Finding Relocation Business
Before the real estate professional can make any money in the relocation business, he/she must find potential clients. This business will mirror the prospecting the real estate license holder conducts to find individual sellers, but on a larger, corporate scale. The following sections give some ideas on where to find corporate relocation business.

Corporate Calling The best and most efficient way to find corporate relocation business is to design a system for corporate calling. Corporate calling involves finding the correct people to phone. A broker should make a list of companies in the brokerages market, along with any state or federal agencies, universities, hospitals, community colleges, and school districts. The broker should check with the local chamber of commerce, search online, do research at the library, visit the economic development council and planning committees, and try to come up with the names, addresses, phone numbers, and email addresses of the people who handle personnel matters for these companies. Once the broker locates the correct people, the broker should phone them.

There are two types of phone calls. The corporate fact-finding phone call is simply to find out information. The broker wants to find out whom to phone and whether that organization has any plans for relocation. The more information the broker obtains, the more versed the broker will be when it comes time to ask for business.

The second type of phone call actually asks for the business or at least sets up an appointment to discuss the possibility of relocation business. The latter would be used when dealing with smaller operations.

Past Clients and Customers Past clients and customers are people with whom the broker has conducted real estate business. All these people with whom the broker and his/her sponsored license holders have had real estate business work somewhere, and businesses are always transferring employees. These past associates may:

- introduce the broker to their human resource department staff and/or the personnel director and possibly help set up an appointment
- allow the broker to use their names as references

The Military All branches of the military transfer and relocate personnel all over, all the time. If there is a military base in the brokerage area, the broker should make a phone call to the base or visit it. The broker might first talk with the commander, who may lead the broker elsewhere. If the base is large enough, it probably has a personnel director. Generally, people in the military are highly professional and structured, but they will allow time to speak with the local businesspeople. Some bases arrange transfers only through third-party companies, but the broker might still obtain a few leads. Also, by making this connection, the broker may reach a local individual in the military who wants to live off base and/or simply move to another residence, neither of which would go through the third-party company.

Commercial Brokers Commercial brokers usually help businesses buy or lease space for their companies but rarely want to help them find a place of residence. The broker should become acquainted with these commercial brokers. They may have the first contact with a new company relocating to the area.

Third-Party Relocation Companies Large organizations with lots of relocations might choose a third-party relocation company to arrange the transfers of their employees. These companies handle the entire relocation move for an organization. Using a relocation company is very expensive but worth the cost compared to handling the move without it. The broker can contact various relocation companies and ask to submit a proposal to be one of their designated brokers in a particular area. If successful, the broker will be required to meet their requirements for the relocation business.

Community Involvement The broker should become active in the local community. Leaders of a community enjoy giving back by joining civic and charitable organizations. People in the civic and charitable arenas are less defensive and will bond with the broker more quickly at a community event than they will if the broker approaches them while they are at work. These people will grow to like and trust the broker more at these functions than any other time and place.

Company Involvement The brokerage's entire staff, including managers, sales associates, and support staff, must be kept aware of the importance of relocation opportunities and of the myriad programs and lead sources of new referral lead sources. The broker should make sure the relocation department is properly introduced to the whole staff. The broker should explain to all managers and sales associates how the relocation department fits into the company's overall business plan and goals.

The broker and/or the relocation director must be aware of current trends in the relocation industry and provide ongoing training for the brokerage's "corporate team" of sponsored licensees. These team members should be full-time and detail-oriented individuals; they should understand the paperwork necessary for the job and always be professionally dressed. They need to be knowledgeable about the area they serve. They should understand the disclosure and buyer/seller representation laws for the state, the minimum knowledge required to answer questions from a relocating buyer or seller intelligently. The broker should establish criteria for the licensees who will be handling these referrals.

First-Time Homeowners

Serving first-time homeowners is an expansion a broker could implement relatively easily. If the broker has a few sponsored license holders who need a boost in production, the broker could make them the "First-Time Homeowners" team. The broker would then need to put that team through training on how to handle first-time homeowners. The broker would arrange to advertise, market, and promote the team through normal media channels. As members leave the team, the broker could promote others.

Fine Homes and Estates
Fine homes and estates are properties that are typically worth at least $500,000 or above, depending on the market. The sellers and buyers of these properties tend to enjoy a little more attention than those in more modest purchases. The "Fine Home and Estates" team would be formed and operated the same as the "First-Time Homeowners" team. The broker would set the criteria for the team before beginning this expansion.

Farm and Ranch
Farm and ranch specialization could be an option for any brokerage that is on the outskirts of a city. A few of the broker's sponsored license holders may want to specialize in farm and ranch brokerage, so to meet that need and the needs of the owners of such property, the broker can add this specialty service as another source of business. Training is the key to adding any new real estate service. Farm and ranch brokerage has issues that the broker and all on the team need to be keenly aware of.

Other types of organic-growth real estate services that could be offered include but are not limited to:

- commercial property
- industrial property
- apartment locators
- leasing
- property management

Of course, the broker should not attempt to be all things to all people, but perhaps adding a real estate service or two would motivate certain sponsored license holders as well as provide another source of income.

Inorganic Growth (Mergers and Acquisitions)

Mergers and acquisitions, considered inorganic growth, should be thoroughly analyzed and debated before the broker spends the capital necessary to make such growth happen. Too many brokers get excited about the inorganic aspect of expanding and then overextend themselves, and consequently the brokerage fails.

> CASE IN POINT—One broker had a superior operation. Within one year, he took the brokerage from the previous owner who didn't think it would last more than three more months, and he turned it into one of the top 10 in production for the entire real estate region. This broker clearly knew how to drive ONE real estate brokerage. Well, the broker thought, if I can do it with one, then three would be better. In time all three offices failed. The reason was simple: The broker's dedication was split three ways, and no single office felt that the broker cared. The broker should have taken more time, first finding a competent manager to handle the first office and then looked for one more office.

Mergers and Acquisitions

One of the best ways to get started or expand in the real estate brokerage business is to merge with another real estate company or simply to buy them out. The start-up headaches are avoided, as are most of the start-up costs. A broker could, in theory, buy today and operate today.

When buying a real estate office, a broker should not make the mistake of paying too much for it. Real estate offices are basically valued on their production. Production is based on the work of the office's sponsored real estate license holders, and license holders are independent contractors who can leave at any time. Brokers have spent a great deal of money for a brokerage and its production to find out after the purchase that the current license holders have all left and taken the production with them.

No matter what the reasons are for the merger or acquisition, license holders will have to adapt and transition into a new work environment, and that is essentially like going to work for a new company. How the license holders are treated and how their lives are affected by the transaction will likely play an important role in license holder retention and the success or failure of the acquisition.

Brokers are also known to want a fortune for their office even though they actually lost money the previous year. They base their value on some hidden future worth or on their so-called goodwill, neither of which makes the new broker/owner money today.

Here are a few questions a broker needs answered before considering buying another real estate brokerage.

Why Do the Owners Want to Sell?
Finding out why a fellow broker wants to sell is as important for a broker as almost all the other information combined. If a broker can truly find out the seller's motivation for selling then the buying broker can structure a very beneficial agreement for both sides.

> CASE IN POINT—The first office one broker bought was for sale in Texas for $50,000 less than the owner had paid for it, and that owner financed the entire amount for the buying broker with nothing down. The owner was more than willing to negotiate. He was in bad health and had a new home waiting for him and his wife in Colorado, where they always wanted to live. The buyer broker did not take advantage of him, but the buying broker did get a favorable deal.
>
> The same buyer broker negotiated with a different broker/owner who wanted to sell but had no real urgency. She wanted $600,000 cash, and the brokerage was worth approximately $80,000 at the most. The lesson: There can be a great difference in sales price depending on the reason to sell and hence the seller's motive to sell.

It is not that easy for a broker to find out the real reason an owner wants to sell. A broker should not believe the first thing that is said. The broker needs to do some research. It is best for the broker to talk with a few of the sponsored real estate licensees in the office that the broker is considering buying. To do this, the broker could ask one of the licensees to lunch and ask about current operations and the things the license holder feels ought to change. The broker can find out helpful, truthful information in a one-on-one conversation.

What Is the Broker Actually Buying?
The broker needs to be sure of what he/she is buying. The broker should look at the accounting books to analyze every detail. It might be best for the broker to hire a mergers-and-acquisitions accountant to help analyze that data to determine if the brokerage would be a sound investment.

CASE IN POINT—One broker was reviewing the records of a potential buyout because the business was showing a profit of more than $150,000. Not bad for a real estate company! After closer scrutiny, however, the broker noticed that there were no salaries being paid even though there were seven people working in the brokerage office (not including sponsored license holders). The owner explained that the seven were his relatives and that they stayed at his home and he paid them directly. This immediately raised two major problems:

1. There could be negative tax consequences from the arrangement. A broker needs to be careful not to buy someone else's liabilities. If the Internal Revenue Service allocates unpaid taxes and penalties for these "unpaid" employees, there could be a huge financial loss.
2. The business was not making a profit but was actually experiencing a loss. Take the $150,000 and divide it by seven (the number of "unpaid" employees), and that means that each employee was paid a little over $20,000 per year. It would be difficult to hire any talent for $20,000 per year, and the broker can expect that the "relatives" will not continue to work if they receive no renumeration.

Without a detailed review of the owner's records, the employment fiasco would have been undiscovered. Needless to say, the broker did not buy the brokerage and was extremely thankful he had reviewed the records.

Owners may want to sell for any of the following reasons:

- A brokerage owner may want to sell because a significant part of the owner's net worth is tied up in the brokerage firm, and the owner may want to free up that capital.
- Few owners have solid succession plans in place or have no involved family members to whom to turn over the business.
- The owner may just be tired of being a broker. Brokerage is constant drain on energy and time, so some owners may just want to be relieved of their responsibility.
- Some owners are ready to retire. They have spent their working life in real estate and recognize when it is time to retire.
- The brokerage is losing money, and the current owner does not know how to stop the bleeding.

A wise broker should be sure to inventory every item involved in the purchase. The broker should not leave anything out of the written inventory or accept only a verbal offer. If the owner tells the buyer broker that the broker gets everything in the brokerage, that is great, but the offer needs to be in writing.

Another discussion that needs to be held is about commissions. Will the owner want the commissions on the current pending sales? Listings? What about the current liabilities? Dues? Deposits? Leases? Every cost or income must be evaluated and agreed to.

Is the Brokerage Currently Well Managed?
Whether the brokerage is being managed as it should be is a key question because if it is being managed properly, then what is the advantage to buying it? If it is not being managed properly, the buyer broker may be able to make adjustments to the current cost structure or revenue flow so that in a short period of time the brokerage will earn a profit.

Once the three key questions—Why do the owners want to sell? What is the broker actually buying? Is the brokerage currently well managed?—are answered, the broker should have a better estimation of whether to move forward with the purchase or to move on to a better project.

Roll-in
Another type of acquisition is the roll-in. A roll-in is buying another real estate brokerage, closing the doors of that office, and "rolling in," or incorporating, the current sales force into one of the broker's existing offices as a way to buy the previous broker's sponsored licensee holders. Real estate license holders are the assets in the brokerage business and are what makes an office profitable. If two real estate companies are competing for the same clients in the same area, it may be wise for one broker to buy out the other and roll the brokerages into one office. With the additional license holders, the brokerage could begin to see additional economies of scale—that is, the brokerage would have the ability to buy large amounts of product at discount.

Valuation of a Real Estate Company
Valuation of a real estate company is completely different from valuation of a residential property. The complexities and uniqueness of real estate companies virtually eliminate the normal avenues available for

comparison. One real estate office is totally different from another office, which may be just down the street. Office space, inventory, and goodwill cannot be adequately compared. However, the basis of all evaluation—the definition used in foundational real estate courses—still applies:

Valuation is what a typically motivated buyer would be willing to pay a typically motivated seller in open-market conditions, with all parties operating in their own best interest and with all pertinent information known.

This definition provides the foundation for rational evaluation of the real estate office. The key point on valuation is that very often real estate is not included in the sale. The only thing the purchaser is buying is the business itself, not the building.

Looking Toward the Future

A broker must consider the future to determine how and when he/she will move out of brokerage. This is not an easy thing to do because the broker is probably concentrating on current operations and not thinking about what should happen 10 or 15 years or longer down the road. However, it is critical for the broker to analyze the potential end of the enterprise at the beginning; otherwise, the broker could wake up many years down the road and have no options but to "give away" the brokerage to some unwanted investor who will destroy those years of blood, sweat, and tears the broker gave to his "baby." This future analysis is called an exit strategy.

Exit Strategy

An exit strategy is a detailed plan on how the broker plans to retire, if that is ever to happen. The key reason a broker should have an exit strategy is to know when to sell. Most brokers stay much too long to be of any real service to the sponsored license holders or the brokerage.

"Old brokers never retire. They just get listless!"

A broker could exit by many means. The broker should analyze each possible strategy and determine the best one for his/her situation. Once a choice of strategy is determined, the broker should work throughout the years to develop the perfect situation for his/her exit. A broker who wants out but has not developed an exit strategy may discover that to get out without losing a great deal of money or equity is nearly impossible.

The following sections offer a few options for an exit strategy a broker could choose.

Sell
Selling the brokerage is the most common exit strategy brokers use. The key to this strategy is to sell at the peak of the brokerage's success. Most brokers ride through the success phase and then try to sell once the brokerage is at the bottom. The broker's job is to buy a successful brokerage or develop a brokerage to success and then operate that brokerage until the broker loses passion. Only then should the broker sell, while the brokerage is still successful.

Bequeath a Legacy
Brokers can give the brokerage as a legacy gift. Brokers love this one: They build a brokerage business and then turn it over to their heirs to continue the family business. This is a great idea, but the heirs must want to take over the business. This exit strategy requires the heirs who will eventually get the business to work in the business and move up through the ranks years before the takeover. The heirs must make this career choice because without the experience, they will not be properly prepared and could cause the brokerage to fail. Also, the broker needs to consider how to address the issue of multiple heirs and how a brokerage is to be distributed among them.

Dissolve
Dissolving the brokerage means that the broker did not create an ongoing business. The broker needs to address this negative situation because if the broker dies before the termination of the brokerage, the heirs could be left with a tremendous burden.

All these exit strategies must be considered many years before the actual execution of the exit strategy. Knowing how the business will end is the best way to begin an enterprise. The ending strategy is for the broker/owner's benefit, not necessarily for the brokerage.

CHAPTER SUMMARY

Horizontal expansion is the act of integrating into the current brokerage other assets and/or entire real estate brokerages.

Horizontal expansion includes expanding into other locations, adding more brokerages, and even enlarging the geographic reach of the brokerage.

Horizontal expansion provides several benefits:

- *economies of scale*—These allow a brokerage to purchase larger amounts of office supplies, office furniture, and office equipment, all on negotiated discounts from the suppliers because of the bulk purchase.
- *vendor discounts*—These allow a broker to negotiate more favorable rates with vendors because of the volume of business the brokerage could provide.
- *better serving customers' needs*—By expanding, the broker can now hire specific staff members who can better serve the consumer.

Real estate brokers could expand their business by adding offices to work in cooperation with the original office.

Brokers could decide on opening additional offices in adjacent areas of the current office.

There could be many advantages to adding offices in a brokerage's current market area, including:

- name recognition
- synergies of distance

There could be many disadvantages to adding offices in a brokerage's current market area, including that doing so may split:

- sponsored license holders
- customers and clients

The broker could open additional offices in an area not around the current office.

There could be many advantages of adding offices in different areas, including:

- larger presence
- referral of a client from one area to the another

There could be many disadvantages to adding offices in different areas, including:

- greater distance and greater loss of control
- loss of market presence

Market segmentation is the process by which submarkets within a larger market are identified and analyzed.

The broker could expand offices located within the same market segment as the current office.

There could be many advantages to adding offices in similar market segments, including that doing so:

- solidifies reputation
- creates redundancies

There could be many disadvantages to adding offices in similar market segments, including that doing so limits:

- market expansion
- out-of-market-segment sales

When a broker adds offices in different market segments, the broker must have or must obtain knowledge in those market segments or risk legal and financial pitfalls.

There could be many advantages to adding offices in different market segments, including that doing so expands:

- market area
- reach within the market area

There could be many disadvantages to adding offices in similar market segments, including:

- lack of specialization
- unfamiliar markets

Vertical expansion is the act of expanding into new operations for the purpose of decreasing a brokerage's reliance on outside ancillary businesses. Ancillary businesses are those that make their money through real estate sales but are not directly involved in the actual transactions. Ancillary businesses include mortgage lending, title searches, property inspections, appraisal, notary functions, property insurance, property repair and remodeling, and appraisal all the way to telephone service and discounts on travel.

Organic growth is the process of business expansion through increased production, adding to the customer base, or the addition of new real estate services. A real estate broker might choose to add land development to the repertoire of services offered to the public. Relocation business ranges from the moving of a sole transferee to the relocation of an entire organization. Serving first-time homeowners is an expansion a broker could implement relatively easily. Fine homes and estates are properties that are typically worth at least $500,000 or above, depending on the market. Farm and ranch specialization could be an option for any brokerage that is on the outskirts of a city.

Other types of organic-growth real estate services include but are not limited to:

- commercial property
- industrial property
- apartment locators
- leasing
- property management

Mergers and acquisitions, considered inorganic growth, should be thoroughly analyzed and debated before the broker spends the capital necessary to make such growth happen.

One of the best ways to get started or expand in the real estate brokerage business is to merge with another real estate company or simply to buy them out.

A roll-in is buying another real estate brokerage, closing the doors of that office, and "rolling in," or incorporating, the current sales force into one of the broker's existing offices as a way to buy the previous broker's sponsored license holders.

Valuation is what a typically motivated buyer would be willing to pay a typically motivated seller in open-market conditions, with all parties operating in their own best interest and with all pertinent information known.

An exit strategy is when a broker considers the future to determine how and when to move out of the brokerage.

CHAPTER QUESTIONS

1. What is the act of integrating into the current brokerage other assets and/or entire real estate brokerages?
   A. horizontal expansion
   B. restructuring
   C. incorporation
   D. second-level expansion

2. Which of the following is a benefit of horizontal expansion?
   A. economies of scale
   B. vendor discounts
   C. better serve customers' needs
   D. all of the answer choices

3. Which of the following is an advantage of adding offices in the current market area of the original brokerage?
   A. splits sponsored license holders
   B. enhances name recognition
   C. splits customers and clients
   D. all of the answer choices

4. What is the process by which submarkets within a larger market are identified and analyzed?
   A. generation
   B. segmentation
   C. integration
   D. disintermediation

5. What is the act of expanding into new operations for the purpose of decreasing a brokerage's reliance on outside ancillary businesses?
   A. vertical expansion
   B. operations initiation
   C. reliability analysis
   D. none of the answer choices

6. What businesses are those that make their money through real estate sales but are not directly involved in the actual transactions?
   A. adjacent
   B. adversary
   C. ancillary
   D. arbitrary

7. What type of growth is the process of business expansion through increased production, adding to the customer base, or through the addition of new real estate services?
   A. phenomenal growth
   B. controlled growth
   C. organic growth
   D. fundamental growth

8. Which of the following is an example of organic growth?
   A. commercial
   B. apartment locators
   C. property management
   D. all of the answer choices

9. What is it called when a buyer broker closes the doors of a newly purchased brokerage and moves all its sales force into the broker's current brokerage?
   A. pirating
   B. roll-in
   C. deceptive practice
   D. market segmentation

10. What is it called when a broker considers the future to determine how and when to move out of the brokerage business?
    A. retraction
    B. consolidation
    C. exit strategy
    D. market strategy

Chapter Review Answer Key

CHAPTER 1

1. C
2. D
3. A
4. A
5. A
6. D
7. C
8. D
9. B
10. A

CHAPTER 2

1. B
2. D
3. B
4. A
5. B
6. C
7. D
8. D
9. C
10. C

CHAPTER 3

1. A
2. C
3. D
4. C
5. D
6. B
7. C
8. A
9. D
10. B

CHAPTER 4

1. A
2. C
3. D
4. D
5. B
6. C
7. A
8. B
9. C
10. B

CHAPTER 5

1. B
2. C
3. D
4. B
5. B
6. A
7. D
8. D
9. C
10. C

CHAPTER 6

1. B
2. D
3. A
4. B
5. C
6. D
7. C
8. D
9. D
10. A

CHAPTER 7

1. D
2. A
3. C
4. A
5. D
6. B
7. A
8. C
9. D
10. B

CHAPTER 8

1. A
2. B
3. C
4. B
5. D
6. B
7. C
8. D
9. A
10. C

CHAPTER 9

1. C
2. B
3. A
4. A
5. D
6. C
7. D
8. B
9. A
10. C

CHAPTER 10

1. B
2. C
3. C
4. B
5. D
6. C
7. A
8. B
9. C
10. D

CHAPTER 11

1. C
2. A
3. C
4. D
5. B
6. D
7. C
8. A
9. A
10. B

CHAPTER 12

1. B
2. C
3. A
4. D
5. B
6. C
7. A
8. B
9. D
10. B

CHAPTER 13

1. A
2. D
3. B
4. D
5. B
6. D
7. A
8. B
9. C
10. D

CHAPTER 14

1. A
2. D
3. B
4. B
5. A
6. C
7. C
8. D
9. B
10. C

Appendix

Referral Salesperson Contact Scripts

This script should be used to get a referral group started.

BROKER: "Mr. Jones?"

REFERRAL SALESPERSON: "Yes."

BROKER: "My name is Dan Hamilton, broker at Acme Realty. Did you receive the information that I sent to you on our exciting new program on how you can earn big money in real estate without ever selling or listing a home?"

REFERRAL SALESPERSON: "Yes."

BROKER: "Well, we've designed this dynamic new program so that people like you, those whose licenses are on an inactive status, can potentially earn thousands of dollars more per year and work your own hours, from the convenience of your own home. Mr. Jones, let me ask you, if you could potentially earn $60, $70, $80 an hour or more, working part-time in real estate, and never have to list or sell, would you be interested in meeting with me at some time in the future to hear about our new program?"

Objection-Handling Scripts

SALESPERSON: "Thanks for calling, but I'm happy where I am."

BROKER: "Understood and I am glad to hear that. Can I offer you the opportunity to attend an upcoming training event that could help you increase your production with no pressure or obligation to you at all?"

Salesperson: "I'm too busy to meet with you."

Broker: "And that is exactly why you should meet with me. We can discuss not only how our company can help you make more money but how we can help you have more time to enjoy your success."

Salesperson: "Let me think about it, and I'll call you later."

Broker: "I hope you do, because we can help your career. Hey, while I have you on the phone, can I offer you the opportunity to attend an upcoming training event that could help you increase your production?"

Salesperson: "I'm just not ready to talk about changing at this time."

Broker: "I understand. A quick question, would an increase in your income with more flexible time for you be of any interest to you?"

Salesperson: "Why should I leave? I'm doing well here!"

Broker: "That is exactly why you should leave. Let me explain. You are doing well because of you and your efforts. What I would like to show you is how our company can actually help you with your efforts. Our programs far exceed any in the industry. By simply meeting me and talking with me, you will see how you can take advantage of those services I am offering."

Salesperson: "Tell me what you have to offer over the phone."

Broker: "If I could do that, I would suggest that you stay where you are. I am offering you countless services that will help you make more money and do it with less effort to you."

Salesperson: "What will you do for me if I join you?"

Broker: "Great question. I am glad you asked that. I would like to explain all the things we can do for you to increase your income with less effort to you. Now we can meet later today, or would tomorrow be better?"

Salesperson: "Can I negotiate commissions?"

Broker: "When we sit down and meet we will discuss all the opportunities that you have with our company to run your business. We can meet later today, or would tomorrow be better?"

Salesperson: "You're a training company."

Broker: "Yes, we are, and thank you for recognizing that. Top quality training is one of the many benefits we offer to our people. I would like to discuss the many other services we also offer our salespeople."

Salesperson: "I don't want to pay franchise fees."

Broker: "I wouldn't want it any other way. Do you know why? Franchise fees are used to give you services independent real estate companies cannot provide. National advertising is not cheap and name recognition is extremely valuable. Let me discuss with you the ways a small fee can return large profits."

Salesperson: "We've got more market share."

Broker: "I truly am concerned about *you*, not your company. You are important, and within our company, we want our people to be successful and will sacrifice to ensure their success."

Salesperson: "I have a private office here."

Broker: "How much money does having a private office actually make you per year? I ask because I can show you how our company can *actually* put more money in your pocket, and you can then spend it however you want; doesn't that make sense?"

Recruited Agent Checklist

NAME: _____

- ☐ Business cards ordered
- ☐ Keys to the office given
- ☐ Announcement to the Sphere of Influence
- ☐ Advertising for new or transferred listings coordinated
- ☐ Farm area chosen
- ☐ Name badge, desk plate, and door plate ordered
- ☐ Passcodes set up for copier, long distance, and security entry codes
- ☐ Name riders and car signs ordered
- ☐ Tour through the office
- ☐ Introduction to working the office equipment
- ☐ Location of forms and marketing materials
- ☐ Introduction to the staff and a description of their functions
- ☐ Gift for joining
- ☐ Letter from broker or manager sent to home address
- ☐ Introduced at office meeting
- ☐ Association of REALTORS® MLS/notified
- ☐ Independent Contractor Agreement signed
- ☐ Personal photo taken
- ☐ Press release written and sent
- ☐ Real estate commission change/license sent
- ☐ Website and email address transferred or set up
- ☐ Telephone system orientation and direct line set up
- ☐ Manager's coaching scheduled

Closing Techniques

BROKER: "If there were a way for you to have a better compensation plan, how would that affect your thoughts about a transition?"

BROKER: "If the bottom line dollars earned with your current company are actually less than what you could earn with our firm, would you think about the idea of a transfer?"

BROKER: "If your actual commission-split with us worked out to be greater than what you currently have, with all of those costs and expenses, would it at least make sense to examine our program in detail?"

BROKER: "Did you sign a contract? For how long? What kinds of obligations and penalties does it contain if you choose to leave? Do you feel that is fair?"

Costs of Associating with a Real Estate Company

COMPANY:_____	COMPANY PAYS?	AGENT PAYS?
OFFICE COSTS:		
Telephone/Long Distance		
Business Cards (1,000)		
Desk Fees		
Copier Fees		
PROMOTIONAL ITEMS:		
Newspaper Advertising		
Internet Advertising/Web Page		
Property Brochures		
Marketing Campaign		
Magazine Advertising		
Just Listed/Sold Postcards		
Post/Stake Yard Signs		
Combo/Electronic Key Boxes		
Name Riders		
Direct Mail Printing/Postage		
MLS SERVICES:		
New Listing Insertion Fee		
Transfer Fee		
TRAINING:		
Sales/Legal Training		
Tuition Reimbursement Program		
TELEPHONE SERVICES:		
Long Distance Charges		
Answering Service		
Voice Mail Services		
High-Speed Internet Access		
Facsimiles		
Total		

Characteristic Profile

Characteristic	Measured	Value	Scale	Total
1.				
2.				
3.				
4.				
5.				
6.				
7.				
8.				
9.				
10.				
TOTAL		100		
			Needs to be	700+

Recruiting Interview Questions

1. Whom else will your decision affect?
2. Do you need a private office?
3. Do you have any special needs that are a concern?
4. How soon would you consider joining our company?
5. Must you settle any matters before making the decision?
6. Do you currently have any listings? Pendings? If so, when will they close?
7. Are you familiar with the procedures for changing real estate companies?
8. Have you interviewed any other offices that you liked?
9. Did you make any written agreements?
10. Are there any other real estate agents who may want to change?
11. Why are you thinking of changing?
12. What do you like best about your present company?
13. What do you like least about your present company?
14. Do you have any special interests or hobbies?
15. What do you (think you will) like most about being in real estate?
16. Do you (think you will) prefer listings or buyers? Why is that?
17. Where do you see yourself in five years? Ten?
18. How do you feel about the market?
19. What is your most successful marketing idea? or How do you plan on marketing yourself?
20. What's most important to you in a real estate company?
21. May I ask why you joined "Competitor Realty"?
22. Have the reasons why you chose the company then and the reasons why you are with them today changed at all?
23. What do you think of the company's overall office policies?
24. Would you like to see any of those polices changed or improved?
25. What are your primary and secondary motivations behind a change?

Real Estate Brokerage Value Package

- Table funding
- Production awards
- Administrative help
- Marketing assistance
- Management expertise
- Team atmosphere
- Unparalleled training
- Top block service
- Career planning
- Ancillary business
- Accounting functions
- National company
- Professional ad writing
- Great location
- Advantageous compensation
- Family culture
- Private office
- Non-competitive managers
- Relocation business
- Social events
- Management advancement
- Community service

Trade Show/Career Day Checklist

- ☐ Parking Pass and Directions
- ☐ Check-In
- ☐ Payment
- ☐ Hotel Accommodations
- ☐ Maps of Area
- ☐ Printed Materials
- ☐ Laptop Computer
- ☐ Computer Power Cord
- ☐ Remote Mouse
- ☐ Extension Cords
- ☐ Data Projector
- ☐ Tablecloth with Company Logo
- ☐ Backdrop
- ☐ Refreshments
- ☐ Registration Forms
- ☐ Handouts
- ☐ Promotional Gifts
- ☐ Pens/Writing Pads
- ☐ Reserve Cash or Credit Cards
- ☐ Mobile Telephone

Questions to be Asked Before You Accept a Speaking Engagement

1. What exactly is the topic to be covered?
2. How many people will be present?
3. How is the room arranged?
4. What audio-visual equipment will be on hand?
5. What is the speaking fee? Reimbursement for costs?
6. What time and for how long are you to present?
7. Are you the keynote speaker or a breakout speaker?
8. What type of audience will be there?
9. What does the audience expect?
10. When can you get to the facility?
11. Who is to pay for the printing of the materials?

Corporate Calling Log

	Date	Time	Number
Calls Made			
Proposals Sent			
Presentations Made			

Relocation Services Offered

Here is a list of some of the services you could offer as a relocation specialist:

- Act as a recruiting partner for the company and promote the new location with the spouse while the company promotes the job opening with the employee.
- Provide a Newcomer's Packet with vital information on schools, housing, taxes, houses of worship, childcare, and much more.
- Offer individual and family relocation counseling.
- Offer assistance with mortgage pre-qualification through a preferred mortgage company.
- If the relocation person needs to rent before buying, provide rental assistance.
- Help with a job search for the spouse.
- Provide national and international assistance for all transferees.
- Provide basic real estate services, like being a professional and competent real estate person. You should provide assistance with selling and buying, plus the ability to manage and coordinate a number of related details, while always keeping open all communication channels.
- You should thoroughly know relocation management company
- operations.
- Be able to offer agency representation to their transferees.
- Make available discounts for their transferees on loans, temporary housing, car rental, and hotels.
- You should be easy to communicate with—be accessible by phone, fax, and email.
- Your company should have the financial ability to pay vendors up front on corporate listings.
- You should possess real estate expertise in the geographic area.
- There should be minimum qualifications for agents, such as the stipulation that they be fulltime with at least three to five years' experience. They should have previous relocation experience, be available at reasonable times, be successful at assessing buyers' needs, as well as be detail oriented and professional in appearance and conduct.
- Offer a home purchase program if the house doesn't sell in a given time frame.
- Help the transferee with moving household goods.

- Offer temporary housing for those who have found a home but cannot move at this time.
- Provide home-finding trips—destination assistance.
- You should present advice on the tax implications of buying or selling real property.

Questions for Selecting an Office

1. Do you have the funds to operate a real estate office? Do you have the funds to buy the infrastructure you need to start up a real estate enterprise? Do you have reserve funds necessary to continue operations for at least six months?
2. Do you have the expertise to manage a real estate office? Be honest.
3. Do you want to operate a single office, or do you want to develop into a multi-office enterprise?
4. What type of real estate do you want to concentrate on? Residential? Commercial? High end?
5. In which geographic areas do you want to specialize?
6. What do you predict as your office market share? Profitability?
7. What is the maximum number of salespeople you want in your office?
8. What are your office policies? Will you be strict or flexible?
9. Do you believe in a family atmosphere or a corporate structure? What type of reputation do you want to project?
10. What are your growth strategies for the business? Expansion? Franchise affiliation? Merger?
11. What type of training do you plan to provide?
12. Are you concerned about name recognition in the market? What will you do to address this issue?
13. Will your company offer ancillary services? Will you charge for these services?
14. Do you plan on being technology proficient, or do you plan to do things the old-fashioned way? How much are you willing to pay for technology?
15. Should you buy an existing real estate company, or should you form your own?
16. Should you buy or lease a location?
17. What business equipment should you purchase?

Expectations of New Sales Associates

1. KNOW YOUR OFFICE INVENTORY.
   A. See all office listings.
   B. Plot active listings on a map in prime market areas of the office.
   C. Route homes by area, and then make appointments to see no more than five homes at a time.
2. FARMING.
   A. Choose a farm area.
   B. Compile all names, addresses, and phone numbers.
   C. Knock on all doors in the farm area.
3. CALL 100 PROPERTIES EACH WEEK.
   A. Call all expireds every day.
   B. Call no more than ten for sale by owners per week.
   C. Call 25 houses on each side of office solds, new listings, and/or upcoming open houses.
4. HOLD TWO OPEN HOUSES EACH WEEK.
5. ATTEND OFFICE SALES MEETINGS AND TOURS.
6. ATTEND ALL TRAINING SESSIONS.
7. GOALS
   A. Put in writing production goals, and discuss with broker.
   B. Put in writing those programs that are going to be implemented in the next thirty days.
   C. Make a weekly planner that details how the action steps will be accomplished.

Expectations of Experienced Full-Time Sales Associates

Personal Production
1. Determine annual production goals and put them in writing.
2. Develop a personal marketing plan in alignment with personal goals. Review and adjust quarterly with manager's assistance.
3. Maintain a minimum activity level of five "Clear Cut" listing appointments per week.
4. Commit a minimum of 5 1/2 days to the real estate business per week.
5. Develop a follow-up system for contacting prospects and clients.
6. Set up a business farm area and consistently work it with mailings, phone calls, and personal contacts.
7. Invest in your business through personal or promotional advertising, mail-outs, giveaways, and so on.
8. Maintain a record of your sales and listing activity to determine your production levels and possible areas of improvement.
9. Meet with a manager each quarter to review activity and plan direction.

Office Participation
1. Conduct floor-time responsibilities professionally.
2. Tour all new office listings weekly.
3. Attend office meetings and company meetings regularly and on time.
4. Process all sales and listings accurately and immediately.
5. Continue calling:
   A. FSBOs
   B. Expired listings
   C. Finish with cold calls
6. Continue to upgrade skills and professionalism.
7. Present a professional image in appearance, attitude, and behavior.

People Who Might Want to be in Real Estate

- personal contacts
- college students
- at-home spouses
- fraternity members
- investors
- sporting goods salespeople
- best friends and family
- school teachers
- travel agents
- children's music teachers
- nurses
- grocery managers
- car salespeople
- interior decorators
- military
- apparel salespeople
- auto repair people
- neighbors
- peers from sports or hobbies
- scout leaders
- pharmacists
- hair stylists
- restaurant managers
- store owners
- doctors
- christmas card list
- previous employees
- interest groups
- spouse's family
- insurance salespeople
- lunch partners
- wedding participants
- bowling team members
- computer programmers
- bank personnel
- attorneys
- veterinarians
- appliance salespeople
- home repair people
- coaches
- cosmeticians
- church members
- civic activities
- bridge partners
- pta members
- civic club members
- small business owners
- spouse's hair stylist
- furniture salespeople
- plumbers
- dentists

Important Office Information

1. Identify All Major Roads:
2. List Any Special Geographical Features:
3. Name and Describe All Area Neighborhoods:
4. Demographics (by neighborhood):
   A. Age Levels:
   B. Income Levels:
   C. Lifestyles:
5. Location of:
   A. Board of Realtors:
   B. Local Government Offices:
   C. City Services:
6. Transportation:
7. Schools:
   A. Elementary Schools:
   B. Middle Schools (or Junior Highs):
   C. Secondary Schools:
   D. Colleges:
   E. Private Schools:
8. Commercial:
   A. Major Shopping Centers:
   B. Restaurants:
   C. Unique Specialty Shops:
9. Recreational Facilities:
   A. Golf Courses
   B. Parks
   C. Entertainment Centers

(Your Office) Tour Sheet

(To be given to each real estate salesperson who is on office tour)

Address: _____

What I noticed most about the property is _____

_____

The kind of person who should buy this property is _____

_____

I believe the price of the home should be _____

_____

Address: _____

What I noticed most about the property is _____

_____

The kind of person who should buy this property is _____

_____

I believe the price of the home should be _____

_____

Activities for New Real Estate Salespeople

1. Review office policies and procedures.
2. Schedule and attend any of your Board and MLS orientations.
3. Schedule and attend computer training.
4. Read your office's computer manual.
5. Familiarize yourself with the MLS computer program.
6. Attend MLS tours for your area.
7. Attend your office tour.
8. Sit in during "opportunity time" at your office's property desk. Learn the procedure.
9. Accompany one of your office's associates on an open house.
10. Research the supply room in your office—read the brochures and forms.
11. Complete envelopes to mail with notes for the announcement of your association with your new company.
12. Visit with a Mortgage Loan Officer.
13. Visit with an Escrow Officer from a neighborhood Title Company.
14. Visit your neighborhood Mortgage Company.
15. Check out tapes and CDs from your local Board office or from various Title Companies.
16. Preview all office listings in your market area.
17. Study a prospect profile form.
18. Complete Sample Contracts.
19. Compile a list of your Sphere of Influence.
20. Read any books about understanding people, their motivation, and so forth.

Commitment Exercises

Full-Time Agents

"EDUCATION WITHOUT APPLICATION IS WORSE THAN WORTHLESS"—To help you practice the skills you have learned today, complete the following assignments during the next week and have your broker check each exercise as you complete it. When you have completed all of the exercises, have your broker sign at the bottom of the page.

1. Get a HUD key.
2. Three days this week make cold calls. Put each lead on a 4" × 6" card. Fill in the following chart as you call. You must call until you get a clear-cut listing appointment to count as a day.

	DAY 1	DAY 2	DAY 3
# OF CALLS			
TIME			

3. Have two outgoing referrals.
4. Schedule at least three listing appointments (clear-cut) by prospecting.
5. Complete the Independent Contractor Agreement.
6. Check out three books or cassette tapes on sales or real estate.
7. Role-play at least five times with another your prospecting call.
8. Have your trainer monitor your prospecting calls and give you feedback for 25 minutes.
9. Put 10 people on your Sphere of Influence. Put them on 4" × 6" cards. Bring the cards to class.
10. Answer these three questions:
    - What do I want? Be specific, in writing, no limitations; dream.
    - What will it take to get there?
    - Am I willing to pay the price?

Commitment Exercises

Full-Time Agents

"EDUCATION WITHOUT APPLICATION IS WORSE THAN WORTHLESS"—
To help you practice the skills you have learned today, complete the following assignments during the next week and have your broker check each exercise as you complete it. When you have completed all of the exercises, have your broker sign at the bottom of the page.

1. Begin a business diary.
2. Three days this week make cold calls. Put each lead on a 4" × 6" card. Fill in the following chart as you call. You must call until you get a clear-cut listing appointment to count as a day.

	DAY 1	DAY 2	DAY 3
# OF CALLS			
TIME			

3. Have two outgoing referrals.
4. Schedule at least three listing appointments (clear-cut) by prospecting.
5. Complete a business budget.
6. Check out three books or cassette tapes on sales or real estate.
7. Role-play at least five times with another your prospecting call.
8. Have your trainer monitor your prospecting calls and give you feedback for 25 minutes.
9. Put 10 people on your Sphere of Influence. Put them on 4" × 6" cards. Bring the cards to class.

Commitment Exercises

Full-Time Agents

"EDUCATION WITHOUT APPLICATION IS WORSE THAN WORTHLESS"—To help you practice the skills you have learned today, complete the following assignments during the next week and have your broker check each exercise as you complete it. When you have completed all of the exercises, have your broker sign at the bottom of the page.

1. Find an investment prospect.
2. Three days this week make cold calls. Put each lead on a 4" × 6" card. Fill in the following chart as you call. You must call until you get a clear-cut listing appointment to count as a day.

	DAY 1	DAY 2	DAY 3
# OF CALLS			
TIME			

3. Have two outgoing referrals.
4. Schedule at least three listing appointments (clear-cut) by prospecting.
5. Develop a marketing manual.
6. Check out three books or cassette tapes on sales or real estate.
7. Role-play at least five times with another your prospecting call.
8. Have your trainer monitor your prospecting calls and give you feedback for 25 minutes.
9. Put 10 people on your Sphere of Influence. Put them on 4" × 6" cards. Bring the cards to class.

My Goal Plan

Name:_____Date:_____

1. Short-Term Goal (less than one year)
   _____

2. Mid-Term Goal (one year to five years)
   _____

3. Long-Term Goal (longer than one year)
   _____

Steps to Reaching Short-Term Goal	Timeline
1.	1.
2.	2.
3.	3.
4.	4.
5.	5.
6.	6.

Steps to Reaching Mid-Term Goal	Timeline
1.	1.
2.	2.
3.	3.
4.	4.
5.	5.
6.	6.

Steps to Reaching Long-Term Goal	Timeline
1.	1.
2.	2.
3.	3.
4.	4.
5.	5.
6.	6.

Goals

Financial-- _____
_____

Career-- _____
_____

Family-- _____
_____

Spiritual-- _____
_____

Physical-- _____
_____

Self-Improvement-- _____
_____

Practices of Conduct

1. Do not divulge prices or terms of any previous or present offer.
2. Do not leave the office alone with someone if you are not sure about him or her. USE YOUR INTUITION.
3. Never present a contract without a signed agreement. Use a one-time listing form if necessary.
4. Never release a check to anyone without having him or her sign for it.
5. Never fail to give copies to buyers and sellers. Always give copies of anything someone signs. Remember to sign all listings, offers, and cancellations.
6. If you are the listing salesperson, request two keys; if not available, make two copies of keys. Make sure the keys fit. Use key boxes.
7. Never give out a key to an occupied house unless it is to another real estate salesperson. Requested keys are signed out in a logbook.
8. When showing a property, never leave doors unlocked unless you found them that way. Don't lock doors between house and garage if the owners use a garage-door opener. Leave the property in the same manner as it was when you arrived.
9. Do not commingle earnest money. Be careful of cash for which you are responsible. Give a receipt for all cash received.
10. Do not advertise real estate for sale or purchase or sell property without signing "real estate salesperson" or "broker" behind your name or phone number. Remember: It's impossible to buy or sell property, even your own, without the company being liable.

11. Never talk real estate commissions with any real estate company or salesperson.
12. Never give out telephone numbers or emails of sellers.
13. Never talk to a seller about contracts, terms, his or her listing, and so forth, unless you are his or her listing salesperson.
14. Never make a verbal offer or present an offer by telephone.
15. You will need insurance to carry people. Be careful: You are responsible for accidents!!!

Office Policies and Procedures

Responsibilities

1. Listing salesperson handles all seller activity.
    a. Estimate of seller charges
    b. Listing agreement

       All listing agreements and associated material must be turned in within 24 hours after the seller signs the listing agreement.
    c. The listing salesperson is responsible for establishing the file and verifying lot size, zoning, square footage, schools, and all other pertinent data.
    d. A Competitive Market Analysis should be included in the listing folder.
    e. The listing salesperson shall not enter any information that has not been verified with the seller. Any errors on the listing data sheet could result in the listing salesperson losing his/her listing commission. The listing salesperson must never underestimate the importance of a properly filled out listing-data sheet.
    f. Call the owner at least every week, starting the first week. Use MLS statistics as a reason to call and point out activity, competition, price reduction, and so forth; keep the owners informed of market activity.
    g. Furnish seller with advertising copy and comments each time property is advertised.
    h. Knock on doors in areas for the purpose of finding a buyer and/or to find other listing leads.
2. Buyer's salesperson handles all buyer activity.
3. Appraisers are handled by either the listing salesperson or the buyer's salesperson.
4. Repairs handled by both.

5. Closing handled by both.
6. Folder information sheet to be kept current and accurate by both.
7. Contract cancellations handled by buyer's salesperson.
8. Listing salesperson handles ads and listing renewals.
9. Broker/sales manager assists in listings upon request.
10. Buyer's salesperson closes out file.
11. Listing salesperson closes out MLS.

Floor Duty

Keep the floor covered for calls and drop-ins from 9 a.m. to 5 p.m. Monday through Saturday and 1 p.m. to 5 p.m. Sunday.

1. All agents shown on floor duty schedule are expected to work during the floor duty hours.
2. It is requested that the person on duty make no appointments during floor duty hours. If a listing or prospect call is received during the floor duty, then these calls should be serviced immediately. It shall be the responsibility of the "duty person" to notify the manager or another salesperson.
3. Floor duty gives you an excellent opportunity to secure prospects. Floor time can be profitable, even when there is little floor activity. It is a good time to bring listings up-to-date, to make telephone solicitation, or to plan work for the following day. It is recommended that on floor duty, salespeople:
   a. Make cold canvass telephone calls
   b. Contact expired listings
   c. Contact "For Sale by Owners"
   d. Call sellers back for updates
   e. Call back current contacts
4. Advise office manager when sickness prevents fulfilling floor duty requirements.
5. COMPANY POLICY: NO SHOWING APPOINTMENTS AFTER DARK!!!!!
6. VACATIONS—Since the sales staff consists of independent contractors who receive no vacation pay, salespeople may regulate their own vacations; however, it is requested that the sales staff use judgment to assure that vacations do not overlap, leaving the office shorthanded.

Salespeople must arrange for another salesperson to look after their business during vacations, illness, or extended absences.
7. USUAL OBSERVED HOLIDAYS: Mother's Day, Father's Day, Easter, Independence Day, Thanksgiving, and Christmas. Office is always open, but the staff will be off on these days.
8. To assure adequate parking space for our customers and clients, all salespeople and employees should park their cars on the side of the building. Leave the spaces in front available.
9. The kitchen/dining area has been provided for the enjoyment and convenience of all salespeople who, on occasion, may want to remain in the office for a meal or snack. Keep the area clean.

Commissions
1. Commission will be negotiable unless otherwise approved by the broker or sales manager.
2. Reducing the commission from time to time may be necessary. In the event a salesperson finds it necessary to reduce a prior agreed upon commission *without management approval,* that reduction will be treated as offering a bonus and will be deducted entirely from the salesperson's share of commission.

Guidelines for Real Estate Professionals to Help Prevent Claims

Real estate professionals do business in an intensely competitive world. In that world we must watch our backs because there are a *few* who would like to take our money. I don't believe all people are nasty, but the few can ruin your day or your career.

You have to be aggressive if you're a real estate salesperson or broker. But it's a good idea to try to move carefully, too. And while you can't really prevent a claim—since claims hinge on the client's perception of what you did or didn't do—there are still some concrete steps you can take to stop a claim from turning into a full-scale lawsuit or a major loss.

Written record keeping is one important measure. Accurate written records make up the only hard evidence you have to prove you acted professionally in a specific situation. Keep conversation notes in your computer file or write them right on the file folder.

DO HOMEWORK: First and foremost, say the experts, is to do your homework.

When you present a property, be sure you know and can point out the accurate properly lines or, better yet, have a survey. Make a check of your own listings and note the obvious defects. Explain these defects to the sellers, telling them that we must disclose these to the buyer. If the seller refuses to fully disclose, you may have to walk away from the listing. The seller should also complete a "Seller's Disclosure Form" that lists most things in a house and then note whether everything is working or not. It may sound like an unrealistic way to behave, but the alternative could be far worse. Case files disclosed to the courts have consistently held that brokers and salespeople have the obligation to know and communicate all pertinent facts as part of their professional responsibility. We are not inspectors, but we do have a standard of professionalism.

DELIVER SERVICE: The second guideline has to do with delivering on your promise of service. In other words, don't encourage your buyer to purchase on a whim, and don't push beyond the limits of reasonable salesmanship. It's not just good business, so make sure you have a satisfied buyer and a sale that will stick—it could help you ward off "buyer's remorse" claims.

Finally, be careful in what you say. When you don't know the answer to a question, say so. Find out the information as soon as possible, but don't guess. One apparently harmless remark during a busy afternoon of home tours could wind up as the basis of a misrepresentation claim letter.

Sixty-Day Fitness Report

Name: _____

Thanks for selecting our company to assist you in developing for yourself a real estate sales career worth having. The letter of expectation that you have studied spells out what you can expect from our team and what is expected of you so that you can become a successful and important member of our professional real estate sales team.

The first sixty days of one's real estate career, as in most careers, are critical. This is normally the time frame when good work habits and professional ethics are established for the rest of one's career. We orchestrate the first sixty days and follow up almost daily as the agent progresses through the remaining thirty days.

This Sixty-Day Fitness Report is a detailed checklist of tasks that you should accomplish and goals that you should attain during this critical time in your career. It is **your** responsibility to make sure that each of these things is accomplished during the prescribed time. Let's develop a successful and profitable business for you and a career worth having. Use this actual checklist to check off accomplished tasks and show to your manager and mentor for periodic review.

During the first sixty days, new salespeople should be physically prospecting or be at the office accomplishing the Sixty-Day Fitness Report tasks. New salespeople will work closely with their managers or mentors (if one is assigned), and other staff members to ensure that the first sixty days are PRODUCTIVE, COMPREHENSIVE, POWERFUL, and ENABLING.

Day 1

Manager *(normally accomplished in the morning)* [Administrative Assistants will review and make sure all paperwork is completed.]

- ☐ Complete Agent Profile Form.
- ☐ Have Salesperson complete and sign Independent Contract Agreement.
- ☐ Have Salesperson read Statement of Understanding.
- ☐ Read and discuss Expectation Letter.
- ☐ Assign desk/workstation.
- ☐ Issue building key.
- ☐ Read and discuss "Also Insured" rider on auto insurance policy.
- ☐ Hand out Sales Meeting schedule.
- ☐ Hand out Floor Duty Policy.

- ☐ Get and complete MLS form.
- ☐ Provide training schedule and location.

(Normally accomplished in the afternoon)

- ☐ Have Salesperson complete Realtor Association Application.
- ☐ Have Salesperson complete Key Card Lease Agreement.
- ☐ Have Salesperson take Application and Key Card Lease Agreement to Association with a check and/or credit card and join board.
- ☐ Schedule Association Orientation and MLS Training.
- ☐ Get supplies for desk: map book, business calculator, and day planner, for example.
- ☐ Set up desk/work station.

Management/Staff Review _____ Date: _____

Day 2
Staff Support

- ☐ Review Salesperson paperwork with Administrative Assistant to ensure it's correct.
- ☐ Explain photo policy and where to order photos.
- ☐ Explain advertising policy.
- ☐ Explain office postage system.
- ☐ Assign mailbox.
- ☐ Order car signs.
- ☐ Order business cards and name tags.
- ☐ Explain printing needs/graphics system.
- ☐ Introduce to all support staff.
- ☐ Explain forms wall.
- ☐ Demonstrate copier equipment use.
- ☐ Demonstrate fax machine use.
- ☐ Enter extension into phone system.
- ☐ Assist Salesperson in establishing voice mail prompts.
- ☐ Explain full capabilities of telephone system.

Manager

☐ Explain Property Management function.
☐ Explain websites.
☐ Explain E&O Insurance and risk management.
☐ Explain Virtual Tours.

Salesperson

☐ Get desk supplies.
☐ Set up desk.
☐ Set up voice prompts on desk phone.
☐ Set up call forwarding.

Management/Staff Review _____ Date: _____

Day 3

Administrative Assistant

☐ Explain agent-billing system.

Manager

☐ Explain commission disbursement.
☐ Explain what happens if the Salesperson's bill does not get paid.
☐ Explain function and support of Marketing Director.
☐ Emphasize need to promptly turn in all listing/sales transaction paperwork.
☐ Referral procedures and qualifications.
☐ Explain referral assignment process.
☐ Explain corporate and third-party business.
☐ Explain agent-to-agent intra-office referrals.

Management/Staff Review _____ Date: _____

Day 4
Manager

☐ Explain auto insurance requirements.
☐ Read and understand all forms in Buyers and Listing Packets.

Allow a full afternoon for reading Policies and Procedures Manual.

☐ Read Policies and Procedures Manual and especially those policies noted below.

Confirm reading and understanding with initials on this form:

☐ Dress Code
☐ Floor Duty/Opportunity Time
☐ Listings
☐ Sales Reporting Procedures
☐ Commissions
☐ Referrals
☐ Property Management
☐ Goal Setting
☐ Operating Charges
☐ Termination
☐ Minimum Standards
☐ Established Agency
☐ Business Cards at Showings and Going Out of Town or Unavailable
☐ Tour

Management/Staff Review _____ Date: _____

Day 5
Manager

☐ Floor Duty Training
- Goals
- Procedures
- Dos and Don'ts

☐ Role Playing for Floor Duty calls

- ☐ Explain importance of Sphere of Influence (SOI) base.
- ☐ SOI homework: complete SOI list by Day 6 to include name, mailing address, work, cell, and home phone numbers, and email address. Minimum of 25.
- ☐ Emphasize that the SOI is the best source of leads.
- ☐ Discuss importance of goals.
- ☐ Working with buyers
  - ☐ Information on Brokerage
  - ☐ Buyer's Representation Agreement
  - ☐ Pre-qualify Mortgage Company
  - ☐ How to show homes
  - ☐ Closing the sale
  - ☐ Writing, negotiating, receipting of the contract
- ☐ Working with sellers (listings)
  - ☐ Elements of a good listing presentation
  - ☐ Graphic aids
  - ☐ Using laptop with marketing presentation
  - ☐ Homework: develop initial listing presentation
  - ☐ Develop notes/scripts/questions for Floor Duty callers
- ☐ Practice listing presentation
- ☐ Role-play for Floor Duty calls
- ☐ Introduce to MLS
- ☐ Explain CMA method
- ☐ Do CMA on computer
- ☐ Practice CMAs and general use of MLS

Management/Staff Review _____ Date: _____

Day 6
Manager

- ☐ Become familiar with real estate websites.
- ☐ Prospecting
  - ☐ Floor Duty (company generated business)—role-play
  - ☐ Sphere of Influence (SOI)—role-play

- ☐ Other types of prospecting
    - ☐ Cold-calling
    - ☐ Phone calls
    - ☐ Walking neighborhoods, door hangers with just-listeds, just-solds, or other types of flyers
    - ☐ Mail-outs—just-listeds, solds, flyers, newsletters, refrigerator magnets with calendars, recipes, sports schedules, and so on
    - ☐ Email—short notes to multiple address lists or notes with attachments with all the above, including e-greetings
    - ☐ Farming
- ☐ Homework
    - ☐ Write a trial offer on a house listed in the MLS.
    - ☐ Use Buyer's Packet and fill out all necessary forms.
    - ☐ Draft Introduction Letter to SOI list.
- ☐ Practice listing presentation with manager or mentor using a listing packet and filling out all necessary forms in packet.
- ☐ Role-play/practice for Floor Duty with manager or mentor.

Management/Staff Review _____ Date: _____

Day 7

Manager

- ☐ FSBO scripts and role-playing with other salespeople
- ☐ Expired scripts and role-playing with other salespeople
- ☐ Cold-calling scripts and role-playing with other salespeople

Management/Staff Review _____ Date: _____

Day 8

Manager

- ☐ Pre-qualifying by the salesperson for client wants and needs
- ☐ Pre-qualifying by Mortgage Company
- ☐ Cold-call for two hours

Management/Staff Review _____ Date: _____

Day 9
Manager or Mortgage Loan Officer

☐ Discuss various types of financing (VA, FHA, and Conventional).
☐ Discuss potential problems for qualifying.
☐ Discuss how to question clients about financing.
☐ Introduce the Mortgage Company.
☐ Prospect for two hours.

Management/Staff Review _____ Date: _____

Day 10
Manager

☐ Sale of Other Property Addendum
☐ Temporary Buyer Lease
☐ Temporary Seller Lease
☐ Back-up contracts
☐ Prospect for two hours

Management/Staff Review _____ Date: _____

Day 11
Manager

☐ How to conduct an open house
☐ How to advertise other listings
☐ Telephone prospect for two hours

Management/Staff Review _____ Date: _____

Days 12–18
Mentor

☐ Explanation of information on brokerage (agency)
☐ Schedule to attend an open house
☐ Conduct an open house (for another salesperson's listing)

- ☐ Goal-setting process
- ☐ Homework: telephone prospect for two hours daily

Manager

- ☐ Demonstrate how to do Net Sheets
- ☐ Homework: practice CMAs, Net Sheets on computer

Management/Staff Review _____ Date: _____

Days 19–25

Mentor

- ☐ Telephone prospect for two hours daily
- ☐ Drive about, learn areas, and team up if possible

Management/Staff Review _____ Date: _____

Days 26–32

Mentor

- ☐ Telephone prospect for two hours daily
- ☐ Drive about/learn areas and subdivisions

Manager

- ☐ Thirty-day follow-up
- ☐ First listing processed

Management/Staff Review _____ Date: _____

DAYS 33–39

Mentor

- ☐ Telephone prospect for two hours daily
- ☐ First contract receipted and in escrow
- ☐ At least 25 SOI names submitted to manager
- ☐ Drive about/learn areas and subdivisions

Management/Staff Review _____ Date: _____

DAYS 40–46
Mentor

☐ Telephone prospect for two hours daily
☐ Twenty-five more SOI names submitted to manager
☐ Drive about/learn areas and subdivisions
☐ Follow up on listings and contracts in escrow

Management/Staff Review _____ Date: _____

Days 47–53
Mentor

☐ Telephone prospect for two hours daily
☐ Discuss how to get more listings/sales
☐ Second listing processed
☐ Drive about/learn areas and subdivisions

Management/Staff Review _____ Date: _____

DAYS 54–60
Mentor

☐ Telephone prospect for two hours daily
☐ Follow-up interviews with management
☐ Drive about/learn areas and subdivisions
☐ Preview new homes
☐ Preview production
☐ Submit 25 more SOI names to manager
☐ Counseling
☐ Sixty-day follow-up with management

Management/Staff Review _____ Date: _____

NEW AGENT CHECKLIST

Sales Associate's Name: _____ Hire Date: _____

To be completed in the first week

	Contact Person	Due	Completed	Sign Off
Learn Operation of Office Digital Camera	Administrative Asst.			
Learn How to Download Photos	Admin Asst.			
Learn How to Send Emails of Homes	Manager			
Input Your SOI into Your Computer	Agent			
Attend MLS Training	Agent			
Review Expectation Letter with Mgr	Manager			
Complete New Agent Application	Manager			
Complete Agent Profile	AA			
Sign Independent Contractor Agreement	Manager			
Complete IRS Forms	AA			
Complete Statement of Understanding	Manager			
RE Commission Sponsorship Form Signed	Manager			
Complete Business Card Application	AA			
Order Name Badge	AA/Manager			
Get Tour of Office and Key	Manager			
Discuss Personal Safety Guidelines	Manager			
Join Board of REALTORS®	Agent/Board			
Complete Key Card Lease Agreement	Agent/Board			
Complete Press Release	Agent			
Review Operational Manual	Agent			
Set Up Voice Mail	AA			
Learn Operation of Phone	Front Desk			
Learn Operation of Fax Machine	AA			
Learn Operation of Copier	AA			
Ensure All Paperwork Is Turned In	AA/Agent			
Send an E-Greeting from Internet	Agent			
Digital Photos for Advertising	AA			
Order Sign Riders	Agent/AA/Manager			
Order Car Signs	Agent/AA/Manager			
Complete-Announcement Cards	Agent			
Discuss Office Meetings	Manager			
Discuss Office Tour	Manager			
Discuss the Office's New Agent Training	Manager			
Discuss How to Turn in Listing Changes				
Discuss How to Turn in Sales Changes				
Discuss How to Turn in Status Changes	AA			

Relocation Policy

1. All referrals will be directed to the Relocation Director or Manager.
2. Relocation Director will contact the client to determine wants and needs and will place with the correct real estate salesperson best suited to work with the client based on the client's wants and needs and the salesperson's knowledge and service area.
3. Referrals will not be assigned on a rotation basis, nor will they be assigned according to which real estate salesperson is on floor duty at the time a referral comes in.
4. To qualify for incoming referrals a real estate salesperson MUST:
   A. Dress according to the Policy Manual.
   B. Maintain a clean car inside and out.
   C. Show only in areas the salesperson is familiar with. If the client desires to look outside of the salesperson's expertise, the salesperson must report to the Relocation Director for guidance.
5. The salesperson must attend appropriate, required training and become a certified relocation specialist.
6. The real estate salesperson must be willing to meet the client at the airport, make hotel reservations, and be of help in a broad range of services.
7. The salesperson must keep progress reports updated regularly. Keep Relocation Department updated monthly until contract and then weekly.
8. If a real estate salesperson is unable to dedicate the necessary time or requirements of a referred client, the salesperson must report to the Relocation Director. Do not ever pass the referral to another salesperson.

Time Management

1. Keep a written and prioritized to-do list.
   - ☐ It should flexible yet thorough.
   - ☐ Ask yourself: What is the most important thing I should be doing at this given moment?
2. Work at work and play at play—a corollary to work is work and home is home. Waste time honestly. If you don't feel like working, just admit it.
3. Have an assistant: If you don't have an assistant, you are an assistant, not a broker!
4. Work only 51/2 days per week: This lessens burnout.
5. Handle paperwork only once: Do it, and then file it or throw it away.
6. Use the phone, fax, mail, email, and scan.
7. Combine activities.
8. Start the day early.
9. Never let your tank go less than half-full.
10. Listen to educational CDs, and always have educational books in your car.
11. Pay to have the things done that take up your personal time, like mowing, washing the car, cleaning the house or office.
12. Learn to say "NO." Refuse to do the other person's job.
13. Track your time.

Credits

Article	"Stop the Revolving Door: Treat Your Agents Like Customers"
Author	Rich Casto
Online mag.	Realty Times
Web address	http://realtytimes.com/rtpages/20040908_revolvingdoor.htm
Published	September 8, 2004
Article	"Recruiting the Experienced Agent"
Author	Rich Casto
Online mag.	Realty Times
Web address	http://realtytimes.com/rtpages/20040420_experience.htm
Published	April 20, 2004
Article	"Why Agents Leave: It Isn't the Splits"
Author	Jon Cheplak
Online mag.	Realty Times
Web address	http://realtytimes.com/rtpages/20040324_agentsleav.htm
Published	March 24, 2004
Article	"Three Keys to Recruiting Better Agents"
Author	Terri Murphy
Online mag.	Realty Times
Web address	http://realtytimes.com/rtpages/20030225_recruiting.htm
Published	February 25, 2003

Article	"Errors and Omissions Insurance for Real Estate Agents"
Author	Janet Wickell
Online mag.	About
Web address	http://homebuying.about.com/cs/errorsomissions/a/errors_omission.htm
Published	no date
Article	"How Do You Measure Up?"
Author	Robert Freedman
Online mag.	Realtor Magazine Online
Web address	http://realtor.org/rmomag.NSF/pages/HowDoYouMeRobArchive1999Sep
Published	September 1, 1999
Article	"The Future of Real Estate Brokerage"
Author	Ellen P. Roche, PhD, Kate Anderson
Online mag.	Realtor.org
Web address	http://www.realtor.org/Research.nsf/files/futurehighlights.pdf/ $FILE/futurehighlights.pdf
Published	No date given
Book	*The Vault Real Estate Career Guide*
Author	Raul Saavedra
Publisher	Vault, Inc.
Address	150 West 22nd St., New York, NY 10011
Published	November 2003
Article	"How to Make a Valuable Office Policy Manual"
Author	Tracey Velt
Online mag.	Planet Realtor
Web address	http://www.planetrealtor.com/Florida/FLRealtorMagazine/ BookSmart0605.cfm
Published	2005

Article	"Will Your Recruits Fit In"
Author	Michael Abelson
Online mag.	Realtor Magazine Online
Web address	http://www.realtor.org/rmomag.NSF/pages/forbrokersJune03?OpenDocument
Published	June 1, 2003

Article	"Make Your Recruiting Mirror Your Market"
Author	Laurie Moore-Moore
Online mag.	Realtor Magazine Online
Web address	http://www.realtor.org/rmomag.NSF/pages/MakeYourReLauArchive1998May?OpenDocument
Published	May 1, 1998

Article	"Do a Reality Check on Your Recruiting Costs"
Author	Laurie Moore-Moore
Online mag.	Realtor Magazine Online
Web address	http://www.realtor.org/rmomag.NSF/pages/DoaRealityLauArchive1998Sep?OpenDocument
Published	September 1, 1998

Article	"Which Brokerage Is Right for You?"
Author	Mariwyn Evans
Online mag.	Realtor Magazine Online
Web address	http://www.realtor.org/rmomag.NSF/pages/feb03brokerage
Published	February 1, 2003

Article	"Recruiting the Best"
Author	Chris Heagerty
Online mag.	Texas Realtor Online
Web address	http://www.texasrealtoronline.com/issues/0900/recruiting/recruiting.html
Published	September/October 2000

Article	"Effective Meeting Tips"
Author	None given
Online mag.	Meeting Wizard
Web address	http://www.meetingwizard.org/meetings/effectivemeetings.cfm
Published	2001–2005

Article	"What's in a Name?"
Author	David Avrin
Online mag.	The Visibility Coach
Web address	http://www.visibilitycoach.com/newsletter/april05.html
Published	April 2005

Article	"The Approachability Philosophy"
Author	Scott Ginsberg
Online mag.	Front Porch Productions
Web address	http://www.hellomynameisscott.com
Published	No date given

Article	"How to Start a Kiosk Business"
Author	None given
Online mag.	Entrepreneur.com
Web address	http://www.entrepreneur.com/article/0,4621,309713,00.html
Published	July 18, 2003

Index

A
acceptance, 210
ACPA (Anticybersquatting Consumer Protection Act), 86
acquisitions, mergers and, 552, 577–580, 585
action awards, 484–486
actual rent, 259–260
ADA (Americans with Disabilities Act), 90–92, 131
ADAAA (Americans with Disabilities Act Amendments Act), 92
addendum, 108
administrative law judge (ALJ), 123–124
advertising, 100, 311. *See also* referral networks
   AIDA steps in, 312–313, 341–342
   in business plan, 165–166
   at career days, fairs, 322–323
   car signs, 320
   classified, 312–313, 341–342
   at conventions, 322
   emotion in, 313–314
   fair housing laws and, 337
   fair housing wording guidelines in, 103–104
   familial status in, 103
   frequency of, 317
   handicaps in, 102–103
   as home improvement shows, 322
   on internet, 11
   magazine, 319–320
   misleading, 98
   name recognition, 292, 339
   name tags, 320–321
   newspaper, 317–319
   policies, 315
   print, 317–320, 342
   prospect-generating, 292–293
   public relations and, 321–322, 343
   race, color, national origin in, 101
   for recruits, 442–446
   Regulation Z in, 104–105, 337
   religion in, 101–102
   sex, gender in, 102
   TREC rules on, 315–316, 337–338
   through word of mouth, 323–324
   writing effective, 312–315
advice, of salespersons, 64
affiliates, 325–327, 343–344
agency, representation and buyer-only offices, 93–94

dual agency, 94–95
intermediary offices, 94
minimum-service requirements, 96–99
non-agency, 95
seller-only, 92–93
agency notice, 109
agent report, 150
agents, 2
business plans of, 519–523
encouraging, 34
foreclosures and, 189
motivating, 34
new, checklist for, 632
sales, 126
agents with other companies. *See* AWOCs
AIDA steps, in advertising, 312–313, 341–342
ALJ (administrative law judge), 123–124
Americans with Disabilities Act (ADA), 90–92, 131
Americans with Disabilities Act Amendments Act (ADAAA), 92
ancillary businesses, 569–571
ancillary services, 552
annual report, of NAR, 82
Anticybersquatting Consumer Protection Act (ACPA), 86
antispam rules, 120, 133
antitrust, 113–118, 133
appraisers, 326–327
arousing interest, 312
art, in real estate offices, 280
assets, 225–226, 248–249.
See also liquid assets
assumed names, 379–380
attracting attention, 312
avoidance, 209
award rallies, 512–513
AWOCs (agents with other companies), 422, 472

action plans, 436–437, 471
calling on, 437–441
fair deal, 439–440
interviews, 450, 453–454
keys to working with, 435–436
offers to, 440–441

B

bait-and-switch strategy, 105
balance sheet, 171, 225–226
bankruptcies, 188
bathroom ad cards, 308
best practices, fair housing laws and, 122–123
billboards, 298, 340
board of advisors, 166–167
bonuses, 401–403, 547
boutiques, 36
boycotting, 116
breaks, 392
bricks-and-mortar building, 265–266
brochures, 302–303
brokerage business, monitoring, 545–550
brokerages. *See also* offices; *specific topics*
business name of, 25
configuring, 48–52
customers, defining, 155–156
dissolving, 582
duties of, 131–132
evidence-of-trust accounts of, 26
existing, purchasing, 32, 34–35, 54
initial planning for, 20–29
lack of focus in, 19
lack of management experience in, 19
lack of specialization in, 20
megafirm, 9, 13
mom-and-pop, 9, 13, 35–36, 54

Index 641

naming, 46–48, 56
outlook, trends, 8–11
owner of, 5–8, 33
planning, 18, 28–29, 54
policies of, 337–338
position, in marketplace, 157–158
profit of, 228–229
protecting, 184
protecting image of, 337–339, 344
purchase of, 227–228
reasons for failure, 18–20
regulations on, 25–28
responsibility of, 83–85, 129–130
rules and regulations of, 25–28
selecting facility, 262–266, 284
selling, 582
starting, 18, 53
start-up, 30–32, 54
undercapitalization of, 18–19
valuation of, 601
virtual, 402
working capital of, 228
brokers, 2. *See also* competitors; license holders; offices; recruiting; *specific topics*
advantages of being, 5–7, 12–13
business goals of, 28–29
business plans of, 28, 54
characteristics of, 20–25
commercial, 574
contracts, 106–108
designated, 354–356, 379
disadvantages of being, 7–8, 12–13
education requirements for, 27
encouraging, motivating agents, 34
failure of, 53
independent, 36–37, 40–41
knowing, 81, 129
license holders choosing, 424–425
looking to future, 581–582
misrepresentation by, 76–81
P&P for, 199, 215
prospecting laws, 100–106
rapport with competitors, 35
regulations on, 4
respect from, 516
responsiveness of, 516
salespersons and, 3–5
teamwork of, 24
unconscionable action by, 80–81, 128–129
watching for events, 441
builders, investors and, 547–548
burnout, 482–483
bus benches, 308
business. *See also* working the business
ancillary, 569–571
description, 158–160
development, 572–573
ethics, 67–71, 125 (*See also* law)
expenses, monitoring, 553–555, 558–559
goals, 28–29
income statement, 224
name, 25–26
practices, unfair, 89–90
business cards, 305
business entity requirements, 355–356, 379
business financials, 224–226, 248–249
business insurance, 211–212, 216
business loan application, 229, 249–251
ability to repay, 230, 234–235
appointment, 240–242
available collateral, 230
business plan in, 233–234

cash flow, 236
credit rating, 231–232
debt and, 237–238
equity, 233
management experience, 232–233, 238
on net worth, 237
presentation, preliminary actions before, 238–240
process, 234–238
profit in, 235–236
business plan
advertising, promotion, 165–166
of agents, 519–523
balance sheet, 171, 225–226
board of advisors, 166–167
of brokers, 28, 54
business description in, 158–160
for business loan application, 233–234
capital requirements, 172
cash-flow statement, 170–171
on competition, 167–169
continuous improvement, 155
cost of services, 172
cover page, 152
defining customers, 155–156
developing, implementing, 150
development status, 161
estimated sales, 165
executive summary, 152–153
on financials, 169
financial statement, 169–170
income statement, 170
location in, 164
management description, 166
on market, 156
marketing plan in, 156–157
method of sales, 164–165
mission statement, 153
operating expenses, 171–172
operations, 160
on outsourcing marketing, 163–164
ownership, 166
personnel development, 161
on position, in marketplace, 157–158
for productivity, 518
on risks, 172–173
service fees, 160
service process, 161–163
strategy, 154–155
table of contents, 152
vision statement, 153–154
writing, 151, 175–178, 520–523, 537–538
business structures
choosing, 42–46, 55–56
corporations, 45–46, 55–56
LLCs, 45, 55
partnerships, 44–45, 55, 376
sole proprietorships, 43–44, 55, 374
buyer-only office, 93–94
buyers, 2–3, 12, 487, 532. *See also* consumers; homebuyers; Notice to Prospective Buyer
disclosures to, 108–113
of existing brokerages, 32
of foreclosure property, 189
market, 143, 174
property insurance for, 112
buyer's market, 542, 556
buying offices, 256–257, 282

C

call nights, 509–511
calls for action, 313
Candidate Handbook, 27
CAN-SPAM Act, 120
capital requirements, 172
career apparel, 336
career days, fairs, 322–323, 602

car signs, 320
cash-flow statement, 170–171, 226, 236
cash on hand, personal, 221–222
Century 21 Real Estate, 85–86
characteristics profile, for real estate professional, 427
city offices, 41–42
civic clubs, 334
civic duty, 64
civic groups, membership in, 333–334
Civil Rights Act, 100–101
claims, preventing, 621–622
classified ads, 312–313, 341–342
Clayton Antitrust Act, 117–118
client care, 62, 67
clients
    closing gifts for, 329–330
    duties to, 131–132
    past, 573–574
    prospecting for, 517
closing gifts, 329–330
closing techniques, 476, 597
    alternate-of-choice close, 462
    appeal to the higher authority, 466–467
    assumptive close, 462
    feedback question close, 463
    if-then close, 467–468
    puppy dog close, 465–466
    reduce-to-the-ridiculous close, 464–465
    similar situation close, 463–464
    take-away close, 466
    tie-down close, 461–462
    trial close, 461
clubs, civic, 334
CMA (competitive market analysis), 93
collateral, 230, 250
collections, 393
"coming soon," 338–339

commercial brokers, 574
commercial lease,
    negotiating, 256
commercial market, 142, 173–174
commercial real estate, 340
commission, 515–516, 621
commission rates, 114, 150
commitment exercises, 614–616
communications and information systems, 281–282
community newspapers, 319
community offices, 41
community programs, of NAR, 82
community property, 193, 213–214
community service, 328–329, 344, 575
company. *See* brokerages
company direction retreat, 508
company events, 511–512
company image, protecting, 337–339, 344
company registration, 26
company website, 300–301
compatible businesses, 357
compensation, 111, 360, 363, 365, 368, 381–382
compensation management, 388, 396–403
competency, 70–71
competition, 248
    analyzing, 146–149
    business plan on, 167–169
competition, in real estate sector, 8
competitive market analysis (CMA), 93
competitors, 357
    broker awareness of, 140
    local, researching, 147–148, 174–175
    outside, researching, 148–149, 175
    rapport with, 35

complaints, 548
compliance review, oversite transaction and, 200–209, 215–216
computer networks, 281–282
computer software, downloads, 548–549
confidentiality, of salespersons, 64
configuring brokerages, 48–52
consumer protection laws, 106
consumers. *See also* Anticybersquatting Consumer Protection Act; Telephone Consumer Protection Act; Texas Real Estate Consumer Notice Concerning Hazards or Deficiencies
  damages, 80
  DTPA for, 76
  ethics treatment of, 67
  financial protection for, 26
contact relation management (CRM), 518, 537
continuous improvement, 155
contracts, 132
  dates in, 208
  homeowners' association documentation in, 207
  keeping neat, 201
  laws and, 106–108
  license holders and, 201–205, 215–216
  mineral clauses in, 112–113
  notices paragraphs, 205
  request for repairs in, 208
  residential service, 297, 340
  special provisions of, 207
  of Third-Party Financing Condition Addendum, 205–206
  TMS for, 209
  on use, misuse of property, 207–208

conventions, 322
copiers, 278–279
copy, writing, 313–314
corporate calling, 573, 604
corporate ethics, 67–71, 125
corporations, 45–46, 55–56
cost of services, 172
costs, of associating with real estate company, 598–599
creating desire, 312–313
credit cards, 245
credit cards, personal, 222
credit rating, 231–232
CRM (contact relation management), 518, 537
CSR (customer service representative), 488–489, 533
current lender, in short-sale transaction, 189
customers, 155–156. *See also* clients
customer service representative (CSR), 488–489, 533

D

damages, 77, 80, 98
DBA (doing business as name), 25–26
debt, 237–238
deceptive practices, 78–79
Deceptive Trade Practices Act (DTPA), 76–81, 127–128, 213
delegation, 518–519
Department of Housing and Urban Development (HUD), 101, 110, 121, 123
designated brokers, 354–356, 379
desk fee, 399
desks, 278–279
direct marketing
  business cards, 305
  company brochures, 302–303

flyers, 304
mail-outs, 304
postcards, 302–303
property brochures, 303
property profile sheets, 303–304
direct marketing companies (DMCs), 301–302
disclosures. *See also* seller's disclosure notice; TILA and RESPA Integrated Disclosures
to buyers, sellers, 108–113
DTPA, 213
of mold growth, 112
of relationships, with residential service companies, 110–111
by salespersons, 63
discrimination, 100–101, 117–118, 120–121, 134
diversification, 211
divorce, 185–187
DMCs (direct marketing companies), 301–302
doing business as name (DBA), 25–26
Do-Not-Call, Do-Not-Fax laws, 118–120, 133
DTPA (Deceptive Trade Practices Act), 76–81, 127–128, 213
dual agency, 94–95
duplication, 211

E

earnest money, 108
Economic Espionage Act (EEA), 87
education requirements, for brokers, 27
EEA (Economic Espionage Act), 87
emotion, in advertising, 313–314
emotional stability, of broker, 21
empathy, 24

employees, 402, 415–418, 480–482
employment
federal guidelines for, 390–391
FMLA and, 391, 413–414
law, 388
process, 409–413
relations, 388–390
state guidelines, 391–396
energy efficiencies, 554–555
English Common Law of Agency, 2, 12
environmental hazards disclosure, 109
E&O (errors and omissions insurance), 77, 212, 215–216
equities, 225–226, 233
errors and omissions (E&O) insurance, 77, 212, 215–216
estates, 142, 174, 258–259, 283, 576
estimated sales, 165
ethics. *See also* NAR Code of Ethics®; Texas Real Estate Commission
business, 67–71, 125
canons of, 60–64, 67
consumers and, 67
defined, 60
law and, 60–61
thoughts, 64–67
event sponsorships, 331–333
evidence-of-trust account, 26
exit strategy, 581–582, 585
expansion, 148
horizontal, 564–569, 583–584
vertical, 569–571
expectation letter, 490–491
expenses
minimizing, 553–556, 558–559
operating, 171–172
experienced license holders, 356–357, 424

F

facilities management, 284–285
  bathrooms, 274–275
  breakroom, 277
  bullpen, 275
  buying office equipment, 277–280
  conference rooms, 274
  day-to-day operations, 268–269
  equipment room, storage of, 276
  landscaping, 270–271
  office cleaning, 269–270
  office identity, 272
  office in general, 271–272
  office layout, 273
  office philosophy, 272–273
  office supplies, 273
  operation office, 276
  private, semiprivate offices, 275–276
  reception area, 274
  utilities, 269
facility, for brokerage, 284
  building types, 263–266
  common areas, total space of, 262
  finish out, 263
  operational hours, 262–263
  signage, 264
Fair Housing Act, 100–101, 120–122, 132, 134
fair housing laws
  advertising in compliance with, 103–104, 337
  best practices, 122–123
  enforcement of, 123–124
  equal treatment under, 133
  familial status protections in, 122
  protected classes in, 121, 133–134
  violations of, 121–122
  wording guidelines, 103–104

false light, 88–89
familial status
  in advertising, 103
  protections, in fair housing laws, 122
Family and Medical Leave Act (FMLA), 391, 413–414
farm-and-ranch market, 141–142, 173
farm and ranch specialization, 576
fax machines, 278
Federal Emergency Management Agency (FEMA), 110
federal employment guidelines, 390–391
Federal Trade Commission (FTC), 90, 118, 130–131
FEMA (Federal Emergency Management Agency), 110
fidelity, 69
fiduciary, 98–99
fiduciary relationships, 2, 12
field training, 495
file cabinets, 279–280
financial controls, 543–545
financials, 169, 220
  business, 224–226, 248–249
  horizontal, vertical, ratio analyses, 221, 247
  personal, 221–224, 247–248
  protection, 26
financial statement, 169–170
financing contingency, 205–206
fine homes, 142, 174, 576
first-time homeowners, 575
fixed-rate loans, 105
floor duty, 620–621
flyers, 304
FMLA (Family and Medical Leave Act), 391, 413–414
focus, lack of, 19

Index

follow-up contacts, for recruits, 434–435
foreclosures, 188–189
For Sale by Owner (FSBO), 39, 184, 197, 300
franchises. *See also* offices
  international, 40–41
  national, 40–41
fraud, 77–78, 88–89, 107
frequency, of advertisements, 317
FSBO (For Sale by Owner), 39, 184, 197, 300
FTC (Federal Trade Commission), 90, 118, 130–131

G

GAAP (generally accepted accounting principles), 224, 248
general fiduciary duties, in Texas, 97–98
general law, 75, 126
generally accepted accounting principles (GAAP), 224, 248
general operating budget (GOB), 246–247, 543–544
general partnerships, 44, 55, 376, 383
gifts, 329–330, 547
giveaways, for marketing, 309–310, 341
goal plan, 617–619
GOB (general operating budget), 246–247, 543–544
Golden Rule, 61
government, 63
grocery store place-card boards, 308
growth. *See also* expansion
  inorganic, 577–581
  opportunities, 564
  organic, 572–577, 585

H

holding companies, 10
homebuyers
  qualifying, 63
  seminars, 310–311
home equity loan, 245
home improvement shows, 322
home inspections, 110
home office, 402
homeowners, first-time, 575
homeowners associations, 207, 333
home seller seminars, 310–311
home warranty, 297
horizontal analysis, 221, 247
horizontal expansion, 564, 583–584
  adding offices, in adjacent areas, 565–566
  adding offices, in different areas, 566–567
  adding offices, in different market segments, 568–569
  adding offices, in similar market segments, 567–568
houses, in divorce, 187
Housing Affordability Index, 145–146
HUD (Department of Housing and Urban Development), 101, 110, 121, 123

I

IABS (Information About Brokerage Services), 316, 342–343
IBD (individual business development) meetings, 491–492, 533
identity, of office, 49, 272

648 Index

income
  maximizing, 551–553
  personal, 222
  statement, 170
  statement, business, 224
independent brokers, 36–37, 40–41
independent contractors, 415
  challenges, 394
  employee versus, 394–395
  managing, 395–396, 480–482
  status, 393
independent offices, 40
individual business development (IBD) meetings, 491–492, 533
industrial market, 142, 174
influence, sphere of, 324
Information About Brokerage Services, 109
Information About Brokerage Services (IABS), 316, 342–343
Information About Special Flood Hazard Areas, 110
information boxes, 295
information management, 550–551, 557–558
information technology (IT), 282
inorganic growth, 577–581
inspections, 62, 78, 571
Inspector Information, 112
insurance, 77. *See also* Texas Department of Insurance
  business, 211–212, 216
  liability, 211–212
  property, 112, 570
  title, 571
integrity, 69
intent, 77, 129
interest rates, 8–9, 11
intermediary office, 94
intermediary relationship notice, 109

Internal Revenue Service (IRS), 394
international franchises, 40–41
international newspapers, 318
internet, 4, 10–12, 50
  for marketing, 300, 340
  virtual office and, 266–268
interviews, with recruits, 473–474
  AWOC questions, 450, 453–454
  closed-ended question, 449
  general interest questions, 450, 453
  introductory discussion, 447–448
  objectives, 451
  open-ended questions, 448–449
  questioning techniques, 448, 600
  wants-and-needs analysis questions, 449, 451–453
intuition, 23
investment groups, 245
investment properties, 8–9, 257
investors, builders and, 547–548
IRS (Internal Revenue Service), 394
IT (information technology), 282

J

JIT (just-in-time) training, 494–495, 533
joint tenants with rights of survivorship, 375–376, 383
joint ventures, 377, 383
just-in-time (JIT) training, 494–495, 533

K

keep it simple and short (KISS), 313
key boxes, 295–296, 339

KISS (keep it simple and short), 313
Kleenex, 87
knowing broker, 81, 129

L

labor code, 391–392, 414–415
land development, 572
landman, 191
landscaping, 52, 270–271
Lanham Act, 85
laws, 60–61. *See also* agency, representation and; employment; fair housing laws; Federal Trade Commission; unfair competition laws
   antispam, 120, 133
   antitrust, 113–118, 133
   consumer protection, 106
   contracts and, 106–108
   Do-Not-Call, Do-Not-Fax, 118–120, 133
   general, 75, 126
   license, 71–75
   passing-off, 86–87
   probate, 193–194
   prospecting, 100–106
   RESPA, 124
   truth-in-advertising, 106
lawsuits, 195
lead-based paint disclosure, 109
leadership, 378
   development of, 353
   by example, 350
   management and, 351–353
lead management program, 488–489
leasehold, 258–259
leases
   clauses of, 259–261
   types of, 258–259, 283
legal consideration, 132

legal law, 60–61
legally competent parties, 132
legal objective, 132
legal paperwork, 26
lenders
   calling on, 239–240
   mortgage, 189–190, 571
   underwriting requirements for, 206
liabilities, 108, 225, 247, 249
liability insurance, 211–212
libel, 88–89
license
   application, 27
   exam, 27–28
   obtaining, 26–27
licensed inspectors, 62, 78, 326
license holders, 126. *See also specific topics*
   as advisors, 423
   choosing brokers, 424–425
   client care by, 62, 67
   contracts and, 201–205, 215–216
   DTPA and, 76
   experienced, 356–357, 424
   managing, 480–481
   moral law of, 61
   NAR Code of Ethics® and, 67–68
   no risk, 62
   number, production of, 147
   in offices, 36–39, 54
   operations, 482–486
   personal interaction with, 508–509
   respecting, 516
   selling own property, 184–186
   staff, presentation of, 61
   TREC Canons of Professional Ethics and Conduct and, 67–71
license laws, 71–75

license-returned people, 424
limited liability corporations
    (LLC), 45, 55
limited partnerships,
    44–45, 55, 376
liquid assets, 221–222, 247
listings, purchase agreements and,
    486
listings taken, 150
LLC (limited liability
    corporations), 45, 55
loans, 206. *See also* business loan
    application
    alternative sources of, 242–246
    from business associates,
        244–245
    from family, friends, 243
    home equity, 245
    from investment groups, 245
    partners and, 243
    from venture capitalists, 245
local competitors, 147–148,
    174–175
local market, 148, 175
local newspapers, 319
local regulations, 75
locations
    in business plan, 164
    number of, 148
loss control, methods of,
    209–211, 216

M

magazine advertising, 319–320
mail-outs, 304
management, 580
    description, 166
    of employees, 480–482
    experience, 19, 232–233, 238
    of independent contractors,
        395–396, 480–482
    of information, 550–551
    of license holders, 480–481
    of people, 354–358
    performance, 486–489
    structure, 348, 374–377, 383
    students, 357–358
    style, 348, 368–373, 381–382
manager development program
    (MDP)
    assistant managers in,
        363–364, 381
    branch managers, 365–368, 381
    compensation, 360, 363, 365,
        368, 381–382
    manager candidates in,
        358–359, 380
    manager trainees in,
        360–363, 380
    monthly performance review
        in, 360–368
managers
    collaborators, 371–372
    commanders, 369–370
    controllers, 372–373
    leaders versus, 351–353
    peacemakers, 370–371
    sources for, 356
market
    analyzing, 144–146
    average days on, 150
    broker awareness of, 140
    business plan on, 156
    buyer's, 143, 174
    changes in, 542–543
    commercial, 142, 173–174
    farm-and-ranch, 141–142, 173
    fine homes and estates, 142, 174
    identifying, 156
    industrial, 142, 174
    local, 148, 175
    residential, 141, 173
    seller's, 143–144, 174, 542, 556
    vacation property,
        142–143, 174

marketing, 290, 339. *See also* advertising; direct marketing; telemarketing
   brokerage plan, 291–293
   budget, 306–307, 340–341
   campaigns, 147–149, 307–311, 341
   general strategies, 291
   giveaways for, 309–310, 341
   internet for, 300, 340
   open houses for, 334–335, 344
   outsourcing, 163–164
   plan, personal, 523–525, 538
   sales and, 156–157
   by salespersons, 63
marketing companies, 39, 54
marketing properties
   commercial, 297–299
   property management, 299–301
   residential, 293–297
marketplace, position in, 157–158
market share, 147
Markovich v. Prudential Gardner Realtors, 98
MDP. *See* manager development program
meetings
   after, 506–507
   agenda, 501–502
   before, 505–506
   business, 500–508
   conferences, rallies and, 556
   during, 506–507
   entertainment at, 503
   introduction to, 502
   office, 495–496, 501–507, 534–535
   presentations in, 502–503
   REALTORS®, 323–324, 446
   sales, 500–501
   tips for, 504–507
   training and, 504
   wants and needs in, 504

megafirm brokerages, 9, 13
mentoring, 499–500
mergers, acquisitions and, 552, 577–580, 585
Metropolitan Median Home Prices and Affordability, 146
military, 574
mineral clauses, in contract forms, 112–113
mineral rights
   background on, 190–191
   determining, 191–192
minimum-service requirements, 96–99
minimum-service transaction, 95
misappropriation of trade secrets, 87
misleading advertising, 98
misrepresentation, by broker, 76–81
mission statement, 153
MLS (multiple listing service), 39, 50, 115, 296–297, 338–339
mold growth, disclosure of, 112
mom-and-pop shop brokerage, 9, 13, 35–36, 54
money, 549–550
monitoring, brokerage business, 545–550
monopoly, 117–118
moral character, 60, 125
moral law, 61
mortgage
   companies, 326
   lenders, 189–190, 571
Mortgage Acts and Practices, 106
movie screens, 308, 341
moving trucks, 308–309
multiple listing service (MLS), 39, 50, 115, 296–297, 338–339
multiple plans, 396
multistate offices, 42

N

name recognition advertising, 292, 339
name tags, 320–321
naming brokerages, 46–48, 56
NAR (National Association of REALTORS®), 61, 67–68, 81–82, 86–87, 125, 129, 145
NAR Code of Ethics®, 67–68, 81, 125, 337
NAREB (National Association of Real Estate Boards), 68
NAREE (National Association of Real Estate Exchanges), 68
National Association of Real Estate Boards (NAREB), 68
National Association of Real Estate Exchanges (NAREE), 68
National Association of REALTORS® (NAR), 61, 67–68, 81–82, 86–87, 125, 129
 Research Resource Guide, 145
National Do Not Call Registry, 118–120, 429
national franchise offices, 40–41
national newspapers, 318–319
negotiation, by salespersons, 63
neighborhood offices, 41
networking groups, 324, 446–447
net worth
 business, 237
 personal, 223–224
new licensees, recruiting, 424
newspaper advertising, 317–319, 342
niche offices, 36, 41
non-agency, 95
non-operating activities, 224
notary services, 570
notices paragraph, of contract, 205
Notice to Prospective Buyer, 110, 133
Notice to Purchasers: Importance of Home Inspections, 110, 133

O

objection-handling
 scripts, 593–595
 techniques, 456–460, 475–476
 worksheets, 460–461, 476
objectives, time versus, 518
OBO (or best offer), 313
occupancy, 100
office buildings, 266
office meetings, 495–496, 501–507, 534–535
offices, 54–56. *See also* facility, for brokerage
 adding, in adjacent areas, 565–566
 adding, in different areas, 566–567
 adding, in different market segments, 568–569
 adding, in similar market segments, 567–568
 buyer-only, 93–94
 buyer-only with seller representation, 93–94
 buying versus renting, 256–257, 282
 city, 41–42
 cleaning, 269–270
 community, 41
 equipment, 277–280, 556
 in general, 271–272
 home, 402
 identity of, 49, 272
 important information for, 611
 independent, 40
 intermediary, 94

landscaping for, 52
layout, 273
license holders in,
    36–39, 54
more than five, 38–39
multistate, 42
national franchise, 40–41
neighborhood, 41
new locations, 148–149
niche, 36, 41
operation, 276
outside break areas of, 51–52
parking for, 50–51
philosophies of, 272–273
physical versus virtual, 266–268
private, semiprivate, 275–276
regional, 42
selecting, 607
seller-only, 92
seller-only with buyer
    representation, 93
signage for, 49–50
single, 36–38
staff, 61, 546
supplies, 273, 546–547
tours of, 335–336, 612
two to five, 38
virtual, 266–268
oil, gas prices, 11
100%, 400
open houses, 334–335, 344
operating activities, 224
operating budget, general,
    246–247
operating expenses, 171–172
or best offer (OBO), 313
organic growth, 572–577, 585
organization, analyzing, 149–150
orientation programs,
    489–491, 533
outside competitors, 148–149, 175
outsourcing marketing, 163–164
overall profitability report, 149
oversite transaction,
    compliance review and,
    200–209, 215–216
owner. *See* brokers
ownership, 166

P

paid workers, 549
parent-teacher associations (PTAs),
    333
parking, for offices, 50–51
partners, 243
partnerships, 44–45, 55, 376
passing-off law, 86–87
past clients, customers, 573–574
penalties, 393
Pending Home Sales Index, 145
people, managing, 354–358
performance appraisals, 491–492
performance management,
    486–489
personal computers, 281–282
personal education, development,
    498–499
personal ethics, 60
personal financials, 221–224,
    247–248
personal income, 222
personal interaction, with license
    holders, 508–509
personal marketing plan,
    523–525, 538
personal production, 609
personnel development, 161
policies and procedures (P&P)
    for brokers, 199, 215
    floor duty, 620–621
    manual, 197–198, 201
    privacy policy, 197–199
    responsibilities, 619–620
    for salespersons, 199, 214–215
    TREC on, 199, 214–215

position, in marketplace, 157–158
postcards, 302–303
P&P. *See* policies and procedures
practices of conduct, 618–619
predatory pricing, 115–116
prelicensed prospects, recruiting, 423
prevention, 210
price-fixing, 114
principle of anticipation, 145
print advertising
  magazine, 319–320
  newspaper, 317–319, 342
printers, 278
privacy policy, 197–199
probate law, 193–194
producers. *See* salespersons
productivity management, 515–519
profit, 228–229, 235–236, 249
profit-and-loss statement, 224
profit sharing, 401–403
promotion, 165–166. *See also* advertising
property
  appraisal, 571
  brochures, 303
  community, 193, 213–214
  inspections, 571
  insurance, 112, 570
  license holders selling own, 184–186
  management, 299–301
  profile sheets, 303–304
  repair, remodeling, 571
  separate, 193–194, 213–214
  use, misuse of, 207–208
  vacation, 142–143, 174
prospect-generating advertising, 292–293
prospecting
  for clients, 517
  laws, for brokers, 100–106
    (*See also* advertising)
  by salespersons, 64
prospective buyers, notice to, 110, 133
protected classes, in fair housing laws, 121, 133–134
PTAs (parent-teacher associations), 333
public relations, 321–322, 343
public speaking, 327–328
purchase agreement, 200, 486

Q

qualifying homebuyers, 63
questions. *See* interviews, with recruits

R

radio, 299, 340
radio broadcasting stations, 336–337
rapport, with competitors, 35
ratio analysis, 221, 247
real estate. *See specific topics*
real estate agents. *See* agents
real estate associations, 81–82
real estate brokers. *See* brokers
Real Estate Center, 146, 174
real estate firms, 4
real estate industry, 2–3, 8–11, 236–237
Real Estate License Act, 26
real estate magazines, 320
real estate-owned property (REO), 188
real estate sellers. *See* sellers
Real Estate Settlement Procedures Act (RESPA), 104, 124, 134, 552, 558
Real Property Records, 207

REALTORS®
  meetings, 323–324, 446
  risk management of, 182
recorded messages about
  properties, 337
recruited agent checklist, 596
recruiting, 148, 422, 469, 551
  actions, 428–431
  best salespersons, 425–427
  bonus, 401
  campaigns, 474–475
  costs of, 455–456
  door to door, 432–433
  leads, 428
  new licensees, 424
  objection-handling techniques,
    456–460, 475–476
  objection-handling worksheets,
    460–461, 476
  opportunities, 446–447
  packet, 455, 474
  prelicensed prospects, 423
  presentation, 454
  telemarketing, 428–429
  ways to improve, 441–442
recruits. *See also* closing
    techniques; interviews, with
    recruits
  advertising for, 442–446
  categories of, 433–436, 471
  follow-up contacts for, 434–435
  retaining, 509–513, 536,
    551–552
  selecting potential,
    423–424
  tips for speaking with, 431–433
reduction, 209–210
referral gifts, 330
referral networks, 324
  affiliates, 325–327, 343–344
  civic groups in, 333–334
  community service in, 328–329
  gifts for, 330

  public speaking and, 327–328
  rules of, 325
referral salesperson contact
  scripts, 593
regulations
  on brokerages, 25–28
  on brokers, 4
  on license holders, 60–61
  local, 75
Regulation Z, in advertising,
  104–105, 337
reliance, 77
relief provisions, 395
religion, 101–102
relocation business, 573–576,
  605–606
relocation policy, 633
rent, 258–260, 283–284
renting offices, 256–257, 282
REO (real estate-owned
  property), 188
representation, 76, 97
residential market, 141, 173
residential service company,
  disclosure of relationship with,
  110–111
residential service contract,
  297, 340
resignation, termination and,
  513–515, 536
RESPA (Real Estate Settlement
  Procedures Act), 104, 124, 134,
  552, 558
responsibility, of brokerages,
  83–85, 129–130
responsiveness, of brokers, 516
retention, of recruits, 536,
  551–552
  award rally for, 512–513
  call nights for, 509–511
  company events for, 511–512
retreats, 508
risk control, 183–184

risk management
  process, 183, 212–213
  of REALTORS®, 182
  theory of, 182–184
risks, 62. *See also* contracts
  business insurance for, 211–212, 216
  business plan on, 172–173
  divorce and, 185–187
  to license holders, selling own property, 185–186
  loss control and, 209–211, 216
  oversite transaction for, 200–209
rollback, 397–398
roll-in, 580, 585
rolling rollback, 398–399
roundtables, 447

S

sales, 2
  agent, 126
  estimated, 165
  marketing and, 156–157
  meetings, 500–501
  method of, 164–165
  number of completed, 150
  short, 188–190
sales associates, expectations of, 608–609
salespersons, 3–5
  activities for new, 613
  bottom producers, 404
  characteristics of, 426–427, 469
  confidentiality of, 64
  dead wood, 409
  kennel dogs, 407
  middle producers, 404
  nesters, 408–409
  new sponsored licensees, 404
  P&P, 199, 214–215

prima donnas, 407–408
  recruiting, 425–427, 469
  referral, 593
  roles of, 422–423
  searches, 406
  shooting stars, 405
  sponges, 409
  top producers, 403
  training, 63, 496–497, 533–534
SBA (small business administration), 246
school programs, 330–331
scope of activities, TREC on, 348–349
scripts
  objection-handling, 593–595
  referral salesperson contact, 593
SDN (seller's disclosure notice), 62, 109, 133, 195–197, 214
self-image, of leaders, managers, 353
seller-only office, 92–93
sellers, 2–3, 12, 487–488, 532
  disclosures to, 108–113
  market, 143–144, 174, 542, 556
  property insurance for, 112
seller's disclosure notice (SDN), 62, 109, 133, 195–197, 214
separate property, 193–194, 213–214
separation, 210
service
  ancillary services, 552
  community service, 328–329, 344, 575
  cost of, 172
  CSR, 488–489, 533
  fees, 160
  minimum-service requirements, 96–99

Index

minimum-service transaction, 95
MLS, 39, 50, 115, 296–297, 338–339
notary services, 570
process, 161–163
residential service company, disclosure of relationship with, 110–111
residential service contract, 297, 340
sharing, 210
Sherman Antitrust Act, 113–116, 133, 396
shopping carts, 308
shopping mall kiosks, 329
short sales, 188–190
shotgun approach, 423
signage, 49–50, 264
sign riders, 294–295
single family, 206
single office, broker, license holders and, 36–38
single plans, 396–397
sixty-day fitness report, 623–631
slander, 88
slogans, 314
slump, 484
small business administration (SBA), 246
Society for Business Ethics, 67
sole proprietorships, 43–44, 55, 374
speaking engagements, 603
specialization, lack of, 20
sphere of influence, 324
splits, 397–399
sponsorships, 330–333, 378
sports team sponsorships, 330
spousal negotiations, 187
staff, of real estate offices, 61, 546
staffing, 555–556

stand-alone building, 264
start-up brokerages, 30–32, 54
state employment guidelines, 391–396
Statute of Frauds, 107, 132
Statute of Limitations, 108, 132
strategy, 154–155
strip center, 266
structural engineers, 327
subagent, 126

T

TAR (Texas Association of REALTORS®), 91–92, 109–113, 133
taxes, 237
TDI (Texas Department of Insurance), 553, 558
teams, 401–402
teamwork, 24
telemarketing, 428–431, 469–470
Telephone Consumer Protection Act, 118
telephone systems, 281
television, 300, 340
tenancy in common, 375, 383
termination, resignation and, 513–515, 536
term of rent, 260
Texas Addendum for Property in a Propane Gas Service Area, 111
Texas Association of REALTORS® (TAR), 91–92, 109–113, 133
Texas Deceptive Trade Practices Act, 87
Texas Department of Insurance (TDI) Procedural Rule 53, 553, 558
Texas Minimum Wage Act, 393, 414–415

Texas Payday Law, 392–393, 414
Texas Probate Code, 193
Texas Property Code, 75
    Texas Real Estate
      Commission (TREC),
      26–27, 44, 97–98,
      100, 108
    Addendum for Reservation
      of Oil, Gas, and Other
      Minerals, 113
    on advertising, 315–316,
      337–338
    on assumed names, 379–380
    on brokerage responsibility,
      83–85, 129–130
    Canons of Professional Ethics
      and Conduct, 67–71, 125
    on designated brokers, 354–356
    environmental hazards
      disclosure of, 109
    on independent contractors,
      393–394
    on mineral rights, 192
    notice to prospective
      buyer, 110
    on P&P, 199, 214–215
    Real Estate Center, 146
    records of, 557
    on responsiveness, 516
    on Rule 531.3 competency,
      480, 532
    on scope of activities, 348–349
    on SDN, 195, 214
    on spousal negotiations, 187
Texas Real Estate Consumer
    Notice Concerning Hazards or
    Deficiencies, 111–112
Texas Real Estate Exam, 423
Texas Real Estate License Act
    (TRELA), 88–89, 96–98,
    126–127, 379
Texas Small Business
    Administration, 246

Third-Party Financing Condition
    Addendum, of contracts,
    205–206
third-party relocation
    companies, 575
TILA (Truth-in-Lending Act),
    104–105
TILA and RESPA Integrated
    Disclosures (TRID), 104
time management, 525–526, 634
    allocating time, 531
    assistants for, 528
    hints for, 527–531, 538
    home, work in, 527–528
    paperwork in, 528–529
    "to do" list for, 527
title companies, 326
title company, 191–192
Title III Public Accommodations
    and Services Operated by
    Private Entities, 91–92
title insurance, 571
TMS (transaction management
    system), 209
top producer training, 497–498
tortuous interference, 89
tracking, 481–482
tracking systems, 208–209
trade groups, 116
trade libel, 88
trademark infringement, 85
trade shows, 298–299, 340, 602
training
    costs of, 493–494
    field, 495
    JIT, 494–495, 533
    meetings and, 504
    mentoring and, 499–500
    office meetings and, 495–496
    personal education,
      development, 498–499
    in production, 517
    programs, 492–500

salespersons, 63, 496–497, 533–534
top producer, 497–498
transaction management system (TMS), 209
TREC. *See* Texas Real Estate Commission
TRELA (Texas Real Estate License Act), 88–89, 96–98, 126–127, 379
TRID (TILA and RESPA Integrated Disclosures), 104
trust accounts, 26
truth-in-advertising laws, 106
Truth-in-Lending Act (TILA), 104–105
turnover, 422

U

unconscionable action, 80–81, 128–129
undercapitalization, 18–19
unfair business practices, 89–90
unfair competition laws
  false light, 88–89
  misappropriation of trade secrets, 87
  passing-off law, 86–87
  trade libel, 88
  trademark infringement, 85
Uniform Trade Secrets Act (UTSA), 87

utilities expenses, 553–554
UTSA (Uniform Trade Secrets Act), 87

V

vacation, 484
vacation property market, 142–143, 174
valuation, of company, 580–581, 585, 601
venture capitalists, 245
vertical analysis, 221, 247
vertical expansion, 569–571, 584
virtual brokerage, 402
virtual office, 266–268
voluntary agreement, 107, 132

W

wages, 392–393, 414–415
waivers, 78
wants-and-needs analysis, 449, 451–453, 504
work, conceptions of, 352
working capital, 228
working the business, 35

Y

yard signs, 293–294